SERIES V   CYCLE A

LECTIONARY PREACHING WORKBOOK
Revised

For All Users
Of The Revised Common,
The Roman Catholic, And
The Episcopal Lectionaries

Russell F. Anderson

CSS Publishing Company, Inc.
Lima, Ohio

*This book is dedicated to Marian Lucille Anderson, my mother,
whose witness, prayers, and teachings have been the primary influence
in my spiritual formation. The light of her faith continues to burn brightly
in the many lives she has touched.*

Copyright © 2007 by
CSS Publishing Company, Inc.
Lima, Ohio

Scripture quotations are from the *New Revised Standard Version of the Bible*, copyright 1989 by the Division of Christian Education of the National Council of the Churches of Christ in the USA. Used by permission.

Revised and reprinted from *Lectionary Preaching Workbook*, Series V, Cycle A, ISBN: 0-7880-0520-0, printed in 1995 by CSS Publishing Company, Inc.

For more information about CSS Publishing Company resources, visit our website at www.csspub.com or email us at csr@csspub.com or call (800) 241-4056.

ISSN: 1938-5552

Cover design by Barbara Spencer

ISBN-13: 978-0-7880-2488-7 Perfect
ISBN-10: 0-7880-2488-4 Perfect
ISBN-13: 978-0-7880-2489-4 Binder
ISBN-10: 0-7880-2489-2 Binder

PRINTED IN USA

Table Of Contents

Preface

Since his seminary days, preaching has been the author's first love. He discovered that God had given him the ability to see the texts in fresh ways and to communicate the gospel in a thoughtful, yet passionate, manner. This book will stimulate your creative juices and enable you to view the lectionary texts from various angles or perspectives. Numerous sermon approaches are presented in each chapter, described in a single paragraph. These paragraphs are preceded by suggested sermon titles that catch the attention of the worshipers, even before the preaching commences. Many of these "Sermon Angles," as they are called, are further developed by sentence outlines, providing a framework onto which you can construct your own creative sermon. This author has expanded the scope of the *Lectionary Preaching Workbook* to include two to four illustrative stories in each chapter, which are fresh and penetrating revelations of the gospel at work in the modern world, not golden homiletical oldies that have been circulating since the middle ages. Another plus is that the various seasons in the first half of the church year, beginning with Advent, include suggestions as to how you can develop the appointed texts into a thematic sermon series for the season, if you choose. In addition, each chapter contains a specially written Prayer Of The Day, which captures the theme of the day in crisp, contemporary language.

May the Holy Spirit guide you in the central task of proclaiming the gospel of our Lord and Savior, Jesus Christ.

— Russell Anderson

Editor's Note Regarding The Lectionary

During the past four decades there has been a movement toward a uniform lectionary among various Christian denominations. Striving toward the goal of increased Christian unity, the Revised Common Lectionary was developed. This established a three-year cycle of scripture lessons to help unite Christians of many faiths. It is believed that if we are reading the same scripture together, our goal of being strengthened and more united would be gained.

CSS Publishing Company has embraced this goal of uniformity and unity. We recognize, however, that some churches are using variations of the Revised Common Lectionary. We are currently using the "semi-continuous" version of the lectionary. If your church uses the "complementary" series form of the lectionary, only the gospel reading for the Sundays after Pentecost should be different.

Our plan is to offer alternative worship material that will encompass those using the complementary series.

— Rebecca K. Allen
Managing Editor

Sermon Planner/Builder

Date: _____ Cycle / Season: _____ Sunday: _____

Cycle/Season/Sunday theological clue: _____

_____

Psalm/central thought: _____

_____

Collect/prayer concern/focus: _____

_____

Sermon text(s): _____

_____

Summary of sermon text(s): _____

_____

_____

_____

_____

_____

_____

_____

Pastoral perspective: _____

_____

_____

_____

_____

_____

Stories/illustrations: _____

_____

_____

_____

_____

Type of sermon: _____

Sermon plan/sketch: _____

_____

_____

_____

_____

_____

_____

Introduction

A Word About The Structure Of This Book

As one might expect from the title, the chapters in this book follow the liturgical calendar. A brief introduction precedes each season in the church year. Each chapter, in turn, divides into three major sections.

The first section, **A Brief Commentary On The Lessons**, concisely reveals the content and context of the lection. The exegesis is far from exhaustive, since there are ample resources to aid you in this task. The intent is to capsulize and summarize the meaning of the text as it was originally spoken. Before we can deduce theological principles applicable to our day, we need to probe the *sitz im leben* of the text. The preacher should also consult commentaries and other exegetical resources, when he or she decides on a text.

The second section of each chapter, **Theological Reflection On The Lessons**, probes the lections for theological themes. We need to ask, "What message about the nature of God relates to the needs of the people? What universal theological principles might we deduce from the lessons?" This provides the bridge from the original context to the contemporary context.

A third section, **Sermon Approaches With Illustrations**, builds on the previous two parts. At this stage, we find a compelling twist for one of the theological themes. We begin with a sermon title that grabs the imagination and sparks interest in the sermon. The **Sermon Angle** comes next for the purpose of briefly explicating the theological theme. The scripture texts are like jewels with many facets. When pondered from various angles, we see differing aspects of the same reality. Outlines further develop the central idea.

Methodology

I don't believe that there is only one right way to preach. Some preachers were taught to develop a three point sermon. Others contend that the sermon should be a development of one major point. Still others insist that expository preaching is the only way to go. Some homilists plan out their sermons months in advance, while many others compose their sermons the week prior to delivery. Multiple styles of preaching can be highly effective when the preacher knows and loves his or her congregation, knows and loves the Lord, is a person of prayer, is a keen observer of human affairs, and is a student of the scriptures who works hard at his calling. Most of my preaching career, I preached from an extended outline, thoroughly thinking through the introduction, conclusion, and major transition points. This served me quite well but when I purchased a computer and started writing my sermons out in manuscript form, I felt that my preaching improved because the whole effort was thoroughly thought out. In so doing, I was kept from redundancy and was able to make the language of the sermon more vivid and visual. Every sermon should be packed with similes, metaphors, and images that make speech pictorial. Two or three short stories or illustrative anecdotes are a must. Contemporary observations from newspapers, magazines, movies, books, and everyday life work best. A good preacher is a keen observer of life, who is able to discern the hand of God in human history. A word of warning: Though it is good to write out your sermons, a preacher should never read a sermon. I find that I must thoroughly familiarize myself with my sermons, so that I can interact with my people during its delivery.

There are only a few instances in this book when I suggest that the preacher might tie together two or more readings for the same sermon. While it may be relevant to show how the gospel theme is also found in the Old Testament, for instance, it is best to concentrate on one text and probe deep therein.

Martin Luther always contended that every sermon should contain law and gospel. The law makes us despair in our human goodness so that we might be more ready to embrace the gospel of new life in Christ. This principle remains relevant, but I believe that we need to go light on the law and heavy on the gospel. Many of the people in our pews are already racked with guilt. They come to church for some hope, some good news. The good news goes beyond the wonderful truth that we are saved by grace through faith to embrace the deeper truth that our lives can be changed, transformed through the gospel. Through the power of the Spirit, we can gain victory over our failures, compulsions, addictions, and especially our sins. However, the power of the gospel to transform must not end with us; Christ would have us challenge the church to let the Spirit use us as agents of renewal and redemption.

Why Lectionary Preaching?

There are many good reasons for lectionary preaching. Here are a few of them.

1. It keeps us in continuity with a tradition of the church that dates back centuries.
2. It prevents the preacher from getting on his or her hobbyhorse and serves to enable him or her to plumb all the mysteries of faith.
3. We are united with sister churches by meditating on essentially the same scriptures.
4. The liturgical calendar, upon which the lectionary derives, helps us remember that all time is sacred and that life is a journey from birth through death to resurrection.
5. We are forced to grow as we struggle with difficult passages.
6. It helps us see how the gospel grows out of the Old Testament tradition and gives us a greater appreciation of our Jewish roots. The first lesson and the gospel usually correlate, while the second lesson, which takes the form of semi-continuous reading from a book of the Bible, often stands alone.

The Church Year Calendar

The Christmas Cycle

Advent	**Color**
Advent 1	purple or blue
Advent 2	purple or blue
Advent 3	purple or blue
Advent 4	purple or blue

Christmas	
Christmas Eve	white
Christmas Day	white
Christmas 1	white
Christmas 2	white

Epiphany	
The Epiphany Of Our Lord	white
The Baptism Of Our Lord/Epiphany 1/Ordinary Time 1	white
Epiphany 2/Ordinary Time 2	green
Epiphany 3/Ordinary Time 3	green
Epiphany 4/Ordinary Time 4	green
Epiphany 5/Ordinary Time 5	green
Epiphany 6/Ordinary Time 6	green
Epiphany 7/Ordinary Time 7	green
The Transfiguration Of Our Lord (Last Sunday After Epiphany)	white

The Easter Cycle

Lent	
Ash Wednesday	black or purple
Lent 1	purple
Lent 2	purple
Lent 3	purple
Lent 4	purple
Lent 5	purple
Passion/Palm Sunday	scarlet or purple
Maundy Thursday	scarlet or white
Good Friday	black or no paraments
Holy Saturday	white

Easter	
Easter Vigil	white or gold
Easter Day	white or gold
Easter 2	white
Easter 3	white
Easter 4	white

Easter 5			white
Easter 6			white
The Ascension Of Our Lord			white
Easter 7			white
The Day Of Pentecost			red

The Pentecost Cycle

The Season After Pentecost

Revised Common / Episcopal	Lutheran (Other than ELCA)	Roman Catholic	Color
The Holy Trinity	The Holy Trinity	The Holy Trinity	white
		Corpus Christi	green
Proper 4	Pentecost 2	Ordinary Time 9	green
Proper 5	Pentecost 3	Ordinary Time 10	green
Proper 6	Pentecost 4	Ordinary Time 11	green
Proper 7	Pentecost 5	Ordinary Time 12	green
Proper 8	Pentecost 6	Ordinary Time 13	green
Proper 9	Pentecost 7	Ordinary Time 14	green
Proper 10	Pentecost 8	Ordinary Time 15	green
Proper 11	Pentecost 9	Ordinary Time 16	green
Proper 12	Pentecost 10	Ordinary Time 17	green
Proper 13	Pentecost 11	Ordinary Time 18	green
Proper 14	Pentecost 12	Ordinary Time 19	green
Proper 15	Pentecost 13	Ordinary Time 20	green
Proper 16	Pentecost 14	Ordinary Time 21	green
Proper 17	Pentecost 15	Ordinary Time 22	green
Proper 18	Pentecost 16	Ordinary Time 23	green
Proper 19	Pentecost 17	Ordinary Time 24	green
Proper 20	Pentecost 18	Ordinary Time 25	green
Proper 21	Pentecost 19	Ordinary Time 26	green
Proper 22	Pentecost 20	Ordinary Time 27	green
Proper 23	Pentecost 21	Ordinary Time 28	green
Proper 24	Pentecost 22	Ordinary Time 29	green
Proper 25	Pentecost 23	Ordinary Time 30	green
Proper 26	Pentecost 24	Ordinary Time 31	green
Proper 27	Pentecost 25	Ordinary Time 32	green
Proper 28	Pentecost 26	Ordinary Time 33	green
	Pentecost 27		green
	Reformation Sunday		red
All Saints	All Saints	All Saints	white
Christ The King	Christ The King	Christ The King	white
Thanksgiving Day, USA			white

Preaching From The Gospel Of Matthew

Cycle A of the three-year lectionary features Matthew's gospel.

Background Of Matthew

Biblical scholars hold that Mark is the precursor of the gospels of Matthew and Luke. Of the 661 verses contained in Mark's gospel, 606 of them are found in Matthew. Tradition ascribes the book to Jesus' disciple, Matthew, the tax collector. Textual studies reveal that it is more likely that it was written by a second or third generation Christian, composed in the region of Antioch in Syria around 85 to 90 AD.

Theological Threads Contained In Matthew

1. *Jesus as the Messiah* foretold in the Old Testament. Matthew quotes copiously from the Old Testament, particularly Isaiah, to show that Jesus is the fulfillment of the Jewish hopes for a Son of David, an anointed one. This gospel writer opens with a genealogy to prove that Jesus is a descendant of King David. Nevertheless, the Gospel is not unconcerned about the Gentiles, as evidenced by the Great Commission contained in Matthew 28.

2. *Jesus as teacher.* Mark records for us what Jesus did; Matthew informs us about what he taught. The Sermon on the Mount (Matthew 5-7) provides the most complete rendering of Jesus' teachings. In addition, Matthew contains five more chapters of Jesus' parables and teachings. Jesus is seen as a new Moses and the Beatitudes are a kind of counterpart to the Ten Commandments.

3. *A strong interest in the apocalyptic.* Matthew has more than the other gospels concerning judgment, the second coming of Christ, and the like. Matthew alone has the parables of the talents, the wise and foolish maidens, and the sheep and the goats, all contained in chapter 25.

4. *A gospel for the church.* Matthew's gospel alone contains the word "church" *(ekklesia).* Peter's confession at Caesarea Philippi that Jesus was the Messiah (Matthew 16:13-23) serves as the foundation of the church. Only this gospel contains instructions for settling disputes in the church (Matthew 18:17).

5. *The kingdom of God.* From beginning to end, Matthew paints Jesus in royal purple. At the beginning of the book, the wise men come seeking the one who is to be born the king of the Jews. In the closing chapter, the risen and exalted Christ, receiving all authority from the Father, commands his disciples to "go and make disciples of all nations." For Matthew, Christ's preaching, teaching, and healing demonstrate his kingly authority.

Brief Background On The Gospel Of Matthew

The Popularity Of Matthew's Gospel

The book of Matthew supplies the bulk of the gospel lessons for Cycle A — 47 out of 52 Sundays. From the beginning, the church has heavily relied on Matthew's interpretation of the gospel. Why? It is very complete, containing an infancy narrative, large blocks of Jesus' teachings, and an expanded section of the resurrection. Its style made it popular in public worship — clear, pithy, and well written. Its structure, with blocks of teaching and narrative material interspersed, lent it to public instruction. Unlike Mark's gospel, Matthew's gospel does not raise questions in the reader's mind, such as: Does Jesus' baptism by John indicate that he needed repentance?

Date And Authorship

Since the gospels of Matthew and Luke employ large amounts of material found in Mark's gospel, which scholars believe to be written about 65 AD, it is thought that they were both written between 80-90 AD. The book of Matthew reflects a period when the church had begun to institutionalize.

While Papias in 150 AD attributes this gospel to the apostle Matthew, modern scholars consign the book to a second or third generation Christian.

The Structure Of The Book

Matthew prominently portrays Jesus as a teacher and the gospel as something of a new law. This emphasis is visible in the structure of the gospel itself. Historical narratives of the life and ministry of Jesus are interspersed with five major teaching discourses by the Lord.

Theological Emphasis Of The Author

A chief concern is Matthew's Christology. Matthew presents Jesus as the Messiah, promised by the prophets of the Old Testament. He is the fulfillment of the hopes of the Jewish people for a Messiah. In this capacity, Christ ushers in the kingdom of heaven, a theme that pervades the entire book. As Messiah, Christ is preeminently the teacher of a new righteousness that interprets the scriptures in a fresh and authoritative fashion. Yet, Christ came not to abrogate but to fulfill the law of God.

Matthew has a good deal of interest in the ethical implications of the Christian faith. He attempts to deal with the tension between the uncompromising demands of Jesus, on the one hand, and human sinfulness on the other. He seems to draw a distinction between being accepted and being perfect (complete), as in the case of the rich young man (Matthew 19:10-12).

Matthew is keenly interested in ecclesiastical matters and seems to almost equate the kingdom with the church. He holds high the authority of the apostle Peter — one reason his gospel is highly regarded in the Roman Catholic tradition.

This is a missionary gospel. Matthew concludes his gospel with the Great Commission, which reflects his keen interest in promulgating the gospel to the nations.

The Advent Season

The Genesis Of Advent

Since the ninth century in the western church, the season of Advent has been commemorated as a period of preparation for the birth of our Lord and the beginning of the ecclesiastical year. It begins on the Sunday closest to the Feast of Saint Andrew (November 30).

In the early church the words "Advent, Epiphany, and Nativity" were employed interchangeably to denote the feast of the Nativity. Advent liturgies first appear in the sixth century in the church of Gaul. Epiphany was observed as a baptismal festival and the period preceding it was utilized as a period of preparation for baptism, much like the season of Lent. Consequently, Advent originated as a type of little Lent. From France the observance spread to England in the seventh and eighth centuries. In the ninth century, Advent was finally incorporated into the Roman rite.

The Meaning Of Advent

The word "Advent" means literally, "to come to." It is a special season when we celebrate the bold assertion that the Lord of the universe has come among us in human form through Jesus of Nazareth. In Jesus, the Christ, we have Immanuel, God with us. Not only do we celebrate that God has come (past tense) to the world in the Man from Galilee but also that God is come (present tense) as a spiritual reality and will come again (future tense) in triumph at the consummation of the ages. Because of the reality to which Advent points, we are not frightened children locked in an indifferent universe. God has, is, and will come to us in Jesus, the Christ.

There is another sense to the definition of Advent, "to come to." Since God has, is, and will come to us, therefore, *we need to come to*. Our task is to become fully awake not only to the significance of the incarnation but also to the many incarnations of Christ in our lives. The apostle Paul expresses this thought well: "It is time for us to awake from sleep. For salvation is nearer to us now than when we became believers" (Romans 13:11). None of us is fully conscious of God's presence; we need to come to, to wake up, and be vigilant for the visitations of God within history and at the end of time when the kingdom is fully realized.

The Mood Of Advent

If God is coming to us and we truly believe that to be true, our mood will be one of excitement, anticipation, and joyful preparation. There is a prominent penitential theme in the lessons, but it ought not make our observance of the season a somber affair. As Christmas draws nearer, most people are picking up on the excitement and joy all about them. When they come to church, they do not want a wet blanket thrown on them but a message of hope and salvation. This good news should be reflected in bright banners, lively liturgy, and a positive gospel message. This is particularly the case during the last two Sundays of the season. The third Sunday of Advent has traditionally been dubbed "Rejoice Sunday," when many congregations have their cantatas and the candle on the Advent wreath is rose colored. This mood is conveyed also through color and light. As the awareness of the celebrative nature of Advent has grown, many congregations have substituted blue for the traditional purple. The brighter blue, the color of the infinite sky, conveys better the bright hope of eternal life in Christ than the more somber purple.

The Message Of Advent

As preachers, our job is to proclaim that God is come to this sin-sick world as Savior and Lord. The Old Testament prophecies are prominent in the season of Advent and so we will want to show how Jesus is the surprising fulfillment of their promises. Going the other direction, we need to hold up the hope of Christ's second advent, the *parousia*. Nevertheless, as those who struggle to find meaning in the interim between the two advents, our most urgent task is to hold up the present reality of Christ's advent. It is fine to celebrate the birth of the Babe of Bethlehem but that incarnation has significance only as it brings to light the God who continues to come to us and for us. As those who speak God's word, we will need to flesh out how Christ comes to humankind now and how we can receive and carry Christ's presence today. We will succeed if we can get our people to come to a new consciousness of the reality of Christ in their life and in the world. To that end, the faithful preacher will hold up for the people certain Advent attitudes found in the Bible — alertness, attentiveness, watchfulness, readiness, joyful anticipation, patience, and receptivity. Our task is to help our people come to full consciousness of the God who comes to us in Jesus Christ and to be a people prepared.

Thematic Framework For Advent

Seasons such as Advent lend themselves to a thematic sermon series. This gives the congregation a handle for receiving and remembering the messages. The suggested title for this Advent sermon series is: **The Advent Attitudes**. Attitude here means more than a mental mindset; attitudes are revealed in behavior. To receive the God who comes to us in Christ we will need to display the following attitudes:

Advent 1 — "The Attitude of Readiness"
Text: "Therefore, you also must be ready ..." (Matthew 24:44).
Advent 2 — "The Attitude of Repentance"
Text: "Repent, for the kingdom of heaven is at hand" (Matthew 3:2).
Advent 3 — "The Attitude of Patience"
Text: "Be patient, therefore, until the coming of the Lord" (James 5:7).
Advent 4 — "The Attitude of Obedience"
Text: "When Joseph woke from sleep, he did as the angel of the Lord commanded him ..." (Matthew 1:24).

Suggested Text For Preaching

This designation is for the benefit of those who want to implement the above outlined thematic emphasis for Advent. If you do not choose to go this route, disregard this designation.

Advent 1

Revised Common:	Isaiah 2:1-5	Romans 13:11-14	Matthew 24:36-44
Roman Catholic:	Isaiah 2:1-5	Romans 13:11-14	Matthew 24:37-44
Episcopal:	Isaiah 2:1-5	Romans 13:8-14	Matthew 24:37-44

Advent Theme: Advent Attitudes

Theme For The Day: The Attitude Of Readiness

Suggested Sermon Text: Matthew 24:37-44

BRIEF COMMENTARY ON THE LESSONS

Lesson 1: Isaiah 2:1-5 (C, RC, E)

Though this passage may have been written by Isaiah, it appears to be out of context. It seems to better reflect the theology and mood of second or third Isaiah. Isaiah 1 is an indictment concerning the sinfulness of the people. The verses following our pericope pick up the theme of judgment. However, our text is a triumphant vision of the distant future when the temple in Jerusalem would be the focal point for universal peace, knowledge, and righteousness. The passage is found also in Micah 4:1-3.

Lesson 2: Romans 13:11-14 (C, RC); Romans 13:8-14 (E)

This text appears in the context of a block of Paul's ethical teachings (Romans 12:1— 15:13) and directly follows a discussion showing how love is lived out in various relationships. Immediately preceding our text, Paul states that love is the fulfilling of the law. However, in our text the ethical imperative receives added emphasis from eschatology. Using the image of day and night, light and darkness, Paul reminds his readers that the *parousia* is imminent. Therefore, believers should strip off the filthy works of darkness — such as drunkenness, debauchery, quarreling, and jealousy — and put on the Lord Jesus Christ. If we are so attired, we will be ready for Christ's second advent, whenever that may occur.

Gospel: Matthew 24:36-44 (C); Matthew 24:37-44 (RC, E)

Our text appears within a block of eschatological material (Matthew 24:1—26:2) which contains several passages on spiritual preparedness. This gospel is straightforward. The disciple is to be ready at all times for the end of the age. The Son of Man will come suddenly and unexpectedly, like a thief in the night, so be ready at all times! Not even the Son of Man is cognizant of that day.

Psalm Of The Day

Psalm 122 (C, E) — This song of ascent expresses a note of joy at the prospect of worshiping God at the temple. "I was glad when they said to me, let us go to the house of the Lord!" (v. 1). This verse would function well as a call to worship. Psalm 122 is also a prayer that Jerusalem would live up to her name and truly be a city of peace.

Prayer Of The Day

Shake us awake, O God, from the lethargy brought on by our sins that we might truly be a people prepared to receive you at your coming. In Jesus' name. Amen.

THEOLOGICAL REFLECTION ON THE LESSONS

Lesson 1: Isaiah 2:1-5

In front of the United Nations building in New York City there is a sculpture of a muscular man beating a sword into a plow point, with an inscription below it from the appropriate portion of Isaiah 2:4, "... they shall beat their swords into plowshares...." The United Nations is a secular embodiment of the vision God gave to Isaiah. The United Nations and its antecedent, the League of Nations, were formed with high hopes that they would provide a forum for nations to work out their differences in a rational manner and usher in the vaunted day of world peace. The usefulness of the United Nations cannot be argued, but we are still light years away from the new world where humanity lives in harmony.

While the vision of Isaiah and of the framers of the United Nations is similar, the source of the vision is radically different. Those who put their faith in the United Nations as the means to the peaceable kingdom are in reality placing their trust in human rationality and good will. Such faith will meet with constant disappointment because it has largely underestimated the depths of human selfishness. In contrast, for Isaiah and for people of faith, the peaceable kingdom is an act of God which will be brought into existence in God's good time. The kingdom which Isaiah dimly sighted is not politically achievable apart from all people submitting to the lordship of the Prince of Peace.

Isaiah's vision of peace is inextricably tied to the concept of God as Judge. "He shall judge between the nations" (Isaiah 2:4a). There is a lesson for us here. Conflict results when we insist on judging things from our narrow perspective, but peace and harmony flow from God's penetrating point of view.

Lesson 2: Romans 13:8-14

Paul's images of light/darkness and night/day must be viewed against the backdrop of the expectation of Christ's imminent second return. God's new day was about to dawn, revealing all the sordid works of darkness. Spiritually, it remained night but there was still time to prepare for the dawn glinting on the horizon. There was still time to rip off those dirty rags of selfishness and put on the robe of righteousness. In Paul's thinking, sin was associated with the darkness and righteousness with the light of day. Then as now, sleep took place at night and the daylight was embraced with wakefulness. It was time to wake up, cast off the works of darkness (some of which Paul names in v. 12), and put on the Lord Jesus Christ.

Gospel: Matthew 24:36-44

As children we would engage in a game of hide and seek. The person designated as "it" would close his eyes, turn his face, and after counting to ten would cry out: "Ready or not, here I come." That is the message of the gospel lesson and of Advent. Christ is "it" but there is no place we can hide from him; ready or not he's coming for us. Are we ready?

"As were the days of Noah ... so shall be the coming of the Son of Man...." There won't be any signs, any warnings. No leaflets will drop from heaven warning of impending crisis. When the rain starts it will be too late to build an ark or even to get aboard someone else's. No, we had better locate our ark long before the deluge drops. The name of the game is perpetual readiness, a life of faithfulness. The same point is made with the example of the thief in the night; the thief's key tool is the element of surprise. Christ is coming; the kingdom is ready. Ready or not.

PREACHING APPROACHES WITH ILLUSTRATIONS

Alternative Advent Series

If you do not want to adopt the thematic framework suggested in the introduction to the Advent Season, here is another sermon series based on the Old Testament lessons for the four Sundays in Advent. The sermon series is titled: **Advent Actions**.

Advent 1 — "Go To The House Of The Lord"
   Text: "Come, let us go up ... to the house of the God of Jacob" (Isaiah 2:3b).
Advent 2 — "Share The Peace Of The Lord"
   Text: The wolf shall live with the lamb (Isaiah 11:6-9).
Advent 3 — "Receive The Salvation Of The Lord"
   Text: "He will come and save you" (Isaiah 35:4b).
Advent 4 — "See The Sign Of God's Son"
   Text: "Therefore the Lord himself will give you a sign" (Isaiah 7:14).

Lesson 1: Isaiah 2:1-5

Sermon Title: The Value Of Public Worship

Sermon Angle: Verse 3 invites the hearer to go up to the mountain of the Lord, the house of the God of Jacob (v. 3). In our era of individualistic spirituality, we need to hear and heed this reminder to engage in public worship. Such worship not only ascribes worth to God but is of real value to the worshiper, too. Your sermon could lift three points from the text which presents cogent reasons why every believer should approach the throne of God's grace in communal worship.

Outline:
Introduction: Come, let us go up to the house of the Lord.
1. So that God may teach us his ways (v. 3)
2. That we might walk in his paths (v. 3)
3. That we might live in peace (v. 4)

Sermon Title: Swords Into Plowshares — Conversion

Sermon Angle: Isaiah speaks of a wonderful thing. He speaks not merely of a time when humankind will abandon the horrible weapons of war. No, he dares to suggest that, under the reign of God, nations will convert the weapons of annihilation into the implements that bring life to the world. That same thing happened when Christ converted the cross from an ugly instrument of execution into the foremost sign of forgiveness, reconciliation, and salvation. Likewise, through the power of the cross God transforms enemies into friends, sinners into saints.

17

Lesson 2: Romans 13:8-14

Sermon Title: Do You Know The Time?

Sermon Angle: Do you know what time it is? Christ's second return is the expected *kairos* that gives us a new perspective on time.

Outline:
1. It's later than you think (v. 12)
2. It's time to wake from sleep (v. 11)
3. It's time to put off our sins and put on Christ (vv. 12-14)

Gospel: Matthew 24:36-33

Sermon Title: The Attitude Of Readiness

Sermon Angle: Noah was ready when the Lord acted but the others were not. Christians need to be ready not only for the second coming of Christ but also for the Lord's ongoing visitations.

Outline:
1. The value of readiness — you can seize the moment
2. The consequence of ill readiness — disaster strikes
3. Be ready for Jesus' coming into everyday existence
4. Be ready for Jesus' coming at the end of time

* * * * *

At the time of this writing, the tornado season has commenced. Several communities have been devastated by the devil twisters. Nothing can stop them, but if you know they are heading your way you can, at least, save your life, together with those you love. Several people have lost their lives because they weren't prepared. Tornados can be tracked on Doppler radar. If warning is issued, heard, and heeded, it can save life. If our ears are tuned to God's warnings, we won't be blotted out by the moral disasters that swoop down on the unsuspecting. Of course, we need to be ready not only to avert the whirlwinds of judgment but to inspire the life-giving gusts from the Spirit of God.

* * * * *

In August 1993, hundreds of thousands of young people gathered at the Roman Catholic youth festival in Denver, Colorado. The big draw was Pope John Paul. One priest from Omaha, in charge of a busload of kids, was left behind. He directed a bunch of the youth to go to the bus, while he searched for the rest of his group. The missing teens found their way to the bus but when the youths' shepherd arrived at the place of departure the bus had already pulled out. Not only evil things but even good pursuits can prevent us from our appointed meeting with the Lord. If you're not ready, for whatever reason, you get left behind. That's the point of the gospel lesson. Christ is coming to take home all who belong to him; be prepared and ready to go.

* * * * *

The author of an article in the *U.S. Catholic* magazine tells of the time when he was not ready for the opportunity of a lifetime. Like many young men, he dreamed of playing baseball in the big leagues but never really thought the opportunity would come his way. Suddenly, it materialized as he was scanning the want ads for a summer job. The Toronto Blue Jays were having tryouts in his hometown. His baseball cleats were rusty and his pony league uniform was layered with dust but he decided to go for it! Why not? After arriving at the try-out site his anxieties soared. He even imagined that he heard some of them sharpening their spikes. "How long ya been practicing for this?" one hopeful asked another. " 'Bout six months. Wished I started sooner," he moaned. Our would-be big leaguer had already struck out. He knew it and it was too late to do anything about it.

People who have their minds set on playing baseball know the importance of readiness. When the opportune pitch comes over their home plate, they are ready to swing for all they're worth. They won't always connect but they are prepared to play the game with gusto. It is the same attitude of readiness that is required of all who would follow Christ. Our spiritual senses must be honed and ready when Christ comes where we live.

*   *   *   *   *

Is it possible to be pregnant and not know it? Apparently it is, if written accounts are to be believed. In one account, an obese woman was experiencing abdominal pain and was taken to the hospital where they discovered she was in the process of giving birth. It blows one's mind to think that a new life could be forming inside a woman and yet she would not be cognizant of it. Does this come about because layers of fat disguise the pregnancy and insulate the mother from the quickening of the infant within? This explanation seems likely, since most of the women that this has happened to were definitely overweight. Whatever the cause, these women probably felt cheated. You see, they didn't have time to get ready for this great event. There was no opportunity to buy clothing and furniture for the baby, because it was not anticipated. There was no chance for the mother's or the father's friends and family to share in the joy and expectation, the waiting and the watching for the precious gift of a new life from God. Most importantly, there was no time for the parents to prepare themselves emotionally and spiritually to properly receive their surprise package.

Many denominations teach that the Spirit of Christ has been conceived in our hearts through baptism. Yet millions of so-called Christians seem to have no awareness of the Christ who dwells so near. Could it be that we are insulated from his heartbeat by spiritual obesity and lethargy? Do our jobs, our families, our amusements, and even our holiday preparations, keep Christ concealed? One day it will be revealed that Christ was within us. How shamed and disappointed we will be if we are caught off guard and unprepared. Pregnancy ought to be a time of active waiting, watching, and anticipating, leading to joyful fulfillment, but so should Advent. The world was not ready for the birth of Jesus. Are we any better prepared now? We need to pay heed to the quickening of Christ within so that we are ready for his appearing.

*   *   *   *   *

Life is designed to flow along at a reasonable pace so that we have time to take in our surroundings. We might compare the flow of existence to one of those people movers which are seen in airports and other places where it is necessary to transport large volumes of people. You know what I mean: it's like an elevator that doesn't go up, just carries us along. Have you ever noticed how quite a number of people are not content with the speed at which this conveyance is moving them along? It's as if the track beneath them is the course for the Grand Prix and they're a super-charged BMW determined to win the race. There may be legitimate reasons for them to race their engines (such as the need to make a connecting flight) but for many it is a way of life.

Such revving of our engines is a common practice for many of us during the Advent/Christmas season. Christmas is seen as a kind of finish line and to get there in time one has to make all the required laps in record time. The gifts, parties, cards, and other activities are the laps. The result of this mind-set is that the peace of God is vanquished from our soul, God's gift of grace is left unwrapped, and we become wound so tightly that we are in danger of breaking. The object of our celebration is not to pass others so that we can get to Christmas in record time but to permit Christmas to get to us in God's good time. We cannot make ourselves ready for Christ or Christmas. God makes us ready as we look to him to carry us along.

Advent 2

Revised Common:	**Isaiah 11:1-10**	**Romans 15:4-13**	**Matthew 3:1-12**
Roman Catholic:	**Isaiah 11:1-10**	**Romans 15:4-9**	**Matthew 3:1-12**
Episcopal:	**Isaiah 11:1-10**	**Romans 15:4-13**	**Matthew 3:1-12**

Seasonal Theme: Advent Attitudes

Theme For The Day: The Attitude Of Repentance

Suggested Text For Preaching: Matthew 3:1-12

BRIEF COMMENTARY ON THE LESSONS

Lesson 1: Isaiah 11:1-10 (C, RC, E)

This text is related to Isaiah 9:1-6. "The people who have walked in darkness have seen a great light" (Isaiah 9:2a). In their original context, both passages are believed to be coronation Psalms for God's Anointed One, the king. It is possible that Isaiah composed today's lesson for the coronation of King Hezekiah. Though a king was held to be a direct link between the people and their God, the prophet realized that the righteous rule envisioned in this passage was beyond the range of human possibility and would be accomplished only through the gift of God's Spirit. Though Isaiah spoke to a particular situation, the prophetic messages he uttered transcend that time and place. From the beginning of the Christian church, believers have viewed such messianic passages in the light of Christ's lordship.

Lesson 2: Romans 15:4-13 (C, E); Romans 15:4-9 (RC)

In these verses Paul is bringing the ethical section of his epistle to a close. He begins this section by making an appeal to an expansive interpretation of scripture, which he viewed as a living book, speaking to each succeeding generation. He appears to go even further by stating: "For whatever was written in former days was written for our instruction ..." (v. 4a). In so doing, Paul makes clear that the sacred writings are not just for the Jews but for all believers. He is also suggesting here that scripture leads us to Jesus Christ and that he is the interpretive key. However, this is not a theoretical discussion of hermeneutical principles. Paul's purpose is to provide hope and encouragement for present and future challenges. The story of God's salvation in former times provides the needed sense of continuity, hope, and endurance which the church sorely needs. In keeping with this communal image, Paul appeals for unity in witness and worship.

Gospel: Matthew 3:1-12 (C, RC, E)

In the wilderness John the Baptist heralds the approach of the kingdom of heaven and the necessary attitude of repentance required to receive it. The word *kerusso*, translated "proclaiming" in the NRSV, means to herald, as would a public crier shouting out some momentous news on the public thoroughfares. Contrary to the method of our Lord, John did not go to the people; they flocked to him to receive instruction for spiritual renewal and be baptized as a sign of their repentance. The crowds indicate that there was a spiritual uneasiness and a readiness to change.

The gospel writer viewed John as the Elijah figure who was expected to precede the Messiah and as the fulfillment of Isaiah 40:3. John views his role as preparatory and points beyond himself to the one who would baptize with the Holy Spirit and fire.

Psalm Of The Day

Psalm 72 (C, E) — A prayer for the king that he might rule in justice and compassion, assuring peace and prosperity for the people.

Prayer Of The Day

Compassionate Christ, by following crooked paths we have become lost in a maze of our own making. We confess our lostness and implore the help of your Holy Spirit in following the way that is straight and narrow and which leads to your kingdom, through Christ our Lord. Amen.

THEOLOGICAL REFLECTION ON THE LESSONS

Lesson 1: Isaiah 11:1-10

Roots and shoots. The nation of Israel confronted perilous times. The foe threatened to hack down their whole way of life. The problems seemed overwhelming for the leaders. In this predicament the prophet held up the promise of new life for the nation. God would send a leader after the likeness of King David, full of the wisdom and knowledge of the Lord. "A shoot shall come out from the stump of Jesse, and a branch shall grow out of his roots" (v. 1). God is Lord of the living and he will cause new life to spring from the stump of the old. The life is in the roots and so life may linger even though the branches wither. Roots and new shoots are needed in every age. Roots speak of who we are and where we have come from, but new shoots point to what we can become. Roots give stability, but shoots provide freshness and hope. At a time of grave uncertainty, the prophet reminded the people of their roots that would eventually produce new shoots, by the power of God.

The Christian tradition proclaims that Christ is the shoot from the stump of Jesse that reconciles us with God and will one day bring harmony to all creation.

Lesson 2: Romans 15:4-13

Harmony and hospitality. The apostle Paul makes an appeal for harmony in the church (vv. 5-6). Why? Because harmony is the outward sign that God's peaceable kingdom is reality. Divisiveness in the church mocks the gospel of peace. Paul appeals to the Romans to glorify God as with one voice. The plea here is not for uniformity (that would be monotony) but rather harmony, the intentional blending of our voices. For a quartet to sing harmony there must be four unique voices with different pitch and timbre uniting in melodious song.

Not only does the apostle appeal for harmony but also for hospitality (v. 7). Harmony speaks of our relationships with those outside the fold, with those who are strangers. Of late, we have heard a great deal about how our worship services need to provide hospitality to the stranger. In the apostolic era, most Christians were acutely aware of the needs of the stranger, having recently been strangers themselves. In many congregations today, the members have belonged for generations and have lost touch with the needs of those outside the walls of the church. Harmony and hospitality are attitudes found in any living church.

Gospel: Matthew 3:1-12

The desert experience. The gospel writer pegs John's ministry in the Judean wilderness; the significance is more than geographical. In semitic thought, the wilderness is a hostile and ominous place. It is the haunt of hunger, thirst, death, outlaws, and demons. It is home for dangerous creatures — scorpions and snakes. The wilderness was considered an area of primal chaos or as cursed by God. John the Baptist went into this dark region to do battle with the force of evil, on his own turf. Jesus did the same thing after his baptism by John. Where is the wilderness today? Where is the primary arena where we have it out with Satan? I doubt whether many of us would choose the wilderness, even a desert place. No, we would probably not identify an uninhabited place as wilderness, spiritually speaking, but rather places teeming with people. Most of our cities have areas of primal chaos and lawlessness. Cities are not evil any more than rural areas are necessarily righteous. It's people who can turn any environment into a wilderness — people who rebel against their maker and have no regard for others. In the last analysis, wilderness is a spiritual state — not a geographical area.

If wilderness is a state of chaos — without sign, pathway, or marker — the spiritual challenge is to find a way out of the wilderness. John offered a baptism signifying repentance as the highway whereby God can enter our lives, as the way out of the wilderness. Unfortunately, repentance alone won't get us out of the wilderness. We need the healing power of the gospel of Christ.

PREACHING APPROACHES WITH ILLUSTRATIONS

Lesson 1: Isaiah 11:1-10

Sermon Title: Roots And Shoots (v. 1)

Sermon Angle: Isaiah promised a shoot from the root of Jesse. Roots and shoots are necessary and interdependent. We need *roots* to know who we are by understanding where we come from. We also need *shoots*. In faithfulness to our heritage, we must branch out in new directions and express our being in creative ways that address today's needs and issues. This is true both personally and corporately as the body of Christ. Here is one possible approach.

1. The importance of our individual roots
2. The importance of our spiritual roots
3. The necessity of new shoots — personal and corporate
4. Examples of roots and shoots we need to nourish

*   *   *   *   *

Years ago we owned a cottage on Saddle Lake in southwest Michigan. Nearby was low land, thickly inhabited by trees. On occasion we would have terrific storms that would blow in off Lake Michigan and topple some of these trees. It seemed strange that such tall and stately trees could not weather the storms more effectively. Looking more closely, I noticed that the root system was wide but not deep. A foot or two beneath the surface was water, which the roots could not penetrate. Until the day of destruction, the trees looked perfectly healthy. They had plenty of limbs and branches, but the roots were too shallow to anchor them for life. How deeply are we rooted in God's love and holy word? Are they deep enough to provide an eternal anchor?

Lesson 2: Romans 15:4-13

Sermon Title: Harmony And Hospitality

Sermon Angle: Paul was very cognizant that our Christian faith is not merely judged on the merits of our beliefs but on the manner of our relationships to others. We are known by the fruit of our lives. Two of those fruits are harmony and hospitality. A sermon on this subject could be developed as follows:

1. Begin by citing an example of how a group of people have worked together harmoniously
2. Admit that harmony is often destroyed by the discord of sin
3. Show how harmony stems from our relationship with Christ
4. Demonstrate how harmony is a powerful witness to the world
5. Make an appeal to go beyond harmony to hospitality so that the stranger might know the love and peace of God

Gospel: Matthew 3:1-12

Sermon Title: The Attitude Of Repentance

Sermon Angle: Though Advent is a joyous season of preparation, there is also a distinct penitential aspect. John the Baptist, who is a prominent figure in this season, identified his ministry as that of preparing his people through repentance for the coming of the Messiah. Admittedly, John's vision of the messianic role was different than that of Jesus; his emphasis had more to do with judgment than grace. Nevertheless, his proclamation of repentance is the necessary prerequisite for life in the kingdom of God. The repentance that John the Baptist proclaims is not merely a formal act, it is an attitude, a way of living that bears fruit (v. 8).

Outline:

Introduction: Start with the story that follows this outline from Dr. Karl Menninger's book, *Whatever Became of Sin.* Make the point that nobody seems to take sin or repentance seriously anymore. Why do we need to repent?

1. Because the kingdom of God is near (v. 2). Point out that we are not only speaking about the kingdom beyond history but the kingdom of God within history.
2. To enable God to enter our lives — God cannot enter if sin is in control (v. 2)
3. So that our lives might be fruitful — Fruitfulness follows repentance (vv. 7-10)
4. So that we might escape God's judgment (vv. 11-12) (God does not desire any to be lost)

Conclusion: End with an affirmation of the positive effects of an attitude of repentance.

* * * * *

In the book, *Whatever Became of Sin*, Dr. Karl Menninger tells of a man who would position himself on a busy street corner in the Chicago Loop and, as workers would scurry to their jobs or to lunch or speed to get in a bit of shopping, the man would solemnly lift his right hand and pointing to the person nearest to him intone loudly but distinctly the solitary word, "Guilty!"

Maintaining the same expression he would resume his former pose for a few moments. Then, as if he were responding to some inward voice, there would once again be the mechanical raising of the arms, the pointing, and the pronouncement of the single word, "Guilty!"

The effect of this odd pantomime on those who passed by was interesting. They would pause, stare, and glance at other people around them with a look that spoke, "When did this guy get into the fermented berries?" Then they would skitter off, sometimes glancing back over their shoulders at this peculiar man.

It is not likely that many of those who encountered this street prophet took him seriously, any more seriously than we would take the likes of a John the Baptist living an unconventional lifestyle and pointing the finger of accusation at each of us with the solemn warning, "Repent!"

*   *   *   *   *

In his book, *Den of Lions*, Terry Anderson, the longest held captive of the Islamic fanatics in Beirut, tells of his spiritual turning in the narrow confines of the prison cell. Living intimately with several other men, there was no hiding from himself. Anderson describes this existence as "living in a hall of mirrors." The theme of guilt runs through the narrative and one of the most touching moments is when Anderson, a fallen-away Catholic, confesses his sins to Father Jenco, a fellow prisoner. Anderson confesses that he has wandered away from the church and that he is not a good man. In fact, he concedes that his drinking and pursuing other women are largely to blame for the failure of his marriage. As the confession proceeded, both penitent and priest found spiritual and emotional release through plentiful tears. The room became littered with tear-stained tissues. That marked Anderson's first confession in 25 years and his turning back to the church and a life of faith. Finally, Father Jenco laid his hand on Anderson's head and pronounced absolution: "In the name of a gentle, loving God, you are forgiven." In the crucible of captivity the Holy Spirit had gifted Terry Anderson with an attitude toward life that leads to freedom — the attitude of repentance.

*   *   *   *   *

There is a theme that has been appearing with some regularity the past few years on the editorial pages of our newspapers and in periodicals: the theme is that we've become a nation of victims. Many people try to push off their problems on to others; it's not their fault because they are simply victims. This is not to deny that there are legitimate victims but to make the point that this rationalization has been gravely abused. People are loathe to accept responsibility for their own actions. This is a problem because there is no growth, no change, without honest self-awareness.

Dr. John Brokhoff, who for years was professor of Homiletics at Chandler School of Theology in Atlanta, Georgia, tells how a man responded to an evangelistic sermon by getting up and confessing: "I've been a sinner, a contemptible sinner. And I've been one for years but I never knew it before tonight." A deacon who was standing next to him in the aisle leaned over and whispered to him, "Sit down, brother, the rest of us have known it all the time."

Advent 3

Revised Common:	Isaiah 35:1-10	James 5:7-10	Matthew 11:2-11
Roman Catholic:	Isaiah 35:1-6, 10	James 5:7-10	Matthew 11:2-11
Episcopal:	Isaiah 35:1-10	James 5:7-10	Matthew 11:2-11

Seasonal Theme: Advent Attitudes

Theme For The Day: The Attitude Of Patience

Suggested Text For Preaching: James 5:7-10 (Matthew 11:2-11 also applies)

BRIEF COMMENTARY ON THE LESSONS

Lesson 1: Isaiah 35:1-10 (C, E); Isaiah 35:1-6, 10 (RC)

A message of promise and hope comes to the captive children of Israel. Yahweh is going to free them from their oppression and open a road through the parched desert to the holy city of Jerusalem. The writer (not Isaiah) poetically pictures the entire creation participating in the redemption of God's people as the desert springs to luxuriant life, free of ravenous beasts. In this second exodus from the land of captivity to the promised land, the redeemed leave their disabilities behind as they joyously make their way back home. This blissful vision is meant to make the prisoners strong and full of hope. God is present with his people and will shortly reveal his saving might.

Lesson 2: James 5:7-10 (C, RC, E)

The expectation of the imminent return of Christ is reflected in these verses. James urges the fledgling church to be patient as they watch for that glorious day, citing the examples of the farmer, who plants the precious seed and patiently waits for the rain to raise it to life, and the prophets who uttered the word of the Lord and patiently anticipated its coming to pass.

Gospel: Matthew 11:2-11 (C, RC, E)

Troubling reports concerning the activities of Jesus cause the imprisoned John the Baptist to have second thoughts about his designation of Jesus as the promised Messiah. Apparently, Jesus is not fulfilling the messianic role in the manner that John expected. John believed in fearlessly facing the truth and so he sent some disciples to ask Jesus, "Are you the one who is to come, or are we to wait for another?" (v. 3). Jesus answers these emissaries by pointing to his deeds: "the blind receive their sight, the lame walk, the lepers are cleansed ..." (v. 5). Did not these signs demonstrate that the kingdom was breaking into the world?

After the emissaries depart, Jesus declares that John is the greatest of prophets; he was even more than a prophet, because he was the promised Elijah. Yet, the humblest follower of Jesus is more privileged than John because he has witnessed the grace and mercy of God in the sacrificial servanthood of God's Son (v. 11).

Psalm Of The Day

Psalm 145:7-10 (C); Psalm 146 (E) — Those who put their hope in God are called happy, because God heals the wounded and executes justice for the oppressed.

Prayer Of The Day

Help us, dear Christ, to hear anew the Advent message that the kingdom of God does not come effortlessly, but with patient preparation. Renew the flickering candle of our faith when assailed by the cold winds of doubt and open your eyes to behold the hopeful signs of your reign all around us, that we may rejoice now and forevermore. In Christ's name. Amen.

THEOLOGICAL REFLECTION ON THE LESSONS

Lesson 1: Isaiah 35:1-10

In Isaiah's poem of God's redemption, he pictures the desert blossoming into glorious life. The threat of the desert was never far from the experience of the Israelites. They were forged by God into his people through their forty years wandering into the wilderness. The nearby desert always threatened to encroach on Israel's fertile valleys, dependent on the seasonal rains. The desert described the psyche of the Jewish captives — lifeless, dry, rocky, lonely, and threatening. Isaiah's promise was that God would pour the water of his spirit into their parched souls and they would blossom and grow into a garden of delight (vv. 1-2). This word from God caused buds of hope to spring up in the desert of the captives' soul.

Where is the desert experience for our people today? Is it sickness, old age, loneliness, poverty, or faithlessness? God has provided the way out of the wilderness of our sinful human situation through Jesus, our Lord and Savior. We can travel on our way rejoicing as we tread toward Zion, the city of our God.

Lesson 2: James 5:7-10

James urges the church to be patient because the Lord was close at hand. The word for patience means, literally, long-suffering. Obviously, if we're feeling fine and enjoying ourselves, we don't need patience, because we are not anxious for our experience to end. The church that James addressed was subject to suffering. They were anxious for their ordeal to end with the second coming of Christ. How different from our pampered existence in affluent America! No wonder most Christians don't get too excited about the prospect of the *parousia.* Most Americans are not anxious for Christ to return, and so the kind of patience which James enjoins is about as well received as a can of soda pop without its fizz. After all, it's been over 2,000 years since James promised the eminent return of Christ in glory. We have no idea how soon or late that advent will be. Nevertheless, suffering is still with us and patience is still needed. The nearness of the Lord can still inspire us to hang in there. Regardless of the date of the *parousia,* Christ is near to strengthen us in suffering and give us the victory.

Gospel: Matthew 11:2-11

Does Christ offend you? Apparently, Jesus offended and scandalized many people in his days in the flesh. He offended his family. At one point, they thought he was a little crazy and sought to spirit him away. He offended the rich young ruler by requesting that he sell all his goods and give the proceeds to the poor. He offended the religious leaders by associating with tax collectors and sinners. And in our gospel lesson he appears to have offended John the Baptist as he languished in prison. Jesus' actions were raising questions in his mind about whether or not Jesus was really the Messiah (vv. 2-3). What actions? Perhaps it was Jesus' dining with Pharisee sinners or with women, like Mary and Martha. Maybe Jesus was merely enjoying life too much, or so it seemed. After all, the Lord was no ascetic like John. At any rate, Jesus was not comporting himself in a messianic manner, according to John's way of thinking. I could have been mistaken, John reasoned. So, he sent some disciples to find out if Jesus is really the Anointed One. In answering John's question, the Lord points to his deeds — healing actions which the prophets identified with the kingdom of God (vv. 4-5). Then Jesus added, "And blessed is anyone who takes no offense at me" (v. 6).

I can understand why John the Baptist was offended, can't you? I too am sometimes offended by Jesus. When he tells us that we should not judge others, lest we be judged for the same sins, it offends my sense of justice. How can Christ see me in the same league with prostitutes and crooks? After all, I'm a rather upstanding person. Christ also offends me when he informs me that I must be as a little child to enter the kingdom of God. I have a mind and there are some questions I want answered first. Christ's teaching that the one who finds the Lord's mercy at the very end of life is going to receive the same reward as those of us who have followed Jesus from our youth likewise offends me. Does that seem fair? Of course not! But you know what really offends me, especially when I'm feeling high and mighty? You guessed it, the cross. Am I really so bad that God had to sacrifice his only Son? What I really want is a Teflon-coated gospel and a non-stick Christ that doesn't burn and isn't messy. I want a Messiah that acts like I think he should.

Then, as I lay in my self-righteous prison, the Lord comes and opens my eyes and says: "Look! The blind receive their sight, the lame walk, the lepers are cleansed ..." (v. 5) and a voice wells ups from deep in my soul saying: "Blessed is the one who takes no offense at me" (v. 6). Forgive me, dear Jesus, I have offended you and you have taken my offense and that of the entire world all the way to the cross, where you nailed it, killing it forever. Thank you, patient Jesus.

PREACHING APPROACHES WITH ILLUSTRATIONS

Lesson 1: Isaiah 35:1-10
Sermon Title: High Way To Heaven

Sermon Angle: The title is a word play, derived from verse six. A road is called a highway because it is elevated above the surrounding terrain. This makes the road visible, facilitates transit, and helps assure the survival of the highway. It is also a word play on Michael Landon's television show by that name. If we want to go to Zion, we had better follow the highway God has prepared.

Outline:
1. God promised a highway for the captive Jews to return home to Zion — the way of salvation
2. There is a difference between man's highway to heaven and God's (Contrast works and/or righteousness with faith)
3. Christ is the only true high way to heaven

Lesson 2: James 5:7-10 (Suggested sermon text)

Sermon Title: The Attitude Of Patience

Sermon Angle: We live in an impatient world with people who have short fuses. We want everything right now! We need to develop the attitude of patience not only because it makes life ever so much more pleasant but because the Lord Jesus is near. He is the prime example of suffering patience. Patience on our part is a sign that the Lord reigns in our hearts.

Outline:
1. In our world of instant gratification, patience has gone out the door (Give examples)
2. Patience or the lack of it reveals our spiritual condition
3. We need to be patient because
   — Christ is near
   — Christ has shown God's patience
   — we are witness to the nearness of God's kingdom

*   *   *   *   *

Our impatience with others is very often based on false assumptions or ignorance. If only we knew the situation of the other person and realized how our impatience hurts others, we might be more patient, like the man in this story.

A group of English folks was traveling by train through the steamy expanses of the subcontinent of India. As the train rattled endlessly onward and day yielded to night, the hot and weary travelers wanted nothing more than to settle in for the night. Unfortunately for them, there was a man situated toward the rear of the car who was cuddling a tiny infant who was becoming increasingly restive and cranky, crying incessantly, or so it seemed. Finally, one man verbalized the annoyance and impatience of the entire group: "Would you please give that baby to its mother!" After a brief pause came the reply, "I'm sorry, I'm doing the best I can. The mother of my child lays in a casket in the car to our rear." There was a long, awkward silence. Finally, the man who voiced the complaint got up and went to the bereft father to offer his apology. Then, he took the infant in his arms and in loving patience cared for her through the night.

*   *   *   *   *

If John the Baptist were a modern day truck driver, this is how he probably would have expressed his patience.

The driver of a sixteen-wheeler pulled off I-80 at an all night restaurant near Omaha, Nebraska. The waitress had just served him his grub when a trio of Hell's Angels-type guys wearing leather jackets and chains swaggered into the establishment. They quickly surrounded the driver. Eager to provoke a fight, one biker took the trucker's hamburger, another captured his french fries, and the third stole his drink. The truck driver calmly rose, proceeded to the cash register where he paid for his meal. The waitress watched as he quietly exited the restaurant, entered his rig, and drove into the night.

When she returned, one of the bikers snarled, "That fellow ain't much of a man, is he?"

"I can't answer that," she replied, "but I do know that he's not much of a truck driver. He just ran over three motorcycles out in the parking lot."

29

Gospel: Matthew 11:2-11

Sermon Title: Does Jesus Offend You?

Sermon Angle: When Jesus walked on earth, he offended many people, good and bad, including John the Baptist, who pictured a more fiery Messiah. Christ continues to offend us. Thank God.

Outline:
1. Christ offended John the Baptist by his gracious dealings with sinners
2. Christ offended the sensibilities of the religious leaders of his day
3. Christ continues to offend us today by saying that we must die to self, take up our cross and follow him.

* * * * *

The book, *The Scandal Of Lent* by Robert Kysar, makes an excellent point. The basic thesis of the book is that we can never truly embrace the Christian faith unless we are first scandalized by it. The word "scandal" can be interpreted as a "stumbling block." That is, the gospel isn't easy to believe; it causes offense. The rich young ruler was offended by Jesus' admonition to sell everything that he had and then come and follow him. Nicodemus was scandalized by the Lord's assertion that he "must be born anew." The Jews were scandalized by a dying Messiah and the Gentiles were scandalized by a God who laid aside his powers that he might enter into human suffering and death. John the Baptist was scandalized by Jesus' behavior: all that cavorting with tax collectors and other sinners. People today are still scandalized when they take seriously Christ's words.

About ten years ago, a couple in my new members' class let me know that they were offended by the very words of our Lord concerning divorce. The woman had been previously married and they both took exception to Jesus' teaching that whoever divorces his wife causes her to commit adultery if she should remarry. I did not deny the offensiveness of this teaching but tried to soften it. It didn't work! The offense could not be erased. Let's face it: Jesus wasn't the expounder of a politically correct gospel that soothed everyone's sensibilities! His words sear our souls and prick our consciences. He makes us feel uncomfortable; he brings us face to face with our dis-ease concerning our spiritual state.

John the Baptist was a fearless prophet who died because he would not compromise his loyalty to God. Yet he was not nearly so radical as Jesus. John admonished that people needed to repent, change their ways, reverse the direction of their lives. Jesus insisted that we must die to self, take up our cross and follow him.

The couple who was offended by the teaching of Christ just might be closer to the kingdom than millions of Christians who no longer feel the offense of the gospel. Soren Kierkegaard's words still ring as true for our age as for his. He believed that in a so-called Christian culture we tend to make pabulum of the faith. We cut out the offending elements in order to make the faith easily digestible. If our faith is to remain vital, we must wrestle with the offense of the gospel and include it in the main course of that which we serve up to our people.

Advent 4

Revised Common:	Isaiah 7:10-16	Romans 1:1-7	Matthew 1:18-25
Roman Catholic:	Isaiah 7:10-14	Romans 1:1-7	Matthew 1:18-24
Episcopal:	Isaiah 7:10-17	Romans 1:1-7	Matthew 1:18-25

Seasonal Theme: Advent Attitudes

Theme For The Day: The Attitude of Obedience

Suggested Text For Preaching: Matthew 1:24 and Romans 1:5

BRIEF COMMENTARY ON THE LESSONS

Lesson 1: Isaiah 7:10-16 (C); Isaiah 7:10-14 (RC); Isaiah 7:10-17 (E)

This selection contains a verse (v. 14) that rings musically in the Christian's ear at Christmas. It speaks of a virgin (*almah* actually means young woman) conceiving and bearing a son who will be called Immanuel. Beginning with Matthew, the church has baptized this as a messianic passage, even though it is not. Consider well the historical context of this saying. King Ahaz is being besieged by an alliance of Israel and Syria. The king intends to repel the threat by forming an alliance with Assyria, which Isaiah warns against. The prophet urges Ahaz rather to trust in the Lord, requesting that the king ask God for a sign of his promise of deliverance. Ahaz refuses to ask the Lord on a pious pretext because he has already decided to go the political route. God gives a sign anyway — the sign of a son. The promise is not of a righteous king for some future time but of a child who will be born in Ahaz's day; by the time this child is able to know what food he likes (age 2 or 3), those countries threatening Ahaz will be deserted.

How then do we handle this text? God gave Ahaz a sign of salvation through Isaiah — the birth of a child. God has given to the world a much more potent sign — the sign of God's Son. As in Isaiah's day, the sign of the son was unsolicited and undeserved. In the midst of a threatening world, the people of God can point to the living sign of hope and salvation, the Son who is Emmanuel, God with us.

Lesson 2: Romans 1:1-7 (C, RC, E)

In this introduction to the epistle to the Romans, Paul identifies himself and his mission. The first title which he assumes is *doulos*, which can be translated as either servant or slave. The NRSV and the NIV prefer to translate this "servant." Actually, "slave" conveys better Paul's sense of necessity and urgency in proclaiming the gospel. This identity is conferred by God through his call (v. 1). What is he called to? To be an apostle, one who is sent as an ambassador, whose authority resides not in himself but in the one who sent him, in God. What is the mission for which he is consecrated or set apart? The gospel concerning the one promised by the prophets; the one who is both human (Son of David) and divine (v. 4); the one through whom we have received grace and apostleship so that others might come to the obedience of faith in Christ, that they might call Christ Lord and experience the freedom of being his slave.

Gospel: Matthew 1:18-25 (C, E); Matthew 1:18-24 (RC)

The first 17 verses of Matthew's gospel consist of genealogy, to establish Jesus' human lineage as a descendent of Abraham and of King David. This week's gospel seeks to reveal our Lord's divine source, that he was conceived by the Holy Spirit without benefit of human father. The story is told from Joseph's vantage point, who, upon discovering that his betrothed was pregnant, was ready to quietly divorce her, until an angel revealed in a dream the true cause of her condition. To reinforce that this is not Joseph's child, the angel reveals the name of this special child. The name indicates role and mission; "Jesus" means "he shall save." As always, Matthew attempts to show how these happenings were a fulfillment of scriptural prophecies.

A central fact that we must extract from this passage is the obedience of Joseph to the voice of God in the face of rather questionable outward circumstances.

Psalm Of The Day

Psalm 80:1-7, 17-19 (C) — "Restore us, O God ..." A psalm of deliverance from national foes.

Psalm 23 (RC) — A Psalm expressing confidence in God's guidance.

Psalm 24 (E) — "Lift up your head, O gates ..." This psalm was probably used in association with processions with the Ark of the Covenant.

Prayer Of The Day

God of glory, thank you for graciously taking on our humanity in the flesh of Jesus. As you revealed the sign of your Son to Mary and Joseph, who bowed in humble obedience to your word, so may we receive and nourish the gift of your Son, our Savior, Jesus the Christ. Amen.

THEOLOGICAL REFLECTION ON THE LESSONS

Lesson 1: Isaiah 7:10-17

Sign language. Human beings are very insecure creatures who continually need reassurance. Many wives complain that their husbands seldom, if ever, say the reassuring words: "I love you." Words help but they must be reinforced by actions. The biblical narrative reveals numerous instances where anxious people sought a reassuring sign from God, but in this text, however, it is God who asks Ahaz if he would like a sign of God's presence. Ahaz refused but God gave the sign anyway — that of the young woman who would bear a son called Immanuel. Jesus chastised his generation for always seeking signs, yet the scriptures indicate that God has often granted signs of his saving presence. In the Noah story, it is the rainbow, and in the Abraham account, it is the sign of circumcision. Moses was granted the rod that transformed into a serpent and Gideon had his fleece. The miracles of Jesus were themselves signs of God's saving presence. The Lord's supper is a poignant sign of divine presence in the valley of the shadows and the cross is the foremost sign of God's triumph over sin and death.

In this holy season, we too are given a sign, the sign given the shepherds when they were informed of the special birth: "This will be a sign for you: you will find a child wrapped in bands of cloth and lying in a manger" (Luke 2:12). The sign of the child is the sign of a new beginning for God, for humankind, for each of us who are willing to become as a little child in order to enter the kingdom of heaven.

Lesson 2: Romans 1:1-7

Slaves of sin or of the Son? In his very first sentence to the church at Rome, Paul describes himself as the *doulos,* translated servant or slave, of Jesus Christ. It seems that "slave" would better fit Paul's sense of call. A servant is hired for wages and is free to quit at any time. A slave has no choice, receives no wages, and is not free to do as he likes. For Paul, being a servant and apostle of Jesus Christ is not an option but an absolute necessity. This does not mean that he served grudgingly; no, he found joy in his willingness to fulfill the mandates of the Master.

This business of freedom is something of an illusion. There are all kinds of forces which impinge on our lives. In the first three chapters of Romans, Paul establishes the truth that no person is free from the power of sin. There is choice but it is limited — to be a slave of God's Son or of sin. Jesus said it well: "No one can serve two masters ... You cannot serve God and wealth" (Matthew 6:24). The irony of it is that it is in this slavery to Christ that we find perfect freedom, the freedom to love and to give.

We are called, in our baptism, to become the slaves of Jesus Christ: his apostles, ambassadors, sent into the world to call others to embrace the obedience of the gospel. This message is the essential antidote for the false notion of freedom being touted today: the heresy that the way to fulfillment is to be free to do as you will. We must hold high the gospel paradox that we are only free when we willingly serve Christ as slave.

Gospel: Matthew 1:18-25

Just Joseph. When Joseph discovered Mary's untimely condition, he decided to divorce her quietly rather than humiliate her. Joseph might have looked at this apparent tragedy from his own selfish perspective but, to his credit, he still cared for Mary and wished to shield her from shame. For this attitude, he is judged as righteous or, as the RSV puts it, just.

Picture in your mind's eye the typical nativity scenes that you have witnessed. Mary often has a glazed-over look of glory on her face but Joseph is just standing there, rather expressionless. Joseph the Just has been transformed into just Joseph, the adopted father of Jesus. A nice guy but who needs him? Joseph is silent in the gospels. We don't know if Joseph ever enunciated any great truths but his actions speak volumes. Try to comprehend what a humbling experience this was for him. He's about to get married and finds out that his fiancée is pregnant but not by him. An angel tells him to go ahead and wed Mary because this child is of the Holy Spirit. Out the window are any visions of connubial bliss. Instead, he's handed the embarrassment of a pregnant fiancée and the thankless job of caring for another's child. Come on, folks, let's hear it once for Joseph the Just, who humbly obeyed the message from God and faithfully discharged his responsibility as husband and father, rather than sluff it off as a bad dream.

PREACHING APPROACHES WITH ILLUSTRATIONS

Lesson 1: Isaiah 7:10-17

Sermon Title: Sign Language

Sermon Angle: Since God is spirit, which cannot be apprehended through our senses, we must rely on signs which point to and convey his presence. Signs are concrete words or actions which convey the divine presence. The only way we can experience God is through sign language.

Outline:
1. At a time of national crisis, Ahaz was given the sign of God's saving presence, a child
2. In Christ, God has given us his special child as a sign of his saving presence
3. Christ comes to us in word and sacrament
4. We are sent into the world as signs of God's love and forgiveness

Lesson 2: Romans 1:1-7

Sermon Title: Set Apart Saints Who Serve And Are Sent

Sermon Angle: Who are we as Christians? Paul defines his identity and that of other Christians as saints, those who are set apart by God for the gospel. As saints, our function is to serve God through the neighborhood and go out as apostles, re-presenting by word and deed the good news of salvation through Jesus the Christ.

Outline:

Introduction: Who are we, Christian friend?
1. We are God's saints
   a. We are not sinless
   b. We are set apart
2. Set apart for what?
   a. For service
   b. For sending (to proclaim the gospel)

Gospel: Matthew 1:18-25

Sermon Title: The Attitude Of Obedience

Sermon Angle: When Joseph was told of Mary's miraculous conception by the angel, he did not hesitate to obey the message from God. He played out his lines in the first act of a drama containing a plot he could not have understood. In our era of individual aspirations and relativism, we need to hold up the virtue of obedience to the word of God.

*   *   *   *   *

The Dotzlers are an interracial couple residing in Omaha, Nebraska. Ron's chemical engineering job enabled them to enjoy a comfortable lifestyle, but in the mid-1980s they became convinced that God was calling them as missionaries. They approached their congregation, Trinity Interdenominational Church of Omaha, with their plan, but were told that they were too old and that their family was too large. Nevertheless, they remained convinced of the Lord's call and moved to the near-north side of Omaha, a predominately poor black community, to await the Lord's direction. Some time later the Lord's directive came: They were already living in their mission field. Eventually, they formed ABIDE Network, a nondenominational Christian ministry whose purpose is to provide practical and spiritual help to churches and ministries in rural and inner-city communities. ABIDE stands for "A Bible In Daily Experience." The ministry also aims to break down barriers between blacks and whites. So far, they have been successful in assisting area churches with construction projects, youth programs, and much more. Like Joseph and Mary, the Dotzlers obeyed the spiritual vision and heeded the voice of God, despite great obstacles.

*   *   *   *   *

Contrast the above with fallen television evangelist, Robert Tilton, who was caught trying to fleece the sheep rather than obey the voice of the Good Shepherd. Tilton spent 84 percent of his airtime on promotion and fund raising. He did not blink at asking listeners to send in $1,000 and send it immediately. The television program, *Prime Time Live*, exposed Tilton's avarice along with allegations of wrongdoing, which led to his ministry's demise.

*   *   *   *   *

Some of the sublime actions of humankind as well as some of the most wicked and degrading have been done in the name of obedience. Thousands of people led millions of Jews to the slaughter, out of obedience to their lord and master, Adolf Hitler. At the same time, others risked their lives to save Jews out of obedience to the Lord of life or, at least, to a transcendent moral imperative.

October 2007 marks the 64th anniversary of the rescue of the Danish Jews during the Nazi occupation. In late September 1943, word leaked out to the Jews of Denmark that they were in imminent danger of being rounded up by the Gestapo. Despite curfews, German patrols on land and sea and the threats of punishment, non-Jewish Danes enabled over 7,300 of the 7,800 Jewish Danes to escape. When the roundup came during Jewish New Year, October 1-2, 1943, most of the Jews were already in hiding in coastal towns, awaiting passage to Sweden. The people of Gilleleje, a small fishing village some forty miles north of Copenhagen, succeeded in getting close to 1,300 of these Jews to safety by the end of October that year.

*   *   *   *   *

After the massacre/suicide of about 1,000 people in Jonestown, Guyana, Russell Baker, a columnist for *The New York Times*, wrote an article in which he compared freaks to zombies. The 1960s was the era of the freak. He defined a freak as a person who has turned individuality into social excess. The freak is so focused on doing his or her own thing that he/she sometimes makes individuality look like a type of insanity. The freak is totally self-involved and obeys only himself.

The zombie, on the other hand, has sacrificed his or her individuality and his or her mind to a master who demands and receives total and unquestioned obedience. In the Moonies cult, individual thought is labeled a "tool of Satan." David Koresh was able to lay claim to the same kind of unblinking devotion from the members of his Branch Davidian cult in Waco, Texas. Most of them were willing to kill and be killed in the name of their leader/messiah and we all are aware of their tragic end. Zombies have no will of their own; their will is manipulated by the one they claim as their master.

There is no place for those who insist on being freaks or zombies in the kingdom of Christ. Christ seeks our obedience, but it is certainly not unthinking devotion. To the contrary, he urges those who would follow him to first weigh the cost carefully. No place for wild and impulsive devotion in the kingdom of God. Christ does not seek to obliterate our will; rather, he gives us the grace to willingly subject our will to that of God's. Another distinction between Christian obedience and that of the zombie variety is that Christ does not seek power or control for self-aggrandizement. Rather, he seeks to focus and channel the power of obedience for the benefit of the neighbor. The mystery is that the way of willing obedience to Christ is also the means of self-fulfillment and happiness.

Christmas Eve/Christmas Day

Revised Common:	**Isaiah 9:2-7**	**Titus 2:11-14**	**Luke 2:1-14 (15-20)**
Roman Catholic:	**Isaiah 9:2-7**	**Titus 2:11-14**	**Luke 2:1-14**
Episcopal:	**Isaiah 9:2-4, 6-7**	**Titus 2:11-14**	**Luke 2:1-14 (15-20)**

Theme For The Day: The Good News Of Christ's Birth

BRIEF COMMENTARY ON THE LESSONS

Lesson 1: Isaiah 9:2-7 (C, RC); Isaiah 9:2-4, 6-7 (E)

The prophet declares the dawning of a new day of light, justice, and everlasting peace for the downtrodden of the Lord. A son is given who mediates the very presence and attributes of God; he is proclaimed the Wonderful Counselor, Almighty God, Everlasting Father, Prince of Peace. There has been a great deal of discussion as to whether this passage is pre- or post-exilic, whether it was composed by Isaiah or a later writer. There is no reason to suppose that this is other than the work of Isaiah and was probably composed to celebrate the coronation of a king. This condition of peace (understood in the Jewish sense of total well being) will not come about through political intrigue but through the action of God (v. 7). The Christian church sees Christ as the one who will bring about this triumph of shalom.

Lesson 2: Titus 2:11-14 (C, RC, E)

In Jesus, the grace of God became visible and accessible for the salvation of all people, not just the chosen few. Christ will return in glory as "God and Savior." This is the only scripture where Jesus is given the title of "God." Ethics flow from theology. Since Christ died to purify us from our sins (his priestly role) and may return at any time, the believer needs to renounce sinful passions and zealously pursue that which is good.

Gospel: Luke 2:1-14 (15-20) (C, E); Luke 2:1-14 (RC)

Luke's wonderful nativity account raises a number of historical and exegetical questions which would be best kept to ourselves. Christmas is not a time for questions but affirmation and celebration. Rather, let us serve as the angel who announced the holy birth and lift our voices with the heavenly chorus in praise of our newborn king. The passage reiterates a chord found often in scripture: God is manifest in the poor and the humble of the earth. Let us savor the miracle of God's incarnation with awe and wonder.

Psalm Of The Day

Psalm 96 (C, E) — "Sing to the Lord a new song ..." (v. 1).

Prayer Of The Day

Glory to you, O Lord. As we gather around your manger, that symbol of your love and grace, our hearts bubble over with awe and wonder at your self-giving surprise. Jesus, be born in our hearts anew, that we may always radiate the glory of your love. Amen.

THEOLOGICAL REFLECTION ON THE LESSONS

Lesson 1: Isaiah 9:2-7

Darkness and light. This is one of the great scriptural motifs, which crops up frequently in Isaiah. This passage is one of the greatest of this genre (v. 2). The people knew of the darkness of corruption and political subjugation, but now their hopes blazed brightly with the advent of a new ruler. Unfortunately, this star soon became a black hole. The Christian community was quick to realize that only Jesus is the sun that will never set; as he claimed, he is the light of the world.

Studies have been conducted on those who were born blind but through the wonders of modern surgery were given new and perfectly healthy eyes. With breathless anticipation, they awaited the removal of the bandages. What do you think they saw when the light first struck their corneas? Almost nothing! A nebulous blob. Seeing is more than light and lenses; one must learn how to see. When we are given the gift of sight at birth, we gradually learn how to see, but when sight comes much later, the difficulties are almost insurmountable. Many of these people found it too difficult to learn how to see, they went back to their ways of perceiving when blind. Some people find it more congenial to walk in the darkness than in the light. When we really walk in the light of God's Son, the Spirit teaches us how to see through the eyes of Christ and walk in the light without stumbling.

Lesson 2: Titus 2:11-14

Grace and glory. We are told here that Christmas is preeminently a celebration of God's grace; salvation is made available to all through the One born in Bethlehem (v. 11). However, Christmas has a face like the god Janus, looking both ways. Christmas is past but Christ is coming again: this time, in glory and power (v. 13). The first advent was hardly noticed but his second advent will be a great manifestation of glory that all will see and tremble. Our God is a God of grace and glory. There was indeed glory in the stable where Christ was born, but it is a glory concealed, a glory apparent only to a few shepherds out in their fields. Let's be honest though: it is God's self-giving grace that draws us to the manger.

The gift goes on and on and on. You've probably seen the Energizer battery advertisements with the little pink rabbit beating a drum in a parade; all the other participants run out of juice but as the commentator says of the Energizer bunny, "It just keeps going and going and going." God gave his Son and the Son gave himself for the sins of the world (v. 14). This is the gift that just keeps going and going and going as it is received and shared countless times down through the centuries. As a delightful Christmas song puts it: The gift goes on, the gift goes on and on and on.

Gospel: Luke 2:1-20

House of bread. Jesus was born in Bethlehem which means "house of bread." It is appropriate that he who multiplied the loaves and who gives himself to us in bread and wine should be born in this place.

Taxes or charity? The emperor Augustus ordered all citizens to register for his tax. Around that same time another king was born, Jesus, the Christ. He demanded nothing but gave everything, even his own life. Oh yes, according to the gospel of John, the night before his death he washed his disciples' feet and then commanded them to love one another.

Good news for the poor. Luke's nativity story makes very clear that the Messiah's coming is good news for the poor and those considered to be of little importance. His birth announcement was proclaimed to humble shepherds whose status was only slightly greater than that of prostitutes and tax collectors. Luke's version of the Beatitudes is addressed to the poor, while Matthew speaks to the poor in spirit. Luke has a special concern to show Christ's compassion for the down-and-outers, for he enters the world as one of them; he comes to us as a naked, outcast alien. How different in the Western world, where many of the churches reach out to the up-and-comers, those who are wealthy, powerful, and successful. Even at Christmas, when our impulse to charity is magnified, we do little more than share a few crumbs with the poor of the earth. Our giving centers on those who have favored us with gifts. God's love in Christ is pure grace, giving himself to those of no repute. Perhaps Christ first appeared to the lowly shepherds because their economic poverty predisposed them to spiritual poverty and humility, which is the womb of spiritual regeneration. Only those who are poor, naked, and blind can receive the message of an infant Savior as good news.

Worship as witness. The response of Mary and Joseph to the revelations of the shepherds was awe and wonder, the underlying attitude of worship, transmitted by the shepherds (vv. 17-18). However, the gospel of the Savior cannot be kept within. When the shepherds returned to the ordinary arena of their existence, their voices lifted in praise of God (v. 20). As we meditate on the mystery of the incarnation, we are filled with awe and wonder at the grace of God but we cannot stay transfixed at the holy place; rather, we must go back to the fields of our endeavor with jubilant songs of praise on our lips, as worship blends into witness.

PREACHING APPROACHES WITH ILLUSTRATIONS

Lesson 1: Isaiah 9:2-7
Sermon Title: Christmas Dawning

Sermon Angle: The prophet announces a new day for those prisoners of political captivity, who dwelt in the darkness of defeat and hopelessness. The light of the Lord's liberation was dawning on the nation. God was sending a Savior/King. The expectations of the Jews are fulfilled in Jesus Christ, who frees us from the captivity of selfishness and sin. Christmas marks the dawning of a new day.

Outline:
1. The Jews dwelt in the dark prison of national captivity
2. God freed them and caused the dawning of a new day
3. We all experience the dark captivity of being sin's slave
4. With Christ, we have the dawning of a new day in which:
   — God will send his Son to govern us
   — It will be a reign of peace and righteousness

Lesson 2: Titus 2:11-14
Sermon Title: Proclaiming The God Of Grace And Glory

Sermon Angle: This passage speaks of the appearing of the grace of God for the salvation of all people and urges us to prepare for Christ's coming again in glory. God is always both a God of grace and a God of glory, but one aspect is more prominent at one time than the other. In the incarnation, the glory is masked but the grace is clearly evident. That God should stoop to infant form is grace; that Christ should die on the cross and rise again is also pure grace. Some day, however, Christ will come again but this time in visible power and glory. If we receive the grace, we will not fear the glory.

Outline:

1. In Christ we see the grace of God
   — In his humble birth
   — In his gracious words and actions
   — In his sacrificial death and resurrection
2. In Christ we will see the glory of God
   — When he comes to judge the earth
   — When we die
3. Our response, through God's grace
   — Turn off our passion for sinning
   — Turn on our zeal for good deeds

Gospel: Luke 2:1-20

Sermon Title: Close Encounters

Sermon Angle: The confirmation class was challenged to find the extraterrestrials in Luke's nativity account. They couldn't believe it, so they searched. One student hesitatingly responded, "Angels?" "Right on," I replied. The sermon title derives from Steven Spielberg's movie, *Close Encounters Of The Third Kind*, which features an encounter between humans and an extraterrestrial being. The first encounter was between a wrinkled little alien and a child. The response on both sides is not fear but fascination. Angels certainly are extraterrestrials and they figure prominently in Luke's nativity narrative. As you know, the word *angelos* means "messenger"; the angels bore the good news of the Messiah's birth through word and worship. The shepherds themselves became messengers (angels) when they joyously shared all that they had heard and seen about the newborn king (v. 17). Every Christian is an angel (messenger) who is called to bear witness to the wonder of the God incarnate.

Outline:

Introduction: Use the close encounters story and follow with the statement that Christmas contains a close encounter with extraterrestrials.

1. A close encounter with angel-messengers
2. A close encounter with God, through the incarnate Son
3. A close encounter with salvation

Conclusion: Like the angels and the shepherds we are to proclaim the good news of Emmanuel, the joyous tidings of salvation.

Sermon Title: Have A Wonderful Christmas

Sermon Angle: Luke states that all who heard the shepherds' story were filled with wonder and awe concerning events which were beyond their understanding. Wonder is a proper response to that which is mysterious and to that which is holy. The gospel of our incarnate God is indeed mysterious. We must not lose our sense of wonder and worship as we celebrate Christmas. Too often, we are filled with worry rather than wonder as we get taken away with the superficial aspects of Christmas. Verse 19 relates that Mary pondered these things in her heart. The Christmas event is like a precious jewel, which we should reverently examine, turning it over and over to see the light of glory reflected from various angles.

Outline:

Introduction: Relate a story of how wonderful Christmas is to children. Then state that we must not lose that sense of wonder.

1. All who gathered around the manger wondered at the news of the shepherds
2. Mary pondered these things in her heart
3. Today, Christmas often produces more worry than wonder
4. Be a child again and be filled with wonder at the mystery of the incarnation, crucifixion, and resurrection
5. Come, let us worship our king — wonder leads to worship

*   *   *   *   *

Babies can bring out the best or the worst in us. The appearance of the Christ Child elicited a murderous rage in King Herod and worship on the part of the shepherds and the wise men. A baby can bond together man and wife or tear them apart.

Ann Landers asked her readers with children: "If you had it to do over again, would you have children?" A surprising 70% replied that they would not. Apparently, these people thought that children brought more pain than gain.

*   *   *   *   *

A young Presbyterian pastor was approached by a taciturn elder, Angus McDonnell. His son was due to arrive in town on Thanksgiving weekend with his newborn son whom they named Angus Larry. How would you like to carry that appellation around with you the rest of your life? Anyway, the elder wanted the pastor to baptize his grandson. The young cleric quickly spirited Angus into his office and inquired into his son's religious affiliation. Well, they hadn't gotten around to joining any church yet, retorted Angus. Then, the pastor tried to convince him that it would be better if the infant were baptized in the community where his son's family lived. The pastor thought he had put across his point when the elder politely thanked the pastor and left. However, Angus knew how to put a fire under this young upstart. He called every other elder and they held a secret meeting, where they voted unanimously that the pastor should baptize the child.

Following the service, a woman by the name of Mildred lingered in the back of the church. Obviously, she had some agenda. She hesitatingly confessed that her eighteen-year-old daughter had a child out of wedlock adding: "Well, it ought to be baptized, shouldn't it?" The pastor said that he would take it up with the board. After some reluctance and a lengthy discussion, the board voted to approve the baptism. The baptism took place the fourth Sunday in Advent. The church was full. This congregation had the custom of asking this question as a part of their baptismal liturgy: "Who will stand with this child?" At this point, the family, friends, sponsors, and so forth, would stand up and remain standing during the sacrament. The pastor and elders were concerned that nobody but the young woman's mother would stand up with her. When the question was raised, "Who will stand up with this child?" it looked as if their worst fears were being realized. Then a man got up; it was Angus McDonnell. Then some other elders rose, followed by a young couple who had recently joined the church. In short order, a host of congregants were standing with the young mother. Tears of joy danced down her cheeks. The word had once again become flesh in fulfillment of the scripture lesson read earlier in the service from 1 John 4: "See what love the Father has given us that we should be called children of God.... If we love one another, God abides in us and his love is perfected in us." (Based on an article by the Reverend Michael Lindvail in *Good Housekeeping*, December 1990.)

*   *   *   *   *

This account is based on a story in *Parade* magazine, titled "The Gift Of The Toy Man." The Toy Man is Eric Hultgren, who was a tool and dye maker for over four decades. Eric's life was turned on its head by his wife's final illness. Shirley was dying of lung cancer, but being a kind and Christian woman she still was concerned for others. Shirley suggested to Eric they should make something for the children. Before Eric had emigrated from Sweden, his father had created for him a wooden truck, his prized toy. Shirley suggested that he construct some toys like that for the children.

Since Shirley's death, Eric has honored her request by utilizing almost all of his free time carving trucks, cars, school buses, and airplanes, carefully crafted toys created out of love. These toys he takes to the local hospitals and personally presents them to children on the pediatrics ward. In just two Christmases, Eric has presented over 700 children with his special toys. He wouldn't dream of asking for payment; apparently, the joy in the eyes of the children is sufficient reward. He doesn't even introduce himself; he is simply known as "The Toy Man."

Eric has given far more than toys; toys have the connotation of that which is fun but not necessary. No, Eric has given and continues to give himself to those who are frightened by brokenness and disease. Isn't that what Christmas is all about?

Christmas 1

Theme For The Day: God enters the human family and leads us through suffering to salvation.

BRIEF COMMENTARY ON THE LESSONS

Lesson 1: Isaiah 63:7-9 (C)

The prophet recalls the goodness of God when the nation was being born. He harkens back to the covenant God made with his people at Sinai and his guiding them through the wilderness. Though God punishes his people for their sins, he continues to love them, care for them, and guide them. God carries on his gracious work of salvation.

Lesson 1: Sirach 3:2-6, 12-14 (RC)

God placed parents in authority over their children and those who honor their parents will be blessed by God.

Lesson 1: Isaiah 61:10—62:3 (E)

The prophet exalts in the restoration of the nation and the cult, which becomes also his personal salvation. The joy he feels is like that of the bride and the groom, as they are cheerfully bedecked with the festal garments. In like manner, the captives are clothed with the robe of righteousness. The Lord's righteous reign is as sure as the springtime. All nations will see the splendor of Zion.

Lesson 2: Hebrews 2:10-18 (C)

Together with Jesus, the pioneer of our faith, we can call on God as Father and Christ as our Brother. Since all believers share a common spiritual parentage, we are all one family through Christ.

Lesson 2: Colossians 3:12-21 (RC)

The behavior and the virtues of those who have died and been raised to newness of life in Christ are here outlined — compassion, kindness, humility, and so forth. Verses 18-21 speak to the responsibilities within the family, which are grounded in love and mutual respect.

Lesson 2: Galatians 3:23-25; 4:4-7 (E)

Being under the tutelage of the law is like being a dependent child. Through faith in Christ, we have come of age and are given all privileges of being God's mature children. We are given the Spirit, which frees us from the strong arm of the law, gives us access to the very presence of God, and makes us heirs of God's promises.

Gospel: Matthew 2:13-23 (C); Matthew 2:13-15, 19-23 (RC)

The Holy Family flees to Egypt to escape the jealous wrath of King Herod, being warned by an angel. After Herod dies, they make their exodus back to Israel but not Judah, since Archaelaus, Herod's son, is equally despotic. They then settle in Galilee, in the town of Nazareth. In the interim, the slaughter of Bethlehem's boys has taken place. The Holy Family encounters the reality of a world often hostile, cruel, and unjust. God protects them but we still have to deal with the painful truth of a world where the humble are often the seeming pawns of the strong and the power hungry. Again, Matthew tries to show that these things are the fulfillment of prophecy but there is no passage that states that the Messiah was to be called a Nazorean (v. 23).

Gospel: John 1:1-18 (E)

The light of the divine *logos* becomes flesh, to bring life to those who dwell in the darkness of sin. All who receive him are given the power to become the children of God, who like the Christ are born not from human desire but through the will of God and by his grace.

Psalm Of The Day

Psalm 148 (C); Psalm 147 (E) — Let all who inhabit earth and heaven praise the Lord.

Prayer Of The Day

Loving God, as you guided the Holy Family — Joseph, Mary, and Baby Jesus — through the perils of this world, so lead us through our present difficulties to the place of safety, and ultimately to our home in heaven. In Jesus' name. Amen.

THEOLOGICAL REFLECTION ON THE LESSONS

Lesson 1: Isaiah 63:7-9

Count your blessings. The prophet exalts: "I will recount the gracious deeds of the Lord, the praiseworthy acts of the Lord ..." (v. 7). The old gospel song tells us to "count our blessings, name them one by one." There is real value in recounting God's gifts of creation and redemption. It makes us happy, healthy, and thankful. As Isaiah looked back at the gracious deeds of God in the life of his people, his heart was filled with thanksgiving and praise. God himself had been with them in all their pain and difficulties and carried them when they had no strength.

Lesson 1: Isaiah 61:10—62:3

The garment of salvation. Clothing makes a statement about who we are or who we would like to be. There is a syndicated column in the newspaper that tells people in the world of business how to dress for success. His advice is that you dress not necessarily for the position you have but for the position you aspire to. This passage states that God has dressed the people for salvation. The gracious God of all does not leave his people naked, exposing their imperfections, but covers them with his salvation. "He has clothed me with the garments of salvation, he has covered me with the robe of righteousness" (v. 10). This spiritual dressing up is compared to the glad attire of the bride and groom at their wedding. The apostle Paul also spoke of salvation as a spiritual garment: "Put on the Lord Jesus Christ ..." (Romans 13:14). The parable that Jesus told of the man who came to the marriage feast without the proper wedding garment also comes to mind. God sent his Son into the world as a naked infant in order to clothe all who desire with the garment of salvation. Let us thank God for his Christmas wardrobe.

43

Lesson 2: Hebrews 2:10-18

Perfect through suffering. The writer contends that it was God's will to make Jesus "perfect through suffering" (v. 10). Perfection here means "to be complete" or "mature" (*telios*). By implication, it could be argued that it is God's will to make us complete through suffering also. After all, didn't Jesus charge that we must take up our cross and follow him? God can also make us perfect (complete) through suffering for the sake of righteousness, though not all suffering is redemptive. Yet, through the blood, sweat, and tears of shared suffering we become one family in God.

Lesson 2: Colossians 3:12-21

Dressing for holiness. This lesson informs us how we might dress for holiness by clothing ourselves with the proper attitudes, especially love (v. 14). See Lesson 1: Isaiah 61:10—62:3, "The garment of salvation."

Lesson 2: Galatians 3:23-25; 4:4-7

All in the family. We are adopted into God's family and given the Spirit of Jesus that we might address God not as stranger but Father and receive our inheritance.

Gospel: Matthew 2:13-23

Guardian angels. It appears that guardian angels were working overtime in the first part of our Lord's life. An angel warned Joseph to flee to Egypt to avert Herod's wrath and informs him when it was safe to return. Likewise, he was warned in a dream not to settle with his family in Judah. These angels seemed to function like intelligence agents, informing the Holy Family of the enemy's intended moves. Yet, there was no guardian angel warning the Lord of the dangers of going to Jerusalem, where he would be handed over to be crucified; of course, Jesus knew what was facing him.

The Bible never really states that each child of God has a guardian angel, though many of us like to think that we do. If so, it is quite clear that these spirits cannot or will not save us from all suffering or even an untimely death. Maybe their function is not to shield us from danger but to cool our feet when we walk through the flames of adversity.

On second thought, haven't all of us who are children of God experienced guardian angels? They need not be winged spirits; they can also be flesh and blood messengers whom God sends to us at just the right time with just the right word: a word of comfort, hope, or wisdom. If we think about it, we can name some of them; but to whom are we sent as guardian angels with a message from the Lord?

Homemaking. According to Matthew, the Holy Family was not able to establish a real home for some time. Verse 23 states that Joseph made his home in Nazareth. Since Joseph was a carpenter, we could interpret that verse quite literally. In our society, women are generally the ones who are given the title of homemaker. Yet, the truth of the matter is that the contributions of both husband and wife are needed to make a home for the raising up of children. Though two loving parents are best, we need to be careful so that we do not denigrate those single parents who are working hard to provide a proper home for their children and doing admirably. A sermon on the attributes that are needed to be a Christian homemaker could be very helpful: such things as caring, forgiving, listening, disciplining, and openness to God's Spirit.

Holy Innocents. The destruction of the children in and around Bethlehem is dubbed "the Slaughter of the Holy Innocents." While some of us are holy, none is wholly innocent of guilt. Yet, this text is a good opportunity to deal with an issue that troubles millions of people. How can a loving God allow the destruction of those who are comparatively innocent? Why is one person taken while another is spared? We cannot, of course, offer a satisfactory explanation to this agonizing problem but we do have something to say to the issue. We must honestly admit the reality of injustice but also point to the reality of a God who suffers with us the outrageous arrows of adversity, injustice, and untimely death. His resurrection offers hope to all.

Gospel: John 1:1-18

See the gospel lesson for Christmas 2 (C, RC).

PREACHING APPROACHES WITH ILLUSTRATIONS

Lesson 1: Isaiah 63:7-9

Sermon Title: Counting And Discounting

Sermon Angle: The prophet writes that he will recount the gracious deeds of God. Great idea! As the gospel song says: "Count your blessings, name them one by one." On the other hand, discount all the grievous things that have happened to you.

Lesson 1: Isaiah 61:10—62:3

Sermon Title: Dressing For Salvation

Sermon Angle: The world knows how to dress for success but the Bible shows us how to be clothed in holy attire by putting on God's righteousness.

Outline:

Introduction: As children, we dressed in our parents' old clothes as a way of getting into the role we would play someday.

1. There is a relationship between who we are and how we dress
2. Changing our appearance can transform self-perception
3. God has clothed us with the garment of salvation. We see ourselves no longer as sinners but as God's dear children.
4. Living out this identity, we will eventually be clothed with the garments of God's glory

Lesson 2: Hebrews 2:10-18

Sermon Title: Scared Of Dying?

Sermon Angle: Jesus took on our humanity, according to the author of Hebrews, so that he might destroy the one who has had the power of death (the devil) and free humans from their lifelong bondage to the fear of death (vv. 14-15). In destroying the power of Satan over death, he attacks death objectively. Death and the devil have not been eliminated but defanged, brought under subjection to God's power. Jesus also attacks death on another front. He frees people from the slavery to their fear of death. This is a subjective liberation. This insight acknowledges the fact that fear can make us slaves to that which has no objective power. To be in Christ frees us from death as an objective reality and a subjective fear.

Outline:

1. The fear of death is common
2. The Bible tells us that the fear of death is connected to the reality of sin and the fear of punishment (Romans 6:23)
3. Jesus has atoned for our sins (v. 17)
4. Jesus' sacrifice frees us from the power of the devil and the fear of death (vv. 1-15)

Lesson 2: Colossians 3:12-21

Sermon Title: Christian Clothing

Sermon Angle: The theme is very similar to that found in the Episcopal First Lesson (Isaiah 61:10). This passage takes the "Clothing For Salvation" theme a step further. Since God has clothed us with salvation, let us make sure that it shows in our attitudes and behavior.

Outline:
1. God has clothed us in righteousness when we put on Christ. Therefore, let it show.
2. Let it show in our attitudes — compassion, kindness, humility ...
3. Let it show in our relationships — "clothe yourself in love"
4. Let it rule in our family relationships (vv. 18-21)

Lesson 2: Galatians 3:23-25; 4:4-7

Sermon Title: All In The Family

Outline:
1. God sent his child into the world (v. 4)
2. That we might become his dear child (v. 5)
3. All who love Jesus are one family and have the privilege of calling out to God as Father and to Christ as brother

Gospel: Matthew 2:13-23

Sermon Title: Homemaking

Sermon Angle: Christmas is the story of God's attempt to make his home with us. It was a struggle. Jesus was not born into a stable home environment but in an animal stable. The fledgling family was displaced by government regulations and then was put to flight once more in order to escape the rage of a cruel tyrant. Eventually, the Holy Family established their home in Nazareth. It is interesting that the one who came into the world so that we might come home to God began and ended his life on earth without a permanent address. What does it take to establish a home? It certainly has more to do with people than with place. A home is an environment where we know others as we are known, love others as we are loved — a place of safety and acceptance. Those who experience the love of Jesus in their families and their church have a true home. Christmas is a time when our hearts turn homeward, but our hearts will only be truly satisfied when we are sheltered in the everlasting arms.

Outline:
1. At Christmas our hearts turn toward home (tell a favorite homecoming story)
2. What is home? What is it that we are seeking to come back to? (Love, acceptance, security, and celebration)
3. God made his home with us in Christ, that we might be at home with God. Have you come home to your heavenly Father?

* * * * *

Christmas produces a magnetic homeward attraction on our hard metallic hearts. Garrison Keillor, in his *Christmas in Lake Wobegon*, describes this phenomena like this: "You're walking along in a shopping mall when all of a sudden a familiar Christmas tune penetrates your subconscious mind which sets off a switch in that part of the brain where memories are stored and then gates open and tons of water thunder through the Grand Coulee, the big turbines spin, electricity flows, and we get in our car and go back, like salmon."

*　*　*　*　*

The fact that Christ was born into the human family sanctifies this basic building block of community. There has never been a better time to highlight this truth than in this day where the family is being constantly bombarded in economic, social, ideological, and even religious forces. To illustrate, a scout troop of 23 boys meets in a church located in a small city in Nebraska. Twenty of the 23 are the products of broken homes. In the same church a support group for such youngsters draws over sixty children. It's called "Rainbows" and it has already spread to 27 states with a waiting list anxious to enter, that they might share their anguish and anger.

Could this disastrous disintegration of our family and community life be a result of our American love affair with the notion of radical individualism? In the action movie, *The Last of the Mohicans*, there is a scene where some buckskin clan colonials are being badgered by a dandified British officer to join in the fight against the French for control of the land. When the passionate entreaty hit an icy wall of indifference, the officer became furious: "You call yourselves patriots and loyal subjects of the Crown?"

Hawkeye, the half-Indian hero of the movie tersely responds, "Don't call myself subject to much at all."

Have we become a nation of Hawkeyes?

*　*　*　*　*

Those who are the casualties of these failed families often experience isolation, especially the children. The movie, *Clara's Heart*, starring Whoopi Goldberg, illustrates this process. Clara is a maid in Jamaica who has herself survived disastrous family crises, making her sensitive to the hurts of others. She befriends a rich woman from Boston, vacationing with her husband. The woman is in severe depression caused by the loss of her baby and a troubled marriage. The short of it is that Clara becomes their live-in maid and the confidant of their son, about ten years old, who at first bitterly resents her intrusion. He hungers for intimacy and warmth from his parents. The problem is that the mother is so caught up in her own grief and the father with his toys that the boy's feelings are totally discounted. For both of them, individual happiness is paramount. The needs of their son will have to wait. He and Clara become best friends. In the end, both parents find other loves and he is confronted with having to choose between living with his father in Boston or his mother in California. He really wants to live with Clara but he is denied this option. He settles with his mother and achieves some modicum of adjustment. The sad fact remains that here is a boy whose name is legion, who has never really had the experience of coming home.

We in the church must point the way. Christ became a part of our human family to turn our hearts toward home.

Christmas 2

Revised Common:	Jeremiah 31:7-14	Ephesians 1:3-14	John 1:(1-9) 10-18
Roman Catholic:	Sirach 2:4-12	Ephesians 1:3-14	John 1:1-18
Episcopal:	Jeremiah 31:7-14	Ephesians 1:3-6, 15-19a	Matthew 2:13-15, 19-23

Theme For The Day: Through the Incarnate Word, we are conceived in love and born anew as God's dear children. As we begin this new year, we look forward to receiving the gifts of his grace.

Suggested Text For Preaching: John 1:1-18

BRIEF COMMENTARY ON THE LESSONS

Lesson 1: Jeremiah 31:7-14 (C, E)
God proclaims through his prophet a message of hope, comfort, and national revival. The time of the Babylonian captivity would come to an end and the people would come back to Zion rejoicing. God lavishes comfort on this people, whom he allowed to be punished.

Lesson 1: Sirach 2:4-12 (RC)
Wisdom, which God created in the beginning, has found a home with the People of God.

Lesson 2: Ephesians 1:3-14 (C, RC); Ephesians 1:3-6, 15-19a (E)
Paul extols the lavishness of God's gifts of grace in choosing us, before the world was created, to be his own dear children. This gift is ours through the redemption which is in Christ. In him, God has revealed the mystery of his will. It is our destiny, as God's chosen ones, to inherit the riches of eternal life. God has blessed us with his Spirit that we might live a life of praise and thanksgiving for the riches of divine grace.

Gospel: John 1:(1-9) 10-18 (C); John 1:1-18 (RC)
See the gospel lesson for Christmas 1 (E).

Gospel: Matthew 2:13-15, 19-23 (E)
See the gospel lesson for Christmas 1 (C, RC).

Psalm Of The Day
　　Psalm 147:12-20 (C) — It is good to praise the Lord for all his blessings.
　　Psalm 84 (E) — It is good to go to the house of worship and praise the name of the Lord.

Prayer Of The Day
　　Oh, God of grace, we, your people, bless you and praise your holy name for the gifts of life and salvation. You are Alpha and Omega, the first and the last, and so we ask that you would inhabit all our beginnings and endings. In Jesus' name. Amen.

THEOLOGICAL REFLECTION ON THE LESSONS

Lesson 1: Jeremiah 31:7-14

The joy of gathering. Jeremiah foresees a time when God will gather together the scattered people of Israel. This is to be a time of comfort, joy, and celebration for the weak and downtrodden; this will be a glorious occasion to praise the goodness of their God. Christmas and the holiday season is traditionally a time of gathering for families and friends. One of the most depressing prospects possible is to be alone at Christmas. The images of Christmas that warm our hearts feature happy faces gathered around a blazing fireplace, faces aglow, or families assembled around the Christmas tree packed with gifts, a table laden with holiday fare, or worshipers massed together in church pews singing "Silent Night." At Christmas there is a homing instinct, but what is it that we desire to come home to? It is not particularly a house or merely a place but a community of love that draws us. In our waywardness, God scatters us or allows our sin to separate us one from the other but God's salvation brings us back together, back home. Holiday reunions, a foretaste of that which awaits us beyond the value of eternity, are sublime times of rejoicing that transcends the season.

Transforming sadness into gladness (vv. 13-14). Jeremiah experienced all the sorrow and pain of his people; he was so smitten that, at times, he wished that he'd never been born. Yet God made known to him that he was not a macabre Deity but the Lord of the dance and the God of all consolation. The Lord would transform their sadness into gladness, their sighing into singing. In a similar vein, in the gospel of John, Jesus refers to the Holy Spirit as the Comforter. The scriptures reveal a God who stands with us in good times and bad, leading us through the "valley of the shadow of death." The gospel makes manifest the shocking reality of a God who not only consoles us in suffering but actually takes our suffering and sin upon himself and nails it to the cross. As Christians, we experience the fact that we dwell in a strange and foreign land but we rejoice because our captivity will soon be at an end.

Lesson 2: Ephesians 1:3-19a

Manifest destiny. In the nineteenth century, the doctrine of manifest destiny was invoked to justify the westward expansion of our country and to make North America our sphere of influence. It was cited as a rationale for the Spanish-American War in 1898. Unfortunately, this motto had imperialistic overtones and, for better or worse, has led to the United States becoming a world power. In our text, we have a much different kind of manifest destiny lifted up for us. "He predestined us for adoption as his children through Jesus Christ ..." (v. 5). It is our divine destiny to live eternally as God's dear children, but this destiny cannot be realized by imperialistic expansion or an impassioned appeal to blood and race; our destiny is a gift of grace that can only be possessed through love and trust. That destiny is extended personally through baptism but can only be received by faith in Jesus, the Christ. It is only this realization of manifest destiny that can save us. Violence has been perpetrated by those possessed by a misguided concept of manifest destiny, but greater and increasing violence is being waged by those who can see no further than the present moment and view the world as a jungle where every creature is merely struggling for survival. In love we were conceived by God for love; that is our destiny which can only be realized in the Beloved.

Signed, sealed, and delivered. "In him you also, when you had heard the word of truth, the gospel of your salvation, and had believed in him, were marked with the seal of the promised Holy Spirit ..." (v. 13). The Spirit is the guarantee that we are the Lord's and is a down payment on our eternal inheritance. As followers of Christ, we have truly been signed, sealed, and delivered. We have been formed by the sign of the cross. In our baptism, the sign of the cross was imprinted on our forehead as a sign of our adoption as God's dear children. God has signed our name to his. Then, we were sealed with the Holy Spirit. The Spirit in us bears witness that we are children of God. Finally, we are delivered, like a letter from God. The Lord sends us out into the world as a love letter written in the precious blood of his Son, Jesus, the Christ. Do others see the gospel in us or are we like a love letter from God left unopened?

Gospel: John 1:1-18

Lord of life. John states that the divine *logos*, the divine word, was already there at the beginning of all creation, the instrument through which God created all things. This tells us not only that God created, but that the creation reflects a pattern of divine wisdom. The universe didn't just happen; it is the product of divine design. John takes pains to point out that God created everything that has being. This was to counter those who maintained that the material universe was evil, the work of an evil god. No, creation is good, Spirit-ordered, and animated, maintains the Evangelist. To yield up this truth would prove disastrous, resulting in a split between the material and the spiritual. God would no longer be the Lord of all life. There are many who would rejoice to exile God to the heavens. Then they could rape and pillage the world, free of conscience; then they could order the world according to their own design. Indeed, many live a practical atheism, holding to the concept of God but denying God any place in their lives or the created order.

"In the beginning was the word." Much meaning is packed into this short phrase. *Word* implies message and meaning, which informs us that our God wills to reveal himself to us, to communicate. There can be no relationship without communication and the more deeply and truthfully we communicate, the more intimate the relationship. Words are powerful means of conveying knowledge and truth but the most powerful and immediate means of communicating is through our bodies, our being. A caress, a pat, a hand on the shoulder, or a facial expression can reveal more than words can ever say. John proclaims that the word became flesh in the person of Jesus. What God did for us in Jesus reveals more than all of his teachings put together. Obviously, God and his ways are still mysterious, but in Christ we have personally seen, felt, and experienced the heart of God. The incarnation is God's supreme means of self-communication. Notice that I use the verb "is" and not "was." The God incarnate in Jesus is also incarnate in those who know Jesus. We, too, are the living word of God through whom God seeks to disclose his love and grace.

Life and light. From the dawn of time, humans have worshiped the light, realizing intuitively what we now understand scientifically, that there is no life without light. Genesis proclaims this truth also; light is the first order of creation. The prologue of John implies that the light was present in the *logos* from the beginning, but the fullness of the light dawned when the word became flesh. "In him was life and the life was the light of all people" (v. 4). This light has not yet overcome the darkness ("the light shines in the darkness ...") but the darkness has not dispelled the light. The light of Christ is different than created light in that it must be received. Those who receive the light become the children of God, who is light. In his epistles, John says that we must not only receive the light but walk in the light. To love our brothers and sisters means to walk in the light (1 John 1:7; 2:8). The Christopher movement within the Roman Catholic church employed as its motto the saying: "If everyone would light just one little candle, what a bright world this would be." How true. Each act of love, however small, is a candle which helps dispel the darkness of ignorance and sin.

Gifts Galore. "From his fullness have we all received, grace upon grace" (v. 16). Our God is rich and generous. God has lavished his bounty upon us. Yet if we dwell in the darkness of selfishness and sin, we do not see these blessings, let alone appreciate them. At Christmas time, we exchange gifts as a symbol of God's gift of eternal life through his Son, but we seem to lose sight of the gifts of God, especially his supreme gift, in all of our frantic festivity. The Christmas season is similar to Thanksgiving Day; it is a time to meditate on all the gifts of God's grace, including those many items we take for granted.

Gospel: Matthew 2:13-15, 19-23

See the gospel lesson for Christmas 1

PREACHING APPROACHES WITH ILLUSTRATIONS

Lesson 1: Jeremiah 31:7-14

Sermon Title: Homecoming

Sermon Angle: Jeremiah warned his people that if they persisted in their sinful ways, they would be wrenched away from their homeland. After this came to pass, he foresaw a time when the exiles would return home with dancing and singing. Those who were scattered would be gathered together in their homeland, their holy city and their temple. At Christmas, God made his home with us that we might come home to God and God's family, with shouts of praise and thanksgiving.

Outline:
1. God gathered the Jews and brought them home
2. They returned with rejoicing and praise
3. God sent his Son to gather all the families on earth to the kingdom
4. Let us return home to God with praise and thanksgiving

Sermon Title: Transforming Sadness Into Gladness

Sermon Angle: The Jewish exiles lived an existence fraught with pain and sorrow. God promised to transform their tears of sorrow to tears of joy as he carried them home. We, too, live in a world where pain and sorrow are strangers to nobody. We have a God who, in Christ, transforms our sorrows by sharing them with us, all the while leading us to our heavenly home.

Outline:
1. Cite examples of pain and suffering
2. Even God's own people suffer
3. We cannot comprehend the reason for suffering
4. We can trust in a God who shares our suffering and transforms it
5. Let us praise our God who transforms sadness into gladness

* * * * *

The meaning of Christmas can be found in the most unlikely places, such as the comic pages in the newspaper. In the *Wizard of Id* strip for Christmas day I found this story.

Hearing a cutting sound from within the cell, the spook in the dungeon was asked by his jailer what he was up to. "Trimming the tree," was the reply. "Very funny," intoned the jailer.

Then the jailer looked inside the cell. The spook had indeed trimmed the Christmas tree. Nothing was left but two sticks — one vertical and the other horizontal. It was a cross. The jailer scolded, "Nice going ... You've ruined the symbol of Christmas." Isn't that what many people think? That Christmas has nothing to do with the cross? No relationship to sin, suffering, or death. The trimmings and trappings of Christmas often obscure the real message. The abundant beauty, joy, and love symbolized in the Christmas tree is built around a cross. One day, we, too, will go home to be with the Father of Lights and the Family of Faith. By grace through faith we have been grafted into the Tree of Life, because God's Son died for our sin on the naked tree that stood on Golgotha.

Lesson 2: Ephesians 1:3-19a

Sermon Title: Manifest Destiny

Sermon Angle: The doctrine of manifest destiny was a guiding principle for our country's westward expansion. It was interpreted to mean that it was our destiny to possess and control the land. In Christ, we are given an eternal destiny, to be God's dear children.

Outline:
1. Explain manifest destiny
2. God has made manifest our destiny to be his children
   a. Personal redemption (v. 5)
   b. To unite all things in heaven and earth (vv. 9-10)
3. Follow your destiny
   a. Some look to the stars (astrology)
   b. We follow the Holy Spirit (vv. 13-14)
   c. That we might inherit the kingdom

Gospel: John 1:1-18

Sermon Title: Word 1

Sermon Angle: If you are familiar with Microsoft Works word processing software, you have seen the suggested sermon title before. When you open up Works, your document is given a default handle: Word 1. Eventually, you will need to give it your own name, but "Word 1" will get you going. Before any of us wrote on the slate of existence, there was a preexisting word created by God called the *logos*. In our computer literate age, we might think of it as Word 1. The main difference is that the divine *logos* is not blank, like the opening word processing screen. Before we were born, the divine word was written large, underlined with the blood of Christ: God created you and all the world; in him is life and light.

Outline:
1. Skeptics say that the world is wordless — without transcendent meaning
2. The gospel tells us that there is a preexistent word — Word 1
   — it is a creative word
   — a redemptive word
   — a word in human form
3. To all who receive the Word, God gives the power to become his children (vv. 12-13)

* * * * *

Some computer games, packed with action and adventure, are so lifelike that they are dubbed *virtual reality*. But is electronic communication really virtual reality? Hardly! Virtual reality is when you have to communicate with people in the flesh, people who are annoying, stubborn, and uninteresting. Virtual reality is walking the floor half the night with a crying baby, frustrated at not understanding what she's trying to tell you. Virtual reality is the commitment to live with and love a person who speaks of a different emotional language. Virtual reality is the language spoken by the God of the Bible who took on human flesh in Jesus Christ. The grace and truth which he manifests is the first word and the last.

The Epiphany Season

How The Season Came To Be

Epiphany is one of the most ancient liturgical celebrations in the church, second only to Easter, observed as early as the second century. The date, of course, falls on January 6th because that was the ancient winter solstice, the celebration of the rising of the sun god and the lengthening of the light of day. The solstice was later moved to December 25, in 331 AD, but the former date continued to be observed. It is plain so see that the church fathers chose the dates for both Epiphany and Christmas in an attempt to overcome the influence of the ancient festivals. It was a rather easy transition from the rebirth of the light to the manifestation of the Light of the World.

Originally, Epiphany commemorated both the birth and the baptism of our Lord. Later, these two events were separated. The eastern church continued to observe Epiphany as the baptism of our Lord, while the western church lifted up the appearing of the Magi. The church of the east probably chose to emphasize the baptism to counteract the gnostic heresy, which claimed that Jesus was designated the Son of God at his baptism.

The Meaning And Message Of Epiphany

Epiphany is a Greek word that can be translated "manifestation." The divine *logos* has become visible in the incarnate Son of God. Light is necessary for anything to become manifest, and so in this season we lift up Christ as the light of the whole world. The light of God's redemptive purpose can be clearly seen, dispelling the darkness of ignorance and sin. This is not a localized light, beaming on one nation, but the "Light of the World." The story of the visitation of the Magi fits nicely into this scheme, since they were Gentiles who followed the star that they too might worship and adore the Christ.

Our problem is that in the imagination of our culture, the Epiphany event has become fused with the Christmas story. That's quite obvious from observing Christmas pageants and crèches, picturing the Magi kneeling by the manger. In fact, the story of the Magi is itself ambiguous. It implies that the Messiah was to be found in Bethlehem but relates that the Magi found the Christ Child in his home, not his birthplace. Consequently, both of the events associated with Epiphany, the search of the Magi and the Baptism Of Our Lord, have gotten buried in the Christmas celebration. Since the festival of the Epiphany falls during the week, six times out of seven, most Protestant churchgoers never really celebrate Epiphany as such. Roman Catholic Christians are obligated to attend a special mass but one can imagine that this duty is taken with decreasing seriousness.

We do need to work to elevate Epiphany to its proper place of importance but we must guard against the opposite danger of isolating Epiphany from Advent and Christmas. Epiphany is part of the Christmas cycle of theologically related holidays. Advent prepares for the celebration of Christ's first advent at Bethlehem and his second advent at the end of historical time, to consummate his kingdom. Christmas is the celebration of the presence of the Christ, the God made flesh. Epiphany is the celebration of the light of God's incarnate and saving presence, made known to the entire world. The Jewish Messiah becomes the Savior of the whole world; we have been transported from the particular to the universal. This is why Epiphany contains a strong missionary emphasis. The Magi followed the light of the star to the Christ; we are called not only to follow the light of Christ but to be transparent to the light, so that it shines through us into the world of darkness. This is seen as a fulfillment of Isaiah's universalistic prophecies that picture the Gentiles coming to the light of Israel's God.

The Epiphany season would be a wonderful time to spotlight the outreach mission of the church. A different aspect of mission outreach could be highlighted each week such as: foreign missions, American missions (church planting), outreach to minorities and the disabled, witnessing at home and the job, the congregation's mission to neighborhood or community, and ministry to the poor and hungry. The focus should be twofold — making known how the light is already shining and considering new ways to penetrate the darkness with the gospel. Consider establishing an Epiphany emphasis committee to develop a concerted missions emphasis for the season. Planning would need to begin in September or October. Possibilities are limitless and this could be a good way to beat the post-Christmas blahs. Unlike the Advent-Christmas seasons, we don't have to counteract or compete with secular expressions.

During the Epiphany season, the manifestation of the Christ increasingly unfolds. The Magi follow the star to the Christ Child, Jesus is baptized and receives affirmation of his messiahship, he proclaims the gospel, is revealed through word and sign, and finally, in the Transfiguration, is permeated with the glow of visible glory. Revelation is not instantaneous but progressive. That, too, is how we have come to know Christ, for the most part — not a sudden blinding light, but a light coming on here and there, as the darkness retreats.

Other Facts About Epiphany

Length: The season begins on January 6 with the Festival of Epiphany, so the starting point is always the same, but it is an accordion season: its length depending on when Easter occurs. If Easter comes early, it is short, and if Easter comes late, the season lengthens to a maximum of nine weeks.

Name: The Roman Catholic lectionary has no Epiphany season as such, although the lessons are basically the same as the other lectionary series; rather, it dubs the Sundays after the Epiphany as Ordinary Time.

Color: The color white represents the mood and meaning of the season. Paraments of that color are used on Epiphany Sunday, The Baptism Of Our Lord (Epiphany 1), and The Transfiguration Of Our Lord (Last Sunday After Epiphany). White is symbolic of the light and connotes brightness, knowledge, and joy. Green is employed for the other Sundays in the season, conveying the idea of growth. We are called to grow in faith and knowledge of the word made manifest in Christ.

Unifying Theme For The Epiphany Season

During this Epiphany season we will focus on the idea of God as Spirit, which permeates the pericopes for the season. Without God's Spirit, Christianity would devolve into lifeless legalism. Each week you could hold up a different aspect of God's gift of the Spirit, which leads us to Christ and illuminates our lives with his light. If you decide to employ this unitive theme for the season, you will want to adopt the Suggested Sermon Text and the Suggested Sermon Title listed toward the top of each week's resources. However, many other approaches are put forth for your consideration. Sermon titles for the series are listed below.

1. The Festival of Epiphany (January 6) — God's Guiding Spirit
2. Epiphany 1/Ordinary Time 1: The Baptism Of Our Lord — God's Favoring Spirit
3. Epiphany 2/Ordinary Time 2 — God's Inviting Spirit
4. Epiphany 3/Ordinary Time 3 — God's Liberating Spirit
5. Epiphany 4/Ordinary Time 4 — God's Spirit of Humility
6. Epiphany 5/Ordinary Time 5 — God's Illuminating Spirit
7. Epiphany 6/Ordinary Time 6 — God's Forgiving Spirit

8. Epiphany 7/Ordinary Time 7 — God's Loving Spirit
9. Epiphany 8/Ordinary Time 8 — God's Renewing Spirit
10. The Transfiguration Of Our Lord (Last Sunday After Epiphany) — The Fulfilling Gift Of The Spirit: Transcendence

(Please realize that this listed sermon series is only one approach and has not been extensively developed in the pages that follow.)

The Epiphany Of Our Lord

Revised Common:	Isaiah 60:1-6	Ephesians 3:1-12	Matthew 2:1-12
Roman Catholic:	Isaiah 60:1-6	Ephesians 3:2-3a, 5-6	Matthew 2:1-12
Episcopal:	Isaiah 60:1-6, 9	Ephesians 3:1-12	Matthew 2:1-12

Seasonal Theme: Gifts Of God's Spirit

Theme For The Day: The Gift Of Guidance. The Magi were guided to the Christ by the light of the star. We are guided to our eternal destiny by the light of the Holy Spirit.

Suggested Sermon Text: Matthew 2:1-12

Suggested Sermon Title: God's Guiding Spirit

BRIEF COMMENTARY ON THE LESSONS

Lesson 1: Isaiah 60:1-6 (C, RC); Isaiah 60:1-6, 9 (E)

The light of God's glory has been shed on the chosen people and all the people who live in darkness will be drawn to the light, together with Israel's scattered citizens.

Lesson 2: Ephesians 3:1-12 (C, E); Ephesians 3:2-3a, 5-6 (RC)

The mystery of the gospel, withheld from former generations, has now been revealed in Christ to all people, including the Gentiles. All believers are members of the Household of Faith and have direct access to God.

Gospel: Matthew 2:1-12 (C, RC, E)

The visitation of the Magi.

Psalm Of The Day

Psalm 72:1-7, 10-14 (C); Psalm 72 (E) — A prayer that God would endow his anointed king with righteousness and caring spirit.

Prayer Of The Day

Eternal God, you have made known the light of your eternal glory in the face of Jesus Christ. Fill us, your children, with the light of your love, so that the darkness of sin might be dispelled in us and in the world around us. In the name of Jesus. Amen.

THEOLOGICAL REFLECTION ON THE LESSONS

Lesson 1: Isaiah 60:1-6

Rise, shine, and give God the glory. A song that our children's chancel choir sang years ago has the above phrase as part of the chorus. The lyrics seem to suggest that the source of light emanates from within us. This text makes plain that God is the source of light and life. "Arise, shine; for your light has come" (v. 1). Darkness may envelope much of the earth, but the glory of God shines upon his people. The question is: What is our position in reference to the light? To illustrate, consider solar panels: in order for the panels to receive the energy from the sun, they have to maintain the proper angle and attitude. Merely being in the sun is not enough, the solar panels must be positioned properly to absorb the sun's rays. To absorb the energy and light of our Creator, we must maintain the right attitude and angle. Prayer provides the proper spiritual position to absorb the saving light of Christ's presence because real prayer means that we assume an attitude of humility — "Thy will be done." To look at it from another angle, prayer is the attitude that allows the glory of the Lord to shine through us. So, do we throw out the children's song as being theologically incorrect? No, once we receive the light of Christ, it is our duty and delight to glorify and praise the Lord in our worship and in our witness.

Lesson 2: Ephesians 3:1-12

Equal access under the gospel. In our society, we have heard a great deal about equal access under the law. The handicapped are deemed to have equal access to public places. Laws framed to maintain privileges for one group over another have been challenged and overturned. Minorities have successfully sued for their rights under the law. When it comes to our relationship with God, there are no rights of equal access or to any access at all. However, the gospel reveals that our God is gracious and grants equal access, not under law, but under grace. In this lesson, Paul makes clear that the Jews were the first to be given such a lofty privilege. Then the light of grace shone upon Saul of Tarsus, and he was commissioned to be Paul, the apostle to the Gentiles. It was his passion to reveal the mystery of God's unsearchable grace. Now, the doors to the kingdom are open to all people. The only thing that can keep a person outside in the darkness is unbelief.

Wouldn't it be great if every congregation would examine its community life to discover those barriers to equal access under the gospel? The building could itself be a barrier. Is the facility attractive, available to all? Is the worship space cheery and inviting? What about the congregational climate? When a new person comes to worship is he/she made to feel welcome? Do worshipers feel comfortable in being themselves or must they conform to certain outward standards of style and dress? Most importantly, does every person who passes through the doors have equal access to the gospel or are the worship, educational, service, and social opportunities directed to our kind of people? It is God's plan that all people might approach the throne of God with boldness and confidence through faith in Christ (v. 12).

Gospel: Matthew 2:1-12

Wise men (and women) still seek him. You have probably seen this motto previously but a good saying bears repeating. The wise men followed the star on a long and arduous journey to pay tribute to the new king. How different from the reaction of Herod, who wanted to destroy this new upstart out of jealousy. Wise people are still seekers. When we think we have life or God or anything else all wrapped up, we stop seeking and growing. Jesus encourages us to seek that we might find. Discipleship is an invitation to follow Christ on a journey of faith. It doesn't matter so much where we are in our life of faith as it does where we are going. Unfortunately, some people are going nowhere because they perceive that the journey is completed. Possessed by fear and foolishness, they refuse to follow the star.

Then, there are the people who are following the wrong star. They are seekers, all right, seekers after power, fame, and fortune. They are ready at all times to bow the knee to their gods. They, too, are foolish because their journey leads nowhere but the grave.

Not theologically correct. When you really delve into the lovely story of the visitation of the Magi, which has inspired numerous artistic renditions, the implications become somewhat disturbing. These Magi were a priestly class from Media and Persia, functionaries of the Zoroastrian religion. Their belief system was not theologically correct; for starters, they believed in two gods — one good and the other, evil. Furthermore, they were magicians, a practice which is bitterly denounced in the Old Testament. The word *Magi* is the plural of *Magus*, from which we derive the words "magic" and "magician." In their priestly role, they practiced the ancient art of astrology, believing that the stars controlled human affairs. Christianity has always looked at astrology with disdain, because it removes the necessity of a personal God and free will. This account raises some interesting points. Does the Lord accept the worship of those who are not members of the Jewish/Christian faith? Does God guide people who follow erroneous belief systems? If not, why do we have this story in Matthew's gospel? Perhaps this is leading us to a great truth: God is much larger than any religion or theological system. Could it also point to the fact that God is sovereign and uses whomever he wills to accomplish heaven's purpose? This pagan priestly group was looking for a sign indicating the birth of the Messiah and were rewarded. On the other hand, the priests in Jerusalem were not actively looking and were not prepared to accept the sign of God's Son. Certainly, more questions have been raised than answered but that seems to be the result when you gaze into the heavens pulsing with mysterious light.

What sign were you born under? Millions of otherwise rational people put some degree of stock in astrology. You certainly have been asked, "What sign were you born under?" Is there anyone who doesn't know his or her sign? Millions search daily for their sign in the newspaper's astrology column in hopes that it might shed some light on their future. What sign were you born under? The same sign that I was born under: the sign of the cross. It is said that when Emperor Constantine was about to engage in battle with a rival, the outcome of which would determine who would rule the might of Rome, he gazed into the heavens and saw the sign of the cross with the message: "In this sign, conquer." He ordered the legion standard bearer to raise the sign of the cross over the troops as they marched into battle and they were victorious. Consequently, Constantine made Christianity the official state religion. The story may be apocryphal but the principle remains: In this sign we were baptized, in this sign we are redeemed, in this sign we will die and, most importantly, in this sign we will conquer. Our destiny is not to be found in the sign of a star but in the sign of the cross on which God opened his hands to embrace the whole world. Perhaps you've seen the poster with this message: "I asked God, 'How much do you love me?' He said, 'This is how much I love you.' Then, he opened his arms and died." Thank God for such a favorable sign.

They opened their treasure chests. When the Magi found the Christ child, they paid him proper kingly homage as they kneeled before him. Then they opened their treasure chests and laid gold, frankincense, and myrrh at the feet of their king. If we have truly witnessed the Epiphany of Jesus Christ in our lives, would it not follow that we would freely lay before him our treasure as an expression of our homage? Jesus taught, "For where your treasure is, there will your heart be also." Is our treasure locked tight or laid at the foot of our Lord and king?

The Baptism Of Our Lord/Epiphany 1/Ordinary Time 1

Revised Common:	Isaiah 42:1-9	Acts 10:34-43	Matthew 3:13-17
Roman Catholic:	Isaiah 42:1-4, 6-7	Acts 10:34-38	Matthew 3:13-17
Episcopal:	Isaiah 42:1-9	Acts 10:34-38	Matthew 3:13-17

Seasonal Theme: The Holy Spirit is prominently featured in the Epiphany Season pericopes. The Spirit does not act in isolation but works to create and sustain the spiritual community. Each week we will examine a different aspect of the Spirit's presence in Christian community.

Theme For The Day: God's grace and favor, which was made known to Jesus at his baptism, is also revealed to us in our baptism.

Suggested Sermon Text: Matthew 3:13-17

Suggested Sermon Title: God's Favoring Spirit

BRIEF COMMENTARY ON THE LESSONS

Lesson 1: Isaiah 42:1-9 (C, E); Isaiah 42:1-4, 6-7 (RC)

The servant people of Israel, themselves oppressed and humiliated, are declared to be God's beloved servants who will gently reveal the light of God's will to the nations. That light of God is as a smoldering lamp among the heathen but God's servant nation is empowered by the Spirit to open the eyes of the spiritually blind and liberate those who languish in spiritual captivity. While this servant of the Lord can be applied to the nation of Israel, Christians have always seen more in this passage. Jesus is the servant of God's favor, anointed with the Spirit at baptism and commissioned to bear witness to the light of God in a world of darkness.

Lesson 2: Acts 10:34-43 (C); Acts 10:34-38 (RC, E)

Peter perceives from his dealings with Cornelius, a Roman officer, that God is impartial and that anyone who serves God is acceptable to him. In his baptism, Jesus is filled with the Holy Spirit and empowered to carry out a ministry of proclamation, exorcism, and healing. Peter then recounts the heart of the Christian gospel — the crucifixion and resurrection. He and the other apostles and disciples witnessed this saving event and broke bread with the risen Savior. Peter understands his role is to proclaim forgiveness and reconciliation through the power of the risen Christ.

Gospel: Matthew 3:13-17 (C, RC, E)

The baptism of Jesus has always proved troubling for Christians. If Jesus was sinless, why was he baptized by John? Matthew is the only gospel in which the Baptist protests Jesus' request for baptism but is told to go ahead so that Jesus could completely identify with those he came to save. John preached that the Messiah would be the one to baptize with the Holy Spirit. When Jesus was baptized by John, the Spirit descended on him like a dove, and the voice of

God proclaimed that Jesus is his beloved Son on whom his favor rests. While the other synoptic gospels make this event an inward spiritual experience of our Lord, Matthew portrays it as an external event, available to all present. "This is my beloved Son."

Psalm Of The Day
Psalm 29 (C) — The Lord is enthroned as king forever.
Psalm 89:1-29 (E) — God is faithful to those whom he has anointed.

Prayer Of The Day
Heavenly Father, as your beloved Son was baptized by John and filled with the Spirit of favor, so too may we be filled with your gracious Spirit, that we may live out our baptismal identity, until we are drawn into your nearer presence in your glorious kingdom. Amen.

THEOLOGICAL REFLECTION ON THE LESSONS

Lesson 1: Isaiah 42:1-9
A servant people. When people go through the crucible of suffering, it often clarifies who they are and what their existence is really about. The ancient Hebrews were no exception. They had long held that they were the chosen people but had lost sight of the purpose of that election. They were more tuned in to the privilege of their position rather than their responsibilities. The prophet of second Isaiah proclaimed powerfully that the Jews were favored by God, but that their privilege rested in being the Lord's servants. This servanthood was to be exercised with great humility and gentleness. "A bruised reed he shall not break, a dimly burning wick he will not quench ..." (v. 3).

The role of the servant people is evangelistic in nature. They are to bring forth righteousness to the nations, to be lights in a world of darkness, so that all people might see and know God's gracious will. In doing this, they are not to assume that God has completely withheld the light of his presence. They are to gently fan the dimly burning wick into full flame by the breath of God's Spirit. Through the gut-wrenching ordeal of captivity in a strange land, the Hebrews' horizons were lifted to a higher purpose, from survival to mission. Years ago I saw a sign in front of a downtown church: "Serving, not just surviving." It is a danger for any church to fall from a mission mindset into a survivalistic modality. As Jesus warned: "He who would save his life will lose it and he who loses his life for my sake and the sake of the gospel will find it."

Prison ministry. Chuck Colson discovered not only Christ in prison, he also found his mission there. Colson's ministry recognizes that those locked behind bars were confined in a prison of another sort long before they were incarcerated — a prison of spiritual darkness. Colson believes that no person can be spiritually free until he or she is free in Christ. The prisoner labors to free other prisoners. We see this same principle at work in this text. Isaiah addressed those who were themselves prisoners. They were commissioned to bring other prisoners — those locked in a prison of power, wealth, and self-indulgence — out of their spiritual dungeon through their witness to the Lord. Those whom God has freed from the shackles of sin must set out to free others, by the affirming power of God's grace. We are all engaged in prison ministry.

Lesson 2: Acts 10:34-43

How big is your God? Peter provides a useful model for all Christians. His concept of God was constantly growing. First off, he became convinced that Jesus was not an ordinary person — he was the Christ. However, his mind is too small to see Christ as a suffering servant Messiah. When the Lord spoke of his coming suffering and death, Peter soundly responded: "Far be it from you, Lord!" After the resurrection, he came to believe that Jesus is the risen Lord and Savior, but only of the Jews. Then he had a vision, and Cornelius, the Roman officer, had a vision, and the Holy Spirit brought these two men together. Peter's concept of God enlarged once again. Peter became convinced that "God shows no partiality but that anyone who fears him and does what is right is acceptable to him." God had really grown! How big is your God?

Gospel: Matthew 3:13-17

A window to heaven. This account states that when Jesus was baptized, the heavens opened. There are sacred moments when the window of eternity and opportunity open. Jesus' baptism was one such time. Through this act, Jesus was indicating his willingness to yield his life in obedience to the Father. In the moment of self-surrender, a voice from heaven confirmed the Father's favor, which was made tangible through the gift of the Holy Spirit.

While Christ's baptism did not have the same significance as our baptism, there are points of commonality. Both baptisms are acts of obedience through which the baptized experience grace and favor. It is an affirmation that is both personal and public. Both the baptized and those who witness the baptism are made cognizant of God's favor. Baptism is a window through which we see the God of grace. The difference here between Jesus' baptism and our own is that Jesus had earned God's favor and we have not. A second point, baptism was the launching pad of our Lord's ministry and so is our baptism. We are commissioned to be God's servant people. A third similarity is that in Christ's baptism, as well as our own, the Holy Spirit is imparted. We are empowered to carry out our divine commission. In baptism, we are accepted, commissioned, and empowered.

PREACHING APPROACHES WITH ILLUSTRATIONS

Lesson 1: Isaiah 42:1-9

Sermon Title: Are We Serving Or Merely Surviving?

Sermon Angle: The prophet helps his people forge a new identity in the furnace of national defeat; they were to be God's servant people to shed the light of the Lord on the nations dwelling in moral and spiritual darkness. They had been compelled to be the slaves of an enemy empire. Now, they were challenged to willingly be servants of the Lord of heaven and earth, to spread the knowledge of his holy will. They were challenged to serve and not merely survive.

Outline:
1. The Jews of Isaiah's day had lost their national identity through defeat
2. Christians today are losing their Christian identity to the prevailing culture
3. Isaiah reminded his people of God's grace and love for them and challenged them to find new purpose in serving the Lord
4. We, too, like the Jews, are the people whom the Lord has shown favor
5. Let us witness to the light of God that shines through the face of Christ

Sermon Title: Prison Ministry

Sermon Angle: Isaiah challenges his captive people to witness to the light of the Lord to those in spiritual captivity. They would find their own freedom through engaging in the Lord's liberation ministry. We, who have been freed of sin's servitude in Christ, are empowered by the Spirit to engage in prison ministry.

Outline:

1. We are all prisoners of sin (give examples of how sin binds us)
2. The Jews of Isaiah's day were offered freedom in God's covenant of grace
3. God offers us freedom through faith in Christ
4. To remain free, we must engage in Christ's ministry of liberation

Lesson 2: Acts 10:34-43

Sermon Title: How Big Is Your God?

Sermon Angle: In this passage we see how God enables human beings to enlarge their concept of God. Consider Peter — his concept of Jesus is greatly enlarged. First, Jesus is merely a man, then the Jewish Messiah, then the Son of God, and finally, the Savior of the world. Consider Cornelius also, his concept of deity must have dramatically transformed from belief in the multitude of Roman gods, to acknowledging the God of Israel, and finally to confessing Jesus as the Son of God. Some time ago, a book was written titled *Your God Is Too Small*. This would be a great opportunity to address the many inadequate concepts of God that people hold today, such as, God as personal therapist or God as Santa.

Outline:

1. Ask your listeners to think about how their concept of God has grown. Explain how your own concept of God has matured.
2. Show how Peter's and Cornelius' concepts of God had transformed
3. Discuss some of the current inadequate concepts of God
4. End by showing how we must settle for nothing less than the loving and saving God we find in the gospel

Gospel: Matthew 3:13-17

Sermon Title: Baptism, Our Lord's And Our Own

Sermon Angle: There are those who maintain that this festival is about the Lord's baptism and is not the proper moment to discuss our own baptism. They have a point, but the analogies between Jesus' baptism and our own are too compelling to ignore. We especially need to emphasize baptism as that identity forming event in which the Lord has bestowed on us his grace. There is no real life or growth apart from God's grace.

Outline:

1. In our Lord's baptism, the Father's favor was conferred on the Son. (Christian baptism is the preeminent sign of God's favor.)
2. In our Lord's baptism, the Father set his seal on the Son's mission — to fulfill all righteousness. Christian baptism commissions us to be Christ's witness.
3. In our Lord's baptism, the Son was empowered by the Holy Spirit for mission. Christian baptism gifts us with the Holy Spirit, that we might accomplish Christ's mission.

Sermon Title: Favor, The Initial Gift Of The Spirit

Sermon Angle: Since holy baptism is the foremost sign of God's favor, a sermon on God's wonderful gifts of grace would be in order.

Outline:

1. At the beginning of his ministry, Christ was baptized and the Father showered his favor on his Son
2. At the beginning of our spiritual life, in our baptism, God has bestowed his favor on us — acceptance, identity, and purpose
3. As security is the basis for human community, so grace is the foundation of the spiritual community. We need to know that we are loved, valued, and cared for before we can accomplish any good.

* * * * *

Ever since our health care institutions have become convinced that our political leaders intend a radical transformation of our health care delivery system, there has been a great deal of dis-ease in those institutions. Nurses, in particular, have been subjected to great pressures. They are expected to do more work, with sicker patients, in a shorter span of time, without engendering any complaints. I know a nurse at one such institution, and there are certainly legions more, who feels devalued and depressed because of the attitude of the administration. They are quick to share with her any minor complaint, even the slightest infraction. If a patient complains, it is always the nurse's fault. Seldom do they ever affirm the basic human worth of their employees. The bottom line seems to be all that matters, and this from a supposedly Christian institution. Have they forgotten that the healers must be whole but that no person can be whole apart from the realization that they are valued as persons and loved?

* * * * *

Radio preacher, Chuck Swindoll, tells of an experience of grace the day he became a teenager. Having attained the ripe old age of thirteen, he really thought he was hot stuff, "something on a stick" is the way he phrased it. He was taking stock of his newfound importance in his bedroom, while lying on his bed. Chuck's father was right outside the window weeding his garden where he requested that his son help him with the task. Chuck sassily refused, saying it was his birthday. His father did not waste any words; it was a time for action as he dashed into the house and up to his son's room. Swindoll claims that he was all over him like "white on rice," as they made a hurried exit to the garden, where the teen pulled weeds until the cows came home.

That same evening the father took his son to a surprise dinner. He gave his son what he deserved earlier in the day but later on, at the dinner party, he gave him what he did not deserve. The son experienced grace.

* * * * *

We have all experienced the pain of not measuring up — the opposite of grace. A young pastor tells of one such experience in his life. It was a big day. Tommy was going to the local amusement park with his family. With joy he anticipated the little boats with the bells, the

64

happy carousel, and the carnival games. But what Tommy really wanted to do was to ride the big one, the roller coaster. What a thrill! He could share it with his friends and it would prove that he was no longer a little boy. So the big day came and he rode the little boats, cars, and carousel. He threw darts at the balloons and baseballs at the bowling pins and all the while, in the back of his mind was the thought: "Today I'm going to ride the big one!" Finally, they got in line for the coaster, a line that appeared to be infinite. Eventually they worked their way to the front and Tommy was ready to board his dream ride. Just as he was about to step down, the gatekeeper pulled him back and over to a measuring post, explaining that he had to be a certain height; it was the regulation. You guessed it. Tommy was three inches too short. He didn't measure up. Thank God that in Christ Jesus we are acceptable to God. Amazing grace!

Epiphany 2/Ordinary Time 2

Revised Common:	Isaiah 49:1-7	1 Corinthians 1:1-9	John 1:29-42
Roman Catholic:	Isaiah 49:3, 5-6	1 Corinthians 1:1-3	John 1:29-34
Episcopal:	Isaiah 49:1-7	1 Corinthians 1:1-9	John 1:29-41

Seasonal Theme: The Holy Spirit is prominently featured in the Epiphany Season pericopes. The Spirit does not act in isolation but works to create and sustain the spiritual community. Each week we will examine a different aspect of the Spirit's presence in Christian community.

Theme For The Day: The Spirit's Call

Suggested Text For Preaching: John 1:29-42

Suggested Sermon Title: God's Inviting Spirit

BRIEF COMMENTARY ON THE LESSONS

Lesson 1: Isaiah 49:1-7 (C, E); Isaiah 49:3, 5-6 (RC)

The prophet of second Isaiah shares his strong sense of being called by the Lord; he was set aside for his prophetic/servant role while he was still in his mother's womb. He was called to relay some painful truths and feels as if his efforts have met with futility, but then the Spirit of God gives him hope and strength for his mission of restoring the wounded and scattered sheep of the defeated flock of Israel. The Spirit gently chides him for his constricted view of his mission and announces that his task is not merely to restore his fallen people to what they were but to challenge them with a glorious calling to be a light for all the nations on earth, that all nations might acknowledge the lordship of God. At a time of great darkness, God renews and magnifies his call to his people.

Lesson 2: 1 Corinthians 1:1-9 (C, E); 1 Corinthians 1:1-3 (RC)

The apostle Paul begins his epistle to the Romans by setting forth his apostolic credentials — not his human gifts but his call by God. He then addresses the church as those who are likewise set apart by God and called to be saints. The one who called them is faithful and would preserve them in faith until the day when the Lord Jesus appeared in kingdom power, supplying them richly with all the spiritual gifts they would need in the interim. All Christians have a call to be God's saints, and some have a further call to be apostles, teachers, and the like, but it is God who supplies the spirit and strength to fulfill that call.

Gospel: John 1:29-42 (C); John 1:29-34 (RC); John 1:29-41 (E)

The gospel continues the "call" theme found in the first two lessons. Here we have a man with a potent sense of call, John the Baptist, who points to Jesus as being the Messiah. Through this act he fulfills his calling, which is to point to the one chosen by God to purify the people. Two of John's disciples heard their teacher point to Jesus and say, "Here is the lamb of God who takes away the sin of the world." These two follow Jesus to the place of his lodging and spend the rest of the day with the Master. Jesus must have communicated a strong sense of being called as the Messiah, for the next day Andrew, one of the two disciples, finds his brother, Peter, and excitedly announces, "We have found the Messiah." Andrew witnessed as one who has been called by Christ. Not only does he make a verbal witness but brings his brother to Jesus. When the Lord lays his eyes on Peter, he calls him by a new name, Cephas, the Rock. All of these men have one thing in common: They are not fulfilling their own inward desires by responding to a call from outside themselves to be and to act as the Lord's servants.

Psalm Of The Day

Psalm 27:1, 4-9 (C); Psalm 139:1-7 (E) — "The Lord is my light and my salvation; whom shall I fear? The Lord is the stronghold of my life: of whom shall I be afraid?"

Prayer Of The Day

Gracious God, in holy baptism you have called us into the fellowship of saints and have equipped us for the work of ministry. Keep us faithful to our calling to be your servant people that we might be found blameless when the Lord Christ consummates his glorious kingdom. In the name of Jesus. Amen.

THEOLOGICAL REFLECTION ON THE LESSONS

Lesson 1: Isaiah 49:1-7

Reach out and touch someone. Is there anyone who has not heard this advertisement? It has been employed in some of the most gripping advertisements on television. The ads touch us because they present realistic situations, usually joyous ones, where people are sharing their real selves with those they care about. We all need to touch and be touched. What the slogan is really saying is: Go ahead and call someone. When God called the prophet Isaiah to be his servant, he was sending him to reach out and touch those who were dear to the heart of God. He wanted to communicate his love for them, to lift them up from their beds of tears, and gather them together. In turn, the Lord called his chosen ones to reach out to those in spiritual darkness, namely the Gentiles, that they too might walk in the light of the Lord. God calls us in baptism to reach out and touch someone with the good news of Christ's love. What are we waiting for?

"I have labored in vain," complained the weary and depressed prophet. How typically human during a time of darkness to look back on our lives and behold only futility and failure. This would be quite a realistic appraisal if we were to view our lives atomistically, in isolation from God and others. Then the prophet remembers, "Surely my cause is with the Lord." If my cause is also the Lord's cause, surely he will vindicate me, the prophet reasoned.

Wouldn't you think that if a person was feeling as if he were a failure that the Lord might relent and say: "That's all right. I'll remove some of your burden and make it easier for you"? But that's not what happened to Isaiah. The Lord gave him and his people an even greater task, "to be as a light to the nations." In fact, the task seems impossible. Maybe that's how God makes great people and faithful people, challenging them with a great task. The task may be too great for us alone, but our God is able.

Lesson 2: 1 Corinthians 1:1-9

"Called to be...." Most of the time when we were called on, it is to do something, but when God calls us, it is *being* that he is concerned about. The Lord's primary concern is who and what we are. As Christians, we are all called to be saints, to live holy lives. We realize such sanctity not by striving to be perfect — that would be self-defeating — but by offering each moment of our lives to the Lord. Perhaps this would be a fitting prayer for a saint to offer to the Lord: "I'm not much, Lord, but I'm yours. Take me and use me as you will. In Jesus' name. Amen."

Gospel: John 1:29-42

A scapegoat or a lamb of God? When John the Baptist spied Jesus coming his way, he turned to his disciples and announced: "Here is the Lamb of God who takes away the sin of the world!" John was intensely interested in holiness. His baptism was a call to be free from the contagion of sin. John was something of an eccentric in his day but his message was widely received, nonetheless. Today, he would be regarded as a raving maniac whose message was hopelessly anachronistic. You see, John regarded sin with the utmost seriousness. He pointed to Jesus as the sacrificial lamb who would atone for the sins of the world. When people mess up today they blame it on their parents, their upbringing, society, or some other convenient scapegoat. Have you noticed, people don't sin any more? They make mistakes, they slip up, they become temporarily insane or ill, but they don't sin. And when they can't figure out who to blame they throw up their hands and intone, "It just happened." I didn't intend to cheat on my wife; it just happened. I don't know how or why I shot him; it just happened. Who knows, maybe aliens from outer space are taking possession of our bodies when things just happen. One woman killed her husband and you know what her defense was? Her menstrual period. Who needs a Lamb of God to take away my sin, when I don't really sin or when others are to blame?

Come and see. When John pointed to Jesus as the Lamb of God, two of his disciples followed him, and when Jesus saw them he asked, "What are you looking for?" They didn't know quite what to say and so they blurted, "Rabbi, where are you staying?" "Come and see," he responded. That was Jesus' first call. A rather low key approach. "Come and see" is an invitation to examine the life of Christ. It is a request that these men might come to know him, to enter into relationship with him. Christ didn't try to sell himself; he merely invited them to come and discover for themselves. They apparently liked what they saw, at least Andrew did, because the next day he found his brother, Peter, and brought him to Jesus.

Andrew could be dubbed the ordinary apostle. He didn't have any spectacular gifts and he wasn't a great leader like his brother, but what he had, he used. His greatest gift was to invite folks to come and see this Jesus. He must have been kind of a self-effacing man who evinced the attitude voiced by the Baptist, "He must increase but I must decrease." Andrew realized that he didn't have the burden of changing people; all he had to do was bring them to Jesus. That is our calling, too, to enthusiastically invite people to "come and see" who this Jesus might be.

PREACHING APPROACHES WITH ILLUSTRATIONS

Lesson 1: Isaiah 49:1-7

Sermon Title: Faith And Futility

Sermon Angle: The prophet laments: "I have labored in vain, I have spent my strength for nothing and vanity ..." (v. 4). Then, in practically the same breath, he adds, "Yet surely my cause is with the Lord, and my reward with my God." It's quite obvious that faith and futility are not mutually exclusive. Some of the greatest saints, called to the most difficult tasks have, at times, felt like they had been abandoned by God and that their labors were in vain. This is quite natural because those who exercise the greatest faith usually meet the most opposition. Also, faith views the world from a different perspective than does futility. If we look backward at our lives from a strictly rational, sense-experience perspective, it may truly appear that we have failed miserably. The outcome may be a drastic departure from what we had hoped. Faith, on the other hand, comprehends that life is far deeper than what we see. Our perception is finite and largely subjective. Faith acknowledges that our lives are in God's hands and that ultimately "all things will work together for good to those who love God" (Romans 8:28).

Outline:
1. Ask if they have ever felt that their lives didn't count for much. Talk about despair, hopelessness, depression, and the like
2. Point out that Isaiah felt this way and explain why
3. Emphasize that it is not unnatural to feel this way. Give examples.
4. Show that futility can only be counteracted through faith in God
5. Urge them to live out of their faith rather than their futility

Lesson 2: 1 Corinthians 1:1-9

Sermon Title: Called To Be

Sermon Angle: Paul addresses the church at Corinth as those "called to be...." Obviously, I have left out the object in this phrase but as Shakespeare so eloquently turned the phrase, "To be or not to be, that is the question." All existence falls into two categories: being and doing. Our society judges us by what we do; we are measured by our accomplishments. The Bible indicates that doing flows from being. Who and what we are is primary. In the Beatitudes, Jesus teaches, "Blessed are the poor in spirit; blessed are the meek," and so forth. Those who are acknowledged by the Lord have met the criteria of being which flows from their being in the Lord. But what is it we are called to be? Saints. Those who are holy or, we could say, wholly the Lord's.

Outline:
1. Ask the question, If you were standing before the pearly gates and Saint Peter were to ask you why you should be allowed to enter, what would you reply? Would the reasons cited have more to do with what you have done or who you are?
2. As Christians, we are called to be, not to do (vv. 1-2). We are saved by grace through faith.
3. Do we take time to discover who we are in God and to live out this identity?
4. If we live as God's saints, we will be blameless as we stand before the throne of God (v. 8).

Gospel: John 1:29-42

Sermon Title: A Scapegoat Or A Sacrificial Lamb?

Sermon Angle: Increasingly people are refusing to accept responsibility for their actions. It's more convenient and less painful, it seems, to blame somebody else — that other racial group, women, men, parents, and the like — than take responsibility onto oneself. The Jews placed their sins symbolically on a scapegoat and drove him out into the wilderness. This may have helped them cope with guilt but it didn't get to the crux of the problem of sin. God did that in the person of his Son. John the Baptist pointed to Jesus and said, "There is the Lamb of God who takes away the sin of the world." Jesus took our sins to the cross where he crucified them. He enables us not only to evade the guilt of our sins for a time, he frees us from their power so that we have victory.

Outline:
1. Explain the concept of the scapegoat
2. Give examples of how people today attempt to evade responsibility for their actions by casting the blame on others
3. Jesus took on himself the guilt of our sin as the Lamb of God
   — Now we can face our sins honestly
   — Now we have the power, through faith, to defeat sin

* * * * *

Those of us who are white cannot fathom the pain of racial prejudice that blacks and other minorities face in our society. This was brought to our attention by the riot that followed the first Rodney King trial in Los Angeles. In that riot a white truck driver was pulled out of his truck and brutally beaten by some young black men. One of them took a brick and threw it with force at the head of the hapless driver by the name of John Denny. The man who threw the brick and Denny were both invited to appear on the Phil Donahue show. Denny is a Christian and does not blame or hate those who attacked him. He even seems to excuse their actions due to the conditions they live in. To forgive them is wonderful, but should he also release them from the responsibility for their actions? The man who threw the brick, Mr. Washington, says that he is sorry for the harm he has caused Denny but also stated that he does not entirely regret participating in the riot. The audience in the studio was agitated with Washington because they felt he wasn't really sorry for what he had done, that he was not really ready to confess that he had done wrong. I think that the audience intuitively understood that Mr. Washington could not rise above his past sins until he owned them and confessed them. This is not a racial issue; it is a spiritual matter. What it boils down to is this: We don't need a scapegoat; we need to lay our sins on the Lamb of God who takes away the sins of the world.

Sermon Title: The Inviting Christ

Sermon Angle: When Andrew and the other disciple of John the Baptist tailed Jesus, he turned to them and asked, "What are you looking for?" They inquired as to where he was living. Jesus responded with an invitation: "Come and see." Our Christ is inviting, urging us to come home to him, that we might get to know him through his self-revelation. No hard sell, just a gracious invitation. Now Christ lives amongst his people. But how inviting are those who have charge of his house, the church? People still inquire, "Where does Christ live?" Can we in good conscience invite them to come to our houses or our churches, saying, "Come and see"?

Epiphany 3/Ordinary Time 3

Revised Common:	Isaiah 9:1-4	1 Corinthians 1:10-18	Matthew 4:12-23
Roman Catholic:	Isaiah 8:23—9:3	1 Corinthians 1:10-13, 17	Matthew 4:12-23
Episcopal:	Amos 3:1-8	1 Corinthians 1:10-17	Matthew 4:12-23

Seasonal Theme: The Holy Spirit is prominently featured in the Epiphany season pericopes. The Spirit does not act in isolation but works to create and sustain the spiritual community. Each week we will examine a different aspect of the Spirit's presence in Christian community.

Theme For The Day: God's Spirit Is A Liberating Spirit

Suggested Text For Preaching: Matthew 4:12-23

Suggested Sermon Title: God's Liberating Spirit

BRIEF COMMENTARY ON THE LESSONS

Lesson 1: Isaiah 9:1-4 (C); Isaiah 8:23—9:3 (RC)

This passage is a portion of the first lesson for Christmas Day. On that occasion it was employed as a fulfillment of the expectation of the birth of the Messiah. In the context of Epiphany it is used as a fulfillment of the promise that the Messiah would be a light for all the nations. This passage was written during a time of great darkness and gloom. The tribes of Zebulun and Naphtali had been subjugated by the Assyrians in 734 BC. Yet, the prophet envisions a brighter future through the aegis of the messianic king.

Lesson 1: Amos 3:1-8 (E)

Of all the nations on earth, only with the Jews has God entered into an intimate relationship. Therefore, they are judged more severely because knowledge equals responsibility. To those whom more is given, more is expected.

Lesson 2: 1 Corinthians 1:10-18 (C); 1 Corinthians 1:10-13, 17 (RC); 1 Corinthians 1:10-17 (E)

Paul receives word from Chloe's people concerning problems in the Corinthian church, the chief problem being a lack of unity. Paul addresses these issues in chapters 1-6, the first four of which deal with the unity-disunity issue. The rest of the epistle deals with various other issues brought to him. The apostle seeks to pour the cool water of unity on the fires of dissension and party spirit. Christians should follow only Christ in whose name we are baptized, rather than give our loyalty to mere humans.

Gospel: Matthew 4:12-23 (C, RC, E)

Matthew seeks to demonstrate how Jesus is the fulfillment of Isaiah 9. The arrest of John is Jesus' signal to commence his ministry. Following his baptism and temptation in the wilderness, Jesus leaves Nazareth and establishes residence in Capernaum, which is situated along the

Sea of Galilee. Jesus is the Anointed One who brings the light of eternal truth to this cosmopolitan, yet sin darkened, region. From that time, Jesus begins the proclamation of the good news: "Repent, for the kingdom of heaven has come near" (v. 17). He initiates the reign of God by calling his disciples together as the nucleus of the redemptive community of witness. Andrew, Peter, James, and John perceive the urgency of the call and immediately leave their worldly pursuits.

Psalm Of The Day

Psalm 27:1, 4-9 (C) — "The Lord is my light and my salvation, whom then shall I fear?"
Psalm 139:1-17 (E) — God knows us completely and there is no place where we cannot be found by him.

Prayer Of The Day

O God of light, when fear and foreboding hold us captive in a prison of oppressive darkness, set us free through the liberating light of your eternal Spirit. In the powerful name of Jesus. Amen.

THEOLOGICAL REFLECTION ON THE LESSONS

Lesson 1: Isaiah 9:1-4

Living in the latter time. Isaiah distinguishes the former time of gloom and sadness from the latter time of light and gladness. There is no evidence that anything has changed politically in his homeland. Yet, in the midst of ignominy and darkness, the prophet envisions through faith a luminous future. We cannot always change where we are physically, but we can live wherever we want to be emotionally and spiritually. Isaiah existed in a bleak political landscape, yet he was bathed in the light of faith and hope. He chose to live in the latter day. For persons of faith, the future is already here. For such, seeds of promise are already producing life-sustaining fruit and rays of light glinting on the horizon have already become bright as the noonday sun. For those who have experienced the radiance of Christ's Spirit, the former things have passed away and the latter day has dawned gloriously.

God's math. "You have multiplied the nation" (v. 3). God may add or subtract from our joys or our sorrows but the sum is never less than what we need to live victoriously. Those who have experienced the goodness of God have discovered that he allows sorrows to be added (1, 2, 3 ...) but multiplies joys (2, 4, 16 ...). One person shares the joy of the Lord with another and that person shares that same joy with two or three others and they share their joy with many others and so on.

Living in a black hole. When the prophet points to those living in the land of "deep darkness" (v. 2), I think of a black hole. In one sense, a black hole might be a grave and a grave can consist of more than a hole in the ground. A grave can be a rut; I once heard a therapist describe a rut as a grave with its ends kicked out. A deep depression can also be described as a grave, and there are many others. There is another kind of black hole, the kind that inhabits far reaches of outer space. Scientists don't completely understand this phenomena but they have observed regions where nothing seems to escape and no light can penetrate. For the captive children of Israel, life seemed to be such a black hole. Isaiah announces that on such the light of God is already shining and will blaze ever brighter. The psalmist captures this truth poetically:

72

Where can I go from your spirit?
If I ascend to heaven, you are there;
if I make my bed in Sheol, you are there.

— Psalm 139:7a, 8

Lesson 2: 1 Corinthians 1:10-18

The state of disunion address. This passage could be called the state of the union address for the Corinthian church or, perhaps, the state of the disunion address. We often idealize the pristine apostolic church as the church's golden era but a reading of the New Testament brings us back down to earth. In the Corinthian church, at least, factionalism was threatening to destroy the unity of the Christian community. The very symbol of their unity in Christ, holy baptism, was the very symbol of disunity. These babes in the Lord were confused concerning whose name they were being baptized into, thinking that they had become disciples of the one who baptized them, bragging, "I belong to Paul" or "I belong to Apollos" or "I belong to Peter" (v. 12). Paul asks, "Has Christ been divided?" (v. 13). Indeed, he had. Already we have the beginning of denominationalism and factionalism in the church. Divide and conquer is one of the oldest and most successful military strategies. Our enemy, Satan, is a master of divide and conquer but in the Spirit we are one.

Living on purpose. For Paul, the way to achieve unity in the church was manifestly clear. Proclaim the gospel. That was his driving purpose. "For Christ did not send me to baptize but to proclaim the gospel" (v. 17). Even baptism was secondary to that central purpose. Many churches and denominations have gotten caught up in a host of other issues, many of which are valid and good, but in so doing have lost focus on the central purpose of the church, to proclaim the gospel through the foolishness of preaching. Every activity in the church, every dollar in the church budget, every committee meeting, and every decision of the congregation or its board must be judged by how well it contributes to this central purpose. Proclamation of the gospel must be viewed in a much wider context than the Sunday morning sermon; all that we do as the church must make known the claims of Christ.

Gospel: Matthew 4:12-23

Liberation movement. Matthew views Jesus as the prophetic fulfillment of the liberation movement spoken of by Isaiah. A universal liberation movement for the entire world would begin in an ancient pocket of political oppression — the land of Zebulun and Naphtali. There is an interesting change in Isaiah 9:2 as quoted by Matthew. In Isaiah, it is the people who walked in darkness who have seen a great light and those who *lived* in the land of deep darkness on whom the light has shone. In Matthew, it is those who sat in darkness and those who sat in the region and the shadow of darkness who have seen a great light. Matthew's image conveys more of a sense of the darkness of prison. People don't so much walk in prison or live there; they merely sit on their perches like birds in a cage. Incarceration immobilizes its victims. In proclaiming the nearness of the kingdom of God, Jesus is initiating a movement of spiritual liberation.

Kairos crisis. This account of the call of Andrew, Peter, James, and John leaves the impression that Jesus suddenly came along, issued his call and these men immediately left what they were doing in midstream. There are other indications that Jesus had previous interactions with these men. The important point is that Matthew was trying to convey a sense of crisis of *kairos.* *Now* was the special time for the coming of the kingdom; *now* was the time to act; it was the

73

crisis moment. That's what Matthew was seeking to impart through the word "immediately" (vv. 20, 22). This sense of urgency is vital for our personal and congregational spiritual growth. The congregations that are growing spiritually and numerically possess a sense of urgency in presenting the claims of the kingdom and those individuals who are alive spiritually are those who are alert to grasp the *kairos* when the kingdom breaks unexpectedly into their lives.

Repentance: stimulus or response? It would seem that the message of John and Jesus were very similar: repentance and the kingdom. Actually, their message differed radically. John taught that people should repent in order to make themselves ready and worthy for the kingdom of God. Jesus proclaimed that people should repent because the kingdom was near. John taught that repentance was a necessary precondition for the kingdom, the stimulus for God to act. Jesus preached that God was already acting, the kingdom was already coming, and that humanity should repent in order to receive what God had to offer. For Jesus, repentance is a response, not a stimulus.

PREACHING APPROACHES WITH ILLUSTRATIONS

Lesson 1: Isaiah 9:1-4
Sermon Title: Latter Day Saints

Sermon Angle: No, this is not a pitch for the Mormons who call themselves The Church of Jesus Christ of Latter-day Saints. Isaiah distinguishes the former day from the latter day. The former day was a day of gloom and oppression but the latter day was a day of joy and freedom. As John stated in his book of revelation: "The former things have passed away. Behold, I make all things new!" As Christians, we know that the world of sin and injustice, though real, is passing away. The latter day represents God's future and we are already beginning to live in that day.

Sermon Title: Salvation: Being Beamed Out Of The Black Hole

Sermon Angle: Isaiah speaks of those who "lived in the land of deep darkness." These were countrymen who languished under political, economic, and spiritual oppression, which in turn precipitated an inward depression. Scientists postulate regions in the universe, dubbed black holes, where no light can penetrate. This may serve as a fitting metaphor for those under the grip of oppression or depression. The message of hope that comes from the Lord is that there is no condition or region where the light of the Lord cannot penetrate.

Outline:
1. Discuss the concept of the black hole and relate this to the condition of those who find themselves surrounded by the darkness of oppression and depression
2. Relate this to the situation in Isaiah's day
3. Lift up hope revealed by God's invasion of the darkness with the light of Christ and his mighty acts of redemption

Lesson 2: 1 Corinthians 1:10-18
Sermon Title: What Is The State Of Your Union?

Sermon Angle: Paul addressed the Corinthian church which was in a state of disunion and pleaded for unity in the spirit of Christ. This sermon could examine some of the factions that divide the church and their damaging consequences. Then the preacher could personalize the subject by asking the listeners: What is the state of our union in Christ as a congregation? Also, what is the state of your union with Christ as an individual? Finally, appeal for unity in essentials without insisting on uniformity in nonessentials.

Gospel: Matthew 4:12-23

Sermon Title: Liberation Movement

Sermon Angle: The arrest of John the Baptist seemed to be a signal for Jesus to commence his ministry, his liberation movement. Oppression and depression indicate a state of being where people are not free to act, they are immobilized. In contrast, genuine liberation is a movement where people discover they are free to act in new ways. Christ initiates this movement by bringing near the kingdom of God. People can join the movement through repentance and faith. Too many churches are no longer tuned into Jesus' liberation movement; they are merely static institutions.

Outline:

1. Get listener's attention by arguing that Jesus never intended to found a church institution but rather a liberation movement. Institutions are governed by rules of order but liberation movements are driven by the Spirit. (This does not deny the necessity of institutional structures.)
2. Christianity is a liberation movement led by Christ, intended to free people from the clutches of sin and oppression
3. Now is the time to join the movement through repentance, faith, and following Jesus

* * * * *

There was a story on the television program, *Unsolved Mysteries,* concerning the disappearance of a seventeen-year-old girl several years ago. She went home before lunch, called her father at work, and then disappeared. Leads came in that she was kidnapped by a notorious motorcycle gang, called The Outlaws. The mother launched a tireless search to find her daughter; she frequented the haunts of such bikers and found some people who had definitely seen her. One biker, on seeing her picture, reported that he had *owned* her at one time. You see, many of the women who rode with the bikers, "the old ladies" as they were called, were bought and sold like property. This man tried to set up a meeting of the mother with her prisoner daughter but got both of his knees broken at the rendezvous. No more help from that source. Eighteen years after the kidnapping, a private detective turned up a lead that the girl was in England. A man tried to sell her to someone. This lead also fizzled but the mother vowed to never forsake the search until her daughter is set free.

We, too, have been taken captive by a hostile power, the dominion of sin and death. We are powerless to free ourselves. God sent his anointed one to free us from the clutches of sin and Satan through the power of the cross. Some have already experienced this liberation through faith while others have not. One thing is certain: God continues to search for ways to find and free his captive children.

* * * * *

75

During the infamous rule of Uganda's Idi Amin, a planeload of Jews was imprisoned at the Entebbe airport. Knowing that this madman might well kill his prisoners, the intelligence of the state of Israel orchestrated a daring raid. A planeload of Israeli commandos swooped down suddenly and within a few minutes rounded up the captives and spirited them to freedom. One of the prisoners was hospitalized at the time and could not be rescued; she was later killed by Amin's goons. Amazingly, all the others were freed. One minute they sat in the gloom of their makeshift prison, their plight was perilous, and the next minute they were being liberated into the light of freedom. The life, death, and resurrection of Jesus was like a lightning raid into enemy held territory. "The people who sat in darkness have seen a great light ..." (Matthew 4:16).

Epiphany 4/Ordinary Time 4

Revised Common:	Micah 6:1-8	1 Corinthians 1:18-31	Matthew 5:1-12
Roman Catholic:	Zephaniah 2:3; 3:12-13	1 Corinthians 1:26-31	Matthew 5:1-12a
Episcopal:	Micah 6:1-8	1 Corinthians 1:(18-25) 26-31	Matthew 5:1-12

Seasonal Theme: The Holy Spirit is prominently featured in the Epiphany Season pericopes. The Spirit does not act in isolation but works to create and sustain the spiritual community. Each week we will examine a different aspect of the Spirit's presence in Christian community.

Theme For The Day: God's saints are humble in spirit.

Suggested Text For Preaching: Matthew 5:1-12

Suggested Sermon Theme: God's Spirit Of Humility

BRIEF COMMENTARY ON THE LESSONS

Lesson 1: Micah 6:1-8 (C, E)

God brings his chosen people to a cosmic court where even the mountains and hills bear witness. The charge: the people had forgotten the Lord's mighty works of redemption and the wealth of past blessings. In verse 3, he puts them on the witness stand to make their case but they apparently have nothing to say. Therefore, God presents his case, detailing his acts of mercy and deliverance as he brought them out of Egypt and into the promised land. Though guilt is established, no verdict is declared or judgment rendered. There is an abrupt change in verse six to the topic of how a person can be accepted by God. Is it the way of sacrifice, as commonly thought? No, the favor of the Almighty cannot be secured through even a multitude of sacrificial gifts accompanied by the proper rituals. The prescription that follows for how one can stand before the judgment seat of God is one of the most exalted in the Old Testament: "What does the Lord require of you but to do justice, and to love kindness, and to walk humbly with your God?" (v. 8).

Lesson 1: Zephaniah 2:3; 3:12-13 (RC)

God's judgment will pass and the remnant left in Israel will be characterized as humble and righteous.

Lesson 2: 1 Corinthians 1:18-31 (C); 1 Corinthians 1:26-31 (RC); 1 Corinthians 1:(18-25) 26-31 (E)

Last week's epistle lesson dealt with the problem of divisions in the church. In today's lesson, Paul digs to the root of the matter, spiritual pride. The Greeks elevated reason and they were at the point of thinking that they could approach God through a correct understanding of spiritual matters. Paul knocks human reason and wisdom off its vaunted pedestal, claiming that God saves not through human wisdom but through the foolishness of preaching. Lest their heads swell with pride, he reminds the Corinthians that very few of them came from educated and noble worldly ranks but rather surfaced from the dregs of human society through the grace of God. No Christian, from whatever societal rank, has the right to boast except in the gospel.

Gospel: Matthew 5:1-12 (C, E); Matthew 5:1-12a (RC)

The Beatitudes were also featured as the gospel lesson on All Saints' Sunday with the emphasis being the blessings that accrue to those who love the Lord. Here the emphasis is on the defining characteristics of those who belong to God — their humble spirit, meekness, gentleness, and so forth. These blessed ones are those who are in tune with their own weakness and realize that they have nothing to boast of and so they place their trust in God. The Beatitudes, a part of a larger collection of our Lord's teachings called the Sermon on the Mount (Matthew 5-7), are not laws of God or a prescription for righteousness; they are a portrait of God's saints. The gospel lesson fulfills the theme of humility and lowliness found in the first two lessons.

Psalm Of The Day

Psalm 15 (C) — Who are those who will remain in God's dwelling? Those who walk blamelessly before the Lord.

Psalm 37:1-8 (E) — The arrogant, proud people will be replaced by the meek, who will inherit the land.

Prayer Of The Day

God of grace, imprint on us the spirit of your Son, who humbled himself and became obedient unto death, even death on the cross. Pry us loose from a false sense of pride concerning human distinctions so that, through the power of Christ, we may do justice, love kindness, and walk humbly before you, our loving God and Savior. In Jesus' name. Amen.

THEOLOGICAL REFLECTION ON THE LESSONS

Lesson 1: Micah 6:1-8

People's court. This passage is framed in a sixth-century BC courtroom setting. The people of God are on the stand and God is the prosecuting attorney. The charges of infidelity and rebellion are brought forward but the defendants remain mute. They have no defense. But did you notice? No judgment is rendered and no sentence is pronounced as is the case in numerous other Old Testament passages. It appears that the ending of the passage has been lost or misplaced and that the verses subsequent to verse five don't fit here because they don't maintain the judicial image of the Lord. Some scholars think that verses 6-8 are editorial additions from a later period, composed by a different author. Could it not also be possible that Micah had a sort of Damascus road experience where he received a radical new concept of God? Could it not be that the Spirit of God enabled Micah to transcend the legalistic image of God with a more personal concept? Or, if not a sudden transformation, perhaps the prophet experienced a gradual but steady growth in his theology so that he came to see that loving and loyal relationships were what God required, not merely obeying the rules.

With what shall I come before the Lord? (v. 6). Ever since the fall of humankind into sin, people have clung to the notion that God cannot be approached empty handed; God must be placated with offerings and sacrifices. Micah came to see that all of us must stand naked before

God, without pockets. It is not what we have that makes us acceptable to God, it is who we are. Those qualities that Micah says will enable us to stand before God — justice, kindness, and humility — stem from who we are and not what we possess.

Lesson 2: 1 Corinthians 1:18-31

The scandal of the cross. I once read a thought-provoking book titled *The Scandal of Lent.* Paul says that the cross is foolishness to the Greeks and a stumbling block to the Jews (v. 23). The Greek word translated "stumbling block" could just as well be rendered "scandal." We wear crosses around our necks as objects of jewelry which belies its original offensiveness. It was an odious blasphemy according to Jewish thinking that the Messiah should meet such an ignominious end. The gospel, as we have often presented it, is pabulum; it has been stripped of its scandalous and offensive character in our attempt to be all things to all people. Not that the church is free of scandal. There is sometimes the scarlet scandal of immorality. Pastors and other church leaders sometimes cause scandal through a wrongful use of their sexuality or an inappropriate exercise of power. A lack of justice, kindness, and humility on the part of rank and file church members also produces scandal. This is the wrong kind of scandal. The gospel of a God who humbled himself, suffered, and died on the cross should cause the scandal, not the practitioners of the gospel.

Consider your own call (v. 26). Paul reminds the Corinthians of their humble roots: "Not many of you were wise by human standards, not many were powerful, not many were of noble birth." Nevertheless, God called them to be his own and to make his name known. In the modern church it seems that only pastors and missionaries are thought of as having a call. This is unfortunate because we are all called to be Christ's ministers in our baptism. Yet, even in the call of the pastor, I really wonder about how much the typical congregation opens itself up to the leading of the Holy Spirit rather than rely on the commonly accepted wisdom of this world. In my experience and observation, humility, kindness, and gentleness are not at the top of the list of qualifications for calling a pastor. Rather, the standards of this world are paramount: charisma, good looks, powerful persona, charming personality, and so forth. As a matter of fact, I have observed some humble servants of God being given the boot because they didn't measure up to standards. But whose standards? Christ's or the world's? Let's be honest, if the Lord has formed an apostolic search committee, none of the twelve would have even gotten an interview. You and I may dismiss ourselves as being less qualified to do a certain task than someone else, but the Lord sees different qualities than people do.

Gospel: Matthew 5:1-12

The be attitudes. These verses describe those who find their being in the eternal God. It's what we are that really counts, not what we possess or have done. All of these characteristics are a result of our being in Christ. The Beatitudes are rather difficult to preach because they go off in different directions. In a sense, the other Beatitudes flow from the first: "Blessed are the poor in spirit." To be poor in spirit does not mean that one is lacking in spirit, rather it is to be bereft of a proud or haughty spirit. Poverty of spirit is roughly equivalent to the word humility. A humble person is one who knows he does not soar in the heavens but is of the earth, like rich humus soil. In other words, such a person realizes that he is dependent on God, the ground of all being, if his or her life is to be fruitful.

Robert Schuller has written a book titled *The Be Happy Attitudes*, based on his interpretation of these verses. I don't mean to criticize this distinguished colleague but I have a problem with this approach. Jesus is not describing those who are necessarily happy. In fact, they have every reason to be unhappy. They are probably not just poor in spirit, but really poor. They are bereft. They are persecuted. Not exactly a felicitous state of being. Happiness is based in circumstances; the root of the word "happy" is *hap*, which means chance. When chance goes our way we may be happy but not necessarily blessed. To be blessed is a gift which God bestows on his own, a state of inward joy and peace, independent of what is or is not going on in our lives.

PREACHING APPROACHES WITH ILLUSTRATIONS

Lesson 1: Micah 6:1-8
Sermon Title: Walking Small

Sermon Angle: You are probably aware of the *Walking Tall* movies, the true story of sheriff Buford Pusser, who almost single-handedly fought the mob in his county. Like Teddy Roosevelt, he believed in carrying a big stick which he used to bash the bad guys. All of the lessons today talk about walking small, that is, walking humble. Micah says it exquisitely, "What does the Lord require of you but to do justice, and to love kindness, and to walk humbly with your God?"

Outline:
1. We look up to those who walk tall and proud (like Pusser)
2. God accepts those who walk small
   — those who do justice
   — those who love kindness
   — those who walk humble with God

Lesson 2: 1 Corinthians 1:18-31
Sermon Title: The Scandal Of The Gospel

Sermon Angle: Paul gloried in the scandal of the gospel; it was utter foolishness to the Gentiles and a stumbling block to the Jews. He realized the crucified Christ was both the wisdom of God and the power of God. In our society we try to package the gospel Madison Avenue style or reduce the truth of the gospel to the lowest common denominator. The way of God is strength in weakness, glory in shame, wisdom in foolishness.

Outline:
1. Understand the scandal of the gospel
   — the cross shows the weakness of God
   — the cross shows the power of God
   — the cross shows the immanence of God
   — the cross shows the wisdom of God
2. Proclaim the scandal of Christ crucified

Sermon Title: Look What God Chose!

Sermon Angle: According to Paul, God chose that which is weak to confound the strong, God chose what was foolish to shame the wise, and God chose what is lowly and despised to bring to nothing the things that are considered great (vv. 27-29). It doesn't seem as if God is very discriminating. That way, it is manifestly clear that God chose us out of grace, not merit.

Gospel: Matthew 5:1-12

Sermon Title: The Being-In-Christ Attitudes

Sermon Angle: The Beatitudes present certain spiritual inclinations or attitudes of being that put one in touch with God. Since Jesus gave them, we might call them the being-in-Christ attitudes. These attitudes are not prescriptive (do this and you'll be this way) but descriptive (those who have the spirit of Christ are this way). When you ask someone what they want out of life, they often respond that they desire happiness. Jesus tells us that it is better to be blessed than to be merely happy.

Outline:

1. Would you rather be happy or blessed? (Discuss the difference.)
2. Who are the truly blessed ones? Those who have discovered how to be
   — humble (poor in spirit)
   — meek (strength under God's control)
   — hungry for the things of God
   — merciful
   — pure in heart

(pick two or three of the above)

3. To be any of these, you must be in Christ

*   *   *   *   *

The chief characteristic of those whom Jesus describes as "The Blessed Ones" is that of humility. The opposite of humility is pride, which the Bible judges to be the root of all sin. It would seem that if we rooted out our pride, we would obtain humility but those who have endeavored to do so have failed, as the following story shows.

C. FitzSimmons Allison relates in his book, *Fear, Love, And Worship*, this story, which I have paraphrased. There was a seminary professor who understood well the problem of pride, that human pride was the source of all that was sinful and that the Pharisees were the most glaring example of this malady. In his preaching and teaching he never tired of exposing the new Pharisees. The professor deemed it his sacred duty to root out this noxious weed wherever he found it.

One day a friend visited the professor, and this zealous man of God related a heated discussion which he had with some colleagues concerning the nature of the gospel. As he related the points he had made, his friend agreed with his position all the way along. Then the friend added this observation: "You know, there is one question which reveals whether or not one is a Pharisee." "What's that?" the professor inquired. "Who killed Christ?" The professor shook his head vigorously in agreement. "That's right! Those damned Pharisees killed him!" The friend said no more for the professor had been accursed by his own tongue.

*   *   *   *   *

The Beatitudes present us with the paradoxical notion of strength through weakness. Let us briefly consider the different types of weakness. An article I read in *Christianity Today* called "Unraveling the Mystery of Weakness and Strength" by Peter Kreeft loosely guided my thinking on this subject.

81

First, there is the weakness of position: the weakness of playing second fiddle of or not making the first team. In our society, as well as many others, to be obedient is a sign of weakness; to take orders marks you as being inferior to the one issuing the orders. In the world, the strong impose themselves on the weak, but Jesus says that this is not the way it is supposed to be with his followers. Christ's disciples must be willing to be servants and give up the striving for positional advantage. Even in the church there are those who possess greater power than others (an assistant pastor is in a weaker position than the senior pastor), but power and position have nothing to do with worth or value. If we accept our positional weakness, Christ promises blessedness.

A second source of weakness inheres in our finitude and creatureliness. My father, Roy Anderson, was a robust man of strength and endurance most of his life. He was diagnosed with cancer, and toward the end of his life the disease completely sapped his vitality. During the last nine days of his life, we had to care for him as we would a baby. I thought he would rail against his weakness but he did not. This grace that God gave him to accept his weakness was a source of strength. It enabled him to accept the ministration of God.

A third source of weakness is moral and spiritual in nature. It is the infirmity of sin and evil. The first two kinds of weakness we would do well to accept so that God can transform them into strength but the debility of sin must not be accepted; it must be overcome through the power of the gospel. Christ took that weakness to the cross and nailed it there. Christ, through his transforming weakness, is the source of our strength. Likewise, Christ can convert our spiritual weakness into strength. The new birth has been compared to a heart transplant. God uses the weakness of our old hearts to get us on the operating table so that he might implant in us new hearts, hearts that no longer lust after things forbidden but long for the living God.

Epiphany 5/Ordinary Time 5

Revised Common:	Isaiah 58:1-9a (9b-12)	1 Corinthians 2:1-12 (13-16)	Matthew 5:13-20
Roman Catholic:	Isaiah 58:7-10	1 Corinthians 2:1-5	Matthew 5:13-16
Episcopal:	Habakkuk 3:2-6, 17-19	1 Corinthians 2:1-11	Matthew 5:13-20

Seasonal Theme: The Holy Spirit is prominently featured in the Epiphany season pericopes. The Spirit does not act in isolation but works to create and sustain the spiritual community. Each week we will examine a different aspect of the Spirit's presence in Christian community.

Theme For The Day: God's children are light in this world.

Suggested Text For Preaching: Matthew 5:13-16

Suggested Sermon Title: God's Illuminating Spirit

BRIEF COMMENTARY ON THE LESSONS

Lesson 1: Isaiah 58:1-9a (9b-12) (C); Isaiah 58:7-10 (RC)

This passage is a dialogue between the pommeled people of Israel and God. The prophet voices the complaints of the people, as well as the Lord's response. This profound passage is from the hand of trito-Isaiah in sixth century BC and the issue is fasting. The people complain that their pious acts of fasting, a sign of sorrow and supplication, are unnoticed by God. God responds that he is looking for a different kind of fasting; instead of appearing sad and lying prostrate, he wants his people to enter into the pain and sorrow of their brothers and sisters. The prophet promises that they will gain the Almighty's attention by showing compassion to the needy and freeing those fettered by the cords of injustice. "Is not this the fast that I choose; to loose the bonds of injustice, to undo the thongs of the yoke ..." (v. 6a). Such fasting dispels the pall of gloom with the light of God's Spirit.

Lesson 1: Habakkuk 3:2-6, 17-19 (E)

This psalm which comes much later than the time of Habakkuk portrays God as showing his wrath against evildoers but saving his chosen people.

Lesson 2: 1 Corinthians 2:1-12 (13-16) (C); 1 Corinthians 2:1-5 (RC); 1 Corinthians 2:1-11 (E)

Many of the members of the Corinthian community made extravagant claims of their special and secret wisdom, which Paul disdains to do. He did not come to them with lofty words of wisdom, but in fear and trembling he proclaimed the message of the crucified Christ. The appeal of the gospel was not in its plausible wisdom but in the power of the Spirit which it unleashed. Paul does not deny that the gospel contains wisdom but it is of a different order and only those who possess the Spirit of God can receive it or understand it. Those who do not have the discernment of the Spirit regard the gospel as utter foolishness. The believer can thank God that he has the mind of Christ.

Gospel: Matthew 5:13-20 (C, E); Matthew 5:13-16 (RC)

Our Lord teaches his disciples the true importance of their role in God's kingdom, which is far out of proportion with their numbers. As salt, we are to make life savory. As light, we are to dispel the darkness and light the way that leads to the Lord. The transforming power of God's Spirit in our lives cannot exist in a closed circuit but goes out into the world. To be a follower of Christ you cannot exist singly but live in community of witness.

Psalm Of The Day

Psalm 112:1-10 (C) — "Light shines in the darkness for the upright" (v. 4).
Psalm 27 (E) — "The Lord is my light and my salvation" (v. 1).

Prayer Of The Day

Luminous Spirit, we thank you for placing in us the glow of your glory that increases in brightness as we commune together and as we share your love. Remove from us the grimy film of sin that the gospel light might shine through. In Jesus' name. Amen.

THEOLOGICAL REFLECTION ON THE LESSONS

Lesson 1: Isaiah 58:1-9a (9b-12)

Ritual and righteous relationships. This passage focuses on the relationship between ritual acts (specifically, fasting) and the relationship of God's people to himself and one another. The people complained that their ritual acts of fasting produced no demonstrable effect in securing God's aid. They mistakenly thought that their ritual acts would obligate God to grant their wishes. Their religion was centered on ritual to the exclusion of relationships. Religion means, literally, that which binds together. Thus, religion is essentially about relationships. The point that Isaiah was trying to make is that relationships are what matter to the Lord. When our actions isolate and imprison people on the borders of society, we can't expect God's favors because ritual and relationships are out of sync. Ritual symbolically portrays the relationship between God and the people and is only valid when it flows from a relationship of trust in God that, in turn, is manifested in relationships of caring for others. Ritual without loving relationships is an attempt to manipulate God.

Urban renewal. This passage was written at the time when the city of Jerusalem, indeed the very fabric of society, lay in ruins. The prophet gives some excellent advice on how to rebuild and repair the nation in a manner that would bring lasting security. He wisely realized that cities are not composed primarily of streets and buildings but of people and relationships. Urban planners often don't understand this. On the south side of Chicago are row after row of large urban renewal housing projects that are virtual crime zones, where most of the residents live in constant fear of harm and want. You cannot renew society architecturally. Isaiah instructs us how to create a world of *shalom*. For starters, liberate those in bondage (v. 6). Then, share with those in need (v. 7). The old adage is true: Society is only as strong as its weakest link. Only a society that cares for all of its people (a just society) will remain strong and secure.

In ancient days, cities would attempt to secure their safety by building walls around it, but the only thing that it did was to deter an external foe. Most civilizations have been undermined from within by moral corruption and unjust patterns of social relationships. The external foe only served to complete the *coup de grace*. Military might alone can never make a society

84

strong and, in fact, often provides a false sense of security. Isaiah challenged his people with the task of reconstructing society with spiritual building blocks using these words: "Your ancient ruins shall be rebuilt; you shall raise up the foundations of many generations; you shall be called the repairer of the breach, the restorer of streets to live in" (v. 12). The breach that the prophet mentions can be taken two ways; the breach in the city walls, which would allow the enemy to enter the city; or it can be better interpreted in light of Isaiah's message, the breach in the structure of society caused by injustice. That is our challenge today: with God's help, to heal and repair the gaping holes in the house of humankind.

Lesson 2: 1 Corinthians 2:1-12 (13-16)

Unsolved mystery. Most people love to read or view a mystery story to see if they can figure out who the villain is. The television show, *Unsolved Mysteries*, which featured real life mysteries, has been aired for years and even as reruns, it is extremely popular. It seems that when confronted with the ultimate mystery, the mystery of God and of being, however, we desire the curtain of transcendence to be drawn aside. In the New Testament, the word "mysterion" can be interpreted to mean an open secret or a secret that will ultimately be revealed. Paul often employs it as a synonym for the gospel. The secret of God's plan in Christ is revealed to the disciples whose mission it is, not to keep the secret, but to make it known. Through Christ we have revealed the mystery of God's plan of salvation but God himself remains something of an enigma. If God were fully transparent to us, he would no longer be God; rather, we would ourselves be divine.

God wants to give you a piece of his mind. That's not a bad title for a sermon based on this text (vv. 12-14). Have you heard this one? I've got good news and bad news. The good news is that the Lord is coming tomorrow. The bad news is that he's really ticked off. The implication being that God is coming in judgment to give us a piece of his mind. Who hasn't gotten angry at someone and said, "I'm going to give that jerk a piece of my mind"? Or, maybe someone has done something to really irk us, but we've kept back from giving him a piece of our minds but we fantasize about really dressing that person down, really giving him a piece of our minds. Paul makes a fantastic statement: "But we have the mind of Christ" (v. 16b). In other words, God has given us a piece of his mind, not in anger but in love. The gift of the Holy Spirit transforms our minds. Only through the mind of Christ can we understand spiritual realities.

Gospel: Matthew 5:13-20

Salt rather than assault. A man gets fed up at real or imagined discrimination and takes out a semiautomatic pistol on a New York commuter train and opens fire, killing and wounding several people. Some teenage gang members get into an argument at an Omaha shopping center. Later, one of the disputants is gunned down in the parking lot by a rival gang member. There has been a dramatic rise in youth violence in the past few years and every day we hear stories of innocent people being victims of random violence. The frustrated, the abused, and the criminally insane observe much that they dislike in the world and respond with assaults. Christians too look at the world and behold a great deal that disturbs us, but if we follow the Lord's teaching, we will respond with salt. Jesus proclaimed, "You are the salt of the earth ..." (v. 13). We don't have salt; we are salt. When we are frustrated, we need to pour out the salt that we are — pour out the patience, the forgiveness, the helpfulness, and the love — which is able to preserve the world and make it a more savory place in which to live. But the salt can lose its savor, according to Jesus, just as Christians can lose their saltiness, by getting mixed up with salt-substitutes. All that looks like salt is not necessarily the real thing.

You are the light of the world (v. 14). Salt is made to be tasted; light is that which enables us to see and to be seen. The "you" that Jesus refers to in these two metaphors are his disciples. The image is communal. Together we are salt and light when we are in Christ. As with the salt, the light is to benefit others; it is not to be hidden but put in the public place so that all can see. The Lord told his disciples: "Let your light so shine before others that they may see your good works and give glory to your Father who is in heaven" (v. 16). The light that we are is a gift from God and not a result of our good works. Strictly speaking, what Jesus is pointing to are good fruits rather than good works. Good fruits are products of the light while good works can sometimes be viewed as attempts to generate the kind of light which makes one noticed. We are called to let the spirit of Christ shine within us so that others can see that the good that we do is an outgrowth of the light of God.

PREACHING APPROACHES WITH ILLUSTRATIONS

Lesson 1: Isaiah 58:1-9a (9b-12)

Sermon Title: Connections

Sermon Angle: Isaiah devalues religious ritual that doesn't make loving connections with other human beings. Relationships are the main issue here. Studies have shown that most Christians are not able to translate their relationship with God to everyday relationships. This sermon will explore how connections can be made between the sacred and the ordinary.

Outline:

Introduction: Do you ever feel that the things we do here on Sunday don't connect with what you do the rest of the week? You are not alone. In fact, Isaiah highlights that very problem. He condemns the isolation of religion from daily life. How can we change this sad state of affairs?

1. Establish a strong relationship with the Lord
2. Express that relationship formally in authentic ritual or worship (ritual that expresses your inner relationship with God and your outer relationship with others)
3. Express that relationship informally through loving, human contacts

*   *   *   *   *

George Gallup discovered that people are less inclined to affiliate with the institutional church today than they were a decade ago, even though more of them confess Jesus Christ as Lord and Savior. He theorizes that one important reason is that most people cannot make the connection between Christian faith and daily life and the churches are not equipped to help them. Gallup holds up the prospect of some significant membership growth if we can help people integrate faith and life.

Lesson 2: 1 Corinthians 2:1-12 (13-16)

Sermon Title: I've Got A Secret

Sermon Angle: Paul speaks of the mystery which he proclaimed by word and deed. The word "mysterion" does not translate to the common conception of the word — a complicated plot, difficult to figure out. The word "mystery" means secret. God's plan of salvation was mainly a secret until Christ came along. Now, the secret is ours but not everybody knows it. Back in the '50s, a popular quiz show was called *I've Got A Secret*. The guests on the show had done something unusual, like swimming the English Channel, and the panel would ask the guest yes or no questions that would enable them to solve the mystery within the allotted time. Everyone loves secrets and we have the greatest secret of all — God loves and forgives you.

Outline:
1. We all have secrets that are often concealments of the dark side of human nature, things that might make us or others look bad
   — for wholeness, such secrets must be exposed and faced
   — some people delight in passing on bad news because of malevolent reasons
2. Good news is impossible to keep secret (Give examples)
3. The church has been entrusted with the mystery (the secret) of the gospel
   — how can we hold back?
   — make the secret known and live in such a way that others will be itching to know our secret

Gospel: Matthew 5:13-20

Sermon Title: An Illuminating Spirit

Sermon Angle: Jesus said that his followers were light and that our function is to shine before others. However, you have to be turned on before you can emit light. Christ has given us his Spirit, an illuminating Spirit. That Spirit is our baptismal gift which we have to share in the present moral and spiritual darkness.

Outline:
1. Talk about the primacy of light, the importance of light
   — no life without light
   — no seeing without light
   — no color without light
2. In order for us to live eternally, we must receive the light of Christ
   — God is the source of light
   — we merely receive and reflect the light
3. Let the light of Christ shine through you

*   *   *   *   *

Some time ago, a television program on the subject of alternative means of healing featured a community in northern California, called Stonecroft. The tiny community was composed of several Roman Catholic priests and nuns who were providing a family for orphaned children with AIDS. To support their endeavor, they raised Christmas trees. This community was dedicated to the proposition that their purpose was to provide life and light in the midst of certain death. They were willing to love even though they would surely lose the objects of their affection. This program does not affect millions; it was a tiny lamp that barely penetrated the darkness, but it was a light. It witnessed to others that they, too, could light up the corners of their world and the light would spread and intensify. Maybe that's what President George H. W. Bush hoped for with his thousand points of light program. Of course, we know where the true light comes from: the Word that became flesh. As we receive Christ, we become torchbearers for God. If every true Christian would light just one little candle, what a bright world this would be.

*   *   *   *   *

Viktor Frankl, the father of logo therapy, had a psychiatric practice in Vienna, Austria, when he was interned by the Nazis for being a Jew. Through his sufferings and by observing the suffering of others he came to the truth that a person can put up with anything if she has some purpose or meaning for which to live. A purpose that kept Frankl going was to write of his experience. In his book, *Man's Search For Meaning*, he tells how a distant light helped him through the hellish darkness of his incarceration. The camp was the picture of ugliness with its squalid dormitories, smoke-spewing crematoriums, and treeless grounds bounded by barbed wire. The apparent hopelessness of the situation caused many to give up the ghost in despair. But in the distance, there was a house surrounded by trees. Early in the morning on cold winter days, the glow emitting from that farmhouse served as a beacon of hope. Frankl envisioned a normal family gathered around the hearth. The lights had not gone out in all the world and one day the present darkness would be overcome by the light.

*   *   *   *   *

In Florence, Italy, over five centuries ago, the architect of a great cathedral built into the edifice a most ingenious device for determining whether the edifice has shifted on its foundation. A brass plate was built into the floor so that when the sun descended through a particular portal at a specific time on June 21 of each year, it would beam for a few minutes off of the plate. Should the sun fail to strike the plate, it would be a sure sign the foundation had shifted. So far, every sunny June 21, the sun has not failed to illuminate the brass plate. If we are in proper relationship with the Son of God, we will reflect the light of his love and grace, not only for a few minutes but every day. If we linger in the darkness, it is a sign that our spiritual foundation has shifted.

Epiphany 6/Ordinary Time 6

Revised Common:	Deuteronomy 30:15-20	1 Corinthians 3:1-9	Matthew 5:21-37
Roman Catholic:	Sirach 15:15-20	1 Corinthians 2:6-10	Matthew 2:17-37
Episcopal:	Sirach 15:11-20	1 Corinthians 3:1-9	Matthew 5:21-24, 27-30, 33-37

Seasonal Theme: The Holy Spirit is prominently featured in the Epiphany Season pericopes. The Spirit does not act in isolation but works to create and sustain the spiritual community. Each week we will examine a different aspect of the Spirit's presence in Christian community.

Theme For The Day: Get right with your neighbor before worshiping God.

Suggested Text For Preaching: Matthew 5:23-26

Suggested Sermon Title: God's Forgiving Spirit

BRIEF COMMENTARY ON THE LESSONS

Lesson 1: Deuteronomy 30:15-20 (C)

The setting of this lesson is the land of Moab. Moses addresses the Israelites as they are about to cross over the Jordan and enter the land of promise. He confronts them with a crucial choice which they must make that day. The choice is life, which flows from obedience to the Lord, or death which follows disobedience. They were entering a land where the people served other gods. Before they are tempted by these gods, they must choose the Lord of their life. To choose Yahweh now would obviate the danger of choosing false gods later on. It's a life or death situation.

Lesson 1: Sirach 15:15-20 (RC); Sirach 15:11-20 (E)

About deciding whether or not to do the will of God.

Lesson 2: 1 Corinthians 3:1-9 (C, E)

Paul has apparently been criticized for preaching in a simplistic fashion by these Corinthians who prided themselves on their wisdom. Paul responds that he had to preach that way because they were still spiritual babes, immature in their attitudes and actions. This is seen in their conflict over status with its concomitant party spirit. Paul maintains that he and other apostles are only servants of God. God alone is worthy of our adulation and praise.

Lesson 2: 1 Corinthians 2:6-10 (RC)

Paul shows that the gospel is indeed wisdom, but not of the world. Only through the Spirit of God can one discern this wisdom and interpret its truths.

Gospel: Matthew 5:21-37 (C); Matthew 5:17-37 (RC); Matthew 5:21-24, 27-30, 33-37 (E)

Verse 17 contains the unitive thread for this entire passage, in fact, for the entire Sermon on the Mount: "Think not that I have come to abolish the law ... I have come to fulfill it." The word "fulfill" can be interpreted as: to complete or to accomplish. The word can also be interpreted: to infuse with new and deeper meaning. The latter exegesis is preferred. The rest of the passage gives examples of how Jesus fills the law and the prophets with new meaning in such areas as sexuality, murder, and vows. Jesus asserts his authority in a remarkable way and, at the same time, challenges the authority of the religious establishment. "You have heard ... but I say unto you."

Psalm Of The Day
Psalm 119:1-8 (C); Psalm 119:1-16 (E) — "Happy are those ... who walk in the law of the Lord" (v. 1).

Prayer Of The Day
Living God, we bless you for faithfully fulfilling all righteousness in Jesus Christ, your Son, that we might be your dear children. So fill us with your Spirit that we might be agents of reconciliation and forgiveness and thereby accomplish your gracious will. In Jesus' name. Amen.

THEOLOGICAL REFLECTION ON THE LESSONS

Lesson 1: Deuteronomy 30:15-20
An easy choice? The Deuteronomist has Moses presenting to the people a clear choice: on the one hand, life and blessing and, on the other, death and curses. Why would anyone think long about this one? No one intentionally chooses death, do they? Not usually. What happens is that people choose that which appears to be life enhancing but is really a death trap. Drugs seem to be a real life enhancer. They make you feel good but once you are hooked, it's hard to choose life again. To bow down to the god of mammon seems like an attractive thing to do, but once prostrate you may never be able to stand tall again. That's why Moses urged the people to choose now, this very day, to serve God, before they are lured into the service of the gods of death.

We live in a society much like the Canaanite civilization that the Israelites entered once they crossed the river. They worshiped the fertility gods and goddesses, and many people in our society try to find ultimate fulfillment and pleasure in sexual license. It is a wonderful idea to ask your people to choose ahead of time, before they cross the river, God's way, the pathway of life. Half the battle is knowing what you are going to say and do when the crisis arises. The way of death is not something we choose up front, but by default. We get sucked into the way of death when we fail to acknowledge and serve the Lord of life.

Lesson 2: 1 Corinthians 3:1-9
Carnal Christians (v. 1). The apostle charges that the Corinthians were "of the flesh." In other words, they were carnal Christians. Their carnality manifested itself in a spirit of rivalry, jealousy, and party spirit. If they had been mature and spiritual Christians, a spirit of harmony would have prevailed. Debating honest differences can be healthy, but factions destroy the ties that bind us.

Lesson 2: 1 Corinthians 2:6-10
Baby talk. Have you noticed how people talk to infants? Highly educated people find themselves conversing in monosyllables through a voice three octaves above their normal range. It

looks ridiculous, but it connects with babies. The Corinthians were complaining that Paul was talking down to them. Paul retorts that he does so because that is the level that they are on. He has to communicate through baby talk (feed them milk) because they were not ready for weightier matters (meat). Their behavior revealed their level of immaturity. Unfortunately, most churches have a majority of members who are at the baby talk, baby food level of maturity, with development arrested. We have two choices — continue to use baby talk or provide opportunities that challenge them to grow in Christ.

Gospel: Matthew 5:17-37

Fulfilling the law. The entire Sermon on the Mount is a fleshing out of the new righteousness ushered in by Jesus. The radical nature of Jesus' righteousness is obvious as he sets his teachings in juxtaposition to the tradition of the elders. "You have heard it said in ancient times ... but I say to you." Yet Jesus insists that his righteousness is not an abrogation of the traditional concept of righteousness as embodied in the law, but a fulfillment of it (vv. 17-19). But what does the Lord mean by fulfilling the law? God's law contains two elements. There is the outward form and the internal spirit of the law. A very immature form of goodness is to obey the rules either to gain favor or avoid punishment. A deeper level of goodness is to obey the law because a person has internalized the command. A further progression in the ethical life is to go beyond the precept because the person has identified the intent of the law and incarnated these values into her life. For instance, such a person not only refrains from killing but sees greater value in every human being as a child of God and will do all that she can to help rather than hurt. Such a state of being could be called living in love. As Paul said, "Love does no wrong to a neighbor, therefore love is the fulfilling of the law" (Romans 13:10). The Lord condemns those who have kept the outward form of the law without the spirit of the law. Form without spirit is lifeless. That's why Jesus warns: "Unless your righteousness exceeds that of the scribes and the Pharisees, you will never enter the kingdom of heaven" (v. 20).

Conflict management. This is a term we hear a good deal about these days. The art of conflict management assumes that conflict is a given in this world and that it isn't necessarily evil. What is good or bad about conflict is the way we handle it. Unfortunately, most people don't manage their conflicts; on the contrary, their conflicts manage them. They attempt to take what appears to be the easy way out and avoid dealing with the troubling issue. Such conflict seldom goes away and usually worsens unattended. The proper way to handle conflict is to bring it out in the open so that one party to the strife can begin to see the perspective of the other party in the strife. When the facts are in the open, a solution is possible.

Jesus has very important advice concerning conflict management. He says, "If you are offering your gift at the altar and there remember that your brother or sister has something against you, leave your gift at the altar and go; first be reconciled to your brother or sister ..." (v. 24). The offering of the gift at the altar is an attempt of reconciliation with God (conflict management) but Jesus insists that we return to the primary arena of that conflict, our relationships with our neighbors, and seek reconciliation there before we offer our gift at the place of worship.

Righteous to the core. People sometimes say: "He's rotten to the core." That pessimistic assessment is not accurate if it means that humans are bereft of all goodness and are completely corrupt. It is accurate if it means that sin emanates from the center of our being. In the same way, righteousness cannot be wholly judged outwardly; true righteousness emanates from the core of our being. Jesus taught that we must be transformed from within. Thus, to abstain from killing does not absolve one from murder. Murder springs from malignant attitudes that must be replaced with the Beatitudes. "You have heard that it was said ... but I say to you that everyone who is angry with his brother shall be liable to judgment, whoever insults his brother shall be liable to the council, and whoever says, 'You fool!' shall be liable to the hell of fire" (vv. 21-22). Jesus applies the same principle to sexual behavior (vv. 27-30). We must let Christ make us righteous to the core of our being; it is there that attitudes are formed which are, in turn, transformed into words and deeds. The goodness of the scribes and Pharisees was inadequate, according to our Lord, because it did not issue from a spiritually transformed heart (v. 20).

PREACHING APPROACHES WITH ILLUSTRATIONS

Lesson 1: Deuteronomy 30:15-20
Sermon Title: Death Trap
Sermon Angle: Every winter one reads in the newspaper about some apartment or tenement that has burned down due to unsafe wiring and faulty furnaces, resulting in loss of life and limb. A place to live has proven to be a death trap. Japanese workers strive so hard making a living that they work themselves to death. A way of making a living has proven to be a death trap. Had these unfortunate folk known, they might have chosen a life preserving place to live or a life enhancing manner of making a living. What is touted as a way of life may actually be the pathway to death. As the people of Israel were entering the promised land, they were challenged with a choice: "life and good" or "death and evil." Moses urges the people to choose life. The new gods and ways of living would appeal as life expanding but they were truly a death trap. Actually, any forms of existence that does not involve choosing to serve the Lord and obey his commands is a death trap.

Outline:
1. Life presents us with two kinds of choices — those that lead to life or death
2. The problem — it is often difficult to discern which is which (Give examples of ways of living that are actually ways of death — individualism, consumerism, and the like)
3. Life (God) has chosen us and so let us choose life

* * * * *

The story of Alice In Wonderland illustrates the difficulty of choosing when one doesn't know where she wants to go.

Alice was treading the path through the forest in Wonderland when it divided in two different directions. As she stood there wondering what to do, the Cheshire Cat suddenly appeared on the branch of a tree. Alice asked him which path she would choose. "Where do you want to go?" asked the cat. "I don't know," said Alice. "Then," said the cat, "it really doesn't matter, does it?"

God has told us that if we would reach the promised land, we must choose the narrow path, the path of obedience that leads to life eternal.

Lesson 2: 1 Corinthians 3:1-9
Sermon Title: Beyond Tribalism
Sermon Angle: Tribalism is the tragic result of humankind's fall from grace. One tribe or clan sees itself not only as unique but superior to other tribes or clans. Paul was battling religious tribalism. We have witnessed the tragic results of cultural tribalism in places such as Africa, Yugoslavia, Russia, and many other places. Multiculturalism seems to be the buzzword

of political correctness. Tolerance and respect for differences certainly is good but one wonders if some of these efforts don't, in fact, foster tribalism. Should the major emphasis be on our differences or on that which we share in common? The same logic applies to the church. Our unity in Christ transcends our human differences.

Outline:
1. In Corinth, religious tribalism was weakening the fabric of the church
2. In modern times, the church has become even more fragmented
3. We have also witnessed a tragic increase of cultural tribalism
4. Overemphasis on our differences is a sign of spiritual immaturity
5. True unity flows from our relationship with the Lord (v. 9)

Lesson 2: 1 Corinthians 2:6-13

Sermon Title: Channeling

Sermon Angle: Those who participate in the new age movement employ pyramids, chimes, and channeling as means of obtaining wisdom and direction. Channeling seeks supernatural knowledge through contact with the spirits of those who have died. Paul tells us that the only way to make contact with God and secure direction is through the agency of God's Spirit.

Outline:
1. We come into this world without wisdom and understanding
2. Parents, teachers, books, and so forth are channels of human wisdom
3. The Holy Spirit is the only channel for receiving the wisdom and knowledge of God, which we receive through the community of faith
4. Our mission? To be channels for the Holy Spirit to flow out to others

Gospel: Matthew 5:17-37

Sermon Title: A Spirit Of Harmony

Sermon Angle: Jesus proclaimed: "I came not to destroy the law but to fulfill it." How is the law fulfilled? When God and humankind live together in a state of peace and harmony. The Jews were reminded of the purpose of God's law every time they greeted one another with *shalom*. The problem was that the law tended to externalize God's intent into a series of pre-scribed behavior patterns. Jesus gets to the crux of the matter. What God really wants is a change of heart, a transformation of attitudes. Without this spiritual regeneration, the law could never be fulfilled even though behavior might be proper. Jesus was realistic enough to know that harmony would be broken by human sin. In that case, reconciliation was the order of the day. Through the power of Christ, we can make peace with our enemies and restore the harmony between heaven and earth.

Outline:
1. Ours is a God of peace and harmony
2. Adultery, divorce, stealing, and murder are actions that destroy the harmony
3. Jesus points to attitudes that destroy harmony
   — underlying adultery is the attitude of lust
   — underlying stealing is the attitude of covetousness
   — underlying murder is an attitude of arrogance and scorn
4. Christ came to reconcile us to God and to give us the Spirit of reconciliation

*   *   *   *   *

Even non-Christians can sometimes teach us a lesson about reconciliation. In the movie *Gandhi*, a Hindu leader appears at Gandhi's bedside to plead with him to end his fast. The emancipator of India has pledged to keep on fasting until the fighting between the Hindus and the Muslims came to an end. The Hindu leader was angered by Gandhi's resolve to continue his fast and vowed to continue the fight against the Muslims. To justify his behavior, he related how his enemy took his young son and bashed his head against a wall. To seek revenge he captured a Muslim child and did the same thing to him. Then he paused and added sorrowfully, "I have been living in hell."

Gandhi reflected for a few moments and then responded, "I think that I know a way out of hell. Go and find a boy similar to the son the Muslims killed, take him into the home as your son, and raise him as a Muslim."

Our Lord taught that if we would worship the Lord, we must first make peace with our enemies. Reconciliation involves three things: contrition, confession, and satisfaction (to attempt to right the situation). Most of us stop after the first or, possibly, the second part of the act of reconciliation. In order for spiritual harmony to be completely restored, the peace making process must be completed.

*   *   *   *   *

Norman Cousins estimated that in the 6,000 or so years of recorded history, there have only been 292 years of world peace. He estimates that 3.5 billion people have been slain through warfare in that span of time, approximately 80% of the current world population.

*   *   *   *   *

In 1913, a young Austrian by the name of Adolf Hitler made Munich, Germany, his home. The Nazi movement was launched from this great city. The Germans in general and the inhabitants of Munich in particular have been remiss in confronting this dark period of their past. However, attitudes seem to be changing. A recent exhibition has opened at the Stadtmuseum in Munich titled "Munich: Capital of the Movement." The display chronicles the city's contribution through art and artifact. The focus of this exhibition is different than others that deal with this dark era in that it points to the reaction of the common people to the rise of Nazism. The curator of the museum, Brigitte Schultz, points out that much attention has been paid to both the perpetrators and the victims, but little has been done to show how the common people participated in the system in so many small but important ways.

If such an exhibit contributes to a regional and national sense of contrition and confession, reconciliation with the past and peace in the future are more likely.

Epiphany 7/Ordinary Time 7

Revised Common:	Leviticus 19:1-2, 9-18	1 Corinthians 3:10-11, 16-23	Matthew 5:38-48
Roman Catholic:	Leviticus 19:1-2, 17-18	1 Corinthians 3:16-18	Matthew 5:38-48
Episcopal:	Leviticus 19:1-2, 9-18	1 Corinthians 3:10-11, 16-23	Matthew 5:38-48

Seasonal Theme: The Holy Spirit is prominently featured in the Epiphany season pericopes. The Spirit does not act in isolation but works to create and sustain the spiritual community. Each week we will examine a different aspect of the Spirit's presence in Christian community.

Theme For The Day: A loving Spirit is the gift of Christ to all who believe.

Suggested Sermon Text: Matthew 5:38-48

Suggested Sermon Title: God's Loving Spirit

BRIEF COMMENTARY ON THE LESSONS

Lesson 1: Leviticus 19:1-2, 9-18 (C, E); Leviticus 19:1-2, 17-18 (RC)

A preeminent characteristic of God, according to the Pentateuch, is holiness. The Lord is in a class by himself; God is righteous, just, loving, and forgiving. God's people are likewise holy — the Lord's. Their behavior must reflect this reality. They must love their neighbor as themselves because all belong to the Lord. Unfortunately, this love was constricted by a narrow definition of the neighbor — a fellow Hebrew.

Lesson 2: 1 Corinthians 3:10-11, 16-23 (C, E); 1 Corinthians 3:16-18 (RC)

Paul attempts to counteract the arrogant individualism of the Corinthians by reminding them that they are God's holy temple, built on the foundation of Christ. The building up of the Christian church is a communal affair and each person should do his part with care. The sacrificial love exhibited in Jesus Christ is the only eternal foundation for faith and life. We hear echoes of the holiness theme found in the first lessons. The church is holy (belongs to God), as is every member, by virtue of the fact that we are possessed by God's Spirit through Christ. The apostle again puts down human wisdom, which prides itself in possessing knowledge. We already possess everything in Christ. "For all things are yours ... and you are Christ's and Christ is God's" (vv. 21, 23).

Gospel: Matthew 5:38-48 (C, RC, E)

In this passage and throughout the Sermon on the Mount, Jesus holds up an aggressive goodness, a righteousness that has no bounds and goes far beyond the limits of the law. The old righteousness of the law instructs that one must love the neighbor but the new righteousness of Jesus puts forward the outlandish suggestion that we must love our enemies. Love for the neighbor and for those who love us is ordinary and expected, but love for those who oppose us is extraordinary, even divine. Jesus teaches that we must be perfect even as our heavenly Father is perfect (v. 48). The word here is *telios* which doesn't mean without blemish, but complete or mature.

To love as our Lord commands marks one who has attained the fullness of spiritual maturity and holiness.

Psalm Of The Day
> **Psalm 119:33-40 (C)** — "Turn my heart to your decrees ..." (v. 36).
> **Psalm 71 (E)** — "But for me it is good to be near God ..." (v. 28).

Prayer Of The Day

O God, we thank you for loving us with your whole being in Christ and for making us wholly yours through the forgiveness of sins. Make us wholly holy that we might love without limit and reach the fullness of the stature of Christ, in whose name we pray. Amen.

THEOLOGICAL REFLECTION ON THE LESSONS

Lesson 1: Leviticus 19:1-2, 9-18

Like parent, like child. The people of Israel were commanded to be holy, just as their God was holy. Children learn by emulating their parents or those in authority over them. It is said, "He's a chip off the old block," because he looks and acts like one of his parents. Sometimes children are named after parents or grandparents in hopes that the character and traits inherent in the parent or grandparent will rub off on the child. God is gracious, kind, forgiving, just, and merciful. So, if we belong to the Lord, we will manifest those same characteristics. Of course, none of us is perfect (fully mature) but as we grow through life we ought to look more and more like our heavenly Father.

"You shall love your neighbor as you love yourself" (v. 18). This command is based on the assumption that it is natural for people to love themselves. If you didn't love yourself you wouldn't care for yourself. You wouldn't eat properly, brush your hair, exercise, and so forth. The opposite of loving is loathing. But loving yourself does not come through the genetic codes; it is taught or caught. In our society, where millions of children are neglected and abused, many people have never learned to love themselves. Rather, they loathe themselves. They also loathe others as they loathe themselves. Both loving and loathing tend to replicate themselves. We must provide an environment where people learn to love themselves that they might also love God and the neighbor.

Lesson 2: 1 Corinthians 3:10-11, 16-23

Builders of the Master. In verse 10, Paul likens himself to a skilled master builder laboring to construct an edifice according to the blueprint of Jesus Christ and the Holy Spirit. We might turn that phrase around a little to state that all Christians are called to be builders of the Master. We are commissioned to build up the church on the foundation of God's grace in Jesus Christ. A foundation of tradition, good works, or the latest psychological or sociological trend will not suffice. We turn the church into a graven image when we attempt to form it according to our will rather than the Lord's. Christ is both the foundation and the architect for his holy temple; we are merely the workmen.

"All things are yours." This phrase found in verse 21 could be misconstrued by those who want to employ the gospel in the service of selfishness and greed. You've heard the slogans. God wants you to be wealthy. God wants you to be successful in attaining that which you desire. However, Paul is not speaking here about worldly success (wisdom), which he regards

as futile. He is merely establishing that in Christ we have the key to the cosmos and all eternity. This is open to us not because of what we have made of our lives but through what Christ has made of our lives. All things are indeed ours because we belong to Christ and Christ belongs to God (v. 23).

Gospel: Matthew 5:38-48

Love without limits. The Old Testament taught that one should love the neighbor but the Lord removes the boundaries of love. Jesus instructs his disciples to love even their enemies (vv. 44-45). Furthermore, he asserts that it isn't enough to do what is required but that one should go beyond those boundaries. If someone takes your cloak, give him your coat as well. If a Roman soldier orders you to carry his pack one mile, go for two instead (vv. 40-41). Such actions are designed to break down the wall of hostility and stem evil's fury. To love those who love us is well within the bounds of what is normal and expected, but to love the enemy obliterates all boundaries. Such love is only possible through the power of the One who demonstrated a love for the world that is boundless. Such love is not defined by feeling but by doing.

You must be perfect (v. 48). The Lord teaches that we must be perfect, like God. Such an expectation seems light years beyond our spiritual capabilities. We have already discussed the meaning of the Greek word *telios* translated as perfect. It does not indicate a state of flawlessness but of maturity or completion. We know that such maturity will never be completely attained this side of eternity. So, are Jesus' teachings above the higher righteousness meant to drive us to despair concerning our spiritual condition so that we might be receptive to his grace? Certainly, "you must be perfect" does not mean that we must attain spiritual maturity before we are accepted by God. You have probably seen the bumper sticker: "Christians are not perfect, just forgiven." How true. Yet, it is this obvious lack of perfection in the church that keeps many from accepting the gospel. We must do a balancing act. On the one hand, we must take Jesus' call to perfection seriously through the power of the Holy Spirit. Yet, on the other hand, we must hold high the promise of forgiveness for all of us sinners who fall so miserably short of the mark.

PREACHING APPROACHES WITH ILLUSTRATIONS

Lesson 1: Leviticus 19:1-2, 9-18

Sermon Title: Like Parent, Like Child

Sermon Angle: The Israelites are commanded to be holy as the Lord, their God, was holy (v. 2). They were to reject the values of the world and reflect the righteousness of their God. This is comparable to what the Lord says in the gospel lesson about being perfect as our heavenly Father is perfect (Matthew 5:48). Children reflect the values of those who raise and care for them; the closer the relationship, the greater the similarity. We are children of the heavenly Father, so the closer we draw to God, the more we will be like him.

Outline:
1. God's people are called to be holy (set apart to reflect the love of God) (v. 2)
2. God's people are charged to love their neighbor by:
    — reasoning out the conflicts (v. 17)
    — relinquishing grudges and offenses (v. 18)
    — treating others as you desire to be treated

Lesson 2: 1 Corinthians 3:10-11, 16-23

Sermon Title: How To Build A Church

Sermon Angle: Paul laid the foundation for the church — the grace of God in Christ, our Lord. Others have built on that foundation. Each succeeding generation of Christians have added to that spiritual edifice. This sermon should give pause to consider how the strength of the future church is dependent on the spiritual integrity of our church building. Only through the direction of holy scriptures and Holy Spirit can a person or a church become a master builder of God's holy temple.

Outline:
1. Jesus Christ is the only foundation for the church (v. 11)
2. The church is not a steeple, but a people (v. 16)
   — a people set apart through baptism
   — a people possessed of the Spirit
3. Those who wreck the church will be judged (v. 17)
4. Therefore, let us take care how we build up the church (v. 10)

Gospel: Matthew 5:38-48

Sermon Title: Love's Limits Lost

Sermon Angle: Both the Old Testament and the New Testament teach that God's people must love their neighbor. However, in the new covenant the boundary between neighbor and non-neighbor is abolished by Christ. Consequently, the limits of love are lost.

Outline:
Introduction: Christ removes all limits to our love.
1. Love is not limited to those who are good. "Do you resist one who is evil" (v. 39)
2. Love is not limited to kin. "Love your enemies ..." (v. 43)
3. Love is not limited to those who love us (v. 46)
Conclusion: Let us love as Christ loves us.

Sermon Title: Unconditional Love

Sermon Angle: My father once told my mother, "I can't love like you do." I think what he meant was that he found it difficult to love unconditionally. The kind of love that Jesus lifts up in our gospel lesson is *agape* love — the unconditional variety. The love of God is of this nature. This kind of love is only possible for those who are rooted and grounded in love. Only those who rest secure in God's love and exhibit a healthy self-love can begin to love unconditionally. We can only give away that which we have received.

Outline:
1. God has loved us in Christ unconditionally
2. Receive this love and grace personally
3. Share the love of God freely with friend and foe alike

*　*　*　*　*

Among the collected wisdom of the Jewish rabbis is a tale of love between brothers who shared a farm. One brother was married with children and the other brother was single. They worked hard and the land yielded its fruit abundantly. The brothers shared both their toils and the rewards of their labors equally, thanking and praising God for his blessings.

98

One night the single brother thought to himself, *It isn't right that I should share the yield equally with my brother. After all, he has several mouths to feed and I have only myself to look after. I can easily get by with less.* So under the cover of darkness he would go out to the barn and remove grain from his bin and put it in his brother's.

That same night the other brother got to thinking to himself, *It is not right that I should divide the grain equally with my brother. I have many children to look after me in my old age and my brother has only himself. He needs to save for the future.* So, this brother went out into the barn under the cloak of darkness and removed grain from his bin and put it into his brother's.

Each night the brothers would give away quantities of their grain and yet each morning they found that their supply of grain was miraculously replenished. Even so, they never revealed the miracle to one another.

Then one night they met each other out in the farmyard and they realized what had been going on. Overcome with laughter and tears, they embraced one another.

On that spot the temple was built.

This story may be apocryphal. Yet, it is certainly true that God's temple is built in the places where brothers and sisters embrace in laughter and tears.

*   *   *   *   *

On the morning of December 23 my sister called.

"Dad is not doing well. You had better get over to the house."

My dad, Roy Anderson, was suffering the last stages of a battle with prostate cancer that had gone on for over five years. We had just brought him home from a ten-day hospital stay. He had taken a turn for the worse that day.

The day before Christmas Eve, his breathing became irregular and his lungs filled with fluid. He retreated into a semi-comatose stage. The end was rapidly approaching. The family was alerted. All day long grandchildren came to say good-bye. Some of them approached fearfully, intimidated by the specter of death. Some knelt, held Gramp's hand, and prayed.

The eldest grandchild strode into the room confidently and proceeded to the other side of the bed. He laid down by his beloved grandpa, cradling his head, talking naturally to him, as if nothing was amiss. Every once in a while he kissed him on the forehead, telling him that he was the greatest, telling him that he loved him.

In seeing this, I beheld Christ. Dad's sick bed was a loving womb, from which he was being birthed into a glorious new existence with the saints in light. Grandpa was a mere shadow of his former self, unable to give. Yet he was being loved unconditionally. Grandpa paused in his passage through death's door, not wanting to leave such love behind. Christmas Eve and Christmas Day, he was much better, able to sit up, take nourishment, and interact with family. The extension of his life was a gift of love. On New Year's Eve, his spirit was received into the realm of love divine.

Epiphany 8/Ordinary Time 8

Revised Common:	Isaiah 49:8-16a	1 Corinthians 4:1-5	Matthew 6:24-34
Roman Catholic:	Isaiah 49:14-15	1 Corinthians 4:1-5	Matthew 6:24-34
Episcopal:	Isaiah 49:8-18	1 Corinthians 4:1-5 (6-7) 8-13	Matthew 6:24-34

Seasonal Theme: The Holy Spirit is prominently featured in the Epiphany season pericopes. The Spirit does not act in isolation but works to create and sustain the spiritual community. Each week we will examine a different aspect of the Spirit's presence in Christian community.

Theme For The Day: Renewal through trusting God for daily needs.

Suggested Sermon Text: Matthew 6:24-34

Suggested Sermon Title: God's Renewing Spirit

BRIEF COMMENTARY ON THE LESSONS

Lesson 1: Isaiah 49:8-16a (C); Isaiah 49:14-15 (RC); Isaiah 49:8-18 (E)

Through the prophet, God speaks words of consolation to his captive people in Babylon. The frightened and defeated people are beckoned from their hiding places. God promises that he will protect them, heal their wounds, feed them, and lead them back to their homeland. The created world joins in the celebration for the redeemed but the downtrodden people find it difficult to receive the good news saying: "The Lord has forsaken me" (v. 14).

Lesson 2: 1 Corinthians 4:1-5 (C, RC); 1 Corinthians 4:1-5 (6-7) 8-13 (E)

Paul pens this passage with a hurting heart because he and his cohorts are judged to be wanting by the Corinthian church. They did not fit their image of what successful leaders should look like. Paul stakes his leadership claim on his relationship with Christ, not worldly standards. He wants the Corinthians to think of them "as servants of Christ and stewards of God's mysteries." In these roles, the crucial characteristic is faithfulness to the gospel. It was of little concern that he should be judged by humans, only the verdict of God mattered. In fact, human beings should leave the judgments to the Lord, who will bring to light the hidden purposes of the heart. One should also refrain from boasting because everything good is a gift of God.

Gospel: Matthew 6:24-34 (C, RC, E)

In this section of the Sermon On The Mount Jesus lifts up the necessity of single minded service of God: one cannot serve two masters. The Lord urges his listeners to trust in God completely. This would release them from anxiety about food, clothing, or shelter. If God takes care of the birds and the flowers, he would certainly care for those created in his image. If one trusted in God and made this relationship a priority, all other concerns would sift into their rightful place. "But strive first for the kingdom of God and his righteousness, and all these things will be given to you as well."

Psalm 131 (C) — "O Israel, hope in the Lord" (v. 3).

Psalm 62 (RC, E) — "For God alone my soul waits in silence ..." (v. 5).

Prayer Of The Day

Gracious Lord, forgive us for not trusting you above all things and for permitting worldly concerns to torment us with worry. Cause us to center our entire being on you and your kingdom. Then open your hand to supply all that we need from day to day. In Jesus' name. Amen.

THEOLOGICAL REFLECTION ON THE TEXTS

Lesson 1: Isaiah 49:8-18

No hunger or thirst (v. 10). The image here is that of a shepherd who lovingly provides for his flock, like the imagery of Psalm 23. Similar images are also found in the book of Revelation. "They shall hunger no more, and thirst no more; the sun will not strike them, nor any scorching heat" (Revelation 7:16). It is God's delight to satisfy the needs of his children. God has created our hungers and thirsts together with the provision for their satisfaction. The most basic hunger and thirst which the Lord has placed within us is that yearning for Christ himself. In the Beatitudes, Jesus states: "Blessed are those who hunger and thirst for righteousness, for they shall be filled" (Matthew 5:6). When Isaiah states that the people of Israel will hunger and thirst no more, he doesn't mean that their hunger and thirst will be eliminated but that they will be satisfied. To hunger and thirst for God and the kingdom is a good thing; God will never eliminate that spiritual yearning. To do so would lead to complacency and self-satisfaction.

Never Godforsaken. God's chastised people felt forsaken by their redeemer. "My Lord has forsaken me, my Lord has forgotten me" (v. 14). Even those closest to the Almighty have felt this way at times. The medieval mystics described this state of existence as the "dark night of the soul." Even the Son of God cried out from the cross, "My God, my God, why have you forsaken me?" Such a sense of hopelessness is the work of the accuser. We must never view our spiritual condition through the lens of our feelings; they can be deceptive. The time we feel most distant from God may be the time when he is doing his best work in our lives. For those times when we do feel Godforsaken, Isaiah pens wonderful words of assurance and hope. "Can a woman forget her nursing child, or show no compassion for the child of her womb? Even these may forget; yet I will not forget you. See, I have inscribed you on the palms of my hands ..." (vv. 15-16a). Like a loving mother, God is attentive to the cries of his hungering and hurting children. God will never forget his children, their names are engraved on his hands.

Verse 16 speaks powerfully to all those who have laid a loved one in a grave. We will carry that cherished person in our hearts as long as we live but in our heart of hearts we know that time will eventually erase the memory of that person from the face of the earth. We vainly attempt to give that person a degree of immortality by engraving a tombstone with his or her name, together with birth date and date of death. Someday we, too, will have that final inscription placed over our grave. Three or four generations after we have died, maybe sooner, there will be no one who remembers us as more than a name. These thoughts are unsettling and so we push them away and deal with something more pleasant. Yet, there is hope. There is one who will never forget his own. God has not merely written, he has engraved our names on the palm of his hands, if we might be permitted an anthropomorphism. God's people can take comfort not that their names are engraved on a piece of granite, but on the Rock Of Ages.

Lesson 2: 1 Corinthians 4:1-13

The peril of prejudice. Paul warns the Corinthians to reserve their judgments for the Judge of the universe. Prejudice is the practice of judging prior to receiving all the facts. Paul concludes: "Therefore do not pronounce judgment before the time, before the Lord comes ..." (v. 5a). Paul experienced prejudice personally from the Corinthians; perhaps he was found wanting in appearance or leadership style, not sufficiently worldly wise. They erred because they were using the wrong criteria for judgment. Paul urges that they must look at his ministry with different leadership lenses and regard him as a servant of Christ and a steward of the mysteries of God. We must resist the peril of prejudice, not only because we are not aware of all the relevant factors but because we often use the wrong criteria for judging. We tend to judge by the accepted standards of worldly wisdom and success, rather than by God's rule.

Servants and stewards. All Christians, including pastors and other church leaders, should regard themselves as, first and foremost, servants of Christ and stewards of the gospel. Yet, how many search committees ask their church leadership candidates about this aspect of their ministry? How many pastors emphasize these roles when preparing their resumes? The key consideration that Paul invites us to look at in a leader is trustworthiness or faithfulness to the gospel (v. 2). Faithfulness is perceived as dull. The wisdom of the age asserts that leaders should have star quality. Even in the church, we take our cue from the world and hold up such things as looks, image, charisma, youth, sex, personality, charm, and fluency. These human qualities are not unimportant, but should they be the defining characteristics for those who would be stewards of the gospel?

Gospel: Matthew 6:24-34

Don't worry, be holy. Years ago, there was a rather whimsical song titled, "Don't Worry, Be Happy." The song seemed to suggest that worry could be turned off and happiness turned on through the exercise of one's will. All that was needed was a positive attitude. Jesus suggests another approach: Don't worry, be holy. Worry is caused by trying to do too many things, be too many things; the trick is trying to balance them all. The antidote for worry is a single-minded devotion to God. Jesus said: "No one can serve two masters." Christ calls us to holiness; to be set apart for God's service alone; to be wholly the Lord's and trust him for all of life's necessities. If we give ourselves wholly to the Lord, as his holy people, we will be spiritually focused and there will be no place for worry which results from a lack of trust.

A priori means literally that which is before. In logic, *a priori* reasoning proceeds from cause to effect. For a happy and well-ordered life, it is necessary to distinguish that which comes before from that which follows. Jesus states that which comes before all else is the kingdom of God. He teaches that there are many things in life that are important and good but there is one thing which precedes all others, the kingdom of God. "But strive first for the kingdom of God and his righteousness, and all these things (life's necessities) will be given to you as well" (v. 33).

Make Today Count is the name of an organization formed by those who had to face catastrophic illness. This phrase provides an important insight for living. We have no certainty about the future. The future is not ours; all we have is today and so we must make it count. Worry is always focused on the future and the problems the future might deal us. Such worry occupies our time, steals our focus, and saps our energy. Jesus counsels us to live in the present and to trust God for the future. "So do not worry about tomorrow, for tomorrow will bring worries of its own. Today's troubles are enough for today" (v. 34).

PREACHING APPROACHES WITH ILLUSTRATIONS

Lesson 1: Isaiah 49:8-18

Sermon Title: The Hunger And The Thirst

Sermon Angle: The prophet consoles the fallen people of Israel with the promise that God would care for their needs, they would hunger and thirst no more. The promise is not that their needs would be eliminated but that they would be satisfied. What satisfaction would food provide if we never experienced hunger? Without hunger, we would not be inclined to eat. Those who have witnessed a loved one die of cancer know that the absence of appetite is often a sign that the end of life is near. The hunger and thirst is the driving force of physical existence. Likewise, God has placed within our souls a hunger and thirst for God. That drive is good because it causes us to seek spiritual satisfaction, which the Lord delights to supply.

Outline:

1. We have witnessed the scourge of starvation
2. Nevertheless, hunger and thirst is a gift of God
3. Without the hunger and thirst for God, we would spiritually starve
4. Trust the Lord to satisfy the hunger of your body and your spirit

Lesson 2: 1 Corinthians 4:1-13

Sermon Title: The Peril Of Prejudice

Sermon Angle: Paul warns the Corinthians about the peril of prejudice, of judging people without first having all the relevant facts. Prejudice not only hurts other people, it hurts the one prejudiced. He is prevented from knowing others and from knowing the truth. The ultimate prejudice is murder. The murderer judges that a certain person does not deserve to exist and renders sentence and punishment. All prejudice is a kind of spiritual murder where the real person is replaced by a false image. Therefore, says Paul, "Do not pronounce judgment before the time, before the Lord comes, who will bring to light the things now hidden ..." (v. 5).

Outline:

1. Paul experienced prejudice in his ministry
2. Have you experienced prejudice? How did it make you feel?
3. Prejudice has led to atrocities (Give examples)
4. It harms not only the victim but the perpetrator
5. We are warned to refrain from judging until the Lord comes

Gospel: Matthew 6:24-34

Sermon Title: Don't Worry, Be Holy

Sermon Angle: We are called to be God's holy people, wholly devoted to the Lord and his kingdom. We all fall short of this goal, refusing to entrust our lives completely to the Lord. In so doing we open ourselves to anxiety and worry. The world says to those riddled with anxiety: Don't worry, be happy. Christ says: Don't worry, be holy.

Outline:

1. Talk about worry as a common malady of our lives
2. Worry is a symptom of a spiritual malady — lack of trust in God
3. The world counsels the troubled, don't worry be happy
4. Christ counsels, don't worry, be holy (seek the kingdom)

Sermon Title: *A Priori*

Sermon Angle: This sermon should be about priorities. To get our priorities straight we must first know that which is *a priori*, namely, God and the kingdom. God is that which comes before all not only in terms of time but importance. If the Lord and his kingdom are our highest goals, all other concerns will assume their proper place. "But strive first for the kingdom of God ... and all these other things will be given to you as well" (v. 5).

Outline:
1. In our world there is a crisis of values
2. The basic problem — self is *a priori*
3. Solution: Make Christ and the kingdom *a priori*
4. Then, other things will fall into place

Sermon Title: Day By Day

Sermon Angle: One memorable song from the musical, *Godspell*, is titled "Day By Day." The title and the lyrics capture the true nature of Christian discipleship. Though Christians are lifted up by the hope of heaven, our primary focus must be our daily walk with Christ. Jesus teaches that we should not be anxious about tomorrow. Permit the Lord to help you deal with today's difficulties and let tomorrow's troubles rest on his shoulders. Today's challenges are more than ample (v. 34).

Outline:
1. Talk about some of the most difficult times in our lives
2. The Lord promises strength only for today's troubles
3. To worry is to add tomorrow's troubles to today's
   — a sure prescription for physical, emotional, and spiritual dysfunction
   — a sign pointing to lack of faith
4. Conclusion: follow Jesus one day at a time

The Transfiguration Of Our Lord
(Last Sunday After Epiphany)

Revised Common:	**Exodus 24:12-18**	**2 Peter 1:16-21**	**Matthew 17:1-9**
Roman Catholic:	**Daniel 7:9-10, 13-14**	**2 Peter 1:16-19**	**Matthew 17:1-9**
Episcopal:	**Exodus 24:12 (13-14) 15-18**	**Philippians 3:7-14**	**Matthew 17:1-9**

Seasonal Theme: The Holy Spirit is prominently featured in the Epiphany season pericopes. The Spirit does not act in isolation but works to create and sustain the spiritual community. Each week we will examine a different aspect of the Spirit's presence in Christian community.

Theme For The Day: The Transfiguration of Christ was an experience of divine transcendence. The Spirit gifts his children with glimpses of the transcendent Christ and the life to come.

Suggested Text For Preaching: Matthew 17:1-9

Suggested Sermon Title: The Fulfilling Gift Of The Spirit: Transcendence

BRIEF COMMENTARY ON THE LESSONS

Lesson 1: Exodus 24:12-18 (C); Exodus 24:12 (13-14) 15-18 (E)

God instructs Moses to ascend Mount Sinai to receive the law of the Lord. The glory of God appeared to the people on top of the mountain as a consuming fire. Moses enters the mysterious cloud and approaches the fire to receive the divine revelation.

Lesson 1: Daniel 7:9-10, 13-14 (RC)

In the vision of Daniel, the Lord God sits in judgment on the heavenly court. All power and glory are conveyed by the almighty to the messianic king who will reign forever.

Lesson 2: 2 Peter 1:16-21 (C); 2 Peter 1:16-19 (RC)

Peter asserts that Christianity is not based on cleverly devised myths but on eyewitness accounts. He himself witnessed the divine glory in the face of Jesus, as the heavenly voice testified that Jesus is God's own dear Son, with whom he is pleased. The written word of God is confirmed by the incarnate Word, who shines as a light in a world of darkness.

Lesson 2: Philippians 3:7-14 (E)

Paul regards all his accomplishments as rubbish in comparison to the value of knowing Christ. It is his passion to share in Christ's sufferings and death, so that he might also share his resurrection. He has not yet completely taken possession of this new life in Christ, but he presses on like a runner straining for the goal line.

Gospel: Matthew 17:1-9 (C, RC, E)

Jesus has just announced that he is going to Jerusalem to face suffering and death. To confirm this course he ascends a mountain to commune with the Father. On the mountain, Jesus is luminous with divine glory. Peter, James, and John are awed and frightened by the sight and sound of it all. Christ's course is confirmed by the appearance of Elijah, the greatest of the prophets, and Moses, the lawgiver. This sight is a foretaste of resurrection glory, but as they leave the summit, the disciples are told not to share their experience until after the resurrection.

Psalm Of The Day

Psalm 99 (C, E) — "Worship at his holy mountain ..." (v. 9).

Prayer Of The Day

God of light, as you revealed your glory through the transfiguration of your Son, so open our sleepy eyes that we might also see your glory and be transformed thereby. In Jesus' name. Amen.

Transfiguration — Bridge Between Epiphany And Lent

The Epiphany season serves to reveal the glory of God in Jesus. In the transfiguration event, the glory reaches its apex, as the divine substance shines through the body of Jesus and the divine voice renders witness to the Christ. This theophany occurs at a crucial juncture in the Lord's ministry. He is going to Jerusalem to suffer and die on the cross as the sacrifice for the sins of the world. The transfiguration is both a strengthening and a confirmation of that decision. Jesus could proceed with the Father's blessing to the cross. The presence of Elijah and Moses indicates that Jesus' decision is a fulfillment of the law and the prophets.

Not all churches observe the transfiguration on the last Sunday after the Epiphany. The Roman Church reads the transfiguration gospel lesson on the second Sunday in Lent, as well as August 6, when transfiguration is observed by both the Roman and Episcopalian churches. The Presbyterian and United Church of Christ churches employ the lessons for Pentecost. If transfiguration is observed, it should be preached in light of the cross. Just as Jesus was preparing for his journey to Jerusalem, so we are preparing for our Lenten pilgrimage. The glory of God is revealed not only on the revelatory peaks but in the valley of sacrificial service.

THEOLOGICAL REFLECTION ON THE LESSONS

Lesson 1: Exodus 24:12-18

Waiting on the Lord. Moses was instructed by God to meet him on the mountain. He instructed the people to wait below. Then he and Joshua went up the mountain. The cloud of God's presence covered the mountain for six days, and finally, on the seventh day, God spoke out of the cloud. Moses remained on Mount Sinai forty days and nights, receiving the commandments of the Lord. One would think that God could have expedited the matter more quickly, but the Lord doesn't operate on our timetable. Being God gives him the wisdom and the power to speak or not, to act or refrain from acting. The important factor is that we are willing to watch, as we wait on the Lord, and that we be in the place where God instructs us to be. Isaiah expresses this thought best: "He who waits upon the Lord will renew his strength ..." (Isaiah 40:31). We know that those who waited at the base of the mountain refused to wait. They constructed a golden calf, and this brought the wrath of God down upon their heads.

Lesson 1: Daniel 7:9-10, 13-14

Transcendent vision. The transfiguration was a transcendent vision for those who witnessed it. The scene described by Daniel was also a transcendent vision. Both of these visions came at a time of duress, a period of struggle with the enemy who appeared to have the advantage. Both visions come to the same conclusion: all people and powers will eventually bow before the awesome majesty of our God. The New Testament goes one step further than the book of Daniel in claiming that God will rule eternally through his Son, Jesus the Christ.

Lesson 2: 2 Peter 1:16-21

Confirmation hearing. Every time the president of the United States nominates someone to head a major governmental body, it requires a confirmation hearing by the Congress. Friend and foe seek to lift up his or her good and bad points. In a case such as the confirmation of Judge Clarence Thomas to the Supreme Court, it turned out to be a bruising ideological battle. Though confirmed eventually, Thomas was wounded by the fray. Friends said he was different than before and he tended to shy away from social contacts. How different than the confirmation hearing that our Lord had on the Mount of Transfiguration. Those present heard an exceedingly confirming message: "This is my Son, my beloved, with whom I am well pleased." This hearing gave Jesus the strength he needed to go on to Calvary, and it later served to confirm the faith of Peter, James, and John, as well as those who heard their message.

Gospel: Matthew 17:1-9

Listening to the clouds. Did you know that clouds speak? Weather forecasters make a living trying to interpret what they are communicating. High and wispy cirrus clouds tell us to expect a tranquil day. On the other hand, ominous cumulus thunderheads warn of imminent storms. These clouds capture our attention with sudden stabs of blinding light, accompanied by earth-shaking thunder. On the mountain where Jesus was transfigured, the disciples there were suddenly enshrouded by a bright cloud. They fell like dead men, quaking with fear of the unknown. Then a voice echoed from the cloud: "This is my Son, the Beloved, with whom I am well pleased; listen to him!" (v. 5).

In the Old Testament, God led his people by a pillar of cloud to the promised land and he gave the law to Moses from the cloud that enshrouded Mount Sinai. The cloud symbolizes the mysterious presence of *Yahweh* — both concealing and revealing. God spoke through the cloud to reassure and to guide his people and the Almighty still speaks to us through the clouds that suddenly close in upon us. Figuratively speaking, clouds may overwhelm us at intervals throughout our lives. The clouds may be of our own making or God-sent. These clouds may appear to be ominously dark and foreboding; they may obscure the horizon or force us to our knees. The important thing is to listen to God's voice in the cloud. He is present to reassure and guide us. God can transform an apparently ominous cloud into a bright revelatory cloud of his gracious presence.

"Listen to him." That is what the heavenly voice told the disciples on the Mount of Transfiguration. What is it that God wants them to listen to? To understand this we must consider the second half of the preceding chapter. This section begins with the confession of Peter that Jesus was the Messiah. He instructs the disciples not to reveal his identity yet and then reveals something that causes them to reel in shock. He is going to suffer and die in Jerusalem and then rise from the dead. Following this, Peter and Jesus exchange rebukes. This notion of suffering and death is anathema to Peter and the others. Then comes the second part of the one-two punch. Not only must their Master suffer and die but they must take up their crosses also. Finally, Jesus

speaks of the Son of Man returning in glory to establish the kingdom, which some standing there will witness before they die (vv. 27-28).

What God wanted the disciples to listen to was the message of the cross, a message alien to their thinking. The glory of the kingdom would not be like the glory of the world. The glory of God is revealed in self-giving servanthood. Truly, some of them would see the kingdom during the transfiguration. Like a strobe image, it would freeze the action in their minds. Many others witnessed the kingdom through the death and resurrection of Christ. To receive the kingdom, we must still listen to the mighty words and deeds of the Christ.

PREACHING APPROACHES WITH ILLUSTRATIONS

Lesson 1: Exodus 24:12-18

Sermon Title: Waiting On The Lord

Sermon Angle: God could have merely dropped the tablets of his commandments from the sky into the camp of the Israelites, but he didn't. It took forty days of waiting, watching, and dialogue. Moses was gone so long the people thought some ill had befallen him and they got into mischief. In order to receive direction from God we must be willing to wait and watch. God is sovereign and will show himself when he is ready. An important aspect of preparing is being in the place where God has appointed.

Outline:
1. Thesis: we are morally and spiritually adrift as a society
2. Moral decay follows from a loss of transcendence
3. The Ten Commandments resulted from a transcendent encounter
4. Like Moses, we need to wait on the Lord to receive the transcendent vision
5. Strategy to accomplish that end
   — recommit our lives to the Lord
   — feed on God's word daily
   — spend regular times in worship and prayer

Lesson 1: Daniel 7:9-10, 13-14

Sermon Title: The Beatific Vision

Sermon Angle: People of faith have received immeasurable strength for the struggles of life because they have caught a glimpse of the beatific (heavenly) vision. In the conflicts of existence, in their battles with the power of wickedness, the eyes of faith allow them to see God's future. All existence will be united under the glorious rule of our God.

Outline:
1. The book of Daniel was written at a time when God's people were struggling for spiritual survival (Highlight the persecution by Antiochus Epiphanes)
2. God's people still struggle with the enemy (examples)
3. The beatific vision of God's triumphant rule gives us strength

Lesson 2: 2 Peter 1:16-21

Sermon Title: Confirmation Hearing

Sermon Angle: A confirmation hearing was held on top of the Mount of Transfiguration; not a hearing to determine whether Jesus was worthy but to make known that he was the one on whom God's favor rested. The Spirit confirmed to Jesus that he was God's Son, the beloved.

God's favor was bestowed simply because he was God's Son. Next, the Spirit made known that he was well pleased with Jesus. Here the Spirit is confirming the conduct of his life and the course of his mission. This experience of the Father's grace and favor enabled Jesus to fulfill the mission that had been given him. Our baptism is such a confirmation hearing. God declares his favor to us and grants us the grace to go to the cross.

Outline:
1. The Father confirmed that Jesus was the Son of his favor
2. The Father also confirmed the course Jesus was taking
3. The disciples heard and witnessed the divine approbation
4. God has confirmed his love for us in Christ
5. Filled with grace, let us confirm our love for God through sacrificial service

Gospel: Matthew 17:1-9

Sermon Title: Just Listen To Him

Sermon Angle: Sometimes when a person says something contradictory or outrageous, a witness may state sarcastically, "Just listen to him!" In a different context, one in which a group of people is seeking guidance for decision making, a person may counsel, "He makes a lot of sense, just listen to him." The Mount of Transfiguration was such a place. The three disciples didn't know what to make of this frighteningly strange event. Peter foolishly proposed making three structures. Suddenly overshadowed by the bright cloud of glory, the divine voice boomed: "This is my Son, the Beloved, (just) listen to him" (v. 5). God is saying, in effect, listen especially to what he is saying about betrayal, suffering, death, and resurrection. It isn't enough to merely hear him — you must listen to him!

Outline:
1. In this world there is often a welter of conflicting voices
2. Problem: How do we distinguish the voice of God?
   — the world rejects suffering, sacrifice, and death
   — Christ lifts up suffering, sacrifice, and death for the sake of the gospel
3. Just hear Christ, listen to him!

Sermon Title: A Breakthrough Of Transcendence

Sermon Angle: The entire ministry of Jesus might be described as a breakthrough of transcendence. Yet the divine Spirit of power and light broke through much more forcefully at certain times. Peter confessed this transcendence at Caesarea Philippi, but on the Mount of Transfiguration, he and the others were bowled over by it. The Western world has come to so worship human reason that we are largely unaware of the transcendent dimension of the Spirit. Yet, at the same time, we hunger to experience the domain of the Spirit. The Spirit of God is never far from the surface of our lives but are we looking and listening for such breakthroughs?

Outline:
1. The Christ event is a breakthrough of transcendence
2. The transfiguration was a special breakthrough of transcendence
3. Our society has lost its sense of transcendence (indications and consequences)
4. Yet, many seek for spiritual experience
   — Belief in angels is one such indication (see below)
   — Other examples: worship, selfless service, prayer

*　*　*　*　*

109

According to *Time* magazine, a majority of Americans believe in the existence of angels (69%) and 46% believe that they have their own guardian angel. Harvard Divinity School has a course on angels and Boston College has two. The subject is so popular that bookstores have established special angel sections and five of the ten top religious books, according to *Publisher's Weekly*, have been about angels. Billy Graham's 1975 book, *Angels: God's Secret Agents* was a best-seller at 2.6 million copies. Yet, how deeply felt is this belief in angels? Do the figures point to a resurgence of interest in the things of the spirit or a mere wistfulness for the realm of the transcendent, without firm conviction? A number of theologians believe that the latter is the case: that this popularity of angels is all whipped cream and meringue. The fearsome seraphim and cherubim have been transformed into benign, accepting beings, who are always there when you reach the end of your rope.

Sophy Burnham wrote a book about angel encounters titled *A Book Of Angels*, where she maintains that angels are all around but invisible. She contends that angels disguise themselves as a gust of wind, a pulse of energy, a thought, and so forth. The heavenly host don't care about being seen; they are only concerned to put across their message. The form and directness of the angelic visitations is dependent on our capacity to receive.

Does this interest in angels reflect a new enthusiasm for transcendence and things spiritual? It's hard to say but, at least, it shows that we are not content with a strictly materialistic, here-and-now world.

*   *   *   *   *

It can be argued that the Soviet Union collapsed not only because the communistic economic model failed so miserably to supply the goods, but more importantly, that it disintegrated because it lost its transcendent vision. Communism was born of a burning vision of an earthly paradise, where all would share equally and injustice would be vanquished. Unfortunately, the vision was usurped by despots as a means of control. When the vision seemed so far removed from reality, it lacked credibility and died.

In the United States, we have had a longer track record of sustaining the American dream, which is a kind of transcendent vision. Dangerously, however, those are signs that the vision is fading under an assault of selfishness, greed, and violence. Some years ago, George G. Kennan, a former ambassador and political scientist, made an observation about the east-west conflict: "I sometimes wonder what use there is in trying to protect the Western world against fancied threats, when the signs of disintegration from within are so striking." The vision has been distorted by those who view the American dream as consisting of unrestrained personal freedoms. We need to temper the personal freedoms with the so-called republican virtues that the founders of our country held high, such as godliness, patience, hard work, and neighborliness.

The Lenten Season

In the Roman Catholic and mainline Protestant churches, the season of Lent has been elevated to the top spot on the liturgical calendar. The western (Roman) church came to dwell on the passion/death of our Lord, while the eastern (Orthodox) church has given greater weight to the resurrection. Lent is the season to not only meditate on the passion of Jesus but also to die spiritually with him. The goal is not greater knowledge but identification with the passion and death of Jesus. The aim of our Lenten journey is the renewal of our faith. The Lenten emphasis on fasting, meditation, prayer, giving, and good works, with the added religious rites and services, has elevated Lent to a position of preeminence. That would prove theologically incorrect, as the resurrection of Christ is the pivotal event for the Christian faith. Lent should be seen as a period of preparation for the celebration of Christ's victory over death. In this season, the believer suffers and dies with the Lord, so that she might also rise to newness of life with him. The passion and death of Christ are not ends for the believer, but means; you cannot enjoy resurrection without first dying. Lent begins with a special day of repentance on Ash Wednesday and concludes with the solemnity of Good Friday, the crucifixion of our Lord. The word used to denote the season (Lent) is not descriptive of its mood and meaning; it derives from the Anglo-Saxon word *lencten*, which refers to the lengthening of the daylight during the time of the year when Lent occurs.

Historical Development Of The Season

The Lenten season, as it is traditionally observed, required 1,000 or so years of development. Lent began as an observance lasting forty hours, in the church of the first century, because the Lord's body rested in the tomb about that length of time between burial and resurrection. Later, the season was stretched to six days of fasting and special observance, called Holy Week. In the fourth century, Holy Week was practiced in Jerusalem by going to the various sites associated with the passion of our Lord, which eventually led to the stations of the cross.

Next, the six days grew into 36 days, a tithe of the number of days in the year. Around the time of Charlemagne, around 730 AD, four days were added, to total forty. The number *four* was considered special, a symbol of completeness as in the four winds, the four seasons, and the four compass points. The significance of the number four can also be found in the forty years the Israelites wandered in the wilderness, the forty days Moses was on Mount Sinai to receive the commandments, and the forty days our Lord was tempted by Satan.

Sundays were never considered a part of Lent, since it was always celebrated as the Lord's resurrection day. That's why the church refers to the Sundays as in Lent rather than of Lent. For this reason, Lent actually begins 46 days rather than forty days before Easter. Of course, some of the trappings of Lent have spilled over into the Sunday observance in such things as the use of the color purple and the deletion of the *alleluia*.

The date of Lent depends on the date of the Resurrection of our Lord, which is derived from the lunar calendar. Easter occurs on the first Sunday following the first full moon after the vernal equinox. Ash Wednesday marks the beginning of Lent. The name for this day was given by Pope Urban in 1099. Ashes are symbolic of repentance. The practice of covering oneself with ashes and tearing one's clothes as a sign of grief or sorrow harks back to Old Testament times and probably much earlier. The ashes that were thrown over the people by the priests were derived from the previous year's palms. Eventually the practice changed to making an ashen cross on the forehead of the penitents, accompanied by the phrase: "Dust thou art and to dust thou shalt return." For centuries, this practice was abandoned by most Protestants, perhaps out of deference to Jesus' instruction: "And when you fast do not look dismal like hypocrites, for they disfigure their faces that their fasting may be seen by men" (Matthew 6:16). In recent years, the practice of imposing ashes on Ash Wednesday has greatly increased in popularity within the liturgical branch of the Protestant churches and has continued uninterrupted within the Roman church.

Lenten Observance Past And Present

In the early church the period of Lent was a time of preparation for baptism, as the candidates were carefully led through the mysteries of the Christian faith. That practice is not widely observed any more but still has much to commend itself. What better time could there be for baptismal instruction, whether to adult converts or parents of infants who are shortly to be baptized? Now, the focus is on the reaffirmation of our baptismal vows. Lent should be a time when the believer renews his or her commitment to Christ, laying hold of God's grace through faith.

Lent is also a period of penitence, where we become not only cognizant of our sins but also die to our sins. Protestants usually acknowledge their sins every Sunday in a general rite of confession, yet seldom are encouraged to make specific confession of their particular sins. This issue cannot be forced but ought to be encouraged. Perhaps, members could be urged to find a Christian partner with whom they can safely confess their wrongs. In addition, the language of the congregational confession of sins could be made much more specific. In this buck-passing, blame-bouncing society, Christians need to set an example by taking responsibility for their sins.

Fasting and alms giving have also traditionally been emphasized during Lent. Since Vatican II, the Roman Catholic church has greatly slackened its requirements on fasting. For example, it is no longer necessary to abstain from meat on Friday or refrain from eating before mass. Protestants have largely done away with fasting, reasoning that since we are saved by grace and fasting smacks of good works, fasting is superfluous, even harmful. Fasting can be useful as a form of discipline over the demands of the body and as a means of entering into a spiritually heightened state of being. If believers do give up something, such as food, it is a good idea to use the money that would have been spent to help the poor. It is more Christian to give to something than to give up something.

Lent is also a special season of prayer and worship. Most churches have special midweek services, prayer vigils, and Holy Week services. It is a good idea to begin and end the season with a congregational prayer vigil, either 12 or 24 hours. Lent is a natural time to emphasize personal and corporate prayer and devotion. The object is not to make points with God but to be filled with the spirit of Christ, in order that we might accomplish his will. Prayer and worship is the doorway to the Spirit. The midweek services ought not to be self-help exercises but focus on God's sacrificial gift of himself. If there is any time when people are going to be responsive to the gospel, it will probably be the season of Lent. This opportunity should not be missed. Members and inquirers alike should be urged to make a decision to commit or recommit their lives to the Lord. Effort should be taken to make all of the services in Lent stimulating and compelling. A Lenten theme for the midweek or even the Sunday services works well, as does a special Lenten theme hymn.

The events of Lent and Holy Week are high drama; the churches' worship services are the stage and the aim should be that every Christian be drawn into the drama. Too many people in the church are content with staying in the audience. However, the aim is not emotional catharsis but transformation and renewal, and not just renewal of the church but of the world that Christ died to save.

Suggested Lenten Preaching Series

The following thematic framework for the Sunday worship services is provided for your consideration. It is called *Christ's Confrontations On The Way To The Cross.*

Lenten Gospel Lessons

Lent 1 — Matthew 4:1-11 — The temptations of Jesus
Lent 2 — John 3:1-17 — Nicodemus visits Jesus at night
Lent 3 — John 4:5-26 — Jesus encounters a Samaritan woman at the well
Lent 4 — John 9:1-41 — Jesus encounters a man born blind
Lent 5 — John 11:17-45 — The raising of Lazarus from the dead
Passion/Palm Sunday (Lent 6) — Matthew 26:14—27:66 — The passion story

The Themes For The Lenten Series

Lent 1 — Christ confronts Satan
    Sub-theme — Temptation
Lent 2 — Christ confronts Nicodemus
    Sub-theme — The new birth
Lent 3 — Christ confronts a Samaritan woman
    Sub-theme — Grace and forgiveness
Lent 4 — Christ confronts a man born blind
    Sub-theme — Seeing with new eyes
Lent 5 — Christ confronts Lazarus
    Sub-theme — Eternal life
Passion/Palm Sunday (Lent 6) — Christ confronts his enemies
    Sub-theme — Suffering and the cross

If you desire to carry this theme over into Holy Week, the following themes are suggested:
    Maundy Thursday — Christ confronts his betrayers
        Sub-theme — Servant-leadership
    Good Friday — Christ confronts death
        Sub-theme — Life through death

Note: These texts and sermon titles will appear under the category of "Suggested Sermon Text" and "Suggested Sermon Title." These designations are for the benefit of those who do adapt this thematic framework.

Ash Wednesday

Revised Common:	Joel 2:1-2, 12-17	2 Corinthians 5:20b—6:10	Matthew 6:1-6, 16-21
Roman Catholic:	Joel 2:12-18	2 Corinthians 5:20—6:2	Matthew 6:1-6, 16-18
Episcopal:	Joel 2:1-2, 12-17	2 Corinthians 5:20b—6:10	Matthew 6:1-6, 16-21

Theme: Ash Wednesday begins our Lenten observance. The first lesson from Joel 2 sets the theme for the day and the season. It is a time of impending crisis and danger. God's people are called to turn from their sins and, from the depths of their being, return to the Lord with fasting, weeping, and mourning.

BRIEF COMMENTARY ON THE LESSONS

Lesson 1: Joel 2:1-2, 12-17 (C, E); Joel 2:12-18 (RC)

The prophet Joel receives a word from the Lord. The ram's horn is to be sounded so that the people might assemble before the Lord. It is a time of crisis but the source of the trouble is not clear. Scholars differ greatly as to when the book was written — anywhere from 800 BC to 350 BC. Nevertheless, the situation calls for swift and forthright action. All of the people (v. 16), without exception, are called to return to the Lord with fasting, weeping, and mourning. They are summoned to turn to their gracious God with all their hearts and beg the Lord for mercy and pardon. The priests are called upon to stand between the sinful people and their holy God, with pleas of intercession (v. 17). The Lord hears the intercessions of the people and assures them of his provision and care of them (v. 19).

Lesson 2: 2 Corinthians 5:20b—6:10 (C, E); 2 Corinthians 5:20—6:2 (RC)

The apostle Paul pleads with the contentious and divisive Corinthians to become reconciled (at one) with God through Christ. Christ became what we are (took on our sin) so that we might become what he is (righteous). The way to accomplish this goal is to accept the grace of God. The situation is serious and the time to act is now (6:2).

Gospel: Matthew 6:1-6, 16-21 (C, E); Matthew 6:1-6, 16-18 (RC)

These sayings from Jesus, contained in the body of his teachings called the Sermon on the Mount, reflect the tension between the Lord and the Pharisees. That same situation was reflected in the church of Matthew's day. While the first lesson calls the people to assemble for public devotion and prayer, the gospel lesson warns of the dangers of public piety. The primary risk is one of hypocrisy, where action is divorced from attitude or intention. The hypocrite is not real; he is just acting in pretense. Grandstand religion is anathema to God. The believer should direct her devotion to God alone. The mark of the true believer is determined by that which he values above all. The things of God are his true treasure, which in contrast to earthly fortune, cannot be taken away (vv. 19-21).

Psalm Of The Day

Psalm 51:1-17 (C) — "Have mercy on me, O God ..." (v. 1).

Psalm 103 or 103:8-14 (E) — "Bless the Lord, O my soul, and do not forget his benefits — who forgives all your iniquity and heals all your diseases ..." (vv. 2-3).

Prayer Of The Day

Merciful God, because you are gracious and compassionate, we are able to confront our dark side and confess, with wounded hearts, that we have sinned and done that which is evil in your sight. Pay heed to the ashes of our repentance and make our hearts clean as newly fallen snow. In Jesus' name. Amen.

THEOLOGICAL REFLECTION ON THE LESSONS

Lesson 1: Joel 2:1-2, 12-18

Lent: A Time Of Turning. This is the title I gave to a Lenten series that I developed some years ago. The prophet Joel called the nation to a time of turning. It was time for them to turn away from their sins and turn toward their God. Return more accurately reflects Joel's thoughts. The people had in past times walked with the Lord but had since strayed. Joel foresees impending doom on the horizon and interprets it as a sign of God's wrath. Yet, the Lord's heart is not flinty, impervious to the repentant cries of his people. Yes, even God can turn and repent of his ordained chastening (v. 14). Isn't that what Lent is about? God has turned his face toward us in Jesus Christ, that we might turn to him in repentance and faith. If God were only a God of wrath, we would turn away in despair or cower at his feet in fear. It is hope that impels us to turn to him. "For he is gracious and merciful, slow to anger and abounding in steadfast love and repents of evil" (v. 13).

A time of tears. Joel instructs the people to return to their God with fasting, weeping, and mourning. The priests and ministers are to be so earnest in their intercessions for God's mercy that their hearts break, their tears flow. Most of us would probably be embarrassed to weep at worship. We must maintain proper liturgical decorum. Some of our African-American brothers and sisters can teach the value of letting our feelings come forth in worship. Repentance means more than just moving our emotions. If we are really heartbroken for our sins and the iniquity of our people, don't you think it would show? Jesus wept over the hardheartedness of the city of Jerusalem; he wept by the grave of his friend Lazarus and was moved to tears by the widow of Nain, as she buried her only son. There's something cathartic and purifying about tears, not that we let it rest there. Notice that Jesus was first moved to tears and then moved to redemptive action.

Open heart surgery. This is what Joel is calling for. "Return to me with your whole heart" (v. 12). Our diseased hearts need surgery, not the clean and calculated incision of the specialist but the impassioned rending of one desperate for wholeness (v. 13). Yet, how much that passes for repentance is *halfhearted*, at best? How often we are like the little boy, who treated his little sister shamefully, and was later made to apologize by his indignant mother. The words choked reluctantly forth with all the sincerity of Trader Tom, the used car dealer: "All right, I'm sorry."

For the biblical writers, the heart was the seat of the will, not the emotions, which was located somewhat lower in the anatomy. We rend open our hearts to God so that he might fill us with his Spirit for the accomplishment of his will.

Lesson 2: 2 Corinthians 5:20—6:10

Ambassadors. Paul pleads with the Corinthians: "So we are ambassadors for Christ ..." (v. 20a). It was the responsibility of the ambassador from Rome to bring the far-flung peoples of the empire into the Roman family of nations, by presenting the terms of peace. Paul conceives of his ambassadorship as having a much greater purpose, to bring people into the family of

God, by making known the gracious terms for the peace offered through the death and resurrection of Christ. He assumed that role with utmost earnestness. We entreat (beseech you, beg) to be reconciled with God. Lenten observance is not about making ourselves acceptable to God through worship, alms, or prayers, but accepting the gracious terms of peace which God offers through the cross of Christ. Nor is Lent solely a time of spiritual introspection. It is an opportunity to exercise the ambassadorship given us in our baptism, to plead with others to become reconciled with God. Are we permitting God to make his appeal for peace through us?

Gospel: Matthew 6:1-6, 16-21

A secret garden. Jesus teaches that the acts of piety — prayer, fasting, and alms giving — should not be displayed in the public arena for show but exercised in the secret place. In the public arena, there is the danger of playing to the grandstand, so as to impart a favorable impression of oneself. When a person is alone with God, the focus is clear. Our relationship with the Lord is not something that others are privy to, unless we share it with others. It is a secret garden. If we spend regular quality time with the Lord, it is a place of beauty and life. If we neglect the secret garden, it becomes overgrown with weeds or, if neglect plays itself out, degenerates into a spiritual wasteland.

PREACHING APPROACHES WITH ILLUSTRATIONS

Lesson 1: Joel 2:1-2, 12-19

Sermon Title: Lent: A Time Of Turning

Sermon Angle: Joel called the people to turn away from their sins and toward God with their whole hearts and with fasting, weeping, and mourning. It was a time of crisis. Swift and decisive action was needed to turn back the anvil of God's righteous judgment. There is no doubt that we have a crisis on our hands as a nation: family breakdown, lack of values, a rash of teen pregnancies, violence on the streets, and so forth. There is little doubt that this condition has come about because large segments of our society have been cut loose from moral and spiritual values. It is imperative that the people of God call the nation to repentance. However, it won't work if we merely point the finger of accusation at others; repentance must begin with us. Let this Lenten season be a time of turning for our nation, our communities, our families, and our personal lives.

Outline:
1. Joel called his people to return to the Lord
2. We need to return to God (corporately and personally)
3. Lent is God's call to return to him

Sermon Title: Lent: A Time Of Tears

Sermon Angle: Jesus said, "Blessed are those who mourn for they shall be comforted." Lent is not a happy season; it is a time to weep and mourn for our sins; it is a time to shed tears as we confess how we continue to crucify Christ. To be able to weep and mourn is a blessing because it shows our sorrow for our sins and indicates an openness to change. This is Ash Wednesday; ashes were considered a sign of repentance, grief, and mourning. This is the time of tears, but it will be followed by an endless era of rejoicing for all who trust the Lord.

Outline:

1. Ashes are a sign of sorrow and grief
2. The value of weeping and mourning
   — it is cathartic (cleansing)
   — it releases us from the grip of pain
   — it releases us from the grip of the past
3. Grieve for the pain we have caused God and others
4. God is gracious and merciful — he will dry our tears

*   *   *   *   *

All pastors are forced by the nature of their calling to deal regularly with grief and mourning. Some years back, one of my parishioners lost her husband to cancer. Ida didn't shed a tear, informing me that when her father died, during her childhood, she cried her eyes out, but that she hadn't wept since then. Ida seemed to be doing all right but I couldn't help but feel sorry for her. She was wounded so badly that she decided to steel herself against further pain. Christians are called upon to feel their own pain, as well as the pain of others. In Christ, we will enter into the pain that God feels for a world adrift, a torment which God fully felt as the Son hung on the cross. This sorrow can redemptively be expressed in fasting, repentance, prayer, worship, and self-giving, the disciplines of Lent.

*   *   *   *   *

This story has circulated in rabbinical circles for some years. A famous rabbi was strolling with some of his disciples, when one of them asked, "Rabbi, when should a person repent?" "You should repent on the last day of your life," was the reply. The student came back, "But how does one know when the last day of life has arrived?" The rabbi smiled and retorted, "The answer is obvious. Repent now!"

The time of repentance and returning to the Lord is not a season; today is the time for turning away from our sins and back to God!

*   *   *   *   *

In England there is a factory that makes the finest stationery. An American was touring this establishment one day when he noticed a huge pile of rags. The plant manager explained to him that the rags were transformed into high quality paper, that the quality of the paper is related to the amount of rag that it contains. After the American arrived home, he received a box of stationery from the factory, with his initials embossed therein. On the top page was written: "Dirty rags transformed."

Lives of spiritual strength and beauty are formed from dirty rags we call sins, shortcomings, and failures. They are taken by the Master, cleansed, and turned into something beautiful for God, where God's love and grace are plainly written.

Lesson 2: 2 Corinthians 5:20—6:10

Sermon Title: Out Of Court Settlement

Sermon Angle: Much of the vocabulary in this passage has legal overtones. In the opening part of verse 20, Paul states that God was making his appeal through the apostles for all people to be reconciled with God. What is being offered here is an out of court settlement. The plaintiff (God) is offering to dismiss the charges against the defendant. God is more interested in reconciliation than he is in justice. Christ has taken on himself our just sentence, so that we might be pronounced righteous and innocent. Every Christian is an ambassador for Christ, his appointed and legal representative, to make known God's gracious terms for peace.

Gospel: Matthew 6:1-6, 16-21

Sermon Title: The Perils Of Piety

Sermon Angle: In today's lection, the Lord warns against the perils of piety, as he does time and again throughout the gospels. What are these dangers? The number one threat consists in externalizing piety into ritual actions, which do not flow from the heart. The action, not the intention behind the action, become paramount. Related to this is the peril that these acts of devotion are played to the wrong audience, designed to glorify self rather than God. A further hazard can be described with the words hypocrisy, self-deception, and dishonesty. Nothing is more contemptuous than a religion which is a charade.

Outline:

1. Peril #1 — ritual is paramount, not relationship (ritual becomes rut-ual)
2. Peril #2 — playing to the wrong audience
3. Peril #3 — hypocrisy alienates us from God, self, and others

* * * * *

Jesus warns us not to lay for ourselves treasures on earth, which are subject to corruption and decay, but in heaven, "where neither moth, nor rust consumes and where thieves do not break in and steal" (v. 20). The ashes of Ash Wednesday are a much needed reminder of the impermanence of all things earthly. "Remember that you are dust and to dust you shall return." It's a hard lesson to learn. A man very dear to my heart died recently. One day, only a few weeks before he died, his wife observed him fumbling around his pockets. He took something out of his shirt pocket and then placed it in his left trouser pocket, only to transfer it to his right pants pocket a minute later. Then he drew out some of the contents of this pocket and put it back in his shirt pocket and so forth. A day or two later, this man was put in the hospital. When his wife examined the clothes he had been wearing, she discovered that it was loaded with money — hundreds of dollars. I'm not sure what was going through this person's mind but I think that the money gave him a sense of security, or at least, being separated from his money made him feel insecure. What a false sense of security! A few weeks later he died and had to leave it behind.

Lent 1

Revised Common:	**Genesis 2:15-17; 3:1-7**	**Romans 5:12-19**	**Matthew 4:1-11**
Roman Catholic:	**Genesis 2:7-9; 3:1-7**	**Romans 5:12-19**	**Matthew 4:1-11**
Episcopal:	**Genesis 2:4b-9, 15-17, 25—3:1-7**	**Romans 5:12-19 (20-21)**	**Matthew 4:1-11**

Theme: Christ confronts Satan.

Suggested Text For Preaching: Matthew 4:1-11

BRIEF COMMENTARY ON THE LESSONS

Lesson 1: Genesis 2:15-17; 3:1-7 (C); Genesis 2:7-9; 3:1-7 (RC); Genesis 2:4b-9, 15-17, 25—3:1-7 (E)

This text derives from the second Genesis creation account. Just prior to our reading, the stage is set. Adam and Eve are created from the dust of the earth and then infused with God's Spirit. They live in the garden, representing a state of harmony between God, humans and all creatures. The Lord delineates humankind's limits or boundaries, marking out of bounds the tree of the knowledge of good and evil. This state of affairs is challenged by the serpent, the tempter. Biblical scholars insist that the serpent not be identified with Satan — it is a creature of God. Nevertheless, this association will not be erased for a majority of Christians. The serpent begins by subtly employing doubt and deception to undermine the loyalty and obedience of Eve and Adam (did God say ...?) but then directly challenges his authority. (You will not die but will be like God....) The fall from innocence into sin is directly related to this desire to be like God.

Lesson 2: Romans 5:12-19 (C, RC); Romans 5:12-19 (20-21) (E)

The apostle Paul has drawn an analogy between Adam and Christ, showing the consequences of one person's actions for all future generations. Sin came to all through the disobedience of Adam but God offers salvation to all through the obedience of Christ. Sin leads to death for all who sin but salvation brings life to all who believe. The actions of Adam brought condemnation to all, because all people share in Adam's rebellion, but all who turn to Christ are justified (acquitted).

Gospel: Matthew 4:1-11 (C, RC, E)

Directly after Jesus' baptism, he is compelled by the Spirit of God to enter the wilderness, considered to be the domain of demons. The time of trial followed quickly on the heels of the moment of exaltation. The forty days and nights of Jesus' ordeal correspond to the period that the Israelites wandered into the wilderness before occupying the promised land. Matthew mentions the forty *nights* to draw a closer comparison to Moses' fast during the period he received the Ten Commandments. The Lord's decision to obey the Father's will needed to be tested and Satan is the one to accomplish that task. The role of Satan has changed from the time of Job from being God's tester to being the slanderer, a malignant force opposed to the almighty. The three temptations which Satan presented to Jesus portray the nature of his spiritual struggle throughout his ministry. In the first suggestion to turn stones into bread, he is tempted to fulfill the popular conception of an earthly Messiah/king. Satisfy the peoples' physical needs and you will be worshiped. "No," said Jesus, "man does not live on bread alone." The second temptation is to jump from the pinnacle of the temple and land unharmed. Be a miracle worker. People like a good show and will be sure to applaud. Jesus answered "no" once again. "Do not put the Lord your God to the test." In the final temptation, the devil takes Jesus to a high mountain and offers him all the kingdoms of the world, if Jesus will fall down and worship him. The offer here is to exercise political power. "Go away, Satan," says Jesus, "for it is written, worship the Lord your God, and serve him only." Jesus withstands the assaults of Satan because he has stored up God's word in his heart. The responses to the Adversary are from the book of Deuteronomy (8:3; 6:13, and 6:16 respectively).

Psalm Of The Day
Psalm 32 (C) — "Happy are those whose transgression is forgiven" (v. 1).
Psalm 51 (E) — "Cleanse me from my sins" (v. 2).

Prayer Of The Day
Living God, as the Lord Jesus was able to withstand the fiery arrows of the evil one with the armor of your holy word, so strengthen us and equip us to prevail against the assaults of our ancient foe. In the powerful name of Jesus. Amen.

THEOLOGICAL REFLECTION ON THE LESSONS

Lesson 1: Genesis 2:4b-9, 15-17, 25—3:1-7
What did God really say? The number one technique of Satan is to get us to doubt God and his word. It is tempting to rationalize away that which goes against our grain. Satan commences his temptation of Eve with a question which raises doubts concerning the content of God's commands. "Did God say...?" The New International Version precedes the word "say" with the adverb "really." That addition "really" captures the intent of this question. Through the centuries people have justified their blatant disregard for God's clear command by rationalizing: It seems that God is saying thus and so, but it isn't really what he is saying. Of course, God didn't really say what Satan suggested, that Adam and Eve could eat of any tree in the garden. It was only the tree in the middle of the garden which they couldn't eat, as Eve pointed out. However, the damage had been done; the seed of doubt had been planted.

The attraction of forbidden fruit. Why is it that we always desire that which is forbidden? Does not the appeal lie precisely in its forbiddance? As a kid, I was forbidden to smoke, so I would steal my dad's cigarettes and light up in some secret place. The allure of that which was off-limits was strong. It's the same with much that passes as erotic or romantic attraction. This points out some other factors that made the fruit of the tree in the middle of the garden attractive. It was good for food (promised to fulfill bodily needs), was pleasant to look at (appealing to aesthetic sensibilities), and was desirable to make a person wise (attractive to the intellectual sensibilities) (v. 6).

Lesson 2: Romans 5:12-19 (20-21)
The power of one. In this era of mass media and mass marketing, we are tempted to discount the power of the individual. Yet, history is laden with examples of solitary individuals

who have impacted the entire planet, either for good or for ill. For example, consider the actions of a simple African-American woman in Montgomery, Alabama, who refused to cede her seat in the white section of the bus. Because of this simple gesture, Rosa Parks ignited the Civil Rights Movement. Paul points out how the sin of one man, Adam, led to the transgression of all humans and, ultimately, to death. On the other side of the ledger, the righteousness of one man, Jesus Christ, has led to the gift of justification and eternal life being offered to all people.

Gospel: Matthew 4:1-11

Your Achilles' heel. If I recall correctly my knowledge of Greek mythology, Achilles was dipped head first into the River Styx, which made him immortal and invulnerable, except for the heel by which he was held, which was not immersed. He later suffered a mortal wound to that very spot, his vulnerable spot. Satan is quick to notice our Achilles' heel where he stoops for attack. Since Jesus had fasted forty days and nights, the devil figured he would be famished and, like Esau, be willing to sell his soul for a pot of stew or loaves of bread. Jesus was ready with the defense: "Man does not live by bread alone, but every word that comes from the mouth of God" (v. 4).

The importance of knowing who you are. All sin proceeds from a deluded or perverted sense of the self. In his baptism, Jesus received affirmation of his identity as the Son of God. In all of these temptations, Satan's tactic is to engender doubt in the mind of Jesus concerning the veracity of this identity. Satan led off his assault, "If you are the Son of God...." When we think that we have to prove to ourselves or somebody else who we are or what we can do, we are already on thin ice.

Text or pretext? It is interesting that in both the temptations and the rebuttal of the temptations, scripture is employed. Satan took certain passages out of context and made them pretexts to deceive Jesus into accepting his point of view. In rejecting the temptations, Jesus also used scripture but in its proper context. Do we use the Bible to support our preconceived ideas and our established behavior patterns or do we permit God's word to shape and inform us?

PREACHING APPROACHES WITH ILLUSTRATIONS

Lesson 1: Genesis 2:4b-9, 15-18, 25—3:1-7

Sermon Title: The High Cost Of Forbidden Fruit

Sermon Angle: The serpent tempted Eve with forbidden fruit. Did God say, "You must not eat any fruit in the garden?" "No," Eve replies, "we can eat from the fruit of any tree except that fruit from the tree in the middle of the garden." The serpent wanted Eve to believe that God was unfairly restrictive. By drawing attention to that which was forbidden, he made it more alluring. The forbidden fruit was attractive and desirable, but the serpent failed to point out the high cost of obtaining it — a loss of innocence, a fall from grace, broken relationships, and death.

Outline:
1. The necessity of forbidden fruit — life has to have its boundaries
2. The desire for forbidden fruit is coveting
3. To take forbidden fruit destroys relationships
4. To take forbidden fruit leaves a bitter aftertaste
5. Live thankfully for what God has given you

Lesson 2: Romans 5:12-19 (20-21)

Sermon Title: The Power Of One

Sermon Angle: Somewhere along the line you have probably received a Christmas card containing a poem called "One Solitary Life," which compares our Lord's humble circumstances with the enormous impact of his life on the whole world. The poem ends approximately as follows: "All the kings that have ever ruled and all the armies that have ever marched have not changed the world as much as that One Solitary Life." As we look at the world with all its enormous problems, it is easy to feel insignificant. We might be tempted to speak out or act out against some problem but then refrain from doing so as we think, what can I do? I'm just a tiny drop in an endless sea. Paul argues that sin came into the world through one person but so did salvation.

Outline:
1. One person can unleash unimaginable evil (such as Hitler)
2. One person can unloose boundless good (examples)
3. Only one person brings eternal salvation (Jesus)

Gospel: Matthew 4:1-11

Sermon Title: Duel With The Devil

Alternative Sermon Title: High Noon

Sermon Angle: Some of you who have been around as long as I have may recall the classic western movie of the '50s titled *High Noon*, starring Gary Cooper, who played the role of the sheriff. The plot is classic western. This little town is controlled by a marauding band of outlaws, who have their way because the people are paralyzed with fear. The bulk of the movie is devoted to the largely losing struggle, which Cooper's character has, to convince the townspeople to join him in taking a stand against the bandits. The ultimate confrontation between good and evil occurs at noon, high noon, but I won't tell you the outcome. Our Lord went unaccompanied into the desert to duel with the devil. He knew that the only way to defeat the evil one was to shoot it out with him, not with guns but the word of God.

Outline:
Introduction — How does one duel with the devil?
1. Know your opponent
2. Know his tactics
   — create doubt about God's goodness
   — appeal to human pride
   — attack a vulnerable spot
3. Know your weapon and how to use it (God's word)

Sermon Title: Your Achilles' Heel

Sermon Angle: Achilles was invincible to attack except for one spot where he was vulnerable, his heel. As humans, we corporately have an Achilles' heel, our desire to play God. The form in which this weakness is manifest varies from person to person, depending on the nature of our own peculiar intellectual, moral, and spiritual vulnerabilities. Satan is quick to attack at the point of our weaknesses. We need to be ready with God's word and Spirit as our defense.

Outline:
1. Satan tried to uncover weakness in Jesus unsuccessfully
2. Satan attacks us in the same way
3. Know your weaknesses so that you might not be caught off guard
4. Employ the weapons of the Spirit that you might stand victorious

*   *   *   *   *

The Last Temptation Of Christ, in my estimation, was not a good movie. In an attempt to portray the humanity of Jesus, they seem to have painted a portrait of a rather weak, confused, and indecisive Messiah. Nevertheless, the last scene provides some fodder for thought. Jesus is on the cross and he is dreaming that he has escaped from the cross to take up a new life as the husband of Mary Magdalene. This is, of course, pure fiction and the mere suggestion that Jesus might have considered such an alternative may strike us as heretical. Yet, it seems reasonable that such a temptation could have been presented to Jesus. Satan planted doubts in his mind and may have argued as follows: Jesus, why do you go around preaching, teaching, and healing, sacrificing your own happiness for them? Those people are just using you. They don't really appreciate what you are doing for them. If you don't give them what they want, they'll turn on you in an instant. Don't throw away your life for the rabble. It will change nothing. Why not just settle down, get married, raise a family, and escape the pain and turmoil of your hectic existence?

*   *   *   *   *

The year that the Berlin Wall was brought down, we took into our home a seventeen-year-old girl from East Germany. She had been raised in an atheistic, totalitarian country and this was her first taste of freedom. It was a little bit like turning loose an alcoholic in a brewery or a child in a chocolate factory. In her country there was not much worth buying. Suddenly, Geesche was surrounded with an abundance of attractive consumer goods. After about seven months of living with us, we received a call from the police. "You had better come on down." "What's the trouble?" I asked. Geesche was caught with stolen goods. When I got there, she averted my gaze, her eyes red with shameful tears. She had walked out of the grocery store with unpaid food. The owner had suspected this previously and was watching her. It turns out that she had been doing this all along, her drawers were chock full of stolen merchandise — mostly earrings.

We were shocked, but in reflecting on the situation it became more understandable. Geesche was an atheist. She had no moral or spiritual principles, no ethical boundaries except that which was imposed from without. She had a sense that it was wrong to steal but this sense was not grounded in any transcendent reality. Without such boundaries, the self comes to encompass all of existence. She probably rationalized her crime away something like this: Look at all this neat stuff. I've been deprived of these things all my life, while these folks here have had an abundance. I deserve these things and so I will just take them.

She learned at least one thing from this ordeal: Sin has its consequences. One has to pay the price of the forbidden fruit. Geesche was looking forward to taking a three-week trip to the west coast with other exchange students. Instead, she was sent home early, with dishonor.

Lent 2

Revised Common:	Genesis 12:1-4a	Romans 4:1-5, 13-17	John 3:1-17
Roman Catholic:	Genesis 12:1-4	2 Timothy 1:8b-10	Matthew 17:1-9
Episcopal:	Genesis 12:1-8	Romans 4:1-5 (6-12) 13-17	John 3:1-17

Theme: Christ confronts Nicodemus — the new birth.

Suggested Text For Preaching: John 3:1-17

BRIEF COMMENTARY ON THE LESSONS

Lesson 1: Genesis 12:1-4a (C, RC); Genesis 12:1-8 (E)

God appears to a man by the name of Abram in what today would be Iraq, about 1800 BC, and orders him to leave his homeland and travel to a land that God would show him. God promises to bless Abram and make of him a great nation. In fact, God's promises make Abram a means of blessing or curse for others. The amazing aspect of this is that Abram was already 75 years of age. Humanly speaking, it didn't seem likely he would see the fulfillment of God's promise, but Abram was a man of faith.

Lesson 2: Romans 4:1-5, 13-17 (C); Romans 4:1-5 (6-12) 13-17 (E)

Paul points out that Abraham was accepted by God as righteous not because of good works but by faith. The law had not even been given. This righteousness is given not only to the Jews but to all those who, like Abraham, trust in God and obey his promptings.

Lesson 2: 2 Timothy 1:8b-10 (RC)

Paul urges his readers to join him in his suffering for the gospel (he is in prison). We are not saved by anything that we have done but by the grace of God.

Gospel: John 3:1-17 (C, E)

Nicodemus, a member of the Sanhedrin, comes to Jesus at night, so as not to be noticed by his friends, to explore some issues. He lets Jesus know of his regard for him but Jesus sees this as a smokescreen and cuts right to the quick. "I tell you the truth, no one can inherit the kingdom of God unless he is born again" (v. 3). Nicodemus doesn't get it and interprets Jesus' remarks literally. Jesus then compares himself to the bronze serpent that Moses set up over the camp of the Israelites. All who were bitten by the fiery serpents (the punishment for disobedience) and looked upon the bronze serpent were saved. So too, those who are stung by the bite of sin, and look to Jesus in faith, will also be saved.

Gospel: Matthew 17:1-9 (RC)

See gospel lesson for The Transfiguration Of Our Lord (C, RC, E).

Psalm Of The Day

Psalm 121 (C) — "My help comes from the Lord" (v. 20).
Psalm 33:18-22 (RC) — "Behold, the eye of the Lord is on those who fear him" (v. 18).
Psalm 33:12-22 (E) — "Happy is the nation where God is the Lord" (v. 12).

Prayer Of The Day

O God of our birth, our baptism and all our beginnings, empower us to fully submit our lives to you, that we might experience the joy of being born anew. In Jesus' name. Amen.

THEOLOGICAL REFLECTION ON THE LESSONS

Lesson 1: Genesis 12:1-8

Faith journey. God told Abram to leave his home, his family, and his country for a land that God would show him. We characterize this move as a faith journey because, as yet, the destination was known only to God. In a sense, we are all called to engage in a faith journey. None of us have seen the promised land, nor are we cognizant of the exact course that we must take to get there. This journey only requires that we stay close to the Lord and follow his leading.

Life begins at 75. Abram embarked on his faith journey at the age of 75. He might have thought that his life was nearly over but God had other ideas. The best was yet to come. We sometimes fail to forge ahead because of human limitations, such as age, but God loves to use people that don't seem to fit the mold. God's power is manifest in our limitations and weaknesses. This passage has much to say to a society such as ours, where the age pyramid is increasingly becoming inverted. God calls senior citizens as well as younger folks to embark on a faith journey. God has something more significant for them to do than shuffleboard or SkipBo. They are now free to follow the Lord into a new avenue of service. One elderly woman I know spends a good deal of her time tutoring elementary school youngsters and serves as a foster-grandmother for children from broken homes. Generativity need not be related to age, as this passage makes clear.

Moving from the particular to the universal. God called Abram, a specific person, at a particular time and place, to embark on a mission. Yet, God has something much greater in mind than showering his favor on one man or nation. God deigned to bless all the peoples of the earth through him. God works from the small to the large, the particular to the universal, from the single scene to the big picture. If life were compared to a movie, God would be the director and each person an actor playing out parts great and small. It's our responsibility to learn our script and perform our role to the utmost of our ability. It is God's role to bring all the parts together in such a way that the plot is powerfully coherent and delivers a blessing to the entire cast. The divine drama is different than a movie, however, because there is no audience, except perhaps the saints in light. Let us play out our parts with passion until that day when we behold the big picture.

Lesson 2: Romans 4:1-5 (6-12) 13-17

The divine ledger. Paul states that Abraham believed God and it was credited to him as righteousness. He was accounted righteous because his faith demonstrated obedience. Picture God placing a deposit in Abraham's account, which canceled whatever debt due to sin that he previously owed. In a similar manner, God put a deposit in our account because of Christ. This deposit was not a wage — something earned — but a gift. If we accept that deposit in our account through faith, God cancels the debt of our sin and declares that we are in good standing with him (justified). Our account has been paid through the generosity of God in Christ.

Gospel: John 3:1-17

Come from the night into the light. The account says that Nicodemus came to Jesus from the cover of the night. He didn't want to be embarrassed by being seen by his friends in the Sanhedrin socializing with Jesus. Night or darkness also describes the condition of his soul. Yet he was beginning to perceive some glimmers of light through the miracles of Jesus. There were things he didn't understand, which didn't fit in with his theological framework, and that is why he came to the Lord. The entire conversation with Jesus revealed a profound confusion of mind and soul. He was looking for intellectual enlightenment but what he received was a challenge to put aside all the baggage and enter into a relationship of profound trust with God, to become as a child. Nicodemus came for a discussion but Christ called for a commitment, inviting Nicodemus to enter the light rather than merely analyzing the light from afar.

"How can a man be born when he is old?" Nicodemus asks. Good question. As we get older, there can be a tendency to get set in our ways. The emphasis for many is preservation rather than generativity. All the more argument for the need to be born anew. Look at our first lesson: Abraham was born anew at the age of 75, when God took him aside and promised that he was going to make a great nation of him. When he showed his faith in God through obedience, God's Spirit entered him and gave him a new life. From his being born anew, a new nation, God's own people, were born. Believe God, trust in his promises, follow in faith and you will be born anew no matter what your age.

Cure for snakebite. Jesus illustrates his saving mission with the story of the bronze serpent. The Israelites bitten by the fiery serpents, sent as a punishment for rebellion, were instructed to look up to the bronze serpent, which was set on a pole in the midst of the camp. The snake on the pole served as an antidote for the snakes in the grass, neutralizing their deadly poison. Similarly, those who were to look up to the one elevated on the cross would secure release from the effect of sin's deadly fangs. Of course, this point would have been lost on Nicodemus, for he had not yet witnessed the Christ crucified, but it makes perfect sense to those of us who look to Christ for salvation. Note John's theology of the cross. The cross is not the symbol of ignominy and shame but of glory and power. The cross is, in effect, Jesus' throne.

"For God so loved the world...." Personal salvation is not the goal of Christianity. God desires to save the whole world. Much the same point was made in the first lesson, the call of Abram. God planned to bless all the peoples of the world through him. We must always keep two great truths in balance — God loves me but he also loves the neighbor. The personal realization of the momentous truth that "God loves me" is the prerequisite for the new birth, but that new birth can become aborted (a stillbirth) if we don't embrace the truth that God loves the world through me and people like me.

PREACHING APPROACHES WITH ILLUSTRATIONS

Lesson 1: Genesis 12:1-8

Sermon Title: Faith Journey

Sermon Angle: God called Abram to depart from the realm of the ordinary and embark on a journey into the misty unknown with only a promise. The destination was not known, nor was

126

it important; the journey was all that mattered. So, too, in our baptism we are summoned to a faith-journey. That is, our entire existence as Christians is a journey with Jesus.

Outline:
1. God called Abram to leave his country and kindred
   — first, he gave a promise of blessing
   — then, he issued the summons to follow
2. Abram trusted God and followed
3. We too are called to journey in faith like Abraham (second lesson)
4. Let us follow in faith

Sermon Title: Sunset/Sunrise

Sermon Angle: We usually speak of sunrise and then sunset but why? A sunset is always followed by a sunrise. Abram was called by God to engage on a journey to who-knows-where during the sunset years of his life. The end of one life was the starting point for another. People sometimes feel, when they reach the end of some phase in their life, that life is over, that there is nothing more to look forward to. Not so for the person of faith. Every sunset is met by a corresponding sunrise.

Outline:
1. God called Abram to venture forth at age 75
2. The sunset years yielded to the rising of the glorious new day
3. You may be reaching some terminus point in your life
4. Discover the journey to which God is calling you and faithfully follow

Lesson 2: Romans 4:1-5 (6-12) 13-17

Sermon Title: The Gospel's Bottom Line

Sermon Angle: The language of this lesson is borrowed from the economic sphere. Paul speaks of credits and wages and freebies. Because Abraham believed God, God forgave his debt and credited the treasure of eternal life in each person's account. All we need to do to collect is to follow Christ in faith. As the apostle declares, the person is blessed whose sins are not counted against him.

Gospel: John 3:1-17

Sermon Title: Come From The Night Into The Light

Sermon Angle: Nicodemus came under the cover of darkness to seek enlightenment. He came to discover who Jesus was but ended up finding out who he needed to become — a new man, born from above. The enlightenment of the mind would issue from a new spiritual birth from on high and not the other way around.

Outline:
1. Nicodemus was in the dark about Jesus
2. He was also in the dark about spiritual reality
3. Jesus appealed to his heart and will — not his mind
4. Spiritual faith is discovered experientially
5. Take the leap of faith

Sermon Title: Cure For Snakebite

Sermon Angle: See Theological Reflection On The Lessons

Outline:
1. The snake has long been a symbol of temptation and evil
2. When the Israelites were bitten, they looked to the bronze serpent for salvation
3. We can overcome sin's deadly sting by looking to the crucified Christ
4. God doesn't want to condemn us but save us (vv. 16-17)

* * * * *

William James, in his book, *The Varieties Of Religious Experience*, distinguishes between the once-born and twice-born believer. His purpose is to bring out the fact that some Christians experience their faith as a process of growth over the entire span of their lives, while others undergo a sudden transformation, which leaves a vivid impression on their psyche. I know a dear Christian lady who declared that she could not recall a time in her life when she was not aware of God's redeeming presence. Most people who feel this way were brought up in a strong Christian environment, where the faith was not only taught, it was caught. Unfortunately, many of the twice-born Christians seem to feel that the manner in which they have encountered God is not only normative but the only way. They place great emphasis on *their* decision to follow Jesus. So doing, they seem to undermine the concept of grace which underlies this passage. When Jesus tells Nicodemus, "You must be born again" (anew, from above), he is not telling him that there is something that he must do in order to be born again. Quite to the contrary, the image of birth preludes the idea of works-righteousness. We don't decide to be born; birth is given to us. There is a heresy prevalent in our culture, which says that we are acceptable because of what we accomplish. This is the basis of *workaholicism* and perfectionism. Nicodemus was an accomplished and respected member of his community, at the pinnacle of power and piety. It's this knowledge that makes Jesus' words so radical and offensive. Jesus was telling this righteous, accomplished man that he needed a new spiritual center. He must abandon his prideful notion of self-righteousness and let God start from scratch with him. It was a hard pill to swallow. No wonder he didn't get it.

* * * * *

Those experienced in Christian life know that we are not only born again, but again and again and again. The most excellent movie, *Shadowlands*, illustrates this point from the life of the English writer and Christian apologist, C. S. Lewis. The movie tells of the story of Lewis' brief love affair and marriage to an American woman by the name of Joy. Joy was a fan of Lewis' writings, which led to written correspondence and, eventually, to their meeting. They became friends, but the relationship was not equal. Joy became attached to Lewis emotionally but he kept himself aloof from intimacy, ensconced in the safe shelter of books and ideas. Joy boldly confronted Lewis, just like Christ confronted Nicodemus with his need to abandon his no-risk mode of relating to persons.

Joy moved to England, with her son, to be near Lewis. One day, she asked him for a favor. Would he marry her so that she could remain in the country? Lewis agreed to a secret marriage of convenience. They continued to live apart. Lewis hoped to live his life as before, untouched by human intimacy and commitment, but Joy became terminally ill with bone cancer. Lewis saw the shallowness of his soul and began to look at Joy through different eyes. He proposed and they married before God and the whole world. Love was born of sorrow and during Joy's brief remission from cancer their life became a love-feast. Unfortunately, their joy was tinged with the knowledge that their relationship would be so brief. Joy died and Lewis was plunged into despair and doubt. He used to teach concerning the meaning of pain and sorrow, acting as if he had all the answers. Now, in his grief, he knew that he didn't. The old, aloof Lewis, loath to lose himself in love because he feared the pain of love lost, died and was reborn.

Gospel: Matthew 17:1-9

See the gospel lesson for The Transfiguration Of Our Lord.

Lent 3

Revised Common:	Exodus 17:1-7	Romans 5:1-11	John 4:5-42
Roman Catholic:	Exodus 17:3-7	Romans 5:1-2, 5-8	John 4:5-42
Episcopal:	Exodus 17:1-7	Romans 5:1-11	John 4:5-26 (27-38) 39-42

Theme: Christ confronts a Samaritan woman — God's grace and forgiveness.

Suggested Text For Preaching: John 4:5-42

BRIEF COMMENTARY ON THE LESSONS

Lesson 1: Exodus 17:1-7 (C, E); Exodus 17:3-7 (RC)

The people of Israel cry out against Moses and God for bringing them out into the wilderness, where there is no water. Moses, fearing for his life, takes the problem to the Lord. God commands Moses to take the staff with which he struck the Nile, when the sea parted before them, and strike a rock. Water would flow forth. This place is called both *Massah* and *Meribah*. *Massah* means "test" and *Meribah* renders "to find fault." The disobedient Hebrew people were guilty of putting God to the test.

Lesson 2: Romans 5:1-11 (C, E); Romans 5:1-2, 5-8 (RC)

In the previous chapter, starting with the example of Abraham, Paul has established how we are justified by faith in Christ. In this chapter, he follows with the blessings that relationship brings. That's why he leads with the word "therefore." What are those gifts that fall from our justification? We have access to God's grace (v. 2a). We rejoice in the prospect of sharing the glory of God (v. 2b). We rejoice in our suffering because it produces endurance, character, and hope (vv. 3-4). Finally, God's love has been poured into our hearts through the Holy Spirit (v. 5).

Gospel: John 4:5-42 (C, RC); John 4:5-26 (27-38) 39-42 (E)

Jesus confronts the Samaritan woman by the well and in so doing tackles head-on some of the prejudices of the day. He confronts the tragedy of racial prejudice, since the Jews would have nothing to do with the Samaritans. At the same time, he also takes on some gender issues. It is not considered proper for a man to publicly speak to a woman, and to engage her in a philosophical conversation was unheard of. The report of this dialogue is rather lengthy and raises several issues. There is grace; the woman has been married five times and the man she is now living with is not her husband. Yet, Jesus is not judgmental. There is witness; the woman leaves her water jar and invites her neighbors to hear Jesus. There is the subject of worship, which Jesus defines not as a matter of place but of spirit. Finally, belief is defined as personal encounter with Jesus rather than merely accepting the reports of others (v. 41). The person who receives Jesus is compared to a spring of flowing water (vv. 10-15).

Psalm Of The Day

Psalm 95 (C, RC, E) — "Harden not your hearts, as at Meribah ..." (v. 8).

Prayer Of The Day

Lord Christ, you are the well that never runs dry, you are the font of our cleansing and rebirth; in you we live and move and have our being. Cause us to drink deeply of your life-giving Spirit, that we might be truly satisfied now and eternally. Amen.

THEOLOGICAL REFLECTION ON THE LESSONS

Lesson 1: Exodus 17:1-7

Job burnout. Job stress and clergy burnout are nothing new. Consider Moses; he has the unthinkable job of leading a rag-tag band of former slaves, over half a million strong, for forty years through a wilderness! Think of all the varying and conflicting role expectations they had of their leader. If this isn't a prescription for frustration and failure, what is? They complained about the diet and in this text they complained about the absence of water. How did Moses deal with the stress? Did he take to drinking or wife beating? No, he turned to the Lord. If the Lord commissioned him for this gigantic task, he would also supply the wisdom and strength required to get the job done. A sure prescription for heart failure is to try to please everyone. Better to turn to the Lord, the Rock from which the water of life flows.

"Is the Lord with us or not?" (v. 7). The sin of the Israelites was not that they complained they had no water; no one can live long without it. Their offense was that they challenged the Lord to prove that he was really with them by providing it. They looked at the Lord like he was a circus performer, whose role it was to satisfy the audience. The potter was put in the untenable position of having to prove his existence to the pots. How human! We're still doing it. God, if you really exist, heal me. God, if you really are sovereign, defeat my foes for me. I'll worship you and follow you if....

Lesson 2: Romans 5:1-11

Salvation in the present tense. Often we think of our Christian faith as a life insurance policy. There are no present benefits; the payoff is in the future. Not so, Paul states: "Therefore, since we are justified by grace, we have peace with God through our Lord Jesus Christ" (v. 1).

Grace and peace. These two words found in verse 1 are so important to Paul that he begins his epistles: "Grace and peace from God...." These two theological symbols are inextricably wedded to one another. Grace is primary; without grace there is no peace. Without grace there can be no forgiveness, no putting aside of offenses, no reconciliation. Without God's grace we would tremble under the sentence of God's condemnation. Through God's grace in Jesus we are set free from fear and condemnation. If we accept the grace, peace begins to flower in our hearts.

Gospel: John 4:5-42

Breaking the ice. Even though Israel possesses a mild climate, the relationship between Jews and Samaritans was extremely frigid. Jesus attempts to break the ice as he is resting by Jacob's well. It is about noon and it is rather unusual that anyone is coming to draw at that hour. This indicates that the woman was probably a social outcast. Jesus asks her for a drink. She is shocked that a Jewish man is asking her for anything (v. 9). If we are motivated by God's grace, we, too, will take the initiative to break the ice in relationships where there is prejudice, hurt, and estrangement.

An inner oasis. Jesus told the woman by the well, "Everyone who drinks this water will thirst again but whoever drinks of the water that I will give them will never be thirsty. The water that I will give will become in them a spring of water gushing up to eternal life" (vv. 12-13). Jesus is speaking of the gift of the Holy Spirit, which God would give to all those who were to believe in him. In the Hebrew language, wind and spirit are represented by the same word. There is also a close affinity between the concepts of water and spirit. The association with wind speaks to the mysteriousness of God's Spirit. The affinity of water and spirit symbolizes the life-giving capacity of the Holy Spirit. We all know that water is essential to life. Likewise, the Spirit is also essential for life in the eternal dimension. The lesson here is that the Holy Spirit, given to all who follow Christ, is like an artesian well that gushes forth eternally. The source of life is not external but internal, since God has placed his Spirit within our hearts. Therefore, the Christian should be like an oasis of life in the midst of a barren and life-threatening desert.

Word and witness. This was the name of a program that ran quite successfully in the Lutheran church for a number of years. The premise was that witness flows from the word. The attempt was made to ground people in the word and, at the same time, discuss ways that the gospel can be witnessed to in daily life. The premise is sound. Once we really hear the word of God through a faith encounter with Christ, we are going to witness. Take the woman at the well: Her encounter with the Word made flesh transformed her relationship with her neighbors. She went to the well at noon so as to avoid her neighbors and their judgments. After she encountered Jesus, she left her water jug and went to witness to her neighbors about Jesus. She wasn't taught by Jesus how to witness; she just did it. A spring of living water was already beginning to gush forth.

Word, worship, and witness. Let's take this process one step further. First, we encounter the word, then we worship the word, and, finally, we witness to the word. Unless we ascribe worth to the word, unless we bow down in submission to Christ as Lord and Savior, we have nothing to witness to. Also, apart from faith we lack the promised Spirit, who empowers and guides our witness.

Have church, will travel. The Samaritan woman tried to divert Jesus into the local argument between the Jews and the Samaritans as to the location of the proper place to worship God (vv. 20-21). Jesus indicates that worship wells up from inside us; the place is immaterial. Like the Jews of the wilderness wandering, we carry our temple around with us. The tabernacle of God is our body where our spirit encounters the Holy Spirit.

PREACHING APPROACHES WITH ILLUSTRATIONS

Lesson 1: Exodus 17:1-7
   Sermon Title: Prescription For Burnout
   Sermon Angle: Moses was given a task that would cause even the most well framed person to collapse — guiding a multitude of ex-slaves to a new land and life. Moses was able to stand up to the terrible strain because he took his burdens to the Lord. In our pressure-cooker society, not only are leaders subject to burnout, but almost everybody is. If we turn to the Lord, we too shall stand.
   Outline:
   1. Moses was near the end of his rope
   2. Many people have trouble coping with stress

3. Here are some coping strategies
   — establish priorities
   — care for your body, mind, and spirit
   — spend time in prayer and meditation
4. Cast your burdens on the Lord and he will direct your path

* * * * *

The people of Israel complained about the rigors of moving from the predictable drudgery of slavery in Egypt into the unforeseen hardships of striving toward the promised land. They aren't any different than any other people who would be thrust into those same circumstances. They didn't like change and uncertainty, and neither do we, much of the time. This reminds me of the story of a woman who bought a needlepoint art piece with the well known saying, "Prayer changes things." The woman hung it over the mantel but noticed a few days later that it was missing. In quizzing her family, her husband confessed to taking it down. "What's the matter?" she exclaimed. "Don't you believe that prayer changes things?" He responded: "I do believe that prayer changes things; I just don't want things to change."

Lesson 2: Romans 5:1-11
Sermon Title: Peace With God
Sermon Angle: "Therefore, since we are justified by faith we have peace with God through our Lord Jesus Christ" (v. 1). Our sins put us in a state of enmity with God, but Christ's death makes peace a reality for all who trust in him. Modern man needs to reckon with the possibility that his or her restlessness and dis-ease stems more from spiritual rather than psychological factors. We only find peace of mind after we have embraced God's peace.
Outline:
1. Our world is increasingly torn by violence and strife (examples)
2. Is your life filled with conflict and restless longing?
3. God offers us peace through Christ
   — accept God's gift of righteousness
   — then you will have peace with God, with self, and with others

* * * * *

A Lutheran pastor from Illinois preached his first sermon after returning home from a retreat/conference. He was anxious to share some of what was on his heart. He preached from a bar stool poised in the middle of the chancel. He confessed: "You know, pastors are sometimes put on pedestals but there are two things that make that very uncomfortable. Number one, it's lonely up there and, number two, there is always someone waiting to knock you down." In so doing, he put his finger on one of the main causes of clergy burnout — isolation. This state of affairs may stem from several sources. The first cause comes from the clergy themselves, who develop unrealistic expectations of what they can do or how they should act. Since they cannot measure up to their own standards, they seek to conceal their failings and weaknesses by staying aloof from the lives of their people. The other source of clergy isolation derives from unrealistic expectations from the congregation or the denominational office. Many clergy try to meet as many of these diverse expectations as they can until they alienate themselves from their family, from their Lord, and their own inner soul. Those of us who preach that the church is the ship/haven in the midst of a tempestuous sea of striving for acceptance, often act as if we were outside the ship attempting to keep ourselves afloat by our own frantic efforts. If we had the humility of that Illinois pastor to admit our isolation and our failure to incarnate the gospel, the church could be a genuine healing community.

Gospel: John 4:5-42

Sermon Title: Christ Confronts The Enemy

Sermon Angle: Christ confronted the enemy in his encounter with the Samaritan woman. In so doing, he confronted prejudice, he confronted hurt and isolation, and he confronted sin. The woman encountered acceptance; Jesus knew all about her and considered her worth saving. At the same time, she encountered her God, herself, and her neighbor.

Outline:

Introduction: Christ confronted an outcast woman and in so doing, faced off a host of enemies that besiege our souls.

1. Christ confronted prejudice
2. Christ confronted a wounded woman
3. Christ gently confronted sin
4. The woman confronted her God, herself, and her neighbor

*   *   *   *   *

The Samaritan invited her neighbors to come to Jesus, "Come see a man who told me everything that I ever did" (v. 29). Did they come out of voyeuristic curiosity thinking that Jesus was going to tell them everything that this woman ever did? Mind you, this woman led a rather colorful life, although unconventional and unsavory. She had five husbands and the man she was now living with was not her husband. Maybe they could experience some vicarious thrills like the voyeurs on *The Jerry Springer Show*. Or did they think that Jesus would tell them everything that they ever did? What's remarkable is that this woman, who stood condemned by the village people and probably felt self-loathing, was willing to stand emotionally and spiritually exposed to the world. She must have been transformed by the grace and forgiveness of God so that she was willing to risk taking off her mask. For the first time in her life, she experienced self-knowledge which set her free. Many of us would rather run away from someone who could tell us everything that we ever did.

Sermon Title: Word And Witness

Sermon Angle: The Samaritan woman encountered the Word in Jesus. It was a word of grace, love, forgiveness, and truth. Next, the woman bore witness to her neighbors concerning Jesus. When we truly encounter the Word made flesh, we are so transformed by grace that we must bear witness to Christ.

Outline:

1. The Samaritan woman didn't know herself or her God
2. She encountered Jesus, the Word, and came to know herself
3. She also came to know her God
4. Her neighbors came to know Christ through her witness

Lent 4

Revised Common:	1 Samuel 16:1-13	Ephesians 5:8-14	John 9:1-41
Roman Catholic:	1 Samuel 16:1, 6-7, 10-13	Ephesians 5:8-14	John 9:1-41
Episcopal:	1 Samuel 16:1-13	Ephesians 5:(1-7) 8-14	John 9:1-13 (14-27) 28-38

Theme: Christ confronts a blind man and heals him. By so doing Christ also confronts the skepticism of the Jewish authorities and each person is confronted with the question: Who is this Jesus?

Suggested Text For Preaching: John 9:1-41

BRIEF COMMENTARY ON THE LESSONS

Lesson 1: 1 Samuel 16:1-13 (C, E); 1 Samuel 16:1, 6-7, 10-13 (RC)

This text presents us with an interesting theological concept that challenges our notions of God's unchangeableness. Here God changes his mind about a choice he had previously made. Saul was no longer worthy to be king and Samuel was to appoint another to take his place. The prophet reluctantly goes to the house of Jesse as directed by God, to select a successor for Saul. When Samuel spies Eliab, who is tall and handsome, he thinks that this is truly the new heir to the throne. God says no, because the Almighty does not judge as humans do, on appearances. God is more interested in what lays inside. Jesse's sons come before Samuel but none are chosen. The prophet inquires if there are any other sons and is told that there is one, David, out in the field tending the sheep. Once again, God does the unexpected and picks the young shepherd boy to be his anointed.

Lesson 2: Ephesians 5:8-14 (C, RC); Ephesians 5:(1-7) 8-14 (E)

Before Christ, a person is not merely in the darkness, he or she is an integral part of the darkness, since there is no source of light within them. Through faith in Christ, we not only walk in the light, we are light, since God's illuminating Spirit is within. While we were darkness, our lives were fruitless, but now that we are light, we produce the fruits of goodness, truth, and love.

Gospel: John 9:1-41 (C, RC); John 9:1-13 (14-27) 28-38 (E)

Jesus heals a man born blind. However, there is much more at stake here than physical sight. This account highlights the dynamics of spiritual blindness and spiritual insight. The blind man receives his eyesight immediately after washing his eyes in the Pool of Siloam, but his spiritual prescription comes more slowly. We see the development in the account, as this man gradually comes to see who Jesus is.

Psalm Of The Day

Psalm 23 (C, RC, E) — "The Lord is my shepherd ..." (v. 1).

Prayer Of The Day

Merciful God, remove the scale from our soul and the film from our eyes that we might see Jesus in the midst of life's joys and sorrows. May the light of his Spirit within us show the way that leads to life eternal. In Christ's precious name. Amen.

THEOLOGICAL REFLECTION ON THE LESSONS

Note: Most of the appointed lessons for this day connect on the theme of seeing and perceiving. In 1 Samuel 16:1-13, God helps Samuel to see beyond the exterior and be a good judge of character. This enables him to pick the right man to replace Saul. In Ephesians 5:8-14, Paul reminds us that we are light in the Lord. No one can see without the light. And in John 9:1-41, Jesus helps a man gain not only physical but spiritual vision.

Lesson 1: 1 Samuel 16:1-13

Learning to see through the eyes of God. When Samuel lived with Eli, the priest, in the house of God, the Lord called him in the night. He had to learn to distinguish the voice of God. When the Lord told him to go to the house of Jesse in order to anoint another king, he needed to learn to look at the candidates, not through the eyes of human perception but through the eyes of the Lord. He needed God's-ray vision to penetrate the heart. Eliab truly impressed the prophet: he was tall and handsome; but David had a heart which sought to please the Lord.

Lesson 2: Ephesians 5:(1-7) 8-14

Fruit of the light. In order for a tree or plant to produce fruit, there must be light. Paul relates that Christians are light and they are to produce the fruit of the light — goodness, righteousness, and truth. Those who do not know the Lord are in the darkness and their lives are fruitless.

Gospel: John 9:1-41

The paradox of suffering. The blind man brought to the fore the questions we all struggle with: Why do some people suffer loss and misfortune and not others? The disciples, products of their society, assumed that such a misfortune must be the punishment for some evil, either on the part of the man or his ancestors. "Rabbi, who sinned, this man or his parents, that he was born blind?" (v. 2). The disciples assumed that there was a neat explanation for everything that happened in this world. They wanted and needed to believe in a rational universe, where there is cause and effect. That's what we want too, isn't it? The factor that really disturbs a lot of people about the epidemic of violence in our society is its randomness. Some punk pulls out a pistol, shoots into a crowd and kills innocent bystanders, who just happened to be there. No more orderly universe. The paradox of suffering can be stated as follows: If God is good, as well as powerful, why do innocent people suffer? God does not explain away the paradox; he merely answers it with another paradox. The God who brings light out of darkness also raises life out of death.

Identity crisis. After Jesus healed the man, there was a question as to whether this sighted man was really the blind beggar. He was known as the blind man, his identifying characteristic, and since he was no longer blind, it must be someone else. If we take the evidence in the text alone, it would appear that this man had no identity crisis. "I'm the man," he boldly proclaimed. Yet this man's life was turned on its ear. He could no longer earn his living as a beggar through the sympathy of bystanders. His world was immeasurably enlarged and transformed — almost like being on another planet. He had to learn how to see and this would take time. Fortunately, he had Jesus to open his eyes not only to the physical world but also to the spiritual world. To know Jesus is to get a handle on our identity crisis.

Seeing Jesus with both eyes. When the blind man received his sight, he did not immediately see Jesus. In the account, we see a growth in his perception of the Lord. When the Pharisees asked who healed him, he responded, "The man they call Jesus ..." (v. 10). Note the impersonality of his designation. As they continue to interrogate him concerning the identity of the man who had healed him, he responded: "He is a prophet" (v. 17). Finally, he encountered Jesus himself. "Do you believe in the Son of Man?" "Who is he, sir?" Jesus replied that he is now looking at him and talking to him. The man formerly blind then confessed, "I believe" and then worshiped Jesus. The restoration of his vision was complete. At the same time, the sighted Pharisees were spiritually blind and would not see the Spirit of God in the actions of Jesus.

PREACHING APPROACHES WITH ILLUSTRATIONS

Lesson 1: 1 Samuel 16:1-13
Sermon Title: Seeing Through God's Eyes

Sermon Angle: Samuel had a tough time seeing why God had rejected Saul as king. When he finally went to the house of Jesse, as the Lord had directed, to discover the next king, he was thoroughly impressed with the eldest son. Eliab was tall and handsome. Surely, this must be the Lord's anointed one. Samuel was warned not to judge by externals, as humans do, but to penetrate to the inward qualities, as the Lord does.

Outline:
1. Humans tend to judge others on exterior characteristics
   — Samuel was ready to choose Eliab as king because of his looks
   — David was initially rejected because he was young, short, and a shepherd
2. Our society judges people based on external qualities — beauty, strength, status
3. God sees the heart
   — not what we appear to be but what we are inside
   — not even what we are but what we can become with his help
4. Let us walk closely with God that we might see others through his eyes

Lesson 2: Ephesians 5:(1-7) 8-14
Sermon Title: Fruit-Of-The-Light Christians
Alternative Sermon Title: Children Of The Night Or Of The Light?

Sermon Angle: Paul informs the Ephesian Christians that they were once darkness but are now light, because of their relationship with the Lord. The darkness produces fruitless works, while the light yields life-giving fruits such as goodness, righteousness, and truth. What kind of fruit is our life producing? Let us constantly turn our faces to the light of Christ's grace and love.

Outline:
1. Both science and faith tell us there is no life without light
   — Genesis describes the pre-created world as a dark, formless void
   — God's first creative act was light
   — Light produces life

2. The ungodly person is a dark, formless void
3. The Christian person radiates the light of Christ
4. Enlightened Christians produce the fruits of righteousness (love, joy, peace, and so forth)

Gospel: John 9:1-41

Sermon Title: The Scandal Of Suffering

Sermon Angle: The disciples assumed that there was a direct link between sin and suffering. Jesus denies this connection in the case of the blind man, without revealing the reason for such misfortunes. Yet, he sees it as an opportunity to display the grace of God. Such misfortune is still a scandal (stumbling block) for those who would believe. Without explaining away the mystery of suffering, we can use it as an opportunity for the Spirit to manifest God's glory.

Sermon Title: Open My Eyes Lord, I Want To See Jesus

Sermon Angle: If you employ this theme and title, use the song by the same name before or after the sermon, as a way of reinforcing the theme. The blind man gradually had his spiritual eyesight opened to the fullness of Jesus. He began seeing Jesus as a man, then a prophet and, finally, as the incarnation of God (v. 38). Do we see Jesus in all his fullness?

Outline:
1. At first, the blind man saw Jesus as a man — we too must acknowledge his full humanity (v. 10)
2. Then, Jesus became larger — a prophet (v. 17)
3. Finally, Jesus confronts him and the man worships him as the exalted Son of Man (v. 38)
4. To be a disciple of Jesus, we must see all three dimensions of Jesus and fall down to worship him

*   *   *   *   *

In the spring quarter of the 1981 *Pulpit Resource*, J. Glendon Harris drew an interesting analogy between Plato's *Allegory Of The Cave* and the state of those portrayed as spiritually blind in our gospel lesson, the Pharisees. In Plato's allegory the majority of humankind is compared to the woeful condition of prisoner in a cave. The den has an opening to the light but the prisoners have their backs to the light, so that they see only shadows. We might think that if these prisoners were released from their dungeon, they would be able to see things as they really are, not mere shadows of reality. The allegory shows that if the dungeon dwellers were free to fully face the light, their sight would be overwhelmed with the painful luminescence of the sin. Their sight would not, at first, be greater but less. They would have to avert their gaze to reduce the stabbing brilliance of the light.

Jesus is the light of the world, but the blind man could not handle the full brilliance of this light immediately. As he admitted more and more light to his soul, he was able to move beyond seeing Jesus as a man, to perceiving him as a prophet and then, the Son of God. The Pharisees chose to linger in their world of shadows, their den of illusions, rather than face the painful process of seeing things as they really are in the light of Christ.

Lent 5

Revised Common:	Ezekiel 37:1-14	Romans 8:6-11	John 11:1-45
Roman Catholic:	Ezekiel 37:12-14	Romans 8:8-11	John 11:1-45
Episcopal:	Ezekiel 37:1-3 (4-10) 11-14	Romans 6:16-23	John 11:(1-16) 17-44

Theme For Lenten Series: Christ confronts Lazarus and raises him from death to life.

General Theme: All of the lessons confront us with the choice between life and death. The first lesson from Ezekiel 37 gives us a foretaste of Easter, with the allegory of the dry bones that are suddenly revivified. The Romans 8 text contrasts sinful humanity, controlled by their natural mind, which leads to death and redeemed humanity, controlled by the Spirit, which leads to eternal life. The Romans 6 passage presents the choice between yielding our lives to be slaves of sin, which leads to death, with submitting our lives to the Spirit, which produces eternal life. The gospel story, the raising of Lazarus, proclaims Jesus as the one who is the resurrection and the life.

BRIEF COMMENTARY ON THE LESSONS

Lesson 1: Ezekiel 37:1-14 (C); Ezekiel 37:12-14 (RC); Ezekiel 37:1-3 (4-10) 11-14 (E)

God instructs Ezekiel to preach to the dry bones scattered over the valley floor, and as he preaches to them they come together, as flesh and sinew cover them. The dry bones represent the people of Israel, who have been taken captive and live hopeless lives in a strange land. The message is that God will carry his people home and fill their lifeless carcasses with his Spirit. This word of hope helps lift the people from their depressed state.

Lesson 2: Romans 8:6-11 (C); Romans 8:8-11 (RC)

The mind of the unregenerate person is slave to sin while the mind of the Christian is controlled by God's Spirit. The former leads to death, while the latter leads to life eternal. If Christ is in control of our lives, our sinful natures, what Paul calls the flesh, are dead. The Spirit of the risen Christ raises us to eternal life.

Lesson 2: Romans 6:16-23 (E)

We are slaves to whomever we yield up our obedience, either to sin, which leads to death, or righteousness, which leads to life.

Gospel: John 11:1-45 (C, RC); John 11:(1-16) 17-44 (E)

According to John, the raising of Lazarus sets the stage for the culmination of our Lord's ministry. By word and deed, Jesus proclaims that he is the resurrection and the life. This sign causes such a stir that Jesus' enemies are galvanized into concerted action against him. He must be silenced forever. The high Christology of John is tinged by feeling touches of the human spirit. Mary expresses consternation that Jesus had not come sooner and Jesus weeps with his friends as they confront the death of Lazarus.

Psalm Of The Day
    Psalm 130 (C, E) — "Out of the depths I cry to you ..." (v. 1).

Prayer Of The Day
    Living God, as you released your friend Lazarus from the confines of death, by your living presence amongst us, free us from fear of death and free us for willing service in your kingdom. Empower us by your Spirit to raise up your resurrected arms over a dying world. In the powerful name of Jesus. Amen.

THEOLOGICAL REFLECTION ON THE LESSONS

Lesson 1: Ezekiel 37:1-14

The power of the word. Ezekiel is commanded to prophesy to the dry bones, symbolic of the discouraged state of the people of Israel, and the bones came together, taking on tendon and muscle. Then he prophesied again and the Spirit of God came into the lifeless corpses and they were truly alive. This is a graphic illustration of the power of the word. This is the same principle witnessed in the Genesis creation accounts: God created life through his spoken word. When the word of God is spoken, the Spirit of God gives fresh hope to the downtrodden and life to the dead.

The Spirit raises up the living dead. There are levels of death, just as there are levels of life. At the point in the vision, when the prophet prophesies to the bones and they come together with flesh and sinew, there is the appearance of life without its reality. We might say that these are the living dead, without soul or spirit. There are millions like them today. Because of hardship, war, and other kinds of abuse, they are little more than breathing corpses. Some have chosen to serve at the altar of the gods of wealth and power and have lost their souls. They, too, are among the host of the living dead. Only through the resurrection power of Jesus Christ are we fully and eternally alive.

"Our hope is gone." This was the lament of the captive people of God (v. 11). No one can live without hope. In tests done on rats, those rodents placed in a situation that was obviously hopeless, died quickly; they gave up. However, when the rats were put into an environment where they were trapped but there seemed to be a possibility of escape, they endured far longer. Our faith, informed by the word of God, buoys us up when we are caught in life's swirling eddies. As children of the eternal one, no situation is hopeless. We are never beyond the pale of God's redemptive grace.

Lesson 2: Romans 8:6-11

Brain-dead sinners and brainwashed believers. Paul describes the natural (unredeemed) mind as being brain-dead (v. 6) because it is hostile to God and unwilling to submit to the will of God (v. 7). Technically, of course, Paul is referring to the mind, the seat of volition, rather than the organ in our cranium. Nevertheless, in the thinking of most people there is a strong relationship between mind and brain. Those who are opposed to the things of God may be brilliant, but they are truly brain-dead because they have short-circuited their God-connection.

Then, there are brainwashed believers. Actually, there are two types of brainwashed believers. There is the bad kind. You know, the person who rigidly holds that he is 100% right and that anyone who disagrees with him is a fool and a sinner. Such a mindset stems from a person who is frightfully insecure. He is afraid that if he permits anyone to challenge his house of dominos, it will all come crashing down. However, there is a good kind of brainwashed believer. This is the person whose mind has been washed by the Spirit of God. Such a believer has freely given over her mind to the flow of the Spirit, trusting that God will lead her to new depths of truth. Her body may be nearly dead but her brain (mind) is alive (vv. 8-11).

Gospel: John 11:1-45

"The one whom you love is sick" (v. 3). This brief statement makes clear that there is no logical connection between illness and God's favor. When illness and other misfortune strike, our first impulse is to think that God has abandoned us or, worse, is punishing us. No, he still loves us. Even when he doesn't seem to spring to our aid, as in the case of Lazarus, even when he appears absent from our lives, our plight is not forgotten.

Sickness unto death. When Jesus was informed of Lazarus' illness, he responded that this sickness would not end in death (v. 4). Lazarus died but death was not his final end because Jesus was his friend and Jesus had shown himself to be the resurrection and the life.

The twice-dead experience. You've heard of the twice-born experience, our natural birth and our spiritual birth, but Christians are also among the twice-dead. We die to our old sinful nature, beginning in baptism, and we die physically. Our spiritual birth would not be possible without our death to selfishness and sin. Our birth into the kingdom of heaven would not be possible without our physical death. Of course, looking at it from another perspective, life involves many births and many deaths. As Martin Luther states, we must, through repentance, die daily to sin so that we might rise to newness of life.

Don't forget about God's glory. We must be very careful about pointing to specific causes for particular misfortunes and it is often not helpful to attribute such things to the will of God. Who are we to say? Nevertheless, we err when we view tragedy strictly from our subjective perspective. Too often, we focus only on the impact that events have on our own lives. Jesus claimed that the reason for Lazarus' illness was to glorify God (v. 4). We should also look at tragedy from God's perspective and ask: How is God being magnified? How is God making himself known to me and others through this event?

Anger and death. About the first thing that Mary and Martha said to Jesus when he arrived at their home was: "Lord, if you had been here my brother would not have died" (v. 21). At first glance, it is a statement of faith. Yet, when we probe deeper, we can sense the underlying hurt and anger. What they may have wanted to say was: "Where were you, Lord? Where were you when we really needed you?" Anger is often a part of the grief process. It isn't wrong; it's just there and we have to deal with it; otherwise, it will fester within our souls. This is the same question that went through Christ's mind from the cross. "My God, my God, why have you forsaken me?"

The compassion of Christ. When Jesus witnessed the sorrow surrounding the death of Lazarus and the pain evinced in Mary and Martha, the text says more than once that he was deeply moved, profoundly disturbed. It also states that Jesus wept. The Greek stoics believed that to show compassion or feeling was a sign of weakness. Therefore, since God is all-powerful, he cannot be moved by human pain or sorrow. Such compassion would prove that humans had power over God. Consequently, God is the unmoved mover, apathetic to human woe. This is not the God we see in Christ, who weeps with his people over their loss and yet still has the power to raise them to newness of life.

PREACHING APPROACHES WITH ILLUSTRATIONS

Lesson 1: Ezekiel 37:1-14

Sermon Title: God Raises The Living Dead

Sermon Angle: Not only does God raise the dead (those who have physically died), he also raises the living dead (those who have broken contact with God or are without hope). This sermon is directed to those who go through the motions of living but whose spirit is dead.

Outline:
1. Ezekiel addressed a people without hope (the living dead)
2. Many people today are in the same predicament
3. The word of God raised them to life and gave them hope
4. The word of the risen Christ raises us and gives us hope

Sermon Title: Body Building

Sermon Angle: God took the parched skeleton of the nation of Israel and gave it tendon and muscle. When I was a child, I was attracted by the Charles Atlas Body Building Course, found in comic books. I even sent for information because I wanted to build up my body. God is in the body building business. God builds up the body of his people, not through their exercises, but through his prophetic word.

* * * * *

At the age of 56, George Fredrich Handel was a pathetic shadow of what he had been. He had incompletely recovered from a paralyzing stroke and was almost broke. For years, his Italian operas were well received but the aesthetic tastes of the public switched to French stage plays rather than Italian operas. For Handel, life had become a soulless shadowland much like the experience of the captive Israelites that Ezekiel addressed. One night, as he was limping home through the dreary London fog, Handel was contemplating his fate. When he got home, he found a piece of mail from a man named Jennings. It was a manuscript that he hoped Handel might develop into an oratorio. As Handel thumbed through the piece, the words suddenly came alive. "Comfort ye, comfort ye, my people ... and the glory of the Lord shall be revealed." Instantly, his depression and gloom fell away as the composer feverishly penned the music that flooded his entire being. He hardly paused to eat or sleep as the melodies and harmonies flowed from his pen. Seventeen days and nights later he was finished. *The Messiah* lifted Handel out of his valley of dry bones and became an instant favorite that has continued to ring out the Christian message of resurrection life down through the corridors of time. (Based on an article from *Pulpit Resource*; March 28, 1993.)

Lesson 2: Romans 8:6-11

Sermon Title: Good News For The Brain Dead

Sermon Angle: There is no worse tragedy than to mate a healthy body with a dead brain. Remember the case of Karen Anne Quinlan, who existed for years in a vegetative state? She was apparently kept alive by medical technology, and her parents had to go to court to obtain an order to free her from the life-support machines. The person who is separated from God, hostile to the claims of her Maker, is indeed brain-dead. Paul says that the mind of sinful man is death (v. 6). Good news for the brain-dead — Christ will give us a new mind through faith.

Gospel: John 11:1-45

Sermon Title: Christ Confronts Lazarus

Sermon Angle: In confronting Lazarus, Christ faced off with the ultimate foe — death itself. In raising Lazarus from the dead, Christ also confronted the hostile powers. He pitted himself against those who were dead and didn't know it yet — the scribes and the Pharisees. This helped precipitate his crucifixion. He also encountered the anger and disappointment of Mary, Martha, and the other mourners. Finally, he came face to face with his own vulnerability.

Outline:

1. Christ confronts anger, pain, and sorrow (the mourners)
2. Christ confronts hostility (the scribes and Pharisees)
3. Christ confronts faith (Martha and Mary)
4. Christ confronts death and wins the victory

Sermon Title: A God Who Grieves

Sermon Angle: Even though this passage highlights the resurrection power of Jesus Christ, the humanity of the Lord is also featured prominently. Jesus was deeply moved and troubled by the death of Lazarus and the pain that it caused. Jesus was moved to tears. Since Jesus is the incarnation of God, we see a very compassionate image of God. Some may find this disturbing because it seems that God is out of control. Most people will find this image of him comforting and reassuring.

Outline:

1. Jesus was deeply moved by the death of Lazarus. This shows
   — that God is touched by human misery
   — that God enters into the human drama
2. God is still moved by the pain and sorrow of humanity
   — what is it that brings tears to Jesus' eyes today?
   — give examples
3. Christ was not only moved in emotion but moved to action
   — he raised Lazarus from the dead
   — he proclaimed hope of resurrection and eternal life
4. Let the Spirit move you to enter the pathos of a broken humanity

Passion/Palm Sunday (Lent 6)

Revised Common:	Isaiah 50:4-9a	Philippians 2:5-11	Matthew 26:14—27:66 or Matthew 27:11-54
Roman Catholic:	Isaiah 50:4-7	Philippians 2:6-11	Matthew 26:14—27:66
Episcopal:	Isaiah 45:21-25 or Isaiah 52:13—53:12	Philippians 2:5-11	Matthew (26:36-75) 27:1-54 (55-66)

Theme For Lenten Series: Christ confronts his enemies. On one level, his enemies are the priests, scribes, and Pharisees. On a deeper level, the enemy is sin and death.

Theme For The Day: The passion and death of our Lord. The evil scheming of human beings, which led to the suffering and death of Christ, are co-opted by God for his redemptive purpose.

BRIEF COMMENTARY ON THE LESSONS

Lesson 1: Isaiah 50:4-9a (C); Isaiah 50:4-7 (RC)

This is one of the five servant songs in Isaiah. The servant encounters shame and derision with fortitude and faith, with the sure confidence that God is with him. The servant's ears are open to the wisdom of *Yahweh* and so he is able to stand against the tide and speak words of comfort to those who are afflicted.

Lesson 1: Isaiah 45:21-25 (E)

The Lord is God alone, to whom every knee shall bow and every tongue swear allegiance. He is the source of righteousness and strength.

Lesson 2: Philippians 2:5-11 (C, E); Philippians 2:6-11 (RC)

Paul is attempting to instill the humility of a servant in the minds of the Philippians and so he points to the example of Christ. This passage contrasts the exalted state of being in the form of God and being equal to God with the servant posture which Jesus assumed. "He became obedient unto death, even death on a cross" (v. 8). Because of his obedience, God has exalted him as Lord of all, to whom every knee shall bow. Paul sees this as the fulfillment of the suffering servant poem in Isaiah 45.

Gospel: Matthew 26:14—27:66 (C, RC); Matthew (26:36-75) 27:1-54 (55-66) (E)

These extensive passages relate the multifaceted events concerning the arrest, trial, suffering, and death of our Lord. Even the shortened version is far too large to preach on, especially when we consider all the other events that are packed into this day. One could, of course, merely read the Passion Story and cap it with a brief time of reflection, deleting the sermon. This is not recommended. A better course of action is to select a specific portion of the account as the basis for a short sermon. A third possibility is to highlight a theme that runs throughout the entire narrative. Let me suggest three such themes. First, there is the theme of political intrigue. The chief priest, the scribes, and the Pharisees conspired to do away with this troublemaker, with the active cooperation of Judas Iscariot. Here we see man's attempt to manipulate events, to play

God. Second, there is the theme of the helplessness of God. It is summed up in the phrase: "He saved others, he cannot save himself" (27:42). This theme forces us to struggle with the mystery of human freedom. God was helpless to save the world from sin and death without sacrificing his Son. A third thematic strand running through the passion account shows Jesus not as a victim but being in control. Christ willingly gave his life for the world. God employs even the forces of evil and human weakness to bring about the salvation of the world. Darkness and death are all around, but humankind, at its worst, can't stop the dawn.

Psalm Of The Day

Psalm 31:9-16 (C) — The servant of God hears rumors of intrigue from those who plot to take his life but he continues to trust in the Lord.

Psalm 22:1-21 (E) — A plea for mercy from one who is mocked and scorned; "Save me from the mouth of the lion" (v. 22).

Prayer Of The Day

Merciful Lord, our hearts are overwhelmed with thanksgiving for enduring the barbs of sinful and foolish humans and for going all the way to the cross in order to save us. May our lives be filled with faith and love and so prove that your suffering sacrifice for us was not in vain. In the name of Christ. Amen.

THEOLOGICAL REFLECTION ON THE LESSONS

Note: The remainder of this chapter will be devoted to the gospel lesson. Since this is Passion Sunday, as well as Palm Sunday, we will focus on the story of our Lord's passion and death. Following the most recent revision of the lectionary, Passion Sunday and Palm Sunday have been celebrated together. Formerly, Passion Sunday was celebrated on the fifth Sunday in Lent. The suggestion has been that our Lord's Palm Sunday entrance into Jerusalem be observed right at the beginning of the service, with the Palm Sunday gospel read from the back of the church, just prior to the procession. Some congregations have confirmation, reception of new members, and other events. On top of that, even the shortened version of the gospel is quite lengthy. Very little time is left for the sermon. The preacher is confronted with the choice of giving an overview of the Lord's passion or focusing in on a single segment of that story.

Text: Matthew 27:11-14

The silence of God. Pontius Pilate was frustrated with the silence of Jesus. He asks a simple question: "Are you the king of the Jews?" Yet, the response is an ambiguous: "You have said so." But when he was confronted by the Jewish elders, he uttered not a word. The governor couldn't comprehend Jesus' reticence to defend himself. The Lord lets each person draw his or her own conclusions about himself; otherwise, there would be no need of faith. There are many times in our lives when God seems mute, when we cry out for God to make himself known. The probable reason that the Lord didn't speak out is that no one was listening; no one really wanted to hear the truth. It took the action of the cross to catch the ear of a world deafened by sin.

Text: Matthew 27:15-26

Which Jesus do you want? It's interesting that Pilate was giving the people the choice between two Jesuses. There is Jesus Barabbas and Jesus Christ. The name *Barabbas* is Hebrew for "Son of the father." Thus, there were two Jesuses, one who was called the son of the father and the other who was called the Son of God, the Father. These were two very different Jesuses. The one was a man of violence, who believed in taking the kingdom by storm. The other, the Christ, was a man of peace, who died on a cruel cross to reconcile the world to God. The one preached judgment and retribution on one's enemies but the other proclaimed love and grace. Which Jesus do *you* want?

Text: Matthew 27:37

Titilus. On the cross the Roman government hung the *titilus*, the sign that contained the charge for which he was convicted: "This is Jesus, the king of the Jews." The charge was false. It can be argued that Jesus never intended to be the king of the Jews, much to the disappointment of his disciples. He said, "My kingdom is not of this world." His goal was to usher in the kingdom of God for all people — a non-geographic, non-temporal realm of the spirit. The king of the Jews was dead and in his place there rose one who would be the Savior of the world. On the cross that hangs in our church, can a *titilus* be observed that reads: "Jesus, king of the Lutherans" or "Jesus, king of the Methodists"? Maybe the sign reads: "Jesus, Savior of the upwardly mobile middle class." Such a Jesus deserves to die, so that the kingdom of God might be open to all.

Text: Matthew 27:39-40

"You who would destroy the temple and rebuild it in three days ..." The enemies of Jesus were taunting him for his weakness. Jesus had made such a claim referring not to the temple in Jerusalem but his body. His enemies did not understand that though the temple of his body was being destroyed, God would raise it up on the third day.

Text: Matthew 27:45-50

A loud shout. Jesus didn't die in the usual way. That is, most people die with a groan, a whimper, a sigh, or a rattle. There is not energy to cry out. Jesus died with a loud shout on his lips. First, there was the cry of dereliction, the shout of despair: "My God, my God, why have you forsaken me" (v. 46). Then, it says that Jesus cried again with a loud shout and breathed his last. Matthew emphasizes the sense of abandonment our Lord felt on the cross. Luke adds a new dimension. He gives content to that last shout of our Lord. Luke 23:46 reports that Jesus cried at the last: "Father, into your hands I commend my spirit." It is a shout of victory. The feeling of abandonment yields to trust; he is convinced that the Father would lead him through the darkness into the light.

Text: Matthew 27:51-53

Open temple, open tomb. The crucifixion was an earth-shaking event that broke the shackles of sin and death. The curtain in the temple was torn asunder, from top to bottom, symbolizing that access to God was now open to all who trusted Jesus. In the temple ritual, only the high priest could enter the holy of holies and that once a year. Through Jesus, our high priest, we can all stand in the presence of God. The earthquake associated with the crucifixion also opened some of the tombs. After the resurrection, some of them came out of their tombs and entered the holy city. The dead were placed in tombs to keep them away from the living. Now, through Christ, the dead are free to begin a new life. Via Jesus' body and blood, our temple, we are able to stand in the holy presence of God. Even death cannot separate us from the love of God; our graves now have an open door.

PREACHING APPROACHES WITH ILLUSTRATIONS

Gospel: Matthew 26:14—27:66

Sermon Title: Christ Confronts The Enemy

Sermon Angle: The enemies that our Lord confronted were many. There was the religious establishment who rejected and feared the Christ. There was the treachery of Judas and the ill-formed faith resident in the other disciples. Let us not forget the devious power of the Evil One. Underlying all these enemies is our mortal foe, sin, which gives dominion to our ultimate enemy, death. Jesus met all these enemies and triumphed over them all.

Outline:
1. Jesus confronts the enemy without — the religious establishment
2. Jesus confronts the enemy within — the faithlessness of the disciples
3. Jesus confronts the enemy of our soul — sin and selfishness
4. Jesus confronts our ultimate enemy — death
5. His victory is ours through faith

Sermon Title: The Crucifixion In 3-D

Sermon Angle: When we examine the passion narrative we can clearly see three dimensions. In the first dimension we see the deviousness of humankind. On this level we can see that our Lord's death was caused by the schemes of blind, evil, and power-hungry humans. Through political intrigue they sought to do away with a troublemaker, in an effort to preserve their way of life. In a second dimension, we are made aware of the weakness of God. In the garden Jesus passionately sought another way but there was no way other than the cross. In the third and deepest dimension, we see that the cross is both the wisdom and strength of God. God takes the devious scheming of humankind and transforms them into a means of saving the world. Those who behold the crucified from the up-close-and-personal perspective are compelled to confess with the centurion, "Surely this man was (is) God's Son!" (Matthew 27:54).

Sermon Title: Grief Work

Sermon Text: Matthew 26:36-46

Sermon Angle: Most Christians underestimate the agony of our Lord's grief because he is the Son of God. As the cross cast its shadow over him, he trembled at the great price he was about to pay. Like a cornered cat, he frantically searched to see if there was any way of escape. He needed someone to stand beside him, someone to whom he could pour out his soul. That's what grief work is all about; being there for the one who is entering the dark night of the soul. We cannot take away the grief of another but we can make it bearable by sharing it. By listening, we demonstrate that we care. That is what our Lord needed. That's what we all need when we enter the valley of the shadow of death.

Sermon Title: Which Jesus Do You Want?

Sermon Text: Matthew 27:15-26

Sermon Angle: Most people meet death with a whimper or a sigh. Jesus met death with a shout. Jesus didn't meet the grim reaper with resignation but with confrontation. He confronted the painful loneliness of death head on and ended his life with a shout. Luke tells us the content of that outburst; it was a shout of faith triumphant. We too can meet death with the shout: Thanks be to God who has given me the victory through my Lord and Savior Jesus Christ.

Outline:

1. Most of us recoil at the prospect of death
   — even Jesus felt the sting of death
2. We cannot choose when we will die but only how we will die
   — we can meet death with fear
   — we can meet death with resignation
   — we can meet death with faith
3. Christ met death with a shout of victory and so can we

* * * * *

God shows his love for us in that he was willing to confront death head-on in the person of his Son. In so doing, God released the faithful from bondage to death. In the movie, *The Deer Hunter*, Michael attempts to free his friend, Nick, from the power of death. They were both subject to combat in Vietnam, but Nick was forced to play Russian roulette by his captors. After his release, Nick remains in Saigon where he lives a life of drugged dissipation. Later, Michael returns to seek out his friend and finds him in a back room of a Saigon bar, playing Russian roulette for the entertainment of a wacky group of gamblers. Michael tries to dissuade his friend from this perilous pastime but Nick is too far into his psychotic stupor to listen. In desperation, Michael decides that the only way to shock Nick into his senses is to also play this senseless game. From a human standpoint, Michael's supreme gesture is the height of foolishness. Yet, it is the ultimate embodiment of incarnational love that is willing to take up its cross for the sake of those in bondage to sin and death.

* * * * *

Death possesses a peculiar power to control our lives. When I was an adolescent, I had the neurotic fear that I might die a premature death if I did something wrong. I have overcome or, at least, controlled this fear by confronting it. The other day I called on a man who was clearly at the very end of his life. He was dying of the same disease that claimed my father less than three months earlier. A niece was sitting there. She admitted the seriousness of the situation. Yet, when we were talking to him (he couldn't speak) she was playing the denial game. "Uncle Evert, we've got to get you better because Hal (her husband) needs surgery, and he can't have it until you're home." Evert died the next morning and this niece called the church office. "Hi, pastor. Well, Uncle Evert (long pause) ... slipped away this morning." She couldn't even say the word "death." Christ has freed us from the fear of death and the power of our last enemy, so that we can stare death in the face and claim our Lord's victory.

Maundy Thursday

Revised Common:	Exodus 12:1-4 (5-10) 11-14	1 Corinthians 11:23-26	John 13:1-17, 31b-25
Roman Catholic:	Exodus 12:1-8, 11-14	1 Corinthians 11:23-26	John 13:1-15
Episcopal:	Exodus 12:1-14a	1 Corinthians 11:23-26 (27-32)	John 13:1-15 or Luke 22:14-30

Theme: Victory feast — the Passover and the Lord's Supper, the Eucharist, are feasts celebrating the Lord's victory over oppression and sin. They are occasions for remembering whose we are.

BRIEF COMMENTARY ON THE LESSONS

Lesson 1: Exodus 12:1-4 (5-10) 11-14 (C); Exodus 12:1-8, 11-14 (RC); Exodus 12:1-14a (E)

The Passover marked the beginning of a new era for the Israelites. "This month shall be for you the beginning of months" (v. 2). The people are ordered to set aside a flawless lamb to be slaughtered, roasted, and eaten on the fourteenth day of the month. Everyone was to be part of the feast. The meal was to be eaten in haste because God was on the move. The people are to be ready to leave as soon as the Lord breaks the bars of slavery. The blood is to be placed on their door posts and lintels as a redemptive sign, so that no plague might come near them. They were to keep this festival in perpetuity, as a remembrance of God's redemptive act.

Lesson 2: 1 Corinthians 11:23-26 (C, RC); 1 Corinthians 11:23-26 (27-32) (E)

Paul dresses down the Corinthian church for their insensitive abuse of the Agape Feast. Some were eating out of turn, while others were getting drunk. The poor and hungry were overlooked. By the time the community was ready for the Eucharist, the abuses worked against the possibility of a holy communion. The apostle tells the story of the institution of the Lord's Supper to instill a spirit of awe and sacredness in the hearts of the rowdy Corinthians. It is this rendition of the Words of Institution that is employed by most churches in their liturgies. Paul concludes by warning against an undiscerning and irreverent reception of the Lord's Supper.

Gospel: John 13:1-17, 31b-35 (C); John 13:1-15 (RC, E)

John has no account of the institution of the Lord's Supper. Instead, he recounts another act of Christ's self-giving love, the washing of his disciples' feet, which takes place at the Passover celebration. This gesture is an acted-out parable that provides a teaching moment. "So if I, your Lord and teacher, have washed your feet, you also ought to wash one another's feet" (v. 14). Since the Lord Jesus had shown himself their servant, they too must be willing to serve the needs of others. The Lord's words and actions were of one piece. The disciples must be willing to follow that example.

Gospel: Luke 22:14-30 (E)

In this version of the giving of the Lord's Supper, we observe an emphasis on the future. Jesus mentions that he will not partake of this feast again until it is fulfilled in the kingdom of God. The disciples will also be given the kingdom and shall become judges of the twelve tribes of Israel. The apostles argue about who is the greatest, but Jesus teaches them that true greatness comes to those who are willing to follow in his steps as servants.

Psalm Of The Day

Psalm 116:1-2, 12-19 (C) — "What shall I repay to the Lord for all his bounty to me? I will lift up the cup of salvation and call on the name of the Lord" (vv. 12-13).

Psalm 78:14-20, 23-25 (E) — "Mortals ate of the bread of angels ..." (v. 25).

Prayer Of The Day

Bounteous God, as you have freely showered your blessings upon us, so also fill us with the bread of heaven, that we might hunger no more, and the cup of salvation, to quench our thirsty souls. In Jesus' name. Amen.

THEOLOGICAL REFLECTION ON THE LESSONS

Lesson 1: Exodus 12:1-14

A meal for sharing. The instructions are that each household is to gather for a meal of roasted lamb. Those households too small or too poor to provide a lamb for themselves are instructed to join with their neighbors who have more than enough. No one was to be excluded because of their economic situation from the appointed feast. However, this feast was not to be a gluttonous affair. Each household is to carefully take a count and apportion the lamb so there is enough but without excess. If anything remained in the morning, it was to be burned. From this, we learn that everyone has a right to share equally in the feast. This also touches on the situation that Paul addresses in 1 Corinthians 11:17 ff, where there was a lack of equality and sharing. In this situation (the Eucharist), all the members of the family of faith are to have equal access to the Lamb of God who frees us from our sins. It is the *Lord's* supper — not our private feast.

Fast food. In verse 11, the Lord instructs the people to eat the Passover meal fully clothed, ready to leave at a moment's notice. The redeemed of the Lord must be ready to follow the Lord toward the land of promise. The ritual meal was not an end in itself but a means of empowerment for the journey of life. Those who shared the meal were to live out their identity as God's people in the world.

Written in blood. God tells the Israelites that the blood, which they were to affix to their doorposts, was to be a sign that God's people lived there. Judgment would not befall them. They were saved by the blood. The old covenant was written in blood but so is the new covenant. When Christ extended the cup to his disciples at the Last Supper, he announced: "This is my blood of the (new) covenant which is poured out for many for the forgiveness of sins" (v. 28). The blood is a sign of redemption, by which we gain freedom and life. In the old covenant, the blood was applied externally; but in the new covenant, it is received internally. The divine life-force is now within the believer, who becomes a redemptive sign in the world.

The gift of remembrance. The Israelites are told to keep the feast as a memorial to God's great act of redemption. Think how great a gift memory is! Without it we wouldn't be human. There wouldn't be any civilization or progress. Through the gift of memory, the past is present. The reenactment of the Passover feast would enable the Jews to remember God's great act of redemption through which they became God's holy people. At the Last Supper, Jesus said, "Do this in remembrance of me." It is essential that we remember the act whereby God claimed us as his own in Christ, through the shedding of his blood.

Lesson 2: 1 Corinthians 11:23-32

His body broken, his blood poured out. Before the Lord gave his disciples the Passover bread, he broke it. The bread had to be broken to be shared. Without breaking, the bread could not give life. As with the bread, so it was with his life. Jesus knew that before he could bestow the gift of life on a dying world, his body had to be broken. The broken bread and the wine poured out sacramentally would proclaim the Lord's atoning death on the cross for all future generations. Food that is kept whole or in its container is not available to give life. We, too, must be ready to be broken and poured out, so that Christ might give life to others through us.

Spiritual gourmets. Paul warns against gluttony and instructs that we must become spiritual gourmets. That is, we must be discerning about what we put in our mouths or our lives. He maintains that it is unhealthy, even damnable, to eat the communion bread and wine without discerning the body of Christ (vv. 28-29). This is a warning against unthinking and careless participation in the sacrament. Unfortunately, some believers have been driven into spasms of anxiety about what it means to receive the body and blood in an unworthy manner. This has kept some away from the Lord's table. We need to remind one another that this is a meal of grace in which the unworthy are invited, not the worthy.

More about discerning the body of Christ. Discerning the Lord's body goes far beyond the confines of the sacramental celebration. The apostle is informing us that we must discern the Lord's body within the community of believers. How we receive our brothers and sisters is more important than the manner in which we receive the communion bread. When we hurt a fellow believer, we do injury to Christ's body. When we fail to see Christ in other believers, even those who have a different theological perspective, we are in danger of profaning the body of Christ. How can we receive Christ without receiving our neighbor?

Gospel: John 13:1-17, 31b-35

Endless love. John tells us that Jesus loved those who belonged to him, to the end (v. 2). Yet, death was no end for him. His resurrection shows that his spirit partakes of the eternal and that we too participate in the realm of the eternal through him. Christ's love is without limits; it is endless love.

The importance of knowing who you are. John portrays Jesus as having it all together. He knew where he had come from and where he was going. That is, that he had come from God and was going back to God (v. 3). Jesus knew who he was. This knowledge is essential if we are to act with grace and purpose. If we know that we belong to the Lord, we don't have to prove anything to ourselves or others. Since Jesus knew who he was, he was free to take the role of servant and wash his disciples' feet. He knew he was somebody; he didn't have to prove it. If we know who we are in Christ, we too are free to serve the needs of others.

It takes grace to be served as well as to be the servant. When Christ approached Peter with the washbasin and towel, Peter brashly declares, "You shall never wash my feet." Jesus responds, "Unless I wash you, you have no part in me" (v. 8). Our pride keeps us not only from being the servant but also from being served. We don't like feeling beholden to any person. We deceive ourselves into believing we are self-made people. No person can follow Christ without the humility to let Christ and others meet his or her needs. Such service cleanses us from pride and the illusion of self-sufficiency.

An exemplary Christian. After the foot washing, Christ informed his disciples that he had set an example which they were to follow (v. 15). An exemplary Christian is not one who does all things perfectly but rather one who incarnates the love of Christ.

PREACHING APPROACHES WITH ILLUSTRATIONS

Lesson 1: Exodus 12:1-14

Sermon Title: A Meal Is For Sharing

Sermon Angle: The Passover meal was to be shared with all the people, without the distinctions of sex, status, or economic position. The Lord's supper was shared with all the disciples, even the traitor Judas. Meals, in general, are meant for sharing, not only food but our very selves. Due to our fast paced and compartmentalized lives, contemporary people are increasingly disengaged from the ritual of the table. Food and fellowship go hand in hand. You can help your people to see the sacramental possibilities for all meals; that we should share our lives along with our food.

Outline:
1. The Passover was a meal of sharing
    — God gave them life and they gave their lambs
    — the well-off shared with the needy
    — the shared meal indicated a shared destiny
2. The Lord's Supper is a meal of sharing
    — Christ gave his life to us
    — we share his life with each other
    — we also share the bread of life with a starving world

Sermon Title: The Gift Of Remembrance

Sermon Angle: The Passover was a memorial feast. The people of the covenant were never to forget God's redemptive actions on their behalf. Unfortunately, they soon forgot. Christ said, "Do this in remembrance of me." Woe to us if we ever forget the great price God paid to redeem us.

Outline:
1. Without the gift of remembrance we are lost
    — we lose sight of who we are
    — we lose touch with the past (Alzheimer's is a tragic example)
2. The Passover is a meal of remembrance
    — the Jews are to remember what God had done for them
    — they are to recall who they were in him

3. Holy communion is a meal of remembrance
   — we remember what Christ has done for us and
   — we remember who we are through him

Lesson 2: 1 Corinthians 11:23-32

Sermon Title: Broken Bread, Broken Lord, Broken People

Sermon Angle: Christ broke the bread in order to share it with his disciples. He let his body be broken on the cross to share it with the world. We are to let Christ break us of our pride and arrogance that he might share us with the world.

Outline:

1. Christ took the Passover bread and broke it and shared it
2. Christ gave his life as bread on the cross, that it might be shared with the world
3. Let your life be broken in repentance and faith, that all might be nourished

Gospel: John 13:1-17, 31b-35

Sermon Title: Role Reversal

Sermon Angle: Jesus took the role of the servant even though he was the Lord and teacher. It was symbolic of the servant role which he assumed throughout his life. Christ's life was one of serving the needs of others even though he was, in fact, Lord and Master. The disciples were treated as the favored guests, even though they were the pupils and workers in the kingdom. In life, we assume both roles, which are frequently reversed. We must always stand ready to be the servant, but there are other occasions in which we must be willing to be served. It takes grace to assume either role.

Outline:

1. Jesus was Lord but gladly assumed the servant role
2. The disciples were the Lord's servants but they shunned this role
3. Christ's foot washing is a living example of self-giving service
   — it was a reversal of role expectations
   — if the Lord assumed this role, how much more should we
4. We must also have the humility to let Christ and others serve our needs
   — we are sometimes the honored guest (example — Lord's Supper)
   — at all times we must be willing to be the servants of the Lord

*   *   *   *   *

There was a chief executive of a large corporation who did a very unorthodox thing. He would arrive at the office an hour before his staff arrived and proceeded to go from department to department brewing warm coffee. When his employees arrived, the hot, fresh coffee would be waiting for them, from the lowliest errand boy to the top executives. At first, they were mystified about the source of this service but soon the word leaked out that the boss was responsible.

It is interesting to note the manner of response to this kindness. Many employees were touched by their boss' action. It made them resolve to be more dedicated in their work and more considerate of their fellow workers. Others, however, reacted differently. They felt that their superior's behavior was highly inappropriate. They were offended that he stepped outside his appointed role and were fearful that they might be expected to manifest the same humility toward those who worked under them. They were suspicious of his motives. What does he want

153

from me? However, among those who responded favorably to the actions of their chief executive, a spirit of community and cooperation developed that transformed the entire organization. (Based on a story from *The Scandal of Lent* by Robert Kysar.)

*   *   *   *   *

The gospel of John shows Jesus to be one who knew who he was. This knowledge gave him the security to step outside his expected role and be the servant. Eric Liddell, the heroic character in the movie, *Chariots Of Fire*, was also a person of power that derived from a clear image of who he was. He was scheduled to race in the Olympiad on a Sunday but refused, based on his Christian principles. He believed that Sunday was the day to worship and honor the Lord. Later, he won the 400-meter race but what really impressed the world was Liddell's shining Christian example on and off the track. His life was imbued with spiritual potency, not because of any innate ability, but because the pattern of his behavior fit the pattern of his beliefs. His life was a glorious example of the Christ's life.

Good Friday

Revised Common:	Isaiah 52:13—53:12	Hebrews 10:16-25 or Hebrews 4:14-16; 5:7-9	John 18:1—19:42
Roman Catholic:	Isaiah 52:13—53:12	Hebrews 4:14-16; 5:7-9	John 18:1—19:42
Episcopal	Isaiah 52:13—53:12 or Genesis 22:1-18 or Wisdom 2:1, 12-24	Hebrews 10:1-25	John 18:1—19:37

Theme For Lenten Series: Christ confronts death.

Theme: The passion and death of our Lord.

BRIEF COMMENTARY ON THE LESSONS

Lesson 1: Isaiah 52:13—53:12 (C, RC, E)

This sublime poem of the suffering servant lifts up an idea that is featured prominently in Christian theology: suffering, pain, and sorrow can be redemptive. Biblical interpreters have traditionally identified the servant in this poem with the nation of Israel. The nation had undergone profound humiliation and disfigurement through their ordeal in Babylon. Yet, the prophet predicts that God's afflicted one will be exalted at some future date (v. 13). While the nation can legitimately be interpreted as the servant in this poem, there are some problems. The description of the servant's sufferings is markedly individualistic and personal. It seems as if the prophet is holding up some specific person. Some contend that Isaiah may have Jeremiah or Job in mind. The Christian church, from the very beginning, have seen Christ as the suffering servant of God. He fulfills the role of the suffering servant much more effectively than does the nation. He was innocent; the nation of Israel was not. He willingly accepted humiliation for the sake of others; the nation had no choice. Isaiah found meaning in the suffering of his people. God was doing his mysterious work of redemption. Yet, as Christians, we discover greater meaning in the suffering and death of Christ.

Lesson 1: Genesis 22:1-18 (E)

God tests Abraham by instructing him to offer his only son, Isaac, as a sacrifice to God. Abraham passes the test and so his son is saved from the slaughter. God himself provides the ram for the sacrifice.

Lesson 1: Wisdom 2:1, 12-24 (E)

Those who maintain that this life is all that there is to reality and conclude that they will squeeze as much selfish pleasure from existence as possible oppose the righteous.

Lesson 2: Hebrews 10:16-25 (C); Hebrews 10:1-25 (E)

The need for continuous offerings for sin proved that they were ineffectual. Christ has offered up himself for the sins of the world, once for all. We can, therefore, approach God with a clear conscience and a pure heart. Believers need to be vigilant, to hold fast their faith, and to inspire one another to loving deeds by regularly meeting together for worship and prayer.

Lesson 2: Hebrews 4:14-16; 5:7-9 (C, RC)

Those who trust in Christ are brought into a state of repose and confidence, that the writer of Hebrews terms the "Sabbath rest." Those who persist in unbelief do not enjoy such a repose (vv. 4-11). The next two verses seem somewhat disjointed, declaring that human hearts will be laid bare by the word of God. Verse 14 picks up the theme of Jesus as our high priest, the source of our salvation, which is carried through the rest of this passage. Since we have such a great high priest, let us hold fast our confession of Jesus.

Gospel: John 18:1—19:42 (C, RC, L); John (18:1-40) 19:1-37 (E)

The passion story according to John. If you have read Matthew's passion account on Passion Sunday, you may not want to read this extensive passage at worship. John 19:17-30 could be substituted in its place.

Psalm Of The Day

Psalm 22 (C); Psalm 22:1-21 (E) — "My God, my God, why have you forsaken me?"

Prayer Of The Day

Lord Christ, you endured the shame, humiliation, and alienation brought on by our sin, so that your soul cried out in bitter agony from the cross. Accept our grateful thanks for your redemptive suffering and death. Through your glorious cross, raise us to newness of life. In your name we pray. Amen.

THEOLOGICAL REFLECTION ON THE LESSONS

Lesson 1: Isaiah 52:13—53:12

(In the interpretations of this lesson, we will interpret the passage in a Christian sense, where Jesus is the servant of the Lord.)

"Nothing in his appearance that we should desire him" (v. 2). Nowhere in the New Testament is there a description of the physical appearance of Jesus. There are probably two reasons for this. It is unimportant, or the Lord's appearance was not attractive or was, at best, average. Both factors may well be the case. God communicated to Samuel, when he was so impressed by the appearance of Jesse's eldest son, "God does not judge by outward appearance but searches the heart." But humans are quick to judge by appearance. Good-looking people have an advantage in this world. Why else would we spend billions of dollars on products that purport to improve our appearance? The usual pictures of Christ that show a ruggedly handsome visage may be far from the mark. This may be his way of telling us to look deeper.

"Surely he has borne our infirmities and carried our diseases ..." (53:4a). The image that the prophet has in mind may well be that of the leper, with his hideously deformed body. Jesus carried the leprosy of our sin in his body on the cross. Those who looked on him turned away in disgust and derision. We who are a part of Christ's body carry the infirmities of a sick society.

The silence of the Lamb. "He did not open his mouth" (53:7b). According to the passion story, Jesus did not respond to the attacks of his tormentors. The Lamb went silently to the slaughter. This was not the usual Jewish manner of dealing with adversity. Consider the loud defense that Job made to his accusers. Christ offered himself up willingly as the Lamb of God that takes away the sin of the world.

"The righteous one, my servant shall make many righteous" (53:11). When we are moved by the love of God we see on the cross, we are declared righteous.

"He poured out himself to death ..." (v. 12). This is similar to the great hymn of Christ's self-giving love found in Philippians 2. Christ poured out his life blood; he emptied himself. God rewarded his generosity by filling him up with his eternal spirit and exalting him on high.

Lesson 2: Hebrews 10:1-25

Hold tight. "Let us hold fast the confession of our hope without wavering" (v. 23). The sentiment found in this verse is repeated time and again throughout the book of Hebrews. Even in the pristine days of Christian faith, many believers were falling away; maybe because the second coming of Christ did not occur as soon as expected. The picture of the roller coaster comes to mind. We believers are those inside the cars, hurtling along with breakneck speed. The sudden dips, spins, and curves threaten to throw us out of the car but we'll be all right if we just hold on and sit tight until the ride comes to a stop.

Lesson 2: Hebrews 4:14-16; 5:7-9

The Islam of Christ. The word *Islam* means submission. Christ cried out to the Father in fervent prayer that he might be spared from the torment of suffering and death. The Father heard his prayer but did not grant his petition. The writer of Hebrews concludes that Jesus learned obedience (submission) through what he suffered. He was made perfect (mature, complete) through what he suffered, so that he might become the source of all salvation.

Gospel: John 19:17-37

Christ the gambler. The soldiers cast lots for the Lord's seamless robe, gambling for the only worldly possessions he has left. In a sense, this is fitting because the Lord was himself a gambler. He was willing to stake all for the sake of God's kingdom. Christ was willing to cash in his life for a world redeemed. Some would say he saw it as a sure bet, but if that were true, what would become of faith? Even Christ had to walk by faith, not by sight.

Standing under the cross. Our Lord's mother, his sister, Mary Magdalene, and John were standing near Jesus, under the cross. These had not forsaken him to his fate. They did not understand what was happening, but love drew them to the place of the skull. We too can never fully understand the meaning of the cross but, as Christians, we take our stand under the cross. Here we stand beneath the cross of Jesus, our feet firmly planted on the rock of our salvation.

Water and blood. John reports that the Roman soldier pierced Jesus' side, out of which flowed water and blood (v. 34). Jesus began his ministry through the waters of John's baptism and he ended his ministry on the cross, where his blood was shed. Both water and blood are also life-giving fluids. John is telling us that eternal life flows from the slain body of Christ.

PREACHING APPROACHES WITH ILLUSTRATIONS

Lesson 1: Isaiah 52:13—53:12

Sermon Title: The Wounded Healers

Sermon Angle: Isaiah describes the Servant as a disease carrier. "Surely, he has borne our infirmities and carried our diseases" (53:4). The affliction of his brothers and sisters has been caught by him. Christ too was afflicted with our common spiritual maladies — loneliness, rejection, failure, and death. Though he was wounded by our sins, he devoted his life to healing.

Christians carry the same diseases as the rest of humankind, but we also carry Christ's healing spirit. Let God work his medicine through us.

Outline:
1. The Jews (God's servant) bore the affliction of a sin-sick world
2. Christ carried the dis-ease caused by our sin (he was the Wounded Healer)
3. Christians carry the dis-ease of our world
4. Christians also carry Christ's healing spirit (we are wounded healers)
5. As we work to heal others, we too are healed

* * * * *

More than a century ago, Father Damien went to Hawaii, the island of Molokai, to minister to those from whom people hide their faces, those who suffer the isolating disfigurement of leprosy. For a long time, his parishioners were reluctant to accept him. They had seen others come and leave in disgust. Why would this man be any different? The mistrust eased as Father Damien persisted in his effort to minister to their needs, but he was not completely accepted until the day he truly became one of them. That Sunday morning, he addressed his congregation as "fellow lepers." He would no longer minister to them from the heights of holiness but from the depths of the disease. He was now their wounded leader. The healing ministry was imbued with mutuality.

Sermon Title: Lonely Is The Night

Sermon Angle: The servant of the Lord was despised and rejected (53:3). In other words, he was cut off, alienated, and lonely. The exiled people of Israel certainly felt lonely, cut off from all that was dear to them. Christ, the one who was wounded for our transgressions, experienced this tragic condition especially during the last week of his life. There was none to share the burden of the cross with him. Loneliness stems from spiritual alienation from God and others. Christians also feel this loneliness, but Christ draws us back into the redemptive community. Lonely is the night, but the day has dawned.

Outline:
1. We live in a world afflicted with loneliness (examples)
2. What is loneliness? — alienation from God and then others
3. Christ shared our loneliness (especially his passion)
4. How to defeat loneliness
   — get close to Christ
   — reach out as part of the community of love and grace

* * * * *

One Saturday, my daughter's dog, Sadie, was taking my wife and me for a walk when we encountered a young couple taking their Schnauzer for a walk. The man handed me a pamphlet and informed us that he was running for Congress. His name was Jon Christianson. His wife told me he had made 17,000 calls since June. They were the very embodiment of the American dream. The individual soars from obscurity to prominence, rags to riches. Here comes the rub: to attain that dream he may have to sacrifice his wife, family, church, and any other relationship. With millions of people following the same kind of dream, is it any wonder we have so many lonely people?

158

* * * * *

The other day, I heard on the radio that a study showed the average male does not have a single friend. He may have plenty of companions or acquaintances. He may meet with those who share his interests, but there are few, if any, with whom he feels free to share his inmost being. Maybe it's because society seems to tell men they must always be in control, always on top. Many men don't feel they can afford the luxury of being vulnerable. That's a really lonely spot to be in.

Lesson 2: Hebrews 4:14-16; 5:7-9

Sermon Title: Under Orders

Sermon Angle: The writer of Hebrews maintains that though Jesus was the Son of God, he, too, had to learn to submit his life to God. Jesus had to learn to submit his will to the Father. He was under orders. He wasn't here to do as his human nature dictated but as God decreed. Prayer is the discipline in which we learn God's will that we might order our lives accordingly.

Gospel: John 19:17-37

Sermon Title: Beneath The Cross Of Jesus — A Place To Stand

Sermon Angle: The mother of Jesus, Mary, the wife of Clopas, Mary Magdalene, and John stood beneath the cross until the bitter end. They must have struggled in vain to understand why this was happening. We can never completely understand why God chose the way of the cross. All we can do is stand under the cross and claim the salvation that it has brought.

Outline:
1. How painful it was for the three Marys and John to stand under the cross
   — they felt our Lord's pain
   — they struggled to comprehend its meaning
   — they died with him
2. We must also stand under the cross by faith
   — to forsake the cross is to forsake the Christ
   — if we suffer and die with him, we will also rise up with him

Sermon Title: The Cosmopolitan Christ

Sermon Angle: Jesus did not live and die in a cultural backwater. His cross was elevated near a cosmopolitan city, the crossroads of many peoples and cultures. The sign placed on his cross read "King of the Jews" in Hebrew, Latin, and Greek. His life and death has universal significance. The sign was in Hebrew, the language of the people of God's promises. He is the fulfillment of humankind's religious longings. The sign was also in Latin, the language of the ruling Romans. All authority to rule comes through him. He is king of the rulers of the earth. Finally, the sign was in Greek, the language of culture and learning. He is the source of divine wisdom and all earthly wisdom falls under his judgment. Christ came not just to save souls but to redeem the world.

Outline:
1. Jesus isn't just king of the Jews
2. He is the fulfillment of humankind's religious yearnings
3. He is the authority of all earthly rule
4. He is the source of all wisdom
5. The cross reveals the cosmopolitan Christ

The Easter Season

The Development Of The Season

The resurrection of Jesus Christ is, of course, the focal point of the Christian faith. In the primitive church there was no special day singled out to celebrate the Lord's resurrection. Every Sunday was a mini-celebration of the Lord's victory. Since the resurrection occurred around the same time as the Jewish Passover, early Christians referred to the church's chief festival as the *Pasca*, the Greek word for the Passover. Jesus became the Passover Lamb who frees us from the bondage to sin and death. The efficacy of his sacrifice is shown in the fact that God raised him from the dead.

There is sparse written evidence for yearly liturgical celebration of the resurrection before 200 AD, but it is likely that it was well established in most churches by 100 AD. The earliest evidence informs us that the *Pasca* consisted of a vigil beginning on Saturday evening and ending on Sunday morning, incorporating a remembrance of the Lord's crucifixion together with the celebration of his resurrection. The vigil was crowned with the baptism of those who had been instructed in the mysteries of the faith. The liturgical celebration not only centered around the baptism of new converts but also the celebration of the Eucharist. Around 300 AD, most churches commemorated the passion and death of our Lord on Good Friday and devoted Easter Sunday to the resurrection. In some churches, the celebration of the resurrection lasted for eight days. The newly baptized were required to attend the daily services until the Sunday following Easter. Since they were required to wear a white baptismal robe, the Sunday after Easter came to be known as "White Sunday."

In the first centuries of the Christian church, there was a good deal of controversy concerning the proper date to observe the resurrection. Those with close affinities to the Jewish faith insisted that it occur on the 14th of Nisan in the Hebrew calendar; this was the date of the crucifixion according to the gospel of John. Most rejected this suggestion because this would mean that most years Easter would not fall on Sunday, the weekly day of resurrection. The Council of Nicea, in 325 AD, established the procedure for determining the date for the resurrection celebration. The formula is based on the lunar calendar. Easter falls on the first Sunday following the vernal equinox. To put it more simply, Easter is the first Sunday after the first full moon following the onset of spring. If the first full moon is Sunday, then Easter is the following Sunday. In the Orthodox tradition, Easter falls ten days later than for the western church because it is based on the Julian rather than the Gregorian calendar.

The celebration of the resurrection is associated, in the minds of many, with the cycle of renewal in nature, since it occurs in springtime. Symbols of fertility and renewal have been associated with Easter and, in some cases, have been baptized as tools for the telling of the story. As an example, the Easter egg has been employed as a symbol of Christ's resurrection. In fact, the name for the queen of all Christian feasts is derived from the name of the Anglo-Saxon goddess of springtime and of the dawn.

The Importance Of The Season

The importance of Easter for the church can be discerned from two facts. First, the entire church year pivots around this event. The length of the Pentecost season is determined by the date of Easter. When Easter falls late, the length of the Pentecost season is shortened. The other fact that indicates the great importance of Easter has to do with what happens just before. The resurrection of our Lord is so crucial that it is preceded by the forty days (not counting Sundays) of Lenten preparation. The problem for the Western church is that the time of preparation

160

(Lent) assumed a life of its own and soon came to eclipse the season of Easter. For many, Easter is a glorious skyrocket that suddenly bursts over our heads a shower of brilliance and joy but soon falls cold to the earth. The memory of its glory lingers for a while but soon fades with the resumption of normal activities. An argument could be made for giving less emphasis to Lent and more to the season of Easter. Yet, we err to even try to define Easter as a season. No, Easter is not truly a season but an event which radically alters the way we view all the seasons of life. Through the resurrection we transcend earth, time, and seasons.

A Preview Of The Easter Season

You will note that the lessons for the Easter season come overwhelmingly from three books of the Bible. The first lesson is based on the Acts of the apostles. The second lesson derives from the epistle of 1 Peter, except for the reading for Easter Day, which is from Colossians. The gospel lections hail primarily from the gospel of John, except for Easter 3. If the preacher were to base the sermons for the Easter season on either the first lesson, second lesson, or the gospel, his or her listeners would see the resurrection from a particular perspective. This would enable the preacher to focus on the theological perspective of that particular biblical witness. If desired, a sermon series could easily be created.

Easter Sermon Series

Series Title: The Rock Proclaims The Resurrection

This sermon series could lift up the resurrection from the perspective of Peter, the one whom Jesus dubbed the "Rock." The witness will primarily come from the second lesson, featuring the epistle of 1 Peter. It is well known that Peter was accorded a position of primacy in the early church. He was the first to confess that Jesus was the Messiah and the first to step into the empty tomb, according to John. Peter was witness to the Transfiguration and witnessed Christ's agony in the Garden of Gethsemane. Peter's bold witness to the risen Christ stands in sharp contrast to the denial of his Lord in the courtyard of the high priest. This series would enable your congregation to view the resurrection through the eyes of one who had died and rose to newness of life, the one whom Christ named the *Rock*. The texts and titles for this series follow. *(The **Suggested Sermon Title** and the **Suggested Sermon Text**, which are listed at the beginning of each chapter in the Easter season, are meant only for those who carry out this series.)*

Lessons For Sermon Series

Easter Day — Acts 10:34-43
Easter 2 — 1 Peter 1:3-9
Easter 3 — Acts 2:14a, 36-47
Easter 4 — 1 Peter 2:19-25
Easter 5 — 1 Peter 2:4-10
Easter 6 — 1 Peter 3:18-22
Easter 7 — 1 Peter 4:12-17

Sermon Titles For Series

Easter Day — The Rock Proclaims The Resurrection
Easter 2 — The Rock Proclaims The New Birth
Easter 3 — The Rock Proclaims The Lordship Of Jesus
Easter 4 — The Rock Proclaims The Good Shepherd

Easter 5 — The Rock Proclaims The Cornerstone

Easter 6 — The Rock Proclaims Purity Of Conscience

Easter 7 — The Rock Proclaims Glory In Suffering

Alternate Sermon Series Based On The Gospel
Series Title: What The Resurrection Reveals
Lessons For The Series

Easter Day — John 20:1-18 — Mary Magdalene encounters the risen Christ

Easter 2 — John 20:19-31 — Thomas' doubt is replaced with faith

Easter 3 — Luke 24:13-35 — The risen Christ reveals himself in the breaking of the bread

Easter 4 — John 10:1-10 — Jesus is the door to eternal life

Easter 5 — John 14:1-14 — Jesus prepares a place for his own

Easter 6 — John 14:15-21 — Jesus promises the Holy Spirit

Easter 7 — John 17:1-11 — Jesus prays for his disciples

Sermon Titles For Series

Easter Day — The Resurrection Reveals God's Eternal Love

Easter 2 — The Resurrection Reveals That Faith Is Stronger Than Doubt

Easter 3 — The Resurrection Reveals Christ In The Breaking Of Bread

Easter 4 — The Resurrection Reveals Christ As The Door To Eternal Life

Easter 5 — The Resurrection Reveals Our Eternal Place In The Son

Easter 6 — The Resurrection Reveals God's Holy Spirit

Easter 7 — The Resurrection Reveals A God Who Sustains Me To The End

Easter Day

Revised Common:	Acts 10:34-43 or Jeremiah 31:1-6	Colossians 3:1-4	John 20:1-18 or Matthew 28:1-10
Roman Catholic:	Acts 10:34, 37-43	Colossians 3:1-4 or 1 Corinthians 5:6-8	John 20:1-9
Episcopal:	Acts 10:34-43 or Exodus 14:1-14, 21-25; 15:20-1	Colossians 3:1-4 or Acts 10:34-43	John 20:1-10 (11-18) or Matthew 28:1-10

Theme For The Day: The Lord's victory over the powers of sin and death.

Sermon Text For Easter Sermon Series: Acts 10:34-43

Sermon Series Title For Easter: The Rock Proclaims The Resurrection

BRIEF COMMENTARY ON THE LESSONS

Lesson 1: Acts 10:34-43 (C, E); Acts 10:34, 37-43 (RC)

Peter testifies to the Lord's resurrection to the household of Cornelius, the Roman centurion who feared God. These two men are brought together by their visions. Through this encounter, God reveals to Peter that the Gentiles are also heirs to salvation. In his sermon, Peter covers the fundamentals of the gospel, Christ's death and resurrection. Peter testifies as an eyewitness, who ate and drank with Christ after he rose from the dead, that Jesus is the one ordained by God to be the judge of the living and the dead. He is the fulfillment of the expectations of the prophets and the one through whom any who believe in him receive the forgiveness of sins.

Lesson 2: Colossians 3:1-4 (C, RC, E)

"If you have been raised with Christ, seek the things that are above" (v. 1). This lesson speaks of the resurrection of believers as something that has already occurred, which has implications for the way that we live out our lives. The believer has been raised up by receiving a new spiritual center. Therefore, the follower of Christ should live out of this center rather than descend to the level of his old sinful nature.

Gospel: John 20:1-18 (C); John 20:1-9 (RC); John 20:1-10 (11-18) (E)

According to John's witness, Mary Magdalene comes alone to the tomb early on the first day of the week. Finding the stone rolled back, she is alarmed and runs to tell Peter and John what has happened. These two disciples then dash to the tomb to investigate. John gets there first, peers into the grave, but does not enter until Peter steps inside the tomb — another first for Peter. The disciples return to their dwelling in puzzlement. Mary remains by the grave, where she peers in and sees two angels. They ask her why she is weeping. "Because they have taken away my Lord and I don't know where they have laid him," Mary replies. Then Jesus appears, asking the same question as the angels. Mary doesn't recognize Jesus, thinking him the gardener, until Jesus calls her name. Finally, she rushes to the other followers of Jesus with the news of her unbelievable encounter with the risen Lord.

Psalm Of The Day

Psalm 118 (C, E) — "I shall not die but live" (v. 17).

Prayer Of The Day

Eternal God, we sing your praises for raising your Son, our Savior, Jesus Christ, from the grave and lifting him up as a sign of salvation for all who trust in his name. Raise us also from the grave of sin and death, that we might join in Christ's victory song, together with the innumerable host who surround your heavenly throne. In Jesus' name. Amen.

THEOLOGICAL REFLECTION ON THE LESSONS

Lesson 1: Acts 10:34-43

The Rock proclaims the resurrection. Peter, the one whom Jesus named the Rock, crumbled into sand during the trial of our Lord, but the resurrection of Christ was the cement that solidified his faith. Peter boldly proclaimed to a Roman officer and his household that this Jesus, crucified as a common criminal, was raised from the dead; not only that, but he is the one designated by God to judge the living and the dead. There is no need to fear his judgment, however, because "every one who believes in him receives forgiveness of sins through his name" (v. 43).

Eyewitness news. The news department of almost every television station dubs itself: Eyewitness News. The apostles were also eyewitness reporters to the greatest news in the history of the universe. Peter tells the household of Cornelius that the apostles were eyewitnesses to the signs and wonders which Jesus performed during his ministry. More importantly, they were eyewitnesses to the risen Christ; they ate and drank with him after his resurrection.

Lesson 2: Colossians 3:1-4

Be high minded. If we have died and risen with Christ, spiritually speaking, we must set our minds on things above, says the writer of Colossians. Where our mind is, there will our body be also. A person can let his mind descend into the abyss or focus it on that which is of God, all that is noble and true.

Gospel: John 20:1-18

Resurrected run. What was it that made Peter and John race to the tomb? Of course, Mary Magdalene reported that the tomb was open and empty, but why the rush? Had they remembered that the Lord said he would rise from the grave after three days? Were they merely curious? On entering the tomb, they observed that the grave clothes had been left behind. If his body had been stolen, why were the burial clothes not taken with the body? Yet their response is rather anti-climatic; they merely went back home.

Is that the way Easter is for us? Temporary excitement? A mad dash to the empty tomb and to a full church? Yet we don't linger long enough to encounter the risen Lord. Mary Magdalene wasn't going to go back home until she had found the Lord. Like Peter and John, we return home empty hearted, full of disappointment. Faith is not formed by witnessing an empty tomb but by encountering a living Lord.

A new outfit for Easter. Peter and John observed that the Lord's burial clothes had been left behind. How appropriate. Jesus had cast off his shroud, his death duds. God had decked him in a new Easter outfit that would not fade or decay. Jesus is Lord.

One of the traditions surrounding Easter is to go out and buy a new Easter wardrobe: a new dress, shoes, suit, or bonnet. Easter should not be an opportunity to show off new clothes, but the custom has some merit. Our new clothes symbolize what God has done for us because of Christ's resurrection. God has removed our burial shroud and decked us with the robe of righteousness.

Why are you weeping? This is the question that Mary Magdalene was asked by the angels sitting on the slab that had held the body of Jesus. Her inconsolable grief kept her from recognizing him, and he asked the same question. "Woman, why are you weeping?" That's a good question to ask in light of the resurrection of Jesus. We may still have reason to weep because life inflicts great wounds but we need to know why we are weeping. Are we weeping for ourselves? Do we feel sorry for ourselves? That's a futile kind of weeping. Do we weep because someone we love has been hurt or has died? Such tears can prove healing if we can get them out and then move on. Do we weep because we feel like an orphaned child? Christ understands that feeling and will come to console us. We may not recognize him, at first, but the living Lord stands ready to speak our names and wipes the tears away from our eyes. Weeping may last the night, but joy comes in the morning.

We're all in the family. The risen Lord instructed Mary Magdalene to tell the disciples that "He was ascending to my Father and your Father, to my God and your God" (v. 17). Most of them had failed him, deserted him, and disappointed him during his hour of need, but they were forgiven. They were still children of God, still brothers and sisters. That's the wonderful news that the risen Christ has to tell each and every one of his disciples.

PREACHING APPROACHES WITH ILLUSTRATIONS

Lesson 1: Acts 10:34-43
Sermon Title: The Rock Proclaims The Resurrection
Sermon Angle: The resurrected Christ solidified the Rock so that he might truly live up to his name. Ever since Christ rose from the dead, Peter proclaimed the resurrection, but here Peter proclaimed the resurrection to a Gentile, an officer of the occupying force in Peter's country. The pre-resurrection Peter proclaimed that Jesus was the Jewish Messiah but the post-resurrection Peter proclaimed that Jesus was the risen Lord of all.
Outline:
1. Peter proclaimed Christ's ministry of healing and peacemaking (vv. 36-39a)
2. Peter proclaimed that God raised Christ from the dead (vv. 39b-40)
3. Peter proclaimed that the disciples ate and drank with the risen Christ (v. 41) (No mere vision but fellowship with the risen Christ)
4. Peter proclaimed that Christ is judge of the living and the dead but that there is forgiveness through his name (vv. 42-43)

Lesson 2: Colossians 3:1-4
Sermon Title: High Minded
Sermon Angle: We see the "already but not yet" dimension of our resurrection. We have been raised to newness of life through faith, but we still live in a corrupt world. Christians have their feet planted in two worlds: the old sinful world and the new world that Christ is ushering in. We are to focus our minds on the new world, on the things that are above. Setting our minds on the values of the world will drag us down, but fixing our minds on the things of God will lift us up. In other words, be high minded.

Outline:
1. We have already been raised to newness of life through Christ
2. Yet we still live in the old sinful world
3. We can choose which world we will focus on
4. To fix our minds on the values of this world leads to death but ...
5. To fix our minds on the world that is coming through Christ leads to life

Gospel: John 20:1-18

Sermon Title: What The Resurrection Reveals — The Long Arm Of God's Love

Sermon Angle: Jesus delivered Mary Magdalene from seven demons (Mark 16:9). She was a very sick person. She experienced the love of God through Jesus' healing as she never had before. In gratitude, that love was returned. Mary Magdalene stayed close to Jesus. She was with him in Jerusalem the final week of his life; she witnessed his crucifixion, his burial, and his resurrection. She was there early Easter morning to prepare his body for burial. She must have been devastated when the one who loved her so much was taken from her. She was frantic when his body was not in the tomb but then, miraculously, he called her name. The long arm of God's love had reached out from the grave.

Outline:

What does the resurrection reveal?
1. Love that reaches beyond the grave
2. Loyalty that is rewarded (Mary stood by Jesus)
3. A God who knows me personally (Jesus called Mary's name)
4. A gospel worth proclaiming (Go and tell ...)

Sermon Title: Good News From The Grave

Sermon Angle: After the risen Christ encountered Mary Magdalene at the grave, he instructed her to tell the disciples the good news; he was alive and was soon to ascend to the God and Father of them all. She must have been delirious with joy and excitement as she relayed the good news to the disciples of Jesus, but they were not inclined to believe her. How frustrated she must have been. Their response is understandable because we don't expect to hear good news from the grave. What a surprise to all who inhabit a grave of sickness, hopelessness, crushed dreams, failures, and opportunities left unseized. It is from Christ's grave and our graves that God raises us to newness of life!

Outline:
1. Good news — Jesus is risen
2. Good news — we are still of God's family (... my Father and your Father, my God and your God ...) (v. 17)
3. Good news — the love of Jesus reigns ("I am ascending ...") (v. 17)
4. Good news — Jesus lives and we can live eternally through him

*   *   *   *   *

Garrison Keillor, author of *Lake Woebegon Days*, relates the true story of a Minnesota farmer who had a resurrection type experience. It was time for spring planting and the farmer was working manure into the soil with his tractor and disc plow. It was a warm day, the field was long, and the farmer was bored. He thought of all the exciting things he could do if he wasn't married to the land. Suddenly, he felt himself falling. He had fallen asleep. In desperation, he reached for the tractor hitch just as he hit the ground. The tractor was the old type with a notched throttle. It kept chugging along at about 5 mph. The distraught farmer was unable to pull himself up. All he could do was hang on for dear life; should he lose his grip, he would be cut to ribbons by the blades of the disc that were doggedly chasing him. The scene would be comic were it not so potentially tragic. Picture this poor soul being dragged through the dirt and manure down the length of the field, up the embankment, and into a grove of trees. The tractor finally came to rest against a tree, the wheels still spinning. It took about ten minutes for him to gather the strength to pull himself up on the tractor seat and turn off the ignition.

It was a new man that sat there pondering what he had just gone through. He had personally experienced the reality of resurrection. The manure-impregnated earth smelled sweet; the sky never looked so blue. That farmer looked at farming and all of existence with new eyes. He had been reborn.

*   *   *   *   *

The Parable Of The Two Parties

It was Good Friday, and my family and I were on our way to worship. As we approached the lane that leads into the church parking lot, we noticed a huge party in the parking lot of a local nightspot across from the church. This is the kind of hangout where the waitresses are required to sport skimpy shorts and halter tops, displaying to the maximum effect large breasts and shapely thighs. The draw was a sandless beach party 1,600 miles from the ocean. In front was the icon for the assembly, a huge, inflatable can of beer, the sacramental beverage of the assembly. The band was blaring and the congregates were getting into the spirits. As we walked to the church door, the noise of the revelry pelted our ears.

I couldn't help but notice the incongruity of these two assemblies — the one in the parking lot and the one in the church. The revelry in the parking lot seemed so out of place in this holiest of Christian holidays. Christ died for all, but this group of revelers couldn't care less. Of course, from their perspective it might seem like the church is a bunch of crepe hangers who have lost the ability to celebrate life. In their way of thinking, the church is out of sync with the world, not the other way around. If they had left the beach party to join the throng who was paying homage to the crucified Christ, it would have struck them as macabre. All this talk of sin, suffering, and death would seem the antithesis of life. Those dancing to the drumbeat of the moment wouldn't understand that Christians are also celebrating life, but in a very different way. The followers of the man from Nazareth have discovered that life and death are not mutually exclusive. As strange as it seems, they have found that the door to the celebration of life is only through death. Christ gave himself to death that we might gain eternal life. As we give our life to Christ and neighbor, we learn to dance with the angels: We are raised up to a new and wonderful level of life and love. The revelers in the parking lot, by and large, are attempting to seize life by fleeing from death. They may be attempting to still the restlessness of their hearts by sating their senses and by pursuing superficial encounters rather than committed relationships.

These two Good Friday gatherings are a parable of life. In the parking lot are those who find death in life but in the sanctuary are those who discover life in death. Be warned! Those in the sanctuary must not look down their noses in judgment on the revelers. We are not better than they. Our challenge is to celebrate life in such joy and love that they will be attracted to our party. The Christ who turned water into wine and transformed death into a dance is the life of the party that has no end. All are invited.

Easter 2

Revised Common:	Acts 2:14a, 22-32	1 Peter 1:3-9	John 20:19-31
Roman Catholic:	Acts 2:42-47	1 Peter 1:3-9	John 20:19-31
Episcopal:	Acts 2:14a, 22-32 or	1 Peter 1:3-9 or	John 20:19-31
	Genesis 8:6-16; 9:8-16	Acts 2:14a, 22-32	

Theme For The Day: The theme of faith and doubt runs through the lessons for today. In the first lesson, Peter attempts to elicit faith on the part of his hearers in the risen Christ. In the second lesson, Peter points out how Christians are born anew through their faith in the resurrected Christ, even though they have to undergo persecution and hardship. In the gospel, we have the story of Thomas, who would not believe unless he would see for himself. This is an account which speaks eloquently to the skeptical age in which we live.

Sermon Series Title For Easter 2: The Rock Proclaims The New Birth. Peter, the Rock, boldly and joyously announces not only the good news of Christ's resurrection, but also its consequence for our lives: "Blessed be the God and Father of our Lord Jesus Christ! By his great mercy he has given us a new birth into a living hope through the resurrection of Jesus Christ from the dead ..." (1 Peter 1:3-9).

Suggested Text For Preaching: 1 Peter 1:3-9 (For sermon series)

BRIEF COMMENTARY ON THE LESSONS

Lesson 1: Acts 2:14a, 22-32 (C, E)

This pericope contains a portion of Peter's Pentecost sermon, as recalled by Luke. It is a good representation of the major themes contained in the early apostolic preaching. The following points seemed to be central to the preaching of Peter and the other apostles and evangelists: 1) the signs and wonders performed by Jesus during his earthly ministry; 2) Jesus was handed over to be crucified by sinful people; 3) nevertheless, the suffering, death, and resurrection of Jesus are a result of God's design; 4) these events are a fulfillment of Old Testament prophecies (Psalm 16 is quoted as a proof that David had foretold the resurrection); 5) the first Christians were witnesses to these events; 6) finally, though it is not contained in this passage, there is an appeal to repent and believe the good news.

Lesson 1: Acts 2:42-47 (RC)

See the first lesson for Easter 4 (C).

Lesson 2: 1 Peter 1:3-9 (C, RC, E)

Beginning today, the second lesson for the entire Easter season derives from the epistle of 1 Peter. The first two verses reveal that this epistle is addressed to a post diaspora church, after the fall of Jerusalem. Though some think this epistle is not written by Peter, it certainly reflects the Rock's emphasis of the centrality of Christ's resurrection for believers. The audience of 1 Peter is different than that of Acts, since it contained few, if any, eyewitnesses of the Lord's passion, death, and resurrection. Yet, these believers have been born anew by the resurrection of Jesus Christ from the dead. They live in hope as they wait for the completion of God's work of salvation in their lives. Even the fiery trials of tribulation and persecution cannot consume their faith but, rather, purify it. These believers have not personally seen Jesus. Yet, through trusting in him they are born anew by their faith in the risen Christ.

Gospel: John 20:19-31 (C, RC, E)

The gospel pericope is in two parts. The first part (vv. 19-23) provides for us the story of the Lord's appearance in the inner circle of the disciples. All but Thomas are present. Christ breathes on them and thereby bestows the Holy Spirit, granting them his peace as he commissions them to go out and proclaim the good news. Here we have John's rendition of Pentecost and Ascension, all rolled into one. In the second part of the passage (vv. 24-29), Christ reappears, but this time Thomas is with the other disciples. Christ challenges him to touch his wounds, to see and believe. Thomas confesses his faith, in light of the evidence. Yet Jesus declares that the ones who have not seen him like Thomas, yet still believe, are those truly blessed. The last two verses of the passage reveal the purpose of John's gospel. That his readers, who have not seen Christ, might believe in him and, thereby, obtain eternal life.

Psalm Of The Day
Psalm 16 (C) — "You show me the path of life ..." (v. 11).
Psalm 111 (E) — "Great are the works of the Lord ..." (v. 2).

Prayer Of The Day
Living God, we bless you that we are born anew through the resurrection of your Son. By the power of your Spirit, enable us to turn our backs to evil and witness to the light of your grace and love, which is ours through the merits of your Son, our Savior, Jesus Christ. Amen.

THEOLOGICAL REFLECTION ON THE LESSONS

Lesson 1: Acts 2:14a, 22-32

The Lamb. In verse 22, Peter maintains that Jesus was handed over to those who killed him by the plan and foreknowledge of God. God offered up his Son as a sacrifice for the sins of the world. God displays not only his love but his power, by harnessing humankind's evil impulses for the salvation of the world.

Humpty Dumpty. "Humpty Dumpty sat on a wall. Humpty Dumpty had a great fall. All the king's horses and all the king's men could not put Humpty Dumpty together again." Nursery rhymes contain truths about life. The Humpty Dumpty rhyme, for instance, reveals the truth that certain actions cannot be undone. It teaches us to be circumspect concerning how we live our lives. Even God cannot undo what we have done, but he can put the pieces back together again. Peter boldly accuses his listeners of killing Jesus but the good news is that God put the pieces together again; he raised Jesus from the dead (vv. 23-24). Yet, according to the gospel lesson, even the resurrected Christ bore the scars of his execution. Thus, there is a twofold message in this passage. Our actions have lasting consequences but God can and does put together the broken pieces of shattered lives. Humans crucify Christ (we are still doing it), but God raises us to newness of life with him through faith.

Lesson 2: 1 Peter 1:3-9

A new birth. We hear a lot of talk about being born again and it has created a lot of confusion. Some people don't know if they've been born anew. They haven't seen any visions, heard any voices, or had any out of body experience. They can't name the day when God became more than a word to them. Yet the Lord is real to them and they trust in him for the forgiveness of their sins. How do we know if we are born anew or born again? Here are some factors to consider. Do we trust in Christ and his resurrection rather than rely on our own goodness? Do we believe that, in him, we have the forgiveness of sins? Do our lives make visible the grace and love of God, which we have received? We need to remind one another that being born anew does not depend on human formulas or feelings.

Hold up the shield of faith. Verse 5 states that we are protected by the power of God through faith. It does not mean that we are spared all adversity because, in verse 6, it speaks of the "various kinds of trials" the believers had to endure. What does faith shield us from then? How about doubt and despair? Believers realize that they will still have to undergo pain and suffering but do not view it as a sign of God's displeasure; rather, they regard it as the caldron in which their faith is strengthened and purified.

A refined faith. In this passage the tested faith of those addressed is compared to gold that is tested by fire. The process by which gold and other precious metals are refined is alluded to here. Suffering, persecution, and other ordeals are like the refiner's fire, which burns away the base elements and leaves that which is precious and imperishable. Thus, a refined faith is not necessarily a faith that is acceptable to the cultural elite but a faith that has been put to the fire and thereby purified.

Gospel: John 20:19-31

Peace for the fearful of heart. The disciples were so petrified with fear that they were ensconced behind locked doors. At first, the Lord's appearance did not calm but rather exacerbated their fears. Jesus was tuned in to their inward condition. Two times he calms them with the words "Peace with you." It is a total peace which Christ extends to them, a peace of heart, soul, and mind. It is a peace that comes from knowing that Christ forgives them, that they have a second chance. What is even a greater source of assurance is that they are no longer bound by the fear of death. Jesus has tamed this great dragon. Death can still take the believer for a ride but cannot destroy those who belong to Jesus.

Apostles of forgiveness. John compresses resurrection, Pentecost, and ascension all into one event. Christ breathes on the disciples, imparting the Holy Spirit, so that they might have the power to carry on God's reconciling work. He sends them out with the authority to pronounce God's forgiveness. They are apostles of forgiveness. Exercising the power of forgiveness is the key to eternal life. Christ gives his followers the power to pronounce his forgiveness on those who will accept it (v. 23). Those who know God's reconciliation experience the joy of eternal life.

Believing is seeing. Thomas wasn't present when Jesus appeared to the other disciples. When they joyously informed him of their Master's visitation, Thomas was skeptical. "Unless I see in his hands the print of the nails ... I will not believe" (v. 25). Seeing is believing. Right? Wrong! We can only see a fraction of that which is real. We can't see microbes, nor can we see distant galaxies. Yet, we've been told by witnesses that have seen them that they exist. We have come to accept the unseen as gospel truth. When we're sick and go to the doctor and he tells us that we have a staph infection, for which he is prescribing an antibiotic, we don't question his judgment. We don't say: "Wait a minute, Doc. How do you know such bacteria exist? I've never seen them. I don't believe in anything that I cannot see with my own eyes. Forget your medicine." We'd think that such a person is very foolish to limit himself to that which he could perceive with his senses. On the other hand, if we accept the physician's judgment that bacteria exist, if we by faith accept his hypotheses, we open the door to life and healing.

Christ did reveal himself to Thomas through his physical senses but he pronounces that those who have not seen him and yet believe in him are the truly blessed ones (v. 29). If we believe in the risen Christ, even though we have not seen him, if we operate on the premise that he lives and forgives, we will come to experience his healing and life-giving power.

PREACHING APPROACHES WITH ILLUSTRATIONS

Lesson 1: Acts 2:14a, 22-32

Sermon Title: The Resurrection Of Humpty Dumpty

Sermon Angle: Peter accused his listeners of killing Jesus but then he added, "But God raised him up." A convicted killer pleaded for mercy saying: "If I could undo the horrible things that I have done, if I could bring her back, I would." Then he tearfully added, "But I can't." Some lives are so badly broken that there is nothing that can be done, humanly speaking, to restore them. The victims of incest, rape, and child abuse, for example, have an arduous journey to reach some semblance of normalcy. But when we take a life, we cannot give it back again. Only God can raise up a life that has been taken, as he demonstrated in the raising of his son. All the king's horses and all the king's men couldn't put Humpty Dumpty back together again. There is a limit to what humans can do to restore that which they have broken, but the Lord can do what humans cannot. Our lives are often shattered, like Humpty Dumpty, but the Lord can put us back together again. God can raise us to newness of life after we have taken even a fatal plunge.

Outline:
1. The crucifixion shows the brokenness caused by human sin
2. The resurrection shows how God restored the One who was broken
3. We're like Humpty Dumpty — there is much brokenness in our lives
4. The resurrected Christ can raise us to newness of life

Sermon Title: Using Evil In The Service Of God

Sermon Angle: The cross is the prime example of how God breaks the back on evil, by employing evil in the service of God. The evil is a result of the misuse of human freedom. God shows his sovereignty by taking that which is opposed to him and using it for his redemptive purposes. We, too, can employ evil in the service of God and good when we show love and forgiveness to the perpetrator of the evil.

Outline:
1. In the cross, God transformed an instrument of evil into an instrument of life
2. We, too, can use evil in the service of good when we
   — forgive those who hurt us
   — labor to eliminate the conditions that spawn evil

Lesson 2: 1 Peter 1:3-9

Sermon Title: The Rock Proclaims The New Birth

Sermon Angle: Peter proclaims the glorious fact that we have been given a new birth through the resurrection of Jesus Christ from the dead. I once saw a sermon title which has stuck with me: "Born Again Believers: Is There Any Other Kind?" How true, but what does it mean to be born again? Some churches teach that we are born again through baptism; others maintain that we are born again when we consciously give our lives to Christ. Still others insist that there must be a special baptism or anointing with God's Spirit. This passage makes plain that we are born again not through human actions but through the resurrection of Jesus Christ. We appropriate Christ's resurrection when we die daily to sin through repentance, after which God raises us to newness of life. Thus, we are not just born again, but again and again and again.

Outline:
1. When Christ died, the faith of his followers also died
2. Christ's resurrection gave the disciples of Jesus a new birth
3. What does it mean to be born anew or again?
   — we die daily to selfishness and sin through repentance
   — we turn the center of our lives over to Christ
   — we no longer live; Christ lives in us
4. Let us bless God for our new birth (v. 3) and rejoice (vv. 8b-9)

* * * * *

Many people, even good Christians, are sometimes filled with anxiety about their forthcoming birth into the kingdom of heaven. This story, "The Parable Of The Twins," might provide a new perspective.

Once upon a time, twin boys were conceived in the same womb. Weeks passed, as the twins developed. As their awareness grew, they laughed for joy: "Isn't it great that we were conceived? Isn't it great to be alive?"

Together, the twins explored their world. When they found their mother's cord which gave them life, they sang for joy: "How great is our mother's love, that she shares her own life with us."

As the weeks stretched into months, the twins noticed how much each was changing. "What does it mean?" asked the one. "It means that our stay in this world is drawing to an end," said the other. "But I don't want to go," said the one. "I want to stay here always." "We have no choice," said the other. "But maybe there is life after birth!" "But how can there be?" responded the one. "We will shed our life cord, and how is life possible without it? Besides, we have seen evidence that others were here before us, and none of them have returned to tell us that there is life after birth. No, this is the end."

And so the one fell into deep despair, saying, "If conception ends in birth, what is the purpose of life in the womb? It's meaningless! Maybe there is no mother after all!" "But there has to be," protested the other. "How else did we get there? How do we remain alive?"

"Have you ever seen our mother?" said the one. "Maybe she lives only in our minds. Maybe we made her up, because the idea made us feel good!"

And so the last days in the womb were filled with deep questioning and fear. Finally the moment of birth arrived. When the twins had passed from their world, they opened their eyes and cried for joy. For what they saw exceeded their fondest dreams. (Author unknown. Taken from the Wayne, Nebraska, Hospice Newsletter)

172

Sermon Title: Putting Faith To The Fire

Sermon Angle: Fire has traditionally served as a symbol of life. Thus, John F. Kennedy's grave has an eternal flame, so called, to symbolize the hope that his legacy would not burn out, but live on. Fire is also associated with judgment. It burns away that which is unworthy and leaves that which is eternal. Peter compares the faith of Christians to gold, which is refined through the fiery furnace (v. 7). Hard times, persecution, and other forms of adversity are like a smelting furnace that purges away that which is temporal or unworthy, leaving that which is precious and eternal.

Gospel: John 20:19-31

Sermon Title: Believing Is Seeing

Sermon Angle: Believing in Christ is like stepping out into the shadows. There is no way to view the distant horizon. But when we launch out in faith, the shadows give way to a wonderful world of life and love, that we could not see before. Thomas came to believe through seeing. For us, the only options are to see through believing or to remain in the darkness.

Outline:
1. Thomas missed seeing Christ because he was absent from the assembly (We run the danger of missing Christ when we absent ourselves from the body of believers.)
2. He refused to believe the report of the other disciples
3. Christ honored his skepticism by appearing to Thomas
4. Faith is seldom free of all doubt
5. Christ will bless those who act out of their faith, rather than their doubts

Easter 3

Revised Common:	Acts 2:14a, 36-41	1 Peter 1:17-23	Luke 24:13-35
Roman Catholic:	Acts 2:14, 22-33	1 Peter 1:17-21	Luke 24:13-35
Episcopal:	Acts 2:14a, 36-47 or Isaiah 43:1-12	1 Peter 1:17-23 or Acts 2:14a, 36-47	Luke 24:13-35

Theme For The Day: The risen Christ is revealed as believers gather together and break bread. The First Lesson describes the resurrection community in Jerusalem as having everything in common. They broke bread with glad and generous hearts, praising God. The Gospel tells how Christ was revealed to the two strollers on the way to Emmaus, when Christ blessed and broke bread with them.

Sermon Series Title For Easter 3: The Rock Proclaims The Lordship Of Jesus

Suggested Text For Preaching: Acts 2:14a, 36-47 (For sermon series)

BRIEF COMMENTARY ON THE LESSONS

Lesson 1: Acts 2:14a, 36-41 (C); Acts 2:14, 23-33 (RC); Acts 2:14a, 36-47 (E)

This is the ending of Peter's Pentecost sermon. He confronts his listeners head-on with their participation in the crucifixion of Jesus, stating that this Jesus, whom they killed, is both Lord and Christ. The crowd is overwhelmed with guilt and asked the question which every good sermon should address: "What do we have to do?" Peter is quick to supply the answer: "Repent and be baptized ..." (v. 7). Some 3,000 responded. The rest of the passage portrays the dynamic Christian community in Jerusalem, where the believers shared their lives, their fortunes, and their food. A eucharistic community of prayer, signs, and witness attracted the positive regard of the wider community.

Lesson 2: 1 Peter 1:17-23 (C, E); 1 Peter 1:17-21 (RC)

This epistle addresses a radically different Christian community than does Acts. In Acts, the Christian community was still regarded with favor by the wider community. But in this letter, the church is subject to persecution. It is no longer centered in Jerusalem but is a church in exile (v. 17). There is a eucharistic theme in this passage, which links it to the other two readings. Christ is presented as the perfect Passover Lamb who shed his blood for the ransom of the world (v. 19).

Gospel: Luke 24:13-35 (C, RC, E)

Two disciples of Jesus are walking away from Jerusalem, toward the village of Emmaus, discussing the events of Good Friday and Easter morning. The risen Christ joins them on their journey, though they do not recognize him. He inquires about the nature of their conversation. They relate the apparently tragic events and then Christ proceeds to explain the true meaning of those events in light of scripture. They stop for the evening and Jesus acts as though he is going further. They invite him to stay with them and suddenly the guest becomes the host. As he breaks the bread their eyes are opened, and they recognize the Lord. Christ reveals himself through word and sacrament.

Psalm Of The Day

Psalm 116:1-4, 12-19 (C); Psalm 116 (E) — "What shall I render to the Lord for all his benefits to me?" (v. 12).

Prayer Of The Day

Lord Jesus, as you revealed your living presence to those disciples on the road to Emmaus and especially in the breaking of bread, so reveal yourself now through Word and sacrament, as we gather in your blessed name. Amen.

THEOLOGICAL REFLECTION ON THE LESSONS

Lesson 1: Acts 2:14a, 36-47

Guilt trip. Peter apologetically and boldly laid a guilt trip on his listeners. "Let the whole house of Israel know with certainty that God has made him both Lord and Messiah, this Jesus whom you crucified" (v. 36). We're reluctant to employ guilt these days, choosing only to proclaim the good news of God's forgiveness and love. The preaching of Peter and the early church employed both law and gospel. Actually, the law cut them to the heart and made them ready to receive the gospel. "Brothers, what shall we do?" (v. 37). Peter replied, "Repent and be baptized every one of you in the name of Jesus Christ" (v. 38). The guilt trip which Peter induced led them to the gateway of grace and a new life.

Courage from conviction. Peter preached with great conviction: "... let the whole house of Israel know with certainty that God made him both Lord and Messiah...." You might say that he gained courage from his conviction that Jesus had risen and was reigning at the right hand of God. There was no doubt in Peter's mind that Jesus was both Lord and Christ. A person is not going to put her life on the line for a theory or probability. No, a person will only stake her life on that of which she is utterly convinced. Preaching that doesn't issue from a firm conviction that Jesus is Lord and Savior is about as appealing as cold oatmeal, but not nearly so nourishing.

"Save yourselves from this crooked generation" (v. 40). For the early Christians, there was no doubt about the opposition of Christ and culture. The values of the Christian faith stood out vividly against the pagan backdrop. Beginning with Constantine, Christ and culture became allies. In recent years, western culture has increasingly rejected Christian values. This has proven disastrous for society, but there is an up side. Now, at least, there is a clear choice between Christ and the values of the culture. We cannot be transforming agents in the world unless we are clear on this.

Koinonia and community. A chief characteristic of the Jerusalem church was *koinonia*, a profound sharing of their entire lives with the fellow believers. It is said that they "had all things in common" (v. 44). They worshiped together at the temple. They celebrated the *Agape Feast* and the Eucharist in their homes. The believers shared freely of their material substance, and the basic needs of everyone were met. In our day, when the bonds of community have broken apart to an alarming degree, people are starving for real community. Yet, the fellowship found at most churches is shallow except for a few Bible study or prayer groups. Instead of ministering to one another's needs, we look to the government or some other institution to do the job. How do we recapture *koinonia*? Not through canned programs but by being channels of the awesome presence of the risen Christ.

Lesson 2: 1 Peter 1:17-23

Confidence through Christ. Verse 21 informs us that we have confidence in God through Christ. We don't have to live in fear and uncertainty because Christ reveals a God whom we can count on to navigate us through stormy and calm seas alike. This passage suggests not only that we can rely on God but also that we can lead confident lives because, through faith, we are in God. For Christians, our positive mental attitude is not the result of some self-help psychological gimmick; it is the outcome of our relationship with the Lord.

Gospel: Luke 24:13-35

Word and sacrament. How do we come to see the risen Christ? The same way that the two travelers on the road to Emmaus saw him: through word and sacrament. They first came to see Christ in the word and then in the breaking of the bread. This passage hints at the various means of receiving God's grace. First, through the mind, then through the heart ("Did not our hearts burn within us") (v. 32) and finally, the senses.

Spend the night with us, Jesus. As they drew near their place of lodging, they begged Jesus: "Stay with us because it is almost evening and the day is nearly over" (v. 29). I always get choked up when I view the final scene from the movie, *Jesus of Nazareth*. The disciples are huddled around Jesus, like a brood of chicks under their mother's wings, and one of them (John, I think) voices the passage above. We are all like children, nervous as the night sets in, longing for the reassuring presence of a parent who will shelter and protect us, as the shroud of darkness sets in. The night is suggestive of mystery, uncertainty, isolation, and finality. As the darkness sets in, we have but to invite the Lord to spend the night with us.

Blessed bread. Jesus took the bread, blessed, and broke it (v. 31). Bread is truly blessed because it is a gift of God, a token of God's love and care for his children. When we take the bread and bless its giver, the one who is the bread of life, that bread is truly holy, like manna from heaven. An ordinary meal can have a sacramental quality, if we receive it as from the hand of God. Bread that is blessed must be broken because, until it is broken, it cannot be shared, and until it is shared, it cannot be received, and until it is received, it cannot produce a blessing. The church is meant to be broken bread through which the world comes to see and receive the bread of life.

PREACHING APPROACHES WITH ILLUSTRATIONS

Lesson 1: Acts 2:14a, 36-47

Sermon Title: The Rock Proclaims The Lordship Of Christ

Sermon Angle: Peter was the first to confess that Jesus was the Messiah at Caesarea Philippi. Jesus declares the rock upon which he would build his church. The rock crumbled under the duress surrounding the cross but was restored and strengthened by the risen Lord. Peter boldly proclaims that Jesus is both Lord and Messiah, to whom every knee must bow.

Outline:
1. Peter was given a name to live up to — the Rock
2. Peter was the first to confess that Jesus is the Christ

3. Peter's faith crumbled when he relied on his own powers
4. After Christ's resurrection, Peter confidently confessed Jesus as Lord
5. Is your life built on the foundation of Christ as Lord of your life?

Sermon Title: Coin-o-nia

Sermon Angle: The sermon title is a play on the Greek word *koinonia*, meaning common or shared: that which binds together. Verses 43-47 describe the form that this *koinonia* or fellowship took. The fellowship of the Jerusalem church was profound because it covered every aspect of life, including the economic sphere. *Koinonia* took the form of coin-o-nia. The believers sold their material possessions and shared them with the community. The sharing of material wealth indicates how profound was the transformation of those first believers. There can only be meaningful *koinonia* when the faith of Christians is so strong that it issues in coin-o-nia.

Outline:
1. The resurrected Christ took the form of a new kind of community
2. *Koinonia* is the word that describes the nature of this community (define *koinonia*)
3. They had all things in common
   — they shared their worship (v. 46)
   — they shared their homes and food (v. 46)
   — they shared their praises (v. 47)
4. That which really set them apart was the generous sharing of money and material goods (v. 45) (Coin-o-nia)
5. We witness to the risen Christ when coin-o-nia is at the heart of our *koinonia*

*　*　*　*　*

There is a pattern in laying bricks that greatly strengthens the structure under construction. It is called the common bond pattern. Every so often a brick (called a header) is laid crossways to the other bricks, so that brick ties together two other bricks. This process creates a bonding that is hard to break. A house or a wall so constructed will endure a very long time.

Bonding is a fact of nature. All things, including the human body, are held together by chemical bonds. For instance, our body is made largely of water and water contains two hydrogen atoms bonded with one oxygen atom. The science of chemistry consists of studying the nature of these bonds and discovering how these bonds can be broken and to what effect.

A major aspect of religion is learning how spiritual bonds are established, maintained, and then reestablished when they are broken. The word "religion" indicates that which binds together. The early Christian community was tied together by its common bond — Jesus Christ. Their love for and loyalty to their risen Lord and Savior tied them to one another. They freely gave of their time, talents, and treasure because they all belonged to God through Jesus Christ, who had redeemed them from the power of sin.

*　*　*　*　*

Some people are too cynical and selfish to feel the common bond with other humans. We see such a character in the person of the king in the *Wizard of Id* comic strip. The king is departing Easter services at the village church and the Padre asks him how he liked the sermon (The topic on the bulletin board is "He Is Risen").

King — "It's a good story, Padre, but face it, Who's gonna believe it?"

Padre — "The peasants believe it."

King — "Peasants ... HA ... What do they know about anything?"

Padre — "They know that if he lives again, they will live again."

King — "Yeah, yeah, right."

In the next scene the king is in bed. He has apparently been thinking about his conversation with the Padre all day long. The king reflects ...

King — "If the little beggars live again ... I'll tax 'em ... (next frame) ... AGAIN." In the last frame, the king concludes: "Our God is good."

Lesson 2: 1 Peter 1:17-23

Sermon Title: Confidence Through Christ

Sermon Angle: Peter maintains that through Christ, the Passover Lamb, we have confidence in God. Contrary to the feel-good gurus, positive mental attitude is not sufficient to produce lasting confidence in the human psyche. Our confidence is grounded in that which is eternal and in the knowledge that our acceptance is not based on our achievements but in Christ's sacrifice.

Outline:

1. Social scientists tell us that self-esteem is essential for human well-being
2. Lack of self-esteem stems from a feeling of worthlessness
3. Our worth is shown by God's gift of Jesus (v. 21)
4. In Christ, we have confidence for this life and hope of glory in the next

Gospel: Luke 24:13-35

Sermon Title: Break Thou The Bread Of Life

Sermon Angle: The above title is the name of a hymn. The Bread of Life referred to here is the Bible, through whom we come to know Christ. According to John, Jesus himself is the Bread of Life. For the two travelers to Emmaus, Jesus broke the bread of life as he expounded the word but also as he blest and broke the bread for their evening meal. Christ has the power to nourish us through word and sacrament, because his life was offered as bread on the cross, where it was broken and offered to all.

Outline:

Introduction: In this text we find the structure of our worship service. It is the service of the word, the eucharistic meal, and the going forth to witness to the risen Christ. The service of the word occurred when Christ expounded the Old Testament to the two distraught travelers. The eucharistic meal took place when Christ broke the bread for the meal. The witness to the world, the third and indispensable part of worship, happened when the two men rushed back to Jerusalem to tell the other followers of the resurrection.

1. The service of the word
2. The service of the eucharistic meal
3. The service of worldly witness

Sermon Title: Jesus, Stay The Night

Sermon Angle: When the travelers got to the place of lodging, they implored Jesus to stay the night with them. He comforted their bruised souls. How desperately we need Christ when we tread the valley of the shadows. In effect, they were asking Jesus to stay with them until the night was passed. There is another sense to the word "stay." In this context it means "to stop" something from happening. Sometimes we implore God to keep the darkness away, to prevent us from being beset by adversity. God never promised to keep the darkness from our doorstep, but he has promised to share our darkness until the day breaks.

Outline:

1. Jesus shared the traveler's journey of grief and sorrow
2. These disciples were hurt and confused because Jesus was overcome by the darkness of suffering and death
3. They were comforted as the stranger pushed back their soul's darkness
4. Jesus accepted their invitation to stay the night
5. Jesus will stay with us during our night and, one day, he will prevent the night from descending

Easter 4

Revised Common:	Acts 2:42-47	1 Peter 2:19-25	John 10:1-10
Roman Catholic:	Acts 2:14, 36-41	1 Peter 2:20-25	John 10:1-10
Episcopal:	Acts 6:1-9; 7:2a, 51-60 or Nehemiah 9:6-15	1 Peter 2:19-25 or Acts 6:1-9; 7:2a, 51-60	John 10:1-10

Theme For The Day: God is our shepherd and guide. In the first lesson, the church appointed deacons to look after the needs of the church members. They were undershepherds, under the leadership of the apostles. In the second lesson, Peter states: "For you were going astray like sheep, but now you have returned to the shepherd and guardian of your souls" (v. 25). In the gospel, Jesus describes himself as the shepherd and door to the sheepfold.

Sermon Series Title For Easter 4: The Rock Proclaims The Good Shepherd

Suggested Text For Preaching: 1 Peter 2:19-25 (For sermon series)

BRIEF COMMENTARY ON THE LESSONS

Lesson 1: Acts 2:42-47 (C); Acts 2:14, 36-41 (RC)

See the first lesson for Easter 3 (C, E).

Lesson 1: Acts 6:1-9; 7:2a, 51-60 (E)

The idealistic picture of the Jerusalem church is beginning to show a crack or two. The Hellenistic Jews complain that the needs of their people are being neglected. The apostles decide to appoint seven men to tend the physical needs of the community. These are the undershepherds of the apostles. Among the seven is Stephen, noted for his demonstration of the power of God, who becomes embroiled in a dispute with Jews from abroad. Stephen hits hard as he points to their ancestors' record of having rejected and killed the prophets of old. In a great outpouring of anger, they drag him outside the city and stone him. As he is dying, Stephen reports that he sees Jesus at the right hand of God, which increases the vehemence of his enemies. Stephen falls to the ground pleading that God might forgive his murderers.

Lesson 2: 1 Peter 2:19-25 (C, E); 1 Peter 2:20-25 (RC)

The church is experiencing real persecution that severely tests the faith of the fledgling believers. Peter reminds his audience that the innocent suffering of the faithful will earn the approval of God. He recalls the example of the Lord Jesus, who suffered persecution and scorn but took it patiently. Christ is likened to the sacrificial or Passover lamb. He bore our sins on the cross that we might die to sin and rise to newness of life (v. 24). His bruises produce salve for our wounded souls. In verse 25, Peter switches the metaphor. Now, the Lamb becomes the shepherd and guardian of our souls.

Gospel: John 10:1-10 (C, RC, E)

Jesus is the good shepherd. In verses 1-6, Jesus describes himself as the good shepherd who enters the sheepfold by the door, in contrast to the thieves who sneak in some other way. He calls to his sheep and they respond to his voice and follow him. In verses 7-10, Jesus uses a related metaphor. He is the door to the sheep. To understand this figure of speech, picture a walled enclosure where the sheep are kept at night. The shepherd lays down in the doorway of the enclosure so that any thief or marauder would have to first pass over his body. Jesus pictures himself as that shepherd and door of the sheep, who is willing to protect the sheep from their enemies even at the cost of his life.

Psalm Of The Day
Psalm 23 (C, E) — "The Lord is my shepherd ..." (v. 1).

Prayer Of The Day
Dear Jesus, our shepherd and guide, when we wander from the safety of the flock that is called by your name, bring us back and protect us from the perils that threaten us from every side. Give us the discernment to hear and the wisdom to heed your voice. In your name we are bold to pray. Amen.

THEOLOGICAL REFLECTION ON THE LESSONS

Lesson 1: Acts 2:42-47; Acts 2:14, 36-41
See Easter 3.

Lesson 1: Acts 6:1-9; 7:2a, 51-60
Leadership in the church. This is the key issue in the first six verses of this lesson. Just as the father-in-law of Moses advised him to select qualified people to share the burden of leadership for the people of Israel, so, too, the apostles hit on the same strategy for the church. The church was no longer an informal band of believers; they were becoming an institution. The demands of growth necessitated a division of labor structure and organization. We have here the first distinction between the ministry of word and sacrament and the *Diaconia*, the ministry of service (v. 2). Certain people are called to the ministry of word and sacrament, while others are called to different ministries. The ministry of the word and sacrament is the progenitor of all other ministries in the church, but this is not to say that those who perform the former are more exalted than the latter. All leadership roles in the church are pastoral ministries. There are merely different fields of service and different styles of shepherding. If the needs of the church are to be met, there must be a division of labor.

Who is qualified to lead the church? Like other institutions, politics is often the prominent factor in deciding who leads the contemporary church. In choosing deacons, council representatives, elders, and the like, the candidate's spiritual qualities are all too often overlooked. It is noted in our text that Stephen, among the first deacons, was a man full of faith and the Holy Spirit (v. 5). These are among the kind of qualities that were paramount for the pristine church of Christ, not family connections, social standing, and the like.

Proclaiming law and gospel. In seminary, many of us learned that preaching ought to contain law and gospel. The law convicts of sin and the gospel declares God's gracious forgiveness. We don't have Stephen's entire sermon but what we do have is mostly law. What he said was true but more than they could take. We might ask: Where is the gospel in Stephen's sermon? It is the conclusion. "Lord, do not hold this sin against them" (v. 60). The gospel ought to be clearly visible in the conclusion of every sermon and at the end of every life. The word that we hear last is often the one that reverberates in our hearts. The gospel was primarily revealed in Stephen's gracious and forgiving spirit toward his enemies. The words that issued from this pure spirit reflect those of our Lord as he breathed his last on the cross (vv. 59-60). This left an indelible impression on a man who held the garments for Stephen's executioners. We know his name was Paul, the apostle of God's grace.

Lesson 2: 1 Peter 2:19-25

Suffering that saves. Secular people scorn the idea that suffering can have meaning or be redemptive. Yet, the gospel is founded on the veracity of this claim. What kind of suffering qualifies as redemptive? Suffering which is not the result of sin: the suffering of the innocent. Also, it is suffering that is an offering to God as a sacrifice or worship. Peter makes the distinction that the sufferer must be "aware of God," while suffering unjustly, if his suffering is to be redemptive.

The wounded healer. Christ has been referred to as the wounded healer. He suffered and died due to humankind's deadly malady, sin. In tones reminiscent of Isaiah 53, Peter states: "By his wounds you have been healed" (v. 24). A psychiatrist struggled with a very difficult patient. "I've done everything I know how to do but you are still the same," she sobbed. "I have failed to get through to you." From that moment, the patient began to show a dramatic improvement. She was moved by the depth of her therapist's love for her. The shared wounds of the healer and the afflicted person proved therapeutic for both. Healing for the soul can only come from the hand of those who have been wounded.

Gospel: John 10:1-10

Christians are doors to eternal life. Jesus speaks of himself as the door for the sheep. He is the entrance into the kingdom of God, the family of faith. As we follow him into a personal relationship with God, we begin to experience the dimension of eternal life. When we exhale our last breath, we will enter heaven through that same door. When we are in Christ we, too, are doors through which others come to know the joys of being members of the flock redeemed by Christ. Persons, not places, are the portal to eternal life.

Lead by example. Albert Schweitzer, I believe it was, said that "example was not the main thing, it was the only thing." Jesus said when the shepherd brings out his flock, "he goes before them." The shepherd did not merely point out the way for the sheep, he showed them the way. That's the way parents teach children, teachers instruct their pupils, pastors lead deacons, and deacons lead the congregation.

PREACHING APPROACHES WITH ILLUSTRATIONS

Lesson 1: Acts 42-47; Acts 2:14, 36-41
See Easter 3.

Lesson 1: Acts 6:1-9; 7:2a, 51-60

Sermon Title: Growing Pains

Sermon Angle: The church was greatly increasing in number, a sign of vitality, but with growth comes problems and pains. With new people, there was more diversity and cultural conflict. The Hellenistic Jews felt that their widows were being neglected. Plus, the greater size meant that the church leaders couldn't personally tend to the needs of all the people. The apostles wisely decided that they needed to share the leadership of the church. They delegated the diaconal aspects of the ministry to seven men chosen by the church at large and this helped alleviate some of the growing pains.

Sermon Title: The Church — Charismatic Institutionalism

Sermon Angle: The church was originally a charismatic community but the growth necessitated greater institutionalism. We might say that the church was, at this stage, a charismatic institution. This is what the church must strive for in any age. If the church is only charismatic, it cannot perpetuate itself and is likely to get carried away by excess. If the church is only institutional, it is dry as dead men's bones. Charismatic institutionalism suggests Spirit-led, yet disciplined communal life.

Outline:
1. The growth of the church led to new demands
2. The leadership task was too large for the disciples
   — they realized that they must share the burden
   — the church picked seven men and the apostles ordained them
3. The church was becoming institutional as well as charismatic
   — charismatic (Spirit-led, free, flexible)
   — institutional (division of labor, well ordered, traditions, procedures)
4. The church must guard against the dangers of being only charismatic or only institutional and become a charismatic institution

Sermon Title: The Legacy Of Leadership

Sermon Angle: The effectiveness of leadership can be discerned from the legacy it leaves behind. Back in the mid-1970s, Richard Nixon, mired in the Watergate scandal, left a legacy of cynicism and mistrust. Other national leaders, concerned only with their selfish interests, have left the same legacy. Stephen, the first Christian martyr, left a legacy of fearless faith and forgiveness. Wouldn't it be wonderful if all church leaders left such a legacy?

Lesson 2: 1 Peter 2:19-25

Sermon Title: The Ecstasy Of Agony

Sermon Angle: No, the title above was not crafted by a sadist. Suffering and pain are no fun, but they can transport us into ecstasy. That is, they can enable us to transcend ourselves. Likewise, the ecstasy of love can raise us out of ourselves and into the soul of the one we love. Our lesson reminds us that suffering for the sake of God or others can be redemptive, lifting us out of ourselves. It merits the Lord's approval (v. 19). Christ's suffering is the prime example of the ecstasy of agony. From the heightened perspective of the cross we can see our God, ourselves, and our neighbor.

Sermon Title: The Wounded Healer

Sermon Angle: "By his wounds you have been healed" (v. 2). Father Damien ministered for years to a leper colony on one of the Hawaiian islands, but without much success. That changed after he contracted the terrible disease and became one of them. Since he carried their sickness, he now knew what they felt and faced. He was now able to be a healing agent, because of his own wounds. If the church is to minister to the sickness of our society, we must do so not from a position above or below, but alongside of.

Sermon Title: The Rock Proclaims The Good Shepherd

Sermon Angle: The epistle proclaims that believers are not alone in their suffering and pain. Christ, the shepherd of their souls, has brought back the strays into God's fold (v. 25). He will protect and keep us until the end. Unlike the gospel, Peter does not use the adjective "good" in front of shepherd but would heartily agree. You might want to employ the psalm and the gospel to help make the following points.

Outline:
1. Christ is the good shepherd because he suffered and died for the sheep
2. Christ is the good shepherd because he died for our sins
3. Christ is the good shepherd because he forgave us our sins
4. Christ is the good shepherd because he guides and guards us (v. 25)

Gospel: John 10:1-10

Sermon Title: Windows And Doors

Sermon Angle: Christians might be compared to windows and doors. A little boy was transfixed by the stained glass windows in the magnificent cathedral. As the light cast its illuminating glow, he asked: "Mom, who are those people that the light shines through?" Her reply, "They are the saints, my son." The people of God are those whom the light of the divine shines through. In the reading from Acts 6, we see the light shining through Stephen as he breathed his last. He shared what he saw, "I see the Son of Man at the right hand of God...." The light of God's love glowed through his being as he pleaded for God to forgive his executioners.

In the second part of the gospel lesson (vv. 7-10), Jesus describes himself as the door to the sheepfold. By faith in him, we enter into the family of God. Some will try to climb in, says Jesus, but they are thieves and robbers (v. 1). We may try to climb in through respectability or by attaining a leadership position in the church or some other way. There is no way other than the door of Christ's forgiving grace. Christ, our door to eternal life, also shuts out those whose aim is to lay waste to God's sheep. We too are doors by which others enter into the fold of faith. How widely is it open?

Outline:
1. Stephen was a window to God's forgiving grace (What the apostle Paul witnessed may have led to his conversion)
2. We are windows to the eternal. How much light shines through?
3. Christ is the door to the family of God. Have we entered by faith?
4. We are Christ's door for others. Are we open?

* * * * *

During the civil rights era of the 1960s, a number of pastors became committed to the cause of social and racial justice. They joined protest marches and sit-ins, as well as preaching and teaching on the topic. In some cases, activist pastors of white congregations alienated their congregations, but in other instances they did not. What made for the difference? Studies have shone that a key factor was pastors. Those pastors who had not established a strong pastoral bond with their congregations, soon found themselves in trouble with their flocks. Other pastors who were equally committed to the cause of racial equality had little trouble. While many of their parishioners may have disagreed with them, they still respected their pastors because they had shown care and concern for them as individuals. They had called in their homes and been there for them in times of grief and trouble. Through their actions, they had revealed themselves to be the good shepherds. The sheep were ready to listen to the voice of their shepherd.

*   *   *   *   *

Leslie Newbigin, in his little book, *The Good Shepherd*, tells of a gathering of bishops which he attended. They were discussing the nature of the office of bishop and the various styles in which that office is lived out. One bishop voiced a rather traditional view of the bishop as Father. Another said that he viewed his job in light of Ephesians 4, that of equipping the saints for ministry. An American bishop cut through all the theological jargon. "I just say, 'Come on, let's go,' and they follow." Another participant commented on that remark. "That's all right if you understand the context in which our Lord said it. It was, as you recall, in the Garden of Gethsemane when he said, 'Arise, let us be going,' " and he went to his passion.

Easter 5

Revised Common:	Acts 7:55-60	1 Peter 2:2-10	John 14:1-14
Roman Catholic:	Acts 6:1-7	1 Peter 2:4-9	John 14:1-12
Episcopal:	Acts 17:1-15 or	1 Peter 2:1-10 or	John 14:1-14
	Deuteronomy 6:20-25	Acts 17:1-15	

Theme For The Day: Come into me. In the Episcopal first lesson, Paul has been secreted out of a couple of Greek towns. He leaves word that Timothy and Silas are to come to him as soon as possible so he can continue the work of building up the body Of Christ. In the second lesson, Peter urges his readers to "Come to Him (Christ), a living stone ..." and become living building blocks in the church. In the gospel, Jesus tells his disciples that no one can come to the Father but by him.

Sermon Series Title For Easter 5: The Rock Proclaims The Cornerstone

Suggested Text For Preaching: 1 Peter 2:4-10 (For sermon series)

BRIEF COMMENTARY ON THE LESSONS

Lesson 1: Acts 7:55-60 (C)

Stephen was the first Christian to be martyred for his bold witness that Jesus is the Christ. He preached both law and gospel. It was the law that enraged his audience because he accused them, as well as their ancestors, of being responsible for the death of Jesus. As he was dying, he saw the beatific vision and prayed that God would forgive his slayers. Stephen demonstrated the gospel with his last breath.

Lesson 1: Acts 17:1-15 (E)

Paul and his message continue to stir up a certain element among the Jews. His life is threatened in Thessalonica, to the degree that his followers spirit him out of the city. Not finding Paul and his entourage, the foes of the faith drag Jason and the other local followers of the *way* to the authorities. The accusation they level against them is really quite accurate: those who have "turned the world upside down." In Beroea, the gospel is well received. At least, the members of the synagogue were willing to consider the claims of the apostle. However, like hornets whose nest has been disturbed, the enemies from Thessalonica stir up the troops in Beroea also.

Lesson 1: Acts 6:1-7 (RC)

See first lesson for Easter 4 (E).

Lesson 2: 1 Peter 2:2-10 (C); 1 Peter 2:4-9 (RC); 1 Peter 2:1-10 (E)

Peter invites his readers to come to the living stone (Christ), rejected by men, but chosen and precious to God (v. 4). The believers are to be built into a spiritual edifice. Briefly, the image then shifts; they are to be a holy priesthood offering spiritual sacrifices. Peter comes back to the stone image, this time it is employed in reference to God, alluding to Isaiah 8:13-14, in which the Lord is the stumbling stone for Israel and Judah. God is the stumbling stone for those who disbelieve but the cornerstone for those who have faith. Peter applies to the church the prerogatives formerly accorded Israel — "a chosen race, a royal priesthood, God's own people...." To what end? "In order to declare the mighty acts of him who called you out of darkness into his marvelous light" (v. 10).

Gospel: John 14:1-14 (C, E); John 14:1-12 (RC)

This is the commencement of Jesus' farewell discourse that extends through chapter 17. He is preparing his disciples for his departure (ascension). He informs them that he will return for them and, in the meantime, he is going to prepare a place for them. Thomas expresses the confusion of the group: "Lord, we do not know where you are going. How can we know the way?" Jesus retorts: "I am the way, the truth and the life. No one comes to the Father but by me" (vv. 5-6). Jesus goes on to point out that they have seen the Father in him. The Father is in him and he is in the Father. Those who believe in him will do even greater things than he has done.

Psalm Of The Day

Psalm 31:1-5, 15-16 (C) — "Be a rock of refuge for me, a strong fortress to save me" (v. 3).
Psalm 33:1-11 (RC) — "Rejoice in the Lord, O you righteous ..." (v. 1).
Psalm 66:1-11 (E) — "Make a joyful noise to God, all the earth ..." (v. 1).

Prayer Of The Day

O Lord, you are the rock of our salvation, you are the foundation upon which we live, move and have our being. Forbid that we should craft our lives on the shifting sands of earthly gain and lead us safely to our eternal home with you. In the strong name of Jesus. Amen.

THEOLOGICAL REFLECTION ON THE LESSONS

Lesson 1: Acts 7:55-60

See Easter 4, Theological Reflection On The Lessons, *Proclaiming Law And Gospel.*

Lesson 1: Acts 6:1-7

See Easter 4.

Lesson 1: Acts 17:1-15

The scandal of the cross and resurrection. Paul always went to the heart of the most thorny issue for those with whom he was sharing his newfound faith, the cross, and resurrection. This mode of operation is evidenced in verse three. The sufferings of the Messiah and his resurrection were a scandal, a stumbling stone. They couldn't see why it was necessary. That is still our task today as we present the gospel to would-be believers. Not only is Christ's suffering a stumbling stone but also the present pain of God's people. What kind of a God would permit this, you ask?

Turning the world upside down. That was the accusation which the mob leveled at Paul and his associates. How true! They were turning the world upside down. Revolutionary stuff, this Christianity. Paul and the other apostles did not try to transform the political system or the institutions of society, but their concept of God and humankind redefined both. Yet for many contemporary Christians, Christianity is the epitome of the status quo.

Lesson 2: 1 Peter 2:1-10

Christ the living stone, the foundation stone, the cornerstone. We often think of rocks as being dead, inanimate matter, containing the skeletons of the past. Thus, the metaphor of Christ as the "living stone" seems strange. Modern science informs us that rock, and other so-called inanimate matter are really a microcosm of whirling subatomic particles. What Peter may be alluding to is that stones become living when they are shaped and formed into an edifice, where living takes place. Christ is that living rock, the cornerstone of the church, the foundation of our lives. As the foundation stone, he is the platform upon which our lives are constructed. Because of the strength and permanence of that foundation, we can rest assured. The cornerstone served the function of knitting the walls together. As a cornerstone, Christ knits together our lives and gives our existence shape and form.

Stumbling stone or precious stone. Peter takes off on Isaiah 8:13-14 and shows how the one stone can differ radically, depending on the attitude of the person. For the nonbeliever, Christ is a stumbling stone of offense. For those who are being saved, Christ is a precious stone. When a builder constructs an edifice out of stone, he may reject a certain stone. In his crucifixion, Christ was rejected but through his resurrection God made him the chief cornerstone (v. 7).

Gospel: John 14:1-14

A place prepared. We normally think that we must get ready for Christ's coming. This passage speaks of Christ preparing a place for us. What does that mean? Is Christ building tract houses in the heavenly realm? Hardly. It has been suggested that he builds our eternal home with the materials that we send him. Actually, does it really make a lot of sense to describe heaven as a place? Isn't heaven and hell determined by our relationship with the Lord? Heaven is any place where the Lord is and hell is any place where God does not dwell. "I go and prepare a place for you." What the Lord is really saying here is that we shouldn't be afraid of death. If we know him, we will always be with him. He is the Lord, but also our gracious host, who opens his arms of welcome to us at the end of our life's journey.

Many rooms. Could this possibly mean that heaven will be an inclusive, rather than exclusive, state of being? Many people think of the heavenly home as hemmed in by all sorts of zoning regulations. Only those who believe as I do will enter the gates of glory, they think. It makes sense that the one who ate with sinners and tax collectors, will welcome many whom we have deemed wanting. What the Lord seeks above all is a repentant and trusting heart.

The way to the Father. Yet the way to God is very specific. Jesus said, "I am the way, the truth and the life; no one comes to the Father but by me" (v. 6). There is no other way to come to God except the way of forgiveness and trust, revealed by Christ, our Lord.

Greater works than Christ? Jesus said, "He who believes in me will also do the works that I do, and greater works than these will he do, because I go to the Father" (v. 12). Jesus did marvelous things but only reached a comparative few during his lifetime. The church has reached, healed, fed, and saved hundreds of millions. It was and is possible not through human might or power but by Christ's Spirit.

PREACHING APPROACHES WITH ILLUSTRATIONS

Lesson 1: Acts 7:55-60

Sermon Title: Shout It Out

Sermon Angle: These verses report two different loud shouts. First of all, the angry shouts of a mob enraged by Stephen's accusations (v. 57). Their shouts, accompanied by the covering of their ears, was intended to drown out the preaching of Stephen. The loud shout came from the mouth of Stephen. He shouted out with a loud voice: "Lord, do not hold this sin against them." The first is a shout for blood, but the latter is a shout for peace. The one shout issues in the death of body and soul, but the other results in life eternal. The one shout incurs guilt, and the other secures release from guilt. It is a natural thing to cry for the blood of our foes. It is a supernatural event when we cry out for God's mercy for our foes.

With this sermon title, you can play on a slogan of a nationally advertised cleaning product. The product is designed to unlock stains from clothing. Consumers are invited to "Shout It Out!" When the world is affronted, it cries out for blood, for revenge. It is a loud, discordant shout, that can boil the blood of those who hear it. Christians need to follow the example of Stephen and shout out even more loudly the glad news of God's forgiveness. Only the Spirit of Christ in us can shout out the stain of human hatred and sin.

Lesson 1: Acts 17:1-15

Sermon Title: When Upside Down Is Right Side Up

Sermon Angle: Paul met very stiff opposition in Thessalonica among the Jews. It got so hot that he was sent huffing out of the city. When they stormed Jason's house, where Paul had apparently been staying, they dragged some of the local believers to the authorities. To the magistrate, they characterized the Christian missionaries as "these men who have turned the world upside down" (v. 6). How true! The truth has a way of becoming upsetting, especially when it challenges our most cherished notions. But sometimes the world needs to be turned upside down, so that it can become right side up. The gospel of Christ turned the world upside down with its notion of human dignity and the equality of all individuals as they stand before God. In our day, when lawlessness is being flaunted and human freedom abused, we need to turn the world upside down. When normalessness is all the rage, we need to point to the *way*, which is Christ. Yes, we need to turn the world upside down so that God and his ways are right side up.

Lesson 1: Acts 6:1-7

See Easter 4.

Lesson 2: 1 Peter 2:1-10

Sermon Title: The Rock Proclaims The Cornerstone

Sermon Angle: The one whom Christ dubbed the "Rock" refers to Christ as a stone: a precious cornerstone (v. 6). The cornerstone helped to knit the walls together and give them strength and substance. The church is a living edifice, composed of individual believers who are the living stones. It is Christ who knits our lives and our church together, not as a dead monument but as a vital and breathing structure. However, what is the cornerstone for us becomes a stumbling stone for those who will not believe the gospel.

Outline:
1. Stone is a symbol of that which endures
   — Christ is the foundation stone of our faith
   — Christ is the cornerstone of the church
   — Christ is the stumbling stone of offense to nonbelievers but precious to those who have faith
2. Come to Christ, the living stone and be
   — an integral part of the living church
   — offer spiritual sacrifices to God — obedience, prayer, praise ...

* * * * *

Michaelangelo would search the quarry near Florence, Italy, for just the right piece of marble for his works of art. A particular sculpture would call for a particular piece of rock. One day, a friend observed Michaelangelo methodically examining a particular block of stone. "What are you doing?" he asked. The master quickly replied; "I am seeking to release the angel within the stone." For Michaelangelo, that stone was truly alive.

* * * * *

The church is strongest when all of her members (the living stones) work together, as one body, for worship and witness. Charles Colson in his book, *The Body*, tells of the struggle of some Polish workers to build a church near their factory in Nowa Huta (New Town). At first, the officials acceded to this demand but later recanted their approval. The struggle commenced. The workers erected a wooden cross on the site of the church and held a mass there every evening. The officials tried to disperse them with water canons. That didn't work, so they destroyed the cross at night. In the morning the workers would erect a new cross. Through their struggle to build the church building, which went on for years, the workers came to realize the true nature of the church. The church is not a place but the people of God, celebrating the presence of Christ in their midst. Eventually, the struggles of those Christian workers bore fruit. Karol Wojtyla, who would later become Pope John Paul II, officiated at the dedication of a place of worship on that field of conflict. The workers were indeed living stones, knit together by Christ, the cornerstone, and their common faith.

Gospel: John 14:1-14

Sermon Title: Room At The Top

Sermon Angle: Jesus said: "In my Father's house are many dwelling places. If it were not so, would I have told you that I go to prepare a place for you?" We live in a day when the competition for the most prestigious and well paying positions is fierce. There is less room at the top than there was a decade ago. Many highly educated and skilled people have to take jobs for which they are overqualified. Jesus assures his disciples that no matter how tough life becomes, there is always room at the top, in the heavenly dwelling place, for those who love him.

Sermon Title: Show Me The Way To Go Home

Sermon Angle: The above phrase is contained in a drinking song: "Show me the way to go home. I'm tired and I want to go to bed. I had a drink about an hour ago and it went straight to my head." This silly song has a serious side to it. Many people are lost. They don't remember

190

the way to go home. In an attempt to override their anxiety, they have drunk deeply of this world's pleasures, which further muddled their sense of direction. Someone needs to show them the way to go home. Jesus offers himself as the way, the truth and the life (v. 6).

Outline:
1. We all need to be at home with others and God
2. Sin has disturbed our homing instinct
3. Jesus offers himself as the way, the truth, and the life
4. Come home to God through him

Easter 6

Revised Common:	Acts 17:22-31	1 Peter 3:13-22	John 14:15-21
Roman Catholic:	Acts 8:5-8, 14-17	1 Peter 3:15-18	John 14:15-21
Episcopal:	Acts 17:22-31 or	1 Peter 3:8-18 or	John 15:1-8
	Isaiah 41:17-20	Acts 17:22-31	

Theme For The Day: Making God known. In the first lesson, Acts 17:22-31, Paul witnesses to the cultured pagans on the Areopagus. Referring to a statue to an unknown god, he declares that unknown God is revealed in Christ. In the second lesson, 1 Peter 3:15-22, Peter encourages the beleaguered Christians to make Christ known through their words and actions. In the gospel, Christ promises that he will make himself known to the disciples through the Holy Spirit.

Sermon Series Title For Easter 6: The Rock Proclaims Purity Of Conscience

Suggested Text For Preaching: 1 Peter 3:15-22 (For sermon series)

BRIEF COMMENTARY ON THE LESSONS

Lesson 1: Acts 17:22-31 (C, E)

Paul alters his approach in an attempt to reach the cultured pagans of Athens by correlating the gospel to the cultural context. Later, in 1 Corinthians, we see that he repudiates this approach in favor of presenting an unvarnished version of the gospel. Rather than quote scriptures, he quotes pagan poets. He begins on a positive note, by observing that they are very religious, even having a shrine to an unknown God. This unknown God was not far from them; he desires that people seek and find him. Paul reveals that this unknown god has been revealed in Jesus Christ. In the past, God overlooked their disobedience but now was calling on all people to repent.

Lesson 1: Acts 8:5-8, 14-17 (RC)

Philip travels to Samaria and exerts a powerful witness to the risen Christ. Many miracles of healing and deliverance are evidenced, and the people gladly pay heed to his witness. Later, Peter and John travel to the region and lay their hands on the believers, so that they might receive the Holy Spirit. Previously, they had only been baptized in the name of the Lord Jesus.

Lesson 2: 1 Peter 3:13-22 (C); 1 Peter 3:15-18 (RC); 1 Peter 3:8-18 (E)

Peter urges the persecuted church to always be ready to give witness to their faith but without bitterness or rancor. By so doing, they will maintain a clear conscience. He calls to mind the example of Christ, who suffered for doing what is right. They too need to be ready to suffer for doing right, not wrong. Peter makes a rather obscure allusion to the spirit of Christ going to Hades or Sheol, witnessing to the spirits of those who were disobedient during the time of Noah and the flood. He correlates this to Christian baptism which saves us by washing our consciences clean.

Gospel: John 14:15-21 (C, RC)

Jesus continues his farewell discourse, urging them to keep his commandments out of love. He will pray to the Father to send them another counselor (to take the place of Jesus), referred to as the Spirit of truth. Those who do not believe cannot receive the Spirit. Jesus speaks of the Spirit as both a present possession and a future gift. Those who keep Christ's commandments will experience the love of the Father and the Son in their lives.

Gospel: John 15:1-8 (E)

Jesus uses the analogy of the grapevine stem with its radiating branches to illustrate that the believer can stay alive only through intimate communion with Christ. Apart from Christ, the believer can do nothing of eternal significance.

Psalm Of The Day

Psalm 66:8-20 (C) — "Bless our God, O peoples ..." (v. 8).
Psalm 65:1-7, 16, 20 (RC) — "Cry to God with joy ..." (v. 1).
Psalm 148 (E) — "Praise the Lord ..." (v. 1).

Prayer Of The Day

Spirit of God, our hearts spill over with boundless praise that you have made yourself known to us through the death and resurrection of our Lord Jesus. By your power, make us always ready to make our witness known to those who dwell in the darkness of unbelief. In Jesus' name. Amen.

THEOLOGICAL REFLECTION ON THE LESSONS

Lesson 1: Acts 17:22-31

We are one. "From one ancestor he made all nations ..." (v. 26). With the so-called ethnic cleansing that took place in what was formerly Yugoslavia and ethical/racial conflicts in many other parts of the world, we need to be reminded that we are one human family. Since God created us all, we are sisters and brothers.

Moral responsibility. Paul contends that God has overlooked the times when human beings disobeyed God's law out of ignorance (v. 30). We might equate this with humankind's age of ignorance. Here is a loose analogy. A child commits a crime but is too young to understand the extent of his offense. He may be released to his parents' supervision or, perhaps, judged in the juvenile rather than the regular courts. Guilt is punishable only if there is sufficient maturity and knowledge of one's actions. Paul further suggests that, in Christ, God reveals the ramifications of our actions, our sins. We are morally accountable. It is time to repent because God has set up Jesus to be our judge.

Lesson 1: Acts 8:5-8, 14-17

Completed Christians. Charismatics make a distinction between water baptism and the baptism of the Spirit. Those who have both baptisms are referred to as completed Christians. Passages such as this one give theological credibility to such a distinction. These Samaritans were baptized in the name of Jesus but not the name of the Holy Spirit. Peter and John finished the job. There are those who believe in Christ and yet their lives lack spiritual dynamism. Their faith doesn't move them. The Holy Spirit is the animating force by which God is able to complete that which he has begun.

Lesson 2: 1 Peter 3:13-22

How to keep a clear conscience? Peter appeals to believers to keep their consciences clear. Their newfound faith was constantly being challenged by unbelievers. It would be quite natural to lash out against those who were critical. Peter says, "No." Be ready to witness to the hope that you have but in a spirit of gentleness (v. 15). What does this mean? Don't attack the person who is challenging you or hurl unflattering names at them. Differences between ideas should not lead to rifts between persons. Don't address your foe with a haughty demeanor but witness to your faith in a spirit of love. Often, the things that weigh heavily on our consciences arise from an outburst of anger when that which is sacred to us is challenged.

Baptism saves us (v. 21). Noah and his family were saved through the waters of the flood. In like manner, believers in Christ are saved through the waters of baptism. Baptism signifies that we have died to sin and been raised with Christ to newness of life. While baptized persons are not free from sinning, we are free from its damning and controlling power. Our consciences are clean and clear because we are forgiven and accepted through our life in Christ.

Gospel: John 14:15-21

Keep your eyes on Jesus. Jesus said: "If you love me, you will keep my commandments" (v. 15). The verb here is *toreo* which means "to watch." It is closely related to another Greek word, which means to guard from loss, by fixing the eyes upon. The Jews quite literally kept their eyes on God's commandments by putting them in little boxes by the doors to their houses and placing them in little leather boxes attached by thongs to their foreheads. Jesus' command is that we love him, first of all, and then love each other. If we keep our eyes on Jesus through prayer and worship, we will be sure to keep his commandments.

Home alone. Perhaps you've seen the movie by this title. A large family grouping goes on a Christmas vacation, accidentally leaving a ten-year-old son behind. When they reach their distant destination they realize their omission but are unable to quickly book a return flight. In the meantime, robbers try breaking into the family house but the youngster is able to foil their schemes. Jesus wanted the disciples to know that when he ascended they would not be left home alone. He would pray to the Father and he would send another counselor (paraclete). Christians are never left home alone; God is present through his Spirit.

Paraclete. The word that John uses for the Holy Spirit is *parakletos*, translated comforter, counselor, advocate, or friend. The underlying idea is to have someone there beside you, to speak on your behalf and to advise you, like an attorney. The major difference is that the attorney works for money, while the paraclete is there out of love.

PREACHING APPROACHES WITH ILLUSTRATIONS

Lesson 1: Acts 17:22-31

Sermon Title: Marketing The Faith

Sermon Angle: Paul was the best salesman for Christianity in the history of our faith. It sounds crass, but it's true. He had a passion for trying to convince people to accept the gospel, not to enrich himself, but them. In our text, we find him on the Areopagus, a hill overlooking the city of Athens, where people traded the latest ideas and philosophies. These learned men had a hard time buying the veracity of the resurrection. It seemed so unreasonable. This is one instance where Paul tried to dress Christianity in the latest philosophical fashion, to make it more appealing and acceptable. This strategy didn't work too well and, as far as we know, he did not try this approach again. He vowed that he would present the gospel of the crucified and risen Lord in all its offensiveness, realizing that the gospel doesn't need to change, people do. In Augustana Lutheran Church in Omaha is a banner with this message: "Proclaim the gospel — with words, if necessary." The best way to sell the gospel is to live it.

Sermon Title: Making God Known

Sermon Angle: Paul's life was devoted to making God known through Jesus Christ. The altar to an unknown God, which he observed in Athens, illustrates the plight not only of the pagan world but of many who call themselves Christians. They have concepts and ideas about God but they do not know him either intellectually or through experience. The task of the church is to reveal the way by which the world might come to personally known God, through his Son.

Outline:
1. The non-Christian world worships some unknown god
   — explain that a god is anything around which our lives revolve
2. Yet, in our hearts we want to know God (v. 27)
3. Through the risen Christ we come to know the unknown God
4. Repent of your sins and trust in the living Christ (v. 31)

You could develop the above theme into a three-point sermon using three different lessons to drive home the theme of *Making God Known*. The texts and the three points are contained in the Theme For The Day.

Lesson 2: 1 Peter 3:13-22

Sermon Title: The Rock Proclaims Purity Of Conscience

Sermon Angle: Peter lifts up the notion of a clear conscience, or a pure conscience, two times in this text: once, in reference to witnessing and once in regards to baptism. In baptism, we have the assurance that our sins are washed away; our conscience is clear, because we are forgiven in Christ. A pure conscience is, first of all, a gift from God. Then, with the help of God, we keep our consciences clear and clean by loving our enemies, returning good in place of evil.

Outline:
1. Because of his denial of Christ, Peter must have had a guilty conscience
2. The resurrected Christ accepted him and cleansed his conscience
3. Baptism is the sign we are accepted and forgiven (v. 21)
4. God will keep our consciences clean if we regularly return to our baptism through repentance

*　*　*　*　*

In the movie, *Casualties Of War*, five American soldiers are on patrol in Vietnam. The sergeant in command decides to kidnap a young Vietnamese woman, so the soldiers can take turns raping her. Two of the group object. One of them has a rosary around his neck, and when the group pressure wears him down, he takes off the crucifix, places it in his pocket, and then takes his turn raping the terrified girl. Only one of the men refused to participate in this despicable crime. Only one listened to his conscience and, thereby, kept it clean. At risk of his life, he reported the crime. This story really happened. To protect his life, he now lives in anonymity.

The account illustrates what can happen when we lose our moral compass, when people believe that the world is devoid of moral values. The conscientious soldier in the story commented that just because they were living in an environment where they could get blown away any second, that they could do anything that they wanted and it didn't matter. He felt that it was the other way around. Precisely because they could get blasted away any second, they had to be extra careful about what they did; what they did mattered even more.

* * * * *

We change language as a means of lessening the burden of guilt, which can weigh heavily on our consciences. We use words like *disinformation* or *misspoke*, which makes lying seem like something that happened by accident. It is an attempt to whitewash our consciences.

* * * * *

In spite of much good that President Nixon did, his administration will always be defined by the Watergate Scandal. He ordered his advisors to stonewall the investigators. The wrong that was done was not as destructive as the attempt to cover it up. The only way to clear one's conscience is to come clean through confession.

Unfortunately, modern culture still teaches the value of concealing one's wrongdoing. In the Woody Allen film, *Crimes And Misdemeanors*, Judah Rosenthal, a successful ophthalmologist goes to the ultimate extreme in trying to conceal an affair from his wife. His lover is determined to reveal their affair and blow apart his comfortable existence. When other efforts fail, he accepts his brother's offer to find someone to kill her, rather than take a rabbi's advice to come clean. At first, he is beside himself with guilt. "Oh, my God, what have I done?"

Eventually, his guilt fades away, after it becomes clear that he is not going to be caught in the web of justice. The modern notion of conscience seems to equate guilty conscience with getting caught rather than doing wrong. It is reasoned: since I didn't get caught, what I did must not have been all that bad.

Gospel: John 14:15-21
Sermon Title: Public Defender
Sermon Angle: If a person is accused of a crime and can't afford a lawyer to defend him, the state appoints and pays for a public defender. No one has to face the judgment seat alone, unless he refuses legal representation. Before Jesus left his disciples, he promised that he would send the Holy Spirit, the Paraclete. This term is variously translated as comforter, counselor, or advocate. We have here a legal image merged with a personal image. Like an attorney, the Spirit is there to speak on our behalf, to represent us before the throne of grace, but the Spirit is more than a legal representative — he is our companion and friend.

Sermon Title: Someone To Watch Over Me
Sermon Angle: No matter what our age, we are still children at heart. We may think that we are completely independent. Not so: we need someone to watch over us, to shepherd and guide us. God has sent such a presence to those who trust in Jesus, the Holy Spirit. The three English

translations of the Greek *parakletos* — advocate, counselor, and comforter — provide the outlines for this sermon. The idea behind *advocate* is that the Spirit is there to speak on our behalf, to defend us from the enemies within and the enemies without. The term *counselor* is similar to the previous title but conveys the sense that the Spirit enables us to make the right decisions and choices. Finally, *comforter* informs us that the Spirit is our friend, who doesn't necessarily tell us what to do, but is there for us when we are hurting.

Outline:

Introduction: When Jesus told the disciples that he was going away, they must have felt like they were being left to the lions. Jesus assures them that they will not be alone. He will ask the Father to send the Holy Spirit.

1. To be our *advocate*
2. To be our *counselor*
3. To be our *comforter*

Conclusion: Let the Spirit also work **through** you to be advocate, counselor, and comforter in the lives of others.

The Ascension Of Our Lord

Revised Common:	Acts 1:1-11	Ephesians 1:15-23	Luke 24:44-53
Roman Catholic:	Acts 1:1-11	Ephesians 1:17-23	Matthew 28:19-20
Episcopal:	Acts 1:1-11 or	Ephesians 1:15-23 or	Luke 24:49-53 or
	Daniel 7:9-14	Acts 1:1-11	Mark 16:9-15, 19-20

Theme For The Day: The risen, ascended, and exalted Christ. Both Acts 1:1-11 and Luke 24:44-53 relate the story of the ascension according to Luke. The account from Ephesians 1 exalts Christ as having all things put under his authority.

BRIEF COMMENTARY ON THE LESSONS

Lesson 1: Acts 1:1-11 (C, RC, E)

In introducing his book, Luke notes to Theophilus that he is taking up where he left off with his gospel. The gospel ends with the witness to the resurrected Christ and Acts begins by bringing to a close this forty-day string of appearances. The disciples are still anticipating a kind of earthly reign (v. 6), but Jesus tells them not to be concerned with God's chronology but to wait for the baptism of the Holy Spirit, which would empower them for witness to the world. Having said this, he rose out of their sight. Two angels ask them why they are gazing heavenward. Jesus would return in the same manner in which they witnessed him go.

Lesson 2: Ephesians 1:15-23 (C, E); Ephesians 1:17-23 (RC)

This poetic passage exalts Christ as the sovereign who is above every authority and power throughout the universe. God has put all things under his feet. Christ assumes this power not just for his benefit but for the sake of his body, the church (v. 22). The power of Christ's resurrection is manifested in the lives of believers and in the church.

Gospel: Luke 24:44-53 (C); Luke 24:49-53 (E)

The risen Christ interprets to his disciples how his ministry, especially his death and resurrection, is a fulfillment of the scriptures. The purpose of this is that forgiveness of sins might be offered to all nations, beginning in Jerusalem. He reminds them that they are witnesses of all these things, but that they should wait until they have received the promised Spirit from on high. Christ led his disciples to Bethany, and while he lifted his hands in blessing, he ascended to the Father. The disciples responded to these events with unsurpassed joy and praise as they worshiped continually in the temple.

Gospel: Matthew 28:19-20 (RC)

Christ claims that all authority has been given to him by the Father. He commands his disciples to go and make disciples of all nations, baptizing them in the name of the Father, and of the Son, and of the Holy Spirit.

Psalm Of The Day

Psalm 47 (C, RC, E) — "God has gone up with a shout ..." (v. 4).

Prayer Of The Day

Mighty risen Lord, you rose above the plane of earthly existence, not to distance yourself from us, but that all who believe might know you and serve you through the gift of the Holy Spirit. Give us the wisdom to yield all authority unto you, that we might discover true fulfillment and joy in your service. In Jesus' name. Amen.

THEOLOGICAL REFLECTION ON THE LESSONS

Lesson 1: Acts 1:1-11

Wait for the promise. That's what Christ told his disciples shortly before he ascended. What promise? The Holy Spirit. We Americans are impatient people. We are reluctant to wait for what we want. We barge ahead and then become tired and discouraged when plans backfire. Jesus told his disciples to wait for the gift of the Holy Spirit, the power of the Spirit, without which their strength would soon flag. Waiting is necessary because it shows that the Lord is in control, not we ourselves. The apostles asked if God was going to restore the kingdom to Israel at that time. He told them that the times and seasons were God's prerogative, and that they needed to wait for him to act. How do we wait? Prayer is waiting for God to instruct, strengthen, and guide us. Isaiah proclaims: "They who wait upon the Lord will renew their strength, they will mount up with wings as an eagle, they will run and not be weary, they will walk and not faint" (Isaiah 40:31).

Times and seasons. When the disciples asked if he was going at that time to restore the kingdom to Israel, he replied: "It is not for you to know the times or the seasons which the Father has fixed...." The Greek words were are *chronos* and *kairos*. *Chronos* is a span of time, measurable time. *Kairos* is that special, God-appointed time. *Chronos* has to do with quantity of time. It is time which permeates all aspects of existence, giving it meaning and purpose. We don't know how much time (*chronos*) we have and we never know when God will invade our time in a special way with his holy presence. Our main task is to witness to the *kairos* (the life, death, resurrection, and ascension), which defines all time and eternity.

Get ready, he's coming back. As soon as Jesus ascended, two angels put a fire under them. What are you standing around gazing at the heavens for? Jesus is coming back the same way you saw him depart. Get about the tasks of the kingdom.

Lesson 2: Ephesians 1:15-23

The eyes of the heart. Paul speaks about having "the eyes of our heart enlightened" (v. 18). In the Bible, the heart is the vital center for human beings. The heart is considered the seat of the physical, intellectual, emotional, moral, and spiritual life in man. So the prayer of Paul is that God may open the eyes of the new believers in their vital center. You might say he's talking about seeing reality through the eyes of God's Spirit in us.

God's power. This passage speaks eloquently of God's power. We must be clear about the nature of this power. God's power is not a type of force by which God seeks merely to dominate us. No, God could do that any time he chose. God seeks to effect his power from *within us*. Verse 19 speaks of the "immeasurable greatness of his (God's) power *in us*" (RSV) but is translated "for us" (NRSV). Both prepositions reveal a different aspect of God's truth. God chooses to display his transforming power "in" us, when we yield him obedience. The proposition "for" us speaks to the qualitative dimension of God's power. God exercises and channels his power for our good.

Gospel: Luke 24:44-53

The Word interprets the word. The risen Christ opened the minds of his disciples to understand the scriptures (v. 45). Christ is the incarnate Word that unlocks and opens the door to understanding the scriptures. We can only rightly interpret the scriptures, and the God of the scriptures, through the gospel of Jesus Christ.

You are witnesses of these things (v. 48). All Christians are called to bear witness to that which they have seen and experienced in their relationship with the Lord. They are to witness to the reality of the risen Lord and the forgiveness offered in his name. Before we can fulfill this command, we must have something to witness to. That is, Christ must be a living reality in and through our lives.

Final blessing. In the television show, *Unsolved Mysteries*, there was the case of the brutal murder of an elderly man in ill health. He was bludgeoned to death with an iron by a vagrant. The son repined how horrible it must have been for his father to end his life staring into the face of a crazed killer, whose bloodied hands were raised in violence against him. In this passage, Luke reports that the Lord raised his hands in benediction as he was taken up into heaven. That image may well have been the final image before those witnesses were ushered into glory. What a comfort for every Christian to know that our Lord's final gesture was one of blessing, which he left behind as he ascended.

Gospel: Matthew 28:19-20

Mandate for mission. These verses disclose the church's reason for being: go, make disciples, baptize, and teach. There is good reason that this is not called the *Great Suggestion* or the *Great Guideline*. There is no option here; it is a command, an imperative. If the church forgets this truth, it becomes a club, a religious society to promote the self-interest of its members, not the living body of Christ.

PREACHING APPROACHES WITH ILLUSTRATIONS

Lesson 1: Acts 1:1-11

Sermon Title: Wait For Reinforcements Before Engaging In Battle

Sermon Angle: Jesus instructed them to wait in Jerusalem until they received the promise of the Father (the Holy Spirit). It's dangerous to engage in battle with a mighty foe until your forces have the edge. Better to wait for reinforcements than to jump presumptuously into the fray. Jesus realized that his modest cadre of troops was no match for the foe. That's why he instructed them to wait for the promised Spirit. This was done for the same reason Gideon, of Old Testament fame, weeded out his recruits by taking only those who lapped water like a dog. It was to show that power resides in the Lord, not in the strength of our army.

Sermon Title: Return Trip

Sermon Angle: The angels asked them why they stood gazing into the heavens. Jesus was going to come back the same way he went. You might think that this comment might have encouraged them to camp on the hilltop, telescope in hand. What the heavenly visitors apparently communicated to the disciples was that they need not worry; Jesus had not abandoned them. Not only had he bequeathed his Spirit to them, he was coming back to receive them into glory. Life is not a one way trip to nowhere but a round trip to our spiritual home.

Outline:

Introduction: When you book a vacation, you don't look for a one way flight but a round trip. The ascension was Jesus' return trip back to the Father. The angels assured that Jesus was going to return, but for what reason?
1. To judge all people
2. To establish the kingdom
3. To receive his own
4. To return us to our spiritual home

Lesson 2: Ephesians 1:15-23

Sermon Title: Dynamite

Sermon Angle: This pericope speaks eloquently of God's power. The Greek word here is dynamis, from which we get the name for dynamite. In the thinking of Paul, the power of God is preeminently revealed in the resurrection of his Son. But what kind of power is it?

Outline:
1. It is power *above* every earthly or heavenly power (vv. 21-22)
2. It is power *in us* who believe (v. 19)
3. It is power *for us* who trust in him
4. It is power *channeled through* and *for* the church (v. 22)

* * * * *

April 26, 1994, was a historic day for South Africa. For over four decades, the majority black population had been on the losing end of a power struggle, but that April 26, they were given the power of the ballot, the power to determine their own destiny. Years ago, Desmond Tutu, the Anglican Archbishop in that country made an ironic comment that I heard on the radio. This is the sense of what he had to say. "Most people would say that I'm a reasonably responsible individual. Yet, I cannot vote. At the same time, a nineteen-year-old man can vote simply because he's white." He shared how demeaning it was to be treated like children. The elderly and the infirm were given the privilege of being the first to exercise their right to vote. The television showed clips of them going to the polls for the first time. They hobbled on crutches, rode in wheelchairs. They got there any way they could, standing in long lines. The joy that they evidenced at the opportunity to exercise their power of franchise was truly inspiring. This happy day has dawned because individuals, Nelson Mandela and others, boldly witnessed to the truth.

Gospel: Luke 24:44-53

Sermon Title: I Witness News

Sermon Angle: Almost every television newscast in the country claims to be "Eyewitness News." They claim this title by virtue of the fact that they send photographers and reporters to the scene of newsworthy events, where they report what they have observed or others have witnessed. Christian witness to the resurrection is not so much *eye*witness news, since we came on the scene almost 2,000 years after the resurrection, but *I* witness news. The world will not know of the risen Lord or his love for us except through "I witness" testimony. Christianity is not as much dogma as it is truth, communicated through persons.

Sermon Title: The Church's Ho Hum Festival

Sermon Angle: Of all the holy days of the church, The Ascension Of Our Lord has to be the least understood. Most Christians regard it with apathy and ignorance. What is the significance of the ascension?

Outline:
1. It concluded Jesus' earthly ministry
2. It expanded the Lord's outreach through the church
3. It made available the Holy Spirit to the church
4. It allowed Jesus to prepare a place in heaven for his own (John 14:1-6)
5. It made forgiveness available to all (v. 47)
6. It shows that glory, not death, is God's final word (Hebrews 2)

Easter 7

Revised Common:	Acts 1:6-14	1 Peter 4:12-14; 5:6-11	John 17:1-11
Roman Catholic:	Acts 1:12-14	1 Peter 4:13-16	John 17:1-11
Episcopal:	Acts 1:(1-7) 8-14 or Ezekiel 39:21-29	1 Peter 4:12-19 or Acts 1:(1-7) 8-14	John 17:1-11

Theme For The Day: Prayer is the golden thread that ties together the three lections. Acts 1:12-14 states that after the ascension the disciples went back to the place where they were staying and devoted themselves to prayer (v. 14). The reading from 1 Peter advises the persecuted Christians to cast all their worries on the Lord (vv. 7-8). In the gospel, we find Jesus' high priestly prayer; as he faces the end of his earthly journey, he prays that the Father will keep his disciples faithful to his teaching.

Sermon Series Title For Easter 7: The Rock Proclaims Glory In Suffering

Suggested Text For Preaching: 1 Peter 4:12-17 (For sermon series)

BRIEF COMMENTARY ON THE LESSONS

Lesson 1: Acts 1:6-14 (C); Acts 1:12-14 (RC); Acts 1:(1-7) 8-14 (E)

The risen Christ orders his disciples to bear witness to him with the promise of the Holy Spirit to enable them to accomplish the same. The newborn community of faith then returns from the Mount of Olives to the place where they were staying in Jerusalem. The eleven apostles are named, together with Jesus' mother and his family. This is the last time in the New Testament where Mary is mentioned. The community devoted itself to the discipline of prayer, while it waited for the guiding and empowering presence of the Spirit. Verses 1-8 are contained in the first lesson for ascension. If no service was held on that festival, you might want to deal with that topic. At any rate, the text ties together ascension, just completed, with Pentecost, which is next Sunday.

Lesson 2: 1 Peter 4:12-14; 5:6-11 (C); 1 Peter 4:13-16 (RC); 1 Peter 4:12-19 (E)

Peter instructs the church not to be caught off guard by their sufferings and persecutions. To endure suffering for the sake of Christ identifies them with the Lord, in contrast to suffering which results from wrongdoing. The suffering referred to might be that which was instigated by Nero, around 64 AD. By this time, the term "Christian" was already in use (v. 16). Peter encourages the church to humbly accept their persecutions and to cast all their anxieties on the Lord (vv. 6-7). The persecutions are an attack of Satan (v. 8) and are to be resisted. Comfort derives from knowing that their suffering is shared by Christians throughout the known world (v. 9) and that, after a time of suffering, God will restore and strengthen them (v. 10).

Gospel: John 17:1-11 (C, RC, E)

This lection is part of Jesus' high priestly prayer, toward the end of the farewell discourse begun in chapter 13. The setting is the Last Supper. In his prayer, Jesus asks the Father to glorify the Son. For John, the glory of Christ is seen in the cross, as it is viewed through the lens of the resurrection. A developed Christology is evidenced here. Jesus refers to himself as Jesus Christ, which we see nowhere else in the gospels. Jesus communicates that he has finished the task that the Father assigned him, to confer eternal life on his own (v. 3) by making God's name and word known. Jesus prays that the Father will sustain the community in unity enjoyed by the Father and the Son (v. 11).

Psalm Of The Day
Psalm 68:1-10, 32-35 (C) — "Let God rise up, let his enemies be scattered ..." (v. 1a).
Psalm 27:1, 4, 7-8 (RC) — "The Lord is my light and my salvation ..." (v. 1a).
Psalm 47 (E) — "God has gone up with a shout ..." (v. 5a).

Prayer Of The Day
Dear Jesus, as you have made suffering glorious by offering up your life to the Father and for the world, teach us how to offer the unavoidable suffering of our lives up to you as our sacrifice of worship. We cast all our anxieties upon your strong shoulders. Lift us up and lead us on. In Jesus' name. Amen.

THEOLOGICAL REFLECTION ON THE LESSONS

Lesson 1: Acts 1:6-14
The upper room. In the same room where Jesus offered his life through bread and wine, which became his body and blood, the disciples returned after his ascension and devoted themselves to prayer. They were a community of pray-ers. There is a well-known and respected devotional booklet called *The Upper Room.* Surely, this title was inspired by this passage. We all need to go regularly to our upper room. It doesn't have to be a particular place, though that is a salutary idea. Our upper room is a space and time in our lives when we make our whole being available to God, praising the Lord and seeking his guidance.

(For other approaches on this text, see The Ascension Of Our Lord.)

Lesson 2: 1 Peter 4:12-19; 5:6-11
The pinnacle and the precipice. Few men have experienced the pinnacles and the precipices of life more than President Richard Nixon. He had an indomitable spirit. One of his favorite maxims was: "Failure is only fatal if you give up." His life began in adversity; his family was so poor that the children had to pass on their shoes to the next one in line. One of his brothers had asthma and so the mother took him to Arizona, leaving the other members of the family in California. In writing to her, he referred to himself as "your good dog." Because of this background, he didn't expect that life should be one continuous picnic. Defeat and adversity are as much a part of life and just as valuable, as are success and victory. Peter tells his readers, "Don't be surprised at the fiery ordeal which comes upon you...." The assumption is that adversity is integral to existence and that if we share Christ's suffering, we will also share his glory. If we don't bear the cross, we can't bear the crown.

The foot to the fire. Fire has traditionally been a symbol of God and, by association, the judgment of God. Fire consumes the impermanent, purges that which is tainted; consequently, it purifies. The "fiery ordeal" (v. 1) is a metaphor for judgment, which Peter mentions later in the passage (v. 17). Ordeal by fire is part of the religious tradition of India and some of the cultures in the South Sea islands. If a person can walk unscathed over a bed of red-hot coals, he or she is regarded as possessing the spirit of the god or gods. That's probably where we get the expression of putting one's foot to the fire. The fire of undeserved adversity and pain is truly an ordeal by fire. If our focus is not on the fire or our pain, but on the Lord, it will prove that we are the Lord's and improve the quality of our faith.

Who cares? When adversity strikes, we are tempted to think that nobody really cares, including God. Peter enjoins: "Cast all your anxiety on him because he cares for you" (v. 7). We forget that caring is not synonymous with sheltering. If we have children, we sometimes have to let them take their knocks. It's part of the learning and character building process. The same applies to our relationship with God.

The eleventh commandment. Years ago, a young woman asked me, "Pastor, you know what the eleventh commandment is?" "No," I responded. She retorted: "Thou shalt not sweat it." Peter is saying something similar in verse seven: "Cast all your anxieties on him...." There is a difference, though. Saying "don't sweat it" isn't very helpful. The cause of the anxiety may not be valid for someone else, but it is for the sufferer. When we enjoin another to cast his anxieties on the Lord, however, we are not dismissing his concerns but merely telling him to put the burdens on the Lord's back. He cares about us and will take our concerns seriously. Peter's advice is a little like the old Greyhound Bus commercial: "Leave the driving to us." God knows where you want and need to go. Put him in the driver's seat. Then relax and enjoy the ride, even when the road is rough and bumpy.

Gospel: John 17:1-11

Eternally yours. As Jesus was preparing to sign off the letter of his life, he spoke and prayed concerning eternal life in the presence of his disciples, of how life could be eternally theirs. Eternal life is more than length of days or duration of time; eternal life is more quality than quantity. Eternal life is life saturated with the awareness of God. Duration of endless time apart from God is hell. Jesus laid out the way to eternal life, to know the Father through the Son (v. 3). Knowing is more than acquaintance. It is a relationship of love, sharing, and intimacy. We need to tell the world that through such a relationship with Jesus life remains eternally theirs.

The shining. The word *doxa* (glory) is employed several times in this passage. God is glorified in Christ and Christ is glorified in those who belong to him. When the Bible uses this word or words closely related, it pictures a luminous presence associated with the holy. For example, the glorious presence of God was revealed to the Jews in the period of wilderness wandering through the pillar of fire. Moses reflected this same glory after his encounter with God on Mount Sinai. In this passage, glory correlates closely with obedience (v. 4). Jesus showed forth the glory of God because he was obedient unto death. Likewise, we are God's shining ones when we yield our lives in obedience to his word and his will.

Jesus is praying for you. My mother is a woman of prayer. I'm certain that she prays for me at least daily. It's wonderful to know that I'm being lifted up to the Lord continually. It's also great to know that we are on Jesus' prayer list. As our high priest, he is offering up the names of all those who belong to him, all who were imprinted with the name of the Holy Trinity at baptism.

The union label. Jesus prays that his disciples might be one just as the Father and the Son are. Their unity would show their union label, their union with the Father and the Son label.

PREACHING APPROACHES WITH ILLUSTRATIONS

Lesson 1: Acts 1:6-14

Sermon Title: The Upper Room

Sermon Angle: The followers of the Lord returned to the upper room following the ascension of the Lord. There, they devoted themselves to prayer. The upper room is that special place of prayer that each Christian must find. More than that, the church is the upper room community, which is strengthened and knit together through common worship of the glorified Christ.

Outline:
1. The upper room — the place where Christ offered his body and blood
2. The upper room — the place of safety and security
3. The upper room — the place where the risen Christ appeared
4. The upper room — the prayer powerhouse of the fledgling church
5. Spend time daily in the upper room

*   *   *   *   *

Billy Sunday, formerly a baseball player for the Chicago Cubs, received the call to become an evangelist. At that time, he held spellbound great throngs of people with his simple gospel message. It was Sunday's practice to pray for the leaders of a community, where he was about to have a campaign. At one point, he wrote to the mayor of Columbus, Ohio, and asked for the names of those whom he should be praying for. The mayor sent Billy a copy of the phone book.

My daughter got a card in the mail informing her that her pastor was praying for her that day. She belongs to a very large and speedily growing congregation, where the pastor knows very few of his parishioners. How can pastors effectively pray for their flocks if they don't know their parishioners? Jesus knew his disciples as he poured out his soul in ardent prayer in the upper room. It's comforting to know that Jesus is praying for us, for all those whose names are recorded in the Lamb's "Book Of Life."

Lesson 2: 1 Peter 4:12-14; 5:6-11

Sermon Title: The Rock Proclaims Glory In Suffering

Sermon Angle: The glory and power of God was ultimately revealed through Jesus' suffering and death. Peter maintains that as we share Christ's sufferings, we should glorify and praise God. Such suffering indicates we belong to the Lord and that we shall also share Christ's glory, when it is revealed in his second coming. To see glory in suffering necessitates seeing beyond the immediate pain to one's ultimate gain. It is difficult for American Christians to conceive how they might have to suffer for the sake of Christ. It needs to be pointed out how our culture is increasingly hostile toward traditional Christian values, as they relate to sexuality, family, and economics.

Outline:

Introduction: Our text was written to a persecuted church to enable them to hang in there. Peter reminds the flock that it is good and glorious to suffer for the sake of Christ. In American culture, Christians are not overtly persecuted, but our culture is increasingly in conflict with our values. (Give examples.) Peter proclaims glory in suffering for Christ; how can this be?
1. Glory and honor are not easily obtained but come to those who are willing to pay the price of suffering and pain

206

2. Such suffering purifies and proves our faith (makes it durable) (v. 12)
3. If we share Christ's struggles, we will also share his victory (v. 13)
4. Suffering for Christ shows that God's Spirit rests upon us (v. 14)

Sermon Title: The Fiery Ordeal

Sermon Angle: Peter refers to the persecutions, which the church was undergoing, as the "fiery ordeal" (v. 12). Fire is a metaphor for God's judgment. Sodom and Gomorrah were deemed so sinful that they were destroyed by fire; only Lot and his family survived. Shadrach, Meshach, and Abednego survived the fiery furnace of judgment because of their faith in God (Daniel 3). Peter predicts that the world will be destroyed through fire (2 Peter 3:7-12). Fire is a fitting metaphor for the judgment of God because it not only destroys, but also transforms and purifies, which is God's ultimate aim. Our English word "purify" derives from the primary Greek word in the New Testament for fire. Paul maintains that the endeavors of our lifetime will be tested "as by fire" (1 Corinthians 3:12-15).

Outline:
1. Fire is a biblical symbol and metaphor for God's presence
2. Fire also symbolizes judgment (v. 12)
3. The early Christians had to suffer the judgment of the world and so must we
4. Only God's judgment really matters
5. The aim of God's judgment is to purify

Gospel: John 17:1-11

Sermon Title: The Glow Of Glory

Sermon Angle: Just prior to his crucifixion, Jesus is praying that the Father would glorify the Son so that the Son might glorify the Father (v. 1). The word "glory" refers to the luminous and awesome presence of the Holy, such as was manifested by Moses on top of Mount Sinai. This luminous glory was shown by Jesus on the Mount of Transfiguration. For John, the glory of Jesus is revealed on the cross. The suffering and death of Jesus are glorious because they show forth the glory of God's saving love. Christians demonstrate God's glory in their suffering for the gospel, according to our second lesson.

Outline:
1. Jesus prayed that the Father would glorify the Son (v. 1)
2. The glory of God is seen more clearly in the cross of Jesus (The glow of God's glory is seen not in pomp and power but in sacrificial love.)
3. Christ's glory is revealed in his obedience, which led to suffering (v. 4)
4. We reveal God's glory in being willing to suffer in obedience to the gospel
5. Some day we will live in the light of God's eternal glory (vv. 10-11)

* * * * *

In the Old Testament, the meaning of the Hebrew word for glory (*kabod*) means literally to "be heavy in weight." A person who receives glory is one who carries a considerable weight of importance. To give glory and praise is to acknowledge the weight that the person carries in the community. We sometimes say of a powerful person: "He's a heavyweight" or "Look at him throw his weight around." On the scale of importance, God carries the greatest weight of authority and honor. That's why he deserves our honor and praise. Christ reveals a God not only glorious in power (though he doesn't simply throw his weight around), but also glorious in goodness and love.

*   *   *   *   *

In October of 1983, a crazed zealot steered a truckload of dynamite into the United States Marine compound, killing over 200 American soldiers. A few saw the face of the terrorist attacker as he gunned his truck toward the mark. They reported that he wore a smile on his face. There he was on a mission of destruction and death, and his face was lit with a smile. Is this the expression of a demented mind? Perhaps. It could also be the face of one who believed supremely in the rightness of his cause. He assuredly believed that he was about to enter the gates of paradise. The smile reflected the glow of misguided glory.

The apostle Paul also witnessed the smile of glory. It was on the face of Stephen, the first Christian martyr. As Stephen was being stoned, he looked up and was transfixed by the glow of glory (Acts 7:55). Paul observed that glory and was eventually transformed by it.

The Pentecost Season

Pentecost — Festival And Season

The festival of Pentecost marks the beginning of the second half of the church year. The first half of the church year, beginning with Advent and ending with The Ascension Of Our Lord, centers around the life of Christ. The Pentecost season is built around the life of the church. The focus is on the life of the believer.

The festival of Pentecost launches the season of Pentecost. The fantastic happenings of that first Pentecost are recorded in the second chapter of Acts. The risen Christ, according to Luke, told the disciples to wait in Jerusalem for the promised Spirit. This promise was fulfilled by the events reported in Acts 2. The Holy Spirit descended on the church with the sound of a mighty wind, tongues as of flame, and the ability to tell forth the gospel in other languages. Jews from many nations heard the gospel in their own tongues. This was a reversal of the Tower of Babel story, where human arrogance led to the breakdown of communication between people. The effect was increased differentiation among humankind, resulting in conflict and misunderstanding. The Spirit, given at Pentecost, is like a magnet that draws together disparate humanity. The Spirit comes as a unifying presence, whose aim is to enable humans and God to speak the same language.

Relationship Between The Jewish And Christian Pentecost

To avoid confusion, we need to differentiate between the Jewish Pentecost and the Christian Pentecost. The Jews observed the Feast of Weeks (Exodus 34:22; Deuteronomy 16:10) seven weeks after the Passover. It celebrated the giving of the law and the birth of the Jewish nation. Pentecost was also an agricultural festival, celebrating the harvest of first fruits (Exodus 23:10). The mood was one of celebration and thanksgiving. The Jewish Pentecost would attract throngs of people from all over the world. That helped make it a fitting setting for the Christian Pentecost. Representatives from all over the known world were galvanized into the new Israel. Pentecost marks the birth of the church, the new Israel of God, in fulfillment of the prophetic expectations that Israel would be a priestly people.

Meaning Of The Word Pentecost

Pentecost is a Greek word meaning fifty. The Jewish Pentecost arrives fifty days after Passover. The Christian Pentecost comes fifty days after the resurrection.

Symbols And Colors

The color for the festival of Pentecost is red, representing the tongues of flame. Fire and light have been associated with the divine from the dawn of time. In the biblical tradition, God called Moses out of the burning bush. God also led the Israelites out of Egypt by appearing as a pillar of smoke by day and a pillar of fire by night. Like the burning bush, the fire of Pentecost blazes as a non-consuming fire. The Spirit aims not to destroy but to create. The fire of Pentecost gave energy to the infant church, driving it out of its cloister and into the world. The Spirit, symbolized by wind and fire, made the disciples of Jesus burn with love and white hot zeal to proclaim the gospel. Three thousand were added to the church on the first Pentecost, after the preaching of Peter. The remainder of the Pentecost season is symbolized with the color green, because the Holy Spirit serves as our counselor, teacher, and guide, as taught by the gospel of John, through whom we grow in faith and love. Green is the color of life and growth.

The dove is also represented in this season, harking back to the baptism of Jesus. The gospel writers relate that the Holy Spirit descended on the Lord like a dove. Water serves as an appropriate symbol of Pentecost because the Spirit descended on Jesus, following his baptism by John the Baptist in the Jordan River. Likewise, the church has taught that God imparts the Spirit through Christian baptism.

Sometimes the number seven combines with the preceding symbols. Seven represents the number of completion, the length of our week. In the Christian church, this number represents the sevenfold gifts of the Spirit. These gifts of the Spirit are variously represented as seven doves, seven tongues of flame, or seven drops of water.

The Day Of Pentecost

Revised Common:	Acts 2:1-21	1 Corinthians 12:3b-13	John 7:37-39
Roman Catholic:	Acts 2:1-11	1 Corinthians 12:3-7, 12-13	John 20:19-23
Episcopal:	Acts 2:1-11 or	1 Corinthians 12:4-13 or	John 20:19-23 or
	Ezekiel 11:17-20	Acts 2:1-11	John 14:8-17

Theme For The Day: The gift of the Holy Spirit, as told by Luke (Acts 2:1-11) and John (the gospel). The 1 Corinthians 12 text has to do with the gifts of the Spirit in the church.

BRIEF COMMENTARY ON THE LESSONS

Lesson 1: Acts 2:1-21 (C); Acts 2:1-11 (RC, E)

The promised Spirit comes upon the church in the midst of the throngs of pilgrims that were making their way to the temple to celebrate the Jewish festival of Pentecost. The believers in Christ received the Spirit in dramatic and visible form, as tongues of flame and the ability to speak in other languages. This is not glossolalia because the pilgrims heard the church speak in their own language. The people are perplexed and amazed, and so Peter interprets the event as a fulfillment of Joel 2:28-29, that God would bestow his Spirit on all flesh, not just a select few. He urges the assembly to repent and be saved.

Lesson 2: 1 Corinthians 12:3b-13 (C); 1 Corinthians 12:3-7, 12-13 (RC); 1 Corinthians 12:4-13 (E)

Paul lays out some of the gifts which the Spirit supplies to the church, such as faith, prophecy, miracles, healing, and the like. He names nine gifts, but this should not be taken to be an all-inclusive catalog. No one has all the gifts of the Spirit, but we each have, at least, one of them.

Gospel: John 7:37-39 (C)

Jesus goes up to the temple unbeknownst to his family and teaches the crowds, assembled for the Feast of Tabernacles. On the last day of the feast, the Lord issues an invitation not unlike the one he issued in Matthew 11:28-30. Those who had a thirst for God were invited to come to him in faith, and from their hearts would flow streams of living water. Through Jesus would come the Holy Spirit after he was glorified. This invitation becomes vivid for those at the temple festivities because, every day during the feast, water would be drawn from the Pool of Siloam and taken to the temple. That practice was to portray God giving the children of Israel water from the rock, as they journeyed through the desert. Water remains the prime symbol of life, and Jesus takes it unto himself.

Gospel: John 20:19-23 (RC, E)

This is John's Pentecost story. The setting is not out in public, as in Acts, but in the upper room, where the disciples were cloistered behind locked doors. Suddenly, the risen Christ stands in their midst, granting peace to their fearful hearts. Christ commissions them to go out and spread the gospel. He then empowers them with the Holy Spirit and the authority to pronounce God's forgiveness.

211

Psalm Of The Day

Psalm 104:24-34 (C, E); Psalm 104 (RC) — "When you send forth your Spirit, they are created ... and you renew the face of the ground" (v. 30).

Prayer Of The Day

O Spirit of wind and fire, breathe into our souls your life giving and life sustaining Spirit. Fan the embers of our feeble faith into full flame, that we might boldly witness to your love and grace, through Christ our Lord. Amen.

THEOLOGICAL REFLECTION ON THE LESSONS

Lesson 1: Acts 2:1-21

Tower of Babel reversed. People of many different nations flooded into Jerusalem to worship God at the temple. It is no coincidence that God selected this time to pour out his Spirit. He desired to counter the divisive effects of race and nation. Pentecost reverses the Tower of Babel story, where humankind became fragmented, as evidenced by the confusion of language. At Pentecost, the believers did not speak the same language but were given the ability to speak the gospel in foreign languages. The Spirit still gives us the ability to speak in such a way that those from different backgrounds can hear the gospel comprehensively.

Word processing the Spirit. Those who witnessed the Pentecost drama were amazed and perplexed. They saw some wonderful things but didn't know what it meant (vv. 7-12). They needed a word processor to make sense of that which had happened. Peter stepped in to interpret the activity of the Spirit in light of the word of God and to call for a response.

Lesson 2: 1 Corinthians 12:3-13

Varieties of religious experience. William James wrote a book on this topic to portray the various ways that humans experience God. No two people worship and serve God exactly the same way. Faith is as unique as each of us. This results not only from our unique genetic makeup but also from the fact that the Spirit has gifted us with a special configuration of spiritual gifts. Paul says that there is only one Spirit but various gifts that flow from the same Spirit. God is not in the business of turning out carbon copies, only first edition masterpieces.

Gospel: John 7:37-39

Well within. Living in a semiarid part of the world, the Hebrews were always concerned that they be near a source of water. Aridity for the spirit is every bit as deadly as for the land. Jesus promises that those who come to him in faith will not only have their spiritual thirst quenched, but also that he will provide an artesian well of the Spirit that will continue to bubble up from within the believer. That promise was fulfilled at Pentecost. With the well within, all would be well therein.

Gospel: John 20:19-23

Pervasive peace. The disciples were still paralyzed with fear, even though in the morning Mary Magdalene reported that she had seen the risen Christ, even after Peter and John witnessed the empty tomb. Their basic sense that the world was a good and trustworthy place had been violated by the brutal murder of their Lord. Then the resurrected Lord appeared in their midst. Twice in our text he confers his peace. The world was still a dangerous and threatening place, but their fear vanished with the realization that they were not alone. Christ was with them, conferring the peace of his presence.

Exorcize your fears by exercising your faith. The way to overcome your fears is not to hide from them but to face them. Christ sent his little band of believers from behind closed doors out into the open to face the very people who had filled them with fear (v. 21).

Breathe on us, breath of God. Luke's version of Pentecost describes the impartation of the Spirit as the sound of a mighty wind. This occurred in a public setting. John's version of Pentecost has Jesus breathing on his disciples to impart the life-giving power of the Holy Spirit. This happened in a private setting. Both breath and wind are related. Sometimes the Spirit comes to us as a gentle breath, filling our inward being with life and hope. Other times, we experience the Spirit as a mighty wind of change that shakes everything in its path.

PREACHING APPROACHES WITH ILLUSTRATIONS

Lesson 1: Acts 2:1-21

This lection can be combined with the gospel from John to form a memorable sermon.

Sermon Title: The "Ps" Of Pentecost

Sermon Angle: The idea of God as Spirit is hard to get a handle on. We can relate to the idea of God the Creator and Jesus, the Son of God, our Savior, but the symbol of Holy Spirit is somewhat vague and mysterious, even dangerous. The other two persons of the Trinity lend themselves more readily to intellectual constructs, but the Spirit has to be experienced to be known. Nevertheless, we can attempt to understand the function of the Spirit by associating it with certain words that begin with "P." Based on the first lesson and the gospel, we will briefly discuss the "Ps" of Pentecost. Luke's Pentecost is different from John's but they both inform us concerning the manner in which Christians experience the Spirit.

From the account in Acts 2, we see how the Holy Spirit came down on the assembled believers in *power*. The Hebrew word for spirit is "wind." Most of us have witnessed the tremendous energy inherent in wind. A tornado can pulverize a house. A hurricane can bend a steel pole at a ninety-degree angle. The Acts account describes the descent of the Spirit as a mighty wind. The demonstration of the power of the Spirit caught the attention of the witnesses. When the Church is filled with the power of the Spirit, old barriers come crashing down, lives are healed and transformed. The greatest power that the church possesses is the reconciling power of forgiveness. This power must not be used to manipulate believers through guilt and fear but instead to free people from the paralyzing grip of sin.

The second "P" of Pentecost is *presence*. When Jesus appeared to the terrorized little band of believers in the Upper Room, as told by John, he lifted their spirits by his presence. They were no longer alone or forsaken. Jesus showed them his wounds that they might know it was him. If we know that God is with us and that his love reaches even the deepest valley of our souls, we can face almost anything.

The third "P" of Pentecost is *peace*. In John's account, Jesus repeats the greeting, "Peace be with you." The peace of Christ is not an absence of conflict but a total sense of well-being.

The fourth "P" of Pentecost is *prophecy*. According to Acts, those who witnessed the in-rush of the Spirit were perplexed. They didn't know what to make of this unusual event. They were even accused of being drunk. Peter stood up to explain what it all meant. He explained it as a fulfillment of the prophecy of Joel. Prophecy actually means "to speak forth or declare."

That's what Peter did, so that others could make sense of the signs and wonders. Such proclamation calls for a response: to repent and believe the good news of Jesus Christ. Any so-called manifestation of the Spirit needs to be interpreted through the lens of the Word Incarnate and the written word. Any manifestation at odds with the life and teachings of Jesus is to be rejected.

The last "P" of Pentecost is *purpose*. The Spirit does not act erratically. Behind the mystery is purpose. Peter interprets that purpose as being prepared for the "Day of the Lord" (v. 20) through repentance and faith. For John, that purpose is to make known the forgiveness of sins, through the power of the Spirit (vv. 22-23).

We could add an additional "P" of Pentecost for *personal*. The Holy Spirit is not an idea but a person. Our major task is not to understand the Spirit but to receive the Spirit into our person. The Spirit is given to all who know, trust, and walk with Jesus.

Outline:
1. Pentecost power
2. Pentecost presence
3. Pentecost peace
4. Pentecost prophecy
5. Pentecost purpose

Lesson 2: 1 Corinthians 12:3-13

Sermon Title: One Spirit, Many Gifts

Sermon Angle: Throughout this passage, Paul emphasizes that there is only one Spirit who bestows many gifts. Gifts can be divisive if we forget that they are gifts. We see this problem in the Corinthian church where, for example, the gift of speaking in tongues was prized more highly than other gifts. Some took pride in their gifts but disparaged the gifts bestowed on their brothers and sisters. Paul's emphasis on the "one" Spirit was a way of pointing to the source of their unity. He reminds them that the gifts of the Spirit are granted so as to promote the common good (v. 7), not to make us stand out as individuals.

Outline:
1. Society encourages us to assert our individuality — get noticed
2. The Spirit would have us realize our unity
3. By the one Spirit we are baptized into one body, in which we drink one cup (vv. 12-13)

Gospel: John 7:37-39

Sermon Title: Water From The Rock

Sermon Angle: The invitation by Jesus to come to him and drink (v. 37) needs to be viewed against the backdrop of the Feast of Tabernacles. The feast commemorated a historical event when God supplied water to his thirsty people from a rock (Numbers 20:2-13). This event was symbolically reenacted during the feast by taking water from the pool of Siloam to the temple. When Moses struck the rock and water gushed forth, it quenched the thirst of the body temporarily. What Jesus offered was an eternal source of water for the soul (the Spirit). Jesus remains the rock of our salvation.

Outline:
1. The feast celebrated God's provision for the natural thirst of the body
2. Satisfying physical needs does not suffice
3. Jesus is the rock (source) of the spring of eternal life (the Spirit)
4. Are you drinking from that rock?

Gospel: John 20:19-23

Sermon Title: Expiration, Inspiration, A New Creation

Sermon Angle: In the creation account in Genesis, it tells that God breathed into the lifeless clay that he had fashioned and it became a living human being. In this account, Christ breathed on the moribund band of followers and they became a new creation. Through God's expiration of the breath of life and our inspiration of his life-giving Spirit, we are re-formed into a new creation. By God's grace, we have not only form but spirit.

Outline:

1. God breathed into our lifeless form and we became an incarnate spirit
2. Sin and death suck out the breath of life
3. If we belong to Christ, he re-animates us with his living Spirit
4. Breathe into others the breath of life. Life is sustained only through a reciprocal process of inspiration and expiration.

Sermon Title: The Peace Process

Sermon Angle: We often hear the term "peace process" in reference to the efforts to reconcile peoples and nations that are in conflict with one another. This tells us that peace is not simple; it usually involves a multi-stepped process in which there is movement on both sides. God's peace is different. It is not negotiated but given freely. Christ granted his peace to his distraught disciples, reassuring them of his love and forgiveness. Christ loves us and forgives us, even when we fail him. An essential part of the peace process is accepting God's peace and then sharing it with others. That's why he sent them out with his message of forgiveness (v. 23).

Outline:

1. Such things as failure and conflict steal our peace
2. When we belong to Christ, he bestows his peace when we need it
3. He commissions us to share the peace and forgiveness of the Lord

* * * * *

Pentecostalism has often been weak in theology, while it has been strong on experience — the opposite of traditional Protestantism. An example is Benny Hinn, prominently featured on the Trinity Broadcasting Network. Hinn, who authored a best-selling religious book titled, *Good Morning Holy Spirit*, preached a television sermon in October of 1990 that elicited numerous charges of heresy. In that sermon, Hinn revealed that each person of the Trinity was a triune being: He boldly proclaimed, "If I can shock you ... there are nine of them." Hinn has since repudiated this assertion. He has also recanted a claim that he has received revelations directly from God. (Information gleaned from *Christianity Today*.)

* * * * *

The modern day Pentecostal movement got off the ground in 1901, during a revival on Azusa Street, Los Angeles, under the ministry of a black evangelist by the name of William Seymour. A reporter wrote disparagingly that "that night was made hideous by howlings of the worshipers." From this modest beginning, Pentecostalism has swelled into a movement that contains well over 100 million devotees and is growing rapidly. The three largest congregations on the planet are Pentecostal. Dr. Paul Cho's Full Gospel Central Church in Seoul, Korea, boasts over 500,000 weekly participants. (Information gleaned from *Christianity Today*; "America's Pentecostals: Who Are They?" by Grant Wacker.)

The Holy Trinity

Revised Common:	Genesis 1:1—2:4a	2 Corinthians 13:11-13	Matthew 28:16-20
Roman Catholic:	Exodus 34:4-6, 8-9	2 Corinthians 13:11-13	John 3:16-18
Episcopal:	Genesis 1:1—2:3	2 Corinthians 13:(5-10) 11-14	Matthew 28:16-20

Theme For The Day: The lessons for the festival of the Holy Trinity have to do with the name of God. Particular attention is given to the symbol of God we call the Holy Trinity, though the term "Trinity" appears nowhere in the Bible. The Genesis text presents God as creator. In the Exodus text, the Lord reveals his name and nature to Moses, in the giving of the two tablets of the law. In the second lesson, Paul closes his epistle with the triune name of God, the Apostolic Greeting. The Matthew text contains the Great Commission, instructing the church to go, make disciples, and baptize in the name of the Father and of the Son and of the Holy Spirit.

BRIEF COMMENTARY ON THE LESSONS

Lesson 1: Genesis 1:1—2:4a (C); Genesis 1:1—2:3 (E)

This is the first of two creation accounts found in Genesis. God creates through the power of his word. This account suggests that God is not quite as close to his creation as does the account beginning in Genesis 2:4b and following, where God takes a hands-on approach to forming humankind out of clay. The word used for God's creative acts is *bara* and is used only in reference to the Lord. God creates from nothing; humans form things from that which already exists.

Lesson 1: Exodus 34:4-6, 8-9 (RC)

After Moses breaks the two tablets of the law in angry reaction to the people's apostasy, God gave the people of Israel another chance. He instructs Moses to go up to the top of Mount Sinai with two tablets of stone and God would inscribe his laws on them. There, God reveals himself as the Lord, the almighty, merciful, and forgiving. Nevertheless, iniquity has its price that future generations have to pay (v. 7).

Lesson 2: 2 Corinthians 13:11-13 (C, RC); 2 Corinthians 13:(5-10) 11-14 (E)

The Corinthian church was one of Paul's greatest challenges. He calls into question several issues of morality and behavior. In closing out his letter, he urges them to mend their ways and live in peace and harmony with one another. The epistle is completed on a positive note with the Trinitarian blessing, known as the Apostolic Greeting in some churches.

Gospel: Matthew 28:16-20 (C, E)

Just prior to this lection, the risen Christ orders his disciples to meet him at a certain mountain in Galilee. They worship him, but some have doubts. Christ announces that God has given him all authority. He commands them to go and make disciples of all nations, baptizing them in the name of the Father and of the Son and of the Holy Spirit. The task seems overpowering, but Christ promises to be with them always.

Gospel: John 3:16-18 (RC)

John 3:16 is sometimes referred to as the gospel in a nutshell. "God so loved the world that he gave his only Son that everyone who believes in him might not perish but have eternal life." God is not in the business of condemning but of saving.

Psalm Of The Day

Psalm 8 (C) — "O Lord, our Sovereign, how majestic is your name ..." (v. 1).
Psalm 150 (E) — "Let everything that breathes praise the Lord!" (v. 6).

Prayer Of The Day

Holy God, in your mercy you have revealed to us your sacred name, that name which is above every name in heaven and earth. We bow before the mystery of the Holy Trinity, one God made visible in three persons. May our lives truly proclaim your precious name by what we say and do. This we pray in the name of the Father and of the Son and of the Holy Spirit. Amen.

THEOLOGICAL REFLECTION ON THE LESSONS

Lesson 1: Genesis 1:1—2:4a

In the beginning, God. This may be the most important verse in the Bible because it asserts that God is the source of all things created. From this fact we conclude that all creation belongs to him and carries his imprint. The cosmos is not a random coming together of various substances. There is mind, design, and purpose underlying all life. God was there in the beginning and is the source of all of our beginnings.

Behold the goodness of creation. At various points in this creation account it states that God looked at what he had made and judged it to be good. This tells us that life is good, all created things are good. Do we take the time to behold the essential goodness of creation? Do we treat the world as God's garden? What does "good" mean in this context? It means that the handiwork of God fulfills the intention of its creator.

Is God vegetarian? Verses 29-30 state that God gave to man and beast alike the fruit of the earth as food. No mention of eating meat, which is a concession to the state of the world following Noah and the flood. This means that it was God's intention not only that God and man live in harmony but also man and beast.

Remember the sabbath. The Hebrews ground their observance of the sabbath day in God's creative act of rest. After God finished his creation, he rested (Genesis 2:2). Rest and work are part of the cycle of creation. Our daily body rhythms are based on this cycle. We work and then we rest. God knows that we also need extended and regular periods of rest and worship. The day of rest and worship for Christians shifted to Sunday, the day of resurrection. Unfortunately, sabbath observance has been relegated to the dustbin of religious history, through our modern obsessions for things material. We need to take a day off, not only to recharge our creative energies but to remember and worship the God of all creation.

Lesson 2: 2 Corinthians 13:(5-10) 11-14

Mend and blend. Paul entreats the errant Corinthians to mend their ways, subdue their contentious manner by blending with their brothers and sisters. "Mend your ways ... agree with one another, live in peace ..." (v. 11).

Greetings from God. Last week's gospel lesson has Jesus greeting his discouraged disciples in the upper room with the sign of peace, the *shalom.* In this lesson, Paul leaves his greetings in the name of the triune God: "The grace of our Lord Jesus Christ, the love of God and the communion of the Holy Spirit be with you all." Grace, love, and fellowship are each linked with one of the persons of the Trinity. Grace, the undeserved gift of Christ, comes first. He is the one through whom we come to know the love of God and fellowship of the Spirit.

Gospel: Matthew 28:16-20

Going home. Jesus directed his disciples to head back to Galilee, to a certain mountain, perhaps the site of the Transfiguration, where he would meet them. Before death, many folks want to go home to familiar surroundings. Jackie Kennedy Onassis, at the latter stages of lymphoma, was told that there was nothing more that could be done for her. She decided to go home to die. Jesus was not dead, but his physical presence was about to be withdrawn. He was going home to be with the Father. Christ commissioned his disciples to point to others the way to go home to God.

Faith and doubt. When the disciples saw the glorified Lord, they worshiped him but Matthew adds, rather parenthetically, "but some doubted" (v. 16). We don't know who doubted but it is interesting to note that no one was chastised for their doubt. Faith and doubt are never completely exclusive one of the other. Even the most substantial faith experiences an occasional doubt. Otherwise, it would not be faith but sight. God honors even the most puny faith, if it is acted upon.

On whose authority? That's the question Jesus was asked time and again. Jesus spoke and acted with great authority. He claimed that same authority as he sent out his disciples with the gospel. In an attempt to be relevant to contemporary culture, has the church lost touch with its fountainhead of authority?

Mission mandate. The Lord commands his disciples to go into all the world and make disciples. Nothing is said about institutions, buildings, and programs. Spiritual replication is still the mainstream of the Church's mission. Our reason for existence can be summarized in four simple mandates: Go, make disciples, baptize, and teach.

Disciples, not decisions. In evangelical circles, great stress is placed upon making decisions for Christ. The believer can then point to a certain point in time when she became a Christian. Thus, becoming a Christian is considered a highly individualistic decision that almost makes the community of faith optional. It can be argued that making a disciple and becoming a disciple is a process, beginning at baptism, and not a one-time event. An integral part of this process is teaching and learning. It took Jesus three years of intense interaction and teaching, capped by his death and resurrection, to form his disciples into a church. Yet, many churches think that they can manufacture disciples during a three-week orientation course.

PREACHING APPROACHES WITH ILLUSTRATIONS

Lesson 1: Genesis 1:1—2:4a

Sermon Title: The Community Of God

Sermon Angle: In verse 26, God says: "Let *us* make man in *our* image." Who is God addressing here? Biblical scholars maintain that it is the heavenly court of angelic beings. Other believers see this as a reference to the Holy Trinity. In any case, the passage suggests that God cannot be imaged apart from community. God is not known in solitary splendor, as Creator or even Father. God can only be known fully in the three persons of the Godhead, who are so closely intertwined as to be one. We come to God through the community of the Godhead and the community of faith.

Sermon Title: A Non-Carnal World

Sermon Angle: Verses 29-31 portray a world where there is no prey. The strong do not feed upon the weak. God gave humans and beast alike the fruit of the earth and green plants for food. It was truly a non-carnal world. Paul, of course, uses the word *carnal* or *flesh* to depict our sinful human nature. So, meat-eating symbolizes humankind's sinful nature. Admittedly, after the flood, God somewhat reluctantly permits humans to eat meat. Is this God's admission that sin cannot be eradicated in this world, without blotting out freedom of choice as well? Perhaps. At any rate, we know that heaven will be a non-carnal existence.

Outline:
1. Eden was a non-carnal existence
   — no beasts of prey or shedding of blood
   — every creature lived in mutuality and freedom
2. Relate carnality to sin and give examples
   (to hurt the neighbor is like tearing their flesh)
3. Establish that the kingdom of God is a non-carnal existence of love
   — Isaiah's peaceable kingdom (Isaiah 11)

Lesson 2: 2 Corinthians 13:(5-10) 11-14

Sermon Title: Mend Your Ways

Sermon Angle: At the crucifixion, the soldiers threw dice to determine the ownership of Christ's seamless robe. They didn't want to tear it. That robe symbolizes the unity of the church. The Corinthians were tearing at Christ's robe through their desire to stand out. This put them in competition against one another and produced a destructive effect. Paul orders them to mend their ways by living in peace. To take the analogy further, we can say that we are strands or threads in Christ's robe. By ourselves we are weak and of little account, but when we are woven into Christ's seamless robe, the church, through baptism and faith, we become a thing of strength and beauty. Then we are able to confer on others Christ's forgiveness and grace.

Sermon Title: God's Name Is Grace

Sermon Angle: The theme for this Sunday has to do with the names of God, especially Father, Son, and Holy Spirit. We could just as well name God grace, love, and community because these characteristics encapsulate for us the nature of God. Paul's greeting in verse 14 links these concepts to the persons of the Trinity. All three concepts — grace, love, and community — reveal to us the essential nature of God. A fruitful sermon could plumb the depths of this trinity of theological expressions. However, to keep this from becoming too abstract, there must be ample illustrations.

Gospel: Matthew 28:16-20

Sermon Title: Absence Of Authority

Sermon Angle: There is a great void in our modern, Western world; it is a void which sends fundamentalists of any religion into an apoplexy of fear and dread. I speak of the absence of authority. The tenure of our time is that God is all right as long as he doesn't make any demands which would infringe on our freedom. The Bible is no longer the authority, even for most who claim Christianity. Most regard with skepticism religious institutions and denominational leaders. The teacher, the policeman, even the doctor, has lost his or her aura of authority. Most of the established Protestant denominations are diminishing because Christ's authority as Savior and Lord has been rejected. This rejection is usually not explicit but by default. Jesus said, "All authority in heaven and earth has been given to me. Go, therefore, and make disciples...." For those who believe and obey Christ, there can be no absence of authority.

Outline:
1. There is an absence of authority
   — in the institutions of society
   — in the family
   — in the church
2. The result — lack of norms, law breaking, and depression
3. Jesus claimed his authority
   — do you believe him?
   — if so, obey him by carrying out his mission

Sermon Title: Copy-Right And Copy-Wrong

Sermon Angle: In the Great Commission, we could say that Christ gave to his disciples his copyright. This means that he gave them his permission to replicate in others the faith he had given them. Actually, Christ's command to replicate our faith goes beyond rights; it's a commission. There is a right and a wrong way to make disciples, however. The right way proclaims and incarnates the grace and love of God, which we experience in Christ. The wrong way lays guilt, bullies, pressures, or judges. The wrong way to witness occurs when we point to ourselves or our congregation, rather than to Christ, as the object of faith. Copy right!

Outline:
1. Christ gave his church the copyright on the gospel
2. Our duty and delight is to transmit the faith in the *right* way
   — to show the love of Christ
   — to walk the walk as well as talk the talk
3. Harm comes from sharing the gospel in the *wrong* way (examples)
4. The greatest harm stems from refusing to share the gospel
5. Share concrete ways of witnessing in the right way

* * * * *

Life is three-dimensional. One of the early Greek philosophers posited that there were three primary elements of life in this world — earth, fire, and water. We also employ the language of the Greeks to describe our humanity — body, mind, and spirit. Jews, Muslims, and Christians picture the cosmos as 3-D — heaven, earth, and hell. Physicists report that the inner world of the atom is composed of three primary particles — protons, neutrons, and electrons. The family has traditionally been constituted of three essential beings, called father, mother, and child. Christians attempt to explain the mystery of God by affirming that God is 3-D, Father, Son, and Holy Spirit.

* * * * *

220

What does God look like? That was the question that Tommy was puzzling over.

"Does he look like us?" his teacher queried.

"No, I don't think so," Tommy responded.

The teacher handed him a piece of drawing paper and requested Tommy to draw with his crayons what he thought God looks like.

The end result was a large yellow circle sun-face, a smaller circle-face to represent the earth, and a large dominating rainbow to personify the Holy Spirit. The sun symbolized the Father, the earth was Jesus, the Son, and the rainbow represented the Holy Spirit. Tommy's picture amazed his teacher with its simple profundity. The sun as God's face, the earth, where God became human in Jesus, the face of the Son of God, and the rainbow, which reflects the rays of the sun, frames the earth with its beauteous glory. (Gleaned from *U.S. Catholic*; "Draw Me A Mystery.")

Corpus Christi

Roman Catholic: Deuteronomy 8:2-3, 14-16   1 Corinthians 10:16-17   John 6:51-58

Theme: The bodily presence of Christ communicated through bread and wine. In the Deuteronomy text, Moses exhorts the Israelites to remember the blessings of God when he sustained them with manna and water throughout their wilderness journey. In the second lesson, Paul reminds the Corinthians that the Eucharist signifies participation in the body and blood of Christ. In the gospel, Jesus feeds the 5,000 and invites his hearers to receive him as the bread of life.

BRIEF COMMENTARY ON THE LESSONS

Lesson 1: Deuteronomy 8:2-3, 14-16

Deuteronomy came to light in the seventh century, during the reign of King Josiah, who instituted a religious revival. It comes in the form of discourses from the mouth of Moses, which bring to mind the goodness of the Lord in leading them through the wilderness and into the promised land. The people are called to respond to God's goodness by ratifying the covenant and serving the Lord. In this text, Moses exhorts his people as they are about to embark into their new land. They are warned against forgetting the Lord when the hardships of their liberation would yield to the pleasures of a prosperous existence. The God who has fed them with manna from heaven and slaked their thirst with water in the desert was worthy of their worship and loyalty.

Lesson 2: 1 Corinthians 10:16-17

In this chapter, Paul warns the Corinthians against the dangers of idolatry. In so doing, he lifts up the example of the rebellious Israelites during the wilderness wandering period. Many of them suffered the punishment of the Lord as a consequence. Paul sees the Israelites' experience as a warning to the Church to serve Christ alone. Christians were constantly being asked by their friends and neighbors to participate in meals that followed sacrifice in pagan temples. Paul warns that such accommodations are forms of participation in the worship of false gods. As Christians receive the communal cup, they participate in the blood of Christ, and as they share in the eucharistic bread, they share in the body of Christ. Though they are many, they are one with Christ and each other through participation in the Lord's Supper. This oneness must not be adulterated by compromise with false gods.

Gospel: John 6:51-58

Jesus calls himself the living bread, which came down from heaven. Jesus compares himself to the bread which the Jews gathered each morning in the wilderness. He also draws out a contrast. Those who ate the manna still suffered eventual death, but those who eat his flesh and drink his blood will live forever. Our lection is part of an extended discourse on the topic of Christ as spiritual bread, which follows the account of the feeding of the 5,000. Following the feeding episode, great crowds dog Jesus. Christ senses that they are attracted by the hunger of their bodies rather than their souls. Christ appeals to the masses to permit him to satisfy the deepest hunger of their souls by receiving him as the living bread from heaven.

Psalm Of The Day
 Psalm 147:12-15, 18-20 — "He has not dwelt thus with any other nation ..." (v. 20).

THEOLOGICAL REFLECTION ON THE LESSONS

Lesson 1: Deuteronomy 8:2-3, 14-16

Time of testing. Moses explains to the Hebrews the purpose of their forty years of wandering, just as they were about to set foot in their own land. God was testing them to determine whether they would be loyal and faithful to him. It is interesting that when our Lord was tempted by Satan in the wilderness, Jesus used a passage from this text to rebut the evil one. When Jesus was hungry because of fasting, Satan commanded him to turn stones into loaves of bread. The Lord replied with a phrase from verse three: "Man does not live by bread alone but every word that proceeds from the mouth of God." It is always a temptation to seek the tangible bread of this earth rather than spiritual bread of heaven. Yet, food for our spirits is far more essential than bread for our bodies.

Our daily bread. Our Lord taught us to pray: "Give us today our daily bread." Physical needs are important and God wants us to petition him for them. The emphasis falls on the word "daily." Jesus instructs us to pray just for our immediate needs, so that we realize that our dependence rests on God, not ourselves or our substance. God was teaching the Hebrews the very same truth through their ordeal in the desert. They needed to trust him for all their needs, to receive the Lord as daily as bread for their body and their soul.

The peril of plenty. The latter part of this passage is a warning about the perils of plenitude. A life of abundance and ease can cause amnesia. Materially possessed people tend to forget the blessings of the Lord and his great salvation. Moses warns the people not to forget the God of their salvation when their possessions would multiply and their bellies would become full. The Passover was instituted by God for the Hebrews so that they would not forget the Lord and his salvation when they got settled in their new land. Likewise, the Eucharist was instituted by Christ so that his people would not forget their great salvation.

Lesson 2: 1 Corinthians 10:16-17

Participation, not observation. Authentic Christian worship is marked by participation, not observation. The Eucharist is participation in the death and resurrection of Christ. "The cup of blessing that we bless, is it not participation in the blood of Christ? The bread that we break, is it not sharing in the body of Christ?" To answer the question posed by the spiritual, "Were you there when they crucified my Lord?" Yes, I was there and am there every time I partake of the Lord's Supper.

Cup of blessing. Paul refers to the eucharistic cup as the "cup of blessing." What a beautiful expression! What specifically are the blessings of the communion chalice? Forgiveness of sins tops the list. Becoming blood brothers and blood sisters through the sacrifice of Christ ranks a close second. Those who drink of the one cup are family. We might also say that we are bread brothers and sisters. Paul explains: "Because there is one bread, we who are many are one body, for we all partake of one bread" (v. 17). This unity stands as one of the real blessings of this sacrament. Exclusionary communion practices militate against the unity signified in the sacrament. A third blessing comes as a renewal of our Christian identity forged in baptism. A fourth derives from the fact that the communion elements are vehicles for the Spirit of Christ to enter our hearts. A fifth benefit is announced in the word "Eucharist." When we truly comprehend what God has done for us, our hearts are filled with thanksgiving.

Christ is bread and so are we. It is the most ancient and most universal of all foods. That's why bread is the symbol for life. Let's plumb this metaphor a bit. First of all, bread begins as a little seed of wheat that is planted in the earth, where it dies but is raised to newness of life as a green plant. Once the wheat bears fruit and matures, it is harvested. Pulverized into flour, it dies again, only to be reborn as bread. Every Christian must be willing to die and be raised to newness of life, not only for his own sake but for the sake of the world. We must also remember that it takes more than a single head of grain to make a loaf of bread. Are we willing to be blended and baked into a community of nourishment? Remember also that bread is not meant to be admired but rather to be broken and shared.

Gospel: John 6:51-58

Wonder bread. When I was a child, Wonder Bread was widely touted. It was supposed to help develop strong bodies eight ways. Don't ask me to name those ways. Jesus, our Lord, is the true wonder bread. He claims that if we eat of him, we will live forever. This tells us that faith is not something external to our being but that which we incorporate into our bodies. Christian faith cannot keep Christ at arm's length; his word and spirit must be as much a part of us as the air that we suck into our lungs. It is not enough to receive Christ into our hearts at some point in time. We must daily take him into our vital centers like bread.

It was too much to swallow. Jesus announced that if his disciples wanted to inherit eternal life, they would have to eat his flesh and drink his blood. These words seemed crassly offensive and literal. What could he mean? To this point, Jesus had been quite popular. The signs and healings made him the buzz of the town squares and meeting places. The multiplication of the loaves aroused huge crowds of the curious. Christ didn't seek mere followers; he desired disciples. Christ's talk of drinking his blood and eating his flesh might have been his way of separating the wheat from the chaff. Indeed, John informs us that many of those who followed Jesus ceased doing so at this point. The spectacle seekers and lookers-on could go packing. Those who chose to remain would have to swallow his gospel completely. They would have to permit Christ to take control of their lives. Is it any wonder that they were confused and offended? The gospel of an indwelling Christ is still too much for most people to swallow. Many people don't want someone else in the driver's seat of their lives.

PREACHING APPROACHES WITH ILLUSTRATIONS

Lesson 1: Deuteronomy 8:2-3, 14-16

Sermon Title: Forward In Remembrance

Sermon Angle: Moses addresses the people as they are going into the promised land. He urges them to remember the Lord and his great acts of love and salvation. He was concerned that when they became materially prosperous, they would have a tendency to forget the Lord. It is not healthy to dwell in the past, but as we go forward, we need to constantly recall from where we have come. Also, at the peril of our lives, we must strive to remember our spiritual origin. As the historian stated: "Those who forget the past are doomed to repeat it."

Outline:
1. In times of prosperity we tend to pat ourselves on the back and forget God
2. Remember God, who brought us through our wanderings to the place of promise
3. Remember the blessings we have received through Christ
4. In the Eucharist, we give thanks and we remember

Lesson 2: 1 Corinthians 10:16-17

Sermon Title: Christianity Is Not A Spectator Sport

Sermon Angle: Two key words in this lection are participation and sharing. Love and caring must be expressed in participation and sharing. Christ participated in our human existence, that we might participate in the life of God. Holy Communion is participation in the life of Christ, including his death and resurrection. Christians express their faith by entering into the joys and sharing the sorrows of the world.

Outline:
1. Spectator sports are becoming enormously popular
2. They offer a type of vicarious identification
3. This attitude can be dangerous if applied to other arenas of life
4. The Eucharist is for participants, not onlookers
5. The Christian life means entering in, not looking on

Sermon Title: Eucharist Is Not A Thing

Sermon Angle: This title comes from a most thoughtful article on the Eucharist written by Father Richard T. Szafranski (January, 1990; *U.S. Catholic*). The article opens with this scene. A woman is seeking the peace of God after a hard day at the office. She arrives at the church but it is too late; the doors are locked tight. She goes to an ATM type of machine by the side of the door and inserts her plastic card that identifies her as a practicing member of the Catholic church, good nationwide. The computer screen asks if she wants only the bread, only the wine, or both. She punches in "both." Out pops a hermetically sealed plastic pouch with wafer and tiny cup. The message on the screen: "Have a nice day." Of course, such machines have not been employed by the Catholic church. This scene illustrates the point of the article. The Eucharist has become a "thing" for many Catholics (other Christians, too, we might add). Father Szafranski maintains that the Eucharist is not a thing to be received but the action of the whole people of God. For centuries, he contends, the Eucharist has been the domain of the priest, who alone has the power to transform ordinary bread and wine into the body and blood of Christ. There was very little sense of the kind of participation, which the second lesson talks about. The author is attempting to lead us to the realization that the people of God are not merely to receive consecrated bread and wine, the body and blood of Christ; we are to be bread and wine. We are to be the body and blood of Christ for a spiritually malnourished world. In other words, Christians are the Eucharist. We are called to be a people broken and poured out for the world, in fulfillment of Christ's mission. We are to bring to the world the real presence of Christ's love, grace, and forgiveness. We have fulfilled Christ's mission if our lives of thanksgiving give others a reason to celebrate.

* * * * *

The Eucharist is a meal of sharing. In our modern compartmentalized world, we have lost, to a significant degree, the sacramental sense of sharing and participation in the lives of one another through a common meal. We hurry into a fast food joint, order our food and drink, and then find a cubicle of space which is hermetically sealed off from the crowd that surrounds us. Eating is not meant merely for consumption but for sharing with others. Saint John Chrysostom taught that we should first feed the hungry and then decorate the table. The temple of our afflicted neighbor's body, he instructed, "is more holy than the altar of stone on which you celebrate the holy sacrifice. You are able to contemplate this altar everywhere, in the street and in the open squares." A non-Christian named Aristides once defended Christians before the Emperor Hadrian employing this apologetic: "If one of them is poor and there isn't enough food to go round, they fast several days to give him the food he needs." The sacramental sharing of the Eucharist extended far beyond the ritual meal; sharing was a way of life. The church, as a eucharistic community of sharing, is called to be a sacramental sign pointing to what the kingdom of heaven is to be like.

Gospel: John 6:51-58

Sermon Title: Wonder Bread

Sermon Angle: The bread on the Lord's table is indeed wonder bread. It is wonder bread because it is the bread of heaven, the bread of life. Jesus claims that whoever eats of this bread will live forever. It is wonder bread because it carries the real presence of Christ and conveys forgiveness, grace, and strength. It is wonder bread also because it evokes wonder and awe. We cannot understand how Christ is present in this bread; we cannot explain it. We can only accept it and receive it. Terms like transubstantiation, consubstantiation, and real presence are but awkward attempts to plumb the mystery of the Eucharist.

Outline:
1. The communion bread is more than it appears; it is wonder bread
2. It is the bread of the earth and, at the same time, the bread of heaven
3. To receive the bread is to receive Christ
4. Let us proclaim the mystery

Proper 4/Pentecost 2/Ordinary Time 9

Revised Common:	Genesis 6:11-22; 7:24; 8:14-19	Romans 1:16-17; 3:22b-28 (29-31)	Matthew 7:21-29
Roman Catholic:	Deuteronomy 11:18, 26-28, 32	Romans 3:21-25, 28	Matthew 7:21-27
Episcopal:	Deuteronomy 11:18-21, 26-28	Romans 3:21-25a, 28	Matthew 7:21-27

Theme: A contrast between the righteousness of obedience and the righteousness of faith. The first lesson from Deuteronomy presents Moses' instruction to obey God's laws by making them an integral part of their daily lives. The first lesson from Genesis shows how Noah obeyed God by building the ark. In the gospel, Jesus teaches that everyone who hears his words and does them is like the person who built his house on the rock. In contrast, the person who hears his teachings and does not do them resembles the person who foolishly builds his house on the sand. Those who obey his teaching will not be swept away.

BRIEF COMMENTARY ON THE LESSONS

Lesson 1: Genesis 6:11-22; 7:24; 8:14-19 (C)

This account of Noah and the flood is the first of twelve lessons from Genesis. Noah was obedient to God's command to build an ark, even when the notion of a flood seemed farfetched and he was probably ridiculed by his neighbors. Noah also demonstrated great faith in the Lord. We have here a perfect synthesis of faith and obedience.

Lesson 1: Deuteronomy 11:18, 26-28, 32 (RC); Deuteronomy 11:18-21, 26-28 (E)

Moses instructs his people to treasure up the word of the Lord in their hearts. Every moment of every day was to be immersed in the awareness of God's word. The Jews were to instruct their children in God's word morning, noon, and night. It was to be a sign on their hands and as a frontlet between the eyes (v. 18). There were blessings for obedience; they would live long in the land. There were also curses for disobeying God's commandments. The Jews were given the choice between the blessings of obedience and the punishment for disobedience.

Lesson 2: Romans 1:16-17; 3:22b-28 (29-31) (C); Romans 3:21-25, 28 (RC); Romans 3:21-25a, 28 (E)

Paul contends that the righteousness of God has been revealed apart from the law; it is the righteousness of those who have faith in Christ Jesus. The former righteousness is not effective because all people are tainted by sin. There remains no room for boasting or pride, since salvation comes as a gift of God received by faith.

Gospel: Matthew 7:21-29 (C); Matthew 7:21-27 (RC, E)

Being acquainted with Christ is not enough to gain entrance into the kingdom of heaven. The deciding issue is not the profession of our lips but the profession of our lives. What we say must be backed by our actions. The warning of Jesus has a sobering effect: "Not every one who says to me Lord, Lord, will enter the kingdom of heaven but he who does the will of my Father who is in heaven" (v. 21). To know the Christ through faith necessarily leads to doing the works of Christ. This teaching bears out the point of Jesus' parable of judgment found in Matthew

25:31-46. It is a wise person who puts Jesus' teachings into practice. That person is like the one who builds his house on a rock. When the storms of life assail, it will not move. The foolish person is the one who fails to put the Lord's words into practice. When the storms of life come, he will be swept away. This passage completes the Sermon on the Mount.

Psalm Of The Day

Psalm 46 (C) — "God is our refuge and strength" (v. 1).

Psalm 31:2-4, 17, 25 (RC) — "Be a strong rock of refuge to me, a strong fortress to save me" (v. 2b).

Prayer Of The Day

O Christ, you are our rock. Deliver us from the temptation to build our lives on the sands of a cheap grace and a superficial commitment to you. Rather, give us wisdom and strength in our struggle to express a lived faith in all that we think, say, or do. In Jesus' name. Amen.

THEOLOGICAL REFLECTION ON THE LESSONS

Lesson 1: Genesis 6:11-22; 7:24; 8:14-19

Questions about creation. The first twelve chapters of Genesis deal with some profound theological issues and raise lots of questions. For instance, did God know that humanhood was going to become corrupt and sinful? If so, why did he go ahead or why didn't he alter his creative plan? Once the world did become corrupt and violent, did he really think that purging the world of all but a remnant would rectify the problem? After all, all humans are from the same stock. These stories raise some disturbing questions, such as: Does God make mistakes? Is God aware of all future events? Is God truly all powerful? I don't claim to know all the answers to these questions, but I do believe that the answers are tied up with the notion of human freedom. God opened himself to pain and frustration when he created us in his image to be free.

Faith made visible. How is faith made visible? It is made visible through obedience. Imagine this dialogue:

God: Noah, do you trust me?

Noah: Yes, Lord.

God: Then build me an ark. I'm going to destroy the world.

Noah: Forget it, God. What do I know about building an ark? I'm no ship builder. I'm a farmer.

God: Noah, I'll direct you. Trust me.

Noah: Forget it, God. I'd be a laughing stock. I believe you but you'll have to find somebody else.

Such a response could not be called faith. Faith is made visible through obedience. To put it another way, obedience is the fruit of faith.

Lesson 1: Deuteronomy 11:18-21, 26-28, 32

Lay away. In verse 18, Moses instructs the people to put God's word in their hearts and souls. The Revised Standard Version translates this "lay up." There is great value in laying away or storing up God's word for future needs. As we lay away or meditate on God's word, it becomes an integral part of the core of our being.

No sacred and secular. Moses commands the people to bind God's commandments on their wrists and between their eyes and fasten them on the doorposts of their houses. They were to teach God's word to their children as they were pursuing their everyday activities. There was no splitting of existence between secular and sacred, worldly and spiritual. The awareness of God and his word was to permeate everything. In the mind of the typical person in the Western world, religion is something that people do at certain times. In the biblical conception of religion, religion defines who we are.

Hand, head, and home. A visible reminder of God's word was to be attached to the wrist, between the eyes, and on the doorpost to the home. The box on the wrist was to remind the Hebrews that all that they did was to be in accordance with God's word. The box between the eyes was to enable the Hebrews to view everything through the lens of God's will, since the eyes are a window to the mind, heart, and soul. The box on the door was to remind them that the home was the primary site for the inculcation of the faith.

Lesson 2: Romans 1:16-17; 3:21-28 (29-31)

Equal before the law. In most older courthouses, you can find the statue of Lady Justice, standing blindfolded, holding out the balance of justice. We are supposed to stand equally before the law of the land. Paul says we all stand equally before the judgment seat of God. "For there is no distinction" (v. 22b). We all stand guilty before God, apart from saving faith in Christ (v. 23).

Are all people justified by grace? Paul's answer seems to be, "Yes." All people are sinners, and all people are offered the gift of justification through Christ. The rub is that not all people receive this gift through faith. Faith is the tool by which we lay hold of the grace of God (v. 25). Paul makes this point in Romans 1:16: "For I am not ashamed of the gospel; it is the power of God for salvation to everyone who has faith."

Gospel: Matthew 7:21-29

Nodding acquaintance or trusted friend? Jesus warns, "Not everyone who says to me, 'Lord, Lord,' will enter the kingdom of heaven but he who does the will of my Father who is in heaven" (v. 21). Being introduced to Jesus or knowing things about Jesus does not bring justification. Jesus does not lack for acquaintances. A friend, unlike an acquaintance, will do almost anything for us. Her words are confirmed by her actions. God will receive those who have demonstrated friendship toward his Son. Their faith is visible through acts of love.

Works without faith are dead. The epistle of James says that faith without works is dead. Jesus teaches that the opposite is also true. Works without faith are dead. In verse 22, Jesus paints a scene of judgment. "On that day...." A group of people are shocked witless by the Lord's denial that he ever knew them. They argue: "Lord, Lord, did we not prophesy in your name, and cast out demons in your name, and do many mighty works in your name?" They demonstrated works, but they did not flow from a heart of faith. They never knew Jesus. They were not moved by their faith but by the desire to glorify themselves. People who lack faith can still be used of God for great things but no personal benefit will accrue to them, because it did not flow from a faithful heart.

Choose wisely your building materials. Jesus contrasts the foolishness of the man who built his house upon the sands with the wisdom of the man who built his house upon the rock. Actually, sand and rock are the same substance. We could say that sand is liquid rock, which has been pulverized by the ceaseless motion of wind and sea. Sand is rock that has taken a pounding. Since it is soft and porous, it is not suitable to serve as a foundation for a house. However, if you take sand and mix it with a hardening agent, like cement, it is most suitable as a foundation and will stand up well against the storms of life. If we construct our lives on the foundation of our own goodness, we will surely be swept away by the torrents of evil. However, if through faith, we add the hardening agent of a living faith in Christ, our lives rest secure on a rocklike foundation.

PREACHING APPROACHES WITH ILLUSTRATIONS

Lesson 1: Genesis 6:11-22; 7:24; 8:14-19

Sermon Title: Noah, Man Of Favor And Faith

Sermon Angle: Noah found favor with God. His life and that of his family were going to be spared in the coming deluge. Noah was the object of God's favor, but his favor cannot be passively received. Noah had to exercise his faith by, first of all, believing God and, secondly, by putting his faith into practice through building the ark. The point could be made that we are objects of God's favor in Christ and that the proper way to receive that gift is through faith active in obedience.

Outline:
1. Noah was the object of God's favor (grace)
2. Noah was a man of faith expressed by
   — believing the word of God
   — acting on that belief
3. God has favored us in Christ with salvation
4. This salvation is experienced through the church (the ship is a symbol for the church — a place of safety)
5. Let us receive this favor through a lived faith

Lesson 1: Deuteronomy 11:18-21, 26-28, 32

Sermon Title: God In A Box

Sermon Angle: During the period of the wilderness wandering, the Hebrews carried the Ark of the Covenant. It was so sacred that it was like having God in a box. Our boxes are labeled religion, denominationalism, and philosophy. It's all part of the process called secularization, pushing God off main stage and into the corners of creation. It's all right to believe in God, but keep him in the religion box. Don't let him into the school, the factory, the boardroom, or the bedroom. Moses commanded the people to make their faith in God integral to every aspect of their existence. They were to treasure God's word in their hearts. They were to integrate it with every daily activity. They were to teach it to their children in their homes. Your sermon can discuss ways of letting God out of the box and into our everyday existence.

Outline:
Introduction: Rework thought expressed above
1. For the writer of Deuteronomy, God was not boxed into the temple or the synagogue. The home was the primary site of religious devotion.
2. God was recognized as Lord in all of life
3. Don't box God into the religious establishment
4. Store the gospel in your heart that it might direct all your doings

* * * * *

230

This lesson raises an issue that is crucial to the state of religion in American culture. How can I connect my faith, my religion, with my everyday existence? The membership in mainline Protestant churches continues to hemorrhage because we have neglected this vital concern. Consequently, church members increasingly feel that the institutional expression of religion is irrelevant to where they live. George Gallup discovered in 1988 that the number of unchurched in America had increased some 3%. This equates to a loss of approximately seven million church members. Does this indicate that Americans are less religious? No, the number of Americans who believe in Jesus Christ increased from 78% to 84% in the same time period.

*   *   *   *   *

The Monday Connection by William E. Diehl is a helpful effort to connect the Sunday experience of institutional worship with the Monday world of the school, business, office, and home. He explores ways in which Christians can connect what they believe with daily behavior. In the first chapter, he makes a very cogent observation; that the denominations that relate to the world primarily through institutional action are losing members, while those denominations that are gaining members relate primarily to society through its individual members. Most Christians would probably agree that Christians need to express their faith both through institutions and individuals. The problem is that mainline denominations channel their energies and resources almost exclusively into institutional expressions, to the neglect of the personal dimension of faith. Diehl hastens to point out that the wrong kind of individualism can be destructive to faith, but individualism is of two stripes. The first kind of individualism that shows up on the Gallup surveys is characterized by statements such as: "One can be a good Christian or Jew without going to church or synagogue." These folks believe that one should arrive at his religious faith independently of the religious institutions. This kind of individualism poses great dangers.

The other type of religious individualism is different. It has to do with how individuals experience their faith. It is not acceptable to this group of Christians to blindly accept theological expression; they have a need to know how these beliefs can be applied to daily existence. These believers have rightly concluded that beliefs are impotent unless they influence our values, ethics, thoughts, and behavior. These individualists don't want to merely talk about God; they want to experience God. Gallup found that 56% of church members thought that churches were too concerned with organizational issues. Denominational leaders have received these findings as a threat rather than a challenge. For instance, the Priorities Task Force of the Presbyterian Church (USA) in reporting to the General Assembly in 1988 expressed the fear that the ministry of the laity was being increasingly oriented toward the area of daily work rather than "churchcraft." Such responses are unfortunate because those who catch the vision of ministry in daily life are among the strongest supporters of the institutional church.

Lesson 2: Romans 3:21-28
Sermon Title: The Righteousness Of God
Sermon Angle: Our lesson starts out: "Now the righteousness of God has been revealed." The biblical religions take great pains to establish the righteousness of God. The gods of the Greeks and Romans were not particularly good. They seemed to be subject to all the corruptions and weaknesses of human beings. They were noted not for their goodness but for their strength. The God of the Bible is holy, just, sinless, and righteous. God's act of self-giving love

through Christ lifts up as never before the righteousness of God. What are the ramifications of worshiping a righteous God? First, we can rest assured that God will not act arbitrarily or cruelly, but in love and mercy. Second, such a God is ethical and expects his children to act in a righteous and responsible manner.

Sermon Title: God's Gift To You

Sermon Angle: God did not send his Son into the world to prove his own goodness but to offer his righteousness to us as a gift (v. 24). The sacrifice of Christ atones for our sins (v. 25). Such a sacrifice is necessary to preserve God's righteousness and, at the same time, offer his righteousness to us as a gift. This gift will only benefit us if we receive it by faith.

Outline:
1. God has a gift addressed not to "occupant," but to you personally — the gift of righteousness and forgiveness
2. This gift must be personally acknowledged and received
   — first, confess your sinful condition
   — second, receive Christ by faith

Gospel: Matthew 7:21-29

Sermon Title: Name Dropper

Sermon Angle: Some people like to drop the names of important and influential people. They may do this to gain entrance or merely to impress others. Jesus warns: "Not everyone who says to me, 'Lord, Lord,' will enter the kingdom of heaven ..." (v. 21a). Many people throw around the name of Christ but they don't really know him. Dropping names around might impress other people but it won't impress God or gain us entrance into the kingdom. We must know Christ through faith. In the arena of faith, it's not just what you know but who you know.

Outline:
1. Some people like to toss out prominent names to open doors
2. It isn't enough to know some things about Jesus
3. We gain entrance into the kingdom by knowing Jesus

Sermon Title: How Firm A Foundation?

Sermon Angle: Jesus teaches that there are two kinds of people. There are those who build their lives on the sands of worldly values. They are the foolish ones because what they have built will be swept away. Then, there are those who build their lives on the rock of Christ. They are deemed wise, for their edifice will stand the test of time and eternity. What kind of a foundation are you building on? What manner of foundation are you laying for your children?

Outline:
1. On what kind of foundation are you building your life?
2. Is your life built upon the shifting sands of worldly values?
3. Or, is your life constructed on the rock of a faith that connects with daily life?

* * * * *

In searching the yellow pages for a reputable auto mechanic, my eye was struck by the company name: Christian Car Care. I reasoned: We have one of three things here. "Christian" could be a family name, much like Anderson. The second possibility was more cynical. This is a fellow who wants to overcome the unsavory reputation of auto mechanics and has adopted the name "Christian" as a marketing ploy. The third possibility was that this company really was trying to integrate Christian faith and values into their business. I decided to test them out. As I walked into the office, there was Christian literature prominently displayed. I wondered if the two owners were going to attempt to verbally witness to their faith. They did not. After three or four dealings with them, however, I have concluded that they did indeed supply Christian care. They were very reasonable, exceedingly honest, and trustworthy. They witnessed positively to their Lord in the course of their daily work.

Proper 5/Pentecost 3/Ordinary Time 10

Revised Common:	Genesis 12:1-9	Romans 4:13-25	Matthew 9:9-13, 18-26
Roman Catholic:	Hosea 6:3-6	Romans 4:18-25	Matthew 9:9-13
Episcopal:	Hosea 5:15—6:6	Romans 4:13-18	Matthew 9:9-13

Theme: The call. The book of Hosea is one long plea for the people to turn their hearts to God. The Genesis 12 text and the second lesson present the call of Abraham. The gospel lifts up the call of Matthew, a tax collector regarded as a notorious sinner. When criticized for dining with sinners, Jesus responds: "I came not to call the righteous, but sinners."

BRIEF COMMENTARY ON THE LESSONS

Lesson 1: Genesis 12:1-9 (C)

God calls Abraham to leave his homeland and go to the country that God had promised him. God pledged Abraham that he would be the father of a great nation. Abraham obeys God by setting out with his aged, barren wife and his nephew, Lot.

Lesson 1: Hosea 6:3-6 (RC); Hosea 5:15—6:6 (E)

Hosea prophesied in the early part of the eighth century BC, a contemporary of Isaiah. Underneath the pronouncements of judgment is an impassioned entreaty for his people to know and love him. God threatens to turn away from his sinful people until they repent. The loyalty of the people is superficial, like the morning cloud or dew (v. 4). God concludes that he would rather have his people know him and love him than engage in meaningless ritual actions (v. 6).

Lesson 2: Romans 4:13-25 (C); Romans 4:18-25 (RC); Romans 4:13-18 (E)

Paul holds up Abraham as an example of saving faith. Abraham was accepted by God not because he kept the law but as a result of his obedience to the Lord. He trusted in God's promise, and it was regarded by God as righteousness. His acceptance by God could not have come through keeping the law, since he had not yet been circumcised, but through faith. Those who likewise have faith in the God of Abraham, the Father of our Lord, Jesus Christ, will also have their faith regarded as righteousness by God.

Gospel: Matthew 9:9-13, 18-26 (C); Matthew 9:9-13 (RC, E)

Jesus calls Matthew, a tax collector for the despised Roman occupiers, to follow him. Matthew accepts his challenge to discipleship and proceeds to invite his old cronies to his house to dine with Jesus. This action scandalizes the Pharisees who are shocked that Jesus was freely associating with notorious sinners. Jesus responds to their criticism with an observation, a criticism, and a pronouncement. The observation: "Those who are well have no need of a physician but those who are sick." The criticism: "Go and learn what this means: I desire mercy and not sacrifice." This ties in directly to the first lesson (Hosea 6:6). The pronouncement: "For I came not to call the righteous, but sinners" (vv. 12-13).

Psalm Of The Day

Psalm 33:1-12 (C) — "Happy is the nation whose God is the Lord" (v. 12a).

Psalm 50:1, 8, 12-15 (RC); Psalm 50 (E) — "Offer to God a sacrifice of thanksgiving ..." (v. 15a).

Prayer Of The Day

Merciful and gracious God, with broken heart and tears we confess to you our moral and spiritual weakness, reflected in a shallow faith and superficial repentance. By your Holy Spirit, free us from spiritual pride and fortify our faith, so that our entire lives might prove to be a sacrifice of thanksgiving and praise to you. In Jesus' name. Amen.

THEOLOGICAL REFLECTION ON THE LESSONS

Lesson 1: Genesis 12:1-9

Blessed for blessing. God instructed Abraham to go to a land that he would show him so that he might bless him and also bless all the people of the earth through him. Like Abraham, God blesses those who journey forth at Christ's beckoning. We are blessed in order to transmit God's blessing to all the world.

Faith of our father. Abraham is the father not only of the Jews, but of the Muslims and Christians, too. He is our father in faith. Unfortunately, not all who belong to Abraham's family share the faith of our father.

Lesson 1: Hosea 5:15—6:6

God, the spurned lover. Hosea paints a passionate picture of God. He is not so much the judge or the sovereign, demanding obedience to the letter of the law. No, he is like the lover who has been betrayed by his beloved. Hosea's painful ordeal with his own wife is a metaphor of God's relationship with his people. Hosea presents us with an emotionally wounded deity who is almost beside himself. "What shall I do with you, O Ephraim? What shall I do with you, O Judea?" (v. 4).

Loyalty due and dew-like loyalty. In verse 4, God bemoans the lack of loyalty on the part of his people. He describes it using the simile of morning dew (v. 4) — ephemeral, fleeting, easily absorbed. God yearns for the loyalty and faithfulness he regards as due him. All he receives is dew-like loyalty.

The kind of sacrifice God desires. In verse 6, God says that he desires steadfast love and not sacrifice. Actually, he yearns for the sacrifice of our love and loyalty as opposed to a superficial sacrifice of a cultic nature. It's not that religious sacrifice was bad but that it was devoid of heart and soul.

Lesson 2: Romans 4:13-25

Faith, the long and short of it. Paul informs us that Abraham was not only a man of faith but of hope, as well. Actually, faith and hope are two aspects of the same reality. Faith is trust directed toward God in the near term, in the present moment. Hope is faith projected into the future. It is faith in the long term. Abraham exercised faith in the near term by going at God's command. He showed forth faith in the long term (hope) by believing that God would make of him a great nation someday, even though he would never live to see it. Now you have the short and the long of it — faith, that is.

235

God is able. Paul states in verse 21 that Abraham didn't waver in his faith, convinced that God was able to do what he had promised. This skeptical generation has partially disabled God. The gospels record that often times, before Jesus would heal somebody, he would ask whether or not they believed he was able to heal them. Their faith seems to have had an enabling capacity for Jesus. Is our faith enabling God to do wonderful things in our life?

The power of praise. Verse 20 states that Abraham "grew strong in his faith as he gave glory to God." In some mysterious way, praise allows us to plug into the power of God. Perhaps, this power derives because in worship God's Spirit enters into our spirit.

Gospel: Matthew 9:9-13, 18-26

Why does Jesus eat with sinners? The Pharisees asked Jesus' disciples why he dined with tax collectors and sinners. This was not a real question, of course; it was a criticism. They could not conceive of any reason why a righteous Jew would ever eat with blatant sinners. Nevertheless, the question remains a good one and a fruitful topic for a sermon. Possible answers: He eats with sinners to demonstrate God's love for them. Because God wants to save them. Because sinners are the only ones open to God. Maybe Christ eats with sinners because that's the only kind of human being available. The Eucharist provides a very special occasion for thanking God that he does indeed eat with and reach out to sinners.

How to know when you're ill. Jesus came to be the physician to the sick. That is, he came to bring healing to those who realize their illness. If a person becomes ill but doesn't know he is sick or denies his illness, that person cannot be helped or healed. How does one know when he is spiritually ill? Anxiety becomes crippling. Relationships break down, starting with one's relationship with the Lord. Life becomes joyless. These are but a few symptoms. The first step to wholeness occurs when the afflicted person acknowledges his diseased condition. The second step is to put your life under the care of a physician you can trust. Jesus said: "Those who are well have no need of a physician, but those who are sick" (v. 12).

PREACHING APPROACHES WITH ILLUSTRATIONS

Lesson 1: Genesis 12:1-9
Sermon Title: How To Secure A Blessing

Sermon Angle: There is no shortage of self-appointed preachers who are ready, willing, and able (they claim) to unleash a torrent of God's blessings. All one has to do is demonstrate faith by sending in a little cash. The Abraham narrative shows us that blessings flow from our relationship with the Lord; they result from faith and obedience.

Outline:
1. God desires to bless us like he did Abraham
2. How did Abraham obtain God's blessing?
   — he believed God
   — he obeyed God
   — he persevered in hope
3. Because Abraham was faithful, he was a font of blessing for others

Lesson 1: Hosea 5:15—6:6

Sermon Title: Levels Of Loyalty

Sermon Angle: God's love and loyalty is as dependable and life-giving as the spring rains, according to Hosea (v. 3). The loyalty of God's people for their Lord is quite another thing; ephemeral as the morning dew on a summer's day (v. 4). The loyalty and faithfulness of God and that of his people are on two entirely different levels. We can always count on God's faithfulness, but can God count on our loyalty to him? God desires that we know and love him as we grow into an ever deepening level of loyalty.

Outline:

1. God's love for us has always been there for us, but our love for God has often been lacking (v. 3)
2. Loyalty is not highly valued in our individualistic culture, leading to brokenness and unhappiness
3. Relationships are more essential than outward actions (v. 6a)
   — God yearns for us to know and love him
   — He also requires faithfulness in our earthly relationships
4. Know the joy of moving to deeper levels of loyalty with God

Lesson 2: Romans 4:13-25

Sermon Title: The Flesh Is Weak But The Spirit Is Able

Sermon Angle: Paul says that Abraham trusted in God's promise of becoming the father of a great nation even though his body was "good as dead" (v. 19). His spirit was able and willing, even though his flesh was weak. In Paul's thinking, the flesh not only represents our body but our propensity to sin. We err by putting too much confidence in our flesh (physical strength) but our God is able and, by faith, we are enabled to do great things through the power of the Spirit.

Outline:

1. Abraham was old and physically weak
2. He was enabled by faith in God's promises to be the father of nations and our father in faith
3. The Spirit of God within us is our vital force, not our physical strength
4. Let God empower you for life's journey

Sermon Title: Generativity For The Geriatric Set

Sermon Angle: In our youth-dominated culture, those of advanced age are marginalized because it is believed that they don't have the capacity or strength to accomplish anything worthwhile. How mistaken they are. God has done great things with older people. Moses was quite advanced in years when he was called of God to deliver the Hebrews from their bondage in Egypt. Abraham was old when the Lord ordered him to leave his familiar surroundings for a new land, a new task, and a fresh identity. Sarah was past childbearing years when she became pregnant. Our God is the creator of all generativity and he can launch new and creative endeavors through people of any age.

Outline:

1. God used Abraham and Sarah in their sunset years to start a new nation
2. God is the source of generativity, not youth (give examples of older people who lead productive and creative lives)
3. To what new thing is God calling you?

237

A great evangelist of the nineteenth century, Dwight L. Moody, describes three different kinds of faith. First, there is struggling faith, which is compared to a person struggling to survive in deep waters. Second, there is clinging faith, which is likened to a person clinging to the edge of a boat while his body is still in the water. Finally, there is resting faith, which finds a person securely inside the boat and is free to reach out to other poor souls who are thrashing in the sea of life.

Gospel: Matthew 9:9-13, 18-26

Sermon Title: Mercy Me

Sermon Angle: After Jesus called Matthew, numbers of other tax collectors came to dine with Jesus. This scandalized the orthodox Pharisees, who were more concerned about maintaining their spiritual purity than in reclaiming sinners into the company of the committed. They indignantly queried the disciples as to why their master ate with sinners. Jesus chides the Pharisees' narrow, egotistical outlook and then quotes from Hosea 5:6: "I desire mercy and not sacrifice." Jesus teaches that the Lord is a God of mercy and he looks for mercy and compassion in those who are his own. As used in the sermon title, *mercy* is a verb, though it is not normally so used. Those who are weak and those who are sinners are crying out, *"Mercy me,"* much in the same manner that the lepers cried, "Lord, have mercy on us."

Outline:
1. There are two kinds of religion
   — a narrow, judgmental religion that separates the believers from others
   — an open religion that issues from gratitude and leads to compassion
2. Jesus denounces the former and demonstrates the latter type of religion
3. Many cry out "mercy me" and the church must invite such ones to Christ's table of grace

Sermon Title: The Call

Sermon Angle: Both Abraham and Matthew got a surprise call from God. The call had nothing to do with moral rectitude. Neither was especially deserving of a call because of past performance. It was an act of God's grace. What is noteworthy is that both of them responded faithfully to the call and followed God's leading. Every Christian has been issued a gracious call from Christ to a new life. To enter that new life requires a response of faith, demonstrated through obedience.

Outline:
1. God called Matthew to a new life
2. His call was not based on merit, only grace
3. What happened before the call doesn't matter
4. Through our baptism, we have all been called to follow Jesus
5. How have we answered that call?

* * * * *

Paul Tournier addresses an essential component of this thing we call faith in his book, *The Adventure Of Living*. It is called surrender. It's what Abraham did and Matthew did when they accepted God's call. Faith is not possible without surrender. In the chapter titled "Surrender," Tournier tells of his best friend who came to faith in Christ. His friend described his surrender as an *ah hah* experience. "Now I understand," he exclaimed. "What I must do is put my signature at the bottom of a blank page on which I will accept everything God deigns to inscribe on it. I have no idea what God is going to write on this blank contract but I have complete confidence in what God will place there." To take this risk is to embark on a life of adventure. So often, the stereotypes that we have of religious types is that of rigid, unimaginative dullness. Can you imagine the life of Abraham being a drag? Do you think Matthew left the fast lane for a life of relentless boredom? Ridiculous! Religion can produce mind-numbing rigidity and sameness but that can never be said of faith which is authentic. Tournier makes a sage observation when he makes the analogy that our attitude toward life reflects our attitude toward God and that saying, "Yes" to life is synonymous with saying, "Yes" to God.

* * * * *

Some years ago, my wife and I set out on a journey of faith. For various reasons, we felt that the Lord was leading us to leave where we were and what we were doing and set out on a new adventure of faith. I resigned my call of almost ten years and we moved to Omaha. I pursued some inklings to write both a worship and a sermonic resource. Just when it appeared that endeavor was seeming less and less viable financially, the Lord secured the contract to write this book. When the part-time pastor position I had was drawing to an end and my three year "on leave from call" status was drawing to a conclusion, the Lord opened up for me a wonderful opportunity to serve him in a fresh way just a few miles from where I live. That congregation was looking and praying for just the kind of leadership I had to offer. By faith, life becomes a wonderful journey into new realms, and God is our trusted tour director.

Proper 6/Pentecost 4/Ordinary Time 11

Revised Common:	Genesis 18:1-15	Romans 5:1-8	Matthew 9:35—10:8 (9-23)
Roman Catholic:	Exodus 19:2-6	Romans 5:6-11	Matthew 9:36—10:8
Episcopal:	Exodus 19:2-8a	Romans 5:6-11	Matthew 9:35—10:8 (9-15)

Theme: God's people are commissioned for mission. God told Moses, as recorded in Exodus 19, that the Jews were to be a kingdom of priests and a holy nation. In the gospel, the Lord empowers the apostles to go out and proclaim the gospel and minister in his name. That is our calling, too.

BRIEF COMMENTARY ON THE LESSONS

Lesson 1: Genesis 18:1-15 (C)

Three men appear to Abraham as he sits by the entrance of his tent in the heat of the day. Abraham extends gracious hospitality to them and one of the men reveals himself to be the Lord and announces that Sarah will have a child. Sarah laughs to herself at the idea of such an old woman bearing a child and is chastised by the Lord for her skepticism.

Lesson 1: Exodus 19:2-6 (RC); Exodus 19:2-8a (E)

Moses appears before God in Sinai to covenant with his people. Through his redeeming presence among his people, he has claimed the Hebrews as his special possession. In response to God's goodness, the people are called to be a kingdom of priests and a holy nation. They are to represent God to the nations.

Lesson 2: Romans 5:1-8 (C); Romans 5:6-11 (RC, E)

Having established the need for justification by grace through faith in the first few chapters, Paul discusses the consequences of our justification. "We have peace with God" (v. 1). He goes on to explain that our reconciliation with God is accomplished as God's initiative through Christ's death on the cross. Humankind had done nothing to merit God's saving action, since all have sinned (v. 8). For Christians, reconciliation is past tense; God is the subject and we are the objects. The believer has but to accept this reconciliation and rejoice.

Gospel: Matthew 9:35—10:8 (9-23) (C); Matthew 9:36—10:8 (RC); Matthew 9:35—10:8 (9-15) (E)

The gospel begins with a summation of the main facets of Jesus' ministry — preaching, teaching, and healing. In this ninth chapter, however, his healing ministry is on display. Jesus acts out of a sense of compassion for the multitudes (v. 36) but seems a bit daunted by the magnitude of human need. "The harvest is plentiful but the laborers are few" (v. 37). At the beginning of the tenth chapter, Jesus commissions and empowers the apostles (whose names are listed) to carry out the ministry of the kingdom. The harvest will be complete when many hands join in the task.

Psalm Of The Day

Psalm 116:1-2, 12-19 (C) — "What shall I return to the Lord for all his bounty to me?" (v. 16).

Psalm 100 (RC, E) — "Know that the Lord is God ... we are his people; the sheep of his pasture" (v. 3).

Prayer Of The Day

O shepherd of our souls, when we are lost, find us and bring us home. When we are wounded, soothe our hurts with the balm of your compassion. And when we are confused, set us on the right pathway, so that we might be equipped to carry out the work of your kingdom. In Jesus' name. Amen.

THEOLOGICAL REFLECTION ON THE LESSONS

Lesson 1: Genesis 18:1-15

Welcoming the stranger. This story is not only a prime example of Abraham's generosity but of near-eastern hospitality. For these nomadic wanderers, living in a harsh environment, hospitality was a way of life. It wasn't just a matter of courtesy, one's life might depend on it. Hospitality to the stranger has been largely lost as the bonds of community break down. The church is the last bastion of hospitality to the stranger. Remember the words of Jesus, "I was a stranger and you welcomed me."

Lesson 1: Exodus 19:2-8a

On eagles' wings. As God prepares to lay out his covenant to Moses, he reminds him of how he has borne them up and carried them along, as on eagles' wings. Those who study eagles have observed that when it is time for the eaglets to try their wings, their mother will nudge them out of the nest. If the little eaglet is not equal to the challenge, she will swoop down underneath her baby, so he can latch on to her back. Time and again, when the sins and weaknesses of the Hebrews led to a precipitous plummet, the Lord swooped down to lift them up and carry them along.

Kingdom of priests. God informs his people that if they keep his covenant, they will serve him as a "kingdom of priests and a holy nation" (v. 6). God had ordained them into a special role and ministry. The people accepted the privilege of their priestly position but usually lost sight of the responsibility of their calling. As a priestly people, they were called to set an example of holy living and to represent God to the nations. In 1 Peter 2:9, this concept of a priestly people is applied to the church. We are called to bring the nations to God and God to the nations.

Listen to your elders. Moses presented the covenant of the Lord to the people through the elders (v. 7). They set an example of spiritual leadership for all the nation. Elders were looked upon as people of sound faith, wisdom, and wide experience. In our culture of youth, we have dismissed the wisdom of our elders as being hopelessly outdated. With the exception of the Reformed tradition, most churches don't even call their leaders elders. Isn't it time we turned back to the wealth of wisdom and spiritual discernment we have in our Christian elders?

Lesson 2: Romans 5:1-11

A religion for weaklings. Paul says that "while we were still weak, Christ died for the ungodly" (v. 6). Christianity has long been accused of being a religion for weaklings, and so it is. Christ does not offer salvation to supermen, only super sinners. Is that the reason that less men are active in the Lord's work than women, because men cannot admit that they are weak and vulnerable, while women can?

What time is it? Paul states that it was at the *right time* that Christ died for the ungodly (v. 6). The kind of time being spoken of here is a translation of the Greek *kairos*, denoting time as special or qualitative. Christ died for us sinners when the time was right and this very moment is the right time to accept God's salvation.

Friends of the Lord? The term friend does not exactly fit the relationship we have with the Lord because friendship implies equality. Paul talks about our being reconciled with the Lord through the cross. Reconciliation doesn't necessarily imply friendship, but how could we characterize our relationship with the Lord? We are no longer enemies. We are much more than mere acquaintances. We are more than servants. So, I guess we really are friends with God. In the gospel of John, Jesus tells his disciples that they are not merely servants but his friends, because he has revealed his heart to them. Friendship involves the grace of accepting the other just as she is. With a friend, we can reveal our true selves without fear of betrayal or rejection. What a friend we have in Jesus!

Gospel: Matthew 9:35—10:8 (9-23)

Ministry on the move. This lection opens with the statement that Jesus went about all the cities and villages, proclaiming the kingdom through word and deed. The Lord did not wait for people to come to him. He proclaimed the good news of the kingdom in the marketplaces and in the synagogues, in the cities and the countryside. Jesus brought the kingdom to bear at the point of human need, rather than expecting the people to minister to the kingdom at the point of its need. Regrettably, the church has often failed to employ this most successful mission strategy of our Lord.

Preaching, teaching, and healing. If the kingdom is the food and the implement that Jesus used to serve it was a fork, the three tines on the fork would be preaching, teaching, and healing. Preaching prevails on the heart, the seat of our will, where decisions are made. One must first decide to follow Christ. Healing ministers to the body and the mind, to effect wholeness. And teaching ministers to the mind, so that the disciple understands the implications and applications of the gospel for daily life.

Christ for the common person. Matthew comments that when Jesus viewed the crowds of needy people coming to him, he had compassion for them because they were so harassed and helpless (v. 36). These were peasant people, for the most part, the lilies of the field rather than the well-ordered flowers in an English garden.

Labor shortage. Christ viewed human need as an opportunity to usher people into the kingdom of God. When God's people satisfy human needs, doors open to the gospel. The problem resides in the gigantic scale of such needs. As Jesus beheld the hoards of hurting folk, he repined: "The harvest is plentiful, but the laborers are few" (v. 37). Who is going to supply the labor shortfall? Those disciples who seem to have it all together? Most of us are more like sheep than shepherds, in that we are all harassed and helpless to some degree. Yet, by God's grace, we can make a difference. The band of disciples that Jesus sent out were far from perfect, yet they did great things in Christ's name.

Mission strategy. The reason so many churches never seem to move out in mission is that either they have no mission strategy or have one that is poorly defined. Jesus was very clear about his as he prepared to send out his disciples. He told them to limit their outreach to the Jews. This doesn't mean that he didn't care for Gentiles or Samaritans, but his mission strategy was to reach the Jews and, through them, the rest of the world.

PREACHING APPROACHES WITH ILLUSTRATIONS

Lesson 1: Genesis 18:1-5

Sermon Title: Incognito

Sermon Angle: God appeared to Abraham incognito in the guise of three strangers. Abraham did not recognize the Lord but welcomed these strangers with profuse hospitality. One never knows when God will appear, but he often takes the form of the stranger, the visitor, or the uninvited guest. In welcoming the stranger, we welcome the Lord.

Sermon Title: Limiting The Lord

Sermon Angle: When the Lord told Abraham that he was going to have a child, Sarah secretly laughed. That she should bear a child in her old age seemed impossible, even humorous. The stranger (God) reproved her by saying: "Is anything too wonderful for the Lord?" (v. 14). We can't be too hard on Sarah for her incredulity. We also limit the Lord to the level of our experience.

Lesson 1: Exodus 19:2-8a

Sermon Title: On Eagles' Wings

Sermon Angle: Before God established his covenant with the Hebrews, he recounted his great acts of redemption. He saved them from the power of their oppressor and bore them up on eagles' wings (v. 4). The eagle is a symbol of strength and majesty; no creature can soar with the eagle, which makes it immune to all predators. Just as the mother eagle swoops down to bear up her young, so the Lord lifts up those who are his own.

Outline:
1. To be human is to experience weakness
2. As God's children, we experience God's strength at the point of our weakness
3. God's strength is like an eagle's
   — he may push us out of the nest to make us strong
   — but he swoops down to lift us up when we are too weak to fly

Sermon Title: A Priestly People

Sermon Angle: Through God's great acts of redemption he ordained the Hebrew people to be a kingdom of priests and a consecrated people. They were to bring the nations to God and God to the nations. In a similar vein, Luther enunciated the doctrine of the priesthood of all believers.

Outline:
1. The Hebrews were called to be a priestly people in response to God's salvation
2. We are called to be a priestly people in response to Christ's sacrifice
   — witnessing to Christ's love
   — offering our lives as a sacrifice of worship
   — extending his forgiveness

Lesson 2: Romans 5:1-11

Sermon Title: Beyond Self-Justification

Sermon Angle: Paul's concept of justification is based on the premise that sin is real and that it needs to be accounted for. That's why Christ died on the cross, to pay the punishment of our sin, so that we might be declared not guilty by God. In our day, many people are more concerned with self-justification than being justified by God. Self-justification is an effort to evade responsibility by constructing excuses and blaming others. Self-justification makes a mockery of justice and righteousness. Justification by grace through faith takes sin seriously. We accept our guilt but hold that Christ has taken the rap for us. God now regards us as righteous and innocent.

Outline:

1. Our society has lost its moral compass
   — sin and wrong are not recognized as such
   — the guilty seek to justify rather than repent of their sin
2. Christ offers another way — justification through the cross (v. 6)
3. Move from self-justification to justification by Christ
   — acknowledge your guilt
   — accept his forgiveness and his righteousness

Gospel: Matthew 9:35—10:8 (9-23)

Sermon Title: The Pillars Of The Church

Sermon Angle: The gospels inform us that Jesus' ministry was divided into three main components — preaching, teaching, and healing. His preaching was to make the kingdom known and call for a response. The teaching was to apply the principles of the kingdom to daily life. The healing was to make known that God's intention for his creation is wholeness of body, mind, and spirit. If we make strong those pillars, the success of the church's mission is assured.

Sermon Title: Itinerant Evangelists

Sermon Angle: Jesus commissioned his apostles to be itinerant evangelists, to take the gospel to the people by word and deed. In our day, itinerant evangelists have gotten some bad press with scandals, affairs, and the like. Actually though, the church is a society of itinerant evangelists. The good news of Jesus is not to be hermetically sealed in the church structure, but proclaimed in the marketplace, the streets, and the back alleys. We are to heal and empower the harassed and helpless through the gospel wherever we go.

* * * * *

In David Buttrick's book, *Homiletic*, he distinguishes two arenas for preaching. There is *in church preaching*, usually performed by an ordained person in the context of the Christian community. When we lift up preaching, this is what we normally have in mind. The other type of preaching he labels *out church preaching*. This proclamation is performed primarily by the laity, and the arena is not the church but the world. Yet, few churches train their laity as to how they can present their faith in an authentically Christian manner, and some lay people do not take seriously their commission to proclaim the gospel out in the world. Instead of witnessing to Christ, many Christian people launch into a sales pitch for their congregation. Oh, you've got to come to our church! Our pastor is so neat! Our choir sings beautifully. We have a bowling

244

league and softball teams. Our Sunday school is super and our youth group goes on all manner of fun outings. We have something for everybody in our church. We've got what you're looking for. Such an approach diverts the attention away from the crucial questions such as: What does Christ mean to me? Where is Christ in my life? What difference does my faith make in my daily existence?

*   *   *   *   *

We cannot assume that the audience for our *in church preaching* is totally Christian. Some of those on the church rolls have not internalized the gospel. Many who have turned a deaf ear to the gospel of grace are living under the law. Furthermore, those who are searching for God are apt to visit the local congregation at worship. Some degree of *out church preaching* must transpire in the *in church setting.* That is, the worship and sermon must address issues cogent to those outside the Christian faith. To use a phrase popularized by Patrick Kiefert, an associate professor at Luther Northwestern Seminary in St. Paul, Minnesota, the church is called to welcome the stranger, to be a community of welcome. In his book, *Welcoming The Stranger,* Kiefert related an experience that occurred on the now-defunct *Dick Cavett Show.* As a distinguished guest was being welcomed to the show, Cavett noticed that the fly on his trousers was unzipped. What could he do without embarrassing his guest? A light bulb went off in his head. He ordered all the guests to stand up and turn around and pull up their zipper, explaining that one of them had his open. Nobody in the audience knew which one of them had their barn door open. Cavett created an atmosphere of hospitality by not forcing his guests to reveal the intimate details of their life. If we want people to come back to our communities of faith, we must provide an environment where they can participate without standing out or feeling odd and embarrassed.

Proper 7/Pentecost 5/Ordinary Time 12

Revised Common:	Genesis 21:8-21	Romans 6:1b-11	Matthew 10:24-39
Roman Catholic:	Jeremiah 20:10-13	Romans 5:12-15	Matthew 10:26-33
Episcopal:	Jeremiah 20:7-13	Romans 5:15b-19	Matthew 10:(16-23) 24-33

Theme: Adversity one suffers in faithfulness to God. In the first lesson, Jeremiah gives vent to his despair brought on by reaction to his unpopular prophecies. In the gospel, Jesus informs his disciples to expect suffering and opposition, similar to that which he had received.

BRIEF COMMENTARY ON THE LESSONS

Lesson 1: Genesis 21:8-21 (C)

Sarah jealously guards the rights of her natural son, Isaac, by ordering Abraham to throw out her slave girl, Hagar, with her son. God speaks to Abraham in his distress about the plight of Hagar and her son, telling him to do as Sarah wished because his descendants would be counted through Isaac. Furthermore, God would also make a great nation through Ishmael.

Lesson 1: Jeremiah 20:10-13 (RC); Jeremiah 20:7-13 (E)

Jeremiah was born about 650 B.C. and began his ministry in the 13th year of King Josiah's reign. As the Babylonian threat mounts, the prophet warns his nation to repent or face destruction at the hand of the enemy. His message is met with great antagonism and consequent isolation. In great distress of soul, Jeremiah accuses God of being deceitful with him and taking advantage of his weakness. The prophet makes a pact with himself not to speak any longer in the name of the Lord, but the word of the Lord is like fire in his bones. We witness in this text Jeremiah's painful struggle to be faithful in his calling to be the Lord's spokesman.

Lesson 2: Romans 6:1b-11 (C); Romans 5:12-15 (RC); Romans 5:15b-19 (E)

Paul views Adam as the pioneer of sin and Christ as the progenitor of salvation. The disobedience of the one man, Adam, unleashes the power of sin. The obedience of the one man, Jesus Christ, makes many people righteous. Just as sin exercises dominion in death, so also, grace exercises dominion through justification. Chapter 6 continues by pointing out that those who have been baptized into Christ have put to death their sinful natures. Since they are now new persons in Christ, they can no longer continue under the sway of sin and death.

Gospel: Matthew 10:24-39 (C); Matthew 10:26-33 (RC); Matthew 10:(16-23) 24-33 (E)

The tenth chapter contains a number of sayings which the Lord spoke at different times in his ministry concerning opposition and suffering, which his disciples ought to expect. The disciples should not expect better treatment than their teacher (v. 25). As Jesus was maligned, so too would be those called by his name. They are counseled not to be anxious about their fate or fearful of their enemies' unwarranted accusations. Truth would triumph. There is nothing hidden that would not be revealed in the judgment of God (v. 26). God cares about the smallest aspect of their existence, so they can commend their lives into his keeping. The only fear that the disciple of Jesus should have is that she would turn her back to the Lord.

Psalm Of The Day

Psalm 86:1-10, 16-17 (C) — "In the day of my trouble I call on you ..." (v. 7).

Psalm 69:1-18 (RC, E) — "Save me, O God, for the waters have come up to my neck" (v. 1).

Prayer Of The Day

Merciful Savior, when the waters of adversity mount up to our necks, threatening to sweep over our heads, hear our cry for deliverance. You are the rock to which we cling, forbid that we ever lose our grip on your grace and love. In the powerful name of Jesus, we are bold to make known to you our every thought or need. Amen.

THEOLOGICAL REFLECTION ON THE LESSONS

Lesson 1: Genesis 21:8-21

God hears the cries of his people. It doesn't seem right that Hagar and her son were thrust out from the protection of Abraham's care. Yet God hears the cries of his people who suffer injustice. When Hagar's provisions ran out, she put her child down on the ground and then went a distance, so that she wouldn't have to watch her child die. The infant cried out and God heard his cry; God encouraged Hagar to care for her son. When she did so, she beheld a wall of water to sustain them.

Lesson 1: Jeremiah 20:7-13

Wrestling with the Lord. Recall the story of Jacob wrestling with God until the break of day. We see the same kind of struggle taking place in Jeremiah. Only this time, it's God who won't let go. The Lord won't permit him to remain silent to avoid the opposition of his friends and neighbors. Jeremiah's complaint was that the match was unfair because God was stronger than he (v. 7). Real faith does not come without a struggle, because our human will often comes into conflict with the Lord's will. It is the struggle that makes us strong. Those who attain a faith like Jeremiah's discover that the Lord is not our enemy but our ally in the struggle of life. When we are on God's side, victory is assured.

Honest to God. No writer in the Bible is more honest in expressing his inward feelings than Jeremiah. He didn't tell God what piety told him to say, he let it rip! He told God exactly how he felt and what he thought of him. Jeremiah informed God that he thought he was unfair, that he had tricked and deceived him. Some of us may have had such thoughts, but we probably didn't share them with the Lord or even other believers. Notice that God didn't strike him dead. God certainly understood the difficulty of what his prophet was going through. Oftentimes we play the good Christian games and deny our true feelings. God knows how we feel. It would be healthier for us to be honest to God.

Lesson 2: Romans 6:1b-11; Romans 5:12-19

The power of one. We often make the excuse: I'm only one person, what can I do? History demonstrates that one person can have a lasting influence on the world. Think of the monumental influence of Alexander the Great, Julius Caesar, Martin Luther, Copernicus, Einstein, and Hitler. Paul maintains that sin entered the world because of the disobedience of the one man, Adam, and infected us all. He also holds that grace and forgiveness have entered the world through the one man, Jesus Christ, bringing life to many.

Gospel: Matthew 10:24-39

Realistic expectations. Jesus wanted his disciples to have realistic expectations about how the world would receive the gospel. They would meet with a good deal of opposition, just like their Lord. Their goodness would be portrayed as evil (vv. 24-25). If we have a realistic view of the challenges that face us, we are less likely to fold when the heat is on.

The focus of your fears. In preparing his disciples for the coming spiritual battles, Jesus instructed them not to fear the enemies of the gospel, because their power was limited. Rather, they should fear God because he had the power to commit both body and soul to hell. It's not that Jesus was trying to convince his followers to relate to God out of fear. Instead, he is attempting to show the inappropriateness of most of our fears, because we fear those who have no power to touch our souls. Fear is appropriate and helpful if it prevents us from risking our lives foolishly. On the other side of the ledger, fear is destructive if it causes us to expend time and energy on that which is no real threat to our being.

Fear, love, and worship. Jesus taught his disciples the proper fear of God. In the Old Testament theophanies, the human witnesses were filled with awe, fear, and trembling as they stood in the presence of God. Isaiah was so smitten with the fear of God that he felt doomed. We moderns don't seem to tremble before the Lord any longer. Either we don't feel that the Lord is a power to be reckoned with any more or we have permitted our concept of the love of God to drive out any vestige of fear, believing that fear and love are not compatible. The Bible teaches that God is to be both feared and loved. Fear represents the vertical dimension of faith. God is above and beyond us. This is not a relationship of equals, because God is the one to whom we owe an absolute obedience. Love apprehends the horizontal dimension of our relationship with the Lord. It tells us that God is alongside of us. We can freely entrust our lives into his care. Some may beg to differ, but I don't feel we can truly worship God without the component of fear as well as love.

God cares about the little stuff. Jesus teaches that God is so interested in us and concerned for our well being, that he even numbers the hairs on our heads (v. 30). Some people point out that they pray to God when they have a really big problem but they don't view it as proper to concern him with the little stuff. But think about it; 99% of life is composed of the little stuff. If we don't share the little stuff with God, we have effectively aced him out of the great majority of our existence. God shows his love for us by urging us to invite him into the totality of our being.

PREACHING APPROACHES WITH ILLUSTRATIONS

Lesson 1: Genesis 21:8-21

Sermon Title: God Hears The Cries Of The Oppressed

Sermon Angle: It's hard to ignore the cry of a child. God made us that way, so that the needs of his helpless children would not be ignored. Can God be any less attentive to the needs of his children? When they cry out in pain or fear, he hastens to respond. He hears the cry of the mother abandoned by her husband and the child abandoned by the mother. In compassion, he saves those whom life has dealt a vicious and seemingly unfair blow. God will bless them and keep them. Our God hears the cries of the oppressed. Do we?

Outline:
1. Recite the story of Hagar and her son
2. The Hagars and the Ishmaels are legion in our sinful world

3. Yet, God is not deaf to their cries and sends angels of mercy
4. Are your ears attuned to hear and heed the cries of the desperate?

Lesson 1: Jeremiah 20:7-13

Sermon Title: The Proper Fear Of God

Sermon Angle: In reading this lamentation of Jeremiah, as well as many other such outbursts, one might assume that he did not have a proper fear of God. In his moments of frustration, and they were many, he accused God of being a trickster and a bully, just for starters. Yet, for all his complaining, he never failed in his commission to be the mouth of the Lord. He never shirked his duty. God judges us more by our actions than our words. To fear the Lord manifests itself in obedience to the Lord.

Sermon Title: Honest-To-God Prayer

Sermon Angle: Prayer that is not brutally honest is just so much pious prating. That's why Jeremiah's prayers are so refreshing; he just bares his soul to the Lord. God accepts us just as we are. It's pretending that puts him off. Recall the parable told in Luke's gospel of the Pharisee and the tax collector. We need to hold up the example of such honest-to-God prayer.

Outline:
1. When's the last time you had an honest-to-God prayer?
2. Actually, there is no other kind
3. Jeremiah is a prime example of such authentic prayer
4. Principles of honest-to-God prayer
   — don't worry about the vocabulary of prayer
   — don't be concerned about what others think of your prayers
   — be honest to God (take off your mask)
   — do what God directs you to do
   — thank God for blessings (Jeremiah sometimes forgot this one)

Lesson 2: Romans 6:1b-11; Romans 5:12-19

Sermon Title: God's Gift Of Grace

Sermon Angle: God offers the world the gift of his grace, forgiveness, and eternal life through Jesus Christ. We have but to accept the gift, open it up, and share it with others.

Gospel: Matthew 10:24-39

Sermon Title: Fear, Love, And Worship

Sermon Angle: The proper end for every believer is to worship God. Worship involves both fear and love: fear, because God is awesome, transcendent, almighty, and mysterious; love, because God has shown his love for us in Jesus Christ and in his provision for our every need. Jesus teaches concerning these two vital components of relationship with God, which inform our worship.

Outline:
1. What part do fear and love play in your worship?
   — if we only fear God, there is no room for love
   — if we only love God, he is not a fitting object of worship
2. Jesus teaches that we should fear God, not people (v. 28)
3. Jesus also teaches that we can love God because he loves us (vv. 29-31)

One of the central reasons for family breakdown in our society is that parents no longer claim, yea, demand, their rightful authority. Children no longer fear God or their parents. Don't misunderstand; I'm not advocating that parents rule with an iron hand or that fear should replace love, but if parents would inject a little dose of fear in their relationships with their children, the health of the family might get a needed boost. If parents would set limits, and children would fear transgressing those limits, there would be less delinquency. If children would mind their manners because they fear hurting their parents or bringing dishonor to the family name, would that be a bad thing? I think not.

William Safire, a *New York Times* columnist, writes that what fathers want most for Father's Day is not designer ties or polo shirts. Fathers want their authority back. He argues that the proper role of father is not that of friend, which seems to be the role so many parents take these days. No, a father is someone a child should look up to. Safire puts forth a thesis with which many would contend. "Motherpower is rooted in love, fatherpower in authority." It's not that nurturing is necessarily foreign to men, some do it very well, but moms are more naturally adept at it. Dads are better suited at laying down the law. At least, this is Safire's opinion. I can't help but wonder if the lack of respect for all authority structures could be traced, in part, to the abandoning of authority by dads. Could it be that some men lash out in violence and abuse against their family out of a misguided attempt to reclaim authority? Has the proper holy fear and respect for fatherly authority been replaced by a hellish fear?

Sermon Title: Truth Or Consequences

Sermon Angle: Back in the '50s there was a television show by the named of *Truth Or Consequences*. I don't remember much about the show except its name, but wisdom is contained therein. If you don't tell the truth and live the truth, there are terrible consequences. Jesus said, "What you have heard in the dark, tell in the light and what you hear whispered, proclaim from the housetops" (v. 27). These words were spoken in an era antagonistic to the gospel; its truth was shared secretly, for fear of punishment. The Lord says to proclaim its truth from the housetops without fear of the consequences. In the judgment of God, those who lived the truth will be revealed. Ultimately, the truth is not a thing but a person, Jesus Christ. If we proclaim the truth, the truth will proclaim us (vv. 32-33).

Outline:
1. In the boardrooms of politics and business, truth is often concealed
2. If we conceal the truth, we must bear the consequences (violence, bondage)
3. Jeremiah told the truth and took the consequences
4. The counsel of Christ is to publicly proclaim the truth (v. 27)
5. If we witness to Christ, he will acknowledge us

Sermon Title: God Of The Mundane

Sermon Angle: When a big problem occurs, the first thing we do is turn to God. Not so with the little, inconsequential concerns of life. Jesus teaches that God numbers the hairs on our heads (v. 30). Such a God is aware of the entirety of our being. We can be confident of his protection and pray to him in all circumstances.

* * * * *

When I was ordained, my father gave me a large diamond ring that he inherited from his father. Sometimes I would take it off at night and place it on the bathroom counter. As we were driving to Wisconsin for two weeks vacation, I noticed I had forgotten to put on my ring but I didn't worry about it because I knew where it was. At least, I thought that I did. When we arrived home, I proceeded to look for the ring. It wasn't on the counter. It wasn't on the dresser or in the jewelry box. I looked frantically. Maybe one of my daughters saw this shiny rock, and picked it up as a plaything. We looked in the toy boxes, in the recreation room, down in the basement where they played, outside. We hadn't the foggiest notion where to go from there. I hadn't prayed about it. I thought, God has more important things to concern himself about than my ring. But one day, in desperation, I decided to petition the Lord. I prayed, "Lord, I know you have other issues on your mind and I don't need this ring really; but it was given to me by my dad and it means a lot to him because it was from his father. I don't want to hurt my dad by telling him I was so careless as to lose his ring. Please, Lord, help me find it. In Jesus' name. Amen."

My eldest daughter stopped by the church and we walked home for lunch. We had just finished eating and my daughter went out to play. Shortly, she rushed in saying, "I found Daddy's ring, I found Daddy's ring!" Apparently, my three-year-old picked it up, took it to the neighbor's and proceeded to drop it in the dirt. My eldest found it half buried. Nobody can convince me that God doesn't answer prayer.

Proper 8/Pentecost 6/Ordinary Time 13

Revised Common:	Genesis 22:1-14	Romans 6:12-23	Matthew 10:40-42
Roman Catholic:	2 Kings 4:8-11, 14-16	Romans 6:3-4, 8-11	Matthew 10:37-42
Episcopal:	Isaiah 2:10-17	Romans 6:3-11	Matthew 10:34-42

Theme: The costs and the awards of following Jesus.

BRIEF COMMENTARY ON THE LESSONS

Lesson 1: Genesis 22:1-14 (C)

God tests Abraham's faith and loyalty by ordering him to sacrifice his son. Just as he is ready to plunge the knife into the child, God stops Abraham, commenting that now he has proven his obedience to the Lord. A ram caught in a thicket substitutes for Isaac as a sacrifice.

Lesson 1: 2 Kings 4:8-11, 14-16 (RC)

A woman from Shunem extends hospitality to Elisha the prophet by serving him meals and appointing a room in her house for the prophet to lodge whenever he is in the area. The prophet reciprocates by praying for a son for this childless woman.

Lesson 1: Isaiah 2:10-17 (E)

The Lord will cut down to size all those who are arrogant and full of pride.

Lesson 2: Romans 6:12-23 (C)

Some people distorted Paul's gospel of grace by arguing that since they were not saved through the law or by good works but by faith, it didn't matter what they did with their bodies. Paul contends that we are either slaves of sin or slaves of righteousness. Since through Christ we are slaves of righteousness, we cannot revert to being slaves of sin. Paul commands the believers to not let sin gain control of their bodies (v. 12).

Lesson 2: Romans 6:3-4, 8-11 (RC); Romans 6:3-11 (E)

"Should we continue in sin that grace may abound?" (1b). Some were using the Gospel as a pretext for libertine behavior. Human sin gave God an opportunity to show his graciousness. So let's sin that grace might increase. Paul's answer to the question posed in verse 1 is an emphatic: "By no means!" He buttresses his argument through his theology of baptism. In baptism, believers are dead to sin and are raised to newness of life with Christ. Consequently, we must consider ourselves dead to sin and alive to God (v. 11).

Gospel: Matthew 10:40-42 (C); Matthew 10:37-42 (RC); Matthew 10:34-42 (E)

Jesus is brutally honest with his followers concerning the cost of discipleship. It will bring strife and division among friends and family. "I have not come to bring peace, but a sword" (v. 34). It is not his intention to bring division; rather, it is a by-product of loyalty to Christ and fidelity to the truth. Some will accept his claims, and some will reject them. The result is division. Yet faithfulness is higher on Christ's scale of values than peace. Those who love their family more than Christ are not worthy of him. The disciples must be willing to suffer for the sake of the gospel and give their lives (vv. 38-39). Yet those who welcome and receive one of his disciples welcome Christ. Whoever receives one of God's servants also receives the same reward as the servant. Those who sacrifice for the sake of the kingdom will not lose their reward. Thus, this passage sums up the costs and the awards of following Jesus.

Psalm Of The Day

Psalm 13 (C) — "But I trusted in your steadfast love" (v. 5).

Psalm 89:1-4, 15-18 (RC, E) — "I will sing of your steadfast love, O Lord, forever" (v. 1a).

Prayer Of The Day

Lord Christ, open our eyes that we might follow you, knowing full well what is required and what it will cost us. But also hold before us the eternal weight of glory that you have promised to those who are willing to take up their cross for your sake. In Jesus' name. Amen.

THEOLOGICAL REFLECTION ON THE LESSONS

Lesson 1: Genesis 22:1-14

The test. God tested Abraham's faith by asking him to sacrifice his son. It seems like God is being cruel here, asking him to offer up the son through whom God was supposed to fulfill his promise to make of him a great nation. God appears to rub his nose in it by emphasizing that it's his only son, whom he loves, that he is asked to give up (v. 2). Did Abraham have such intimate knowledge of God that he knew it was a test? Who knows? We do know that Abraham trusted God implicitly, knowing that God would not ask him to do anything cruel or irrational. Abraham had the trust to pass God's formal test because God had passed Abraham's informal test of reliability.

The sacrifice. The same Father who restrained Abraham from sacrificing his son offered up his Son on the high place of the cross. This time, there was no one to stop the oblation, no substitute for this ultimate sacrifice. It was a sacrifice on top of a sacrifice. Christ had already offered his life to the Father in a perfect sacrifice of obedience. It's not that God needs our sacrifices or even desires them. What God does desire is a sacrificial spirit within each one of us. The supreme sacrifice of Christ was not offered to placate an angry God, but to elicit within us the willingness to give freely of ourselves and our substance.

Lesson 2: Romans 6:12-23

Choose well your master. Starting in verse 20, Paul employs an analogy from slavery to refute those who were saying that his gospel of grace was promoting sin. He points out that before faith in Christ, they were slaves to sin. Such bondage results in destruction and ultimate death. After faith, the believer becomes a slave of righteousness. but such allegiance yields the fruits of holiness and eternal life. We do not have the choice of not serving any master. We have only to choose whether we will be slaves of sin or of Christ. Choose well whom you will serve.

Lesson 2: Romans 6:3-11

The problem with grace. One of the early Jewish arguments against the gospel of grace was that it would destroy morals. There would be no incentive for righteous behavior. Indeed, that very doctrine was used as a pretext for immoral behavior. Let us sin, that God's grace might abound. Grace can indeed transform behavior but only for those who have been truly born anew through the Gospel. The unredeemed world in which we live operates primarily under the rubric of law, not grace. The law punishes and restrains evildoers, maintaining order, but cannot change sinners into saints. Only the gospel can do that.

Born anew in baptism. The image of death and resurrection which we see in this passage equates to being born anew in baptism. Paul's point is that those who have put on Christ have died to the slavery of sin through their baptism. In addition, just as Christ was raised from the dead, so we shall be raised to newness of life. Notice that the new resurrected life is in the future tense (v. 8). Christians have already begun to enter that new life, but the fullness of the Christ-life in us will not be realized until we enter into glory. Nevertheless, believers must already consider themselves dead to sin and alive to God (v. 11). We must now live the new life that is to come.

Gospel: Matthew 10:34-42

Something greater than peace. The words of Jesus shock us. "I have not come to bring peace, but a sword" (v. 34). Doesn't Isaiah call him the Prince of Peace? Didn't the Hebrew prophets foretell that the Messiah would usher in a reign of peace? Once again, Jesus doesn't fulfill the common expectations of the faithful, but we must be cognizant that Jesus is employing hyperbole here — strong and exaggerated language that strives to make a point. What is the point? There is something greater than peace, namely, truth. Jesus claims to incarnate the truth of God. Some will accept this claim while others will not. The result is division, hostility, and strife. With Christ, there can be no compromise with falsehood.

Focus on the family? Dr. James Dobson's organization, Focus On The Family, is an understandable, even laudable, reaction to the continuing disintegration of the American family. Yet, I wonder, is that really where our ultimate focus ought to be? The family? I know what the Jesus of the gospels would say: that our focus ought to be the kingdom of God and his righteousness. Family harmony is secondary. As Jesus pointed out, if our ultimate loyalty is to him and to the kingdom, family strife might increase if other family members are antagonistic, even apathetic, to the claims of Christ. However, if Christian faith is shared within the family, it can't help but cement those basic relationships.

Messianic expectations. The pious Jews of Jesus' day shared the expectation that God's Anointed One would be ushered into the world during a period of war, strife, and family disharmony. Jesus seems to identify himself with these messianic expectations. It's not so hard to understand why strife would increase at such a time. When God's forces are the strongest, the reaction of the Evil One becomes more active to meet the challenge. Good and evil, like oil and water, do not mix.

Be a high roller. Jesus proclaims, "He who finds his life will lose it but he who loses his (her) life for my sake will find it" (v. 39). His counsel is to forget about playing it safe. Be a holy gambler, be a high roller, and take the risk of following Christ. We may lose the life we had, but Christ promises in its place a life that is eternal.

Equal pay for the supporting cast. Jesus said, "He who receives a prophet because he is a prophet, will receive a prophet's reward and he who receives a righteous man because he is a righteous man, will receive a righteous man's reward." The supporting cast for Christ's kingdom will receive the same pay as the stars, the main actors.

PREACHING APPROACHES WITH ILLUSTRATIONS

Lesson 1: Genesis 22:1-14

Sermon Title: Giving Back To God

Sermon Angle: The writer of this account states that God asked Abraham to sacrifice his son as a test (v. 1). It seems like a very cruel test. How do we reconcile this order with a loving and merciful God? The heathens sacrificed their children to their gods, but the Lord? Yet we must admit that God had the right to make such a request. Isaac, like all children, was a gift of God. Abraham was not being asked to give up merely his own son but God's son. As the offertory states: "We give thee but thine own ... All that we have is thine alone...." After all, doesn't Jesus urge us to sacrifice our lives to him by taking up our cross?

Sermon Title: Substitutionary Sacrifice

Sermon Angle: The Old Testament sacrificial system was for two primary reasons. The first was to atone for human sin. The animal was a substitute for the guilty party. The second was to demonstrate that God is the Lord of all. The sacrifice was a token of giving back to God what was rightfully his. Both concepts of sacrifice underlie the sacrifice that Abraham was requested to make. God provided the ram in substitution for the life of Abraham's child. God has also provided a substitutionary sacrifice for you and me in the person of his Son.

Outline:
1. Jewish worship centered around substitutionary sacrifice
2. We are all beneficiaries of substitutionary sacrifice
   — soldiers gave their lives on our behalf, to preserve our freedom
3. God desires not our death but our lives
   — God provided a sacrificial substitute for Abraham's son
   — God sent his Son to die for our sins

Lesson 2: Romans 6:12-23

Sermon Title: Yield!

Sermon Angle: You pull your car onto the ramp for the freeway, and the sign says "Yield." This means that you are not to bully your way into the main traffic flow but to yield to it. Some of us don't like to yield. We want to get ahead, to assert ourselves. Yet, what chaos and destruction results when we refuse to yield! Actually, we have no choice but to yield to someone or something. If our lives are not yielded in obedience to the Lord, we are automatically under the power of the evil one, whose tools we become. When we yield our lives to righteousness we become the "carpenter's tools," building for eternity (v. 13).

Outline:
1. Refusing to yield sets lives on a crash course
2. Jesus yielded his life to the Father (the cross)
3. Our choice — yield to sin or to righteousness (v. 13)
4. To be a Christian is to choose righteousness because we have already been chosen by God for salvation (v. 22).

Lesson 2: Romans 6:3-11

Sermon Title: Baptism And Behavior

Sermon Angle: Paul asks a crucial question: "How can those who died in sin still live in it?" (v. 1). In baptism, Christians die to sin and are raised to newness of life with Christ. If this is so, how indeed can we live in sin? Paul is talking about behavior here. If we are new creatures in Christ, we will demonstrate this through the fruit of our actions.

Gospel: Matthew 10:34-42

Sermon Title: The Hour Of Decision

Sermon Angle: To understand Jesus' instructions to his disciples as he sends them out on their mission, one must realize that this is not business as usual. This is a time of crisis, an hour of decision. A new order is being ushered in as Jesus holds up the kingdom of God. The world has to decide between Jesus and the claims of the world, the old order. The kingdom of Jesus will, at first, bring dislocation and dissension. People will have to decide between the old order and the kingdom of Christ.

*　*　*　*　*

The upheaval that Jesus told his followers to expect bears some likeness to what happened in the former Soviet Union. During the old regime, there was certainly order. People didn't have any freedom, but they knew what to expect; the state would take care of their basic needs. With the abandoning of communism, great upheaval occurred. Community, as it was known, had broken down. No one ought to claim that the advent of a free market economy will usher in the kingdom of God for the Russian people. Yet, like in Jesus' day, it was and is a time of crisis. People must decide if they are going to support the new Russia or strive to go back to the old order. A new order is not born without suffering, sacrifice, and death.

*　*　*　*　*

Wolfhart Pannenberg warns that if Christianity is to make an impact, churches will need to steer clear of fundamentalism, on the one hand, and acceptance of secular values, on the other. So warned the University of Munich professor of theology in a speech May 11, 1994, at the annual "Erasmus Lecture" at St. Peter's Lutheran Church in New York City. This lecture was sponsored by the Institute on Religion and Public Life. In an increasingly secularized world, Pannenberg asserted that the church will have to model such values as tolerance, morality, and objective truth. The idea "that society could survive without religion is a delusion," he says. Mainline Protestant churches are no longer equipped for the task of lifting up the truth of the gospel because they are too accepting of contemporary culture and are not defending Christian claims to truth in secular settings. Pannenberg predicts that mainline churches will be eclipsed by Roman Catholic, Eastern Orthodox, and evangelical churches unless they distance themselves from secular culture and regain their Christian identity. (Based on an article in *The Christian Century*, June 15-24, 1994.)

Sermon Title: Ambassadors For God

Sermon Angle: In sending out the disciples, Jesus taught that any person who received them received him, and anyone who received him received the one who sent him, that is God himself (v. 40). The image here is of ambassadorship. To receive the ambassador of a country is to receive the president of the country. To welcome the representative is to honor the country or the leader he or she represents. As Paul reminds us, we are ambassadors for Christ, God making his appeal through us (2 Corinthians 5:20). We must always keep in mind that we are Christ's ambassadors but also stand ready to receive other ambassadors for Christ.

Outline:

1. God doesn't usually come to us in pure spirit form, but enfleshed
2. Jesus said, "He who receives you, receives me ..."
   — we are ambassadors for Christ
   — those who reject our witness, reject Christ, not us personally
3. We must also receive others who come in Christ's name

Proper 9/Pentecost 7/Ordinary Time 14

Revised Common:	Genesis 24:34-38, 42-49, 58-67	Romans 7:15-25a	Matthew 11:16-19, 25-30
Roman Catholic:	Zechariah 9:9-10	Romans 8:9, 11-13	Matthew 11:25-30
Episcopal:	Zechariah 9:9-12	Romans 7:21—8:6	Matthew 11:25-30

Theme: Freedom from oppression. In the first lesson (Zechariah 9:9-12), it is freedom from political oppression. In the second lesson, it is freedom from our sinful human nature, and in the gospel, we are offered freedom from the oppression of the law and of man-made religious regulations.

BRIEF COMMENTARY ON THE LESSONS

Lesson 1: Genesis 24:34-38, 42-49, 58-67 (C)

In his old age, Abraham sends his trusted servant back from the land of his origin to secure a wife for his son, Isaac, from his own people. He discovers Rebekah, daughter of Bethuel, who was Abraham's brother. When Isaac lays eyes on her, he is immediately smitten with love. The story assumes that all these events are due to divine design.

Lesson 1: Zechariah 9:9-10 (RC); Zechariah 9:9-12 (E)

Chapters 9-12 of Zechariah are believed to be penned by spiritual disciples of Zechariah a couple of centuries after the prophet, during the Greek period, 3rd and 4th centuries BC. The author holds up the brilliant hope of the messianic king coming in peace, to usher in an era of peace and prosperity.

Lesson 2: Romans 7:15-25a (C); Romans 7:21—8:6 (E)

Paul speaks vividly of his inner spiritual conflict. In his mind, he desires to do what is right, but he cannot because of the presence of his sinful (carnal) nature. He does the very thing that he hates. In designating himself as carnal (v. 14), he is not just referring to his physical body but to his entire being, though it is in this present bodily existence that this spiritual war is waged. Paul poses the question as to how we might be liberated from this sorry state (v. 24). The answer: Jesus Christ, our Lord (v. 25).

Lesson 2: Romans 8:9, 11-13 (RC)

True believers are not to live according to their sinful nature (the flesh) but according to the Spirit of the risen Christ. If we live according to the flesh, we will die, but if we order our lives through the power of the Spirit, we will live.

Gospel: Matthew 11:16-19, 25-30 (C); Matthew 11:25-30 (RC, E)

Chapters 11-12 seek to establish Jesus' authority. Jesus invites the people who are burdened by the excessive demands of those who claimed to interpret God's law. The rabbis spoke of the yoke of the law, which for many, was a burden they could not carry. Jesus offered another kind of yoke: not one that is easy in the usual sense, but a yoke that does not chafe because Christ offers his love and grace to help carry the burden. When Jesus said: "My yoke is easy," the word is *chrestos*, which means better, good, gracious, and kind. It is not that Christ is less demanding than the rabbis but that he graciously helps his followers carry the load and get the job done.

Psalm Of The Day
Psalm 45:10-17 (C) — "The people will praise you forever and ever" (v. 17).
Psalm 145:1-2, 13b-21 (RC, E) — "I will extol thee, my God and King" (v. 1a).

Prayer Of The Day
Loving Lord Christ, we confess that we have permitted ourselves to remain captive to the power of sin, selfishness, and Satan, though in our hearts we long to be truly free. Empower us by your Spirit to live in the liberating light of the gospel. In the powerful name of Jesus we are bold to say. Amen.

THEOLOGICAL REFLECTION ON THE LESSONS

Lesson 1: Genesis 24:34-38, 42-49, 58-67
The Lord's leading. When Abraham sent out his servant to secure a wife for his son, the servant was given a task that would have long-lasting consequences. When this servant got to his destination, he did not trust in his own judgment but sought and received the Lord's guidance. When this servant brought Rebekah home and she first spied her intended, he was meditating in a field. Perhaps he was praying that the Lord would guide Abraham's servant to make the right decision. When we come to important crossroads in our lives, do we rely on our own judgment or seek the Lord's guidance?

An extraordinary woman. When the servant asked Rebekah for some water, she also served the rest of his party. Not only that, she watered the camels, which was a big job. Here is a woman who graciously received strangers in the midst of her busy schedule and went beyond that which was asked of her. The servant knew that he had found a truly extraordinary wife for his master's son. It is through such people that God does great things.

Lesson 1: Zechariah 9:9-12
Your king comes to you. Most often, the king doesn't come to the people; the people are summoned, by invitation only, to the king. The writer of this passage lifts up the prospect of the Messiah as a humble king who comes to his people in peace. In Jesus, we also have a king who comes to us in peace, offering forgiveness and reconciliation.

Signed in blood. The prophet declares that God will restore and establish his people in peace because of the blood of his covenant (v. 11). Likewise, Jesus offered the world a new covenant of reconciliation and peace when he instituted the Lord's Supper. It was signed and sealed with his blood.

Lesson 2: Romans 7:15-25a; Romans 7:21—8:6
Seeking self-understanding. In frustration, Paul laments that he does not understand his own actions (v. 15). His desires and actions are out of sync. Sigmund Freud came up with a similar analysis, postulating that humans are driven by unconscious forces. To become well, one has to get in touch with this caldron of desire, the id. Paul's analysis is, of course, far

different. We experience this sense of being out of touch with ourselves because we are out of touch with God and dominated by our sinful human natures. What is the solution? It is to know ourselves in relationship with the Lord.

The war within. The dynamics that Paul describes is indeed a war within. God has placed in our hearts a knowledge of that which is good, even a desire to do what is good, yet, there is an alien force, the power of sin, which thwarts our good intentions. Christ has won that battle and, when we yield our lives in obedience, that victory is ours.

Gospel: Matthew 11:16-19, 25-30

The simple truth. Jesus thanks the Father that he has revealed his truth not to those who seek to know God through their own efforts or intellect but to those who simply trust in the Lord as a baby trusts her parents (vv. 25-26). Jesus had scathing things to say about the clergy of his day, the religious intelligentsia. Their knowledge became a straightjacket rather than a tool. The simple folk, the babes, were willing to learn and to walk by faith.

The claims of Christ. Jesus claimed a special relationship with God. "All things have been handed over to me by my Father, and no one knows the Son except the Father and no one knows the Father, except the Son and anyone to whom he chooses to reveal him" (v. 27). Either Jesus was a megalomaniac or he was the Son of God. He leaves us no middle ground, such as teacher, example, or prophet.

Rest for the over-burdened. When Jesus bid the weary and burdened to come to him (v. 28), he was addressing those who were weighed down by onerous religious rules and regulations. They were weary of trying to find acceptance by God and some had given up trying. When he claimed that his yoke is easy and his burden is light, he meant that he could release them from the man-made accretions to God's law, not the righteous demands of the law itself. Read what Jesus said in this regard in Matthew 5:17-20. A second reason that his burden is light follows from the personal relationship with God that Jesus offers us. Since we know God personally, Christ gives us his Spirit, who empowers us to fulfill God's will out of love, not because of the external threat of the law.

A well-fitting yoke. Being a carpenter, Jesus undoubtedly made many yokes. He knew how important it was to make the yoke fit well. A beast beset with an ill-fitting yoke could not effectively do the job. It would chafe and burn too much. Christ doesn't free us from the service of God, but he makes a yoke for us that fits so well that the task seems easy.

PREACHING APPROACHES WITH ILLUSTRATIONS

Lesson 1: Genesis 24:34-38, 42-49, 58-67

Sermon Title: Soul Mates

Sermon Angle: Abraham sent his servant back to his homeland to find a wife for his son, because he didn't want Isaac to get tangled up in the worship of the Canaanite gods. Abraham's main concern was not social status or wealth but spiritual compatibility. He desired to find a real soul mate for his son and was successful in this endeavor. Isaac loved her (v. 67). On the contemporary scene, driven by the ideal of romantic love, physical appearance is paramount for many. We would have many less divorces if those wanting to marry gave priority to shared values and a common faith. Shared faith in God is the soul of marriage, making us soul mates.

Sermon Title: Love And Marriage

Sermon Angle: The last verse of this text states that Isaac took Rebekah as his wife and he loved her. The marriage commitment came first, love followed. In the Western world, we have reversed that process. Romantic love and emotional ecstasy are considered the absolutely necessary precondition for marriage. Yet romantic ecstasy will eventually cool down. Unless romantic love yields to a more mature love, the relationship will falter. Love is not a feeling but a decision, a commitment. There's a song from the '50s called: "Love And Marriage." The verse goes, "Love and marriage, love and marriage, go together like a horse and carriage ... Dad was told by Mother, you can't have one without the other." Boy, has society changed! Millions don't believe that there is a necessary relationship one with the other. Those who do hold to the connection universally believe that love precedes marriage. Not necessarily so. Marriage may well be the horse and love the carriage.

Outline:

1. What is the relationship between love and marriage?
   — modern society, love first, then marriage, maybe
   — throughout most of history, marriage came first
2. Isaac married Rebekah and then learned to love her (v. 67)
   — the future of the clan had a higher priority than personal happiness
   — real love comes when we are committed to something more than self
3. The priorities of marriage are
   — first, let the love of God be the foundation
   — then, commit yourself to the marriage
   — finally, grow in love

Lesson 1: Zechariah 9:9-12

Sermon Title: Our Triumphantly Humble King?

Sermon Angle: Verse 9 describes the Messiah as a triumphant and yet humble king, who comes to his people not on a powerful warhorse but a lowly donkey. "Triumphant and victorious is he, humble and riding on a donkey...." We don't normally associate the adjectives triumphant and humble. It seems as if it is the strong, the aggressive, even the brutal, who win the victory, not the humble. Yet Jesus said, "Blessed are the meek, for they shall inherit the earth" (Matthew 5:5). The humble are going to have their day because Jesus, God's anointed one, was humbly triumphant over the powers of sin and death on the lowly cross of Calvary.

Lesson 2: Romans 7:15-25a; Romans 7:21—8:6

Sermon Title: The Bondage Of The Will

Sermon Angle: In describing the struggle of his soul, the apostle states: "I can will what is right, but I cannot do it." Willing ourselves to do what is good is not sufficient because at the core of our being we are in bondage to sin. Is this a hopeless predicament? No, "For the law of the Spirit of life in Christ has set us free from the law of sin and death" (8:2).

* * * * *

The book, *Life 101*, authored by John Roger and Peter McWilliams, has a chapter that poses the fundamental question: Are human beings fundamentally good or evil? Their answer? Good. How do they come to this conclusion? They ignore holocaust, war, and violence and focus on the baby. They ask: When you look at a baby, do you see fundamental evil radiating from him or her? No, you see purity, joy, sparkle, brightness, and happiness, they conclude. From just casual observation, they appear to make a point. Yet, aren't babies totally turned in on themselves? For the first few months of their lives, they do not even distinguish between themselves and the environment. Mother is just an extension of their own bodies. This may not be evil in them, but is this not the condition that disintegrates into evil later on in life?

Gospel: Matthew 11:16-19, 25-30

Sermon Title: Brain-bound

Sermon Angle: In verse 25, Jesus thanks his Father that he has revealed himself not to the intellectual elite, the religious superstars, but to babes. The scribes, Pharisees and priests were strong on theoretical knowledge of God but weak on experience. When a person has over developed his muscles, he is said to be muscle bound. We might say that the religious elite of Jesus' day were brain-bound. Their knowledge of God made them rigid and inflexible. Babes or infants, on the other hand, have no such constraints. They are content to experience a God they can never comprehend with their minds.

Sermon Title: Lite Religion

Sermon Angle: Where I live, there is a radio station called Lite 96, which I often listen to. They don't play hard rock, just the soft melodies of the '70s, '80s, and '90s. There is also lite cuisine, which can either mean that it's low on fat, calories, or sodium. Why not lite religion? Isn't that what Jesus offered when he bid folk to come unto him saying, "My yoke is easy and my burden is light"? The religion of the scribes and Pharisees was oppressive with its panoply of rules and regulations. Jesus makes the service of God lite, not by removing all obligations, but by helping us carry the load; also, by giving us a new starting point. We serve God not to earn acceptance but to express our love and gratitude.

Outline:
1. Lite cuisine is enormously popular for health-conscious people
2. People also seek lite religion (no obligation to serve or sacrifice)
3. Jesus offers a yoke of service to God
   — the yoke isn't easy or lite
   — it is made to seem lite because of the love of Jesus

* * * * *

In speaking of God's grace, R. Lofton Hudson, in his book, *Grace Is Not A Blue-Eyed Blond*, tells of a teacher who would, whenever one of her pupils misbehaved, draw an angry face and hand it to the guilty party. Sometimes the angry face would be sent home to parents. However, whenever the pupil did what was right, there would be no smiling face, thinking that the student would remember her smiling visage. Such a teacher would have made a great Old Testament prophet.

When our eldest daughter went to the first grade, her teacher believed that she had learning problems. So, she put her in a cubicle in the very front of the room, cut off from the rest of the class. Our daughter despised school because of the harsh judgment of that teacher, who saddled unnecessary burdens on her. The second grade teacher, however, gave her special attention, making her Cinderella in the class play. Lu blossomed under her loving care. Love and understanding can lighten any burden.

Sermon Title: Saddle Ready

Sermon Angle: You can't just hop on a wild horse and ride into the sunset. First of all, you couldn't catch him. Secondly, you couldn't mount him if you did catch him. Thirdly, if you did mount him, you'd get bucked off. A horse has to be trained to get accustomed to a saddle and then a rider. Until then, he's not fit for work or riding. The saddle for the horse is roughly equivalent to the yoke for the ox. The object is to bear a burden, to get the job accomplished by responding to directions from a higher power. As Christians, we cannot accomplish anything good until we are ready to wear the saddle of obedience to Christ and respond as he tugs on the reins.

Proper 10/Pentecost 8/Ordinary Time 15

Revised Common:	Genesis 25:19-34	Romans 8:1-11	Matthew 13:1-9, 18-23
Roman Catholic:	Isaiah 55:10-11	Romans 8:18-23	Matthew 13:1-23
Episcopal:	Isaiah 55:1-5, 10-13	Romans 8:9-17	Matthew 13:1-9, 18-23

Theme: The productivity of God's word. When we sow God's word, God will certainly bless it so that it yields richly. Nevertheless, some good seed will not take root.

BRIEF COMMENTARY ON THE LESSONS

Lesson 1: Genesis 25:19-34 (C)

Once again, God seems to linger in fulfilling his promise to make a great nation of Abraham's progeny. Isaac is forty by the time he married Rebekah. Another twenty years expire before his wife gives birth to the twins, Esau and Jacob. Perhaps the Lord wants to demonstrate that this business of nation building is his doing, not a human accomplishment. Esau, being firstborn, earns the birthright, but foolishly sells it to his scheming brother for a pot of stew.

Lesson 1: Isaiah 55:10-11 (RC); Isaiah 55:1-5, 10-13 (E)

Second Isaiah concludes his prophecies by expressing his joy at the prospect of the imminent return and restoration of his people. The prophet extends the Lord's invitation for the people to come to him, the font of all blessing. They are to look to him for sustenance; they are to listen to God's word. Verses 10-13 compare God's word to the rain and the snow, which nourishes and sustains life. The believer can take heart; God's word is potent; it does not return empty.

Lesson 2: Romans 8:1-11 (C); Romans 8:18-23 (RC)

Paul speaks to a persecuted church. He declares that the suffering of the present time cannot compare with the glories that await us in God's kingdom. The whole creation shares in the futility of natural existence, subject to decay and death, but the creation too will share in our freedom from the power of death. It is this hope of redemption that saves us.

Lesson 2: Romans 8:9-17 (E)

The apostle reminds us that Christians do not live according to the flesh (their sinful human nature) but in the Spirit. The Spirit gives life to our mortal bodies.

Gospel: Matthew 13:1-9, 18-23 (C, E); Matthew 13:1-23 (RC)

This well-known text is traditionally called the Parable of the Sower. However, it would be better termed the Parable of the Soils, since the main point revolves around the receptivity of the soil. This parable helped the disciples to understand why some people received the word of Christ and others did not. It took the burden off the shoulders of the sower. As long as the sower scattered the seeds, his job was complete. He could not be held accountable for the germination of the seed. The last section of this lection is the interpretation of the parable, which many scholars believe was composed by the early church. The explanation allegorizes the parable, and Jesus seldom used allegories. Most parables have only one key point.

Psalm Of The Day

Psalm 119:104-112 (C) — "Your word is a lamp unto my feet and a light unto my path" (v. 105).

Psalm 65 (RC, E) — "You crown the year with your bounty ..." (v. 11a).

Prayer Of The Day

God of seedtime and harvest, you have generously sown the good seed in our hearts. May what you have planted not only take root, but flourish, producing abundant fruits of faith and love. In the name above all other names we pray, Jesus, our Lord. Amen.

THEOLOGICAL REFLECTION ON THE LESSONS

Lesson 1: Genesis 25:19-34

Persistent in prayer. Verse 21 states that Isaac prayed for his wife because she was barren. The inability to produce children was considered a curse. It must have weighed heavily on Rebekah's heart. We see here Isaac's love for God and his wife. He was forty when he married her and twenty years later she gave birth to twins. That's a good deal of persistent praying. Such praying does not merely seek favors; it is a relationship of dependency and trust in the Lord. Prayer is the lifeblood of God's people.

The struggle. Life is a struggle which yields its fruits to those who know what they want and hang in there. According to our text, the struggle of existence began for Jacob and Esau in the womb. Esau came out first, but Jacob was clutching his heel, which symbolized Esau's weaknesses. (Recall the myth of Achilles.) Jacob was a scrapper. He wasn't satisfied with second best; he wanted God's optimum blessing. He struggled with Esau for his birthright; he wrestled with the Lord as he fled from the wrath of his brother; he contended with his uncle Laban for Rachel's hand in marriage. Esau chose the easy way and his brother supplanted him. God rewards those who will not quit until the war is over.

Lesson 1: Isaiah 55:1-5, 10-13

Come to the waters. The image in verse 1 is of a hawker in the city streets who sells fresh water and other beverages. Only now it is the Lord who is crying out to his people and what he offers is free. The Lord is an ever-flowing stream of grace, the wellspring of life, without whom nothing can live.

Choose your foods wisely. "Listen carefully to me and eat what is good" (v. 2). There has been a blitz of material about how to choose a healthful diet, low in fat and sodium, high in fiber. All that we take into our minds is food for our souls. Do we carelessly consume garbage, for example, in the books we read and the movies we watch? Do you consume a healthy serving of God's word?

You can be sure of the seed. God's word is the seed that is guaranteed to grow and bear fruit (vv. 10-11).

Lesson 2: Romans 8:1-11

Sin and death are doomed! Paul employs the word "condemnation" in verses 1 and 3. In verse 1, he means that there is no "doom" for those in Christ. In verse 3, he indicates that through Christ God has "doomed death." Theologically speaking, sin and death are inextricably connected (Romans 6:23). In dooming sin, God also dooms death to eventual non-being. Sin and death continue to exert their deadly influence, but their fate remains sealed.

Lesson 2: Romans 8:9-17

Water and Spirit. Isaiah 55:1 invites us to come to the waters, while this text bids us to let the Spirit of God take possession of our lives. God's Spirit is the water of our souls; without it, we die (v. 10). Fittingly, the water of baptism is the entrance of Christ's life-giving Spirit.

Adoption. Though we are all created in God's image, we have all become slaves of selfishness and sin. The good news proclaims that through Christ we are adopted into God's family. We can call on God as Father (v. 15). This means that God has chosen us as his own dear children, inheritors of eternal life and recipients of his Spirit.

Lesson 2: Romans 8:18-23

Perspective. In verse 17, Paul makes it clear that suffering comes along with being adopted into God's family. In this passage, he goes on to indicate that we must view this suffering with an eternal perspective. The temporary pain is a small price to pay for eternal gain (v. 18).

Birth pangs. The image that Paul presents is of a world *in utero*, a womb-wrapped world that is struggling to be born. Labor pains are the necessary prelude to new life. It is the pain that makes leaving the confines of our old world easier, even desirable. As the contractions of pain squeeze us, we are propelled into the light of a painful process of letting go of the old life and embracing the new life to which the Lord is calling us. In this role, we must help our sisters and brothers to focus on the future gain rather than their present pain.

Gospel: Matthew 13:1-23

From synagogue to seashore. Jesus began his teaching ministry in the synagogues, but in chapter 13 we see a shift. He was no longer welcomed by the leaders of the synagogue nor the religious hierarchy. Yet thousands of simple folk were anxious to hear him, so they gathered at the seashore. Jesus took the message to the people, rather than call the people to message. Christ calls his church to take the Gospel to the highways and byways, wherever there are receptive souls.

What was the secret of Christ's attraction? Verse 1 says that Jesus went out of the house and sat along the seashore and great crowds gathered around him. What was the draw? The gospel writers note time and again that Jesus spoke and acted with authority. His stories were original and powerful. He began where the people were, with images drawn from everyday life, and correlated his message to those images. Those stories allowed his hearers to see themselves and to draw their own conclusions. There was no legalistic listing of dos and don'ts. If the church would follow her Lord's example, she would prove to be an irresistible magnet.

Finding fertile soil. The point of this parable is the receptivity of the soil. It is taken for granted that the seed is good. Farming methods are not questioned. Why does the gospel take root in some lives and not others? It's hard to tell. Just keep on sowing; God will cause the seed to find fertile soil.

Soil testing. Farmers have their soil scientifically analyzed to find out what ingredients are lacking. With that knowledge, some toil, and money, we can make the soil receptive to the seed; we can make it fertile. Wouldn't it make some sense to follow the same procedure in planting the seeds of the kingdom? Market surveys and the like can inform us concerning which groups of people would be most receptive. They can help us to find an opening for the seed. While such information might be helpful, we must remember that God can open the hardest and most impenetrable heart.

God's soil testing. How does God test the soil? He plants seeds in our hearts and waits to observe the results. Those seeds that sprout up to produce a rich harvest are the ones that fell into the good soil (v. 23).

PREACHING APPROACHES WITH ILLUSTRATIONS

Lesson 1: Genesis 25:19-34
Sermon Title: Selling Your Soul For The Sake Of Your Stomach
Sermon Angle: Jacob was a cunning man who understood his brother's weaknesses. He prepared a pot of stew, knowing that his brother would sell his birthright in exchange for some hearty food. How many people are so driven by their immediate physical appetites that they would be willing to sacrifice their souls to satisfy them?

Sermon Title: God Uses Stinkers, Too
Sermon Angle: Sometimes God uses people of exceptional holiness to accomplish his will, but sometimes he uses stinkers. Jacob was a schemer, a manipulator, a trickster. Yet God blessed him and used him for his righteous purposes. In the process, Jacob was transformed into a true person of faith. That's good news for us stinkers!

Lesson 1: Isaiah 55:1-5, 10-13
Sermon Title: The Real Thirst Quencher
Sermon Angle: What's the real thirst quencher? Not Sprite, Coke, or Pepsi but the Holy Spirit. "Ho, everyone who thirsts, come to the waters" (v. 1). What's more, it's free! That's the same message that the Lord communicated to the Samaritan woman by the well, as told by John. "Those who drink of the water I give him will never be thirsty again" (John 4:14). Why? Because those who trust the Lord have the Spirit, the wellspring of life within them.

Sermon Title: The Power Of The Word
Sermon Angle: The prophet holds up the prospect of national revival to a skeptical audience. In verses 10-11, he assures them that God's word is potent; it will surely accomplish its purpose. A word can be very powerful, whether it be a word of condemnation or of hope. We should guard well our words. God's word has special power to create, to restore, to give hope to the despairing and life to the dead.

Lesson 2: Romans 8:1-11
Sermon Title: The Two Modes Of Existence
Sermon Angle: In verses 5-11, the apostle contrasts the two modes of existence. On the one hand, there are those whose lives are dominated by the "flesh," who are controlled by their selfish drives and compulsions. Then, there are those who are redeemed by Christ, who live according to the guidance of the Holy Spirit. Life in the flesh puts a person at odds with God and other human beings, resulting in isolation. Life in the Spirit leads a person ever deeper into the community of the faithful. To live in the flesh leads to an atomistic existence, while life in the Spirit results in a truly communistic (authentic community) mode of being.

Outline:
1. Explain the two modes of existence
2. The fleshly mode leads to alienation and death
3. The spiritual mode leads to communion with God and others
4. In which mode of existence do you experience life?

Lesson 2: Romans 8:18-23

Sermon Title: Birth Pangs

Sermon Angle: Do you know what it's like to give birth? That's only possible for a woman, right? Wrong. Anyone who has had an idea that possesses him so thoroughly that he must create it, knows birth pangs. Such new life involves sacrifice, failure, disappointment, anxiety, and so forth. The battle between our sinful natures and the Spirit within, is a birth process involving pain. Our sinful natures resist the birth process, because it means death to our old lives. The Spirit pushes us along the birth canal to the light of a new life.

Gospel: Matthew 13:1-23

Sermon Title: The Gospel Story

Sermon Angle: Jesus communicated the gospel entirely through the medium of story. That's what a parable is, a story with a key point of comparison between God's kingdom and our lives. Fertile soil is found when his story intersects with our story.

Outline:
1. How do we communicate the gospel?
2. We try to get inside the other person's story
3. We share how God's story has connected with our story and then relate it to their story

*　*　*　*　*

Miss Jean's Story Time has been on television ever since I was a child, not a few years ago. Miss Jean asks the children to help her tell the gospel story by having them send in drawings. She tacks up the drawings on a storyboard and uses them to tell her story. The children are eager to listen because they can see themselves in Miss Jean's story, which is really God's story. This is not unlike the method of Jesus. He looked about for stories and then related them to the kingdom of God. They weren't particularly important stories. In fact, they were very ordinary. That's why they were so potent. Folks could see themselves in the stories. The gospel is still best communicated through story.

Sermon Title: Understanding The Yields In The Fields

Sermon Angle: This parable is an attempt to explain why the gospel yields such vastly different results. In some lives it produces abundantly; in some, it grows for a time and then dies back; in the hearts of others, it doesn't germinate at all. Different yields for different fields. The explanation lies with the soil.

Outline:
1. Why does the yield of God's word (the seed) vary so much?
2. It's not the seed (cross reference: Isaiah 55:1-11)
3. It is the soil (assuming that the seed has been scattered abroad)
4. However, we must not judge the soil infertile as an excuse for not planting
5. Scatter freely and don't worry about yields

Sermon Title: Increasing Our Yield

Sermon Angle: What kind of yield are our lives producing? Have we analyzed what kind of environment we are producing for the seed? Is it hard like cement? Is our spiritual depth shallow? Are we allowing the cares of this world to crowd out God's word? We can increase our yield by making our lives more open to God's word.

* * * * *

What makes for fertile soil? When it comes to the environment needed to produce a healthy and well-adjusted human being, there are many necessary ingredients, but none is more important than love. We see the connection between love and growth in the Helen Keller story. When Anne Sullivan came to live with the Keller family as her live-in teacher, Helen was out of control. Being deaf and blind, she was locked in a solitary prison. Love freed her, fertilized her, and caused her to grow, as she testified.

"The most important day of my life was when my teacher, Anne Sullivan, came to see me. On the afternoon of the fateful day I stood on the porch, dumb and expectant. I guessed vaguely from all the going to and fro in the house that something unusual was about to happen ... I felt approaching footsteps, I held out my hand. Someone took it and I was caught and held close in the arms of her who was to reveal all things to me, and above all things, to love me."

Proper 11/Pentecost 9/Ordinary Time 16

Revised Common:	Genesis 28:10-19a	Romans 8:12-25	Matthew 13:24-30, 36-43
Roman Catholic:	Wisdom 12:13, 16-19	Romans 8:26-27	Matthew 13:24-43
Episcopal:	Wisdom 12:13, 16-19	Romans 8:18-25	Matthew 13:24-30, 36-43

Theme: The mystery of good and evil. In Genesis, Jacob tricks his brother and flees from his wrath. In Romans, Paul bemoans human moral weakness. The gospel parable deals with the mystery of the weeds growing together with the wheat.

BRIEF COMMENTARY ON THE LESSONS

Lesson 1: Genesis 28:10-19a (C)

Upon hearing of Esau's plan to kill Jacob after Isaac's death, Rebekah spirits Jacob back to her relatives in her native land. It is an unsettling time for Jacob, leaving home as a fugitive. Jacob stops for a night at Bethel and in his dream God reaffirms the covenant he made with Abraham and Isaac. In the dream, Jacob views a stairway to heaven, probably a ziggurat, with the angels of God ascending and descending. This establishes Beth-el (house of God) as a sanctuary until the time of Josiah.

Lesson 1: Wisdom 12:13, 16-19 (RC, E)

God's sovereign rule and power.

Lesson 2: Romans 8:12-25 (C); Romans 8:18-25 (E)

See the second lesson for Proper 10 (RC).

Lesson 2: Romans 8:26-27 (RC)

The Spirit of God helps us in our weaknesses by interceding with God on our behalf.

Gospel: Matthew 13:24-30, 36-43 (C, E); Matthew 13:24-43 (RC)

The gospel continues the parables of Jesus, which serves as a logical progression from last week's gospel where we dealt with the mystery of germination and growth. This week, we are presented with the mystery of the weeds. The parable does not explain the mystery. We still don't know the origin or purpose of the weeds. Thus, this parable does not offer an explanation for the mystery of evil. It's considered a fact of our present existence, though it will be abolished at the harvest time, when the kingdom of God fully comes. Humans cannot uproot the evil without destroying the good; that job must be left to God.

Psalm Of The Day

Psalm 139:1-12, 23-24 (C) — "Where can I go from your spirit?" (v. 7).
Psalm 86:11-17 (RC, E) — "I will glorify your name forever" (v. 12b).

Prayer Of The Day

We thank you, gentle Lord Jesus, that you do not deal harshly with us, uprooting the good with the evil, but tenderly cultivate the shoots of faith and love. In Jesus' name. Amen.

THEOLOGICAL REFLECTION ON THE LESSONS

Lesson 1: Genesis 28:10-19a

The Lord stood beside him (v. 13). In Jacob's dream, he saw God standing beside him. Jacob was a fugitive from justice, cut off from home, with dim prospects for the future. God came to reassure him that he had nothing to fear because the Lord would be his protector and would bring his promised blessings to fruition.

A portable God. The ancients had it that each place and people had its god. Gods were considered to be tied to the real estate. Not so, the God of Abraham, Isaac, and Jacob; he was God of heaven and earth; wherever his people would go, he would be with them to guide and protect (v. 15).

Lesson 2: Romans 8:12-25

See the second lesson for Proper 10.

Lesson 2: Romans 8:26-27

Prayer beyond words. Many people conceive of prayer as talking to God while employing certain vocabulary, syntax, and style. In this text, Paul informs us that the Spirit of God prays in us and for us, and that the form that those intercessions take are not always verbal. God is less interested in our words than our hearts, and when we get to the end of ourselves, the Spirit takes over.

Gospel: Matthew 13:24-43

The church is not an English garden. Have you ever seen an English garden? They are so beautiful. The flowers are carefully arranged in rows, fanciful configurations, and geometrical designs. You won't see a weed or an unclipped shrub. The garden is striking because it fits the design of its creator, and all the parts fit together as one body. The garden is also notable because there are no weeds to detract from the flowers or suck out their life. The world which we inhabit is not an English garden; weeds are everywhere.

How to tell a weed. What makes one plant a weed and another a useful plant? Weeds are wild. You don't have to plant them or cultivate them. What's more, they're prolific. However that alone is not enough to classify a plant as a weed. What makes a weed a weed is that they just take up space. They produce no fruit to eat, generally, no flower of notable beauty. They monopolize space that could be better occupied by a more useful plant. Nature abhors a vacuum. It would rather have weeds than nothing at all.

The grim sower. Death is pictured as the grim reaper, a hooded skeleton figure, with scythe in hand. This parable pictures the devil as the grim sower, who covertly plants weed seeds where there ought to be wheat.

The evil is a facsimile of the good. Evil is often pictured as a wart-faced monster. Actually, evil often puts on a glamorous face. The word in Jesus' parable that is interpreted *weed* should actually be *tare*. The tare was the bearded darnel plant. In its immature stages it looked almost identical to the wheat. Only when the tare put on its seed could it be distinguished from the wheat. Jesus said, "You will know them by their fruit."

The danger of pulling weeds. In my flower garden this spring, all kinds of little plants were popping up. I knew that some of them were flowers that had seeded themselves from last year and that others were weeds. The trouble was, I wasn't always sure which were weeds and which were flowers. There was a danger in pulling up what I thought might be a weed; I could have

271

easily been mistaken. We may see some people as weeds and attempt to remove them from our lives, only to find that some of these were actually productive plants in God's field.

Holocaust. According to the interpretation of the parable of the weeds and the wheat (vv. 36-43), the weeds will be separated from the wheat at harvest time. The wheat will be gathered to God and the weeds will be consumed in a holocaust. The holocaust by the Nazis destroyed some of the most fruitful of God's garden, but this holocaust, at the end of time, will destroy only the unproductive and the useless weeds.

PREACHING APPROACHES WITH ILLUSTRATIONS

Lesson 1: Genesis 28:10-19a
Sermon Title: The God Of The Past And The Future
Sermon Angle: In Jacob's dream, the Lord identified himself as the God of his fathers (Abraham and Isaac), representing the past, and the God who would go with him wherever he went (the God of his future). Like Jacob, we are inheritors of the faith of our fathers and our mothers. This gives us a sense of identity and continuity. Yet the Lord is not a static God; he leads us boldly into the unknown future. This provides a sense of mission and purpose.

Lesson 2: Romans 8:12-25
See the second lesson for Proper 10.

Sermon Title: The Gain Of Glory
Sermon Angle: Paul tells persecuted believers that the suffering and loss of the present are not worth comparing to the gain of glory (v. 18). They could avoid the pain but would not receive the gain. Like the champion athlete, we need to subject ourselves to a harsh training regimen now to gain the crown of glory.

Lesson 2: Romans 8:26-27
Sermon Title: I Need A Little Help From My Friend
Sermon Angle: There are times for all of us when we come to the end of our ropes and we need a little help from our friends. Paul suggests that the Spirit is our friend, who takes over when we are weak and intercedes with God on our behalf.
Outline:
1. A friend is someone who is there for us during our time of need
2. The Holy Spirit is our friend, helping us in our time of need
3. The Spirit intercedes on our behalf
4. The Spirit sustains us when words do not come — "sighs too deep for words"

Gospel: Matthew 13:24-43
Sermon Title: Enemy Unawares
Sermon Angle: In the parable, when the servants of the farmer came and asked him where the weeds came from, he pointed the finger at an enemy. This enemy had caught him unawares, working covertly under the cover of darkness. If you know your enemy, you can guard against him, but not one that operates incognito. Jesus clearly taught that there is a spiritual foe, the prince of darkness. His best strategy is covert attack.

Outline:
1. The mystery of the weeds (evil) perplexes us
2. The parable points to an enemy (Satan)
3. The enemy plants his weed seeds under cover of darkness
4. If their servants had been vigilant, they could have prevented the sabotage
5. Be cognizant of the devil's covert and silent method of attack

*   *   *   *   *

Surprise is a key tactic for military strategists. In the early summer of 1944, the Germans were expecting the Allies to attack. The problem was, they didn't know from where. There were rumors of an attack from the northern flank, in Norway, though it was more probable the Allies would storm some of the beaches of France. The shortest route would put them in Calais, just across from the cliffs of Dover. To keep them guessing, the Allies created mock armies, circulated false information, and made the Nazis believe that buildups were occurring in areas where there was no army. Since the Germans didn't know where the invasion would originate, they had to be prepared everywhere. This stretched their resources far too sparsely. When, on June 6, 1944, the Allies did attack, it was on Normandy, believed to be an unlikely place. Since the weather was so stormy, the Nazi general, Rommel, didn't think it likely they would attack at that time. He went home to be with his wife on her birthday. Without the successful element of surprise, the battle and the war might have turned out quite differently. We, too, must know our enemy, his strategies, his tricks, and his subterfuge.

Sermon Title: Live And Let Die

Sermon Angle: When the servants asked their master what to do about the weeds, he told them to let them grow until harvest time, when the weeds would be gathered in bundles and burned, but the wheat would be gathered into the barn. His advice: let the weeds live until harvest, because in pulling up the weeds, one would also uproot some wheat. The weeds will be destroyed by the Lord of the harvest, at harvest time, after the weeds have borne their bitter fruit and the wheat their good fruit. Life and death is determined by the nature of the fruit.

*   *   *   *   *

There's good reason marijuana is called "the weed." It grows wild, though it is also cultivated by growers for greater productivity. Marijuana is symbolic of all drugs to which people become addicted. You pull up a weed here and there but they keep rearing their ugly heads. Our government has embarked on a policy of interdiction, trying to weed out the illicit drugs before they reach our shores. Drug agents have sprayed fields of poppies and marijuana with herbicide. They have attempted to stop the flow of drugs through the transportation networks. Thousands of pounds of drugs have been destroyed or seized. Yet the drug problem has not abated. It appears we are losing the drug war. It seems that illicit drugs cannot be weeded out. Perhaps we should give more attention to prevention. Weeds grow best where there is an emptiness, a vacuum. Millions of our young men and women, boys and girls, experience a spiritual emptiness within. The pursuit of materialism, the breakdown of the family, the exaltation of the notion of free self-expression to the neglect of community, have created a huge void in the lives of our young. Nature abhors a vacuum and will soon fill it. Also, Satan and the forces of evil thrive in such circumstances. We are not going to solve the weed problem by attacking them directly, but instead by nourishing the good plants, so that they might grow and fill all the empty spaces. If our young people know the Lord, if they are allowed to grow in an environment of love, they will become so strong that there will be no room for the weeds.

*   *   *   *   *

Is the world like your lawn? It all depends. If you have the kind of lawn which I have, the answer is, "Yes." My lawn is not like those from which all weeds and watergrass have been banished. You've seen the perfectly manicured outdoor carpets that you're afraid to even walk on. Overall, my lawn looks presentable. There is a fairly luxuriant strand of grass, and, when it is cut, it looks quite nice. However, when it gets long, you can see the panoply of dandelion and a variety of other outlaw plants. The fertilizer/herbicide I put on once or twice a year doesn't seem to faze the weeds. Last year I tried to zap the weeds individually with some toxic stuff that's on the market but my dandelions just wouldn't die. I think I did manage to send one or two weeds to their eternal reward, but twenty more weeds took the place of those who had gone to meet their maker. I've decided to call a truce. Why drive yourself to distraction with perfectionistic tendencies? That's the way the world is, weeds and grass growing together. I just try to care sufficiently for the grass to enable it to live a good life. You people who possess those picture perfect lawns, get real!

Proper 12/Pentecost 10/Ordinary Time 17

Revised Common:	**Genesis 29:15-28**	**Romans 8:26-39**	**Matthew 13:31-33, 44-52**
Roman Catholic:	**1 Kings 3:5, 7-12**	**Romans 8:28-30**	**Matthew 13:44-52**
Episcopal:	**1 Kings 3:5-12**	**Romans 8:26-34**	**Matthew 13:31-33, 44-49a**

Theme: Laying hold of the true treasure. Solomon sought the Lord's wisdom rather than material riches and was commended by God. In the gospel, the parables of the treasure hidden in the field and the pearl of great price make the point that those who realize the exceeding value of the kingdom of God are willing to sacrifice everything else for its sake.

BRIEF COMMENTARY ON THE LESSONS

Lesson 1: Genesis 29:15-28 (C)

Jacob the trickster gets tricked. He is smitten with Rachel and agrees with her father, Laban, to work seven years to obtain her hand in marriage. On the wedding night, he gets an unexpected wedding present, Rachel's sister, Leah. Jacob agrees to work another seven years for Rachel because she is the true treasure of his heart.

Lesson 1: 1 Kings 3:5, 7-12 (RC); 1 Kings 3:5-12 (E)

God appears to Solomon in a dream, telling him to ask for his heart's desire. Solomon recounts a litany of God's blessings to his father and himself. He humbly confesses his inadequacy to lead his people and asks that the Lord give him a wise and understanding heart to discern good from evil. The Lord is pleased with Solomon's request and grants him power and riches in addition to the wisdom and understanding.

Lesson 2: Romans 8:26-39 (C); Romans 8:28-30 (RC); Romans 8:26-34 (E)

This lection includes Paul's greatest expression of faith: "We know that in everything God works together for good to those who love him ..." (v. 28). The new Christians were facing hardships and persecutions but these evils would be transformed into good. The Spirit of God strengthens the saints in their weakness by lifting to the Lord their unuttered needs (v. 26). Furthermore, the evils of their present experience will be used by God for their ultimate good (vv. 38-39). Angelic and demonic powers, associated with the stars in New Testament time, were even powerless to alienate the believers from their Lord.

Gospel: Matthew 13:31-33, 44-52 (C); Matthew 13:44-52 (RC); Matthew 13:31-33, 44-49a (E)

The gospel continues with the parables of Jesus. Each of them points to a different aspect of the kingdom of God. The mustard seed points to the kingdom's small beginnings (vv. 31-32). The leaven (v. 33) shows how the kingdom can transform the world. Verses 44-46 contain two parables that make a similar point. The kingdom is the hidden treasure or the pearl of exceeding value that the wise person will sell all to possess. The parable of the dragnet (vv. 47-50) is similar to the parable of the weeds and the wheat (vv. 24-30): at the end of earthly existence, God is going to gather the good (his treasure) unto himself and dispose of the evil. The person truly trained in the kingdom will incorporate the new wisdom of Jesus with the treasures from the old covenant (v. 52).

Psalm Of The Day

Psalm 105:1-11 (C) — "Seek the Lord and his strength ..." (v. 4).
Psalm 119:129-136 (RC, E) — "The unfolding of your words gives light ..." (v. 130).

Prayer Of The Day

Lord Jesus, we have found in you our true treasure. Why then do we strive after that which is clay, rather than eternity's gold? Free us from the pursuit of that which glitters, so that we might obtain the treasure of your kingdom, which is hidden in you. Amen.

THEOLOGICAL REFLECTION ON THE LESSONS

Lesson 1: Genesis 29:15-28

A work of love. Jacob worked fourteen years for the hand of Rachel, so great was his love for her. This shows that love is more than a feeling; it is a matter of commitment. In our society we have been conditioned to believe that love is without effort; it just happens. Such is not the case; love is a labor, not a labor lost.

Lesson 1: 1 Kings 3:5-12

From wisdom to foolishness. Solomon asked for wisdom to govern the people, but when it came to matters of the heart and of the state, he didn't rule very wisely. His harem of wives led him to compromises in the worship of God. He imposed heavy taxes, probably due to overexpansion, which later led to the division of the kingdom. Solomon was given the gift of wisdom, but he didn't always use that gift.

Lesson 2: Romans 8:26-39

The Spirit's intercession. Paul states that, because of our weakness, the Spirit lifts our needs to God. The picture here seems kind of odd — God in us praying to God above us. We see here the immanence and the transcendence of the almighty. This is another way of saying that God knows our needs even before we ask; even when we cannot verbalize our needs, God hears and responds.

Using evil in the service of good. Paul states that "in everything God works for good for those who love him ..." (v. 28). This shows God's power. He takes the garbage that life throws our way, and recycles it into something good. This is far different from saying that *everything* that happens to us is good, nor is it the same as saying that everything will turn out for the good for everyone. Note the qualifying phrase: "for those who love him."

The eternal bond. Paul eloquently makes one of the greatest affirmations of all times to the effect that absolutely nothing can separate us from God's love (vv. 38-39). Nothing in this world or the next, nothing in the realm of human or even demonic powers can pry us loose from the Lord's loving embrace. If we really hold to this affirmation, we have a shining hope even in the darkest hours.

Gospel: Matthew 13:44-52

Treasure. Who hasn't dreamed of finding a fabulous treasure? The lure of treasure prompts people to enter contests and sweepstakes. Publishers Clearing House ads appeal to that fantasy by highlighting the reaction of a family who has just won millions of dollars. They are delirious with joy. Jesus teaches that the kingdom of God is the ultimate treasure. The first parable (v. 44) tells of a man who accidentally found a treasure buried in a field. He goes home and sells everything that he has so that he might purchase that field. His discovery was a serendipity, something valuable he surprisingly discovered in the process of doing something else. For many, the kingdom is not a treasure we have sought and found but that which has fallen in our laps by virtue of birth and baptism and God's grace.

The next parable (vv. 45-46) features a merchant in search of the perfect pearl, the pearl of great price. When he finds it, he too sells all that he has in order to purchase that one pearl. For this man, the treasure was the result of diligent searching. Jesus taught: "Seek and you shall find...." Contrary to the first parable, where the treasure finder had no point of comparison, this merchant had seen plenty of pearls and chose this one above all the others. The first man intuitively recognized the value of his treasure, while the second was convinced of its worth by shopping around.

Old and new treasure. In verses 51-52, Jesus teaches that the kingdom of God is composed of treasure old and new. The wise person resembles the scribe that Jesus mentions; he or she integrates the treasure of the Old Testament with the new teaching of Jesus.

God gathers his treasure. The parable of the dragnet (vv. 47-50) seems out of place. This parable of judgment would fit better with the parable of the weeds and the wheat. However, there is a connection. Jesus teaches that at the end of time God will gather his treasure to himself by receiving those who are his own and discarding the rest.

PREACHING APPROACHES WITH ILLUSTRATIONS

Lesson 1: Genesis 29:15-28

Sermon Title: Keeping Your Focus

Sermon Angle: When Jacob woke up on his wedding morning with Leah rather than Rachel, he must have been more than a little surprised and upset. Some men might have said, "Forget it! I'm not going to work another seven years for Rachel," and then stormed off. But he loved her, and she alone was the prize that he sought. Jacob kept his focus not on the seven years of additional labor or the injustice of his father-in-law but the beloved.

Lesson 1: 1 Kings 3:5-12

Sermon Title: The Test Of Wisdom

Sermon Angle: When God appeared to Solomon in the dream and told him that he could ask for whatever he desired, Solomon confessed that God had given him a monumental task as king for which he was not equal. Solomon admitted to being a little child (v. 7). This was a modest way of saying that he was not wise enough to wear the mantle of leadership. He asks for a wise and discerning mind that he might know the difference between right and wrong, good and evil. God was pleased with this request. Solomon had already passed the wisdom test. He knew that he didn't know very much and that he required the Spirit of God within him if he were to rule justly. The wise person realizes the limits of his knowledge. That the young Solomon realized his inadequacies testifies to his youthful wisdom.

Lesson 2: Romans 8:26-39

Sermon Title: Hope For Weaklings

Sermon Angle: Most young boys desire to be strong and virile. When I was a boy, I read an ad in a comic book for the Charles Atlas body-building course. The ad pictured a scrawny little runt of a guy being humiliated by larger males, who were throwing sand in his face. The caption read: "I was a 97-pound weakling." The next panel showed this same boy, a virile package of rippling muscles, being adored by a coterie of lovely girls. I never had the money to send for the course but I still remember its appeal. Paul says that the Spirit helps us in our weakness (v. 26). We all experience weakness, whether we're young or old, male or female. God doesn't help us by turning us into a muscle-bound brute but by lending us his strength.

*   *   *   *   *

Those of you who have witnessed a loved one die of cancer know of its debilitating weakness. One of the hardest things for me was to observe the helplessness of my once strong dad. He couldn't stand up or sit up by himself. He couldn't go to the bathroom and so he had to be changed like a baby. Such weakness drives home our human creatureliness and weakness. We are utterly dependent on God for life and strength. There are many circumstances that we cannot control. These are times to let go and let God. "The Spirit helps us in our weakness...."

Sermon Title: Sentence Overturned

Sermon Angle: Paul raises an interesting question: "If God is for us, who can be against us?" (v. 31). Let me name a few possibilities. Other people can be against us. Our conscience can be against us. God's law can testify against us. Of course, what the apostle is getting at is that it doesn't matter who is against us if God is our advocate. God has declared us not guilty because of Christ; our sentence of guilty has been overturned.

Outline:
1. Do you ever feel that the world is against you?
2. You may have done things to cause others to be against you
3. Circumstances may make it seem the world is against you
4. Christ has acquitted you — your sentence is overturned (v. 33)
5. Christ intercedes for you

*   *   *   *   *

I once saw a show on television about a young man by the name of Kevin who had been drunk and killed a young woman. He was given a rather unique sentence. Every Friday for the next eighteen years, he was required to write a check to this girl's parents. This sentence kept the memory of his offense fresh in his mind, which it was intended to do. Some folks thought that he was let off too leniently, that he should have been sentenced to prison. But which is really the harsher punishment: to serve a year for your offense and then try to pick up the pieces of your life, or to be reminded for the next eighteen years that you have killed another human being?

Gospel: Matthew 13:44-52

Sermon Title: The Cost Of Buried Treasure

Sermon Angle: In Jesus' parable, the man who found the buried treasure sold everything that he had so that he might buy the field where the treasure was hidden. The treasure cost him everything that he possessed. That same message was communicated to the rich young ruler, whom Jesus told to sell all that he possessed, give it to the poor, and then come and follow him. Christ also warned: "He who would come after me must deny himself, take up his cross and follow me." The treasure of the kingdom doesn't come cheaply.

Outline:
1. The man in the parable sold everything to buy the field of treasure
2. If a person values something highly, she will sacrifice for it
3. The kingdom of God is our treasure
4. Are you willing to give all to possess it?

*   *   *   *   *

Mel Fisher is a man who has not only sought but found a fortune in buried treasure. In 1963, Mel staked all his worldly resources on a gamble. He sold everything and brought his family and crew to Florida, in search of some incredibly rich Spanish ships that were lost in storms. These vessels contained tons of gold and silver. The partners in this venture, called Treasure Salvors, Inc., agreed to work without pay for a year or until they found treasure. Near the end of the year, he struck pay dirt, as he began to uncover a treasure trove of Spanish coins. After the supply of coins dropped off, he set out to find one of the richest vessels ever to go down in the Caribbean, the *Atocha*. Thousands of silver and gold coins, ingots, bronze cannons, and other treasures were found.

All was not sweetness and light, however, not for very long, anyway. Mel Fisher's family had to pay a high price for their buried treasure. Their fabulous find did not lead to instant wealth. The state of Florida laid claim to the treasure and so the Fishers became embroiled in years of costly litigation. But that wasn't the worst of it. One night, there was a terrible accident. The boat that they were sleeping in quietly began to take on water, listed, and suddenly capsized. Dirk Fisher, his wife, Angel, and another crewman were trapped below, where they drowned. Mel Fisher's search for buried treasure cost him dearly. Yet Fisher has no regret.

*   *   *   *   *

How is it that a person comes to possess the treasure of the kingdom? The parable of the buried treasure and the parable of the pearl of surpassing worth present two sides of the question. In the first parable, the man stumbled across the treasure buried in the field. It appears to be blind luck from a human vantage point, though God's hand was certainly involved. Many of us come into the kingdom in this fashion. We haven't searched out the kingdom. We did not lay claim to it through blood, sweat, and tears. It was given to us. Many of us were raised in Christian homes where we came into possession of the treasure of the kingdom of Christ at an early age. Others do not come to faith so easily. They are seekers and pilgrims. They want to believe, to know the truth, but for them it is a struggle. These folks are like the merchant searching for the perfect pearl. He kept on searching until he found it.

These two ways of coming into possession of the treasure of the kingdom are really two sides of the same coin. The man who stumbled upon the hidden treasure exemplifies grace — the kingdom is a gift. The merchant who was seeking the pearl of great price, portrays the reality of faith — we must desire the kingdom of Christ above all else. On the one hand, God finds us and offers us the treasure of his grace. On the other hand, we must have the faith to recognize and accept the treasure as our highest good, forsaking all else to possess it.

Sermon Title: Blended Treasure

Sermon Angle: Christ did not come to do away with the treasure of the Old Testament. Christ makes that clear in verses 51-52. There is much there of surpassing worth. A Christian is one who should see the treasure of the new covenant as a fulfillment of the treasure of old. An Old Testament scribe, who has accepted the treasure of Christ, integrates the old treasure with the new. In the same way, the church is a repository of things old and new. We must draw on both.

Proper 13/Pentecost 11/Ordinary Time 18

Revised Common:	**Genesis 32:22-31**	**Romans 9:1-5**	**Matthew 14:13-21**
Roman Catholic:	**Isaiah 55:1-3**	**Romans 8:35, 37-39**	**Matthew 14:13-21**
Episcopal:	**Nehemiah 9:16-20**	**Romans 8:35-39**	**Matthew 14:13-21**

Theme: God provides for our need if we but trust him.

BRIEF COMMENTARY ON THE LESSONS

Lesson 1: Genesis 32:22-31 (C)

Jacob returns home with his wives, children, and flocks but, fearing the wrath of his brother Esau, he sends them on before him, remaining by himself. He wrestles with an angel of God until daybreak. The angel cannot overcome Jacob and asks to be let go. Jacob refuses until he receives a blessing. The heavenly visitor notes that Jacob has striven with God and man but has prevailed.

Lesson 1: Isaiah 55:1-3 (RC)

Like a hawker on the street, God bids his people to come to him for spiritual food and drink, which will satisfy the deepest longing of their souls.

Lesson 1: Nehemiah 9:16-20 (E)

The people have returned from captivity in Babylon to rebuild Jerusalem and its temple. In this passage, Ezra, Nehemiah, and all the people assemble to reaffirm the covenants that God established with Abraham and Moses. The story of God's redeeming love is read to the people. The people confess their sins and the sins of their forebears and pledge to be loyal to the Lord.

Lesson 2: Romans 9:1-5 (C)

Paul expresses his anguish for the salvation of his fellow Jews. If possible, he would even exchange his own salvation for that of his people.

Lesson 2: Romans 8:35, 37-39 (RC); Romans 8:35-39 (E)

Paul writes words of encouragement for the besieged Christian church. No one or no thing can separate us from the love of God in Christ: not even the seven forms of sufferings and the ten demonic powers which Paul names. Therefore, we are more than conquerors through the power of Christ. The Christian is not free from suffering or death but is given the spiritual resources with which to wrestle and prevail against these dark powers.

Gospel: Matthew 14:13-21 (C, RC, E)

Jesus tries to find some solitude, but the crowds of needy folks find him. His compassion prompts him to heal the sick, but it is getting toward evening and the disciples want to dismiss them so they can find food for supper. Jesus asks them to do the apparently impossible, provide food for all these people. "You give them something to eat" (v. 16). Astonished, they reply: "We have only five loaves and two fish" (v. 17). Jesus commands that they be brought to him. He blesses the food, and the disciples distribute it to the multitudes. All are fed, with twelve baskets left over. The miracle not only shows the miraculous power of Jesus but God's compassion for the needs of people. It also demonstrates that all needs can be met if we but share with God and with one another that which he has placed in our grasp.

Psalm Of The Day
Psalm 17:1-7, 15 (C) — "I shall behold your face in righteousness" (v. 15).
Psalm 78:1-29 (E) — "Mortals ate of the bread of angels; he sent them food in abundance" (v. 25).

Prayer Of The Day
Gracious God, you have lavishly spread your bounteous table before us, that we might eat our fill, and you have given your Son as food for our souls. Free us to share from your great storehouse that all people might eat, live, and return thanks unto you. This we ask in the name of the Bread of Life, Jesus, our Lord. Amen.

THEOLOGICAL REFLECTION ON THE LESSONS

Lesson 1: Genesis 32:22-31
Wrestling with God. The text indicates that Jacob was wrestling with God or an angel of the Lord, but I wonder if he wasn't also wrestling with his conscience. He had tricked his brother and seized the birthright and his father's blessing. Esau acted stupidly, but he had justification for his anger against his brother. Our struggles with God are directly tied to our wrestling with moral and ethical issues that surround our relationships.

Clinging to God. Jacob would not let go of the angel that he was wrestling with until he secured a divine blessing. The believer needs to be persistent in his or her endeavor to lay hold of the Lord's blessings.

Lesson 1: Isaiah 55:1-3
Come to and through the water. The prophet issues God's invitation to come to him, the water of life. Jesus picks up this metaphor when he says: "I am the fountain of the water of life." Water is to the body as God's Spirit is to the soul. In another sense, we come to God through the waters, the waters of baptism. God is the goal and the way to eternal life.

Be a picky eater. The Lord urges: "Listen carefully to me and eat what is good" (v. 2b). We consume a lot of things that aren't food, which don't satisfy: countless material gadgets and trinkets, music which arouses our aggression, magazines which fill our minds with garbage. God's word is that which truly satisfies our deepest hunger.

God's word is what we need. In verse 1, we are encouraged to let the Lord satisfy the thirst of our souls. In verse 2, we are invited to come to God for food. In verse 3, we are told to turn the inner ear of our souls to God and heed the word of the Lord, so that we might live. When Jesus was tempted by Satan, after he had fasted, he rebuked Satan by saying: "Man shall not live by bread alone but by every word that proceeds from the mouth of God" (Matthew 4:4). When we listen to the word of God, we have all that we need to live.

Lesson 2: Romans 9:1-5

See second lesson for Proper 14 (RC, E).

Lesson 2: Romans 8:35-39

A nonbreakable bond. Christ is the cement that binds us to God. When we are baptized into Christ, that bond cannot be broken by any external force. No demonic powers, earthly powers, or misfortunes can separate us from God's love.

More than conquerors? Paul claims that Christians are more than conquerors through the power of Christ. How can one be *more than* a conqueror? We think that being the victor, the one who comes out at the top of the heap, is the ultimate experience. What could be more important than beating someone else or even accomplishing your cherished goal? Experiencing God's love and grace and sharing the same with others.

Surpassing victory. After listing a litany of dark powers that afflict believers, Paul makes what to some seems like an absurd statement. He says, "No, in all these we are more than conquerors through him who loved us" (v. 37). In the eyes of the world, there can be no greater attainment than to be a conqueror. We are taught that winning the victory is everything. How can one be more than a conqueror? Think about it. A conqueror is one who imposes his power on somebody else; he gets to write the rules because of his superior strength or skill. However, he will not enjoy an open and free relationship with another; he can never know what it means to give oneself in love, for that would make him vulnerable. God could overwhelm us with his power at any time, but in Christ he has chosen a course that surpasses victory.

Gospel: Matthew 14:13-21

Send the crowds away. Jesus was attempting to get away for a period of rest and spiritual recharging by going to a lonely spot across the lake, but the crowds followed him. There was no escape. Rather than feeling exasperation, as many of us might, he felt only compassion. Later on, the disciples came to Jesus and wanted him to send the crowds away. Put the needy ones out of sight and mind, so that we might get some needed rest. Jesus would not dismiss them until they had been fed, physically and spiritually.

The responsibilities of being a host. The disciples wanted to send the crowd away, forgetting that the people were their guests and they were the hosts. That's why Jesus told them: "You give them something to eat" (v. 16). You don't ask your guests to go out and obtain their own food. When the needy ones come to the church of Jesus Christ, it is up to us to do what we can to feed them, heal them, and provide for their needs.

Excuses, excuses, excuses. "We have only five loaves and two fish" (v. 17). The disciples were looking for an excuse to send the crowd away. Their meager provisions did look woefully inadequate, but had they not recently witnessed miraculous things from the hand of Jesus? Our excuses keep us from investing our talents in the lives of others.

Offer it to Jesus. Jesus asked that the five loaves and two fish be brought to him. If we offer up to Jesus all that we have, whether it be much or little, Christ blesses it and multiplies its effect.

God's generous gifts of grace. Everyone ate until they were full, and still there were twelve baskets of bread left over. God doesn't merely supply a maintenance diet but feeds us until we are full. There is nothing stingy about God's grace.

PREACHING APPROACHES WITH ILLUSTRATIONS

Lesson 1: Genesis 32:22-31

Sermon Title: A Tenacious Faith

Sermon Angle: Jacob had a tenacious faith in himself, his future, and, finally, his God. He entered the world clinging to the heels of his brother. Esau had the privilege of being firstborn but Jacob wrestled it away from him. He worked and struggled hard with his Uncle Laban for his wives and flocks. Now, as he returns home, he wrestles with God and comes out the victor. Jacob had a tenacious faith that would not let go until he won a blessing.

Lesson 1: Isaiah 55:1-3

Sermon Title: Real Food For Real People

Sermon Angle: The Lord invites his people to come to the supermarket, which would satisfy the deepest hunger of their soul. Much of what they consumed was junk food; it could not satisfy (v. 2). God and his word could build them up if they would but partake. The eats which God offers, free of charge, remain real food for real people.

Outline:
1. We are warned against the dangers of junk food
2. Junk food fills without satisfying or nourishing
3. All that we take into our hearts and minds is food
   — some of it is junk food
   — God and his word are real food for real people

Lesson 1: Nehemiah 9:16-20

Sermon Title: Renewing The Covenant

Sermon Angle: As the Jews reforged their nation, their leaders realized the necessity of ratifying the covenant that Abraham had established with the God of their forebears. They recited the history of God's acts of liberating his people. In response to God's blessings and gifts, the people were asked to reaffirm their loyalty to the God of their ancestors and to the covenant. As Christians, the covenant that forms us into a people was written with the blood of Christ. Each generation must reaffirm their loyalty to that covenant, if our faith is going to continue to live.

Lesson 2: Romans 9:1-5

See the second lesson for Proper 14 (RC, E).

Lesson 2: Romans 8:35-39

Sermon Title: The Unbreakable Bond

Sermon Angle: The bonds of relationships are broken with regularity in our culture. Studies show that one of every two marriages will eventually end in divorce. Our mobility makes for plug-in and plug-out relationships. Yet there is one bond that can never be broken, except if we would completely turn our backs on God: namely, the bond of faith which God established with us in our baptism. It is a bond of unbreakable love. What good news in a Teflon (nonstick) society!

Outline:
1. Do you seek a love that will last eternally?
2. Such love is difficult to come by
   — tribulations and hardships can separate us from each other (v. 35)
   — demonic powers try to destroy our relationship with God (vv. 38-39)
3. The love of God stands as an unbreakable bond (vv. 38-39)

Sermon Title: Beyond Winning And Losing

Sermon Angle: The church of Paul's day had won some great victories, but it faced some formidable foes. Because of persecutions and hardships, they were in constant danger of losing everything. Paul throws out the worst that life can mete out and then concludes that nothing in this world or beyond this world can separate us from God's love. Winning and losing do not ultimately matter; they are among the passing things of this world. Loving, grounded in God's eternal love, remains the only thing that lasts.

Gospel: Matthew 14:13-21

Sermon Title: When Compassion Isn't Enough

Sermon Angle: When Jesus saw the crowds that had tailed him, the gospel writer says that he had compassion for them (v. 14). Compassion means feeling the pain of other people, entering their sorrows. Many of us feel the pain of others but we don't act on it. Jesus shows us that real compassion issues in acts of love — healing, feeding, and the like.

Outline:
1. Great crowds were attracted to Jesus' compassion
2. For Jesus, compassion went from feeling to action
3. Jesus also went beyond what was expected — fed the multitudes
4. If Christ is in us, we will go beyond feeling to action

Sermon Title: God's Mathematics

Sermon Angle: The disciples added up the resources, five loaves and two fish, and came up short. We do the same. We add up one plus one and get two, concluding that we don't have enough resources with which to act. God is not limited to simple addition or subtraction. He can multiply that which we give manyfold.

Sermon Title: Eucharist

Sermon Angle: When the five loaves and two fish were brought to Jesus, he blessed and broke them; then gave them to the disciples who distributed the food to the crowd. This was a Eucharist and Jesus was both the celebrant and the bread. The foundation of Jesus' power rested on the conviction that God was the giver of every gift, so we must give thanks to him and bless his Holy Name. Once God blesses something, it must be broken and shared.

Outline:
1. Jesus gave thanks to God for the loaves and fish
2. When we offer our loaves and our lives in thanksgiving, God blesses
3. Holy communion is a Eucharist (meal of thanksgiving)
4. Christian life is also one continuous Eucharist

(For other approaches on the theme of the gospel and for illustrations, see Corpus Christi, Roman Catholic.)

Proper 14/Pentecost 12/Ordinary Time 19

Revised Common:	Genesis 37:1-4, 12-28	Romans 10:5-15	Matthew 14:22-33
Roman Catholic:	1 Kings 19:9, 11-13	Romans 9:1-5	Matthew 14:22-33
Episcopal:	Jonah 2:1-9	Romans 9:1-5	Matthew 14:22-33

Theme: How to overcome a contrary wind. The disciples faced a fiercely opposing wind on the Sea of Galilee. So, too, did Elijah, after his victory on Mount Carmel. Queen Jezebel was after his life. In both instances, they felt overwhelmed. Then, God came to still the storm.

BRIEF COMMENTARY ON THE LESSONS

Lesson 1: Genesis 37:1-4, 12-28 (C)

Joseph, who was given a long robe with sleeves as a sign of his father's favor, was deeply resented by his brothers. One day, Jacob sent Joseph out in the field to find his brothers and they seized the opportunity to get rid of him. They sold him to a caravan and informed their father that he had been killed by a wild beast.

Lesson 1: 1 Kings 19:9, 11-13 (RC)

Elijah quickly plummets from the precipice of victory to the pit of defeat. He defeats the prophets of Baal but quickly flees from the wrath of Queen Jezebel. Finding a cave in the wilderness he battles a deep depression. In the stillness, he hears God's voice of calm and assurance.

Lesson 1: Jonah 2:1-9 (E)

Jonah flees from the Lord's mandate to preach repentance to Nineveh, a heathen city, and is swallowed by a large fish. He prays to the Lord, who hears his plea. The fish vomited him up on the seashore.

Lesson 2: Romans 10:5-15 (C)

Salvation does not come through the law because nobody can live up to it (v. 5). We are redeemed through Christ when we accept him in our heart and confess him with our lips (v. 10). Salvation by grace through faith is available to all (vv. 12-13).

Lesson 2: Romans 9:1-5 (RC, E)

Paul experiences a profound anxiety in his soul because the Jews have not, by and large, accepted Christ. He feels so strongly that he would give up his own salvation if it would purchase the salvation of his people. He had hoped that they would accept the gospel because they had been given the law, the prophets, and the covenants.

Gospel: Matthew 14:22-33 (C, RC, E)

Jesus sends the disciples to the other side of the lake, as he dismisses the crowd. He goes to a high place to pray, and then he observes the disciples' boat struggling against the wind. He walks on the water, and the disciples are terrified, thinking that they are seeing a ghost. Impetuous Peter asks Christ to bid him come to him on the water. When he looks at the waves around him, he sinks in fear, calling to Jesus. Jesus saves him, and when they enter the boat, there is a great calm, both on the sea and in the boat. Overcome with awe, the disciples confess that Jesus is the Christ.

Psalm Of The Day
Psalm 105:1-6, 16-22, 45b (C) — "Seek the Lord and his strength ..." (v. 4a).
Psalm 85:8-13 (RC) — "Righteousness and peace will kiss each other" (v. 10b).
Psalm 29 (E) — "The voice of the Lord is over the waters" (v. 3).

Prayer Of The Day
Prince of Peace, when the storms of life assail us and the winds of opposition threaten to capsize our well-ordered existence, still the raging fear within us and bring us safely unto yourself. In the name of Jesus. Amen.

THEOLOGICAL REFLECTION ON THE LESSONS

Lesson 1: Genesis 37:1-4, 12-28
Murderous jealousy. Joseph's brothers were so jealous of Joseph they were ready to kill him. Jealousy is truly murderous. Yet who of us has not committed murder in our hearts? It is common for a brother or a sister to wish that the other one were dead or had never been born. This is often the case with the firstborn child; he or she monopolizes the parents' attention until a sibling pushes him from the throne. When I was a young child, my mother once prevented my father from taking me to the movies, I yelled at her, "I hate you! I wish you were dead!" I felt terrible about it afterward and sobbed to sleep. Yet the dark side of my soul had unexpectedly reared its ugly head. We cannot stand in judgment of Joseph's brothers while most of us have desired, perhaps for an instant, the destruction of one who vies for what we cherish.

Lesson 1: 1 Kings 19:9, 11-13
Knowing when to throw in the towel. When does a person quit? When do you say, "Enough!"? Elijah was going to quit out of fear. That's the wrong time to throw in the towel. A person should quit when the job is completed or when others are in place to take over where he left off. If God has given us a task, he will also give the wherewithal to complete it.

Listening to the whispers of God. Sometimes God may speak through cataclysmic events or in a booming voice that demands recognition. However, most times he speaks in a whisper, in a "still, small voice," as he did with Elijah. Praying effectively means being a good listener.

Lesson 1: Jonah 2:1-9
Crying for help. Jonah cried out to the Lord for help from the belly of the fish and the Lord heard his plea for mercy. He experienced anew the glorious fact that deliverance comes from the Lord (v. 9). Jonah was swallowed by a God that was too big for him; he is the Lord of all nations. In our day, millions are swallowed whole, not by God, but by forces at play in the world. Government, business, and technology tend to swallow the individual whole. God is still the only one who can save us from the belly of these whoppers. We are still important to him, as is each and every person.

Lesson 2: Romans 10:5-15

Moving faith from the private to the public. Many Christians emphasize the importance of believing from the heart without stressing the necessity of confessing Christ with our lips and our lives. Encasing Christ in the private domain makes him available when needed without the discomfort of having our faith challenged in the public arena. Yet, according to scripture, authentic faith always becomes a matter of public record. Believing with the heart always leads to profession with the lips (v. 9) and our lives. Christian faith is never purely a private matter.

Lesson 2: Romans 9:1-5

The witness of conscience. Paul uses an interesting statement when he is trying to establish the credibility of his concern for the spiritual well-being of his people. He states: "My conscience confirms it in the Holy Spirit" (v. 1). Paul connects his conscience to the Holy Spirit which informs it. If conscience is to point to that which is good and true, it must be informed by the word of God and the Spirit.

Salvation is for sharing. Paul was less concerned about his own salvation than that of his fellow Israelites. He passionately affirms that he would forfeit his own salvation if it would mean that they would accept the Lord. The church contains many people who are interested in their own salvation and spiritual growth but have no sorrow in their hearts for those who are lost. They have not learned that salvation is for sharing.

Gospel: Matthew 14:22-33

Alone in good company. Many people avoid aloneness. If they are by themselves, they turn on the radio or television. To be alone, for them, is to be in doubtful company. The person who has made peace with God and herself, when alone, is in good company. After ministering to the crowds all day, Jesus went up to the mountain to pray, to be alone in good company. It's ironic that the basis of Christian community rests on commitment to regularly encounter God in the aloneness of prayer.

From a distance. While Jesus occupied his mountain of prayer, he viewed the distress of the boatload of disciples in the distance (v. 24). Prayer gave Jesus a unique vantage point from which to view the problems of the world and their solutions. To truly see things, we need to put a little distance between ourselves and our lives. Prayer affords us the spiritual perspective and space to see things from God's viewpoint — close, yet from a distance.

The wind was against them. Vicious storms quickly boil up the waves of Lake Galilee, without warning, as in our text. The disciples were being overcome by the wind and the waves. Jesus came to their aid. We all experience such storms in our lives. Jesus watches out for his own and is already there, even before we cry out to him. He may or may not quell the storm without but will always subdue the storm of fear within.

Keep looking up. There was a minister on a Chicago radio station every night for many years who always ended his meditation: "Keep looking up." That's good advice. Peter got into deep water (pardon the pun) when he got out of the boat and proceeded to walk to Jesus on the waves; instead of focusing on the calm face of Jesus, he was distracted by the winds and waves, and his heart flooded with fear.

PREACHING APPROACHES WITH ILLUSTRATIONS

Lesson 1: Genesis 37:1-4, 12-18

Sermon Title: Sibling Rivalry

Sermon Angle: Jacob loved his youngest son better than the rest. Predictably, this led to jealousy and hatred on the part of the other brothers. There is bound to be a certain amount of rivalry for parents' attention, but when parents clearly favor one child, it is a prescription for disaster. Though the brothers did an evil thing to Joseph, the father must also share some of the blame. Though parents can't help their feelings, they can shun obvious favoritism. A sermon on this ever-timely topic might prove healing for many.

Lesson 1: 1 Kings 19:9, 11-13

Sermon Title: Buried Alive

Sermon Angle: Elijah, a great man of faith, fell into a pit of depression, every bit as real as the pit that Joseph was tossed into by his brothers. His faith had faded, his spine had melted, and he was overcome by a black cloud of self-pity and failure. Elijah was depressed! It's comforting that even the giants of God's kingdom are immobilized by such spiritual forces. Elijah was in a cave, symbolic of his state of mind; he was truly buried alive. The Lord raised him from his grave and can do the same for us.

Sermon Title: Jail Break!

Sermon Angle: Elijah had confined himself to a prison. The bars of fear and failure robbed him of freedom. When you're in the slammer, it's very difficult to break out by yourself. You need some outside help. In Elijah's case, that help came from the Lord who spoke to him in a voice of calm. God's presence made him realize that he was not alone: God was with him. God showed him that things were not as bleak as he imagined.

Outline:
1. There are many kinds of prisons (physical and spiritual)
2. When we are in an emotional/spiritual jail we must
   — admit to that which imprisons us (fears)
   — seek help
   — remember that the Lord is with us and can free us
   — focus not on failures but on God's future

Lesson 2: Romans 10:5-15

Sermon Title: Beautiful Feet

Sermon Angle: Not many cultures pay much attention to the feet as an object of beauty. Yes, the Chinese traditionally bound the feet of women to keep them small, which was considered comely, but, all in all, feet aren't given much press. How many feet have you ever seen on the cover of a glamour magazine? Verse 15b lifts up for our consideration the ideal of beautiful feet. What makes these feet so beautiful? They are mobile feet. They are merciful and loving feet. They are feet that carry the good news of God's love to the places of human need, discouragement, and darkness. How beautiful are your feet?

Lesson 2: Romans 9:1-5

Sermon Title: Do You Give A Damn?

Sermon Angle: In the next to the last scene of the movie, *Gone With The Wind*, Scarlet O'Hara begs Rhett Butler, her ex-husband, to come back to her. She had treated him like dirt and now she wanted him back. His response is a classic: "Frankly, my dear, I don't give a damn." What Rhett was trying to communicate was that he didn't care for Scarlet any more. Rhett might have more accurately stated, "I won't receive a damn for you. I won't let you take advantage of me any more." Christ was willing to be damned on the cross for our sins, that we might rise with him to newness of life. Some people may be offended by such strong language, but do we give a damn? Would we be willing, like Paul, to be damned for the sake of others? Do we really passionately care about the spiritual well-being of others? Would we, like Paul, be willing to receive a damn, rather than dish out a damn?

Sermon Title: Legacy Lost

Sermon Angle: Paul recites the rich spiritual legacy of his nation (vv. 4-5). God had established his covenant with the Jews out of love and grace, but this had been turned into a tedious system of rules and regulations. The legacy of an immediate relationship with the Lord had been lost in the maze of laws and tradition. Many Christians seem to have lost touch with their spiritual legacy as well. Tradition can point a way but it cannot save us; only Christ can. Faith is the way to get in touch with our spiritual legacy.

Gospel: Matthew 14:22-33

Sermon Title: Heart Of Darkness

Sermon Angle: The disciples encountered the storm during the fourth watch (3 to 6 a.m.), the darkest part of the night. Christ's watchful eyes pierce the heart of darkness. He sees and he responds to our distress.

Sermon Title: Countering A Contrary Wind

Sermon Angle: Matthew comments that the wind was against the boatload of disciples (v. 24). Nature sometimes dishes out a contrary wind and sometimes society is to blame. The source of the contrary wind does not matter so much. How we handle the contrary wind does. Do we see the contrary wind as a challenge or a rout?

Outline:
1. The experience of contrary winds is universal
2. What contrary winds do you fear?
3. God may not still the winds without but will bring peace within
4. Faith in Christ will enable us to overcome the contrary wind

Sermon Title: A Study Of Hands

Sermon Angle: We can imagine that the hands of the disciples trembled in dread as they tossed on turbulent seas and especially when they thought the form of Jesus was a ghost. They must have been relieved when they realized that it was the Lord. Then Peter asked if he could come to the Lord on the water. Jesus may well have beckoned him with a wave of his hand. When Peter started to sink, he shot up pleading hands, begging: "Lord, save me!" (v. 30). Christ reached down immediately with a helping hand.

Outline:
1. The disciples cried out to heaven with trembling hands
2. Jesus responded to Peter with a beckoning wave of his hand
3. As Peter sank, he cried out with pleading hands
4. Jesus reached down with a helping hand to save him

Sermon Title: Focus And Fear And Faith

Sermon Angle: Whether we are driven by fear or faith depends on our focus. Peter focused on Jesus and walked on the water. Then he focused on the storm and he was overwhelmed by fear, sinking into the sea.

Outline:
1. Faith is a matter of focus
2. The disciples and Peter focused on the storm and were overwhelmed by fear
3. When Peter focused on Jesus (faith) he could walk on water
4. Keep your eyes on Jesus

*   *   *   *   *

Franklin D. Roosevelt's oft-quoted attempt to calm the nerves of the citizens of the United States in a time of war, "we have nothing to fear but fear itself," may not be entirely accurate. Yet, it is extremely insightful. Usually, the fear of that which we dread is more painful and destructive than the thing itself. Fear can literally kill us. The *Pulpit Resource* (July, August, September 1992) reported the apparently true story of a Russian railroad employee who accidentally locked himself inside a refrigerator car. Without success he attempted to attract outside attention. Since he knew of no way that he could extricate himself, he came to accept his fate. As his life ebbed away, he scribbled notations on the wall of the car such as: "I'm becoming colder." Then he wrote: "I'm becoming still colder ... I'm freezing to death ... I'm so numb I can barely write ... I'm getting sleepy, these may be my last words."

When the car was opened they found him dead, even though the temperature in the car was 56 degrees. The cooling coils in the car were inoperable. There was no physical reason why this poor soul should have died. The temperature was bearable and the air supply was ample. His fear was fatal.

*   *   *   *   *

This is the true story of some dear friends of ours. Ed, a childhood friend of my dad's, is married to a woman named Marie. Marie is a sweet gal but a little on the nervous side. Marie was driving as they pulled to a stop in their driveway, so Ed could open the garage door. Had they not been a happily married couple, I might have had suspicions about what was soon to ensue. As Ed was opening the door, Marie's foot slipped from the brake to the accelerator. Ed found himself attached to the car like a giant hood ornament as the car proceeded to punch through the rear cement wall of the garage and into the backyard, where he was flung free of the vehicle. Unfortunately, he still wasn't out of harm's way. The accelerator pedal was still depressed and the car continued to careen wildly in the backyard, barely missing him as it shattered a fence. Mercifully, the car came to a sudden halt as it butted heads with a tree. Miraculously, Ed walked away with only a few bruises, while Marie was finally extricated from the driver's seat with only her pride injured. I think that this episode made more of an impression on Marie than it did on Ed. Every so often, she brings up this time of terror with the exclamation: "Oh my gosh, I could have killed him!"

In thinking about that harrowing experience, I have often wondered: Why didn't Marie jam on the brake? Or, if the pedal was stuck, why didn't she put the transmission in neutral or turn off the ignition? Of course, such questions come from an armchair quarterback, far removed from the field of battle. She was obviously paralyzed with mind-numbing fear, much like that which the disciples felt in the storm-tossed Lake Galilee boat.

That kind of fear can make havoc of our lives, too, if we lose our focus on the presence of Christ. Then, the terrors of the storms of life can take us for a harrowing ride.

Proper 15/Pentecost 13/Ordinary Time 20

Revised Common:	Genesis 45:1-15	Romans 11:1-2a, 29-32	Matthew 15:(10-20) 21-28
Roman Catholic:	Isaiah 56:1, 6-7	Romans 11:13-15, 29-32	Matthew 15:21-28
Episcopal:	Isaiah 56:1 (2-5) 6-7	Romans 11:13-15, 29-32	Matthew 15:21-28

Theme: The ever-expanding circle of God's love. The second portion of the book of Isaiah envisions God's covenant reaching out to include Gentiles. God's house shall be a house of prayer for all peoples (v. 7). Paul pictures God's grace extending to all through the Jewish rejection of Jesus. The gospel has Jesus healing the daughter of a Canaanite woman.

BRIEF COMMENTARY ON THE LESSONS

Lesson 1: Genesis 45:1-15 (C)

Joseph reveals himself to his brothers, who have come to Egypt to secure food during the famine. Rather than seeking revenge, he sees God's gracious hand in his brothers' treachery. Joseph openly weeps for joy and reveals his plan to provide for his entire family in Egypt. This ends the cycle of stories from Genesis.

Lesson 1: Isaiah 56:1, 6-7 (RC); Isaiah 56:1 (2-5) 6-7 (E)

The prophet foresees a time when foreigners would be included in God's covenant. God's holy temple will be a house for all peoples (v. 7).

Lesson 2: Romans 11:1-2a, 29-32 (C); Romans 11:13-15, 29-32 (RC, E)

Paul identifies himself as the apostle to the Gentiles. The Jews have rejected Christ and so the gospel has been extended to the Gentiles. This does not indicate that God has rejected his people, for God's call is irrevocable. It is through the same gospel that the Jews will come to Christ. It is God's intention to shower his mercy on all people.

Gospel: Matthew 15:(10-20) 21-28 (C); Matthew 15:21-28 (RC, E)

Jesus and his disciples leave the land of Israel for the region of Tyre and Sidon, northwest of Galilee on the Mediterranean coast. Perhaps Jesus is seeking some rest. His fame precedes him, as a Canaanite woman comes shrieking after them that he should heal her daughter, possessed by a demon. She addresses Jesus as the Jewish Messiah, "Son of David" (v. 22). Jesus acts as if she were not there but she persists in seeking his help. The disciples want her dispatched quickly. Jesus responds that he was only sent to the Jews. This correctly defined the scope of his earthly mission. Then, she kneels before him and begs: "Lord, help me" (v. 25). The next part of the encounter is what really disturbs a lot of people, because Jesus seems offensive and cruel. He said, "It is not fair to take the children's bread and give it to the dogs" (v. 26). The woman will not be put off: "Yes, Lord, yet even the dogs eat the crumbs that fall from their masters' table" (v. 27).

Some have tried to take the sting away by changing "dogs" to "little puppies." They point out that he may have been employing a little humor, that he is likening her to a puppy yapping at his heels. Others contend that he was merely testing the woman's faith or that of the disciples.

I find all of these interpretations lacking. The point of our interpretation should be persistent faith. This desperate woman sparred with the Lord and won. She conquered him with her unsinkable faith. Jesus commended her faith and instantly healed her daughter. Whether they be outsider or insider, Jew or Gentile, Christ stands ready to help those who cry out to him in faith.

Psalm Of The Day

Psalm 133 (C) — "How very good and pleasant it is when kindred live together in unity" (v. 1).

Psalm 67 (RC, E) — "Let the people praise you, O God; let all the peoples praise you" (v. 5).

Prayer Of The Day

Gracious God, we, your needy children, cry out to you for help, not on the basis of race or class or sex, but because of your great love for all your children. Lord, have mercy upon us all! In Jesus' name. Amen.

THEOLOGICAL REFLECTION ON THE LESSONS

Lesson 1: Genesis 45:1-15

A cry of joy rather than a cry for blood. When Joseph observed his brothers standing before him, he could not contain himself; he cried loudly. Considering that his brothers sold him into slavery, one might think that he would cry out for vengeance. Not Joseph: he cried for joy at the prospect of being reunited with his family.

Let bygones be. Joseph told his brothers not to be angry with themselves for what they had done to him (v. 5). God was able to use their evil for good. Besides, one cannot change the past. We must stand ready to let go of our mistakes and move on.

Move closer. The brothers stood at a distance, not only out of deference to Joseph's exalted position, but because they were afraid and full of guilt. Fear and guilt keep us apart from one another and from God. Joseph bid them to come closer (v. 4). A forgiving spirit draws us closer to our God and to one another.

Lesson 1: Isaiah 56:1 (2-5) 6-7

Good news for outcasts. This lesson speaks to two sets of outcasts. The Israelites were outcasts and God was promising to bring them back to their homeland and the holy city. The Gentiles were also outcasts, as far as the Jews were concerned. The prophet foresees a time when they will be part of the family of God, ministering to the Lord and worshiping him in the holy temple. Both Jew and Gentile, those on the inside and those on the outside, are outcasts. The common denominator is sin. God intends to gather all who desire to be a part of God's covenant people.

Joyful worship. Isaiah proclaims that those who assemble in God's house of prayer will be joyful in their worship. The heart of worship is praise and thanksgiving as we respond to God's gracious acts of liberation. How unfortunate that so many people picture worship as something perfunctory, dull, and boring.

The gathering place. The Lutheran church developed an outreach emphasis titled: The Welcome Place. The purpose was to communicate to insider and outsider alike that Lutherans were a welcoming people, that all people could joyfully gather in God's holy temple.

Lesson 2: Romans 11:1-2a, 13-15, 29-32

When people close doors, God opens another door. Paul indicates that it was the Jews' rejection of the gospel that led to his ministry to the Gentiles (v. 15). The apostle holds out the hope that the door which the Jews closed would someday swing open again. It is God's will to show his mercy to all humankind. As Christians, we should never curse a closed door or despair because some door of ministry is closed off to us. If one door is closed, God will certainly open another.

God is not fickle. Paul contends that the gifts and call of God to the Jewish people is irrevocable (v. 29). When the Lord makes a commitment, he does not vacillate. The apostle must have been specifically thinking of the covenant with Abraham, rather than the Mosaic covenant, which was conditioned by the obedience of the people. God's covenant with us through our baptism into Christ is also irrevocable, as far as God is concerned. It is not based on our faithfulness, but God's will.

Gospel: Matthew 15:(10-20) 21-28

Strategic withdrawal. The early portion of chapter 15 features the ongoing dispute which Jesus had with the Pharisees and others in the religious establishment. Conflict is very trying, consuming lots of energy. Jesus needed to get away from the battle for reflection and spiritual renewal. Such a withdrawal would give him perspective and strength for the coming fray. The cross was looming on the horizon, and he needed time to discern the Father's will. All those in Christ's army need such times of renewal and vision.

Dealing with interruptions. It seems like almost every time Jesus would retire to some lonely spot for prayer, someone would be begging for his attention. Even in this non-Jewish region, he could not go unnoticed. A Canaanite woman came crying after him, raising quite a ruckus. The disciples wanted her sent away. Most of the time, Jesus responded immediately to the need. This time he needed a little persuading. Could it be that this was the Father's way of helping him to see that his messiahship had broader applications? The point that we need to make here is that God often comes to us during the interruptions of our plans rather than in the plans themselves.

Cry for mercy. The woman cried after Jesus: "Have mercy on me, Lord" (v. 21). She wasn't asking for herself but for her daughter. There is not one instance in the gospels where our Lord did not respond positively to a cry for mercy. We need not be embarrassed to issue such a cry.

The silences of God. At first, Jesus was silent to her desperate plea. Her prayer was not immediately answered. Sometimes God seems mute to our pleas. We hear only an echo of our petition rather than an answer, it seems. When this happens, we ought not give up but keep on storming the gates of heaven. God responds to the entreaties of those who continue to seek his mercy. This is not to say that God will always give us what we ask but that he will help those who approach him with a persistent faith.

PREACHING APPROACHES WITH ILLUSTRATIONS

Lesson 1: Genesis 45:1-15

Sermon Title: The Joy Of Reunion

Sermon Angle: Joseph was overjoyed when he was reunited with his brothers. He wept tears of joy as he embraced and kissed them. He experienced the joy of reunion through forgiveness and reconciliation and so can we.

Outline:
1. Joseph was forcibly separated from his family
2. God brought them back together
3. Togetherness is not reunion — reunion comes from reconciliation
   — God brought them together
   — God gave Joseph a forgiving heart
4. Are you separated from others by sin?
5. Let God show you the joy of reunion

Lesson 1: Isaiah 56:1 (2-5) 6-7

Sermon Title: Open House

Sermon Angle: The prophet speaks the word of the Lord, announcing: "For my house shall be called a house of prayer for all people" (v. 7). God's house is an open house, open to all people of faith.

Lesson 2: Romans 11:1-2a, 13-15, 29-32

Sermon Title: Merciful Lord

Sermon Angle: Paul states that the Gentiles, who were once disobedient, have now received mercy (v. 30). The theme of mercy is a common thread that runs through all the lessons. The story of Joseph's reunion with his brothers was affected through his merciful treatment of his brothers. The Isaiah text states that God will mercifully receive the worship of all people of faith. Finally, the gospel lesson features a desperate woman who cried for mercy and received mercy. Our Lord is merciful, and so are his followers.

Outline:
1. The Gentiles have received the mercy of God in Christ (Romans 11)
2. The Isaiah text — God mercifully accepted the worship of Gentile believers
3. The gospel — Christ shows mercy on the Canaanite woman

Gospel: Matthew 15:21-28

Sermon Title: The Cry Of A Stranger

Sermon Angle: The Canaanite woman cried the cry of a stranger, an outsider. She addressed Jesus by his Jewish messianic title: Son of David. She recognized that she wasn't one of the Chosen People, that she was a stranger to the promises of God. Her plea was not on the basis of race or religion; she presented her grave need as a suppliant woman seeking grace. Because of her insistent faith, Christ heard her cry.

Outline:
1. The Canaanite sought mercy as an outsider
   — because of her great need
   — and Christ's reputation for healing compassion
2. Christ heard her cry and helped her
3. Are we sensitive to the cries of those who are strangers to the grace of God?
   — do we hear and do we help?

Sermon Title: What Kind Of Beggar Does Christ Listen To?

Sermon Angle: The Canaanite woman approached Jesus as a beggar, seeking mercy for her daughter. The disciples were also beggars, asking that their Lord send this troublesome woman out of their sight. The first beggar was imploring him to respond to a valid need. The other beggars were asking that they not be troubled by the insistent need of a sister human being. They probably justified their hardness of heart on the basis of race, religion, and sex. God does not honor the prayers of those who beg to be spared the pain of their brothers and sisters. He listens to those who implore him out of the poverty of their spirit.

Outline:
1. The Canaanite woman begged for healing mercies
2. The disciples begged to be sheltered from human need
3. Christ grants the petitions of those who seek God's mercies
4. We are all beggars, who have no right to demand, only beg, for mercy

Sermon Title: The Language God Listens To

Sermon Angle: I don't know what language the Canaanite woman employed in her encounter with Jesus. Perhaps Aramaic. It doesn't really matter what tongue she spoke; her faith spoke eloquently. Though Jesus seemed not to hear at first, the persuasiveness of her faith won him over. God doesn't listen because of certain phrases and formulas, no matter how pious they sound. It is faith that connects with the almighty, though we speak like a babbler.

* * * * *

In the book, *Preaching Through The Church Year*, Robert E. Luccock asserts that, if he had it within his power to fulfill his fantasies, one of the first things he would do is place the image or the statue of the Canaanite woman of Matthew 15:21-28 in every house of worship. Perhaps it would be situated on or by the door of the church to remind us, as we leave the sanctuary, that the world is filled with those crying out in pain for God's mercy. Or, maybe a statue could be placed in the worship area of the church to save us from a smug coziness that turns a deaf ear to the world.

This woman is an important icon because she is the first woman that Jesus ministered to outside of the nation of Israel. She and the centurion, who asked Jesus to heal his servant, are the first Gentiles that Jesus ministered to. This humble woman is significant because Jesus' ministry to the whole world commences with her. As her cries shattered Jesus' tranquility long ago, so may she serve as an icon for all those who would break through our comfortable religious traditions.

* * * * *

When the Canaanite woman came crying after Jesus, he referred to her as a dog, not a complimentary term. What he may have been referring to was her annoying persistence. Dogs generally bark when their security is threatened. The world is filled with barking dogs. Thousands of Haitians flee the abject poverty of their island and bark at our shoreline for a chance to enjoy freedom from want and oppression. Packs of Rwandans bark in terror, as they flee slaughter in tribal warfare. Multitudes in our cities are barking because their lives are torn with violence. The starving millions in our world are too weak to bark; they merely whimper quietly. Tens of thousands of abused women and children in America bark all but silently, for fear of reprisal. Barking dogs, so to speak, may be annoying, even threatening. Yet the right way to still their barking is not to plug our ears but to listen to the bark and respond to the need that led to the bark in the first place. Humans may bark sometimes to scare people away but, more often, to try to draw attention to their needs.

Proper 16/Pentecost 14/Ordinary Time 21

Revised Common:	Exodus 1:8—2:10	Romans 12:1-8	Matthew 16:13-20
Roman Catholic:	Isaiah 22:19-23	Romans 11:33-36	Matthew 16:13-20
Episcopal:	Isaiah 51:1-6	Romans 11:33-36	Matthew 16:13-20

Theme: Deliverance from bondage. The Old Testament readings, with the exception of the Roman Catholic, focus on God's great acts of deliverance. God sends prophets to announce their approaching freedom. We see the completion of God's intent in the gospel, where he gives to the church the power to deliver people from the bondage of sin.

BRIEF COMMENTARY ON THE LESSONS

Lesson 1: Exodus 1:8—2:10 (C)

Generations after Joseph, the Israelites have multiplied and are regarded as a security risk. The period referred to here is from about 1308-1224 BC. The Hebrews are afflicted with harsh burdens, and the Pharaoh orders the midwives to destroy the infant boys, as they are born. This they refuse to do. To avert destruction, the mother of Moses places him in a sealed basket, which she floats in the river. The infant is found by the Pharaoh's daughter, nursed by his natural mother, but adopted by the Egyptian princess. The next ten readings will transport us from the birth of Moses to the Exodus and the wilderness wanderings.

Lesson 1: Isaiah 22:19-23 (RC)

Shebna, the right hand man for King Hezekiah, had apparently misused his authority and was to be replaced by Eliakim, who was to be given the key to the house of David; "he shall open and none shall shut; and he shall shut and none shall open" (v. 22).

Lesson 1: Isaiah 51:1-6 (E)

The Hebrews who were looking and longing for salvation from their captivity in Babylon are urged to hark back to the foundation of faith, the covenant with Abraham. This is referred to as the rock from which they were hewn (vv. 1-2). God will be faithful to his covenant and will free his people from bondage.

Lesson 2: Romans 12:1-8 (C)

Christians are to present their lives to God as a living sacrifice, as opposed to the slain sacrifices placed on the altar in the temple. We are not to be conformed to the world but transformed by the Spirit of Christ. This new existence is expressed in community, in the body of Christ, where each individual has her role to play.

Lesson 2: Romans 11:33-36 (RC, E)

Paul concludes this section of his epistle in which he details God's plan of salvation through Christ. He rhapsodizes about the mystery of God's ways; his judgments are unsearchable and his ways inscrutable. Mere humans cannot completely comprehend the things of God.

Gospel: Matthew 16:13-20 (C, RC, E)

In the district of Caesarea Philippi, Jesus seeks feedback from his disciples. What are folks saying about him? Who do they think he is? The response: John the Baptist, Elijah, Jeremiah, or one of those prophets. The really important question, however, was the opinion of those who were closest to him, "Who do you say that I am?" Peter speaks for the others: "You are the Messiah, the Son of the living God" (v. 16). Jesus blesses Simon and announces that his name shall become Peter (the rock). Roman Catholics and Protestants differ in their interpretation of verses 18-19. Roman Catholics maintain that the church is built on Peter himself and that it is to Peter that the keys of the kingdom were given. This becomes the bases of apostolic succession. Protestants claim that it is the confession of Peter that Jesus is the Messiah on which the church is built. Thus, the keys of the kingdom are given to the whole church. This is the power to proclaim God's forgiveness to the penitent and withhold it from the unrepentant.

Psalm Of The Day

Psalm 124 (C) — "Our help is in the name of the Lord ..." (v. 8).
Psalm 138 (RC, E) — "You preserve me from the wrath of my enemies" (v. 7).

Prayer Of The Day

Liberating Lord, you have come that we might be free from the powers that hold us captive, especially the tyranny of sin. As you have freed us from the grip of sin and Satan, so make us agents of liberation and hope. In Jesus' name. Amen.

THEOLOGICAL REFLECTION ON THE LESSONS

Lesson 1: Exodus 1:8—2:10

Fleeting fame and fortune. Joseph rose from obscurity to eminence, second only to the Pharaoh in power. Verse 8 reminds us how fleeting earthly glory really is: "Now a new king rose over Egypt who did not know Joseph." They had forgotten how God empowered this man to save the country from starvation. This sober realization should prompt us to devote ourselves to God and the things that are eternal.

The plots of men and the plans of God. The Pharaoh and his administrators feared the growing strength of the Hebrew people in their midst, and so they thought they would deal shrewdly with them. They would oppress them and keep them securely under their thumb. Without this negative pressure, God would not have been able to muster enough support for his plan to liberate them from Egypt and bring them into their own land. God even uses evil in the service of good. Humankind attempts to rule, but God overrules.

Lesson 1: Isaiah 22:19-23

Keeper of the keys. The mantle of authority in King Hezekiah's house is to pass to Eliakim. He will control access to the king. He shall shut and no one will open; he shall open and no one will shut. The keys to the kingdom of God are passed on to the church. Christ has given us the mission of unlocking the door of access to all who sincerely seek the Lord. God forbid that our actions should lock the door of access.

Lesson 1: Isaiah 51:1-6

Built on the rock. The captive Jews are told to remember their beginnings as a people, when God established his covenant with Abraham. This is the rock from which they were hewn (v. 1). This correlates with the gospel lesson, which reminds us Christians that we are hewn from the rock of the confession that Jesus is the Christ.

Lesson 2: Romans 12:1-8

See the second lesson for Proper 17.

Lesson 2: Romans 11:33-36

God is an unsolved mystery. In much of contemporary Protestantism, there is a penchant for explaining away the mystery of God. We have tried to contain God in the confines of our puny rationality. The Bible reveals God but does not explain away the mystery. Paul waxes poetic about the mystery of God in Christ. "O the depth of the riches of the wisdom and knowledge of God! How unreachable are his judgments and how inscrutable his ways." If we could comprehend the mind of God, we would be gods ourselves. The mystery of God's being remains unsolved.

Gospel: Matthew 16:13-20

The rock from which the water flows. Caesarea Philippi was situated by the headwaters of the Jordan River. The Jordan flows out of a rock wall, from a subterranean pool of unmeasurable depth. These are the waters which sustained the Israelites and the water in which our Lord was baptized. It is interesting that it is here that Jesus quizzed his disciples about his identity, in light of the Lord's affirmation about Peter and his confession. The affirmation of Jesus as the Christ is the rock on which the Christian church is built. It is out of this church that the baptismal waters give life to all who are washed in its flow.

Who is this Jesus? Jesus conducted a public opinion survey about who people thought him to be. There were various opinions, though most thought of him as a prophet. As Jesus conducted his ministry, witnesses were constantly asking the questions: Who is this man? Where does he get the power to conduct miracles? Where does his authority to teach come from? It's the question that troubled Pilate. What do you have to say about yourself and the charges against you? Jesus remained an enigma to many people and remains so today. The question can never be answered philosophically or solved as one might investigate a crime. Only through faith in Jesus as Lord can we begin to answer this question.

Not through flesh but through the Father. When Peter made his historic confession, Jesus commented: "For flesh and blood has not revealed this to you but my father who is in heaven" (v. 17). Knowledge of God comes not through human striving but is revealed by God.

Binding and loosing. The binding and loosing that is referred to in verse 19 is technical rabbinic jargon for forbidding and permitting, referring to the commandments. We might look at it another way. When we are bound to Christ as Lord, we are set loose from the power of sin and death.

PREACHING APPROACHES WITH ILLUSTRATIONS

Lesson 1: Exodus 1:8—2:10

Sermon Title: Pro Life

Sermon Angle: The Pharaoh wanted the Hebrew midwives to kill all baby boys as soon as they were born. They chose to obey God and their consciences rather than the authorities. God blessed the midwives and the Israelites increased despite the king's plot (1:20). God continues to bless those who exert themselves to extend life rather than destroy it.

Sermon Title: Children On Loan

Sermon Angle: Imagine going to your local rental store and renting a baby for two or three years and then having to return it. When a monstrous thought! Yet, babies are not ours to keep; they are lent to us by God. We had better be sure we return them to their maker in good condition. We must answer to God for carelessness or abuse of one of his little ones.

Lesson 1: Isaiah 22:19-23

Sermon Title: The Keeper Of The Keys

Sermon Angle: This lesson should be linked to the gospel story of Christ consigning the keys of the kingdom to Peter and company. This lesson shows that God consigns the keys of authority on whom he wills. He took them away from one man and gave them to another. It appears that Shebna, the king's steward, was utilizing his authority for his own glory rather than in service of his king and of the people. He tried to create immortality by carving out a pretentious tomb for himself (v. 16). Because he used his delegated authority for self-glorification, he lost the keys of the kingdom. God is the keeper of the keys.

Lesson 2: Romans 12:1-8

See the second lesson for Proper 17.

Lesson 2: Romans 11:33-36

Sermon Title: God Is Deep

Sermon Angle: Paul extols the depth of the riches of the wisdom and knowledge of God. We do not meet God by scaling the heights. Rather, we descend to the One who is immeasurable depth. We meet God in the depth of weakness, poverty, ignorance, and grief. All of these realities force us to reach beyond our own superficiality and find God in the depths of faith, hope, and love. God is not so much high as he is deep.

Outline:

1. God cannot be known through philosophy or theology — his thoughts are too deep for us (v. 33)
2. We experience God in the depths of suffering, weakness, and self-abandonment, where God reveals his love and grace

Gospel: Matthew 16:13-20

Sermon Title: How Would You Answer This Question?

Sermon Angle: Jesus had a question and answer session with his disciples at Caesarea Philippi. He started with a more general question and then moved to the personal. "Who do you say that I am?" Peter responded that Jesus was the Messiah and even more, the Son of the living

God. If someone were to ask us, "Who is this Jesus to you?" could we readily respond? Even more significantly, what does our life say about who Jesus is to us individually and corporately?

Outline:

1. Ask the people on the street what they think about Jesus and you'll get a variety of answers
2. The important question is personal: "Who do you say that I am?"
3. What does your theology say about this question and what does your life proclaim?

Sermon Title: The Keys Of The Kingdom

Sermon Angle: Christ gave to Peter and company the keys of the kingdom of heaven. That means that the church is the gatekeeper to those who would gain entrance into the presence of God. The text mentions keys (plural), indicating more than one. What are they? Confessing Christ as Lord is the main key. A second essential key is forgiveness. Other important keys are faith, hope, love, and humility.

* * * * *

The past twenty years have given us an explosion of Christian rock music. The message of the gospel has been wedded with the medium of contemporary music. Actually, Christian rock goes back to the beginning when Christ said to Peter, after his confession, "... you are Peter and on this rock I will build my church." The Christian community is built on the rock of that confession. Then, during the early years of Roman persecution, believers worshiped in rock catacombs underlaying the capital of the empire. During the middle ages, believers expressed their faith in Christ by constructing huge rock cathedrals, situated in the very center of their cities and villages. Rock is a fitting symbol for our Christian faith, because it suggests permanence and strength. Yet stone and mortar do not a congregation make. The hymn "Built On A Rock" says it best: "We are God's house of living stones made for his own habitation...."

* * * * *

In the neighborhood next to me, million dollar houses are being constructed. One edifice particularly caught my eye; I'd have to be blind for it not to. The place is enormous, with an eight-car garage. Giving it an unmistakable aura of permanence and strength are four gigantic pillars made of cement. They may or may not be weight-bearing pillars. Dating back before the glory of Greece, pillars were used to support the weight of the building. That's why Paul uses it as a term to describe those members of the Christian community that lend the church strength and support (Galatians 2:9). They are load-carrying Christians, without which the church would be in danger of crumbling. A pastor once said, "The church contains two kinds of people: pillars and caterpillars. Pillars support and caterpillars merely come in and go out."

Proper 17/Pentecost 15/Ordinary Time 22

Revised Common:	Exodus 3:1-15	Romans 12:9-21	Matthew 16:21-28
Roman Catholic:	Jeremiah 20:7-9	Romans 12:1-2	Matthew 16:21-27
Episcopal:	Jeremiah 15:15-21	Romans 12:1-8	Matthew 16:21-27

Theme: Suffering for righteousness' sake. Both Jeremiah and Peter rebelled against the idea of suffering for the sake of the kingdom of God; both of them had to be reprimanded by God and brought back into a state of obedience.

BRIEF COMMENTARY ON THE LESSONS

Lesson 1: Exodus 3:1-15 (C)

Moses observes the mysterious burning bush on Mount Horeb and draws closer for an examination. An angelic presence is seen in the fire and then the voice of God calls out to Moses. The voice identifies himself as the God of Abraham, Isaac, and Jacob, telling him that he has heard the cries of oppression coming from the Hebrew slaves in Egypt and has determined to bring them into their promised land. God chooses Moses for the task, who straightaway makes excuses. God assures Moses of his presence and aid in accomplishing this Herculean task.

Lesson 1: Jeremiah 20:7-9 (RC)

The prophet laments the unpleasant task of preaching judgment to those who will not repent of their ways and return to the Lord. He covenants with himself to quit speaking the Lord's word, but its burning within him is impossible to contain.

Lesson 1: Jeremiah 15:15-21 (E)

Jeremiah laments the unhappy consequences of his having to proclaim the word of the Lord; it has caused pain, derision, and loneliness. He accuses the Lord of being deceitful with him. The Lord retorts rather firmly that he should repent of his feeling sorry for himself and utter what is precious, not what is worthless. God promises to deliver him.

Lesson 2: Romans 12:9-21 (C)

Paul gives a survey of the behavioral characteristics exhibited by the person who has consecrated his or her life to God. Such a life will be marked by the fruits of the Spirit, like love, joy, peace, and enthusiasm. The believer will also refrain from judging others and seeking revenge, leaving that sphere to the Lord.

Lesson 2: Romans 12:1-2 (RC); Romans 12:1-8 (E)

In response to the justification which God has effected, Paul urges believers to present their lives as a living sacrifice to God. According to Pauline theology, the life of faith has definite ethical consequences. Christians are not to conform to the pattern of this present world but are to be transformed by God. They are not to think too highly of themselves but exercise their gifts in the community of faith for the building up of the body of Christ. For the Christian, worship is not just a liturgical act; it is a way of living a consecrated life.

Gospel: Matthew 16:21-28 (C); Matthew 16:21-27 (RC, E)

Christ attempts to prepare his disciples for his passion and death by warning that he is going to be betrayed, handed over by the religious officials, crucified, and then raised. Peter stoutly opposes Jesus' plan since it did not fit in with the traditional messianic expectations. Jesus strongly puts Peter in his place by saying: "Get behind me, Satan!" In opposing Jesus' plan, Peter is siding with Satan, the adversary, and is making it more difficult for the Lord to fulfill his mission. It is interesting to see that Peter, the first to confess Jesus as the Messiah, cannot understand the implications of his profession. Jesus then announces that if anyone would be his disciple, he must be willing to take up his cross and follow him. In other words, the follower of Jesus must be willing to suffer and die, if need be, for the sake of the kingdom. True life comes only to the person willing to give to the Lord.

Psalm Of The Day

Psalm 105:1-6, 23-26, 45 (C) — "Seek the Lord and his strength ..." (v. 4).

Psalm 63:2-6, 8-9 (RC) — "So I will bless you as long as I live" (v. 4a).

Psalm 26 (E) — "O Lord, I love the house in which you dwell" (v. 8a).

Prayer Of The Day

O Lord, keep us faithful to our calling to be your witnesses in a world that is often times hostile to the gospel. When we suffer reproach and scorn, enable us to bear it patiently, knowing that we cannot inherit the crown without bearing the cross. In Jesus' name. Amen.

THEOLOGICAL REFLECTION ON THE LESSONS

Lesson 1: Exodus 3:1-15

Non-consuming fire. Moses turned aside to behold the wonder of a bush that burned but was not consumed. God is often represented as a fire, light, or energy source. God, in his judgment, can destroy the unrepentant, but he aims not to destroy but to purify. Jeremiah found that the Spirit of God only consumed him when he tried to hold it in. (Refer to the Roman Catholic first lesson.)

Turn aside, come closer. God entered the burning bush so as to get the attention of Moses. When he approached the bush, the voice of God bid him come closer. God cannot call us or use us until he gets our attention. Like Moses, however, we are attracted and repelled by the holy presence of God. We realize our insignificance and our sinfulness. We want to observe in awe from a distance. At such a time, God graciously bids us to come closer that we might know and do his will.

Lesson 1: Jeremiah 20:7-9

Smolder or burn. Jeremiah tried to contain the word of the Lord within himself but could not. It was too hot to put a lid on. You might say that when the prophet held in God's message, he was smoldering, giving off more smoke than light or heat. But a fire will not smolder forever; it will either go out or burst into flame. Jeremiah just had to let it burn. He was the Lord's burning bush, a sign of God's holy presence.

Lesson 1: Jeremiah 15:15-21

Chafing under the cross. The cross was not used as an instrument of execution in Israel during Jeremiah's day. Nevertheless, Jeremiah had to bear a type of cross; he had to suffer for God's sake. Jeremiah didn't bear up very well under the duress of his cross bearing. He demanded that God bring down destruction upon the heads of his tormentors and even accused God of tricking him. How different from Christ, who bore his cross quietly and willingly.

When we turn back, God will take us back. God communicated to Jeremiah that his attitude was contrary to God's will and that he must repent (v. 19). The Lord said that if he turned back, God would take him back. Who of us has not railed against God, life, or fate? Like the prodigal son, the Lord stands ready to take us back when we repent.

Lesson 2: Romans 12:1-8, 9-21

Non-consuming sacrifice. In the burning bush and the prophet Jeremiah we see two examples of God's non-consuming fire. In this lesson, Paul urges us, in gratitude to God for his salvation, to offer our lives as a non-consuming sacrifice. In the Jewish temple ritual, the sacrificial victim was consumed either by fire or by eating. Here, the believer is to offer himself or herself to God as a living sacrifice. Only the dross will be consumed; what is essential and good will remain, fit to be employed in the daily service of God.

Give to others what they do not deserve. Evildoers treat people in ways they do not deserve. No one deserves to be shot or raped, for instance. Paul takes the lead from Jesus in preaching that we should give others the love and goodness they do not deserve. "Bless those who persecute you ..." (v. 14). Do not repay anyone evil for evil ... (v. 17). "If your enemies are hungry, feed them; if they are thirsty, give them something to drink" (v. 20).

Burning coals on their head. Paul maintains that if we return good for evil we will pour burning coals on the heads of our enemies. What kind of coals does he mean? Guilt, shame, remorse? According to the wisdom of the age, that's a horrible load to dump on someone else. Such coals of white hot love can purify our soul and turn us back to the Lord.

Gospel: Matthew 16:21-28

The messianic secret. After Peter's great confession, featured in last week's gospel, Jesus charged the disciples not to tell anyone that he was the Messiah. This is known as the messianic secret. Why didn't he want this information out of the bag? Because they didn't understand the implication of that accolade. They were still thinking in the categories of glory and power, rather than suffering servanthood. In this week's gospel, the secret unfolds. Jesus is going to be betrayed, maltreated, and crucified, but he would rise again. Peter's astonished reaction to Jesus' pronouncement shows where the disciples were coming from.

Undercover. When Peter sternly rebutted Jesus' announcement of his coming passion, Peter replied: "God forbid it, Lord!" (v. 22). Jesus then slapped him in the face with the "Get behind me, Satan" retort. Peter was unwittingly serving as the undercover agent for the Prince of Darkness. Satan rejoices to use as his undercover agents those who think they are serving the cause of God.

A scandalized Christ. Christ accuses Peter of being a stumbling block to the purposes of God. The Greek word is *skandalon*, which can mean snare trap or stumbling block. Thus, it refers to a cause of offense. How often our attitudes and behavior are a stumbling block to those outside the fold of Christ. Many times Christians are a scandal to the non-believing world. Some time ago, I was listening to an interview of an author on National Public Radio. This woman had been an agnostic, as well as a drug addict. However, she found acceptance at a little church in California and was now a believer. The interviewer made a statement that really scandalized me. He said, "You know, you are the only person I know and respect who goes to church." I thought, is he saying something about himself or the state of the Christian church? I know plenty of churchgoers whom I know and respect. Perhaps he has kept such folks at arm's length, so that he can judge them from a distance. Maybe he didn't respect any churchgoers because his value system was different from theirs. Yet it happens that persons such as this are scandalized by the lack of integrity they observe in Christians. I'm sure that Christ continues to be scandalized by the lack of faith, vision, and integrity he observes among Christians.

Get lost. Jesus states the greatest of contradictions. "For those who would save their life will lose it and those who lose their life for my sake will find it." We only find life when we have the courage to give it away, after the pattern of Jesus.

PREACHING APPROACHES WITH ILLUSTRATIONS

Lesson 1: Exodus 3:1-15
Sermon Title: Are You Hearing God's Call?
Sermon Angle: Before Moses could hear God's call, the Lord had to get his attention through the blazing bush. Once Moses turned aside from his flock to see what this was, God spoke to him and called him to lead his people out of slavery into the promised land. In what ways has God tried to get our attention as we pursue our daily activities? Through sickness, burnout, or desperation? Through a co-worker, a spouse, or a friend? The holy God blazes into our consciousness through special or even ordinary events and people, calling us to obedience.

Sermon Title: God, Apathetic Or Empathetic?
Sermon Angle: The Stoics taught that God was apathetic; that he could feel no pain nor sorrow. They reasoned that if God could be touched by human sorrow, then humans could influence God and, thereby, have power over him. Our text says that God knows the sorrows of his people and has heard their cries of oppression. He sends Moses to free them from their taskmasters. Thus, from the beginning of the Old Testament to the end of the New, we see a God who is empathetic, entering into the joys, pains, and sorrows of his children.

Lesson 1: Jeremiah 15:15-21
Sermon Title: One Is The Loneliest Number
Sermon Angle: Jeremiah chafes under the burden of having to proclaim God's judgment. He complains that he is denied the company of merrymakers and must sit alone, racked by pain (v. 17). The prophet has a bad case of loneliness even though he is not really alone. Though he felt quite abandoned, God was with him.
Outline:
1. Describe the conditions that led to Jeremiah's loneliness
2. Explain that loneliness stems from alienation from God
3. Describe the symptoms of this alienation in our society
4. Explain that loneliness feeds on self-pity, such as Jeremiah showed
5. Conclusion: When we return to God, we are no longer just one, the loneliest number — we are one with God

Lesson 2: Romans 12:1-8

Sermon Title: Presentable Bodies

Sermon Angle: Americans spend millions of dollars trying to make their bodies beautiful and, if not beautiful, at least presentable. Diet foods, body building equipment, and weight loss programs abound. Some are literally obsessed with body image. Paul suggests that we present our bodies (lives) to God as a living sacrifice. That which makes our bodies presentable is not our appearance but the end toward which our bodies are dedicated. If our bodies are idols, they are not presentable, no matter how lovely, but if they are dedicated to God, they are not only presentable, but beautiful.

Outline:
1. Millions of people are dedicated toward making their bodies presentable to the world — weight loss, cosmetics, clothes, exercise, and so forth
2. Paul tells us that we should make our bodies presentable to God, not to the world or ourselves (v. 1)
3. A life dedicated to God is truly beautiful

Gospel: Matthew 16:21-28

Sermon Title: At The Cross Purpose

Sermon Angle: After Peter's confession, Jesus dedicated himself to explaining to his disciples the meaning of his messiahship. He told them that he was going to Jerusalem where he would suffer and die before being raised to newness of life. Jesus' purpose of offering himself on the cross was contrary to the disciples' notion of the Messiah. The ultimate purpose for Jesus was the cross, which put him at cross purposes with those closest to him.

Outline:
1. Jesus lived on purpose — to give his life completely to God
2. God's purpose led Jesus to the cross
3. This put him at cross purposes with his disciples (v. 22)
4. Are we dedicated to the cross of Christ or are we at cross purposes with him?

*   *   *   *   *

The movie, *Forrest Gump*, starring Tom Hanks, is a study on the topic of purpose and destiny. Forrest Gump, the main character in the movie, was born mentally deficient. Yet most everything in his life seemed to fall into place. As a boy, he had to wear braces on his legs, but when he was chased one day by his tormentors, the braces suddenly fell free and he could run like a deer. His fleetness of foot made him a star football player in college. He went to Vietnam and became a hero for saving the lives of several wounded men. One of these men was his superior officer, who felt it was his destiny to die with his men in battle. He was angry with Gump for robbing him of his destiny. In Vietnam, Gump also became a champion table tennis player. In endorsing equipment from that sport, he made a lot of money. He bought a fishing boat and got rich when his boat was the only one to survive the hurricane. When his lifelong sweetheart left him again, he started running across the country and back again. He ran for three years. People started running behind him, thinking that he knew something they didn't: that he had some purpose in mind. But he didn't have any purpose in mind. The movie started and ended with a feather being blown about. It was symbolic of his life. Was it driven merely by the whims of the wind or was there a guiding purpose directing its course? Those who belong to Christ know that they are guided by a destiny that is tied up with the purpose of the cross.

Sermon Title: Whose Side Are You On?

Sermon Angle: In our Lord's stinging rebuke of Peter, he told him that he was not on the side of God but of the adversary, Satan. None of us intend to serve Satan, but if our lives are dedicated to avoiding pain and maximizing pleasure, we are really on his side. A good look at the way we live will reveal whose side we are on.

Sermon Title: A Scandalous Faith

Sermon Angle: The word in verse 23 that is translated *hindrance* is the Greek word *skandalon*, from which we get the English word scandal. The cross was a scandal to the disciples and Peter's rejection of the cross was a scandal to Christ. In the past decade or so, the church has been rocked with one scandal after another concerning the deportment of pastors, leaders, and church officials. It's right that the world should be scandalized, but by the cross and not by our immorality.

Outline:
1. Explain the meaning of the word *skandalon*
2. The cross is a scandal to the world as it was to Peter
3. Our reluctance to embrace the cross is a scandal to Christ
4. Let us abandon the scandal of unchristian conduct and embrace the scandal of the cross

Proper 18/Pentecost 16/Ordinary Time 23

Revised Common:	**Exodus 12:1-14**	**Romans 13:8-14**	**Matthew 18:15-20**
Roman Catholic:	**Ezekiel 33:7-9**	**Romans 13:8-10**	**Matthew 18:15-20**
Episcopal:	**Ezekiel 33:(1-6) 7-11**	**Romans 12:9-21**	**Matthew 18:15-20**

Theme: A word of warning. The Ezekiel 33 text is a word of admonition by God to Ezekiel that he must warn the people of their sins or else he will be held accountable. The gospel lesson contains the procedure for dealing with sin in the church. A three-step procedure is outlined for warning the wrongdoer and bringing him back in communion with the church. In the second lesson, Paul warns Christians to obey the government officials because they are agents of God.

BRIEF COMMENTARY ON THE LESSONS

Lesson 1: Exodus 12:1-14 (C)

The Hebrews are instructed by God to make ready for the Passover. They are to assemble in household groupings, slaughter an unblemished lamb, roast and eat it, applying the blood of the lamb on the lintel and doorposts of their houses. God promises to pass over the houses marked with the blood and effect judgment on the houses of the Egyptian people, who are holding them captive. The Hebrews are to keep this feast as a remembrance of the Lord's great act of deliverance.

Lesson 1: Ezekiel 33:7-9 (RC); Ezekiel 33:(1-6) 7-11 (E)

God reminds Ezekiel that he is his watchman, whose charge is to warn the evildoers to repent. If he warns them and they refuse to change their ways, their sins remain, but the prophet is not held accountable. If he fails to warn the people and they continue in their sin, their sin will be on their own heads, and the prophet of God will also be held accountable.

Lesson 2: Romans 13:8-14 (C); Romans 13:8-10 (RC)

Paul instructs the church to obey the governmental officials, as agents of the Lord. Those who live righteously have no reason to fear state officials, but this is not true of lawbreakers, because the state holds the right to punish wrongdoing. Believers are to pay taxes and whatever else they owe their government. On the other hand, Christians are to owe nobody anything except to love one another. Love fulfills the law. This passage reflects a generally favorable view of the Roman government and must have been penned during a time of tranquility.

Lesson 2: Romans 12:9-21 (E)

See the first lesson for Proper 17 (C).

Gospel: Matthew 18:15-20 (C, RC, E)

Most scholars do not believe that this passage, as it stands, is directly from the lips of Jesus. It seems to reflect a later period, after the church had been well organized. During Jesus' lifetime, there was no church. Furthermore, some of the instruction does not reflect the spirit of Jesus. The admonition, "let him be to you as a Gentile or tax collector," doesn't square with the Lord's loving approach to such outcasts. Yet the instruction for dealing with sin among the faithful is certainly based on Jesus' teachings. (For further discussion of this three-step formula, see Theological Reflection On The Lessons.) This lection concludes by asserting the power of communal prayer and worship. Christ is present where two or three gather in his name.

Psalm Of The Day

Psalm 149 (C) — "Sing to the Lord a new song" (v. 1).
Psalm 95:1-2, 6-9 (RC) — "O come, let us worship and bow down" (v. 6).
Psalm 119:33-40 (E) — "Turn my heart to your decrees" (v. 36).

Prayer Of The Day

O God of mercy, you do not want your children to die in their sins but to turn to you and live. Help us to heed the warnings of your prophets and teachers and find renewed joy in your service and in the worship of your holy name. Amen.

THEOLOGICAL REFLECTION ON THE LESSONS

Lesson 1: Exodus 12:1-14

A new calendar. In verse 2 it states that this month (the month in which the Passover occurred) was the beginning of a new year for the Jewish people. Nisan occurred during March/April, replacing the old calendar, when the new year began in autumn. Not only was God's great act of deliverance a *kairos* moment, it marked a new starting point for measuring chronological time for the Hebrew people. Much the same thing happened when Jesus Christ became our Passover Lamb. His sacrifice marked a new beginning point for humankind, a fresh way of measuring time.

Serving pilgrim style. The Hebrews were to eat the Passover in preparedness, with their cloaks and sandals in place (v. 11). They were to be ready to move out when God gave the signal. They ate the Passover pilgrim style. Some churches serve the sacrament pilgrim style, though some call it continuous communion. At churches that I have served, quite a number of people don't like the pilgrim style. They prefer to pause before the altar and ponder. There is nothing wrong with that, unless it serves to make us forget that we are a pilgrim people who must always stand ready to follow the Lord.

Lesson 1: Ezekiel 33:(1-6) 7-11

A watchman. God told Ezekiel that he had made of him a watchman. The watchman was one who stood in the towers, perched on the walls of the fortified cities. His duty was to watch for enemies and warn of danger. What if the watchman would fall asleep? The enemy might breach the fortifications and enter the city to lay waste to it. Even worse than that, what if the watchman saw the enemy coming and remained mute? Maybe he didn't think that any enemy could pierce the fortifications of the city and lay siege to it. Perhaps he just didn't care what happened to the city, being so disillusioned that he desired the demise of his city.

In a sense, we are all watchmen for both church and society. This passage warns us that if we are negligent in issuing warning to those for whom we are responsible, we will be held responsible for lives that are destroyed.

Lesson 2: Romans 13:8-14

The locus of authority. Paul maintains that Christians should obey government authorities because they are instituted by God. God is the ultimate locus of authority, and he has delegated his authority to governing officials. This seems to be a rather utopian view of government, especially in light of the grave abuses of government authority we have witnessed in this century. Paul saw the Roman government as a protector of the budding Christian community; he himself was a Roman citizen. If we are to sustain the belief in a God active in the world, we must maintain that all governments derive their rightful authority from God. Yet, we cannot claim that all governments are an expression of God's will. Christians have a duty to obey their government only if it is founded on God's laws. Peter said it well: "We must obey God rather than man."

Pay what you owe. The apostle instructs that Christians must pay the government what is owed — respect, honor, and taxes. Furthermore, Christians are not to be indebted to any person. There is only one debt we cannot pay: the debt of love. Since love does no wrong to a neighbor, love is the fulfilling of the law.

Gospel: Matthew 18:15-20

Dealing with disputes. The gospel of Matthew was written at a time when the young church was having to deal with conflicts. Members were stepping on one another's toes, saying and doing hurtful things to one another. If conflicts aren't properly dealt with, they can splinter the church. Let us look at the conflict resolution process, which is grounded in the wisdom of Jesus.

First, nip the problem in the bud before it escalates. If someone offends you, go to him privately and share your feelings. The human tendency is to let problems fester rather than deal with them at the source. Going directly to the person gives opportunity to clear up any misunderstandings and enables the two parties to understand the perspectives of the other. Also, once a dispute goes public, it can get out of control, and the person accused of wrongdoing is embarrassed in front of others.

Second, if the private meeting doesn't work, bring a witness or two. These should be people noted for their wisdom and fairness. They can help the two adversaries see the problem from a third perspective. This is similar to the role of an intermediary or counselor.

If this step is ineffective, then we have no recourse but to bring it to the attention of the congregation. This does not mean that the offense should be aired at a congregational assembly. A deliberating body would do. This is based on the premise that the Holy Spirit offers guidance and effects healing when the whole people of God seek his will.

If the whole church cannot bring about repentance or forgiveness, verse 17 states that the offender should be to them as a Gentile or tax collector. This verse is troubling. It seems to suggest that we should give up on people or exclude them. This does not reflect Jesus' attitude toward sinners. He was accused by his enemies of associating with such people rather than the good people. Thus, this is not an injunction to leave sinners to roast in their juices but to regard them as Jesus regards them. Jesus never tired in reaching out to the outcasts and the lawbreakers; he never gave up on any person. The church must do the same.

Strength beyond numbers. We live in the day of the mega-church. Bigger is considered better. Small to medium sized churches are having trouble surviving. Jesus reminds us that our strength does not rest in numbers but in his presence (vv. 19-20).

PREACHING APPROACHES WITH ILLUSTRATIONS

Lesson 1: Exodus 12:1-14

Sermon Title: Fast Food

Sermon Angle: In the mad dash of our Western world, we often tend to grab food at a fast food restaurant and eat on the run. We are not the first to do this. The Hebrews were instructed to hurriedly eat the first Passover fully clothed and ready to depart (v. 11). The meal was a sign of the old life of slavery they were about to leave behind and the new life to which the Lord was leading. They were to be prepared to follow at a moment's notice. The Lord's Supper is also fast food; it is not designed to fill us forever but to strengthen us in our spiritual journey as the Lord's pilgrim people.

Outline:
1. Discuss the popularity of fast food
2. Why do we crave fast food? Are we frantically searching for meaning?
3. Passover was fast food for the redeemed of God — strength for the journey
4. Holy communion is fast food for our Christian journey

Lesson 1: Ezekiel 33:(1-6) 7-11

Sermon Title: Blood On Our Hands?

Sermon Angle: God informs Ezekiel that the watchman who does not warn the citizens of impending danger will have the victim's blood on his hands (v. 8). From time immemorial, humans have tended to deny responsibility for the harm they have either caused or allowed to happen to their neighbor. Cain denied his responsibility for his brother Abel, whose blood cried out for justice. Through the ages, God reminds his people that they are indeed their brother's and their sister's keeper.

Lesson 2: Romans 13:8-14

Sermon Title: The Patri In Patriotism

Sermon Angle: This passage from the pen of Paul has been used for centuries as a justification for governments and the established order. It provides good rhetoric for patriotic fervor. The root word for patriotism is *patri*, Latin for father. Patriotism might be defined as love and devotion for the Fatherland. According to biblical thought, our Father is God. If the Father is not reverenced in the Fatherland, that government has no legitimate authority.

Outline:
1. How does God rule?
   — through the gospel and the church
   — through governments and earthly authority (our text)
2. Paul's teachings tend to promote patriotism
   — this can be a source of strength or evil
   — we must not dilute the Patri in patriotism
   — no government has authority apart from God
   — if government opposes the rule of God, we must obey God

Sermon Title: Debt Free

Sermon Angle: Paul says to owe no one anything except to love one another (v. 8). A week doesn't go by that I don't receive one or two applications for another credit card. There is intense pressure to spend beyond our means and to immediately gratify our desires. Our economy is hamstrung by a monstrous debt that threatens to bring us to our knees. The gospel presents another way to live, free of debt. Christ has canceled the debt of our sins so that we might be free to live in love.

Gospel: Matthew 18:15-20

Sermon Title: Dealing With Difficult People

Sermon Angle: This passage is designed as a procedure for dealing with conflict and sin in the church. A couple of the principles presented can be applied to any relationship, however. Principle #1: Deal immediately with the offense and the offender. Go to her and talk it out. Letting the conflict ride only makes matters worse. Principle #2: If you can't work it out among yourselves, get help. A third party often enables us to see the real issues.

Sermon Title: Eternal Consequences

Sermon Angle: Matthew reiterates the power of the keys; the declaration of forgiveness for the penitent and the absence of forgiveness for the unrepentant. "Whatever you bind on earth shall be bound in heaven ..." (v. 18). This is not a whip to make the recalcitrant obey. Rather, it is a reminder that our actions have eternal consequences. Many of the things we do have the permanence of chalk, but when we extend or retract the hand of forgiveness and love, we may well have etched something into eternity with indelible ink. The church is about the task of erecting the eternal city of God.

Outline:
1. Christ reminds us that the decisions we make for or against the kingdom can have eternal consequences (v. 18)
2. This is both an encouragement and a warning
3. Let us build on the foundation of God's grace and love

Sermon Title: Prayer Is We, Not Me

Sermon Angle: Jesus promises that if two believers agree in prayer about anything, it will be granted. Not necessarily that the thing prayed for will be given but that God will answer the prayer. Prayer that is me-directed is not Christian prayer. We must pray always as a part of the community, the we. This is a counteractive to selfish prayers, which do not have the best interest of others at mind. The Holy Spirit guides us through the Christian community as to how we should pray.

Sermon Title: In His Name

Sermon Angle: In verses 19-20, Jesus twice uses the qualifying phrase, "in my name." In verse 19, he states that if only two of his disciples ask anything in his name, they will receive it. In verse 20, he instructs that if two or three are gathered in his name, he is in their midst. The significance goes beyond the familiar "in the name of the Father, and of the Son, and of the Holy Spirit." To pray in Jesus' name means to pray for that which Jesus would pray. To gather in his name signifies that all that this fellowship says and does derives from the awareness that Jesus is present in the gathered Christian community.

Outline:
1. We are baptized into the church in the name of the Holy Trinity
2. Our worship and prayers are in Christ's name
   — that means that we seek his will, not our own
   — are our worship and prayers truly in his name?

* * * * *

Some pastors have substituted authoritarianism for authority. I have used the first term to denote power that is taken coercively from the people, while the latter is used to describe the power which the people give their leaders. A pastor whom I respect revealed to me the greatest compliment of his pastoral career. A person, who at first was not supportive of a building proposal backed by the pastor, came up to him after the meeting in which the proposal was approved and told him: "Pastor, I want to thank you for giving us our church back." That pastor had wisely empowered the people to make the decisions affecting the congregation's life and future.

* * * * *

Methodist Bishop Gerald Kennedy outlined the basis of authority in an address to the clergy of the Southern California and Arizona Conference some years ago. His first point was that authority cannot be taken by force. Revolutionaries can seize power but they cannot command authority by force. Secondly, authority cannot be given. A company can give its president all the trappings of power and authority — a fancy office, limousine, and so forth — but this does not bestow authority on him. Thirdly, authority springs from character and integrity. Because of dishonest dealings, citizens withhold authority from elected officials. The most important source of authority is saved for last. Quite simply, God is the locus of all authority, being the author of all things.

Proper 19/Pentecost 17/Ordinary Time 24

Revised Common:	Exodus 14:19-31	Romans 14:1-12	Matthew 18:21-35
Roman Catholic:	Sirach 27:30—28:7	Romans 14:7-9	Matthew 18:21-35
Episcopal:	Sirach 27:30—28:7	Romans 14:5-12	Matthew 18:21-35

Theme: Forgiveness. Jesus teaches that as God has forgiven us, so we must forgive those who sin against us.

BRIEF COMMENTARY ON THE LESSONS

Lesson 1: Exodus 14:19-31 (C)

The presence of the Lord in the pillar of fire, that normally went ahead of the people to lead them, moved to the rear of the community as an obscuring cloud, a kind of buffer between them and the army of the Pharaoh. The Lord caused a strong wind to dry up a pathway through the sea so that the Hebrews passed to the other side. The pursuing Egyptians became mired in the mud and the waters closed in upon them. Thus, the Lord delivered his people from their enemies.

Lesson 1: Sirach 27:30—28:7 (RC, E)

A warning against harboring wrath. A person must forgive others the wrong that they have done if she expects to have her own sins pardoned.

Lesson 2: Romans 14:1-12 (C); Romans 14:7-9 (RC); Romans 14:5-12 (E)

A warning against senseless disputes and judging one's neighbor. Divisions were forming in the church about fasting and other such matters. A believer must show tolerance and respect for fellow believers who hold different views. Each person must answer to God, and God alone, for the conduct of her life. Our lives are not our own; whether we live or die, we are the Lord's.

Gospel: Matthew 18:21-35 (C, RC, E)

Once again, Peter is the spokesman for the disciples, asking if a person should forgive another as many as seven times. Jesus replies: "Not seven, but seventy times seven." There is no limit, no equation when it comes to forgiveness. This becomes a springboard for the parable of the unforgiving servant. A servant asked his lord to forgive him his astronomical debt of 10,000 talents (the talent was equivalent to wages for fifteen years) and was granted his petition. Shortly thereafter, this same servant saw a man who owed him about 100 denarii (the denarius was one day's wage). He seized him by the throat and demanded payment. The debtor begged for time to pay his debt but this heartless man refused. Fellow servants observed this and reported to their master. The master called in the unforgiving servant and, after chastising him, threw him into debtor's prison. The point? We cannot receive God's forgiveness until we share this forgiveness with others.

Psalm Of The Day

Psalm 114 (C) — "Why is it, O sea, that you flee?" (v. 5).

Psalm 103:1-13 (RC, E) — "The Lord is merciful and gracious, slow to anger and abounding in steadfast love" (v. 8).

Prayer Of The Day

God of mercy, when we contemplate the scope of your forgiving grace, our hearts overflow in thanksgiving. To show our gratitude, help us to share with others what we have so freely and undeservedly received from you. In the name of Jesus. Amen.

THEOLOGICAL REFLECTION ON THE LESSONS

Lesson 1: Exodus 14:19-31

Protecting the rear flank. The angel of the Lord led the Israelites by being a pillar of fire in front of them and, as they approached the Red Sea, the angel of God retreated to the rear flank to provide protection from the Egyptian army approaching from the rear. When we have no place to flee from danger, the Lord is there to shield us from danger and deliver us from our enemies that are close behind.

Lesson 2: Romans 14:1-12

Passing judgment. Paul warns against passing judgment on another person, since that is God's province (v. 4). Rather we should pass up giving judgment on those who are different than we. Each person is entitled to his opinion.

Motion sustained. A person of integrity, whose actions flow from a sincere love of the Lord, will be sustained at the judgment seat of Christ, even if he makes mistakes. God will make him stand by his grace (v. 4b).

Connections. On The Learning Channel, there were two programs called *Connections* and *Connection 2*, which endeavored to show how various thoughts, inventions, and technologies lead from one thing to another. Nothing happens in a vacuum. Our lives are not unconnected atoms. We are a part of a community of love and grace. "None of us lives to himself and none of us dies to himself" (v. 7).

Unbroken connection. Paul states something great and wonderful. "Whether we live, we live to the Lord, and if we die, we die to the Lord; so then, whether we live or whether we die, we are the Lord's" (v. 8). Our connection with the Lord can be broken by no outside force, only by ourselves. Nothing in this world can disconnect us from the love of God. What a promise!

Cross connection. In verse 9, Paul states that it is through the death and resurrection of Christ that we have this eternal connection as God's dear child. Because of sin, we are slaves, but by his grace we are brought back into the fold of faith. This connection does not come through creation but through Christ.

Gospel: Matthew 18:21-35

Love without limits. Peter's attempt to try to quantify or limit forgiveness showed that he hadn't yet comprehended the true nature of God's grace and forgiveness. God's forgiveness is not predicated on the quantity of our sins, as humans so often assume. We think: Well, I'm not as bad a sinner as that scoundrel, surely God will recognize my comparative goodness. The bean counting mindset shows that we are still living under law, not grace. Love is without limits.

Mercy me. The debtor of Jesus' parable begged for mercy as he and his family were about to be thrown into debtor's prison. He ought to be the object of mercy, but when he came upon his fellow debtor who owed him a little money, he was unwilling to be the subject of mercy. If I ask God to mercy me, I must also be willing to mercy thee.

Getting more than we bargained for. The servant did not request that his debt be canceled but that his master would be patient and give him more time to pay it back. He got far more than he asked for: the cancellation of the entire debt. God gives us far more than we deserve; he gives us forgiveness.

There's no comparison. The unforgiving servant was forgiven an astronomical sum. If a talent equaled the wages of a laborer for fifteen years, a debt of 10,000 talents equals the laborer's wages for 150,000 years, with no days off. The debt that was owed him was equal to the laborer's wage for 100 days, about 1/500,000th of the size of his own debt. The debt that others owe to us is minuscule compared to what God has forgiven us.

PREACHING APPROACHES WITH ILLUSTRATIONS

Lesson 1: Exodus 14:19-31
Sermon Title: Baptism — A Life And Death Matter

Sermon Angle: In his epistle to the Romans, Paul refers to the passage of the Israelites through the Red Sea as a type of baptism, which imparts life through death. In this baptism, there was the death of the Egyptians. For the Israelites it was also a death, the death of the old life of slavery. This death was necessary so that God could raise them to newness of life. In Christian baptism, the believer also dies to his old life of sin, so that he might be raised to newness of life in Christ.

Lesson 2: Romans 14:1-12
Sermon Title: An Affair Of The Heart

Sermon Angle: The church of Paul's day was already beset by contention stemming from disparate spiritual practices. Some held certain days to be holy; others did not. Some abstained from certain foods to honor God; others did not. The apostle does not take sides. He seems to suggest that there are many ways to serve and worship the Lord. He counsels to be convinced in your own mind (v. 5). That what you're doing is right for you, without judging the neighbor who approaches God differently. In theology he is quite focused, but in practice he is very broad. The assumption underlying Paul's advice is that our relationship with Christ is not a matter of externals; it is an affair of the heart.

Outline:
1. The church is often preoccupied with externals
   — in Paul's day, they were issues like fasting and holy days
   — in our day, there are things like decor and so forth
2. Christianity is not a matter of externals but an affair of the heart (Everything we do should express our love for God and one another)

Sermon Title: Passing Judgment

Sermon Angle: This text is centered on passing judgment. Paul asks the question: "Why do you pass judgment on your brother or sister?" This sermon could address that question coupled with a warning of dangers of passing judgment on others. If we are to pass God's judgment, we must refrain from passing judgment on others.

Outline:
1. Why do we judge others?
   — it makes us feel superior
   — it keeps us from facing our own sins
2. Why should we not pass judgment on others?
   — we are not God and don't see the big picture
   — we cannot see inside another person's heart
   — God has forgiven us, we must forgive others
   — we are individually accountable to God (vv. 11-12)

Sermon Title: Endless Love

Sermon Angle: Paul holds up a great truth when he says that whether we live or die, we are the Lord's (vv. 7-8). God's love for us is endless; he will never let go of those whom he claims as his own. That longing for everlasting love is frequently expressed in love ballads, but can only be realized in Christ (v. 9).

Outline:
1. We all have a need to belong and to be loved
   — without loving relationships, life unravels
2. The Bible says that we belong to God
   — Christ claims us as his own through his death and resurrection (v. 9).
3. Death cannot separate us from God's love
4. We must live for the Lord

Gospel: Matthew 18:21-35

Sermon Title: Three Strikes And You're Not Out

Sermon Angle: In baseball, it's three strikes and you're out. In former president Clinton's crime bill, there was a "three strikes and you're out" provision for habitual serious offenders. Supposedly, they were out of circulation for life. That was the same notion in Old Testament times; you give a person three chances but not four. Peter is being generous when he asks Jesus if seven times is the limit of forgiveness. Jesus' response indicates that there is no limit to divine forgiveness. If a brother or sister seeks forgiveness, we are obligated to grant it.

Outline:
1. We confuse the realms of law and grace
   — the world lives by law (three strikes and you're out)
   — God relates to us also through grace (the 70 x 7 principle)
2. In personal relationships, Christian forgiveness knows no limits
3. As we have been forgiven an infinite debt, so must we forgive without limit
4. The church must model the realm of grace for the world

Sermon Title: Love Does Not Keep Track

Sermon Angle: Jesus' "70 x 7" response to Peter's question about forgiveness makes clear that God's love and forgiveness is infinite. Keeping track of offenses is the province of the law, but in God's realm of love and grace, there is no keeping track, no accounting, for those who by faith accept his grace.

Outline:
1. In the world, people calculate, measure, and record wrongdoing
2. Since we have been accepted and forgiven, we do not keep track of wrongs
3. God's love is not an equation but a relationship

* * * * *

A man had more than a little bit too much to drink at an office Christmas party, where his wife was also present. He made a complete fool of himself and embarrassed his wife to tears. The next day, he was not only extremely hung over but deeply remorseful. He apologized profusely to his wife, asking her to forgive him and forget that it ever happened. She did promise that the whole matter would be forgiven and forgotten. However, several times in the next few months, she referred to his hour of shame. Finally, he could take it no longer. "I thought you promised to forgive and forget!" he charged. She replied: "I have forgiven and forgotten, but I just don't want you to forget that I have forgiven and forgotten."

* * * * *

Dr. Norman Vincent Peale related this story years ago in *Guideposts* magazine. It was about a well-loved shopkeeper in the Bronx of New York by the name of Milton Cohan. One night the gentle man was killed by hoodlums who made off with $6.50. His son found the body and became obsessed with the notion of finding and killing his father's murderers. He got appointed to the New York Police Department and night after night he roamed the streets of the Bronx, driven by a blinding hatred. His wife wept as she saw the light of life extinguished in the man she loved.

One night he caught one of the men he had vowed to kill. He pointed the gun at the man's head but his finger was paralyzed. He could hear the gentle voice of his father speaking in his heart. With his baton, he knocked the knife from the man's hand, cuffed him, and brought him into the station for booking. Afterward, he went home to his wife.

"I had that guy," he recounted to her, "but I couldn't shoot." Then he paused before speaking again, "Father's hand was on the gun, and you know, honey, I feel free and happy again."

"You are now worthy to be your father's son," she said haltingly. "You have been set free."

* * * * *

Clara Barton, the founder of the Red Cross, was reminded one day by a friend of an especially cruel remark that someone made to her years before. When Clara didn't seem to respond, the friend queried, "But don't you remember?" Barton replied: "No, I distinctly remember forgetting it."

Proper 20/Pentecost 18/Ordinary Time 25

Revised Common:	Exodus 16:2-15	Philippians 1:21-30	Matthew 20:1-16
Roman Catholic:	Isaiah 55:6-9	Philippians 1:20-24, 27	Matthew 20:1-16
Episcopal:	Jonah 3:10—4:11	Philippians 1:21-27	Matthew 20:1-16

Theme: The grace of God. Isaiah 55 calls on the people to turn to God for mercy and forgiveness. The second lesson has Paul commending the Philippians to the grace of God from his prison cell. The gospel parable of the laborers in the vineyard teaches us that God rewards us not according to our deserving but according to his generosity.

BRIEF COMMENTARY ON THE LESSONS

Lesson 1: Exodus 16:2-15 (C)

In the hardships of the wilderness, the people complain to Moses. They protest about the lack of food, as they remember the plentiful and well-seasoned fare they enjoyed in Egypt. The Lord hears their murmuring and sends quails in the evening and manna in the morning. Most likely, the manna was a fine, honeydew like excretion of insects that feed on twigs of the tamarisk tree. The term "manna" is interpreted by the question: "What is it?"

Lesson 1: Isaiah 55:6-9 (RC)

As the prophet anticipates the coming restoration of the nation, he issues a call for the people of God to repent and put their trust in God's grace and mercy. They should not presume on God's goodness through further delay. The door of opportunity was now wide open and they are invited to enter. "Seek the Lord while he may be found...."

Lesson 1: Jonah 3:10—4:11 (E)

Jonah is angry when the Ninevites repent and God withholds destruction. He parks himself under a broom tree to see what would become of the city. When the tree is wilted by a hot wind, God uses this as a parable of forgiveness and mercy. Jonah mourned the loss of a tree he did not grow; should God have pity on this great city?

Lesson 2: Philippians 1:21-30 (C); Philippians 1:20-24, 27 (RC); Philippians 1:21-27 (E)

This is the first of four lessons based on Philippians, which provides the preacher with an opportunity to preach a series on one complete book of the Bible. Paul writes from prison in Ephesus. He is extremely fond of this church and begins his letter by expressing his appreciation for their partnership in the gospel. His life hangs in the balance. He doesn't know if he is going to be executed or set free. He is torn between wanting to die and be with the Lord and wanting to live so that he might continue to minister to the churches. He concludes that discussion by asserting that he is confident that he will live and come to them again. In the meantime, they were to lead lives worthy of the gospel, united in faith and spirit.

Gospel: Matthew 20:1-16 (C, RC, E)

This passage is commonly referred to as the parable of the laborers in the vineyard. In this parable, Jesus makes a strong statement about the grace and mercy of God. Workers are hired as day laborers at the crack of dawn and at various intervals throughout the day, the last laborers being hired an hour before quitting time. When those who were hired last are paid the denarius, the customary daily wage for a laborer, those hired at the beginning of the day think they will be paid more, since they worked longer. They grumble when they, too, are paid the same wage as those last hired. It isn't fair, they cry, that you have made these equal to us; we have toiled all day and they have worked only an hour. The owner of the vineyard asserts his right to be generous. After all, he paid them all what he said he would. In so doing, Jesus draws a radical distinction between the way this world is expected to operate and the way that God operates. In this world, we have a right to a fair wage, but the kingdom of God is an undeserved gift.

Psalm Of The Day

Psalm 105:1-6, 37-45 (C) — "O give thanks unto the Lord, for he is good" (v. 1).
Psalm 145:2-3, 8-9, 17-18 (RC, E) — "The Lord is gracious and merciful" (v. 8).

Prayer Of The Day

God of grace and glory, we thank you that you do not reward us according to our deserving, but favor us with the gift of forgiveness and mercy. Give us a new heart that we might not grumble at the extravagance of your grace but rather rejoice. We pray in the saving name of Jesus, our Lord and Savior. Amen.

THEOLOGICAL REFLECTION ON THE LESSONS

Lesson 1: Exodus 16:2-15

Give us our daily bread. Buffeted by the hardships of the wilderness experience, the Israelites waxed nostalgic about the fleshpots and the abundance of bread in Egypt. God heard their complaint and gave them the manna. They had to pick it up off the ground each morning, enough for that day (v. 4). This ties in the fourth commandment in the Lord's Prayer. Christ taught us to pray for that which we need now, not to ask for a storehouse of bread. God wants us to trust in him for our needs and not in the things of the earth that we have stored away.

Bread from heaven or of the earth? There are those who view the passing through the Red Sea and the provision of the manna as a natural phenomenon (see the Brief Commentary On The Lessons). The Bible clearly describes it as supernatural. Yet the Lord is God of both the natural and the supernatural. He designed the laws of nature and uses them to provide for his people. Viewed in this light, the store-bought bread we place on our table is also the bread from heaven. Instead of trying to demythologize the Bible, so as to make it palatable to moderns, we should be about the task of re-sacralizing the things of the earth.

Lesson 1: Isaiah 55:6-9

Window of opportunity. The prophet invites the people to "seek the Lord while he may be found, call upon him while he is near." This is not to suggest that there are times when God capriciously removes himself from our presence, but there are times in our lives when, due to circumstances, a window of opportunity is opened for us to enter into the nearer presence of God. It's not that God is any closer, but rather that we are more open to his presence. It may be an unhappy event, such as death or divorce, or a time of joy, such as a wedding or the birth of a baby. We need to take advantage of those windows of opportunity to let the Spirit enter our lives.

A time of turning. Isaiah invites the captives to "return to the Lord, that he may have mercy on them." The captives were about to be released. God had turned to his people in mercy; they were invited to also return to their God. When is it a time of turning? Anytime, but especially right now. Now is the acceptable time. This is the day of salvation. Today is all that we have. Tomorrow is only a promise.

Awesome God. Isaiah points out that God's thoughts and ways are far above and beyond our own. Though the Lord invites his people to draw near, he is still an awesome, holy God. We dare not approach the Lord with back-slapping familiarity but with reverence and respect. This sense of God's holiness is needed to produce a proper attitude of humility.

Lesson 1: Jonah 3:10—4:11

Begrudging God's goodness. Jonah was angry that his mission was successful and that the people of Nineveh repented. He wanted them to roast in the caldron of God's judgment. Jonah was resentful at God's softness toward sinners. It's obvious that he thought that they didn't deserve it, and he was right. They didn't deserve it! What he failed to see was his own sin, his disobedience of God, his unloving and judgmental attitude. His blindness to his own need of God's grace made him begrudging of God's goodness to others.

Lesson 2: Philippians 1:20-30

An exalted body. So very many people are preoccupied with their body image, some pathologically. Anorexics and bulimics look at their emaciated images and see disgustingly fat people. So, they starve themselves. Millions have bought into the myth that happiness comes when you attain the exalted body beautiful. Paul's aim was not to exalt his body but to exalt Christ in and through his body.

One life to live. Paul states that, for him, to live is Christ (v. 21). What if you were to put a piece of paper in the bulletin of a typical church and ask the people to complete this phrase: "To live is _____"? What responses would you likely get? To live is to golf? To fish? To travel? To be rich? To eat? I doubt seriously if many people would respond as Paul did: "To live is Christ." Do we merely give lip service to serving Christ while seeking happiness through self-fulfillment? The saying may seem trite, but it's true: "One life to live, will soon be past, only what's done for Christ will last."

Living and dying. The apostle expresses his unsinkable faith in a kernel fashion in verse 21, when he says: "For me, to live is Christ and to die is gain." If the average church member were honest, she might turn this around: To live is gain and to die is Christ. That is, we devote our lives to personal gain, knowing that we must one day leave these things behind. In death, we hope to gain Christ, his righteousness, his salvation, and his victory over death.

Euthanasia. "Euthanasia" means "good death." Paul speaks of death as something good, a profit. Most of us do not think of death in positive terms. We conceive of it as an end or a defeat. Only when our faith and hope in Christ is alive and well can we conceive of death as good. Because of Christ's victory, death is not a defeat; it is a victory, a good death.

Gospel: Matthew 20:1-16

Working without a contract. The workers that the farmer hired at the crack of dawn had an informal contract. They agreed to work the day for the usual daily wage, a denarius. Those hired later in the day were merely told: "You go into the vineyard and I will pay you what is right." He didn't promise any certain amount, only that he would be fair. Those hired later were working without a contract. Their employment was strictly a matter of trust. At the end of the day, those hired last were paid first. They were given the denarius. When those hired early in the morning saw this, they were very distraught. They didn't think it fair that those who worked less got the same pay as those who worked all day. When we relate to God through contract, we get what we have coming, but when we trust in God's grace, we get far more than what we deserve. God rewards those who trust him.

Receiving what doesn't belong to you. When those hired early in the day complained, the owner told them to take what belonged to them and go. "I choose to give to these last the same as I give to you." It takes a humble person to rejoice in the neighbor's good fortune. Those who have this begrudging attitude are living under law, rather than grace.

Losers are winners. The world rewards her winners: those who excel, triumph, or bully their way to the top. Jesus lifted up the poor, the meek, and the merciful as the real winners. Those who the world rewards as being the first shall be last in the kingdom, and those whom the world regards as the dregs will be the first to inherit the crown of glory.

PREACHING APPROACHES WITH ILLUSTRATIONS

Lesson 1: Exodus 16:2-15
Sermon Title: A Complaining Congregation
Sermon Angle: Moses and Aaron had their hands full. The people were not happy with their leadership. The old days seemed golden compared to the present hardships. Moses took their complaints to the Lord, and he answered their complaints by bringing them food. Many congregations have faced similar situations. The leadership needs to hear those complaints and then take it to the Lord in prayer. If there is a valid need, God will supply it.

Lesson 1: Isaiah 55:6-9
Sermon Title: Seek And Find
Sermon Angle: Children enjoy playing Hide-and-Seek. God doesn't play games with us, but he does invite us to engage in a "seek-and-find" operation. The prophet invites the people to "seek the Lord while he can be found ..." (v. 6). It's just another way of saying seek the Lord now. God is now near. We have no assurance that we'll even be here tomorrow. We dare not take God's presence for granted. If we seek him now, while we are able, while we have the inclination, we are sure to find him. As Christians, we know that the way to find God is through faith in Christ. We need to urge our people to accept God's gracious offer.

Lesson 1: Jonah 3:10—4:11
Sermon Title: When Is It Right To Be Angry?
Sermon Angle: Twice God poses the question to Jonah. Is it right for you to be angry? (vv. 4, 9). The first time God posed the question was after the Lord relented from his threatened punishment. The second time occurred when the Lord destroyed Jonah's shade tree. In the first instance, Jonah becomes incensed with God because of his mercy and forgiveness, even to the undeserving (v. 2). In the second instance, he waxes angry about a personal affliction. It is not fitting for a child of God to harbor resentment because of God's mercy on the Gentile Ninevites. When something we value is taken away, it is quite natural to be angry, at least, at first. Nevertheless, even here, anger must yield to acceptance if we are to be sound in body and spirit. A third kind of anger, directed toward injustice, can be creative if it forces us to take corrective measures.

Lesson 2: Philippians 1:19-30

Sermon Title: A Labor Of Love

Sermon Angle: Paul doesn't know which he prefers, to die and be with the Lord or a life of fruitful labor in God's vineyard (v. 22). Fruitful labor is what makes life worthwhile: to know that our efforts fashioned through Christ are coming to fruition. Not only is the work of the pastor, evangelist, or teacher fruitful labor, but also that of the clerk, salesperson, and the brick-layer, when their work is an expression of their commitment to Christ.

Outline:

1. Paul didn't know whether life or death was preferable
   — death meant being with Christ, but life meant productive work
2. What is fruitful labor?
   — labor begun and ended in Christ
   — labor offered in love
   — labor which produces disciples not merely profits

Gospel: Matthew 20:1-16

Sermon Title: Receiving What Doesn't Belong To You

Sermon Angle: Consult the Theological Reflections On The Lessons

Outline:

1. Those hired at the beginning got what belonged to them (the wage)
2. Those hired toward the end of the shift got what didn't belong to them (a gift of grace)
3. We, too, have received a salvation and reward we have not earned

Sermon Title: No Seniority Perks In Heaven

Sermon Angle: Those hired last were paid first at the end of the day and they were paid the same as those who labored through the heat of the day. It doesn't seem fair, and it isn't fair: it's God's grace. It's what someone has dubbed the "unjust goodness of God." No seniority perks. It's no way to run a business, but it's God's way of doing things.

Outline:

1. The world awards, based on merit and position
   — those who have gone the furthest with the most wins
2. The kingdom of God is based on grace — all are equal

Sermon Title: Sour Grapes

Sermon Angle: Those hired at the beginning of the day complained about the injustice of the latecomers receiving the same as they. They were sour grapes in the Lord's vineyard. The church still has to contend with sour grape members who expect to be rewarded for everything they do and are jealous of their fellow church members. Sour grapes need to be reminded of God's graciousness and not be allowed to set the teeth of the church on edge.

* * * * *

The gospel lesson has far more to do with the grace of God than wages. Nevertheless, we need to remember that the world of business and industry operates more under the banner of law and justice than grace. While the Lord gives us what we do not deserve, earthly wages ought to be fair and equitable. Many are calling for the end to affirmative action, yet, studies

324

show that the gap in wages between black/Latino workers and white workers, with all other factors being equal, has not narrowed much.

Christians need to work for justice, on the one hand, so that all people receive justice and fairness; on the other hand, we dispense God's grace in the arena of our relationships, giving others what they do not deserve.

Proper 21/Pentecost 19/Ordinary Time 26

Revised Common:	Exodus 17:1-7	Philippians 2:1-13	Matthew 21:23-32
Roman Catholic:	Ezekiel 18:25-28	Philippians 2:1-11	Matthew 21:28-32
Episcopal:	Ezekiel 18:1-4, 25-32	Philippians 2:1-13	Matthew 21:28-32

Theme: God judges us not based on what we were but what we are. If a sinner turns away from his sin to the Lord, he is accounted as righteous. This is the point of Ezekiel 18. The gospel makes a similar point, if the rebel turns to obedience, he is accounted as righteous.

BRIEF COMMENTARY ON THE LESSONS

Lesson 1: Exodus 17:1-7 (C)

The Israelites complain loudly to Moses that they had no water. They question whether the Lord was really with them. In desperation, Moses cries out to the Lord, fearing that they might stone him. God commands Moses to strike a rock on Mount Horeb, and he would cause water to gush forth. The place is called Massah and Meribah (possibly two different springs at the same site), meaning "Test" and "Quarrel" respectively.

Lesson 1: Ezekiel 18:25-28 (RC); Ezekiel 18:1-4, 25-32 (E)

Ezekiel teaches individual responsibility. "The soul that sins shall die." This is to refute the notion apparently voiced by the people that they were suffering unjustly because of the sins of previous generations. Guilt for sin is not automatically passed down from generation to generation, and neither is righteousness.

Lesson 2: Philippians 2:1-13 (C, E); Philippians 2:1-11 (RC)

Paul encourages the church to be united in spirit and love. Though he does not say so, there must have been a problem with divisions and party spirit. The members of the church are not just to look after their own interests but also the needs of others. A hymn which lifts up Christ's self-emptying humility is cited as an example for the Philippians to emulate. Following the hymn, they are encouraged to humbly work out their own salvation, as God is working in their lives to accomplish his will (vv. 11-12).

Gospel: Matthew 21:23-32 (C); Matthew 21:28-32 (RC, E)

It is best to follow the lead of the Revised Common Lectionary. The parable of the two sons is part of the confrontation the Lord had with the Jewish religious authorities in the temple (vv. 23-27). Jesus was asked by what authority he conducted his ministry. Jesus answered their question with his own query about the source of John the Baptist's ministry. They could not reveal their true feelings about John and so they had to reply that they did not know whether John's baptism was of God or not. Jesus also refuses to tell the source of his authority and then tells the parable of the two sons. The son who said he would do his father's bidding and did not represents the Jewish authorities. The son who, at first, refused to obey his father and then changed his mind stands for the tax collectors, prostitutes, and other sinners who heeded God's call for repentance. Jesus' statement that these would go into the kingdom of God ahead of the religious leaders was grossly offensive to them. Thus, the parable is something of an allegory.

Psalm Of The Day

Psalm 78:1-4, 12-16 (C) — "Give ear, O my people, to my teaching ..." (v. 1).
Psalm 24:4-9 (RC) — "Lord, make me know your ways ..." (v. 6).
Psalm 25:1-14 (E) — "To you, O Lord, I lift up my soul ..." (v. 1).

Prayer Of The Day

O Lord, you know our weaknesses and our shortcomings. We pray for your grace and strength to overcome them and turn away from sin. Guide us on the path of righteousness. In Jesus' name. Amen.

THEOLOGICAL REFLECTION ON THE LESSONS

Lesson 1: Exodus 17:1-7

Water from the rock. The Israelites cried out for water. God told Moses to take the staff with which he parted the Red Sea and strike the rock. Water would gush forth. Paul identifies that rock with Christ. From that Rock, the water of life, beginning with baptism, flows into your arid souls through faith.

Lesson 1: Ezekiel 18:1-4, 25-32

Suffering for the sins of our forebears? Ezekiel is very emphatic that a person will not be punished by God for the sins of her forebears. Each person must personally answer to the Lord. At the same time, we must be clear to point out that one generation does indeed suffer for the sins of those who came before. A daughter or son does indeed suffer for the sins or the neglect of a father or mother. This suffering is not a judgment from God but a natural consequence of running afoul of the laws of the universe. What the prophet is trying to establish is that God will only hold someone accountable for his own sins.

Quit the blame game. It appears that the Jews of Ezekiel's day were blaming their forebears for their present problems. This notion was embedded in a proverb: "The parents have eaten sour grapes, and the children's teeth are set on edge" (v. 2). Ezekiel pulls the rug out from under that kind of thinking. Each person needs to accept responsibility for his actions. Though it is certainly true that we bring pain and hardship to one another, it does us no good to engage in the blame game.

Lesson 2: Philippians 2:1-13

The source of your ambition. Paul enjoins the Philippians to do nothing from selfish ambition (v. 3). Ambition can be good or evil depending on what fuels it. Ambition to gain power over others, to make oneself look good at the expense of others, or to gain riches usually results in evil. The apostle doesn't rule out ambition, but it needs to be directed to a righteous end. The Lord calls us to be ambitious in pursuing the things of the kingdom.

A humble spirit. Paul holds up Christ as an example of a humble spirit. He was in the form of God but poured out himself unto death. He is called "The Man For Others." Humility is the ability to get outside of ourselves and into the heart and soul of others (v. 4).

Lord of all. The apostle claims that every knee will bow and every tongue confess that Jesus Christ is Lord. He envisions humans, as well as spiritual powers, uniting in worship of Christ (vv. 10-11). Does he mean to suggest that all those opposed to Christ will repent and turn to him? Or, is it more likely that he is suggesting that even those who continue to oppose him will be forced to acknowledge his Lordship?

A salvation that works. You've heard the saying, "Pray as if everything depends on God and work as if everything depends on you." That seems to be what Paul is saying in verses 11-12. Work out your own salvation, for it is God who is working in you. Faith never operates in a vacuum; it only grows as you exercise it.

Gospel: Matthew 21:23-32

Not the talk but the walk. In the parable that Jesus told, the first son initially refused to obey his father but later repented and did as he was asked. The second son agreed to go right away but he didn't follow through. The first son did his father's will. God judges us not by our talk but our walk.

Seeing yourself in the story. Jesus told this parable against the religious leaders of Jerusalem, as the opposition closed in around him. They came up with the right answer to Jesus' question but they didn't see themselves in the story. They couldn't imagine that they were the disobedient sons of God who said all the right things but failed to follow through. The prostitutes and the tax collectors saw themselves in the preaching of John the Baptist and Jesus and repented.

How to get ahead. Jesus shocked the scribes and Pharisees with the claim that the tax collectors and prostitutes would enter the kingdom of God ahead of them. As Jesus taught, those who are considered last will be first and those who are considered to be first will come out last. Humility and repentance are the qualities we need to come out ahead.

PREACHING APPROACHES WITH ILLUSTRATIONS

Lesson 1: Exodus 17:1-7
Sermon Title: Between A Rock And A Hard Place
Sermon Angle: Moses was literally between a rock and a hard place. He was responsible to lead a pack of desperate people through a barren wilderness. There was no water, and the people bitterly complained to their leader. At wits' end, Moses cried out to God for help. The Lord commanded him to strike a rock, from which water flowed. When we are at wits' end, we can always count on the Lord to refresh our lagging spirit.

Sermon Title: The Secret Of Leadership
Sermon Angle: When Moses sought God's help he instructed him to go on ahead of the people and take some of the elders with him. The Lord would be with him. The secret of leadership is to lead. Go ahead of the people, but don't get ahead of the Lord.

Lesson 1: Ezekiel 18:1-4, 25-32
Sermon Title: Sour Grapes
Sermon Angle: You've probably heard of breastfeeding mothers who have to stay away from certain foods because it gives their infants gas. The Jews of Ezekiel's time apparently held that something like that was happening to them. They believed that they were being punished for the sins of their forebears. They would quote a proverb to this effect: "The parents have eaten sour grapes and the children's teeth are set on edge" (v. 2). To always be looking for scapegoats is sour grapes, which makes one a sourpuss.

Sermon Title: Bringing God To Trial

Sermon Angle: The Lord is accused of being unfair by God's suffering people (v. 25). Many times God's children are gripped by the feeling that the Lord hasn't dealt fairly with them. Like Job, they would like to bring God to trial, to make him defend some action that he has taken which doesn't seem fair. C. S. Lewis wrote a book that deals with these thorny issues titled *God On The Dock.* However, it's one thing to consider these issues from a detached philosophical perspective and quite another to have to struggle with them in our personal experience. When Lewis' wife of only months died, he had to struggle with the gut feeling that her death was unjust. As he struggled with these issues, his faith attained a new maturity. God is not bound to explain his ways to us, but getting our honest feelings out in the open can bring healing and cause us to see things in a new light.

Lesson 2: Philippians 2:1-13

Sermon Title: Being Of One Mind

Sermon Angle: In verse two, Paul urges unity upon the Philippian church by encouraging them to be of "the same mind" and "of one mind." His wish for them was that each of them would have the mind of Christ and so find their being in the one mind of Jesus Christ. When the mind of Christ controls us, we are united in love and service.

Outline:
1. In America, we emphasize independent thought and doing your own thing
2. Christianity emphasizes having Christ's mind and unity of spirit
3. Being of one mind is expressed in Christlike self-giving love (vv. 6-11).

*   *   *   *   *

I am always suspicious of those couples who claim that they have never had an argument or a cross word. Yet, I must admit that my Uncle Herman and Aunt Lotti Anderson, as far as I could tell, fell into that exalted category. Some women's liberationists might scoff at this relationship, in that he coordinated their efforts. She looked to him for leadership and he gave it. He looked to her for support and he got it. Their joy was to make one another happy. Every action was directed by love and consideration. They were truly of one heart and mind, the mind of Christ.

Sermon Title: Don't Mind Your Own Business

Sermon Angle: Paul expands on the meaning of Christmindedness by saying that Christians should not only look after their own interests but also the interests of others. This is contrary to the notion of personal individualism, which has it that each person should mind her own business. Paul contends that we must take an interest in others (v. 4). We are not like isolated atoms but complex molecules; we are bonded together by the Spirit of Christ.

Outline:
1. Everyday people suffer and die in isolation (mind your own business)
2. Contemporary society is an association of individuals, not a true community
3. Christianity is meant to be a community that flows from the mind of Christ
4. A sign of this community is empathy for others and mutual support
5. How well are we taking a Christlike interest in others?

Sermon Title: Therefore

Sermon Angle: Paul links Christ's humble obedience with his exaltation by God with the preposition "therefore." Then, after his poem dedicated to the humble yet exalted Christ, he applies its significance for the believer also with the word "therefore." We are, therefore, to work out our salvation with fear and trembling, for God is at work to will and to do what is pleasing to him. Therefore is indicative of prior action which has consequences for the present and future. God has acted mightily in Christ, therefore ... Christ is risen, therefore ... God has shown his love for us, therefore ... We are inheritors of eternal life, therefore....

Gospel: Matthew 21:23-32

Sermon Title: What Do You Think?

Sermon Angle: Christianity is the thinking person's religion. Christ usually employed inductive reasoning to get people to see the truth for themselves. The parable in this week's gospel is prefaced with the question Jesus posed to the religious leaders: "What do you think?" Christ doesn't want us to sit on our minds or accept things without reflection. He wants to see the truth of God as it is revealed in life's story. Our minds are limited, but God wants us to go as far as we possibly can in the pursuit of divine truth.

Outline:
1. Jesus asked the religious leaders about what they thought
2. Christ does not teach dogmatically but inductively
   — he helps us to see God's truth in life's story
   — he helps us see God's truth in our own story
3. What do you think about Christ?
   — Who is he to you? Is he Lord?
   — Are you seeing Christ's truth in the world around you?

Sermon Title: Rebellion In The Vineyard

Sermon Angle: The first son in this parable was guilty of the sin of overt rebellion. He, at first, refused to obey his father's request that he work in the vineyard, but later repented. The second son showed outward respect for his father and said he would go, but he didn't. He was guilty of the sin of covert rebellion and didn't repent. The first son was rebellious but, at least, he was open and honest about it. The second son perhaps didn't have the guts to say, "No." His was a cowardly and dishonest kind of rebellion. The first type of rebellion was practiced by the tax collectors and prostitutes. The second type was practiced by the religious breed. The overt sinners could more readily see their sins and repent of them, while the religious sinners disguised their rebellion under a religious cloak.

Outline:
1. Both sons in the parable were rebels but with a difference
2. The first son rebelled overtly and openly (criminal behavior is of this stripe)
3. The second son rebelled covertly (the most common variety)
4. Overt rebellion is easier to confront than covert rebellion
5. The primary distinction is that the first son repented

*   *   *   *   *

"Almost all your faults are more pardonable than the methods you think up to hide them." (La Rouchefoucauld, a French moralist)

330

In John Steinbeck's epic novel, *East Of Eden*, Adam Trask is left to raise his two sons by himself. The one son, Aaron, was always obedient and pure. The other brother, Cal, was something of a wild hair. Yet, more than anything, he craved his father's love. To gain this love, he earned a great deal of money in the commodities market and presented it to his father on his birthday. Adam had lost a lot of money on a failed business and Cal's gift would make up the difference. In so doing, he hoped to earn his father's love. When his father rejected his gift, Cal lashed out at Aaron. Cal knew a horrible truth that would shatter his brother. He discovered that their mother was not dead, as they were told, but that she ran a brothel in a nearby town. Cal brought his brother to the brothel and confronted him with the mother. Aaron's image of who he was shattered like falling ice. Aaron cracked, went off to war, and got killed. Cal was racked with guilt, and the father got a stroke from the shock of it all and became mute. In the end, the rebel son and the stricken father are reconciled by Lee, their Chinese housekeeper, who pleaded with Adam.

"Your son is marked with guilt out of himself .... Don't crush him with rejection. Don't crush him ... Adam, give him your blessing."

With extraordinary effort, Adam was able to utter a word which was a blessing; a word which conferred the father's forgiveness on his rebellious son.

Whatever the cause or nature of our rebellion, the Lord stands ready to take us back as soon as we repent. Jesus Christ, who pleads with the Father of lights, is our bridge builder.

Proper 22/Pentecost 20/Ordinary Time 27

Revised Common:	Exodus 20:1-4, 7-9, 12-20	**Philippians 3:4b-14**	**Matthew 21:33-46**
Roman Catholic:	Isaiah 5:1-7	**Philippians 4:6-9**	**Matthew 21:33-43**
Episcopal:	Isaiah 5:1-7	**Philippians 3:14-21**	**Matthew 21:33-43**

Theme: God's judgment on those who do not produce the fruits of righteousness. In the Isaiah text, God pronounces Israel an unfit fruit and votes to let it go fallow. In the gospel parable of the unfaithful tenants, the Lord promises to take the kingdom away from Israel and give it to a nation producing the fruits of righteousness.

BRIEF COMMENTARY ON THE LESSONS

Lesson 1: Exodus 20:1-4, 7-9, 12-20 (C)

God had, in his grace, freed the Hebrews from their slavery in Egypt and was leading them into the promised land. To govern their life together, he gives them the Ten Commandments. God's laws, too, are a sign of his grace. God loves his people so much that he wants to steer them away from the path of death into the path of life.

Lesson 1: Isaiah 5:1-7 (RC, E)

Isaiah recites a poem that allegorically refers to Israel as the Lord's vineyard, which has turned wild and unproductive. Instead of producing the fruits of righteousness, it has yielded violence. The Lord threatens to abandon his beloved vineyard and let nature take its course.

Lesson 2: Philippians 3:4b-14 (C); Philippians 3:14-21 (E)

Paul's goal is to attain union with the crucified and resurrected Christ. He doesn't claim to have already attained this exalted state but he presses on like a race runner straining for the finish line. This striving for spiritual maturity is promoted by God's prior redemptive actions (v. 12). Paul urges his disciples to imitate him in training toward Christlikeness. Some have chosen to be enemies of Christ by devoting their energies toward consuming this world's goods. Such are to be avoided because the Christian's true homeland is in heaven.

Lesson 2: Philippians 4:6-9 (RC)

Paul is winding down his letter to the Philippians and leaves them some valuable advice. They are not to worry but to make their needs known to God in prayer. God will give them his peace. They are to focus not on the dangers of the present world but on whatever is pure, honorable, and true. They are to continue in the gospel that they have heard and observed in Paul. What faith Paul had in the integrity of his faith and life!

Gospel: Matthew 21:33-46 (C); Matthew 21:33-43 (RC, E)

The parable of the wicked tenants. In this allegorical parable, a man plants a vineyard and equips it with watchtowers, walls, and a wine press. Having prepared all, he rents out the vineyard and leaves the area. At harvest time he sends servants to collect the rent, but they are beaten, robbed, and killed. He then sends his own son, thinking that the tenants would respect his son, but these wicked persons slay the son, reasoning that they can now have the vineyard for themselves. But this is sort of an open-ended story. Jesus asks the religious leaders what they think should be done with such wicked people. They respond that such tenants should be put to a miserable death and the vineyard rented out to someone who would yield up the fruit in season. Once again, they fail to see themselves in the parable. Jesus makes clear the point. Israel, especially their leaders, are those wicked tenants and the vineyard is the kingdom of God. The servants who are mistreated and killed represent the prophets, and the son who was slain is Jesus. Jesus makes the same point that Isaiah made: the kingdom of God would be taken away from them and given to those who yielded the fruit of obedience. Jesus was the stone that the builders rejected, which would form the cornerstone of a new spiritual community (v. 42).

Psalm Of The Day

Psalm 19 (C) — "Let the words of my mouth and the meditation of my heart be acceptable to you, O Lord, my rock and my redeemer" (v. 14).

Psalm 80:7-14 (RC, E) — "Restore us, O God of hosts; let your face shine, that we may be saved" (v. 7).

Prayer Of The Day

Gracious God, you have made us caretakers not only of the bounty of the earth but of the treasure of the gospel. Ground us ever more securely in our relationship with Christ that our lives might abound in fruitfulness. In Jesus' name. Amen.

THEOLOGICAL REFLECTION ON THE LESSONS

Lesson 1: Exodus 20:1-4, 7-9, 12-20

Declarative-imperative. God establishes the foundation from which he issues his commandments. He declares that he is their God, who has saved them from slavery in Egypt. He begins in the indicative mode of expression. From this base, he issues his imperatives. Thus, the commandments are conceived as a response to God's grace and redeeming actions.

Don't defame the name. The people are commanded not to misuse the Lord's name (v. 7) and told that he would not acquit anyone who did so. While the fourth commandment is the only one with a blessing attached, the second commandment is the only one that has a type of curse attached to it. This should have a sobering effect on anyone who takes God's word seriously. All children of God bear his name, but who among us has not misused or misrepresented that holy name? We're not just talking about language here; we're talking about lifestyle and values.

Lesson 1: Isaiah 5:1-7

God as lover. You can feel Isaiah's passion for God, his beloved. He feels the pain of his beloved's pain at being spurned by his own people. When you love someone, her hurts are your hurts. Do we feel the pain of God as we observe a world in rebellion?

Wild world. God threatens to let his vineyard go wild. Without cultivation, nature reclaims everything; it goes wild. Wild means survival of the fittest. Wild means lack of fruitfulness, which is achieved through cultivation, work, and discipline.

Lesson 2: Philippians 3:4b-21

Straining toward perfection. Paul uses the image of the runner straining toward the finish line as an analogy of the Christian life. God has already laid claim to him, but he was pushing ahead with all due effort to attain all that God had in mind for him. Paul was straining for perfection or maturity. The word for maturity, *telios*, sometimes translates as "perfection." In this sense, perfection means completion, not sinlessness. Accepting God's salvation is only a beginning point for a life that strains for maturity in Christ.

Looking forward. Constantly looking back on mistakes and failures is a sure prescription for coming in last. Paul was focused on the future goal. "Forgetting what lies behind ... I press on toward the goal ..." (vv. 13-14).

Hold your ground. "Only let us hold fast to what we have attained" (v. 16). The history of the world is full of examples of societies which have attained great sophistication and knowledge before regressing and, in some cases, becoming extinct. It has been said that we are one generation away from the extinction of Christianity. We must hold on tight to our faith and pass it on to our children. Faith does not remain static; if we aren't pressing toward the life hidden in Christ, our faith is losing steam due to spiritual entropy.

Gospel: Matthew 21:33-46

Violence in the vineyard. The tenants not only refused to pay the rent but did violence to the landowner's servants. What is the source of the violence? Lack of respect for authority, lack of respect for life itself, and greed. The tenants weren't satisfied to be tenants; they wanted to own the vineyard. What violence we do when we forget that we are God's tenants on this earth! Greed leads us to try to possess the vineyard rather than care for it, which pits us against the Lord and our neighbors.

Losing the lease. In preaching on this text, we need to be careful to avoid even the appearance of anti-Semitism. In its original context, the parable is one of judgment against the nation of Israel. They had not lived up to the covenant or rendered the obedience which was owed God. They would not be able to keep their special designation as the exclusive caretakers of God's kingdom. That designation was given to the church, made up of those who render repentance and the fruit of faith. It's not that the Jews were more sinful than other people, nor is it true that they were excluded from God's kingdom. All people are now a part of the kingdom of God through the obedience of faith. The institutional church could also lose its lease if we become bereft of the fruits of Christ's Spirit (v. 43).

PREACHING APPROACHES WITH ILLUSTRATIONS

Lesson 1: Exodus 20:1-4, 7-9, 12-20

Sermon Title: Watch God's Copyright Law

Sermon Angle: The electronic revolution has led to a flood of stealing the thoughts and labors of other people. The Roman Catholic church in Chicago once paid a large penalty for copyright infringements on music. With the acknowledgment of a copyright, it is assumed that the material we are using comes from us or our business or institution. The second commandment states that we should not wrongfully use the holy name of God. Through baptism, we bear his name. Anytime that name is associated with that which is harmful or unjust, we infringe God's copyright law. God comes to represent that which is alien to him.

Lesson 1: Isaiah 5:1-7

Sermon Title: Does God Give Up?

Sermon Angle: According to Isaiah, God expected more from his people than he received. It was a bitter harvest. It seems that the prophet is claiming that the Lord was abandoning his people, letting them go a-wilding. It appears that God is giving up on his people. The Old Testament suggests that God does reach a point where he gives humankind over to their own devices. For a time, it may be true that the Lord has to sit back because there is nothing more that he can do (v. 4). Yet the holy history reveals that God is only biding time until an opportunity for salvation presents itself.

Lesson 2: Philippians 3:4b-21

Sermon Title: Debits And Credits

Sermon Angle: Paul discusses his gains accrued in his former life in Judaism (4b-6). Yet these apparent gains he now regards as loss because now he has inherited the treasure of knowing Christ. The ultimate and eternal credit on the ledger of eternity is to know the crucified and resurrected Christ.

Sermon Title: Why Are You Running?

Sermon Angle: You can't live in Western culture without running, it seems. But why do we run? Where is it that we are so intent on getting? Some run to give themselves a sense of self-worth or accomplishment. Some run merely to keep ahead of others, while others exalt in the speed of the race. Why did Paul run? Not to lay claim to the gift of salvation; that was already his. No, because Christ had claimed him, he wanted to lay claim to all that his relationship contained. It was the sheer joy of running with Jesus to the heavenly prize.

Outline:
1. Does your life seem like an endless race? Where are you running and why?
2. Are you running because you are
   — afraid of being left behind?
   — trying to stay ahead of the pack?
   — doing what everyone else seems to be doing?
3. Paul gives us some guidelines for our running
   — don't look back (v. 13)
   — have a worthy goal and keep it in front of you (v. 13)
   — run for the joy of it (v. 12)
4. We are motivated by grace, not propelled by fear

Sermon Title: Pressing Toward The Prize

Sermon Angle: To win a race requires, among other things, a single-minded purpose. All other items are blocked out except the goal. What is the goal, the prize? Oneness with God in Christ, which is heaven. It's not that we strive to earn heaven; that's impossible for us. In Christ, we have been given heaven as our inheritance, and we are pressing on to take possession of the gift. When Paul speaks of his mystical vision, he mentions that he was caught up in the seventh heaven. Does this allude to degrees of glory? Is it possible that even in heaven we will need to press on to full possession of the prize?

Outline:
1. What is your goal?
2. Paul's goal was to know Christ ever more completely
3. In heaven, we will know God fully
4. Heaven can't wait — we seek to lay hold of it now through Christ

Sermon Title: Heaven Can't Wait

Sermon Angle: Some time ago, there was a movie about the exploits of a man who suffered a premature death through accident and was ushered into the host of heaven. It was titled *Heaven Can Wait*. That's the attitude most of us have, until we're very ill or feeble. I suppose if heaven were too alluring, we would try to cut this life short. The fact of the matter is that heaven can't wait. As Christians, we are to be pressing on toward complete union with Christ, which is heaven (v. 14). We are called to bring the love, joy, and peace of heaven to bear on this earthly life.

Gospel: Matthew 21:33-46

Sermon Title: Is God An Absentee Landlord?

Sermon Angle: Most parables have one central point, and so the details of the story ought not to be imputed with symbolic meaning. However, this is an allegorical parable. The tenants are the Jewish nation. The servants of the householder are the prophets and Jesus is the Son. It would follow then that the householder would be God. If so, is God an absentee landlord? It is certainly true that he gives an enormous amount of freedom to us tenants. God doesn't stand over our shoulders to impose his will. Yet it's not biblical to suggest that God is absent from our daily affairs. Perhaps it's more accurate to say that God roams his vineyard but often incognito.

Outline:
1. The earth belongs to God and the church, his beloved vineyard
2. But is God an absentee landlord? (Is he, like the householder in this parable, in another country?)
3. No, but he keeps his distance so that we might have the freedom to demonstrate our faithfulness and fruitfulness

Sermon Title: God Don't Get No Respect

Sermon Angle: Comedian Rodney Dangerfield was always complaining that he "don't get no respect" (excuse the grammar). That seems to be God's predicament. God sends prophet after mistreated prophet but, no respect. Not much, not for long anyway. Finally, he sends his Son, thinking that his people will respect the Son. They kill him in hopes of taking over the vineyard. God could, of course, command respect if he would use force. Instead, God chooses to win his people's love rather than command their respect.

Outline:
1. God's people do not often give God the respect he deserves
2. In Christ, he suffered the ultimate in humiliation
3. God could demand respect by force, but it would not be heartfelt
4. Through the cross, we worship a God we can respect, love, and serve
5. Let us show the Lord the respect he deserves through obedience

Sermon Title: Pronouncing Your Own Sentence

Sermon Angle: Jesus asked his hearers, the Jewish leaders, to render a verdict on the unfaithful tenants of his parable. Their sentence was that those wretches should be put to a miserable death and the vineyard rented out to those who would pay the rent. In so doing, they were unwittingly pronouncing their own sentence. Isn't that the way it always is? We pronounce our own judgment by the way that we live and the manner that we judge other people. God takes no delight in judgment, only in mercy.

Outline:

1. The religious leaders did not see themselves in Jesus' parable
2. The verdict they rendered on the tenants was the judgment they themselves deserved
3. In judging others, we judge ourselves
4. If we live in Christ, we are freed of all judgment

Proper 23/Pentecost 21/Ordinary Time 28

Revised Common:	Exodus 32:1-14	Philippians 4:1-9	Matthew 22:1-14
Roman Catholic:	Isaiah 25:6-10	Philippians 4:12-14, 19-20	Matthew 22:1-14
Episcopal:	Isaiah 25:1-9	Philippians 4:4-13	Matthew 22:1-14

Theme: The importance of accepting God's gracious invitation to the feast of life.

BRIEF COMMENTARY ON THE LESSONS

Lesson 1: Exodus 32:1-14 (C)

Moses is meeting with the Lord on Mount Horeb and is away from the people for a long time. The people suspect that something perverse has happened to their leader, and so they petition Aaron to make gods for them. Taking their jewelry, he fashions a gold calf and proclaims it the object of their worship. Seeing this unfaithfulness, God wants to destroy the people and make a nation from Moses. Moses pleads with God to restrain his anger, reasoning that the Egyptians would say that God took his people out in the wilderness only to destroy them. The Lord changes his mind about the intended destruction.

Lesson 2: Isaiah 25:6-10 (RC); Isaiah 25:1-9 (E)

This text was selected because it picks up the banquet theme contained in the gospel. The prophet foresees the day when Jerusalem will be a place of feasting for all peoples. God will remove the shroud that keeps all people from seeing God truly. He will dry up grief and obliterate death. God's formerly sorrowing people will rejoice in the presence of their Savior.

Lesson 2: Philippians 4:1-9 (C); Philippians 4:12-14, 19-20 (RC); Philippians 4:4-13 (E)

The Philippians are commanded to rejoice in the Lord. This joy was heightened by Christ's return, expected to be very soon (v. 5). Instead of worry, the believers are commended to prayer. Also, Paul urges them to focus on that which is lovely, honorable, and true (v. 8). The apostle rejoices that the Philippians have sent a gift to him, to help alleviate his needs. Nevertheless, he is content in whatever state or condition he is in because of the strength that Christ supplies.

Gospel: Matthew 22:1-14 (C, RC, E)

This lection contains two parables which continue the theme contained in last Sunday's gospel. The Jews' rejection of Jesus leads to God embracing the Gentiles. In the first parable, a king issues an invitation to a wedding banquet prepared for his son. The king notifies the guests that the banquet is now ready, but they go about their business instead, while some mistreat and even kill the king's messengers. Verse 7 tells of the king sending an army to destroy those who have spurned his invitation, but this verse was probably added by Matthew. This is indeed what happened in the destruction of Jerusalem in 70 AD by the Romans. Then the king dispatches his servants to go to the public thoroughfares and invite all who are willing to come so that the banquet hall might be filled.

The second parable in our lection is closely related to the first. The king comes into the banquet hall and observes a man who isn't attired in a wedding garment. It might be supposed that such garments were issued to the guests. Because he was not properly prepared for the occasion, he is ordered to be thrown out into the "outer darkness," where he would weep and bemoan what he had lost. External appearances are not the issue here but rather the inner attitude. The man knew what was required for the occasion and yet failed to prepare himself. That attitude, which is needed in order to enter into the king's presence, is faith. Christ will accept all sorts of people into the banquet hall of heaven, but all who enter must have on the garment of faith. The rejection of the Jews should not be the point emphasized, but rather, the grace of God that issues an invitation to all who will humbly and joyfully receive it through faith.

Psalm Of The Day
Psalm 106:1-6, 19-23 (C) — "O give thanks to the Lord" (v. 1).
Psalm 23 (RC, E) — "You prepare a table before me in the presence of my enemies" (v. 5).

Prayer Of The Day
Gracious God, we thank you for the table you have set before us, unworthy though we are. Make us ready with the garment of faith and obedience to celebrate the banquet of life, love, and forgiveness. In the name of Jesus, we accept your invitation. Amen.

THEOLOGICAL REFLECTION ON THE LESSONS

Lesson 1: Exodus 32:1-4
Come make gods for us. This is what the Hebrews asked of Aaron, in the absence of Moses. So Aaron sculpted the golden calf, representative of one of the old Egyptian gods. However, he may have rationalized that he was merely making a visual symbol of Yahweh. Humans are not made to be godless. If we don't know the true God, we will make our own deities.

Moses as priest. Yes, I know that Aaron was the designated priest. However, in this text we see Moses in the role of intercessor, pleading to God to have mercy on his sinful people. Aaron, on the other hand, failed in his priestly role by giving in to the demands of his people.

Lesson 1: Isaiah 25:1-10
Party time. Isaiah foresees a time when God will hold a huge banquet for all the people of the earth. All the stops will be pulled out; nothing will be spared. This banquet will be a celebration of life, love, and peace. The banquet is a metaphor for the joyous community which all people of faith will enjoy with one another and the Lord.

Lesson 2: Philippians 4:1-14, 19-20
God's happy people. The epistle to the Philippians radiates joy. We should read this book often as a corrective to the notion that religion should be dour. If the Lord is with us, and he is, and we have good news of grace, and we do, then we should be happy Christian campers. Christian joy is contagious. Are our friends and neighbors catching joy from us?

Antidote for anxiety. Paul offers prayer, saturated with thanksgiving, as the best antidote for anxiety (v. 6). Anxiety is produced by the feeling that we're all alone and helpless, probably ground in some early childhood trauma. Prayer is made possible by the notion that we are not alone; the Lord is near. Not only is he near, but he has pledged himself to help us. When we truly comprehend this truth and share all our burdens with the Lord, anxieties go out the door and the "peace which passes understanding" comes in to stay (v. 7).

A can do attitude. "I can do all things through him who strengthens me" (v. 13). Volumes have been written about Positive Mental Attitude (PMA). Believe you can achieve it and you will. A positive mental attitude has even been equated with faith. This is where the problem comes in. PMA can aid one in accomplishing her goals, but this is not faith. Faith is trust in God, not in a person's own abilities. Faith, not PMA, was the source of the apostle's *can do* attitude.

Gospel: Matthew 22:1-14

Not fasting but feasting. In the parable, the king invited guests to a feast, the marriage feast of his son. The wedding feast was the epitome of joy because it meant the continuance of his reign through his progeny. Jesus describes the kingdom of God as a feast which has no end. However, the religious leaders thought of the kingdom as a fast rather than a feast. They believed in sacrifice and righteousness but had no room for joy and celebration. Jesus was so fond of eating and drinking with sinners that he was called a drunk and a glutton. If we radiated more of the joy of the feast, we might win more disciples.

Why were the invited guests so indifferent to the invitation? Think of the incongruity of the situation. The indifferent and rude attitude of the invited guests boggles the imagination. The king of the land invites these people to the most auspicious banquet that can be imagined. Instead, most spurn the invitation in favor of pursuing their business. Others add injury and murder to insult. Who would rather go to work than to the most stellar social event of a lifetime? You'd have to be a fool! Either that, or they thought that the feast was bogus and the invitation a joke.

Who's getting married? I know that the king's son is getting married but to whom? If Jesus is the Son spoken of in this parable, then it is the church which is the bride of Christ. Our faith relationship with God through Jesus is not merely a lifelong commitment but one for all eternity. In this relationship, we enjoy the mystical union of God's Spirit with our own.

Those invited were not worthy (v. 8). Why weren't they worthy? Because they spurned the gracious invitation. Those others who were later invited from the highways of life were actually no more worthy. Both good and bad accepted the invitation (v. 10). The only difference between the first group and the second was the fact that the second group had the good sense to accept the invitation. God invites us to the marriage feast of life not because we are good and worthy but because we have accepted his invitation through faith in God's Son.

PREACHING APPROACHES WITH ILLUSTRATIONS

Lesson 1: Exodus 32:1-14
Sermon Title: The Power Of Intercessory Prayer
Sermon Angle: When God's anger waxed heavy against the Israelites, Moses passionately interceded with the Lord, that the nation might be spared. At that very time, the cavorting Hebrews at the base of the mountain had no idea of the grave danger they were in. They were not cognizant that Moses was pleading on their behalf. Let us never underestimate the power of intercessory prayer.

* * * * *

When you worship at Holy Cross Church, one of the aspects that really stands out is the length of the intercessory prayers. Scores of sick and needy people are lifted up to the Lord every Sunday. These are not just members of the congregation but friends, family, neighbors, and others. Probably thirty or forty people are prayed for. Some members complain that this makes the services too long. "Imagine," said the pastor, "some folks think that we pray too much. What an indictment to make against your church." A visitor to the church told an evangelism caller: "Your intercessions show that you really are a caring church, which believes in the power of prayer."

Lesson 1: Isaiah 25:1-10

Sermon Title: A Feast For All

Sermon Angle: Isaiah envisions a feast for all peoples being held at the temple in Jerusalem. Usually, when a feast is held, there is a very specific guest list — friends, family, and significant others. God invites all people to feast together in his presence. Regrettably, many will decline the invitation.

Lesson 2: Philippians 4:1-14, 19-20

Sermon Title: Always, Anything, And Everything

Sermon Angle: Paul enjoins the Philippians: "Rejoice always"; "have no anxiety about anything but in everything let your requests be made known" (vv. 4, 6). This is a great prescription for living victoriously in Christ.

Outline:
1. A Christian is to rejoice in all circumstances
2. A Christian ought not to be overcome with anxiety
3. A Christian ought to share everything with the Lord in prayer

Sermon Title: A Living Lesson

Sermon Angle: Paul makes a most incredible and dangerous statement. "Keep on doing the things that you have learned and received and heard and seen in me ..." (v. 9). He is setting up himself as a living example of what it means to be in Christ. He commends them not only to his verbal instruction but to the lesson of his life. He has complete confidence that he has incarnated the Spirit of Christ. He is saying, "Watch me, follow me." Every Christian needs to be a living lesson on the Christian faith.

Gospel: Matthew 22:1-14

Sermon Title: Joy Is Not A Private Thing

Sermon Angle: The king in the parable wanted the banquet hall to be filled with guests. This was not for the purpose of showing off but for sharing the joy of this special occasion. Joy, by its very nature, must be shared. To have to keep it to oneself tends to burst the joy bubble. Thus, we begin to comprehend the king's hurt and disappointment when his guests received the invitation with disdain. So that he might have a house full of guests to share his joy, he commands his servants to go out and invite everyone they could find. It should be our highest joy as Christians to invite others to banquet with our Lord and Savior.

Outline:
1. The king wanted to share the joy of his son's wedding
2. Joy cannot be self-contained; it must be shared (examples)

341

3. God has shared his joy with us in Christ
   — the joy of acceptance, forgiveness, and new life
   — the wedding feast which has no end
4. If we have experienced this joy, let us share it

Sermon Title: Guess Who's Coming To Dinner!

Sermon Angle: In the '60s movie by the above title, starring Spencer Tracy, Katherine Hepburn, and Sidney Poitier, the daughter invites her fiance home for dinner. There's only one problem. The fiance is a black man (Poitier). Her mother is able to accept this arrangement, but both mother and daughter fear the reaction of the man of the house. The movie deals with the struggle for acceptance of the relationship by both sets of parents. Who is it that we normally invite to dine or banquet with us? Our friends, family, and those who are most like us. We do not invite strangers or those who appear to be alien to us. To become one with someone of a different social, economic, or racial group is unthinkable for many people. The king in this parable, who represents God, invites all manner of people to be his guests. In most churches, there is little guessing about who is coming to the Lord's supper. Imagine what would happen if we were to invite strangers!

Outline:
1. The king's family found themselves feasting with strangers
2. God's invitation is to all people, even former strangers, to the covenants
3. Are we an inviting church? Are we willing to permit strangers to join our family?

Sermon Title: Feast Of Saints And Sinners

Sermon Angle: The king's servants filled the banquet hall with people both good and bad. Consider what this might mean. Who are the good people? Are the good people those who try to live by God's laws? Are they religious types? Or are they the people who have a genuine love for God, even though they haven't been taught the full counsel of the Lord? Jesus did commend the faith of Gentiles several times, according to the Gospels. Who are the bad folks? The law-breakers? Those who didn't practice the Jewish religion? Those controlled by their selfish nature? Perhaps the good and the bad are one and the same. The New Testament teaches us that we are both saint and sinner at the same time. That's what the church is, sinners who have put on Christ and have been designated as saints. We see the nature of our Christian fellowship most clearly when we participate in the holy supper.

Outline:
1. The wedding hall was filled with good and bad people
2. The church is also composed of good and bad people
   — the good trust in Christ; the bad do not
   — Christians are both saints and sinners
3. Let us invite other sinners to the feast of life.

Sermon Title: Dressed For Salvation

Sermon Angle: The second parable is closely related to the first. The king comes into the banquet hall and spies a man who does not have on the proper wedding attire. He is not prepared to enter into the celebration. Some interpreters wonder how this man can be faulted for not having on the festal garment, since they were brought in from the highways and byways. The king must have handed out garments to all who were invited. For whatever reason, this

342

person didn't put it on. This showed a lack of respect for the host. The festal garment is a symbol for faith. No one can remain at the king's feast unless she or he is properly attired with the robe of righteousness (faith).

Outline:
1. Society teaches the importance of being properly dressed
2. The man who came to the wedding without the proper garment was tossed out
3. We need to be properly dressed to feast with God
   — the robe of Christ's righteousness
   — the garment of faith
4. The world dresses for success; we dress for salvation

* * * * *

A nationally syndicated column was called "Dress For Success." The author of this column tried to help people be more successful in their careers through appropriate dress. For those who want to move into executive suites, he recommended conservative attire, such as grey suits and white shirts. The thesis behind this column was that clothes project a certain image, and a person would want to make sure that she projected the right image. The garment of faith, on the other hand, is not an *image* but a *reality* that is more than skin deep. This garment is given to all who put their trust in God's Son. The right attire really can open doors.

Sermon Title: Tears Of Regret

Sermon Angle: The man without the wedding garment was tossed into the outer darkness, where people weep and gnash their teeth (v. 13). These are not tears of torture but tears of regret. The man is weeping for what he could have had but lost through his own error. I cannot believe in a God who inflicts pain on anyone. I do believe in a deity that makes us bear the consequences of our own actions and decisions. Weeping and gnashing of teeth is a proper image of hell, because hell is eternal regret for not heeding the invitation to the feast of eternal life.

Proper 24/Pentecost 22/Ordinary Time 29

Revised Common:	Exodus 33:12-23	1 Thessalonians 1:1-10	Matthew 22:15-22
Roman Catholic:	Isaiah 45:1, 4-6	1 Thessalonians 1:1-5	Matthew 22:15-21
Episcopal:	Isaiah 45:1-7	1 Thessalonians 1:1-10	Matthew 22:15-22

Theme: The rule of God. In the Isaiah text, God rules through a heathen king, Cyrus. In the second lesson, he claims us through the gospel. In the gospel lesson, Jesus reminds us that God's rule includes the power structures of this world, yet transcends these structures.

BRIEF COMMENTARY ON THE LESSONS

Lesson 1: Exodus 33:12-23 (C)

The Lord is still stung by the golden calf episode and is threatening to withhold his presence. Moses pleads that God would go with him and the people as they made their way to the promised land. Their uniqueness as a people lay in the fact that they were God's unique people. Moses finds favor with the Lord and requests that he might see the glory of God. God promises that he could see his glory from behind, as the Lord passed by.

Lesson 1: Isaiah 45:1, 4-6 (RC); Isaiah 45:1-7 (E)

God calls and uses Cyrus, the Persian potentate, who doesn't even know the Lord, to conquer nations for the sake of his chosen people. God intends that Cyrus know that he is the Lord of the universe. God addresses him by a title reserved for the kings of the covenant and, especially, David and Solomon. He refers to him as "his anointed." This text shows that God can employ all people, believer and skeptic alike, for his redemptive purposes.

Lesson 2: 1 Thessalonians 1:1-10 (C, E); 1 Thessalonians 1:1-5 (RC)

Today we commence a series of six lessons taken from 1 Thessalonians, which was composed about 50 AD from the city of Corinth. Paul thanks the Thessalonians for their work of faith and their labor of love. God had chosen them through the gospel, which was manifested not only in words but in demonstration of the Spirit's power.

Gospel: Matthew 22:15-22 (C, E); Matthew 22:15-21 (RC)

The Lord's confrontation with his enemies continues. The Pharisees try to entrap him, but Jesus is aware of their malice. They confronted him with a political question. "Is it lawful to pay taxes to Caesar, or not?" They thought that they had the perfect trap. If he responded, "Yes," he would make himself opposed to the widespread nationalistic sentiments, which yearned to throw off the dominion of Rome. If he responded, "No," he would set himself up as a revolutionary and a *persona non grata* with the state. In so doing, he would also alienate the powerful Herodians and Sadducees, who had a vested interest in keeping things as they were. Jesus wisely maneuvered out of the trap by having a coin brought to him. He asked whose image it was. They replied, "The emperor's." Then came the pronouncement: "Give therefore to the emperor the things that are the emperor's and to God the things that are God's" (v. 21). Jesus does not thereby split existence into realms of sacred and secular. All earthly powers derive their authority from God. In rendering obedience to rightfully constituted earthly authority, one is also submitting to God's rule.

Psalm Of The Day
Psalm 99 (C) — "Extol the Lord our God; worship at his footstool" (v. 5).
Psalm 96 (RC, E) — "O sing to the Lord a new song, sing to the Lord, all the earth" (v. 1).

Prayer Of The Day
Sovereign Lord, you rule in justice and love, so that all people may know your redeeming goodness. May we in all things render to you the obedience of a faithful life and so bring glory to your holy name. In the name of Jesus. Amen.

THEOLOGICAL REFLECTION ON THE LESSONS

Lesson 1: Exodus 33:12-23
Finding favor. God told Moses that he had found favor in his sight. This might have led some to ask for riches and power. Instead, Moses asks that the Lord might show him his ways and that he might know the Lord (v. 13). Moses wanted fellowship with the Lord, not mere favors. Such an attitude on our part will secure God's continued favor upon us.

A peculiar people. Moses makes the point that it is their identification as Yahweh's people that makes them distinct (v. 16). The Hebrews took pride in their peculiarity, their distinctiveness. More often than not, people want to blend in with the prevailing culture. Some surveys have shown that the behavior of Christians is very little different than that of society in general. Some churches have merged in the name of ecumenism and lost their identity, their peculiarity. We Christians must see our distinctiveness in God's going with us.

Lesson 1: Isaiah 45:1-7
The God who goes before. In the first lesson from Exodus, Moses pleads with God to go before the people and lead them to the promised land. In this reading, God promises to go before Cyrus to bring him victory. Jesus, too, reveals a God who goes before us in suffering, death, and resurrection. If we are to be successful, we must let God take the lead.

God knows our name. The Lord tells Cyrus, "I call you by your name" (v. 4). God knows his own; he calls them by name. God shows us his favor by taking a personal interest in each of us. None of us are numbers; we are known and loved. God's knowing of us precedes our knowing of God.

Lesson 2: 1 Thessalonians 1:1-10
Labor of love. Paul mentions the Thessalonians' "*work* of faith" and their "*labor* of love." Both words imply that faith and love require effort. Faith and love are not merely qualities that we are smitten with but are achieved as we give ourselves as instruments of God's grace.

Chosen of God. Paul reminds the Thessalonians that they are *chosen* by God and dearly loved. How wonderful it is to be chosen as a friend, a lover, or for some special task. To be chosen confers a sense of belonging and worth. The Jews were God's chosen people, and we, too, are chosen in Christ to live and labor as God's dear children.

345

Gospel: Matthew 22:15-22

Levels of loyalty. The Pharisees and Herodians wanted to catch Jesus in an either/or trap. Is it right to pay taxes to Caesar or not? They thought that loyalty to God and to the state were mutually exclusive. Jesus taught that both had a claim on our loyalty but on much different levels. As citizens of this world, we owe support to our government. But we are also citizens of God's kingdom, which lays on us a much more basic claim to our loyalty. Caesar and God are not on the same level of loyalty. God is the foundational loyalty on which all others are based.

In whose image are you coined? The denarius that Jesus had brought to him bore the image of Caesar. This implies that it belonged to the emperor. All humans are coined in God's image because God has created us all. Even more importantly, we have been stamped "in the name of the Father, and of the Son, and of the Holy Spirit" at baptism. We bear his image, which means we belong to God. His children are the units of his value. Gold and silver are worthless in his sight.

Hypocrites. The charge that Jesus leveled against his enemies more than any other was hypocrisy. In today's lesson, the Pharisees and Herodians try to catch Jesus off guard by first buttering him up with phony accolades. What they said was true but it was uttered in an insincere manner (v. 16). Jesus would have respected them more if they would have hit him with a full frontal attack.

PREACHING APPROACHES WITH ILLUSTRATIONS

Lesson 1: Exodus 33:12-23

Sermon Title: Finding Favor

Sermon Angle: The Hebrews and Moses had found favor in God's eyes. God had shown them his grace. Moses wanted to know God's ways, that he and the people might continue to find God's favor (v. 13). God's initial favor is completely a gift, but if we are to continue in God's good will we must walk in God's ways. The proper response to God's favor is to return his favor.

Sermon Title: A People Apart

Sermon Angle: Moses did not envision the Hebrew nation blending into the surrounding cultures. He realized that his people needed to be unique, set apart, holy to the Lord (v. 16). The distinctness of the Jewish people made them the object of misunderstanding and hatred but it also assured their survival and gave them their identity. If Christianity is to remain a strong and vital force, we will need to recapture a sense of distinctiveness. We must not be blindly identified with the common culture.

Outline:
1. The Hebrews' relationship with God made them distinct (v. 16).
2. God was leading them on a journey — their uniqueness lay in God's continued presence and leadership
3. At times they turned their backs on God to blend in with the common culture, with dire results
4. We, too, have been claimed by God as his people
   — but are we not in danger of losing our distinctness?
   — journey with God
   — find your identity in Christ, not the world

We stopped at a very busy McDonald's drive-thru in North Platte, Nebraska, one sultry August day, and as we were eating our ice cream, a group of very peculiar people crowded the restaurant. The men sported beards, white shirts, and suspenders; the women wore white bonnets and long dresses. They were a group of Old Mennonites. Their dress derives from religious convictions, which regard the outside world with suspicion. Some people might regard them as odd (they are something of an anachronism), yet their distinctiveness is a source of their strength. No matter where they go, they can never forget who they are as God's people and that they are in the world but not of the world.

Lesson 1: Isaiah 45:1-7

Sermon Title: God Calls Us By Name

Sermon Angle: God called Cyrus, the Persian king, to free his people from bondage (v. 4). This was true even though Cyrus didn't know the Lord. God knew each one of us long before we knew him. God can even enlist heathens to do his will, because he is Lord of all creation. Yet, his aim is that we know him and serve him with a willing heart. The reason for God's call is so that all people may know God as Lord (v. 6).

Lesson 2: 1 Thessalonians 1:1-10

Sermon Title: Faith Works

Sermon Angle: Paul thanks God for the Thessalonians' *work* of faith and *labor* of love (v. 3). To say that faith works might mean that faith shows results or gets the job done. People of faith have discovered this truth. Such a statement might also be interpreted to mean that faith does not stand idle waiting for God to act. Faith works; it is active in concrete acts of doing, sharing, and loving.

Outline:

1. The Bible shows that faith is rewarded — brings concrete results
2. Faith is also demonstrated in labors of love
   — faith is active and dynamic
   — faith moves us to serve and to help
   — faith is active not only in words but in the power of the Spirit (v. 5).
3. How well is your faith working?

Sermon Title: The Power Of Christian Conviction

Sermon Angle: Three words are closely linked together in verse 5: power, the Holy Spirit, and (full) conviction. The person with strong convictions exerts a powerful influence. The lack of strong conviction leads to a tepid existence that excites no one. Of course, if convictions are turned in a negative direction, the results can be destructive. God used Paul to birth Christianity into a worldwide faith community because he was a man of compelling convictions. Many Protestant churches are languishing because the marrow has been sucked from the churches' skeletal structure. There is no compelling vision that is strong enough to move them and to spark a response from the non-believing community. Only a deeply experienced faith in Christ as Savior and Lord has the power to move mountains. That type of faith only comes through the Holy Spirit.

Outline:
1. Words have little effect when drained of conviction, passion, and love
2. We are bombarded with meaningless words
   — radio, television, advertising
   — the message of many a church is divorced from the power of the Spirit
3. The words of the gospel are filled with the power of the Spirit (v. 5).
4. Submit to Christ, who will give you the courage of an abiding conviction

Gospel: Matthew 22:15-22

Sermon Title: Tripping Over Your Tongue

Sermon Angle: The Pharisees and Herodians approached Jesus with the intent of tripping him up in his own words (v. 15). They failed. While it is easier to trip up a liar and a deceiver, it is very difficult to tongue trap a person of integrity and truthfulness. Such a person has nothing to hide and doesn't have to remember which lies he told to whom. Jesus, on the other hand, caught on to the phoniness of his inquisitors right away (v. 18).

Sermon Title: Paying Taxes

Sermon Angle: Paying taxes to the government has never been popular. It has sparked revolutions, such as in our own country. The rally cry was, "No taxation without representation." Such an attitude was prevalent in Israel during Jesus' day. That's why the Lord's enemies brought this issue to him. The Pharisees held that it was right to pay taxes only to God and to the government only in the context of a theocratic state. Jesus maintains the right of governments to levy taxes for services but also insists that a person must pay God what is owed him: namely, ultimate allegiance and devotion.

Outline:

Introduction: Who likes to pay taxes?
1. We resent taxes because
   — we regard our money as our own
   — we think it is wasted
2. Roman taxation was a divisive issue in Jesus' day, and Jesus' enemies wanted to catch him in this trap
3. Jesus teaches that we must pay the state and God what we owe
   — we owe our government taxes and support
   — we owe God our very lives
4. All that we have is a gift to be shared

*   *   *   *   *

Paul Revere has established the kingdom of Heaven in Oregon. Getting into Heaven is quite easy; it's getting out that is difficult. Two times in the past year, Revere has been jailed for issuing his own license plates with the word HEAVEN embossed thereon and for failing to pay property taxes. At one time, he owed the state over $10,000. Revere maintains that the kingdom of Heaven is not of this world. He claims that it is impossible to serve both God and the state. Revere's 200 followers have renounced their worldly identities and function only as citizens of Heaven, insisting that Jesus did not pay taxes. He further contends that the state is the antichrist and the courts, dens of Satan. He further teaches that the black robes of the judges indicate that they are henchmen from hell, conducting Satanic rituals. Revere urges his followers to become "unyoked" from the governments of this world. Throw away state-issued driver's licenses and Social Security cards and cancel car insurance, bank accounts, and so forth. Revere regards his outpost as a sovereign nation. He has also set up embassies of Heaven in the "foreign lands" of Oregon, Utah, and Texas but plans to go worldwide. The citizens of Heaven remain accountable only to God. (Derived from an article in the *Omaha World Herald*, August 27, 1994)

Paul Revere's argument is essentially that of the Pharisees and religious zealots in Jesus' day.

Proper 25/Pentecost 23/Ordinary Time 30

Revised Common:	**Deuteronomy 34:1-12**	**1 Thessalonians 2:1-8**	**Matthew 22:34-46**
Roman Catholic:	**Exodus 22:20-26**	**1 Thessalonians 1:5-10**	**Matthew 22:34-40**
Episcopal:	**Exodus 22:21-27**	**1 Thessalonians 2:1-8**	**Matthew 22:34-46**

Theme: Loving God and neighbor.

BRIEF COMMENTARY ON THE LESSONS

Lesson 1: Deuteronomy 34:1-12 (C)

Moses goes to the top of Mount Nebo in the land of Moab, where God shows him the promised land. Then he dies and God himself buries him. Joshua inherits the spirit of Moses and the mantel of leadership. He will bring the people into the fulfillment of God's promise. The Deuteronomist summarizes the life of Moses by commenting that there has never since been such a prophet who knew God face to face.

Lesson 1: Exodus 22:20-26 (RC); Exodus 22:21-27 (E)

The people are warned against sacrificing to any other god and oppressing the resident aliens. They are to remember that they were once aliens in the land of Egypt. God is compassionate and listens to the cries of the oppressed.

Lesson 2: 1 Thessalonians 2:1-8 (C, E)

The opposition and suffering that Paul and his co-workers encountered in Philippi did not discourage them from sharing the good news with the Thessalonians. They did not use flattery or deceit but were gentle, like a woman nursing a child. In communicating the gospel, they also shared themselves.

Lesson 2: 1 Thessalonians 1:5-10 (RC)

The Thessalonians became wonderful examples of faith for all the people of the region. It is reported to Paul how they turned from idols to serve the living God and wait for the coming of his Son.

Gospel: Matthew 22:34-46 (C, E); Matthew 22:34-40 (RC)

Still trying to trap Jesus, the Pharisees have one of their experts ask Jesus which is the greatest commandment in the law. Jesus responds that the first and greatest commandment is to love the Lord God with all one's heart, soul, mind, and strength. He adds a second commandment related to it: "You shall love your neighbor as yourself." The first commandment derives from Deuteronomy 6:5 and the second from Leviticus 19:18. Once again, Jesus answers correctly. The new dimension to Jesus' interpretation comes from the close connection of the first and second tables of the law. The love of neighbor is not added to the first commandment, but flows from it. After his answer, Jesus asks the Pharisees a question concerning the Messiah, which they could not answer. This marks the end of the questions. The opposition goes underground.

Psalm Of The Day

Psalm 90:1-6, 13-17 (C) — "Lord, you have been our dwelling place in all generations ..." (v. 1).

Psalm 18:2-4 (RC) — "I call upon the Lord, who is worthy to be praised" (v. 3).

Psalm 1 (E) — "Their delight is in the law of the Lord" (v. 2).

Prayer Of The Day

Gracious God, make us mindful of those things which are of first importance. Then give us the strength to love you above all else and love our neighbor as our self. In Jesus' name. Amen.

THEOLOGICAL REFLECTION ON THE LESSONS

Lesson 1: Deuteronomy 34:1-12

Seeing the land of promise. God took Moses on top of Mount Nebo that he might see the land of promise. Moses could not enter that place, but God had even a more glorious dwelling place in mind. Those who walk closely with God, as Moses did, are able to see both the earthly land of promise and to glimpse by faith the heavenly dwelling place.

Mountain vista. Moses viewed the land God was leading them to from the mountaintop. The mountaintop is symbolic of the place where we meet God, where we can view existence in perspective. When you're in a valley, you can't see the promised land; all you can perceive is the immediate horizon and the problems at hand. If we walk closely with the Lord and converse with him regularly, as Moses did, we will have the elevation to see God's promises.

Laying on of hands. The text says that Joshua, Moses' successor, "was full of the spirit of wisdom, because Moses had laid his hands on him" (v. 9). This is the idea behind apostolic succession, that the Spirit of leadership can be passed on from one generation to another, as symbolized in the laying on of hands. If only we would all pass on the Spirit of the Lord to the next generation, if only we would all take the time to convey the principles of divine wisdom and leadership, we would soon reach the promised land.

Lesson 1: Exodus 22:20-27

Survival of the compassionate. The strong are not to take advantage of the widow, the orphan, or the alien. God threatens destruction of those who abuse such vulnerable folks (22:24). In God's eternal perspective, life does not evolve through the survival of the fittest but survival of the compassionate, who are, in effect, the fittest.

Lesson 2: 1 Thessalonians 2:1-8

Godly courage. Though Paul and party met severe opposition in Philippi, they still had courage in God (v. 2). Godly courage comes from the faith that if a person lives out the will of God, the Lord will ultimately bring his efforts to a successful end. The person who is filled with godly courage relies on God's strength, not his own.

Nurturing presence. The Pauline missionaries did not come to milk the converts for personal gain; rather, they came to feed and nourish them like a mother with child (v. 7). The leaders in the church should not assume the hierarchal power structure of the world, whose aim is to dominate, but tenderly nurture those whom they are trying to teach.

Incarnated gospel. Paul did not only share ideas and beliefs with his converts, but his very self. The message of the gospel was incarnated. Actually, there is no other way to authentically share the gospel than through our own being. Faith is more apt to be caught than taught.

Lesson 2: 1 Thessalonians 1:5-10

Affliction and joy. The Thessalonians received the word with affliction and joy comingled. We don't normally speak of affliction and joy in the same breath. Christians can have joy in affliction because we have the Spirit of God and the good news of Jesus Christ.

Imitation of Christ. The Thessalonians became imitators of the apostolic party and of Christ. It is fine to emulate the example of other Christians so long as they are imitating Christ. The problems arise when those whom we look up to for an example no longer reflect Christ. Like children, we learn from the example of those whom we respect. The more visible our position in the church, the more impact our example has on others.

Gospel: Matthew 22:34-46

Passing the test. All the religious and political groups, the Sadducees, the Pharisees and the Herodians, tried to make Jesus flunk out. He did not plead the fifth amendment or seek to evade their queries. He answered directly and passed with flying colors. The Christ of the gospels has stood the test of time and will not wilt under cynical scrutiny.

Essence. The Jewish teachers of the law tended to move in one of two directions. Either they attempted to further explicate some particular law through increased particularity, or they tried to distill the many laws down to their basic essence. The distillation process underlies the question put to Jesus. That's what the gospel of Jesus does: it distills all the demands of the law into its love essence.

Strength to love. In summarizing the law and the prophets, Jesus uses the word "all" three times to modify the word's heart, soul, and mind. We are to love God with everything that we have. This is a tall order, demanding a superhuman strength. Knowing the essence of the law and the prophets is not enough. It must be put into practice. The gospel of Jesus gives us the strength and the motivation to move toward loving God above all other things, but it also grants forgiveness when we fail.

PREACHING APPROACHES WITH ILLUSTRATIONS

Lesson 1: Deuteronomy 34:1-12

Sermon Title: The Rest Of The Story

Sermon Angle: Before Moses died, God showed him, from a distance, the land to which he was leading the Hebrews. Moses had devoted forty years of his life to bringing them to this point but would not be allowed to finish the job. Isn't that an allegory of our individual lives? We strive hard to accomplish something lasting with our lives, but when our end comes, the story of our lives is incomplete. Perhaps this is to keep us humble and to remind us that we are one small chapter in the unfolding saga of existence. Paul Harvey, the radio news commentator, likes to lead us along with an interesting story and then take a commercial break. After the break, he finishes the story with something of a surprise ending, signing off with the phrase that identifies him: "Now you have the rest of the story." Our hope is that one day we will see the "rest of the story" revealed.

352

Sermon Title: The Secret Of Dying Young

Sermon Angle: The text says (v. 7) that when Moses died, his "sight was unimpaired and his vigor had not abated." He died young even though he was 120 years of age. What is the secret of dying young? Live as Moses did. Walk and talk daily with the Lord and have a great task which spurs you onward.

Lesson 1: Exodus 22:20-27

Sermon Title: God Of The Oppressed

Sermon Angle: God orders his people to be compassionate toward the oppressed and the downtrodden so that they might reflect the compassion of their God (v. 27). Like a parent who seeks to protect and defend the disadvantaged child, so God's heart reaches out to the weak.

Lesson 2: 1 Thessalonians 2:1-8

Sermon Title: The Real Thing

Sermon Angle: How do you tell authentic Christian faith from that which is phony? The bogus variety seeks to please humans, so as to gain power and personal advantage. Bona fide faith, the real thing, only strives to please God. Another differentiation: the real thing stays above board, open, and honest, while counterfeit religion seeks to disguise its base motives.

Outline:
1. Paul defends against the charge of being fake
2. The authenticity of their faith is shown in the fact that
   — they did not deceive but were open (v. 3)
   — they did not seek to win favor with humans but only with God (v. 4)
   — they demanded nothing (v. 7)
   — they were gentle (v. 7)
   — they gave themselves with the gospel (v. 8)

Lesson 2: 1 Thessalonians 1:5-10

Sermon Title: Faith That Takes Flight

Sermon Angle: The faith of the Thessalonian Christians took flight; it became widely known in that whole region of the world. "But in every place your faith in God has become known" (v. 8). The best advertising for the church is a transforming faith that turns us from idols to the true God.

Gospel: Matthew 22:34-46

Sermon Title: Credo

Sermon Angle: The first part of the response that Jesus made to the lawyer was the Jewish *Shema*, their creed. "Hear, O Israel, the Lord is our God, the Lord is one, and you shall love the Lord your God with all your heart, with all your soul and with all your mind" (Deuteronomy 6:5). So very simple and compact. It doesn't say much about the nature of God, as our Christian creeds do, except that he is one. The emphasis is on our response and duty to this God: to love and serve God with our entire being.

Sermon Title: Keep It Simple, Stupid

Sermon Angle: Life has become increasingly complex and people are looking for something which is basic and uncomplicated. In the area of religion, people are not looking for esoteric mystery religions; they are seeking a religion which is simple and to the point. The religion of Abraham, Isaac, and Jacob was simple, but through the centuries it became more and more complex. This was to satisfy the desires of the religious bureaucrats, but it had the result of making the Jewish religion more inaccessible to the uneducated. Jesus reduces religion down to the basics: loving God and the neighbor. He made it simple, and so must we. God has shown his love for us in Jesus Christ. We are called to return this love with our whole beings. That's all that really matters.

Outline:
1. The Jewish religious leaders couldn't see the forest for the trees
2. We, too, lose sight of essentials in our harried lives
3. Jesus focuses the core of religion — love God through the neighbor
4. Jesus gives us his Spirit to enable us to love God from our hearts.

* * * * *

In the movie, *City Slickers*, Billy Crystal and two of his middle-aged friends found a new lease on life at a dude ranch. At that point in his life, Billy's character was not deriving much joy out of his job and viewed his life and future in tones of grey. Curley, played by Jack Palance, was a seasoned, old cowpoke who became a mentor for Billy. Under his direction, Billy was compelled to deliver a calf. Curley offered the benefit of his wisdom. Holding up his index finger, he declared that the key to life was knowing the "one thing." Of course, cowboys tend to be close-lipped and Billy doesn't know what the "one thing" might be. Curley's sudden death forces him to struggle with the question.

With Jesus, the "one thing" is never in doubt: to love the Lord God with all our heart, soul, and mind.

* * * * *

Dr. Frank Laubach, noted for his pioneering efforts in literacy, recorded in his book, *Channels Of Spiritual Power*, that it is much easier to love God than humans. God is the most lovable Being in the universe, but people are often disagreeable, even contemptible. He advised that we need to teach ourselves to love people not because they are lovable but because they need to be loved.

Reformation Day

Jeremiah 31:31-34 **Romans 3:19-28** **John 8:31-36**

Theme: There is freedom from the power and penalty of sin through the grace of God in Christ.

BRIEF COMMENTARY ON THE LESSONS

Lesson 1: Jeremiah 31:31-34

God will establish a new covenant with his people, not written on parchment or etched in stone, but written on the human heart. God will bestow not only the desire but the power to do his will. This new covenant will be intrinsic rather than external. It will also be inclusive rather than exclusive, not just reserved for the righteous few (v. 34).

Lesson 2: Romans 3:19-28

No person will be accounted righteous by keeping the law of God. He who breaks part of it is guilty of all. The good news proclaims that the righteousness of God is available to all people as a gift of grace. This righteousness becomes possible through Christ's atoning sacrifice. Through faith we are accounted righteous and, thus, acceptable to God.

Gospel: John 8:31-36

Jesus tells the Jews that they shall know the truth which will make them free. They misunderstand and reply that they have never been in bondage to anyone. Jesus retorts that anyone who sins is in bondage to sin. Jesus, the Son, is the only one who can make people truly free.

Psalm Of The Day

Psalm 46 — "God is our refuge and strength ..." (v. 1).

Prayer Of The Day

O Lord, our God, you are our refuge and strength, the source of our hope and, through Christ, the object of our faith. Free us from our self-righteous attempts to earn your salvation and ground us in your grace. We ask this in the name of our blessed Redeemer, Jesus Christ. Amen.

THEOLOGICAL REFLECTION ON THE LESSONS

Lesson 1: Jeremiah 31:31-34

New covenant. Jeremiah, the prophet of doom and gloom, the weeping prophet, declares that the Lord will do a new thing. It will not be an act of destruction but a creative act. God will establish a new covenant with his people, not like the old one which they were unable to fulfill. This time, God will inscribe it on the human heart. The old covenant had served its purpose, to make the people aware of the holiness of God and of their own sinfulness. Now they were ready for something new.

New Testament in the Old Testament. The new covenant concept of Jeremiah is closely related to Christianity's concept of inward or personal conversion. Through faith in Christ, God is able to effect the obedience which the law demands.

A marriage analogy. God says that the new covenant will not be like the old covenant, when he took Israel by the hand to lead her out of Egypt, a covenant which they broke even though God was their husband (v. 32). Both marriage and the relationship of God with his people are covenants of trust, promising a mutual relationship of self-giving. The Jews were unfaithful to the covenant. Nevertheless, God promises to restore the relationship through a new covenant (marriage) of forgiveness and grace.

The forgetfulness of God. God promises to forgive the iniquity of his people and remember their sin no more (v. 34). When we leave our sins with the Lord, he forgets where he put them.

Lesson 2: Romans 3:19-28

Accountable to God. The law of God serves the purpose of making persons accountable to the Lord. Sin and evil exist apart from the law, but without knowledge of God's will, no person can be held accountable. And without accountability, sin goes unchecked.

Justification. A big word but an essential concept. Justification is a legal term, and, in the theological context, it means to be declared righteous by God because of his gift of grace in Christ. This status of justification is accepted or received through faith. Paul maintains that no person will be justified through human endeavors (the works of the law) (v. 20). This is the heart of the Reformation message.

The righteousness of God (v. 21). Pauline theology holds central the righteousness of God. In the cross, we see the divine righteousness. It is not the uprightness of an implacable judge, who only acts in accordance with the letter of the law, but a compassionate righteousness that strives to lift up fallen sinners. God sees that imputing his own righteousness is the only way to save his lost children.

Sin is sin. In the world and certainly in the courts of law, we make fine distinctions in determining the relative merit or demerit of a particular action. When it comes to our acceptability to God, no distinctions matter (v. 22). All sin separates us from God. The way that God looks at sin is radically different from the way that the world views the infractions of its laws.

Sole Gratia! Sola Fide! This was the war cry of the Protestant reformers. Grace alone! Faith alone! They passionately supported Paul's position: "For we hold that a person is justified by faith apart from the works prescribed by the law" (v. 28). Christ alone saves us. Critics of the doctrine of justification point out that it removes any incentive for righteous living. If we're already accepted by God, why endeavor to be good? The answer is: We shouldn't endeavor to be righteous. If we have accepted Christ's righteousness, good and loving deeds will be the fruit of our faith.

Gospel: John 8:31-36

Continuing in Christ. According to John, many of Jesus' followers dropped away, offended by the difficulty of his teaching and his demands. It is in this context that Jesus informs them: "If you *continue* in my word you are truly my disciples ..." (v. 31). It simply isn't true that once you're Christian, always you're a Christian. Those who were once saved can be lost if they choose not to continue with Christ.

Continuing in the truth. To take the preceding idea a step further, Jesus taught that if we continue in his teaching, we will know the truth. Truth does not come easily. It takes struggle and perseverance.

Liberating truth. Every tyrant has sought to hold power by concealing the truth from his subjects. They know the liberating power of truth. Psychotherapy also seeks to free clients by assisting them in unveiling personal truth. The Jews of our gospel lesson were unaware of their bondage to sin; even Christ couldn't free them apart from their acknowledgment of this truth.

PREACHING APPROACHES WITH ILLUSTRATIONS

Lesson 1: Jeremiah 31:31-34

Sermon Title: A New Day Is Dawning

Sermon Angle: Jeremiah promises that a new day is about to dawn, a new era in God's relationship with his people. This new day would usher in a new and better way for God to relate to his people, a new covenant. In Jeremiah's day, this prophecy was only a hope. In Christ, that new day has already dawned. God has found a way to transform the human heart. We are children of the dawn and witnesses to the light of that new day.

Outline:
1. The old day of sin and selfishness is passing away
2. Jeremiah promised a new day for Israel and a new covenant
3. In Christ (second lesson) a new day of salvation has dawned for all
4. Let us not linger in the shadow of the old day of sin but walk in the light of the new day ushered in by Christ

Sermon Title: Salvation Is An Inside Job

Sermon Angle: The old covenant sought obedience through laws, threats, and punishment. Obedience was to an outside authority. Jeremiah saw that this was not sufficient. He concluded, through divine inspiration, that God needed to transform people from within: thus, the new covenant of transformed hearts. Christian faith is an inside job, beginning with a new heart and mind. God re-creates us in his image.

Outline:
1. The old covenant sought obedience to an outside authority (God's law)
2. This made people aware of sin but could not make them righteous
3. Jeremiah foresaw that God was going to transform people from within
4. The gospel transforms us from within but is visible in our lives

Sermon Title: God's Spot Remover

Sermon Angle: When God forgives, he doesn't file the offense away for future reference; he blots it out. Though sin may leave a stain, the result of our sin, God doesn't see it or remember it; it is obliterated (v. 34). This is a model for the kind of forgiveness which we are called to exhibit toward one another.

Lesson 2: Romans 3:19-28

Sermon Title: Held Accountable

Sermon Angle: Paul states that the law was given that the whole world might be held accountable (literally, under sentence) for its actions. Without knowledge of sin, no one can be held accountable. We live in a day when humans are seeking to be extricated from personal responsibility. Attempts are made to blame our wrongs on our genes or our environment. On the cover of a recent *Time* magazine, the caption suggested that perhaps infidelity in marriage might be due to a genetic trait. What a wonderful excuse and rationalization for immoral behavior! Without accountability, sin blazes out of control, incinerating whatever is in its path.

Outline:
1. God's law holds an accountable for our actions (v. 19)
2. Modern man seeks freedom from guilt through denial of accountability to God's laws
3. Modern philosophers assert man is only accountable to himself
4. Only by accepting our accountability, can we be transformed by the gospel
5. Confess your sin and ask Christ to free you from the power of sin (gospel lesson)

Sermon Title: Self-Justification Vs. Justification By Grace

Sermon Angle: We humans have a natural bent to justify ourselves; that is, to make ourselves appear righteous when we really aren't. Paul asserts that no human can justify herself through the works of the law (v. 20). Self-justification is self-defeating. It's like being in quicksand — the harder you try to get out, the deeper you descend into the mire. Without God's liberating grace, reaching out to save us, we would all surely perish. The apostle further asserts that we are only justified by God's grace through faith in Christ's sacrifice (vv. 24-25).

Outline:
1. It's hard to live with guilt; it condemns and destroys
2. We seek freedom from guilt through self-justification
   — I'm not as bad as other people
   — Everybody is doing it
   — It's my genes or environment
3. Christ frees us from guilt through his justifying sacrifice (vv. 24-25)
4. Accept Christ's justification through faith

Sermon Title: How To Enter The Holiest Place

Sermon Angle: In verse 25, the word interpreted "expiation" (*hilasterion*) refers literally to the lid of the mercy seat found on the Ark of the Covenant, which rested in the holy of holies in the temple. On the Day of Atonement, the high priest would go into the mercy seat, the seat of God's presence, and sprinkle blood there. This was to absolve his sin and the sin of the people. This suggests that Christ's blood was the sacrifice for the sins of the world and that Christ himself is the mercy seat. Now, all believers have access through faith. To pick up on Jeremiah's concept of the law being written on the human heart, we can see that the holy place has shifted from a certain geographical location to the arena of relationship, our relationship with God through Christ. The holy place can only be entered through faith.

Outline:
1. Explain the concept of freedom from sin through sacrifice
2. Explain the meaning of expiation, holy of holies and mercy seat
3. Christ is both the sacrifice and the mercy seat
4. Let us enter the holiest place through faith

Gospel: John 8:31-36

Sermon Title: To Be Continued

Sermon Angle: All of us have had the experience, I'm sure, of getting engrossed in a good story on television only to see the words pop on the screen: "To be continued." How frustrating that is! We want to know how the story ends and we want to know now! When it comes to our Christian faith, the story cannot be told in a single segment. Our relationship with God is ongoing; it's a serial story. What matters to God is not what happens in the first installment of our walk with the Lord. What counts is that we grow in love as we continue in Christ. Our relationship with Christ remains healthy if we continue in his teachings (v. 31).

Outline:

Introduction: How do you feel when you're engrossed in an exciting story on television and are finally getting to the crux of the plot, when all of a sudden there's a station break, followed by the words: "To be continued"?

1. We want our stories and the episodes of our lives presented in short segments
2. Jesus' admonition for us is encapsulated in the word "continue"
3. Our relationship with Christ is more like a Mitchner novel than a short story
4. Continuing involves discipline, devotion, and commitment
5. If you continue with Christ, you are truly his disciple

Sermon Title: Invisible Chains

Sermon Angle: When Jesus told the Jews addressed in this story that if they continued in his word would be his disciples and be free, they rejected the notion that they were in bondage. They could not see the chains which bound them, chains of selfishness and sins. They responded: "We have never been in bondage to anyone" (v. 33). Jesus tried to make them see. "Everyone who commits sin is a slave to sin" (v. 34).

Outline:

1. Imagine the horror of being someone's slave!
2. It's even more awful to be a slave and not know it (alcoholics and drug addicts are examples)
3. Some of Jesus' followers were this type of slave — they couldn't see that they were in bondage to sin (v. 33)
4. Knowing the truth of our bondage can free us, if we turn to Christ in faith

Sermon Title: Ignorance Freezes Us But The Truth Frees Us

Sermon Angle: Back in my seminary days, one of the books that was required reading was titled *God's Frozen People*. So very often that is true. We see it in the gospel for today. "We are children of Abraham and have never been in bondage to anyone." They were freezing in tradition, deriving confidence from a nominal relationship with Father Abraham. The church, too, gets frozen in its approach to the world. It is safe to be frozen in ignorance but risky to be free in Christ. Only the truth of sin and grace through Christ can free us.

Outline:

1. Ignorance freezes us. People with mental problems are often frozen in mind and impervious to the truth
2. Jesus' followers are often frozen in spiritual ignorance (v. 33)
3. Christ, the truth, frees us from slavery to sin (vv. 34-36)

*　　*　　*　　*　　*

I read of a doll without a face that was marketed years ago. In place of the face, there was a mirror. Thus, when the doll's owner looks into the face of her doll, she beholds herself, her twin. Some claim that this can serve as an effective teaching device, but what lesson is going to come through? Isn't our world full of people who, in beholding other people, see only themselves? When we focus only on the law, we see only ourselves, our successes, and our failures. But, when our lives are centered on the gospel of grace (God's truth), we see only Christ reflected in others.

All Saints

Revised Common:	**Revelation 7:9-17**	**1 John 3:1-3**	**Matthew 5:1-12**
Roman Catholic:	**Revelation 7:2-4, 9-14**	**1 John 3:1-3**	**Matthew 5:1-12**
Episcopal:	**Sirach 44:1-10, 13-14**	**Revelation 7:2-4, 9-17**	**Matthew 5:1-12**

Theme: The saints of God, past, present, and future. The lessons from Revelation hold up the future hope and joys of the kingdom of God. This helps to sustain believers during their ordeal of suffering. The 1 John passage reminds us that love is the sign that we are children of God. The Gospel beatitudes paint a picture of what a saint is like and connects these with future blessings. The emphasis for this occasion has usually been the blessed dead, but we need to also hold up the concept that all baptized believers are his saints.

BRIEF COMMENTARY ON THE LESSONS

Lesson 1: Revelation 7:9-17 (C); Revelation 7:2-4, 9-14 (RC)

This is an interlude between the sixth and seventh seals. The saints are marked with the seal of God which affords protection from the plagues and coming judgment. During this period of great persecution under the Roman Emperor, Domitian, about 96 AD, John encourages the struggling church with a heavenly vision of light and glory. A great throng of believers are gathered around the throne of God for worship and praise. They are clothed in white and are waving palm branches, symbolizing righteousness and victory. The heavenly vision of the victorious Lamb of God and the host arrayed in white gives the persecuted church the courage to risk death by offering up their lives to God. God will comfort and sustain his own.

Lesson 2: 1 John 3:1-3 (C, RC)

God reveals his love for us by making us his children. The non-believing world does not recognize our status because it does not know the Lord. The future remains a mystery, but Christians know that they are God's children, who will be transformed into Christ's likeness at his return.

Lesson 2: Revelation 7:2-4, 9-17 (E)

See the first lesson for All Saints (C, RC).

Gospel: Matthew 5:1-12 (C, RC, E)

This text is also featured in Epiphany 4, where the emphasis was more on the present state of blessedness. For All Saints, the accent is on the blessedness of those who die in the Lord. The reward of the blessed dead is summarized in the first beatitude: "Blessed are the poor in spirit, for theirs is the kingdom of heaven" (v. 3). Furthermore, they will be comforted, they will inherit the earth, they will be filled, they will receive mercy, they will see God, and they will be called children of God. The future hope gives strength in the present moment to live joyous lives.

Psalm Of The Day

Psalm 34:1-10 (C) — "O fear the Lord, you his holy ones ..." (v. 9).

Psalm 24 (RC) — "Who shall ascend the hill of the Lord? And who shall stand in his holy place? Those who have clean hands and pure hearts ..." (vv. 3-4).

Psalm 149 (E) — "Let the faithful exalt in glory ..." (v. 5).

Prayer Of The Day

Holy God, we give you thanks for the blessed dead, whose lives have borne witness to your love and grace. As your living saints, give us strength to hold to our confession of the true faith, until you receive us into your kingdom of light and peace. In Jesus' name. Amen.

Suggested Hymn For All Saints

"For All The Saints Who From Their Labors Rest"

THEOLOGICAL REFLECTION ON THE LESSONS

Lesson 1: Revelation 7:2-4, 9-17

United Nations. In his heavenly vision, John sees people from every language, tribe, or nation composing the redeemed, who surround the throne of God (v. 9). John sees the nations united in the common worship of the Lord God. The League Of Nations, which eventually evolved into the United Nations, has attempted to bring the peoples of the earth together in the pursuit of peace and justice. This is something of a secularized version of the kingdom of God here on earth, where every nation has a voice. The United Nations organization may help contain some hostilities, but the nations will never truly be united until we bow down in worship to the same Lord and God.

Tribulation. As the vision unfolds before John, he sees the host clothed in white and is asked to identify them. He throws the question back to the heavenly speaker, who responds: "These are they who have come out of the great ordeal" (v. 14). In older versions, the word translated "ordeal" is "tribulation." John penned his book in an era of intense persecution, toward the end of the first century AD. Persecution and suffering for the faith was normative and expected. The reward of eternal life is offered to those who endure in their confession of Christ. The faithful have always had to endure periods of persecution by a hostile world, something which modern Americans have lost sight of. As the forces of secularism increase their onslaught on Christian values, a period of intense persecution for Christians is predictable.

Lesson 2: 1 John 3:1-3

Seeing God real (v. 2). None of us sees God as he really is. As Paul said in 1 Corinthians 13, "Now we see through a dark glass...." John speaks of the kingdom of heaven as the time when we will begin to see God as he really is, unobscured by human limitations.

Family resemblance. People seem to take delight in discerning family resemblance. "Oh, you look just like your father." John exalts in our status as children of God and concludes that when the kingdom comes in glory, we will look like God because we will see him as he really is (v. 2).

Gospel: Matthew 5:1-12

Blessed. The word *makarios*, translated "blessed" is used often in the New Testament. Jesus never tires in lifting up the joy that comes to God's children, frequently attributing spiritual blessedness to those with earthly limitations, weaknesses, and sorrows, as in this familiar passage. He contrasts God's attitude with that of the world. Frequently, they are at opposite poles. Those whom Jesus claims as the blessed are cursed in the eyes of the world and vice versa.

Spirit of poverty (v. 3). In Luke's beatitudes Jesus states simply, "Blessed are the poor." Some suggest that Matthew has spiritualized Jesus' message to make it more palatable to the wealthy. I don't think so. A person of little means can let material things occupy the prime spot in his life. A person of many possessions can relegate these things to a subsidiary role in his life. Such a person does not use wealth to assess his own worth or that of others.

Meek, not weak. The word "meek" has often been understood to mean weak. Actually, the concept signifies controlled and disciplined strength. Brute strength is common in our world. Truly, this is not strength but force. When someone hits or hurts you, and you have the power to strike back, but refrain from doing so, this is real meekness.

Full is not the same as satisfied. In the NRSV, fullness is the blessed state of those who hunger and thirst for righteousness (v. 6). The older RSV employs the word "satisfied." The old translation is superior. One can be full and yet not be satisfied. There are countless examples of those whose lives are filled with pleasure and all the good things of life, and yet, they are not satisfied. They have an emptiness within. Those to whom Jesus refers in this beatitude are certainly not full, but they are already satisfied.

Blessedness in the present tense. In all of the beatitudes, the disciples are deemed blessed at the present time, even though their award awaits in the future kingdom. The exceptions are verses 3 and 10, where even the award is put into the present tense. For the believer, the future blessings have already commended. The kingdom has already come, though is not fully come.

PREACHING APPROACHES WITH ILLUSTRATIONS

Lesson 1: Revelation 7:2-4, 9-17

Sermon Title: From Little Band To Great Throng

Sermon Angle: In John's vision, he sees a vast heavenly throng bowing in worship to the Lord, around his heavenly throne. Jesus had gathered just a little band of believers. By the time of the persecutions at the end of the first century, the church had established a beachhead in the region of the Mediterranean, but the numbers were not huge. This was a vision of hope which told him that the kingdom would thrive and grow in spite of the onslaughts of Caesar and Satan. The little flock or band would grow into an innumerable throng.

Sermon Title: Role Reversal

Sermon Angle: The Lamb at the center of the throne becomes the shepherd (v. 17). The victim becomes the victor. A kind of role reversal. In the gospel, we also see role reversal. Those cursed by the standards of this world become those blessed by God. Those who are victimized because of their allegiance to Christ become the victors. They inherit the kingdom. The tables are turned; the roles reversed.

Outline:
1. Role reversal — the Lamb becomes the shepherd
2. Role reversal — the poor in spirit inherit the kingdom and so forth

Lesson 2: 1 John 3:1-3

Sermon Title: What Do You Know?

Sermon Angle: My dad would often use this phrase as a greeting. I wonder what he would have done if someone had really attempted to tell him what they knew? This is a question we should not throw out flippantly, but what do you know? What do you know about who you are? What do you know of God and his ways? One thing we know for sure: In Christ we are God's children, who are dearly loved.

Outline:
1. What do we know for sure?
2. We know we are God's beloved children (v. 1)
3. We know Christ will return (v. 2: "When he is revealed ...")
4. We know that we will be recreated in his image (v. 2)

Gospel: Matthew 5:1-12

Sermon Title: Becoming Saints

Sermon Angle: Sainthood is both a divine act and a process of becoming. In baptism, God declares that we are his holy ones, his saints. This is an accomplished fact by the action of God. However, sainthood is also a process of becoming. Theologians refer to it as sanctification. They are those who hunger and thirst for righteousness. If they had a lock on righteousness and goodness, they wouldn't hunger and thirst for it. A saint is one who is humble enough to plead: "Please be patient with me; God isn't through with me yet."

Outline:
1. Saints are not perfect, just holy
2. Luther stressed that we are saint and sinner at the same time
3. In baptism, we are made God's saints
4. As we grow in grace, we come to realize that identity
5. Sainthood is a process of becoming

* * * * *

I grew up in a largely Roman Catholic neighborhood in south Omaha and was secretly envious of my friends in Catholic school. It's not that I felt that the education they were receiving was superior to mine. That wasn't even an issue. But the Catholics had a host of saints, whom they would honor on the anniversary of the saint's death by dismissing school. They were out free and having fun when I was locked away in a classroom. It just wasn't fair! Of course, at that time, I didn't know a saint from a Saint Bernard, but I knew they had to be quite powerful and wonderful if they could free kids from school.

* * * * *

George Gallup and Timothy Jones wrote a book titled *Uncovering America's Hidden Saints.* From surveys, they discovered a subgroup of Christians whom they defined as deeply religious. They dubbed these the hidden saints. The most outstanding quality these saints possessed was *a personal relationship* with the Lord. They didn't just know *about* the Lord, they *knew the Lord* through their own experience. These people revealed that they have had times of powerful spiritual awakening or insight, which profoundly influenced their lives and service.

Jesus preached that those who know and love God are the blessed ones, the happy ones. This is contrary to the popular image of deeply religious people as lemon-sucking killjoys. The survey referred to above revealed that 93% of the deeply committed were very happy and contented with their lives. Like the song says, "I've got a joy, joy ... down in my heart ... I've got the love of Jesus ... I've got the peace that passes understanding down in my heart." We have this in spite of sorrow, pain, and adversity, because the joy of the believer is not based on having things go her way but on the unshakable conviction that God is with us in all the chances and changes of life. That's why Jesus could make the paradoxical statement: *"Blessed are the poor in spirit ... Blessed are those who mourn ... Blessed are the meek ... Blessed are those persecuted for righteousness' sake ..."* Do you get it? Our joy is in the Lord!

Proper 26/Pentecost 24/Ordinary Time 31

Revised Common:	Joshua 3:7-17	1 Thessalonians 2:9-13	**Matthew 23:1-12**
Roman Catholic:	Malachi 1:14—2:2, 8-10	1 Thessalonians 2:7-9, 13	**Matthew 23:1-12**
Episcopal:	Micah 3:5-12	1 Thessalonians 2:9-13, 17-20	**Matthew 23:1-12**

Theme: Warning against religious hypocrisy. The conflict continues between Jesus and the religious leaders (Matthew 23:1-12).

BRIEF COMMENTARY ON THE LESSONS

Lesson 1: Joshua 3:7-17 (C)

The Hebrews are ready to cross the Jordan to take possession of the new land, under the leadership of Joshua. God commands the priests to take the Ark of the Covenant and walk into the river. When they do so, the waters heap up so that the people can cross over on dry land. This is a repeat of the crossing of the Red Sea under Moses at the start of their journey, and it serves as a sign of God's deliverance.

Lesson 1: Malachi 1:14—2:2, 8-10 (RC)

The prophet condemns the priests because they have turned aside from the way of the Lord, leading the people astray. The passage ends on a very thoughtful note: "Have we not all one father? Has not one God created us? Why then are we faithless to one another, profaning the covenant of our ancestors?" (v. 10).

Lesson 1: Micah 3:5-12 (E)

The prophet lashes out against the leaders of the people and the prophets who are ravishing the people. Micah foresees the coming of a time of great darkness and gloom.

Lesson 2: 1 Thessalonians 2:9-13 (C); 1 Thessalonians 2:7-9, 13 (RC); 1 Thessalonians 2:9-13, 17-20 (E)

Paul lifts up his example and that of his companions, while they were with the Thessalonians. They worked night and day so that they might not be a financial burden on anyone. Their conduct is likened to that of a loving mother with her children (v. 7) and an encouraging father (v. 11). He urges them to follow their lead in living a life worthy of the gospel.

Gospel: Matthew 23:1-12 (C, RC, E)

Jesus warns that the essential ethical teachings of the scribes and Pharisees should be followed, but the example of these leaders should be avoided. The crowds should do as they say but not as they do. Jesus condemns them for making religion a burden, hedged in with endless rules. The leaders are accused of practicing their piety so that they might be seen and praised by others. These are not acts of worship but ostentation and show. They should not seek to be addressed as rabbi because all are learners, nor father, because there is just one Father of us all. The truth of the Beatitudes is reaffirmed: the humble will be exalted and the exalted will be humbled.

Psalm 107:1-7, 33-37 (C) — "O give thanks to the Lord ..." (v. 1).

Psalm 13 (RC) — "I will sing to the Lord for he has dealt bountifully with me" (v. 6).

Psalm 43 (E) — "Hope in God, for I shall again praise him ..." (v. 5).

Prayer Of The Day

O God of grace, through the gospel, free us from all pretense and show. Because we are loved, grant us courage to strip away all hypocrisy, that we might worship you with a pure and open heart. In Jesus' name we are bold to pray. Amen.

THEOLOGICAL REFLECTION ON THE LESSONS

Lesson 1: Joshua 3:7-17

Change of command. Moses had died, and Joshua took over the task of bringing the people to the land of promise. Would the people follow? They were so used to Moses' style of leadership, and this young leader might not command their respect. To help Joshua in his new role, God shows forth his presence with his people by stopping the flow of the Jordan. This demonstrates that religious leadership isn't just a matter of personal leadership skills but, more importantly, the leader's faithfulness to the Lord. This didn't happen in a vacuum. Moses modeled leadership for Joshua and gave him on-the-job training. When Joshua stepped into the river he didn't get cold feet, nor did he get into water over his head. He had been equipped.

Lesson 1: Malachi 1:14—2:2, 8-10

Blessing and curse. Malachi relays a word from God to the priests. They must obey the word of God and "lay it to heart." Otherwise, God will turn their blessings into a curse (v. 2). So very often our blessings do become a curse when we divorce God from the thick of our lives. Material things are a blessing, but when they dominate us, they turn into a curse. Careers are a blessing, but when they lead us to neglect our families, they become a curse. To be born into a Christian heritage is a blessing, but when we fail to appropriate it to our personal lives, it becomes a curse.

Lesson 1: Micah 3:5-12

Night vision. Micah has a dark vision of what the future holds for the people of Jerusalem. The city will become uninhabited because her leaders have prostituted themselves to the god of mammon. Justice and religious services are bought and sold like a leg of lamb to the highest bidder. Therefore, the prophets will see no vision of the Lord but grope like blind men (v. 6). They have a form of religion but it is only that, a form with no substance. They think that no harm will come to them because the Lord is with them (v. 11b), but they will soon wake from their daydream only to find they are living a nightmare.

Lesson 2: 1 Thessalonians 2:7-13, 17-20

Nurturing Christians. Paul maintains that his party was gentle in sharing the gospel, like a nursing mother with her children. Christian nurture is not accomplished through exercise of force but through giving of oneself. A mother feeds her infants from her own body; she gives of herself and this helps establish a lasting bond. Paul was right on when he closely links the sharing of the gospel with the giving of ourselves. The gospel is always incarnational.

The gospel is free. The apostle reminds the church that he worked long hours so that he might not have to ask for money from them (v. 9). He didn't want them to think that they were paying for the gospel.

Worker-priests. Following World War II, the worker-priest movement started in France. These priests were committed to working out in the secular world, so that they might bring the gospel to people where they were. It was also the tradition for rabbis in the Jewish religion to gain their living while working with their hands. The dangers of earning one's living from religion are amply illustrated in the Old Testament lessons for today, except the first lesson for the Revised Common Lectionary. Such religious leaders are exposed to the danger of materialism and of telling people what they want to hear. I'm not suggesting that we can or should do away with religious professionals but we do need to recapture the concept of the priesthood of all believers. We are called to mediate God's presence in whatever we do.

Gospel: Matthew 23:1-12

Religion as burden. Jesus criticizes the scribes and Pharisees for laying heavy burdens on the shoulders of people, without helping them carry the load (v. 4). These are the burdens that Jesus has in mind when he entreats: "Come to me all who are weary and are carrying heavy burdens and I will give you rest" (Matthew 11:28). The Master teaches that true religion frees us from burdens or, at least, makes them easier to carry. The Christ came not to impose more religious burdens but to help us carry our load.

Religion as performance. Jesus also criticizes the scribes and Pharisees for making a spectacle of their religion. They wear their religious symbols large (the phylacteries and fringes) so that all people might recognize their piety (v. 5). They seek the best seats at feasts and pray ostentatiously in the marketplace. Who is the audience? Other people. Instead, the performance of our lives should be directed toward God.

PREACHING APPROACHES WITH ILLUSTRATIONS

Lesson 1: Joshua 3:7-17

Sermon Title: Up-Front God

Sermon Angle: God went before his people as he led them to the promised land. The priests carried the Ark into the river and, as God promised, the flow stopped. The people followed on dry land. Do we still worship an up-front God who leads us into the unknown, or do we worship a God who confirms the road we've already taken?

Lesson 2: 1 Thessalonians 2:7-13, 17-20

Sermon Title: A Faith That Works

Sermon Angle: Paul recounts how hard he and his party worked among them to plant the gospel (v. 9). Theirs was a working faith. They were able to effect in the Thessalonians a faith that worked. How do we communicate such a faith? We find clues in this lesson.

Outline:
1. Through acts of self-giving (v. 8)
2. No obstacles must obstruct the gospel (v. 10)
3. Faith and life intersect (vv. 11-12)

*　*　*　*　*

The Baby Boomers' penchant for style, image, comfort, and success have been much discussed. The Baby Busters, those born between 1963-1977, appear to hold quite contrary values. According to an article in *Christianity Today*, Busters hold divergent values. They prize authentic relationships characterized by honesty and transparency. A young believer in the Washington DC area stated that they didn't want any "dog and pony show, no dancing girls gospel." What they want is unity, love, and acceptance. They desire more than honeyed words and glitzy packaging. They have been burned so often that they desire truthfulness over politeness. Though this generation is extremely hesitant to make commitments (the average age of first marriage has gone from 21 to 26 in the last four decades and continues to go up), they may be ready to commit to Christ if the churches' witness is authentic and sincere.

The Baby Busters don't give a care for a religion that is image and show; they demand a faith that works. (Thoughts gleaned from "Reaching The First Post-Christian Generation" by Andres Tapia, *Christianity Today*, September 1994)

Gospel: Matthew 23:1-12

Sermon Title: Religion — Burden Or Blessing?

Sermon Angle: Jesus accused the scribes and Pharisees of imposing an intolerable burden on the backs of people. The weight of all their prohibitions was staggering. They could not bear the load themselves, and yet they imposed it on others. Christ showed that true religion results in blessings when we put God first and love our neighbor as ourselves. He died on the cross to help lift the burden of sin and death. Religion of only law is a burden, but when the law is fulfilled in the gospel, it is a true blessing.

Outline:
1. The religion of the Pharisees was a great burden because of legalism
2. Jesus came to remove the burden of the law through the gospel
3. Is your religion a burden or a blessing?

Sermon Title: Closet Pharisees

Sermon Angle: The Pharisees in Jesus' day were very proud of their religious identity. Because of the teachings of Jesus, the religion of the Pharisees is now synonymous with sham, show, and hypocrisy. This is, of course, not totally accurate since many Pharisees really were trying to love God in their own way. In the church there are many closet Pharisees, who live not by the gospel but the law. Surveys indicate that about 30% of church members are of this disposition. A sermon contrasting the gospel with modern manifestations of the religion of the Pharisees might wake some people.

*　*　*　*　*

Jesus is not the only one critical of the Pharisees; so too is the Jewish Talmud, the body of authoritative Jewish teachings. Here are a few of the seven different types of Pharisees described in the Talmud.

1. The shoulder Pharisee. He wore his good deeds on his shoulder where they could be seen and admired by others.

2. The self-afflicting Pharisee. He wouldn't think of even looking at a woman in public. To avoid merely the appearance of evil he would keep his head down and eyes shut in crowded places. Consequently, he was always running into obstacles and bruising himself.

3. The humpback Pharisee. He made such an exaggerated attempt to display his humility that he looked like a humpback.

4. The wait-a-little Pharisee. This one sounds very contemporary. He always had some good excuse for postponing the doing of that which was good.

(Taken from *The Gospel Of Matthew*, vol. 2, by William Barclay)

Proper 27/Pentecost 25/Ordinary Time 32

Revised Common:	Joshua 24:1-3a, 14-25	1 Thessalonians 4:13-18	Matthew 25:1-13
Roman Catholic:	Wisdom 6:12-16	1 Thessalonians 4:13-18	Matthew 25:1-13
Episcopal:	Amos 5:18-24	1 Thessalonians 4:13-18	Matthew 25:1-13

Theme: Living in readiness and anticipation of the second coming of Christ.

BRIEF COMMENTARY ON THE LESSONS

Lesson 1: Joshua 24:1-3a, 14-25 (C)

Joshua is now an old man, and so he gathers the tribes of Israel together at Shechem to renew the covenant. In the first part of the passage, Joshua recounts the origin of the covenant which the Lord initiated with Abraham. The second portion of the passage calls for a response from the people. Idolatry is still a problem, because he calls on the people to cast off the foreign gods and serve only the Lord. The people promise to do so. Apparently, he isn't convinced of their sincerity for he tells them that they cannot serve the Lord, for he is a holy and jealous God (v. 19). The people reaffirm their commitment to be devoted only to the Lord of Israel.

Lesson 1: Wisdom 6:12-16 (RC)

True and false friendship.

Lesson 1: Amos 5:18-24 (E)

God despises the religious assemblies of the people because they have divorced them for righteousness and justice.

Lesson 2: 1 Thessalonians 4:13-18 (C, RC, E)

Concern arose in the Thessalonian church when the expected imminent *parousia* did not materialize as quickly as envisioned. Some of the believers were dying and there was concern for their salvation. Paul writes that those who have died will rise first when Christ returns and then those who are living. All believers will be caught up in the air to be with the Lord. Believers are to comfort one another with this hope.

Gospel: Matthew 25:1-13 (C, RC, E)

This is the parable of the ten virgins or ten bridesmaids. The ten bridesmaids were waiting for the groom to come with word that the wedding feast was now ready. Five were foolish (they had no oil for their lamps) and five were wise (they had flasks of oil). When the groom finally came, the foolish wanted the wise to share their oil with them but were refused, being told that there wouldn't be enough oil for all of them. By the time the foolish bridesmaids obtained oil and knocked on the door of the feast site, it was too late. They were denied entrance. The suddenness of the *parousia* is a key element, but this is primarily a parable of faith and hope. It teaches that faith cannot be parceled out at the last minute, and that we must continuously live in hopeful expectation of the inbreaking of Christ's kingdom.

Psalm Of The Day

Psalm 78:1-7 (C) — "Give ear, O my people, to my teaching" (v. 1).

Psalm 63:2-8 (RC) — "So I will bless you as long as I live ..." (v. 4).

Psalm 70 (E) — "Let all who seek you rejoice and be glad in you" (v. 4).

Prayer Of The Day

O Lord Jesus, shake us from our sleepwalking to spiritual wakefulness, that we might be prepared at all times to celebrate with you and all the saints the wedding feast which has no end. In your precious name. Amen.

THEOLOGICAL REFLECTION ON THE LESSONS

Lesson 1: Joshua 24:1-3a, 14-25

Therefore. In the first part of chapter 24, the redemptive acts of the Lord, from Abraham up to the entry into Canaan, are recited. This demonstrates God's prior love and grace in redemptive actions. On the basis of what the Lord had done, the people were called on to make a response. In verse 14, beginning with "Now therefore," Joshua suggests a proper response in terms of putting away their other gods and serving only the Lord.

Choose your god. In verses 14-15, Joshua gives some options for gods that the people could serve. The gods of the Egyptians, the gods of the Canaanites, or the God of Israel. He does not offer the option of choosing no god at all or of remaining neutral. That to which we give our ultimate allegiance is our god, who is revealed more through our actions than our confessions. And if we don't choose consciously, we select by default. Joshua was wise to this reality and so he urges his people to make a conscious decision to serve the Lord, in response to God's redemptive acts.

Choose this day (v. 15). This matter of choosing one's god has an aura of urgency surrounding it. Today is all we have. Tomorrow is only a hope. We are called to choose while we still have the freedom to do so. There is another aspect here. It is not enough to choose the Lord just one day. This choice we must render every day we live.

Lesson 2: 1 Thessalonians 4:13-18

Day of the Lord. In Amos 5:18-24, the Day of the Lord is presented as a time of gloom and judgment, a scene more horrible than the worst science fiction flick. The day of Christ, the *parousia*, on the other hand is portrayed as a day of light and triumph, when believers will experience the glory of God. Which picture is the true one? It depends on your vantage point. If we are trusting in the efficacy of our religious acts, it will be a day of gloom. If, however, we are covered by Christ's righteousness, it will be a day of triumph and glory.

Good grief. The Thessalonians were concerned about those believers who died before the *parousia*. Paul assures that they need not grieve as those who have no hope. Good grief has to do with expressing our grief openly, and talking about the relationship we had before our loved one's death. However, the key factor that makes grief good is our hope in Christ.

God does not forget his own. In Isaiah 49, God promises that he will never forget his people, that he has formed them on the palm of his hand. One of the major fears that children have, when they first venture from the nest, is that their mom or dad will forget about them and they will be all alone. I remember a scene in which our youngest child was in tears. We were delayed in picking her up at school. The same concern is addressed here. Some believers were concerned that those who died in Christ before his return would lose out on eternal life or be forgotten. Paul assures that the dead will rise first and then the living. God does not forget his own.

Gospel: Matthew 25:1-13

Wise and foolish. That which distinguishes the wise from the foolish in this parable is preparedness. The wise were ready for the bridegroom and the marriage feast; the foolish were not ready.

Dead batteries. If Jesus were telling the parable today, he would probably replace lamps with flashlights. Have you ever noticed that whenever you really need a flashlight, the batteries are dead? The oil for the lamps is faith, and faith is something that takes constant recharging.

Faith is nontransferable. The wise bridesmaids wouldn't share with the foolish bridesmaids. It seems so selfish. As was previously stated, the oil is faith, and while faith can be shared with others, it cannot be transferred from one person to another. Our faith must be our own. The faith of our mother, father, or Sunday school teacher won't save us unless it is incorporated into our own.

PREACHING APPROACHES WITH ILLUSTRATIONS

Lesson 1: Joshua 24:1-3a, 14-25

Sermon Title: Serve With Sincerity

Sermon Angle: Joshua urges the Hebrews to serve the Lord in sincerity and faithfulness (v. 14). Most of them gave lip service to our Lord but supplemented their religious capital by investing part of themselves in other gods. Divided loyalties made their pledge of allegiance insincere. A religion of sincerity is not enough; millions are sincerely wrong, but authentic faith is not possible without sincerity of conviction. Sincerity cannot be measured by the tone of voice but through a comparison of actions with convictions. There is little doubt that the Lord values a sincere atheist over a pious fraud.

Sermon Title: Our Holy Jealous God

Sermon Angle: Joshua made it very clear that Yahweh would brook no competition, describing him as a holy and jealous God (v. 19). In modern parlance, the word "jealous" has very negative connotations. We think of a jealous person as being insecure. Theologically speaking, when jealousy is used to describe God, it indicates that he has no peers, that his holiness demands utter faithfulness from his covenant people. Here, jealousy is not a sign of weakness, but strength. This is not a popular concept in our syncretistic world, where God is only one of the options.

Lesson 2: 1 Thessalonians 4:13-18

Sermon Title: Ignorant Of The Lord's Coming

Sermon Angle: Paul starts this lection by saying that he would not have them ignorant of those who have fallen asleep (died). The concern was that the dead would miss out on Christ's kingdom. The apostle gives some detail concerning the events of Christ's second coming. The dead would rise first and then the living would be caught up in the air to be with the Lord. There is a good deal of ignorance concerning the *parousia*. Some try to describe the events before and after the *parousia* in extraordinary detail. That's one kind of ignorance. Other Christians have little or no knowledge of the second coming and live only for the present moment. That's another kind of ignorance. We would be wise to continue to hold up our hope in Christ, without saying more than scripture warrants.

Outline:
1. The early church lived in eager anticipation of the Lord's coming again
2. There are misunderstandings about it (explain)
3. Are you ignorant of the Lord's coming?
4. Let us live as those who eagerly await Christ's return

Sermon Title: Good Grief

Sermon Angle: Grief is integral to human existence, but the grief of a believer is markedly different than that of an unbeliever. A valuable sermon on the subject could, first of all, discuss the universal aspects of human grief and how to healthfully deal with loss. This would be followed by a proclamation of how Christ's death and resurrection transforms the way in which we view death. Hope is the key difference.

Outline:
1. Paul confronts the problem of death and grief — a universal dilemma
2. How do we deal with death from a human perspective? (Kubler-Ross' stages of grief might be referenced)
3. How death is viewed differently by Christians — we have hope because of Christ's death and resurrection

* * * * *

Victor Frankl ends his pioneering book on logotherapy, *Man's Search For Meaning*, with a warning for humankind. He says that we must be alert in a twofold sense. Since Auschwitz, we know what man is capable of, and, since Hiroshima, we realize what is at stake. Frankl, who experienced the horrors of human depravity, places his hope for an improved humankind in our valiant effort to try harder. Yet, if life is a parentheses between actualized moral breakdown and potential annihilation, where is the motivation, the power to attain moral excellence? To live fully in the present, we need a great hope. We need something or someone positive to live for. For Christians, the kingdom of God, the hope of heaven, the return of Christ, has provided a burning hope. The content of these symbols may differ, the images will vary but we cannot live without this hope. Paul was wrong about how that hope was to be fulfilled (in his lifetime) but we believe that his underlying conviction continues to be true. That's why Paul's admonition is as valid today as it was then. We should not grieve as those who are without hope. For we have experienced the crucified yet resurrected Christ in our lives. If God raised Jesus, will he not also raise those who belong to Jesus?

Gospel: Matthew 25:1-13

Sermon Title: The Wise And The Otherwise

Sermon Angle: The difference between the wise and the foolish (otherwise) bridesmaids was the level of their preparedness. They were ready, at a moment's notice, to march to the wedding feast. They weren't going to miss out on what was of great importance to them. The foolish bridesmaid's lack of oil demonstrates an uncaring attitude toward the marriage feast

374

(the kingdom of God). They were foolish because they were concerned only with the present moment. What can be done to increase the number of the wise and reduce the number of the otherwise in your congregation?

Sermon Title: Are You Ready To Party?

Sermon Angle: A wedding feast was and is one of life's most joyous occasions. In Israel, the wedding was a solid week of joyous celebration, a party par excellence, in which the bride and groom were queen and king. Jesus compares the kingdom of God to a wedding celebration. Are we ready to party? Are we ready for Jesus' party, the wedding feast which has no end?

Outline:
1. Are you ready to party?
2. Not the wild revelry of the spiritually dead
3. The celebration of the kingdom — the wedding feast of Christ and the church
4. Those who keep the lamp of faith will be ready for the kingdom's party

Proper 28/Pentecost 26/Ordinary Time 33

Revised Common:	Judges 4:1-7	1 Thessalonians 5:1-11	Matthew 25:14-30
Roman Catholic:	Proverbs 31:10-13, 19-20, 30-31	1 Thessalonians 5:1-6	Matthew 25:14-30
Episcopal:	Zephaniah 1:7, 12-18	1 Thessalonians 5:1-10	Matthew 25:14-15, 19-29

Theme: Being ready for Christ's kingdom. To be prepared, a person need only walk in the light of God's love and invest her/his talents.

BRIEF COMMENTARY ON THE LESSONS

Lesson 1: Judges 4:1-7 (C)

The Israelites were oppressed by the Canaanites. The Hebrews cried out to God, who sent Deborah as prophetess and judge. Deborah sent Barak and a horde of Hebrews against the Canaanite king, Jabin, and his general, Sisera. The Hebrews triumphed over the technologically superior enemy army.

Lesson 1: Proverbs 31:10-13, 19-20, 30-31 (RC)

The ideal wife, faithful to her husband, industrious, wise, and compassionate.

Lesson 1: Zephaniah 1:7, 12-18 (E)

Zephaniah prophesied prior to Josiah's reforms in 621 BC. He predicts the Day of the Lord, a day of judgment for the sins of people.

Lesson 2: 1 Thessalonians 5:1-11 (C); 1 Thessalonians 5:1-6 (RC); 1 Thessalonians 5:1-10 (E)

The images of light/darkness and waking/sleeping are used extensively here. Believers should not be caught off guard, since they are children of the light and of the day. The *parousia* will come suddenly, like birth pangs, and unexpectedly, as a thief in the night. Soberness and vigilance are the order of the day, so that we are not caught off guard by the powers of evil as we await the coming of the kingdom. Our destiny is not damnation but salvation in Christ.

Gospel: Matthew 25:14-30 (C, RC); Matthew 25:14-15, 19-29 (E)

The parable of the talents. Before going away, a man calls his servants and entrusts his money to them. One servant gets five talents, one servant gets two talents, and the other receives just one talent. The money is parceled out according to the ability of the recipient. When the master returns and calls his servants to make an accounting for his money, the first two servants present their master with double his money. He profusely commends them. They have wisely invested the little he gave them; he sets them in authority over a great deal. The first two servants are bold and venturesome. They are willing to take on greater risk for greater gain. The third fellow is a timid sort. He was afraid to take a risk and so he buried the talent, believing his master to be a hard man (vv. 24-25). The master gives this timid fellow a severe dressing down. This sends spiritual shock waves over us because we identify more with him than we do with the ten-talent wizard. "If you thought I was this sort of man, you should have taken the money and, at least, invested it with the bankers," the master chides (v. 27). The master orders that the talent be taken away from this "worthless" servant and given to the servant who had the ten talents. This poor steward is to be tossed into the outer darkness. Through the blazing and uncomfortable light of this parable, we see the truth about the standard by which we will be judged. It will not be so much a question of what we've gained or lost but what we've ventured for the sake of the master. The timid servant is condemned because his misjudging of his master caused him to bury his talent, rather than invest it. The truth is that the person who ventures with his master's talents will always reap a return.

Psalm Of The Day
Psalm 123 (C) — "To you I lift up my eyes ..." (v. 1).
Psalm 128:1-5 (RC) — "Happy is everyone who fears the Lord ..." (v. 1).
Psalm 90 (E) — "Lord, you have been our dwelling place in all generations" (v. 1).

Prayer Of The Day
Lord Christ, you have shown us that the road to discipleship is never easy or safe. Your commitment to the Father led to a cross. Give us the boldness to fully invest ourselves and our abilities in the cause of your kingdom, for the sake of Jesus. Amen.

THEOLOGICAL REFLECTION ON THE LESSONS

Lesson 1: Judges 4:1-7
God hears the oppressed. When the Hebrews cried out to God because of their oppressors, God answered and sent a deliverer, Deborah the judge, to spearhead their deliverance. The Canaanites possessed superior technology in war, 900 iron chariots, but God gave the victory to a citizen army organized by a woman.

Lesson 1: Proverbs 31:10-13, 19-20, 30-31
A working wife. This is a picture of the proverbial wife. She is faithful to her family, hard working, involved in business and in the marketplace, yet compassionate to the poor. Working wives are nothing new; they are women trying to juggle family responsibilities and worldly involvements. Such women carry a tremendous burden and richly deserve the praise of their husbands and their children.

Lesson 1: Zephaniah 1:7, 12-18
God the impotent. The hearts of the people had grown complacent in their worldly pursuits. Their notion was that God was impotent, not able to reward or punish. "The Lord will not do good, nor will he do harm" (v. 12). For many modern believers, God the omnipotent has been replaced by God the impotent. These folks want to marginalize God so that he might not interfere with their selfish pursuits.

Lesson 2: 1 Thessalonians 5:1-11
Knowing the times and seasons. Paul addressed the Thessalonian church concerning the second coming of Christ as if they should have known these things. Actually, nobody knows God's timetable. Paul didn't. All he said was the kingdom would come at a time that people

didn't expect, without warning. Since Christ could come at any time and season, a person needed to always be prepared.

Children of the light and of the day (v. 5). Since Christians are children of light, we should not be caught off guard. We can discern that which is good from that which is evil.

Asleep to Jesus or asleep in Jesus? Sleep is used in three different senses in this passage. In verse 6, sleep is used in the spiritual sense of not being tuned into God and the Lord's ways. In verse 7, sleep is used in the ordinary sense. In verse 10, sleep is employed as a metaphor for death. It is a bad thing to be spiritually asleep because we will not be prepared for Christ's visitation. However, it is good to sleep in Jesus, to die in Christ, because God will awaken us to the blazing light of his new day.

Future hope. Faith, love, and hope are spoken of as defenses against the penetrating projectiles let loose by sin, death, and the devil (v. 8). Faith and love are present realities, but hope is projected into the future. Hope protects us by enabling us to view reality from the future to the present rather than the present to the future. Hope is glimpsing reality from God's viewpoint, and for God, the future is already present. Without future hope, present reality is of little value.

Gospel: Matthew 25:14-30

Each according to his ability (v. 16). The three servants were each given a different number of talents. When the time came for an accounting, they were not judged on an absolute scale but in accordance to what they had been allotted. The important factor is not what we have or what we have gained but what we've done in relation to what we have been given.

Action orientation. The servant who received the five talents went "at once" and traded his talents (v. 16). He wasn't afraid of risk or failure. The two-talent servant was of the same bent. The one-talent servant buried his talent thinking that maybe later he would discover some business in which he could invest his master's money. Of course, he never found any venture free of risk, so he never acted.

Is the master extravagant or stingy? The first two servants perceived the master far differently than the one-talent servant. They saw him as a person who would appreciate bold and daring action. He liked to give a great deal of freedom to his servants and he expected them to be self-starters, to take initiative. Should they give it their best shot and yet fail, he would be fair and understanding, for some of his own ventures garnered no profit either. The one-talent fellow viewed the master as hard and calloused. Should he lose the talent, the master would be unmerciful, because he is a stingy and exacting man. The image that we have of God or others guides our behavior. Sometimes, as in the case of this servant, our perceptions are distorted, which leads to self-defeating behavior.

Was the one-talent servant right about his master? This man believed his master to be a hardhearted man and after hearing what happened to him, a person wonders if he wasn't correct in his assessment. The master seems overly severe. This poor sap of a servant was no wiz, but at least he returned his master's talent. Why should it be taken from him and given to the servant who already had ten talents? Then, to be judged worthless and thrown out into the outer darkness where people weep and gnash their teeth, an image of hell (v. 30), seems totally unfair. Is the master a hard man? For the first two servants, he certainly wasn't a hard man. He was generous, to the point of extravagance. He was hard on the guy who buried his talent. He requires that his servants invest the talents with which he has endowed them.

The rich get richer. "For to all who have will more be given ..." (v. 29). It is a well established fact that the rich get richer, and the poor seem to be getting poorer. Richness and poorness are often a legacy, passed on from one generation to another. But how do some people get rich to start with? They know how to invest. Jesus is suggesting here that those who have spiritual riches are those who have freely invested the talents that they have been given in the service of the master. The more they invest, the more they receive. The spiritually poor, on the other hand, keep getting poorer because they are too selfish or fearful to fully invest. The spiritual rich keep getting richer, and the spiritually impoverished keep getting poorer.

PREACHING APPROACHES WITH ILLUSTRATIONS

Lesson 1: Judges 4:1-7

Sermon Title: A Liberating Woman

Sermon Angle: In this text we see a picture of a strong woman in a key leadership position. The Bible does present roles for women other than that of wife and mother. She was a liberated woman and a liberating woman. God used her to inspire the Hebrew force to victory over the Canaanite oppressors. Many women may need liberation, but personal liberation isn't enough. God calls us to be liberating women and men. No woman is truly free unless she is a liberator. The same applies to men. We can only find personal freedom when we take the risk of freeing others.

Lesson 1: Proverbs 31:10-13, 19-20, 30-31

Sermon Title: A Portrait Of The Perfect Wife

Sermon Angle: This chapter contains one man's view of the perfect wife. It's not a pretty picture if you're looking for glamour and beauty. No sex object here. She's too busy caring for her family, making and selling clothes, and buying and caring for her vineyard to consider her appearance. To do all that is suggested in this passage would require a wonder-woman. I'm not suggesting that you should put forth this ideal of the perfect wife for today's stressed-out women. There is, of course, no such thing as a perfect wife or husband, but this passage could provide a context for getting in touch with our ideals of the perfect wife and society's, so they can be held up to the light of reason and revealed truth.

Lesson 2: 1 Thessalonians 5:1-11

Sermon Title: No Rude Awakening

Sermon Angle: The day of the Lord should not surprise the spiritually alert Christian (v. 4). It should be no rude awakening, for we are not children of the night but of the day. In Christ, a new day has dawned. We are now children of light, fully awake to the presence of Christ. We should not meet the fate of the one-talent servant in the gospel, rudely surprised by his master's severe reaction to his stewardship.

Outline:
1. Relate an occasion of rude awakening
2. The Bible warns that many are asleep to the presence of God (v. 6)
3. Christ's coming will prove a rude awakening to them but not to those who are alert to the presence of Christ (v. 4).

Sermon Title: The Omega Point

Sermon Angle: In the Revelation of Saint John, Christ refers to himself as the Alpha and the Omega, the beginning and the end. The passage deals with the Omega point, that occasion when time yields to eternity, and worldly existence, as we know it, comes to an end. In hope, we see reality from the Omega point, the second coming of Christ. Everything comes together at this point.

Outline:
1. To try to understand who we are, we go back to our beginnings
2. To truly comprehend life is to know its ending
3. Christianity helps us see the meaning of life in the Omega point, Christ's second coming
4. At the Omega point, time yields to eternity

*   *   *   *   *

Frank Tipler, a distinguished physicist, has written an interesting and controversial book titled, *The Physics Of Immortality.* Tipler predicts that intelligent life will fill the universe, growing to infinite intelligence and knowledge by the time of the Omega point, when time curves into eternity, trillions of years from now. The scientist equates the Omega point with God. Tipler postulates that intelligence will be so high that it will recreate all former forms of life and we will live together in a type of heaven.

Christianity does not view its Omega point from the perspective that man will become God, through attaining infinite knowledge, but that God has already become man in Jesus, who died, rose from the dead, and ascended into heaven. The time when Jesus returns, as he promised, is our Omega point, the end point where past and future merge into the eternal present.

Gospel: Matthew 25:14-30
Sermon Title: Reverse Capital Gains Tax

Sermon Angle: When a person sells an asset for more than he paid for it, he has to pay a very substantial capital gains tax. The rules for investing ourselves in the kingdom of God are radically different. The person who makes a clear gain on that which the Lord gives him or her, pays no tax but is given a reward. On the opposite side of the coin, the person who makes no gain on that which is entrusted to him will be harshly penalized.

Sermon Title: Christ The Gambler

Sermon Angle: The master in the parable is Christ, and we are those to whom he has entrusted his substance. We are richly endowed with that which is his. What a chance he is taking! Quite a gamble! That seems to be Christ's way. In his earthly journey, he invested his love in those whose lives were out of control, such as prostitutes and tax collectors. He scattered the seed of the gospel wildly, letting it fall where it may and take root where it was able. The cross was the biggest gamble of all, as the devil whispered in his ear: "They aren't worth it." Some of those wagers paid off; others did not. But those who are his own have caught the gambling fever, and they know the excitement and joy of wagering their life for the redemption of the world.

Sermon Title: Use It Or Lose It

Sermon Angle: Talents are like muscles, if you don't use them, you lose them. The servants given five and two talents, respectively, used their talents and received again as much for their efforts. The one-talent servant refused to use his and lost not only his talent but his life.

Christ The King/Proper 29

Revised Common:	Ezekiel 34:11-16, 20-24	Ephesians 1:15-23	Matthew 25:31-46
Roman Catholic:	Ezekiel 34:11-12, 15-17	1 Corinthians 15:20-26, 28	Matthew 25:31-46
Episcopal:	Ezekiel 34:11-17	1 Corinthians 15:20-28	Matthew 25:31-46

Theme: Christ our king. In the Ezekiel lesson, God is the loving shepherd-king of Israel, gathering the lost, comforting the injured. In the 1 Corinthians text, Christ triumphs over his enemies, especially the power of death. In the gospel, Christ judges and separates those who are his sheep from those who are not. The key determinant consists of attitudes and actions toward the weak and needy ones.

BRIEF COMMENTARY ON THE LESSONS

Lesson 1: Ezekiel 34:11-16, 20-24 (C); Ezekiel 34:11-12, 15-17 (RC); Ezekiel 34:11-17 (E)

The people of Israel were destroyed. The nation was no more — the holy city was defiled and decimated and the sacred temple was ravished. All hope had vanished. In this environment, Ezekiel spoke words of hope to God's captive people in Babylon. The image employed was that of the shepherd. God himself would shepherd the lost sheep of Israel and bring them back to their own land. God would again find them, feed them, and heal their wounds. The Lord would set over them a shepherd-king, descended from David. *Yahweh* was still their loving king, the source of their hope.

Lesson 2: Ephesians 1:15-23 (C)

God has put all things in subjection to Christ, who rules over all things in heaven and on earth and serves as head over the Church, his body.

Lesson 2: 1 Corinthians 15:20-26, 28 (RC); 1 Corinthians 15:20-28 (E)

Chapter 15 of 1 Corinthians establishes the centrality of Christ's resurrection for the Christian faith to counter those who would deny it. Christ has defeated the powers of sin and death and now reigns as the king of eternal life, the first of those to be raised to life. The resurrection is asserted as a fact to be received by faith (v. 20). The first man, Adam, brought death into the world through sin but the first born from the death, Jesus Christ, offers life to all who have faith. When Christ is totally victorious over the legions of sin and death, then he will deliver the kingdom over to God the Father.

Gospel: Matthew 25:31-46 (C, RC, E)

The parable of the sheep and the goats points to the glory of the future kingdom of God, when the Son of Man will separate the sheep from the goats. The shepherd-king gathers his sheep and culls out those who are not: the sheep on the right hand, the goats to his left. The basis for determining who falls into each group has nothing to do with appearance. They are judged on the basis of their attitudes and actions toward the needy, the poor, and the powerless. In serving these little ones, they minister to Christ. Judgment is based not only on the evil that we do, but the good that we could have done, but didn't. Some interpreters would understand "the least of these my brothers" (v. 40) as Jesus' disciples. Many others would opt for a more universal identification of "the least" with all sufferers.

Psalm Of The Day
   Psalm 100 (C) — "Know that the Lord is God" (v. 3a).
   Psalm 23 (RC) — "The Lord is my shepherd" (v. 1).
   Psalm 95:1-7a (E) — "For the Lord is a great God, and a great king above all gods" (v. 3).

Prayer Of The Day
   O Lord God, many lords and powers contend for our ultimate allegiance, but you alone are king of our conscience and Lord of our lives. Hasten the day when every knee will bow and every tongue confess that Jesus Christ is Lord, to the glory of God. In his name we pray. Amen.

THEOLOGICAL REFLECTION ON THE LESSONS

Lesson 1: Ezekiel 34:11-17, 20-24
King of caring. Ezekiel holds up the image of God as a gentle and loving shepherd. He brings back the scattered and strayed to their homeland. God will bind up the wounds of the injured, strengthen the weak, feed the hungry, and stand guard over the strong and the well-fed. The shepherd-king chooses to serve his flock rather than be served by them.

The hound of heaven. The bloodhound searches out the prey for destruction but the hound of heaven, our Lord and shepherd, searches out his sheep in order to preserve them and care for them. God never gives up on his straying children, and neither should we.

Watching over the weak and the strong. It's easy to see why the weak need watching over, but verse 22 states that the Lord also watches over the fat and the strong. Can't the strong ones take care of themselves? Not really: they might be tempted to ravage the weak and vulnerable ones. The Lord watches over the mighty ones so that they employ their strength in the service of life, not death.

Lesson 2: Ephesians 1:15-23
Power in us (v. 19). The New Testament does not so much proclaim the power of God *over* us as the power of God *in* us. We plug into Christ's power through the church. Free-floating power is, at best, unavailable; at worst, destructive. God's power is channeled by the gospel through the community of believers.

Decapitated churches. Have you ever lost your head? Like a decapitated chicken, it's not a pretty sight. Many moderns have cut themselves loose from all authority and power. They are decapitated and jerk aimlessly about until their end. Decapitated churches and Christians are even more pathetic because they have cut themselves loose from Christ, the head of the body we call the church.

Lesson 2: 1 Corinthians 15:20-28
Christ the victor. The kingdom of Christ has many enemies. The cross and resurrection prove to be the fatal blow to the power of the *enemy*, Satan. At the end, this victory will be complete. Without the protection of our victorious king, we are easy prey for the forces of evil.

Gospel: Matthew 25:31-46

The final roundup. Back in the days when cattle roamed the range, owners would put their brands on the calves. When roundup time came about, the cattle owners would separate their own cattle from the herds into which they had dispersed. A similar image is observed in the first lesson from Ezekiel. God, the shepherd, promises to seek out and bring back those who have strayed.

Who are Christ's brothers and sisters? (v. 40). Who are those Christ identifies as the least, his brothers and sisters? Are they exclusively those named on the roster of his disciples or does Jesus identify himself with all downtrodden people everywhere? An argument can be made either way. However, if the brethren are only those called by his name, then we have something of a parochial, rather than a universal, deity whom we worship. We are then implying that God reserves his concern for less than 25% of the world's population. My reading of scripture says that Christ identifies with the weak and wounded, no matter what they call themselves.

Sheep and goats. It seems that Jesus has a bias toward sheep and against goats. Why? An argument could be made in favor of the superiority of the goat species. Goats are more independent than sheep, they can feed on a greater variety of food and are generally more hardy than sheep. While sheep are led, with the shepherd out front, goats must be driven from behind with a stick. Is it this pathological independent streak that makes the goats unacceptable in the community of heaven?

An affair of the heart. The righteous asked the king: When did they see him hungry, thirsty, and so forth? He replied, "Just as you did it to the least of these who are members of my family, you did it to me" (v. 40). The service of their king was not an affair of the head, but of the heart. They responded to the needs of those around them instinctively. It was not that compassion was a function of their genes, but they had been transformed from within by the love of God.

The danger of doing nothing. The verdict of guilty was pronounced by the king not on the basis of what they had done but, rather, on what they hadn't done. "As you did it not to one of the least, you did it not to me" (v. 45). Some of us think that we can preserve our innocence by retreating from action in the world. Not possible, according to the teaching of Jesus. To act and to err is more forgivable in God's eyes than to refrain from action.

PREACHING APPROACHES WITH ILLUSTRATIONS

A three-point sermon on the kingship of Christ, each point based on one of the lessons, could be framed as follows:

Outline:
1. Christ is the shepherd-king, caring for his fold (Ezekiel 34:11-16, 20-24) (Jesus appropriates this image to himself in John 10)
2. Christ is the king of the enemies of our soul (1 Corinthians 15:25-26)
3. Christ is the king of the keys of the kingdom (Matthew 25:31-46)

Lesson 1: Ezekiel 34:11-16, 20-24

Sermon Title: Rescue 911

Sermon Angle: Rescue 911 was a television show that consisted of true-life stories where various rescue units of police and fire departments throughout the nation focused their energies on saving lives. A shepherd often found himself in the rescue business. This lesson presents God as such a shepherd-rescuer, who goes to great lengths to find his sheep and bring them back into the fold. The shepherd of our souls takes the initiative in the rescue operation; he doesn't wait to be called (vv. 11-12). So, too, Christians are called to seek out the lost and the strayed.

Sermon Title: Our Compassionate Shepherd-King

Sermon Angle: Some rulers try to fleece their flocks rather than care for their needs. Our shepherd-king cares for his flock, seeking the lost, feeding the hungry, bandaging the wounds of the injured (v. 16). Jesus appropriates unto himself the role of shepherd-leadership in chapter 10 of the gospel of John. The same compassionate leadership must issue from those who lead in his name.

Outline:
1. Many rulers seek only personal power
   — they don't identify with those they seek to lead
   — they see those under them as objects rather than real people
2. God seeks to minister to those who belong to him
3. Jesus assumed the role of servant leadership, which the church must also incarnate

Lesson 2: Ephesians 1:15-23

Sermon Title: The Kingdom And The Power

Sermon Angle: The word "power" (*dunamis*) stands out in this text. God, the creator of all things, is the source of all power. That power could be employed in a cataclysm of destruction to blot out us sinners. Rather, God harnessed that power in Christ. "God put this power to work in Christ when he raised him from the dead ..." (v. 20). Christ is like the engine that channels God's power to convey us through life to heaven. This text further states that God has put all things under Christ for the benefit of the church. Christ is the head of the church, his body, through which comes the kingdom and the power (v. 22).

Outline:
1. Do we know and experience the power of God?
2. The power of God works through Christ (v. 20)
   — in his resurrection (v. 20)
   — in the church (v. 19)
   — not to subjugate but save
3. The church is the engine through which he accomplishes his will (v. 22)

Lesson 2: 1 Corinthians 15:20-28

Sermon Title: Christ The Conqueror

Sermon Angle: The crucifix suggests that the man hung thereon is a victim. The resurrection proclaims the unbelievable news that the victim has become the victor. Chapter 15 of 1 Corinthians brings to center stage *Christ the Conqueror*. He conquers his enemies, he conquers the powers of evil, and he conquers death, our last and greatest foe.

Outline:
1. The resurrection is the enthronement of the Christ (v. 20)
2. Christ conquers death (vv. 20-22)
3. Christ defeats and destroys the demonic powers (v. 24)
4. Christ subjects all enemies under his feet (vv. 25-27)

Sermon Title: The Kingdom Has Come

Sermon Angle: From the onset of the church, there has always been a great deal of speculation concerning end things and the coming of the kingdom. Premillennialists teach that Christ will come, receive his own into heaven, and then reign for 1,000 years here on earth, until he has subjected all of his enemies. However, such an interpretation does violence to this text. We need to counter this notion with the assertion that the kingdom is come with the resurrection of Christ and the advent of the church. When Christ returns (the *parousia*) the kingdom will be fully come. The battle of Christ and the forces of the adversary will continue until the second coming. Are we fighting on the Lord's side so as to hasten the fulfillment of the kingdom?

Gospel: Matthew 25:31-46

Sermon Title: Estate Planning

Sermon Angle: To leave a legacy to those people and causes we cherish requires some estate planning. This parable states that God engaged in estate planning from the foundation of the world. He set out in his will those who were to inherit the kingdom (v. 34). These blessed ones embody the traits incarnated in the shepherd-king of the first lesson — compassion and mercy for the weak and the lost — thus demonstrating that they are his true children.

Outline:
1. God has bequeathed the kingdom to his children
2. Who are God's children?
   — the least and the lost
   — those who forget themselves in the service of others

Sermon Title: Rex Reckoning

Sermon Angle: No, Rex is not a German shepherd but the Latin word for king. This parable paints a vivid picture of the time when our king will call us to his reckoning, when he will separate unto himself those who are his own. Those judged worthy of the kingdom consist of the ones who reflect the compassion of their king.

Sermon Title: Is The King Dead?

Sermon Angle: Years ago, I read a book titled *The King Is Dead.* The point made therein has it that the day of authoritarian structures is dead for both the world and the church. A large measure of truth adheres to this statement, yet, how can we, as Christians, agree to this adage? The central message of Jesus holds that the kingdom is at hand. The church operates not as a democracy but as a kingdom where Christ reigns. There can be no kingdom without a king.

Outline:
1. Americans pride themselves for throwing off the shackles of monarchy
2. Society remains adrift without adequate structures
3. The church is the kingdom of Christ
4. Christ will come in glory to receive those who have served him as king

* * * * *

America does not stand alone as a society cut loose from authority structures. Since the death of communism, the eastern block has experienced a painful vacuum of authority and power. Such a society is ripe for those who would be king. In Russia, a right-wing extremist by the name of Vladmir Zhirinovsky longed for the day when he could assert the might of Russia against all its foes. His party captured a surprisingly large percentage of the vote in one election. In early October 1994, 1,000 monarchists gathered in the ancient hall of the nobility, near Red Square, in order to further their cause of restoring the monarchy. "The Russian state needs a czar," roared one ultranationalist from a podium decorated with a two-headed Romanov eagle, as black-robed Orthodox priests and men decked in cossack uniforms thundered their approval.

The monarchists are not likely to be successful in their quest to restore the monarchy. However, we observe here an illustration of the truth that a society cannot operate long or well in the absence of a supreme authority.

* * * * *

In the demonstrations that were a part of the so-called Velvet Revolution, which led to the bloodless overthrow of the Communist government in Czechoslovakia, enthusiastic demonstrators chanted: "You have lost already, you have lost already...." The victory was not yet won but in sight. Faith realizes that all creation does not yet acknowledge the kingship of Christ but, envisioning his final victory, acts as if it were already a reality.

Thanksgiving Day

Revised Common: Deuteronomy 8:7-18   2 Corinthians 9:6-15   Luke 17:11-19

Theme: God has blessed us with the good things of creation, with healing and other benefits. Therefore, our lives are to be a sacrifice of praise and thanksgiving to God.

BRIEF COMMENTARY ON THE LESSONS

Lesson 1: Deuteronomy 8:7-18 (C)

The people of Israel must remember God's goodness in leading them through the wilderness into the promised land. Since God has blessed them by bringing them into a rich and fruitful land, thankful lives are called for. When the people enjoy prosperity, the children of God must resist the temptation to pat themselves on the back and take credit for all their good fortune. They must render thanksgiving to the Lord, for he is the source of all blessing. The Lord is the one who led them through the perilous wilderness, supporting them in those difficult times. Thanksgiving is the only proper response.

Lesson 2: 2 Corinthians 9:6-15 (C)

Paul encourages the Corinthian church to generously support the offering that he is taking up for the Jerusalem Christians. The apostle reminds them that those who sow sparingly will reap sparingly and vice-versa. Generosity is a prime mark of the Christian life, which will be richly rewarded by the Lord, not materially but spiritually. Their liberality will bring a rich harvest of praise and thanksgiving to God from others. This giving spirit comes from the grace of God, who favors us with the gift above all gifts, Jesus Christ our Lord.

Gospel: Luke 17:11-19 (C)

Of the ten lepers whom Jesus healed, only one returns to give thanks to God, and he is a Samaritan outsider. Jesus instructs the lepers to show themselves to the priests, who alone could declare them fit to associate with the rest of society. On the way, they are healed. Their going demonstrated their faith, which made them well. While ten were healed of their leprosy, only the one leper was truly whole, for his spirit was filled with thanksgiving.

Psalm Of The Day

Psalm 65 (C) — "Praise is due to you, O God, in Zion" (v. 1).

Prayer Of The Day

God of grace, you have blessed us beyond our knowing with gifts great and small. Give us but one thing more, a grateful heart, eager to return thanks for your continued bounties. In Jesus' name. Amen.

THEOLOGICAL REFLECTION ON THE LESSONS

Lesson 1: Deuteronomy 8:7-18

Remember. The people of Israel are urged to remember all the long way that the Lord has led them (v. 2) during the days of struggle and to refrain from forgetting the blessings of the Lord when life becomes prosperous (vv. 11, 14, 18). They must remember to give thanks.

Credit where it is due. The Deuteronomist warns of the very real danger of giving the credit to oneself rather than the Lord (vv. 14, 17). A person cannot lift up holy hands to God in praise and thanksgiving while, at the same time, reaching around to pat himself on the back. Recall that God rejected the prayer of the Pharisee who prayed: "God, I thank you that I am not like other people ... I fast twice a week, I give a tenth of all my income" (Luke 18:11-12). A thankless heart is discrediting to God and a sign of a soul out of touch with God's Spirit.

Lesson 2: 2 Corinthians 9:6-15

The law of farming. "The one who sows sparingly will also reap sparingly and the one who sows bountifully will also reap bountifully" (v. 6). Sowing and reaping are proportional. The more you sow; the more you will reap. This principle applies not only to farming but to life itself. The more a person hoards the gift of life, the less life will reward her. It's a law built into the structure of things, which is equally valid for those who sow through the Spirit of God.

Hold things lightly. The Corinthians were instructed to give freely and cheerfully (v. 7). In other words, hold on to things very loosely; don't clutch them tightly, so as to keep them from others. Material possessions are meant to be shared with those in need, not put in a safe.

Why God loves a cheerful giver. The grudging giver regards possessions as his own, while the cheerful Christian giver knows that everything comes from God. Who wouldn't be cheerful when you're giving somebody else's money or possessions away? The cheerful Christian giver focuses on the human dimension, the needs of people. The grudging giver loves things more than people. The cheerful Christian giver concentrates on the object of his giving, while the grouch preoccupies himself with what he has given up. The cheerful Christian giver has the faith to entrust his or her future to the Lord; the grudging giver believes that he must shape his own future. The cheerful Christian giver uses his money to empower others; the grudging giver strives only to strengthen his own position. The cheerful Christian giver worships God with his money; the grudging giver worships money as his god.

Gospel: Luke 17:11-19

Equality in suffering. The region through which Jesus was traveling, the border of Samaria and Galilee, contained a mixture of races. The text does not explicitly state the composition of the group of lepers, except that the man who returned to give Jesus thanks was a Samaritan. From Jesus' comment, "Was none of them found to return and give praise to God except this foreigner?" (v. 18), we must assume that some of the ten lepers were Jews. Without their affliction, they would have nothing to do with one another. Their disease was an equalizer. Suffering seems to break down barriers and create a community of the afflicted. Note that when they sought Jesus' healing power, they didn't pray, "Jesus, have mercy on *me*," but, "Jesus, master, have mercy on *us*!" (v. 13). They saw themselves as a community and sought healing not just for themselves but for the community. Unfortunately, once healed of their disease, they ceased functioning as a community. Only one man was changed.

As they went, they were made clean (v. 14). Going to the priests was a demonstration of faith. The priest was the one who could declare that they were now clean and ready to re-enter regular society. The healing was not instantaneous but occurred on the way. As we obey the commands of the master and do his bidding, we are made clean.

Returning thanks. Only the Samaritan returned to praise and thank God for his healing. Giving thanks entails returning to the source of our blessings. It also involves returning something to the ones who have gifted us. This provides recognition not just of the gift but of the giver. To return thanks communicates that the giver is precious to us, a necessary part of our lives.

Resounding thanks. The man who returned thanks to Jesus lost himself in praise and thanksgiving. He praised God with a loud voice, prostrating himself before Jesus (vv. 15-16). He was oblivious to the reactions of others. When we really become aware of Christ's healing and cleansing grace, we become like those about God's heavenly throne, lost in wonder, love, and praise.

PREACHING APPROACHES WITH ILLUSTRATIONS

Lesson 1: Deuteronomy 8:7-18

Sermon Title: Living In Remembrance

Sermon Angle: The book of Deuteronomy calls the people of Israel to remembrance, and our text is no exception. They are called to remember God's great acts of salvation and providence. Thanksgiving necessarily focuses on past deeds and requires that we recall our blessings. We must not be so focused on where we are going that we forget those who have helped us get this far. When Jesus instituted the Lord's Supper, he told his disciples to live in thankful remembrance of his saving grace. Living in remembrance begins at the foot of the cross.

Outline:

1. The Israelites were called to live in remembrance
   — of God's leadership in difficult times
   — of God's provision in prosperous times (v. 14)
2. We are to live in remembrance
   — of material gifts (v. 14)
   — of God's gift of salvation through Christ
3. The Eucharist reminds us to live in thankful remembrance

Lesson 2: 2 Corinthians 9:6-15

Sermon Title: What's The Point?

Sermon Angle: Paul provides a rationale for the cause of giving to the needs of others: in this case, the church in Jerusalem. He addresses the underlying fear that to give generously will cause the giver to come up short. What is the point? The more we give; the more we receive. The more we sow; the more we reap (v. 6).

Outline:

1. Our misconception has it that giving impoverishes the giver
2. The Bible teaches that giving enriches the giver and the receiver (v. 6)
3. Give freely and God will provide for your needs and bless you (v. 8)

Sermon Title: Planned Giving

Sermon Angle: The Corinthians were to give great thought to their giving (v. 7). They were not to be pressured into giving but to contribute freely, according to their own decision. This suggests that giving ought not be haphazard but well thought out. Unplanned giving usually leads to giving God our leftovers, but planned giving enables us to make our giving an expression of our faith.

Sermon Title: Seed Money

Sermon Angle: Verse 10 asserts that not only will God supply that which we need to live (the seed), but we will multiply that seed if we freely sow it. Sometimes groups are given so-called seed money to get a new venture off the ground or sustain an existing one. Comparing money to seed is very biblical. Money, like seed, can be consumed and then it's gone or it can be invested (planted) in hopes of a greater return. God promises that if we invest our seed money, we will reap a bountiful harvest.

Gospel: Luke 17:11-19

Sermon Title: From A Distance

Sermon Angle: Luke states that the lepers kept their distance as they begged for healing (v. 12), in accordance with Jewish law. These pathetic sufferers observed all of life from a distance, except that of their companions. They were all healed physically, but only one, spiritually. Only the Samaritan drew near to Jesus to render thanks for his cleansing. Were the others so alienated from society and God that even after their skin was restored, their souls remained leprous? Were they still outsiders, outcasts, who could not draw near to God in worship and thanksgiving? To live in sin is to be an outcast, looking at life from a distance.

Sermon Title: Returning Thanks

Sermon Angle: The Samaritan, when he noticed that he was healed, turned back to render thanks to God (v. 15). The head of the household sometimes prefaces a meal with the words, "let us return thanks." *Returning* is a wonderful choice of words to use with *thanks*. Thanksgiving causes one to stop and go back to the source of blessings to return thanks, especially to the Lord.

Outline:
1. The Samaritan stopped to return thanks to Jesus
2. Returning thanks completed the healing process
3. Thanksgiving involves returning to the source of blessings (God) and to others through whom God blesses us
4. Who are those to whom you need to return thanks?

*   *   *   *   *

Let me tell you about Gertrude, a pillar of our little Swedish Lutheran church on the south side of Omaha, Nebraska, who lived for decades with her son, since being widowed. Both mother and son were full of the joy of life, oozing with warmth. I was reunited with Gertrude at the congregation's 75th anniversary. Her eyes were aglow as she vigorously pumped my hand and exclaimed: "We're so proud of you!" I was the rebel miscreant whom they never dreamed would become a pastor, one of the three in the history of the congregation. Her love lifted me. I was one of her children, whom she loved unconditionally. My wife, who is a nurse, happened to meet Gertrude's son at a nursing home. Gertrude had recently been admitted. "Maybe you could visit my mom," he suggested, "though I don't know if she'll remember you." Those last words set off alarm bells. Fran and I went to visit Gertrude a week later. She was sitting at the dining room table, soup was spilled in front of her. "Hi, Gertrude, remember me?" She said yes, but there was no spark of recognition. She only complained of her back and of wanting to get back to her room. We spoke of the old days but they were dead to her. We were dead to her. The past was dead to her. Without remembrance, there is no life, humanly speaking. I thank God that Gertrude lives, not only in my mind, but in the hearts of those who loved her and continue to love her. I thank God that he remembers Gertrude and will raise her to newness of life. Thanks be to God for the gift of remembrance and of life eternal.

Sermon Title: Prostrate Trouble

Sermon Angle: Have you noticed how many people, when referring to the male sexual gland called the prostate, refer to it as the prostrate? They bemoan, "I have prostrate trouble." No, they really have prostate trouble; prostrate trouble is a spiritual disease that afflicts us all. The Samaritan was so overwhelmed with thanksgiving that he fell on his face (prostrate) at the feet of Jesus. When is the last time you were so overwhelmed with thanksgiving to God that you fell prostrate at the feet of Jesus, as you shouted out your praise and thanksgiving to God?

US/Canadian Lectionary Comparison

The following index shows the correlation between the Sundays and special days of the church year as they are titled or labeled in the Revised Common Lectionary published by the Consultation On Common Texts and used in the United States (the reference used for this book) and the Sundays and special days of the church year as they are titled or labeled in the Revised Common Lectionary used in Canada.

Revised Common Lectionary	Canadian Revised Common Lectionary
Advent 1	Advent 1
Advent 2	Advent 2
Advent 3	Advent 3
Advent 4	Advent 4
Christmas Eve	Christmas Eve
The Nativity Of Our Lord/Christmas Day	The Nativity Of Our Lord
Christmas 1	Christmas 1
January 1/Holy Name Of Jesus	January 1/The Name Of Jesus
Christmas 2	Christmas 2
The Epiphany Of Our Lord	The Epiphany Of Our Lord
The Baptism Of Our Lord/Epiphany 1/Ordinary Time 1	The Baptism Of Our Lord/Proper 1
Epiphany 2/Ordinary Time 2	Epiphany 2/Proper 2
Epiphany 3/Ordinary Time 3	Epiphany 3/Proper 3
Epiphany 4/Ordinary Time 4	Epiphany 4/Proper 4
Epiphany 5/Ordinary Time 5	Epiphany 5/Proper 5
Epiphany 6/Ordinary Time 6	Epiphany 6/Proper 6
Epiphany 7/Ordinary Time 7	Epiphany 7/Proper 7
Epiphany 8/Ordinary Time 8	Epiphany 8/Proper 8
The Transfiguration Of Our Lord/ Last Sunday After Epiphany	The Transfiguration Of Our Lord/ Last Sunday After Epiphany
Ash Wednesday	Ash Wednesday
Lent 1	Lent 1
Lent 2	Lent 2
Lent 3	Lent 3
Lent 4	Lent 4
Lent 5	Lent 5
Passion/Palm Sunday	Passion/Palm Sunday
Maundy Thursday	Holy/Maundy Thursday
Good Friday	Good Friday
Easter Day	The Resurrection Of Our Lord
Easter 2	Easter 2
Easter 3	Easter 3
Easter 4	Easter 4
Easter 5	Easter 5
Easter 6	Easter 6
The Ascension Of Our Lord	The Ascension Of Our Lord
Easter 7	Easter 7
The Day Of Pentecost	The Day Of Pentecost
The Holy Trinity	The Holy Trinity
Proper 4/Pentecost 2/O T 9*	Proper 9
Proper 5/Pent 3/O T 10	Proper 10
Proper 6/Pent 4/O T 11	Proper 11
Proper 7/Pent 5/O T 12	Proper 12
Proper 8/Pent 6/O T 13	Proper 13
Proper 9/Pent 7/O T 14	Proper 14

Proper 10/Pent 8/O T 15

Proper 11/Pent 9/O T 16

Proper 12/Pent 10/O T 17

Proper 13/Pent 11/O T 18

Proper 14/Pent 12/O T 19

Proper 15/Pent 13/O T 20

Proper 16/Pent 14/O T 21

Proper 17/Pent 15/O T 22

Proper 18/Pent 16/O T 23

Proper 19/Pent 17/O T 24

Proper 20/Pent 18/O T 25

Proper 21/Pent 19/O T 26

Proper 22/Pent 20/O T 27

Proper 23/Pent 21/O T 28

Proper 24/Pent 22/O T 29

Proper 25/Pent 23/O T 30

Proper 26/Pent 24/O T 31

Proper 27/Pent 25/O T 32

Proper 28/Pent 26/O T 33

Christ The King (Proper 29/O T 34)

Proper 15

Proper 16

Proper 17

Proper 18

Proper 19

Proper 20

Proper 21

Proper 22

Proper 23

Proper 24

Proper 25

Proper 26

Proper 27

Proper 28

Proper 29

Proper 30

Proper 31

Proper 32

Proper 33

Proper 34/Christ The King/
Reign Of Christ

Reformation Day (October 31)

All Saints (November 1 or
1st Sunday in November)

Thanksgiving Day
(4th Thursday of November)

Reformation Day (October 31)

All Saints' Day (November 1)

Thanksgiving Day
(2nd Monday of October)

*O T = Ordinary Time

394